Debating Muslims

A. Rippin
Nov. 91
SSHRCC grant
$28.20

New Directions in Anthropological Writing
History, Poetics, Cultural Criticism

GEORGE E. MARCUS
Rice University

JAMES CLIFFORD
University of California, Santa Cruz

GENERAL EDITORS

Nationalism and the Politics of Culture in Quebec
Richard Handler

The Pastoral Son and the Spirit of Patriarchy: Religion, Society, and Person among East African Stock Keepers
Michael E. Meeker

Belonging in America: Reading Between the Lines
Constance Perin

Himalayan Dialogue: Tibetan Lamas and Gurung Shamans in Nepal
Stan Royal Mumford

Wombs and Alien Spirits: Women, Men and the Zār *Cult in Northern Sudan*
Janice Boddy

People as Subject, People as Object: Selfhood and Peoplehood in Contemporary Israel
Virginia R. Domínguez

Debating Muslims: Cultural Dialogues in Postmodernity and Tradition
Michael M. J. Fischer and Mehdi Abedi

Sharing the Dance: Contact Improvisation and American Culture
Cynthia J. Novack

DEBATING MUSLIMS

Cultural Dialogues in Postmodernity and Tradition

Michael M. J. Fischer and Mehdi Abedi

The University of Wisconsin Press

The University of Wisconsin Press
114 North Murray Street
Madison, Wisconsin 53715

3 Henrietta Street
London WC2E 8LU, England

5 4 3 2 1

Printed in the United States of America

Library of Congress Cataloging-in-Publication Data
Fischer, Michael M. J., 1946–
Debating Muslims: cultural dialogues in postmodernity and tradition / Michael M. J. Fischer and Mehdi Abedi.
600 pp. cm. – (New directions in anthropological writing)
Includes bibliographical references.
1. Shī'ah – Iran. 2. Shiites – United States. 3. Iran – Social life and customs. 4. Shī'ah – History – 20th century. 5. Iranians – United States – Social life and customs. I. Abedi, Mehdi. II. Title. III. Series.
BP192.7.I68F56 1990
297'.82'0904 – dc20 89-40531
ISBN 0-299-12430-4
ISBN 0-299-12434-7 (pbk.) CIP

Chapter 7 is reprinted by permission from *Cultural Anthropology,* volume 5, number 2

Contents

Illustrations

Note on Transcription

Arabic, a Semitic language, and Persian, an Indo-European language, both are written in the Arabic alphabet, and share much vocabulary, but the sounds—the phonemic systems—of the two languages differ. The Persian version of the alphabet has a few extra characters (پ *p*, چ *ch*, ژ *zh*, و *v*, and گ *g*); and although it uses all the Arabic characters, Persian does not phonemically distinguish between a number of them. The same sound in Persian can often be written with one of two or more Arabic characters, though spelling has gradually been standardized, and schoolchildren do have to learn the correct spelling of Arabic words. Still, dictation exercises plague Iranian schoolchildren, for instance, when teachers dictate *kār-e savāb savāb dārad* ("there is merit in good deeds"), and expect the children to know that the first *savāb* is spelled *ṣawāb* ("good, right"), while the second is *thawāb* ("merit, divine reward"). To a Persian speaker there is virtually no difference in sound between ع ('ayn) and ء (hamza); nor between what is usually transliterated from Arabic as *s* (س), *ṣ* (ص), or *th* (ث). Likewise Arabic *t* (ت) and *ṭ* (ط) sound the same in Persian. In Arabic ض (*ḍ*), ذ (*dh*), ز (*z*), and ظ (*ẓ*) are quite different sounds, but not in Persian. In most of Iran, there is no difference between ق (*q*) and غ (*gh*); Tehranis laugh at Yazdis whose dialect does distinguish between the two, but not always between *f* and *p*.

Thus, insofar as transcription should indicate both pronunciation and also the written form, Persian and Arabic must be differently transcribed. The difference in transliteration can help the reader distinguish to which of the two languages a term belongs. Thus we transcribe the title of the famous mystical poem of Rumi, *Masnavi,* as it is pronounced in Persian, because the poem is written in Persian; the alphabetic or Arabicized transliteration would be *Mathnawi. Riḍā* is the Arabic equivalent of *Rezā* in Persian, so *Imām Riḍā,* but *Shah Rezā Pahlavi. Ramaḍān* is the Arabic month, and is so adopted into English (or also by an older system *Ramadhan*), but in Persian it is pronounced *Ramazān. Anjuman-i Dhidd-i Bahā'i* would be Arabicized, *Anjoman-e Zedd-e Bahā'i* is Persian, the language of that organization. Arabs do a *woḍu* ablution, Persians do *vozū.* Persians have a sermon form they call *rowzeh;* in Arabicized transliteration this would be *rawḍa. Wilāyat-e faqīh* ("guidance by the clergy") is Arabic, *velāyat-e faghīh* is Persian. In Arabic one says *al-ḥukūma al-islāmīyah* ("Islamic government," the subtitle of one of Khomeini's books), but a Persian would say *hokūmat-e eslāmī.*

To reduce the variation between the two spoken languages and the written forms, we have tended to leave technical terms, most of which are Arabic, in Arabic transliteration, albeit without imposing unnecessary prefixes and suffixes. Some names like Ali and Abbas are now simply English names and do not require the initial ʿayn. Words like *muezzin, ḥadīth, sunna,* and the months *Muharram* and *Ramaḍān* are also now English. *Khomeini* too now is an English name, and is used here rather than the less familiar *Khumaynī.* Oddly enough *Murtaḍā Muṭahhari,* a Persian cleric (*Morteẓā Motahharī*), is normally referred to in English in the Arabicized form, perhaps because he is known to English readers only as a textualized, transliterated figure, rather than as a voluble Iranian person; and we have accepted that. The connective *-e* in Persian and the connective *-i* in Arabic are both here usually standardized into *-e,* except in Arabic formulas such as *bismillāh-i rrahmān-i rrahīm.* We prefer *Islāmi* to *Eslāmi* as the transcription of the Persian word for "Islamic," as being less exoticizing in English.

Those familiar with the languages we use—Arabic, Persian, and occasionally local Persian dialects—should have no trouble in identifying the correct reading of our *taṣ-ḥīf* and *laḥn.* It has become a tiresome sport among Orientalists to claim that every book they review is full of "mispellings" and inconsistent transcriptions. Language traditions which are not as fetishized by their foreign scholars—Hebrew for instance—manage to live with a riot of transcriptions without anyone being misled or offended. T. E. Lawrence began his *Seven Pillars of Wisdom* with a hilarious riposte to the transcription fetishists, which we heartily recommend. But the best riposte was that of the Prophet Muhammad. When Muhammad chose the Abyssinian Bilāl as his muezzen, the now popular proverbial story goes, there were complaints that Bilāl mispronounced *sh* as *s,* so that he would say *as-hadu* ("I deprive [people] of sleep") rather than *ash-hadu* ("I bear witness"). "No problem," Muhammad replied, "God hears the *s* of Bilāl as *sh.*"

Calendars

Anno Hejirae or *Qamari* ("lunar"), the Islamic calendar, is dated from the month of Muḥarram of the year Muhammad withdrew from Mecca to Medina, 622 C.E. The year 1979 C.E. was A.H. 1400 or 1400 Q. The months are Muḥarram, Ṣafar, Rabi' al-Awwal, Rabi' al-Thāni, Jamādi al-Awwal, Jamādi al-Thāni, Rajab, Sha'bān, Ramaḍān, Shawwāl, Dhī al-Qa'da, Dhī al- Ḥajja.

Shamsi ("solar"), the Iranian civil calendar, is derived from the pre-Islamic Zoroastrian calendar, beginning each year on 21 March. The year 1979 was 1358–59 Sh. The months are Farvardīn, Ordibehesht, Khordād, Tīr, Mordād, Shahrīvar, Mehr, Abān, Āzar, Dey, Bahman, Esfand.

Chronology of Significant Dynasties

	Muslim Dates (A.H.)	Christian Dates (C.E.)
Pre-Islamic		
Achaemenians (Cyrus to Alexander)		558 B.C.–331 B.C.
Sassanians (Ardashir to Yazdigird III)		224–651
Early Islamic		
Twelve Imāms (Shi'ite)	11–260	632–872
Rashidun (first four Sunni caliphs)	11–40	632–661
Ummayyads	41–132	661–750
Abbasids	132–656	750–1258
Buyids (Shi'ite)	320–447	932–1055
Seljuks and Il-Khanids (Sunni)	429–754	1037–1353
Iran since establishment of Shi'ism as the state religion		
Safavids	907–1135	1501–1722
Afshars and Zands	1148–1210	1736–1795
Qajars	1200–1342	1785–1925
Pahlavis	1342–1399	1925–1979
Reza Shah		1925–1941
Mohammad Reza Shah		1941–1979

Preface: Notes Toward Anthropology as Cultural Critique

There are times, increasingly, when we need touchstones, reminders, and access to the humanism of others. The following essays are intended to explore genres of access. The opening essay is a response to requests for reading material on lives of people in the Middle East, lives that can reach through the numbing opaqueness of news accounts of confrontation, ideological war, and endless killing; through the reifying opaqueness of histories of political regimes, kings, dictators, coups, and revolutionary masses; through the idealizing opaqueness of theologies of Islam or symbolic analyses of ritual. Lives that make narrative sense, that are not just sentimental soap operas, that do not tell us that people everywhere are the same. Lives that have stories to tell, stories that open up cultural worlds, worlds of difference, worlds of experience, worlds of sense, worlds that can draw their own limits, that illuminate their limitations as well as their depths, that localize and situate their knowledge, their thresholds of change, and their paths of transformation.

Storytelling comes in many genres. Renewed attention to the relation between these forms or genres and the information conveyed has reinvigorated recent thinking about ethnography in general, and about the need to make use of cultural idioms, concepts, tropes, and discourse styles as epistemological guides, not just as ethnographic objects to be described, or reduced to the ethnographers' own categories and forms. Autobiographical storytelling of the sort employed in this first essay depends upon units of narrative, not always told the same way each telling, not always linked the same way together to other stories or contexts. Tellings depend upon audiences. Such storytelling is an oral form, open to digression, expansive elaboration, or brief lapidary reference to oft told familiar incidents, diverting in both senses (entertaining, rerouting according to audience interest). The chronological and topical stringing together of these narrative units, by contrast, is a linear textual device designed for outsiders who do not share the experiential background listeners in other contexts might have.

The use, here, of these stories is intended to invoke and involve the reader in the oral life world of Iranian Shi'ites. This oral life world provides both a structural parallel and a context for the following essay on the Qur'an. The Qur'an is a similar collection, if different genre (having different functions, constructions, uses), of storytellings, and is received by most believers in oral modalities. The first essay is also intended to introduce readers to the socialization, psychology, class dynamics, politics, folk religion, clerical styles, and social changes of provincial Iranians in the 1960s and 1970s. The particular life employed in this endeavor covers an unusual cross section of Iranian experience, running across class divisions, religious and political factions, village, city, metropolis, and international settings. It is a life unusually sensitive to both folk Islam and scholarly Islam, a relative rarity among Iranians in the United States, the majority of whom are of middle-class backgrounds with rather attenuated understandings of Islam in either modality (albeit often rich in mystical, modernist, or other interpretations of Islam), and others of whom may come from folk or working-class experiences of Islam but may not be versed in scholarly Islam. This life might be read together with other sets of Iranian and Shi'ite life histories: Agha Najafi-Quchani's picaresque and humorous autobiography of his life as a cleric in the earlier part of this century, which presents the anxieties, gullibilities, theological disputations, and machinations of his fellow students and teachers in the seminaries, and which is fondly regarded by contemporary clerics as an amusing yet sympathetic insight into their own lives (Fischer 1982c); Roy Mottahedeh's *The Mantle of the Prophet* (1985), which uses the life of a moderate cleric who now teaches in the United States to introduce a series of essays on Iranian culture; Fuad Ajami's (1986) excellent account of Musa Sadr, the clerical activist organizer of Shi'ites in Lebanon during the 1960s and 1970s, which explores both the sociological changes and the politics that refashioned both the Shi'ite community and the larger polity; Shusha Assar Guppy's *The Blindfold Horse* (1988), a memoir by the granddaughter of two well-known early twentieth century religious leaders, which is sensitive, as we hope our account is, to the forms of oral storytelling that preserve, mediate, and turn into vehicles for reflection memories of people, patterns of behavior, disagreements, psychological reactions, folkways, and the impact of social changes upon Iran; Erika Friedl's (1989) evocative vignettes of twelve village women, and Rheinhold Loffler's (1988) complementary interviews with men from the same village; and what is perhaps the most magisterial of all life histories produced in the Islamic world, Louis Massignon's (1975/1982) extraordinarily detailed, and vivid reconstruction of the personality, social cleavages, politics, and ideologies structuring the life, trials, execution, and legacies of al-Hallaj.

We hope that the first essay will be of easy access to all readers, that it can serve as an introduction, for instance, for college students with no background in Islam or in the historical and political crosscurrents of contemporary Middle Eastern turbulence. We would hope that such students would gain from it a feel for the sociological as well as cultural texture of a world hard to appreciate if approached only through the more instrumental policy categories of "modernizing backward, dependent, underdeveloped nations," or if approached only through essentializing categories of intellectual or political history, Islamic theology, or other nonsociologically informed "humanities." We hope that the essay will ring chords of familiarity for Iranians, both those living in America and Europe and those living in Iran; and for the small but gifted group of American Peace Corps volunteers and graduate students who lived in Iran during the 1960s and 1970s, we hope that it will find its place among the other richly textured accounts of that group's experiences in Iran, such as Terry O'Donnell's stories and the novels of Dick Bulliet and Colin McKinnon, as well as that group's more scholarly accounts and those of Iranian writers and film makers. Perhaps it also can serve the children of Iranians raised in America, to give them a sense of the land from which their parents came, and the extraordinary degree of multiple changes in social direction that land has undergone in the last decades. It attempts, at least, to integrate Iran's recent religiopolitical history with life seen on the ground, from the bottom up.

The second essay is both more playful and more serious. It can be used as simply an introduction to the Qur'an, to how it is read and how with the hadith literature it is interpreted. But it also takes on the Qur'an not just as another scripture, but as a premier "text" of poetic enigma, a text that can speak to all the mysteries of contemporary (postmodern) literary criticism, thereby arguing both that such literary criticism is not a passing fad but (understood properly) has deep cultural roots, and that Islamic culture can be an intellectual interlocutor in the modern world scene, as it was in the days when it gave form to the nascent modern "Western civilization."

It was, after all, the brilliance of Andalusian and Sicilian Islamic civilization that was "high culture" for Europe in the eleventh to fifteenth centuries. European courts and scholars looked there for rational philosophy that challenged faith (Aristotle via Ibn Rushd [Averroës]), for science and math (our numeral system, algebra, geometry, astronomy, the medicine of Ibn Sina [Avicenna]), for the arts (the *sic et non* dialectical disputation method, epistolary forms of fiction, dialogic forms of philosophy that became popular in the Renaissance, and vernacular poetry). Not only was troubadour poetry modeled on Arabic forms from Spain, but also Dante's *Divine Comedy* might well be seen as a countertext by a Christian nativist to the *mi'rāj* (mystical journey to heaven and hell) traditions of Muhammad. Some of Dante's fears might be seen as being much like today's Iranian fears of Westernization, as being a Christian nativist fear of Arabization, of cosmopolitan Islamic civilization, Dante not so much borrowing the *mi'rāj* traditions as rather trying to compose a poetically more powerful counterform.[1] Think of the worlds of word borrowings we still have in English from Arabic and Persian: paradise, picnic, algebra, sherbet, sherry, sheriff, pyjama. Ironically, of course, that Islamic civilization was threatened by fundamentalist Islam as is cosmopolitan, liberal Islam today, and for not entirely dissimilar reasons. The interaction in later times through Venice and the Balkans with the Ottoman Empire may perhaps not have been quite so elevated, though tulips, coffee, oriental carpets, arabesque designs, architectural forms, and pottery lusters are some of the elements of civilized elegance that came that way. To reduce these interactions to religious hatreds and crusades for the sake of journalistic, quick-fix "background" for contemporary anti-imperialist rhetoric is not just a lamentable display of historical ignorance, but blocks access to rebuilding grounds for understanding, by essentializing, cartoonizing, and distancing. Even European crusaders sometimes settled down as Muslims, or returned speaking Arabic and teaching things learned abroad.

Intercultural dialogue recently has become a topic of renewed interest among anthropologists, both as a rubric for acknowledging the ways in which cultural information is gathered and, more importantly, as a modality of communication that surrounds texts and that is ill represented by texts. Too often this interest in dialogue has been diverted to the relationship between the individual anthropologist and the people she or he interviews in the field, becoming mere confessional or quest styles of personal story, rather than focusing on the modality of communication, on the other culture's categories, discourses, cultural linguistics, and hermeneutical means of understanding, and on the tracking back and forth between those categories and others (whether conceptualized as "theirs and ours," "emic and etic," "experience-near and experience-far," or different "perspectival" systems).[2] The second essay attempts to contribute to a righting of the balance. It insists on a threefold understanding of dialogue: as internal to the communicative situation (intentions and understandings of parties to communication); as setting arguments one against another (rational reconstruction); and as political (e.g., fundamentalist versus liberal interpretations, but also third-world ideologies against first-world assertions of ownership of "rational" or "universal" truth). The stress is on discourses, on the way interpretive positions structure understanding, rather than on individual interactions, texts isolated from the other texts to which they refer, or arguments separated from their contexts of use.

By the use of epigrams from contemporary theorists, this essay and the one following attempt to set up resonances and dialogue across cultural traditions. Of these, it may be well to remember that Edmond Jabès and Jacques Derrida, although of Jewish background, come more generally from North African Muslim environments, and their exposure of dialogue and disputation in ostensibly monologic texts is explicitly, if only partly, grounded in Judeo-Muslim hermeneutical sensibilities. Emanuel Levinas also comes from a Jewish (albeit Eastern European) background and, like Derrida, is systematically engaged in dialogue with those who would construct modern philosophy on the ruins of Christian hermeneutics (Heidegger, Gadamer), as well as those like Jurgen Habermas and John Searle less sensitive to hermeneutics who attempt to ground dialogue and meaning in social science theories of symbolic interaction (G. H. Mead) or speech act sociolinguistics. James Joyce is a key figure in this play of juxtaposition and dialogue, both for his "seriocomic" humor and for his engagement with Catholic hermeneutics. Joyce incorporates Jewish and occasional Islamic references, but he also is a focus of considerable interest to Derrida and other modern analysts of the "postmodern" linguistic and dialogic condition. Insofar as we invoke the postmodern in these essays, it is in the sense that the world today is one of multilinguistic and multicultural interreference that throws into question the utility of the notion of bounded "cultures." The global political economy deeply structures local events, so that cultural understandings are saturated with borrowings, comparisons, and references to others, drawing partly upon traditionally evolved stereotypes and partly upon contemporary experiences of the media, of labor migration, of mass politicization, and of internationally organized social stratification. Perspectival truth becomes ever more necessary to recognize, and thoroughly antiquates the debates over "relativism" versus "universal reason."

The Islamic emphasis on the oral or dialogic over the textual might be compared with that of eighteenth-century Japanese "nativism."[3] In neither case does the oral exclude the literate; rather, the literate is problematized and kept from being a tyrannical authority. Both cases involve deep historical traditions, and develop discourses that attempt to re-cognize a more pristine past that might act as a moral critique of the ill effects of hegemonic discourses (Chinese textualism in the Japanese case; Arabic textualism, but also "Westernization" with its development schemes, and harnessing to the industrial, capitalist machinery, in the Iranian case). The search for native categories and hermeneutics, and their juxtaposition to other discourses or systems of hermeneutics, can lead ideally to a kind of critical hermeneutics, where the point is not to unpack in ever greater detail a given cultural system, but rather to create through juxtaposition a space for comparison and critical evaluation. We attempt to illustrate these potentials of critique in three ways: by juxtaposing Islamic, Jewish, Christian, and secular interpretations and hermeneutical styles (pursued especially in the epigrams and footnotes of chapter 2 and the *ḥajj* section of chapter 3); by showing how the dialectical disputation internal to Islamic hermeneutics deeply contests Khomeini's political agenda (chapter 2); and by pointing to generational strata or class-linked ideological positions such as the obliviousness of many upper- and middle-class Iranians to Khomeini until the revolution broke out (and in some cases their continued denial even today that Iranians knew anything about Khomeini before the revolution),[4] and the competing generational experiences represented by Murtaḍā Muṭahhari and Ali Shari'ati in chapter 3.

The rationale for detailed comparisons of Islamic argumentation (dialogical-dialectical, exegetical-theological, anecdotal-parabolic) with similar Christian, Judaic, Greek, Buddhist,[5] secular, and other argumentation is not merely to identify historical and cultural environments within and against which it developed. Cultural interreference (*interférence,*[6] transference, and [inter]dependence on cultural alter egos) is basic to the evolution of any tradition. More importantly, it is a way of eliciting alternative meaning structures or interpretations of rituals, myths, tropes, dialogic moves, and connections between stories. Insofar as Muslims, Jews, and Christians draw upon the same biblical stories, their interpretations form families of resemblances. Tracing such differences has affinities with both Lévi-Strauss' style of structuralist analysis of myth (no myth can be understood alone, without its variants) and Derrida's deconstruction (paying attention to the alternative meanings carried within a text). The point is neither to reduce one tradition to another as derivative, nor to reduce interpretations to essential formulae, but on the contrary to recover and enrich our understanding of the utility of rituals, myths, tropes, and allegories for modeling and thinking through complex and ambiguous moral phenomena, and to chart the historical or sociological horizons of how these forms change with social context.

We wish thereby to counter the arrest of interpretation by fundamentalists, makers of state ideologies, or those caught in the everydayness of oblivious repetition. The trope of oblivion and repetition has gone through many variants: repetitive rebirths (Plato, Pythagoras, Buddha, Firdausi),[7] the animality or "false consciousness" of the "rabble" enforced by seductive ideologies and dynamics of the "return of the repressed" (Hegel, Marx, Nietzsche, Freud, Hedayat),[8] and the caughtness of distracted Being[9] in a hyperreal world of commodities and simulacra where reproductions are experienced and desired as more real than originals (Martin Heidegger, Jean Baudrillard, Umberto Eco, Christopher Lasch). Anti-Western Islamic rhetorics draw upon these tropes, accusing Westerners of being consumer automatons without moral soul, but also worrying that Muslims have become appendages of the West, driven by envy, feelings of belatedness, and fear of being locked into subordination. Islamic modernizers, as well as secularists, similarly talk about Muslims as caught in oblivious repetitions of stultifying myths, and of the need for liberation and renewal.

Chapter 3 is an introduction to the *ḥajj,* one of the five pillars of Islam. The first part of the chapter can be read simply as such, but the chapter also attempts to show the role of the ḥajj in the political debates of Iranians over their Islamic and national identity. The second part of the chapter is thus a contribution to the recently revivified literature on nationalisms and collective identities powered by cultural paradoxes. It uses the debate, triggered by the 1968 ḥajj, between Professor "Ayatullah" Murtaḍā Muṭahhari (an important student of Khomeini who was, until he was assassinated in May 1979, chairman of the Revolutionary Council which ran the state from behind the scenes in the first year of the revolution) and Dr. Ali Shari'ati (the most popular ideologue of the 1970s among the youth) as an access to two competing discourses, both constructed as Islamic shields against Western cultural imperialism. It also uses the biographies of Muṭahhari and Shari'ati as tokens of competing generational experiences that are the carriers of grounds for these two discourses. More generally, chapter 3 may be seen as an inquiry into Islamic "work on myth,"[10] and as a continuation of the exploration in chapter 2 of the ethical grounds of the kind of critique sometimes called "postmodern" (Derrida, Levinas, Irigaray, Lacan, Joyce, et al.). "Fear of *différance*" is not only an anxiety attending Muslim fundamentalists; more troublesome is that it is also an anxiety attending cultural conservatives in the American academy who fear the need both to learn about other cultural traditions and to learn from them the alternative interpretations available within our own "Western" culture.

The three historical "horizons" ("traditional," "modern," "postmodern") of the oblivious repetition trope, invoked above, may serve to raise comparative questions about "work on myth" in Islam over the generations: while many believers would deny any historicity to Islamic self-understanding—Islam is a complete and static cosmos—the growth of Muslim scholarly investigations of the meanings of the Qur'an over the generations points to changes in understanding linked to historical horizons of consciousness.[11] Can one trace how Islamic myths change over time, historically and sociologically? Chapter 3 explores interpretations of the hajj as a primal scene in Islam that has been inflected with political meaning in the efforts to shape Shi'ism into a modern revolutionary ideology. Modernist secular thought often dismisses religion as retrogressive and reactionary, and thus Fred Halliday poses the paradox:

> The novelty of the Iranian Revolution resides in a central contradictory paradox: on the one hand, its leadership and ideology were . . . the first ones in the history of modern revolution to be unequivocably religious . . . on the other hand, the social context in which the Iranian Revolution took place . . . [was] far more "modern" than that of any other comparable upheavals. . . . [It] took place exclusively in the cities, the first Third World revolution to do so. Its means of struggle, the mass demonstration and political general strike, were those normally associated with conflict in the developed capitalist countries. . . . [Iran,] over 50 percent urbanized and with a per capita income of more than L 2000, was in socio-economic terms more "developed" than Russia in 1917, or China in 1949. (Halliday 1983: 94–95)

But even in Marxist historiography, there are alternative accounts of the role of myth and religion: Marx's notion of the "time-honored disguises and borrowed language" that revolutions use to give themselves confidence, and his notion that some "revolutions" (e.g., 1848 in France) appear retrogressive, their interest groups may act in self-defeating ways, yet they may be clearing space for the next step forward; Walter Benjamin's notion of the traditions of oppression that provide revolutionary impulses; Mikhail Bakhtin's notion of folk cultures as repositories of resistance to hegemonic forces; Louis Althusser's notion of ideologies as semiautonomous structures; and Antonio Gramsci's notion of "organic intellectuals" and their "wars of position" against hegemonic ideologies. We do not intend to repeat here an account either of the way religion was used to mobilize the masses during the Iranian revolution (Fischer 1980*a*) or of the way religious idiom can be used to formulate class interests (Fischer 1982*b*). Rather, we wish to focus on the contestation over the mythic resources of Shi'ism in the process of turning it into a revolutionary ideology during the 1970s, what Hans Blumenberg in a slightly different context has called "work on myth."

Myth too has its histories and developments. Myth speaks of origins—in the Islamic case, of God, the *hijra,* the Islamic conquest of Iran—but, in fact, "it is more prudent to speak of the 'pluperfect' [*Vorvergangenheit*], the past's past, rather than of origins." Myth, says Blumenberg, names those things that are humanly unmastered, makes metaphors of them, and tells stories about them, that the terror of the unknown, of evil and injustice, of the unresolvable paradoxes of life may be familiarized, circumscribed, placed, and worked through. As human societies gain more (or lose) control over nature and themselves, myths change to deal with what remains wild or frightening, threatening or mysterious. The Faust story no longer can be told the same way by Goethe as it was by Marlowe; the Prometheus myth of Romantic genius changing the conditions or understanding of existence peaked with Napoleon and then lost power.[12] The Prometheus-Faust myth, like the variations on the Antigone myth,[13] serves as a projective screen for the moral dilemmas of submission to convention/authority versus self-assertion, social revolution, and moral growth. Qur'anic (and biblical) versions of these may be discovered in the commentaries to the stories of Abraham-Isma'il-Hagar, Satan-Adam-Cain, and Muhammad, ritually encoded for Muslims in the annual ḥajj pilgrimage to Mecca.

At issue in particular in this chapter, in the Iranian Islamic work on myth, is contestation over nationalism and pan-Islamic transnationalism. Khomeini speaks always of Islam, not of Shi'ism, and insists that Islam is universal. It took considerable persuasion to get him to speak of Iran during the revolution to mobilize people, and to agree that the president of the new republic must be Iranian, not just Muslim. And yet, of course, true Islam for Khomeini means *Ithnā'Ashari* or twelve Imām Shi'ism. For most of his followers, this has something centrally to do with Iran.

Shari'ati is a key figure in recent Iranian work on myth. He attempted to transform traditional interpretations in existentialist, socialist, and modern directions. He was the most explicit of recent Iranian writers to argue that ever since the Safavid dynasty in 1501 made Shi'ism the established religion in Iran, "Safavid Shi'ism" has been a discourse appropriating popular Islam into scholarly Islam for the purpose of subordinating the masses. The work of such academics as Said Arjomand (1981) has supported this interpretation: Arjomand points to Muhammad Baqir Majlisi as a preeminent figure in the Safavid period who did precisely this. Khomeini, like Majlisi defends shrine worship, icons, and other popular forms of worship. He and the revolution of 1977–79 used popular religious forms—*rowzeh, ta'zieh* processions, *dastehs* of young men—to mobilize the masses. In 1978 he sent messages in preparation for the massive marches of Muḥarram that were to crack the illusion that the military would have the stomach to crush the revolution, directing the traditional mourning for Husain to be replaced with active witnessing through political demonstration (this was the true meaning of Tāsū'a and 'Āshūrā: to take up the cause of Husain, not to weep for an event long past). Two years later, after the revolution had succeeded and Muḥarram 1979 had been used to pass the new constitution and deepen the break with the United States, in an effort to demobilize people, Khomeini directed that people return to the traditional, local neighborhood, mourning rituals for Muḥarram 1980. This incorporative, hegemonic style of Islamic discourse plays an important role in the debate over Iranian identity as well. Murtaḍā Muṭahhari, following Āyatullāh Sayyid Hasan Sadr in the previous generation,[14] argues not only that Islam transcends the evils of nationalism, but that Iranian leadership has been essential in the formulation of Islam throughout history.

Shari'ati attempted to counter the Majlisi-Khomeini-Muṭahhari encompassing discourse by calling for a return to "Alavi Shi'ism," the Shi'ism of Imām Ali. It was to be a "protestant reformation," purging Shi'ism of superstitions, of corrupt manipulations by the clergy, and of the restriction of religious authority to the clergy, by means of which the clergy bolstered their role as a political elite often in alliance with the royal elite, but at other times in pursuit of their own goals. He, moreover, engaged in a cultural-linguistic, philological-mythic revaluation of words, symbols, and mythemes, encouraging enlightened (*rowshan-fekr*) contemporaries to take control of their ideological discourse. The struggle between Shari'ati and the clerics (Khomeini, Ṣadūqi, Muṭahhari, et al.) was bitter and mortal. Shari'ati died just before the revolution, and the clerics were able eventually to seize control of the revolution. But despite the efforts of the clerics (and their allies in California and Texas)[15] to reedit and domesticate Shari'ati's writings, Shari'ati's wordsmithy and revaluative play with mythemes has had a pervasive influence upon the generation now in its thirties, and perhaps also upon the younger generation.

Shari'ati and Muṭahhari represent two sociological types of the 1970s, and the debate between them over Iranian national identity, triggered by the 1968 ḥajj, may serve to illuminate the struggle between those with a more secular, cosmopolitan education, who wished to use Islam to construct a shield against subordination to the West by incorporating key Western ideas, and those with a more traditional background, who feared both the marxism of the USSR and the modernism of Europe and America as equally corrosive to such a shield.

The fourth essay is a tribute to a victim of the Iranian revolution, a man who insisted on attempting to live in a conservative provincial city as if he was living in the twentieth century. The essay plays off five rhetorics—political millenarianism, syncretism, rationalism, tragedy, and irony—and their social positioning over the past century in the evolution of Bahā'ism as a mirror or prism of such rhetorics more generally in Iranian society. The introductory section of this essay provides a very brief characterization of the town of Yazd in central Iran which is the primary setting for chapter 1 as well; further material on this town, its four religious communities (Zoroastrians, Muslims, Jews, Bahā'īs), and the struggle over discourses of Iranian identity may be found in *Zoroastrian Iran between Myth and Praxis* (Fischer 1973). On a simpler level the chapter may serve as an introduction to Iranian Bahā'ism, a religion that began in the mid nineteenth century as a schism within Shi'ism, nearly causing a civil war in Iran, attracting among its leaders many Shi'ite clerics, but also attracting individuals from other religious groups who found their religions equally hidebound and resistant to modern education, equality between the sexes, and other modernizing ideals. The virulence of Shi'ite hostility and anger toward contemporary Bahā'īs cannot be understood without an appreciation of this history. The treatment afforded minorities often becomes the index of morality by which a society may be judged; for Iran and Shi'ism, Bahā'ism is a particularly acute test and mirror of conscience.

In the fifth essay, Islam is explored in a new, quintessentially modern context: Houston, a postmodern city, which has nurtured Islamic fundamentalists for the Middle East as well as provided a haven for refugees from traditionalist worlds. Ritual form, a standard anthropological genre of exposition, is explored once again as a frame that breaks out of itself, but that in so doing explores cleavages, hopes, and anxieties of a major new group in American life. The first part of the chapter continues the style and story of chapter 1, focusing on how persons in a strange environment attempt to (re)create and negotiate the emotionally charged rites of passage of marriage and death. The second part of the chapter is a diary of the communal rites of the month of

Ramaḍān, revealing the crosscurrents of opinions, national styles, sectarian custom, and politics that work beneath the surface of attempts to maintain and create Muslim brotherhood and Islamic unity. An account of 1984 with an eye to the activities of Iranians and the effects of the Iranian revolution, it should not be overly hypostasized as a fixed image of what is a changing and evolving mix of Muslims in such communities generally or in Houston in particular, but it should make readers aware of such crosscurrents of opinion, style, custom and politics.

Finally, chapter 6 attempts to reflect on the themes of intercultural dialogue and transnationally extended discourse systems, using as a vehicle some of the visual graphic arts of the revolution. Anthropologists are increasingly aware that their ways of ethnographic writing are being challenged quite dramatically by the scale and complexity of contemporary social change. Neither local community studies nor nation-state frames, nor static cultural codes nor key symbolic forms are sufficient to capture the contemporary struggles over the nature of global integration, and the modalities of local autonomy and transnational connectivity. One of the "pleasures of the text" in trying to construct new ethnographies concerned with such issues is the interplay of spatial, temporal, and voice or perspectival forms that in earlier texts were handled more simply. The interpretation of the Qur'an, the politics of a modern state, and poetics once were separate domains handled by separate specialists: interesting to set these domains in play with one another. Similarly, Houston and Yazd could not be more different, and yet how many lives overlap both settings and in what different ways: interesting to keep track of what has happened to acquaintances from chapter 1. And, of course, in an international world of oil resources, hostage taking, construction contracts, regional warfare dependent on a global arms market, satellite broadcasting, educational and economic migration, what gets said, and how it gets said, in one world is no longer isolable from what gets said, and how, in other worlds.

The title of the volume, *Debating Muslims,* makes indirect reference to a companion volume, *Iran: From Religious Dispute to Revolution* (Fischer 1980*a*). *Disputation* and *debate* are key words, referring to dialogical and dialectical genres traditional in Muslim life worlds, as well as to renewed interest in them in the ethical literatures of contemporary Europe and America. The earlier volume provides a full account of the Karbala story that provides the paradigm of existential tragedy for the Shi'ite view of the world. While we hope that our references to the Karbala story are sufficient for comprehension in this volume, readers who wish a fuller account should turn to that volume, as should those who would like an account of the Shi'ite seminary system in Qum, the class-linked discourses of Shi'ism in the 1970s, and the revolutionary process. Thus, for instance, while we use the metaphor of "primal scene" for the ḥajj, Karbala provides the Shi'ite frame for recognizing it as a primal scene.[16]

The title of this preface refers to another companion volume, *Anthropology as Cultural Critique: An Experimental Moment in the Human Sciences* (1986), written by Fischer together with George Marcus. The phrase *critical anthropology* which might be the more obvious parallel to *critical theory* (a now widely used term adopted from the "Frankfurt School" of Max Horkheimer and Theodor Adorno) is awkward, suggesting mere criticism, when in fact critique is what is meant, critique moreover that is not one-sided, ex cathedra—either from ethnocentric parochialism or from theoretical prejudgments—but that grows out of juxtaposition of multiple, ethnographically grounded perspectives, a modern version of the comparative method (Fischer 1982*a*, 1977*a*). *Critical hermeneutics* works better, referring both to the unpacking of cultural linguistics and to the creation of a space for critique (Fischer 1988). The lineage of these ideas for Fischer goes back to Weber's ideals of a *verstehendes Soziologie,* as well as the Frankfurt School's *critical theory,* and Eric Fischer's liberalism (chapter 5; E. Fischer 1984), more recently enriched both by Gadamerian and Derridian hermeneutics (Fischer 1986).

Postmodernism, insofar as it is used in these essays, is simply a cover term for three ideas. First, temporally, it focuses attention on late twentieth-century modernism as opposed to earlier modernisms. (Following Jean-Françoise Lyotard's [1979/1984] terminological usage, *postmodernism* is a moment of modernism that defines itself against previous modernisms, thus allowing for cycles of modernism that decay and renew and for a historical consciousness of modernism.) Second, substantively, it invokes the increasing pervasiveness of global interaction, and thus the debates over conflicting moral grounds caught in the shifts from small-scale communities to international networks of migrants and social strata. While what Nietzsche called "weightless" cultural choice, and what now is being called "postmodernist play," affects elites, and while belatedness in all its virulent anxieties and political economic inequities affects the proletarianized masses—think for instance of the global recruitment of labor forces in the Persian Gulf—in both cases, there is an increasing cultural interreference, or cross-cultural reading, or play between hegemonic cultural forces and counterdiscourses of resistance, subversion, and alternative realities. The conflicting moral grounds of globally extended social strata are nowhere more dramatically evident than in the 1989 book burnings, pressures on governments to ban (and publishers to withdraw), and invective against Salman Rushdie's *Satanic Verses,* staged by Muslim fundamentalists in England, South Africa, India, and Pakistan. Third, *postmodernism* refers for us to the centrality of America as the type case of modernity, as a vortex of expansive mature industrial capitalism, consumer-driven market forces, and postindustrial information society. The use of the term *postmodern* does not imply any necessary apolitical, amoral, or acritical stance as alleged by various conservative or marxist critics of "postmodernist" theorists.[17]

A word about the nature of the collaboration(s) this volume represents. The book is written in two "I"s and a bifocal or stereoscopic "we." Just as closing one eye makes the triangulation of two eyes rise to consciousness, so too the two "I's" shift perspective. This at first bothered a reader or two, but upon reflection, some of them agreed it was a better device than hyperreal, but false, omniscience. There are obvious places where the "I's" mark perspective (Abedi's eye in chapter 1, Fischer's in chapter 4), and other places where they mark rather a difference in textu(r)al voice; elsewhere, such markers fade (we hope) into unnoticed stereoscopic coordination. We have worked together on a variety of projects since 1970 when Fischer as a young graduate student in Yazd hired Abedi, still in his late teens, to translate Islamic texts. We helped each other to learn the other's language and culture. What began as Abedi's effort to convert Fischer, and Fischer's use of Abedi's argumentation as an anthropological access into the world of Shi'ism, gradually turned into a deep friendship and genuine set of collaborations. Abedi's autobiography (chapter 1) consists of stories Abedi has shared over the years: some he wrote down at Fischer's urging, some were elicited orally in rich memory laden "bull sessions." We had fun retelling them and shaping a chapter around them, Abedi reminding Fischer about Yazdi places, people, events, and practices. Yazd was home to Fischer for some two years (1969–71), and he helped celebrate the birth of Abedi's first son, Reza, there. In 1975 Fischer spent the academic year in Qum, and Abedi came with wife and child to live with him for three months, and to work as a research assistant on the project that eventuated in the book *Iran: From Religious Dispute to Revolution,* or "The Qum Report" as it was originally called in the form it circulated between 1976 and 1980. In

1981 Abedi came with Fischer to Rice University to pursue a Ph.D. in anthropology, and as we completed this manuscript, we also celebrated the birth of Abedi's second son, Maysam Morad.

The chapter on the Qur'an (chapter 2) in part continues the work of "The Qum Report," as does chapter 3. But it more importantly grows out of a response to interests in the Department of Anthropology at Rice in questions of orality and literacy, representation and evocation, hermeneutics and rhetoric, the visual and the performative (e.g., Tyler 1977, 1988; Biesle and Tyler 1986; Taylor 1982; Clifford and Marcus 1986; Marcus and Fischer 1986; Fischer and Abedi 1984; Maranhão 1987, 1990; Traweek 1988). An abbreviated version of this chapter was prepared for the Maranhão edited volume, *The Interpretation of Dialogue* (1990), © 1990 by the University of Chicago, which helped shape the form of the chapter here. We are grateful to Tullio Maranhão for his stimulation and encouragement, and to the University of Chicago Press for permission to use this material.

The chapter on the Shari'ati-Muṭahhari debates grows out of Abedi's translations of these authors: both Muṭahhari's *Mutual Services of Islam and Iran* and Shari'ati's *Return to Self* should appear shortly in Abedi's English translations under the imprint of the Houston-based Institute for Research and Islamic Studies.

The chapter on the Bahā'īs of Yazd was originally prepared for the Symposium on the Relation of the Bahā'ī Faith and Islam, held at McGill University in March 1984, and eventually will be printed in the proceedings. We are grateful for permission to use the article here.

The chapter on Houston stems from some preliminary ethnographic forays. The section on Ramaḍān is taken from Abedi's M.A. thesis; the sections on funerals and marriages are based on oral and written accounts by Abedi somewhat in the manner of chapter 1. We hope these sketches will encourage others in other American and European cities to provide richer accounts than are presently available. We particularly want to thank Hamid Naficy for allowing us to quote from his unpublished work on Iranian television and video in Los Angeles.

The "Postscriptural Parergon" evolved out of an essay Fischer was drafting on the work of writers and filmmakers from Iran, Pakistan, the Levant, and the Subcontinent who live in Europe and the United States, an essay that was to provide a postmodern contrast and counterpoint to an earlier essay on modernist film and story in the Persian culture area (Fischer 1984). Rushdie was always a reference figure along with James Joyce and Thomas Pynchon for notions of encyclopedic postmodern novels. *Satanic Verses,* published in September 1988, after most of the present volume had been written and submitted for publication, appeared as an astonishing coda to our work, astonishing as much for its Shi'ite nuancings (underscoring the play of difference in Islamic interpretations) as for its detailed use of ḥadīth. The section on Rushdie in the projected essay began to outgrow its subordinate role there. Increasingly, the essays here seemed to provide important background in understanding the furious struggle for political appropriation and interpretation of Rushdie's book; and inversely, the Rushdie literary imagination seemed to complement our own intercultural crossreadings, providing one powerful example of the various sorts of hybridization we see emerging. The present essay was presented at the Center for Psycho-Social Studies in Chicago, and at the Conference on Social Text at the University of Maryland, and first appeared in print in *Cultural Anthropology.* We thank the participants of the two presentation forums for commentary and feedback, and the American Anthropological Association for permission to reprint the essay here.

Hybridization in visual idiom is a vehicle in chapter 6 for demonstrating the forceful contemporary nature of the Iranian revolution. It is not hybridization itself which is the mark of the contemporary period, of course, but the elements and modalities of combination. To illustrate other chapters we have selected not only documentary photographs that register the temporal passages of our own lives, but also paintings from earlier horizons of Islamic civilization that have contributed enduring iconic perceptual frameworks. Among the most striking of such intercultural horizons are, for instance, the wonderful drawings of Socrates and Solon engaged in debate with their students, clad in turban and cloak, adorning al-Mubashshir's *Mukhtār al-Ḥikam wa Maḥāsin al-Kalim* ("Best Maxims and Sayings"), along with various Islamic figures drawn in Byzantine style according to classical Greco-Roman conventions (see Ettinghausen 1962). Equally striking are scenes from early Islam depicted with Mongol or Turkomen characters, as in the illustrations for Rashid al-Din's *Jāmi 'al-Tawārīkh,* that the University of Edinburgh has allowed us to reproduce here: a group of Mongols seated in a circle depicting the Quraish tribesmen debating whether to expel Muhammad from Mecca, or Muhammad and Gabriel depicted with Mongol faces. Again, how refreshing to reconsider Joseph in Egypt depicted in Chinese-Mongol style, or Noah's ark in Indo-Persian miniature style. I would like to thank Glen Lowry of the Sackler and Freer Galleries for helping me locate paintings and contact those who kindly gave permission to reproduce them. I would also like to thank Edward Jajko of the Hoover Institution who told me about the British

World War II posters in the Yale University archives, one of which we have reproduced here.

Most of the manuscript was drafted at Rice during 1987–88; the finishing touches were done by Fischer while at the Woodrow Wilson Center for International Scholars during 1988–89, and he gratefully acknowledges the support and congenial atmosphere of that lovely institution, as well as the help of his assistant there, Kris Palmer, who ran down a number of references in chapter 3 and the Rushdie essay. Fischer is grateful, as well, to Rice University for the leave and financial support during 1988–89 that made the completion of the manuscript possible.

The ideas explored in *Anthropology as Cultural Critique,* as well as those in the present volume, have been evolving in the supportive and nurturing environment of several discussion groups at Rice, now under the umbrella of the Rice Center for Cultural Studies. Fischer would like to thank, in particular, the members of the Rice Circle, the Feminist Reading Group, and the Seminar on Moral Sensibilities in Historical and Cultural Context, for their disputatious, but always incisive, engagement with the cross-cultural provocations toward settled humanistic and social scientific assumptions that anthropologists are charged with testing.

We very much hope this book will be read with pleasure and interest by Iranians, both those in the States and in Iran. While we take a critical stance against fundamentalist Islam, it should be clear that we affirm the richness of Islamic tradition, its cultural, emotional, and intellectual resources. Abedi would like to thank the warm Iranian community in Houston that has served as his extended family for the past seven years.

Finally, we would like to thank the various people who read and commented on the manuscript, especially the readers for the University of Wisconsin Press who identified themselves to us, and whose suggestions (whether or not we adopted them) were extremely welcome and helpful: Edmund Burke III, Valentine Daniels, Stephen Humphries, and Marvin Zonis. Also thanks to those who read and commented on particular chapters: Bruce Grant, Tullio Maranhão, Paul Rabinow, Dennis Schmidt, and Susann Wilkinson (who also provided unwavering love and support through months of husbandly distraction and despair over a manuscript that seemed ever more baroquely, and with a telos of its own, to have no end). A very special word of thanks is due to colleague, friend, chairman, and coauthor George Marcus, for his support, friendly critique, suggestions, and constant encouragement.

Note for Teachers

As indicated above, we hope this book can be of use to classes of several different levels. For undergraduates or those with little background, one might take selections from chapter 1, the opening sections of chapters 2 and 3, the last section of chapter 4, and selections from chapters 5 and 6. One might relabel the table of contents for these purposes in the following three alternative ways:

Chapters	Topics
1, RE-ENTRIES AND HIS-STORIES (Islam for Beginners)	circumcision, purity, marriage, 3 life histories
2, QUR'ANIC DIALOGICS (Hermeneutic Islam)	how to read the Qur'an
3, FEAR OF *DIFFÉRANCE* (Islam as Cultural Shield against Imperialism)	the ḥajj; nationalism and Islam; feminism and Islam; 2 life histories
4, WITNESSING/MARTYRDOM (Schisms and Sects)	Bābīs and Bahā'īs; martyrdom and rhetorics of conversion
5, DIASPORAS (Islam in America)	Ramaḍān; temporary marriage; Islam and Afro-Americans; feminism and Islam
6, AUTOGRAPHICALLY CHANGING IRAN (Art and Revolution)	posters, cartoons, and emblems

Thus one might read the ḥajj section of chapter 3 with some students as a straightforward ritual analysis, without worrying about it being either a cultural shield against imperialism or a scene of *différance*. Alternatively, with other students, one can read the politics of cultural shield without worrying about *différance,* especially in the senses of deferring, displacing, supplementary metonymic chains.

Part 1
Oral Life Worlds

The real revolutionary media during May [1968 in France] were the walls and their speech, silk screen posters and the hand painted notices, the street where speech began and was exchanged—everything that was an immediate inscription given and returned, spoken and answered, mobile in the same space and time, reciprocal and antagonistic. The street is, in this sense, the alternative and subversive form of the mass media . . . the frayed space of the symbolic exchange of speech—ephemeral, mortal. . . .

—Jean Baudrillard, *For a Critique of the Political Economy of the Sign*

. . . in October of 1939 . . . I recall . . . we all, professors and students, as by common consent had trooped out to listen to the loudspeaker set up in the street. It was a speech from Hitler . . . strident, vehement, staccato sentences clanged out and reverberated and chased each other along, series after series, flooding over us, battering us, half drowning us, and yet kept us rooted there listening to a foreign tongue which we somehow could nevertheless imagine that we understood. . . . I have sometimes wondered whether McLuhan as a young man in Toronto at that time would have heard the same speech, shared the same experience. . . . I would hazard the guess that Lévi-Strauss might have listened to those accents on the air. . . . Did he sense then a revival of a mythology of the spoken word? Could one guess that Ian Watt, a prisoner of war in the jungles of Burma . . . would have come under a comparable spell through the camp transmitter. . . .

—Eric Havelock, *The Muse Learns to Write.**

*Hypothesizing a generational experience behind the almost simultaneous publications on orality and literacy by himself (*Preface to Plato*), Marshall McLuhan (*The Gutenberg Galaxy*), Jack Goody and Ian Watt ("The Consequences of Literacy"), and Claude Lévi-Strauss (*The Savage Mind*).

1

Shi'ite Socialization in Pahlavi Iran

Autobiographical Sondages in a Postmodern World

Life histories are often used to chart the characteristic formative experiences of persons in particular cultures: either to focus on stages of the life cycle with its typical phases and events or to document the cultural construction of personhood and the quality of experience in a culture through the deeply probed life of a particular individual or to provide a narrative device for exploring how historical changes in the sociopolitical or political economic structure work themselves out in experiential terms. Normally, life histories are constructed by an investigator out of interview, documentary, and commentary materials; and recently, there has been a growing sophistication in cross-cultural contexts of the degree to which native idioms, concepts, genres of discourse are incorporated, as well as of the degree to which attention is paid to the assumptions of the investigator's own culture in the composition of the final written life history. Autobiographies constitute a subclass of life histories: usually they are written to pass on to the next generation memories of the past. Some are didactic, carefully structured as moral exemplars for the next generation; others are more like a Bildungsroman, meant for self-clarification of the ways in which moral consciousness evolves both through personal growth and through changes in historical circumstances; still others, of course, are primarily chronological efforts to define a sense of identity and place in the world. For readers, autobiographies are often rich historical documents of times past, providing not merely personalized accounts of how events were effected by individuals but, at their best, insight into how people thought and felt. In contemporary autobiographies, readers increasingly desire a rich account of interiority.

The autobiography that follows is unique and somewhat experimen-

Fig. 1.1. Yazd: Friday Mosque, Vaziri Library to the left. Photo by M. Fischer.

tal in several ways, although it attempts to perform several of the functions listed above. First of all, it is an account of a life of unusual range: a childhood in an Iranian village, where literacy was restricted and folklorically elaborated religiosity was not; a youth in a provincial city known both for its industriousness (Iran's second most important textile center, with industrial mills as well as traditional looms) and for its conservative religiosity, one of those crucibles of conflict between ideologies of modernization and defense of Islam that would generate the Islamic Revolution of 1979; a somewhat postponed final high school year in Tehran amid the debates of marxists and islamists; a college education in Kansas and graduate work in Houston amid the worlds of exiles and Americans. It is a Bildungsroman, if one likes, of transition from a fundamentalist to a cosmopolitan consciousness, by an individual whose experiential strata cross class as well as cultural boundaries and who thereby has access to multiple worlds of interpretive nuance, and who therefore has been able to serve exiles of various sorts in their dilemmas of readjustment.

Second, it is written as an ethnographic document of worlds that are barely, if at all, accessible in books. Indeed, as the folklorist, historian, and librarian Iraj Afshar one day in Yazd jokingly but quite seriously commented to an American geography graduate student for whom Abedi was translating a local history, collecting marketing data, and serving as a translator, cultural broker and protector from mishap: the real book is to be found in such bright young boys, not in texts. For that world was—and to a large extent remains—an oral life world. It is thus experimental in trying to combine into a meaningful mosaic, in one volume, autobiographical recall, scholarly exposition, and dialogic participant observation.

Third, insofar as this chapter and the volume as a whole may become part of Iranian scholarship, autobiography is itself a relatively novel genre.[1] Writing life histories, traditionally, has been both rare and didactic, apart from the restricted entries of the *rijāl* literature (noting birthplace, parentage, teachers, and perhaps scholarly trips in search of manuscripts) used as part of the critical apparatus in knowing what sources in the ḥadīth literature to trust. Inevitably, this chapter is not as rich as it could be; for posed as setting, it has no clear bounds: it could be expanded to incorporate all of Abedi's knowledge, including (importantly) the contexts in which materials from books are received by their readerships. For the moment, however, the task is to provide one life as an "archeological" sondage back into the strata of the life worlds of provincial Iran of the 1950s, '60s, and '70s. The bracketed annotation is meant to highlight analytic themes, especially those which will be taken up in subsequent chapters. The intent of this chapter is to set up resonances from the lived-in world of contemporary experience to bring to life the worlds of scholarship familiar from texts.

Scenes of a Village Childhood

[Villages are all too often thought of as communal pieces of time immemorial. Villages on the Iranian plateau, however, all have histories, often traceable in the histories of the digging of irrigation systems by governors, merchants, landowners, and others.[2] There is movement, historically, in and out of villages, bad times and good. Hill villages often serve as summer retreats for the better-off urban folk, and cities as places to make money for villagers who come and go. Upstream (or at the top of the irrigation system) is where the better-off folk live.

In the oral life world, information comes with linguistic markers of relative reliability. There is a rhythm of attribution to witnesses. Documents are often suspect as being eminently forgeable and alterable, and so themselves are witnessed with seals around their margins. (These issues of the oral having priority over the written will be taken up further in chapter 2.) Experience, on the other hand, tends to be shared knowledge encapsulated in stories that everyone can recognize. The situation is the reverse of the world of declining shared experience where novels and autobiographies attempt to rebuild experience as information, and where information is replicable. The following autobiography stands between the two worlds.

Villages, interestingly, have a way of etching characters. Experience may be shared, knowledge may be limited, but role and personality take on a heightened salience, and become part of a familial homespun commentary and anecdotal philosophy. Such familial language is a basic stratum in Iranian contemporary existence, providing a backdrop and warming contrast to more sophisticated strata of bureaucratic, professional, or mercantile life. A richness of familial language provides a basis for much literature and film, a characteristic of the phase before cosmopolitan modernism and postmodernism take hold: modernism in this sense (say, Ibsen, Becket, or Ionesco) is easily translatable (who would read Norwegian or Gaelic or Romanian seemed to be the question); while postmodernism in this sense (say Joyce, Pynchon, or Rushdie) is intercultural (encompassing multiple languages and perspectives).[3] The richness of the early modernizing phase registered in idiom and nuances of familial language causes members of such cultures to despair or romantically celebrate that their literature and life worlds are not really translatable. But see for instance the accounts of the Iranian films *Āghā-ye Hālu, Doroshkeh-chī,* and *Gāv* in Fischer (1984).]

Place and Character: The Folkloric Life World

Dareh ("valley") is the name of the little village in which I was born. In the legal documents it is called Dareh-e Miyankuh (Dareh of the middle mountains). It is a poor hill village in a narrow valley of the middle ranges of the Shirkuh mountains, above the basin plain on which sit the larger villages Mehriz and Manshad, to the south of the city of Yazd in central Iran. Not even many Yazdis have heard of it: from Yazd you take the road to Kirman as far as the Abdul Malik Coffee House, then turn right onto a gravel road past Mehriz toward the mountains, and when you come to a branch in the road, you can see the bottom of the village. Villagers distinguish three neighborhoods or *maḥalleh:* upper, lower, and middle. We lived in the middle.

The people of the village tell stories about the good past, the days when water was plenty, much wheat and barley was produced, melons were grown, and everyone was happy. By the time I was old enough to know the village, it was extremely poor, and more than a third of its population had left to work in Yazd or Tehran. (A village near Tehran, Hassanabad, was largely populated by people from Dareh.) Its primary produce was dried mulberries. My memories are of famine conditions of the postwar and post-Mossadeq period, when children were told to fill their bellies by foraging for berries (*angūr-e kūhi* and *panīrok*).[4] American wheat was sent, but it was often spoiled and uncleaned.

Among the spiritual or religious features of the village were, beginning in the lower neighborhood: the *ḥusaynieh* (arena for the passion plays on 'Āshūra),[5] the graveyard and a hyena's grave for curing sick animals, a mosque and public bath house, and on the hillside behind the bath house a rock formation that was said to be an imprint of the sword of Imām Ali. In the middle neighborhood, there was a somewhat holy tree, in our yard. In the upper village, there was a second mosque and a older holy tree. Above the village was a cave where the Imāms were said to have left their footprints (*qadamgāh*) and a mountain ridge in the shape of a camel led by a man and pushed by another. All these sites were visual reminders of moral lessons. The camel shape of the mountain went with the legend that during a time of drought and famine, two villagers decided to declare war on God, and so they set out with their camels to reach the highest point so they could talk to God. God turned them to stone, and so they remain as a constant warning to people against blasphemy; big brother brooks no revolt. Similarly, the sword of Ali was a warning against those who express animosity toward the first Imām: the story was that an enemy had tried to ambush Ali; Ali drew his sword, it hit the mountain, Ali killed the enemy, and the print of the sword remains on the mountain as a warning sign to all enemies. People often kissed the sword, as they did a nearby "camel footprint" which was said to be of the camel of the fourth Imām (associated with the sick). The hyena grave (*qabr-e kaftār*), at the desert's edge, was used for animals as saints' tombs (*imāmzādeh*s) were for humans: when animals fell sick they were circumambulated seven times[6] around this grave, and sacrifices, offerings, and vows were made.

The bathhouse was used both for cleanliness and for ritual purity: menfolk used it before dawn, womenfolk afterwards. Menfolk were less concerned with bathing, and more that they be ritually pure before going off to the fields. Womenfolk enjoyed spending time in the bath house socializing and picnicking. But the bathhouse was also associated with jinn, perhaps through an association with moisture, and so one was never supposed to go there alone. Jinn were said to attack neither those who were totally fearless nor those who were extremely timorous, but only the majority in between. They did not attack the timorous lest they have heart attacks and die; all jinn in this village were Muslims and did not want to have the blood of anyone charged to them; and they feared the totally fearless lest they be seized and have their necks wrung. There was a woman, Zan-e Ḥajji Daqqāq (Wife of Ḥajji the Cloth Finisher), who lived between the *ḥusaynieh* and the mosque who was possessed by jinn and who served as an example to all of what might happen if you failed to exercise caution (*parhīz*). She was constantly talking to the jinn, screaming at them, cursing them, calling on Hazrat-e Abbas to get them to leave her alone. Her sons had to lock her in when they left for the fields. She must have done something to a jinn. And so she was a living reminder that whenever you pushed a stone down a hillside, as kids loved to do, or whenever you threw out hot water, or even whenever you stepped somewhere, you should first call out to warn any invisible jinn in the way: *bismillāh-i rraḥmān-i rraḥīm,* or *parhīz o bismillāh-i rraḥmān-i rraḥīm,* or just *parhīz* ("beware"). If you did get tormented by a jinn, a *jin-gīr* (jinn catcher) would come to divine its name.

The holy tree in our yard had a story that I helped produce. People believed that trees have senses and understanding, so that one could talk to them. If a fruit tree stopped bearing, if one had tried fertilizers and transplanting and nothing else seemed to work, one might try a ritual called *bebor-nabor* ("cut, don't cut"). One placed a saw at its base, and one person pretended to begin cutting it down. A second person would then plead for the tree: "What are you doing, don't you realize this is an apple tree?" First person: "You mean it looks like an apple?" "No, it gives apples" (thus suggesting to the tree its duties). First person: "Why then does it not give apples, looks like a simple plane tree to me." Second person: "Please, I beg you, give it one more year, and I guarantee it will bring forth fruit." We had a tall apple tree in our yard that gave pleasant shade but no fruit. My brother was working in Tehran and had promised to bring us some special black cherry seedlings. My father decided to cut down the apple tree to make room for the new seedlings, but for some reason I jumped at him and began a kind of *bebor-nabor* dialogue with him, and Amū Ali, the village *muezzen* (caller to prayer) joined me. My father relented. Sometime later I happened to kill a snake in the mountain, and I buried it at the base of the tree because snakes were thought to be excellent fertilizer; and I would whisper to the tree: "Please, I want to be proud of you, do your duty and bear fruit." Miraculously, the next year the tree produced an overabundance of apples, but the following winter, as if exhausted by its effort, it died, and did not sprout again in the spring.

Near the mosque in the upper neighborhood there was an ancient plane tree that was even more venerable. Someone on an 'Āshūrā day had said he had seen it bleeding in sympathy with the martyrdom of Husain. And so people believed that if you attempted to cut its branches, especially on 'Āshūrā, something terrible would befall you.

[Such folklore provides the weft in the rich anecdotal tapestry of the village's sense of itself: both its sense of place and its social composition through the lives of its highly individualistic characters. It is a humane tapestry viewed with much humor, as well as suspended judgment: only God knows what is possible; and in a materially hard world, folkloric elaboration provides humane comfort and endless material for storytelling sociability. A few characters may serve to illustrate.]

At the top of the upper village lived a wealthy ḥajji and usurer (*nozūl-khor*), who had connections with both the police and the clergy. (Ayatullah Ṣadūqi of Yazd used to stay at his house.) One day a truck delivered a bag of melons for him; the driver called out to Ḥajji that he was dropping off the purchase, and left. I and some other boys stole the largest melon on top. When Ḥajji discovered his loss, he cursed us and our parents at the top of his lungs. We waited until very late to return home, hoping our parents would be too tired to beat us. They weren't. We were beaten soundly enough so that our cries wafted through the village to Ḥajji. The next day we planned revenge on Ḥajji. We decided to stone his windows. Ḥajji's house was the only one that had glass windows. We did not realize that when the lights were on he could not see out, so we waited until he turned out the lights before throwing stones. When the lights came on we stopped. Ḥajji's house was the highest up the mountain slope, so we simply climbed above it to throw stones. Ḥajji could not figure out what was going on: somehow he did not think it was us. Instead he yelled at his two wives that the one of them who was a *ṣīgheh* (limited term wife) had thrown hot water carelessly on the heads of the jinn, and he read out the prayer against the jinn. He then called a diviner. We were afraid the diviner would discover us, and I was very close to confessing to my mother, but fortunately I held back, figuring there would be time if he actually knew. The diviner, however, concluded it must indeed be the jinn, and that the house was haunted. As a result, Ḥajji almost sold his house and moved to town. It was not until years later that I told my father what had happened, and was surprised to learn that none of the boys had told their parents.

Among the other characters of the village, there was, first of all, Hasan Kadkhodā, the headman, with his pipe and handmade tobacco pouch. He used to be the servant to the previous *kadkhodā,* Ḥajji Mirzā Āghā, I was told. By comparison, it was always pointed out, he was a "nobody." Ḥajji Mirzā Āghā had had fourteen wives and many sons. Being a large landowner, he needed cheap labor. Instead of hiring labor, he married many women, mostly widows, who were happy to be assured daily bread. Hasan Kadkhodā had only one wife, and she had only one eye. She was a bitch, and we children were terrified of her loud mouth.

Then there was Robābeh, the midwife. She was about seventy, and lived with an unmarried daughter who had been blinded by smallpox in childhood. Robābeh was the female healer of the village, curing with herbs. She also baked the most delicious bread. She had a saintly reputation for her piety, her healing, her religious knowledge, and for helping bring so many babies into the world. She herself was also the mother of several men of solid reputation.

There was also Maryam, the female washer of the dead. She was even older than Robābeh. Most children feared her because of her occupation, but I was used to her since she visited our house frequently. My mother liked her, and my father would tease her by asking her to be his concubine. She was always murmuring prayers, and there were stories about the times God had answered her prayers immediately. Before falling asleep at night, I was told, she repeated the principles of her religion (*oṣūl-e dīn*) and the names of the Imāms, so that should she die while asleep the answers for the questions of the angels of death would be ready.[7] Whenever there was a drought, people would ask her to pray for rain. I once asked how she did it, and my father suggested that we kids go with her up the mountain to the cave where the Imams had left their footprints. So one day, two of my sisters and I went with her. This pilgrimage (*ziyārat*) was my first "long trip." Since it was the middle of summer, I knew that Maryam could not ask for rain: there are proper times for asking things of God. But at the cave Maryam began to shout and cry. As her voice echoed in the mountains, I experienced a mixture of fear, excitement, joy, and awe. We then entered the cave: there was a puddle of water and some birds flying about. Maryam said the birds were messengers of God. We sat down for a meal, and departed before sunset. My father admired Maryam and would say she was worth more than several men. He would frequently tell the story of the year Muḥarram fell in wintertime and he tried to cancel the annual passion play, which he supervised, because of the snow. Maryam objected, saying snow was a blessing, and if we abandoned the religious activities of Muḥarram, next year there would be no snow, and hence also no water in the spring for irrigation. She took a shovel in hand and shamed the menfolk into helping her clear the village for one of the best Muḥarram *ta'ziehs* (mourning rites) ever held.

Ali Dallāk, the barber, shaved the men, pulled bad teeth with his pliers, and ran the village bathhouse. During his military service he had learned to read and write, and so was something of a religious authority. He circumcised all my age mates. I was circumcised when I was two. I remember he came to me, calling me *'amū* (reciprocal for paternal uncle and nephew): "Come here, let me see your little dodo and how it has grown." Then snip with a razor. I was so scared I pissed on him. I was then handed over to a woman. My mother was not there, but my father was. There was no ceremony, and certainly no talk of being a man. Children were not supposed to know about sex. The foreskin is supposed to go to an unmarried woman, who grinds it up in a mortar and pestle and eats it to help her catch a husband. Ali Dallak also was the one who cut off the tumor that grew on my face, after various horrible poultices of folk remedies had been put on it. This must have been when I was four. (Folk remedies were often not pleasant. I got whooping cough so bad it gave me a hernia, and a neighbor woman told my mother to give me some *torbat,* the earth from Karbala, to eat. This frightened me, because I had heard the dying were given *torbat,* as a final medicine. But I knew I was not going to die: only other people die, I thought.)

And of course there was my father, who always bragged about his calligraphy, his ability to understand religious issues, and his ability to cure illnesses with talismans. If a girl could not find a husband, if a woman's husband no longer liked her and wanted another wife, for any ill, my father had the book of talismans and prayers. He was the male healer for the village, combining herbs, powders, liquids, and tablets, as well as talismans and prayers. For curing, in most cases, he did not charge. He had a shop in which he also sharpened knives, sickles, and saws, repaired broken china and stone cooking pots. For this he was paid by the villagers in kind: eggs, yoghurt, dried nuts, and other agricultural products. Even peddlers from outside the village often took payment for their wares in kind.

My father was also the supervisor of the passion plays for some forty years, and people would gather at our house from both the upper and lower village on 'Āshūrā. From there a grand procession of floats and *dasteh sīneh-zanī* (flagellants, mainly boys and young men) would go to the ḥusaynieh down at the bottom of the lower neighborhood.[8]

For two months before 'Āshūrā (the tenth of the month of Muḥar-

Fig. 1.2. Yazd: Mir Chaqmaq reviewing stands for Muḥarram processions, with an undecorated *naql* used until 1936, when Reza Shah banned processions in the city, after which major processions moved to such large villages as Meybod, Zarch, and Ardekan. Photo by M. Fischer.

ram, the day of the martyrdom of the third Imām, Husain, on the plains of Karbala) my father would prepare, collecting clothing for costumes, carpets and props for the floats, and reserving particular horses to be ridden. Many items were stored at our house, endowed by the villagers for the passion plays. But no one would refuse a request to lend a fine carpet or *chādor* (veil) or animal: the villagers firmly believed that ill would befall anyone who did not participate in the 'Āshūrā events. The best horse in the village was reserved for Shemr, the evil general of the Sunni Syrian army, because he had to be able to catch Husain. The second best horse was reserved for Ali Akbar, the elder son of Husain, because it took time for Shemr to catch him; and traditionally Ali Akbar would fall from his horse so that he could be caught by the aging Shemr. The laziest horse in the village was used to carry the fourth Imam, the only male who survived the massacre at Karbala because he was sick and did not fight. For a month or so, my father would supervise rehearsals of the chief actors. Shemr had to be tall and have a loud voice with which to frighten people; he was dressed from head to toe in red. When he was available (because he lived in the city), Shemr would be played by my eldest sister's husband's brother, because he had blue eyes (as Shemr is said to have had). Else Shemr was played by my eldest sister's husband. Husain had to be a man in his forties with a full beard. Imam Sajjad, the fourth Imām, was played by a sick old man, in many villages an opium addict. In our village there were no opium addicts—almost no one was rich enough to support an opium habit—so he was played by a man addicted to a *qalyūn* (hubbly bubbly using a potent form of tobacco).

There were only so many lead roles. Most men participated as porters for the heavy floats. In other villages, floats might be carried by trucks, but our village was too steep and narrow. Some twenty floats might be made illustrating all the events of the ten days leading up to 'Āshūrā and the days immediately following, when the women and children were taken off as prisoners to Damascus. Other men were in the black-shirted lines of men beating their breasts with hands or chains and chanting rhythmic dirges mourning the fate of Husain; they all wore Arab kifayas (*chofiya*) or headbands (*'aqqāl*). Only the sick and disabled stood on the sidelines with the women and girls.

For several years, beginning when I was four or five, I played the barely nubile bride of Qasem (the son of Hasan, the second Imām, who wedded the daughter of Imām Husain just before entering combat and giving his life to the cause of Husain). I was given this role partly no doubt because I was the son of the producer of the show, and partly

Fig. 1.3. 'Āshūrā, Yazd: people gather outside town like the armies at Karbala.

as a reward for (or out of my father's pride in) my already being able to recite the Qur'an; also perhaps because I was part city boy, cleaner, better dressed, and better behaved than other village boys in torn clothes, a boy who might be trusted not to blow his nose in the finest silk chādor reserved for the wife of Qasem. The role was intended to make especially the young girls cry, identifying with the tragic fate of this young widow. I had little white sugar balls (*noql*) to hand out, received as blessed sweets. In second grade, I finally refused to play a woman any longer. What triggered the refusal I no longer exactly remember, but I remember bursting into angry tears at either being pinched, winked at, or obscenely teased as if I were a girl.

Such teasing and humor had a regular place: the man who played Zeinab (sister of Husain, who led the women and children after the massacre until the sickly fourth Imām could assume his leadership role) always had a big mustache, and when someone would make a rude comment to him, he would show his mustache from under his chādor. Typically, he had an obscene tongue as well, and would respond to propositioning with such retorts as, "Yes, I'll sleep with you; bring your mother too." There was less humor of this kind during the actual passion plays than I sometimes saw in the city, but afterwards there would be a lot of ribald mockery of the *ta'zieh* ("mourning," passion plays). Shemr and Zeinab would replay their repartee from the passion play in obscene

Fig. 1.4. 'Āshūrā, Yazd: partially decorated *naql* (bier of Husayn). Photo by M. Fischer.

variations, e.g., Shemr: *Agar to Zeinab-i, pas doldolat chīst?* (If you are Zeinab, then what's that penis?) Zeinab: *Khodā dānad ke īn gūsht-e ziādīst.* (God knows it is an extra piece of meat.) And indeed some of the acting could stick to the actor: thus someone named Mahmad who played the role of Shemr might come to be called Mahmad Shemr, even if it caused him to bristle and see red.

Once the procession of floats reached the lower village, it would enter the husainiyeh and circumambulate counterclockwise around the *klak,* a large platform for fire or light. The men were the actors on the husainiyeh floor, while the women sat on the walls (*ghurfeh,* "reviewing stand"). Shemr would gallop into the center calling for Husain to show himself, and announcing to the audience, "I'm not Shemr, nor is this the land of Karbala; I'm just playing the role." This formula was partly used to fend off the danger that the onlookers would become so enraged at his killing of their beloved Imām that they would kill him ("in some villages," goes the archetypical Iranian comment, "people actually killed the person playing Shemr"). Partly, the formula was to allow Shemr to shed tears, to empty himself as it were, so that he could then take on the hardhearted role. Then Husain would enter, crying to the people, "Is there no one to help me?" Ali Akbar would then gallop in, dressed in a white shroud stained with blood and sewn with the arrows

Fig. 1.5. 'Āshūrā, Meybod-e Yazd: *dasteh* of young men flagellating with chains.

Fig. 1.6. Āshūrā, Meybod-e Yazd: passion play in *husainiya,* showing the good Christian monk (with umbrella, often done humorously as a tourist in pith helmet with sunglasses, camera and binoculars) amazed at Husain's severed head reciting the Qur'an.

that had penetrated his body; he always was played by someone of draft age, and was the heartthrob of the girls.

The time frame of the passion play was in fact mythic, rather than chronological, for, of course, all the events were presented on the floats simultaneously prior to and during the theatrical action in the center of the husainiyeh. Thus the head of Husain was already on a pole, and the good Christian who attempted to intercede on Husain's behalf was seated on a chair, dressed in safari khaki shirt and shorts, pith helmet, with binoculars, watching the events. The climax of the play came first with Shemr killing Ali Akbar: the lad would fall off his horse and roll in the dust as Shemr cut off his head, while Husain stood by and cried or pretended to cry. (Both actual tears and pretense at tears on the part of contemporary believers has merit, *savāb.*) And then Shemr would kill Husain, at which point everyone would rush into the middle, beating their heads in grief.

Afterwards, people rushed to eat the blessed wheat stews (*āsh-e gandom*) that were cooked in massive caldrons. These communal meals were supplied either from perpetual endowments, from vows made during the year, or by richer villagers.[9] They usually contained meat of a freshly slaughtered lamb. I remember with amusement scenes of people eating stew communally off big trays, jockeying to make sure they were sitting next to someone relatively clean with whom to share their dipping.

Such communal meals were also important during the month of Ramaḍān (the month of fasting from dawn to dusk). The month was known as the month of God, a time when there was double merit for good deeds, when the rich paid their debts to God by cooking caldrons of stew to distribute, sharing the meat of a slaughtered lamb, and sending gifts of dry provisions (e.g., rice) to their neighbors. My father's father served in his day as the village timekeeper: he was one of the first in the village to have a pocket watch, and just before dawn he would sing hymns of praise to the first Imām (*monājat*) to waken people. Traditionally, villagers would start their fast with the rooster's crow. (Any rooster with an untimely crow was a bad omen and had its throat cut.) The first pocket watches did not change things much, since people could tell time only when the two hands came together at noon and midnight. Thus, watches were called *zohr kūk* and *ghorūb-kūk* (noon winding, midnight winding). Just before dawn my father's father would sing out the formula, "*Ābast o teriāk*" (only time for a "sip of water and a pull of opium"). It is said that my father's father (he died before I was born) would often substitute the phrase, "*Kāseyé tūt-e khōshk o kūzeh āb*" ("only time for a bowl of dried mulberries [the main produce of our village] and a jug of water"). And then he would conclude, "*Tanbal khānā yā allāh*" ("get up you lazy bums"). After he died, this role was taken over first by 'Amū Ali (Uncle Ali), of whom it is said, the first time he saw a radio, he recited the *shahāda,* the credo of Islam, and in mock surprise exclaimed, "So here is the proof of what the preachers say, that at the end of time people can hear each other no matter what the distance." (Radios were enormously popular, and after the first one came to the village, everyone else immediately had to have one, although the mullās, perhaps fearing competition, said that radios caused drought, illness, and poverty.) Then Akbar-i e Ramazan took over the role of calling people to the fast: he eventually became the father-in-law of my father, when my father took a second wife after the death of my mother.

Villagers took the fast of Ramaḍān quite seriously, and I remember that my mother, when we lived in the city, worried about their poverty and nutrition and would send tea and sugar to the village.

On Genealogy, Naming, and the Judaicizing Anxiety

My mother was a city girl, the daughter of Gholām-Husain Vāsel, a shopkeeper, sufi, *zur khāneh* (traditional gymnasium) master, popular storyteller, wit, and interpreter of Rumi's *Masnavī* (the great thirteenth-century mystical poem in Persian that many Muslims call "the Persian Qur'an").[10] He had married the daughter of a rich merchant, Ḥajji Muhammad Karīm Esfahāni, who had come to Yazd from Isfahan. Ḥajji Muhammad Karīm's wife was Maryam, and her father was Yūsuf Āghāii, a Jewish rabbi who had converted to Islam in a striking episode.[11] My mother would often say, "The children of Yūsuf Āghāii are scattered throughout the world; but we do not know very many of them." What she meant was that children of converts assimilate among Muslims without leaving much trace, but they carry a certain kind of character legacy.

Several other morality plots also interlace in her invocations of my great great grandfather. But let me first tell the story of Yūsuf Āghāii's conversion. As you know, Jews were not allowed into the produce bazaar during the day, but only at the end of the day. Being *najes* (carriers of pollution), they could not touch the produce lest it be declared polluted. To ensure that Muslims got first pick as well as religiously pure food, Jews had to wait until the end of the day to shop. Yūsuf Āghāii at the end of one day went to buy some yoghurt. He dipped his finger in it to see if it was still good, and rejected it as sour. The shopkeeper raised a ruckus, crying that Yūsuf had defiled the entire container of yoghurt. A crowd gathered and started to turn ugly. Yūsuf, in an effort to escape, said, "I may be as good a Muslim as you." The shopkeeper retorted, "Let us go to the *mujtahid* (expert in the law) and see." So the crowd took Yūsuf to the *mujtahid* who publicly forced him to eat some yoghurt and meat together, thereby violating Jewish dietary rules. It is said that thereafter the Jews rejected him, but that his father, also a rabbi, asked to be allowed to name Yūsuf's first child: it was a girl, and the name chosen was Maryam. Now Yūsuf had studied both Hebrew and Arabic in Jerusalem, and so, it is said, when he became Muslim he did not need to study any Islamic jurisprudence: he knew it all, and was as learned as any *mujtahid.*

[The anecdote illustrates a very interesting anxiety reflected throughout Islamic literature about the jurisprudential competence and influence of Jewish converts to Islam. The anxiety begins already with accounts of early Islam and the influence on the compilation of ḥadīth and rules of interpretation of the Jewish convert Ka'b al-Aḥbār,[12] and of Wahb ibn Munabbih. The latter was a particularly important conveyer of *Isra'iliyyat* (i.e., Jewish) traditions into early Islam. Well versed in Hebrew, the Torah, Psalms, and Talmud, he himself was a Yemeni, originally either of Jewish (some traditions identify him only as *ahl-e kitāb,* of the "People of the Book," i.e., Jewish or Christian) or of Persian descent (some accounts call him an *abnā,* i.e., descended from troops sent to Yemen by the Sassanian shah, Khosrow Anushiravan [Duri 1983]). But the anxiety continues in the texts of the contemporary Mortadā Muṭahhari regarding also such key figures as the philosophers Abu al-Barakāt Baghdādi or Rāzi and Isḥāq ibn Ya'qūb al-Kindi; the first compiler of Qur'anic recitation styles, Hārūn ibn Mūsa; and even the father of Qur'anic exegesis Ibn 'Abbās because of his title "Ḥibr al-Umma." Muṭahhari wants to prove they all were not only Muslim but Shi'ite (see chapter 3). Jews as omnipresent cultural "others" and predecessors are widespread also elsewhere in Muslim oral life worlds: for Upper Egypt, see Slyomovics (1987: 48, 62).]

My mother, moreover, would say that once a Zoroastrian or a Christian converted to Islam, that was that; but when a Jew converted there was always danger of reverting back for up to seven generations.

One day when I came home as a child, very upset that I was not a sayyed (descendant of the Prophet, entitled to wear a green or black turban), she consoled me by saying that we were another kind of sayyid, that through Yūsuf Āghāii we were descended from Hārūn (Aaron), the brother of Moses, and that this could be seen in our entire family's gift of gab and rhetorical flair. Hārūn, of course, was known for his silver tongue, and the story is well known[13] that when the baby Moses was brought to Pharaoh, Pharaoh tested him by placing before the child some dates and some red hot coals. The diviners had suggested that if it were just an ordinary child it would be attracted to the bright red objects, but if this were the future prophet it would know better and take a date. The child in fact began to reach for the date, but the angel Gabriel took its hand and caused Moses to pick up the coal and put it on his tongue. Hence Moses stuttered, and when he went to plead his people's case before Pharaoh, he asked God to make Hārūn his vizier and spokesman. And so, the majority of Jews are relatively quiet types, but the descendants of Aaron are loquacious and persuasive. And hence, "the children of Yūsuf Āghāii [Jewish converts] are scattered throughout the world, but we do not recognize them as such."

Jews, of course, were ambivalent figures in my mother's discourse: she would use Yūsuf Āghāii both as reproof when she scolded me and as explanation when I did something intelligent. In the negative vein, she used to cite the popular ḥadīth, *al balā li al-awliā* ("catastrophe/sadness befalls only friends of God"), identifying Jews as not friends of God:[14] when Jews raised their faces to God, the angels would immediately demand that God grant their wishes so that the stench of the Jews would disappear; but when the faithful prayed, the angels would tell God to delay granting their wishes so that they might look longer on their faces. Thus it was often repeated that Fatima, the daughter of the Prophet, had to wait eighteen years for her wish (the death of the caliph Umar) to be granted.

My mother had a similar discourse about Zoroastrians,[15] albeit one less complicated by negative elements. When we moved to Yazd, we lived in Pir-e Borj neighborhood near some coppersmiths who made the distinctive tinned copper *mashraba* water pitchers used by Zoroastrians. And so I would see Zoroastrians go by, dressed in their distinctive pyjamas with elastic at the ankles, and the women with the colorful red and green *maqna'a* headcloths instead of somber black chādor veils. My mother explained that people called them *gowr* or *gabr,* but that they did not like these names; that they respected fire and had fire temples as we had mosques; and that they were relatives of Imām Husain, because the daughter of the last Zoroastrian emperor of pre-Islamic Iran, Yazdegird III, had married Imām Husain.[16] She said, one could often see Zoroastrians crying outside the Muslim mourning memorials on 'Āshūrā, because Husain was their son-in-law. All our ancestors, she would say, were *gabr.* Although there were no Zoroastrians in our village, my *pesar 'ammeh* (father's sister's son) who married my elder sister (and played Shemr in the village passion play) also thought well of the Zoroastrians, and would go from the village to their mountain shrine, Pīr-e Nāraki (see Fischer 1973, section 5.3.6 and pp. 213–14) to work for them on their annual pilgrimage (*ziyārat*), doing butchering, selling fruit, and helping set up. School books also stressed the Zoroastrian heritage of pre-Islamic Iran, and as a child, I did not feel any particular contradiction between pride in that heritage and Islam. (On my father's side, I am Mehdi, son of Mahmud, son of Gholam-Husein, son of Ahmad, son of Reza, son of Ḥajji Ahmad, son of Rustam, a Zoroastrian.) Zoroastrians in general had a reputation for honesty and charity, in sharp contrast to Muslims and Jews. There is a famous story in Yazd that one Ramaḍān, only two persons sighted the moon, signaling the end of the fasting, a Muslim and a Zoroastrian. Two reliable witnesses are required, and non-Muslims normally do not count as a full witness. People went to Ḥajji Agha Lab-i Khandaqi, a mujtahid of the Modaressi family, and he said to bring the Zoroastrian. He asked him, "What is the color of the inside of your skullcap?" and the man took it off to look at it before answering, "Red." Ḥajji Agha said his witnessing of the moon could be accepted.

My mother's father, Gholām-Husain Vāsel, must have been a prosperous young man to have married the only daughter of Ḥajji Muhammad-Karīm, but he was, particularly in my mother's stories, a sufi in the true sense, spending all he had, and not valuing the material world. Originally, he was a *māzār* (a processor of henna). He owned a factory and helped others to establish similar factories in Yazd and Ardakan. [Yazd is still known as a center of henna processing. The raw material comes from farther east in Kirman province.] He had traveled a great deal, and composed an epic poem about his adventures, which ended:

> Abul Qasem [his son] sits like a mouse
> Creditors raise hell:
> One claps his forehead;
> Another beats his breast
> Most upset of all is the broker.

Indeed, Gholām-Husain had to sell the business to pay off his debts. He later bought a small grocery; it caught fire and burned down one night. The way my mother used to tell the story, at dawn a neighbor came to her father to break the news about the fire. Bad news is never conveyed directly; one breaks it slowly lest the sudden shock cause the blood to boil (*jūsh kardan*) and overwhelm the addressee's ability to cope. *Jūsh kardan* can kill a person, especially if the shock comes while eating something acid, something made with vinegar, or when the bodily humors are skewed in a particular way. So the man said to my grandfather, "You forgot to lock your shop." To which my grandfather responded, "A shop that has burned down needs no lock."[17] The way the story is told hints at a double meaning: my mother meant to illustrate that her father was detached from the cares of the world; more mystical listeners often were amused by the hint that he had knowledge from the unseen.

There is a second story about a fire and my grandfather. He went blind toward the end of his life. He lived alone, some five minutes from my parents. It was winter, and he was warming himself under a *korsi,* the traditional heating device: a brazier is placed under a low table, over which there are quilts; one sits with one's legs under the quilts. He lit a cigarette, and a few minutes later smelled something burning. He felt around for the fire under the quilts and could not find the fire. By the time he located it, he could not get it put out. So he left the house, hoping someone would come and help. But it was late, and the alleys remained empty. There he sat until morning, when my father on his way to the mosque, smelled the burned house. He ran back to my mother: "Your crazy father has let his house burn down." When my mother asked her father, "Why didn't you come and let us know?" he replied, "The house was not worth the shock (*jūsh kardan*) of waking up a human being." Again, my mother's story was intended to illustrate his equanimity, his detachment from things of this world.

For the last fourteen years of his life, he was blind, and he died destitute. He seemed not to mind: the world was but a passage to the real life. But I think it was after the death of his young wife that he lost interest in the world. He raised his son and three daughters with great difficulty, managing to educate them and marry them, albeit none lived up to his mark. His son, Abul Qasem, a tailor, married the daughter of a mulla, but had no offspring. His youngest daughter, Khojasteh, married a coppersmith, and had three sons and a daughter, all of whom are educated and relatively prosperous. The eldest daughter, Marziyeh, married a sugar shop employee, who suddenly disappeared for seven years, then reappeared with a good education from India and became a customs clerk in Ahwaz. They had a daughter, Rakhshandeh, and three sons: Muhammad-Ali Sirjani became a physician and major in the army and died a suspicious death in the recent revolution; Mahmud became a high school teacher; and Mehdi died at age eighteen shortly before I was born, contributing to the conundrums of my own naming. Rakhshandeh earned a Ph.D. in education and worked as an educational adviser until the revolution. A feminist, she always refused to wear a chādor except for prayer.

My mother's father's death is among my earliest memories: I was only one. When I related this memory to my mother many years later, she was quite surprised. His bed was in the middle of the summer room, and everyone sat around him. The barber came and trimmed his grey beard, but when he touched the mustache, grandfather stopped him, waving his hand to say, not this part. (Large mustaches are sartorial signs of devotion to mysticism.) Then a few minutes later (my mother corrected me: it was a few days later), when I was crawling near the courtyard pond (*ḥowz*) with a little bell around my neck, my mother suddenly came into the courtyard wailing and tearing her dress.

My mother, Farkhondeh, was the middle daughter. Beautiful with thick black hair down to her knees, always braided and hanging down her back, she was witty, an encyclopedia of poetry, a *ḥāfiẓ* of the Qur'an (a *ḥāfiẓ* is one who memorizes the entire Qur'an), a weaver, and a professional dressmaker. The neighborhood women loved her and called our house *bāgh-e delgoshā* ("garden of the open heart") because she had a way of making even the saddest person laugh, and because despite our poverty she was the most generous of souls.[18] She had her most beautiful moments with God, when she melodiously sang the Qur'an and prayers. Despite my love for my father, I must say, she was a world wasted in his house. Once I asked her why she had married him. She said it was her fate (*qesmat*). (She was twelve when she married; he was twenty-eight.)

My father, the spoiled, only son of a relatively well-to-do farmer, had been encouraged by his parents to marry a city girl. My father's father owned a house in Yazd in the same neighborhood as my mother's family; and so periodically, he would come from Dareh to collect the rent and to sell dried mulberries. My mother's family had fallen on hard times, and so were happy to give their daughter to a villager who could at least guarantee steady food. Otherwise, a villager could never have dreamed of marrying a granddaughter of Ḥajji Muhammad-Karīm. In the village, my father owned some land and was well connected: his sister had married the eldest son of the then headman, Ḥajji Ismail, who must have owned half the village. (My eldest sister eventually married a grandson of Ḥajji Ismail, our paternal aunt's son, the man who played Shemr in the passion play. My second sister married the son of a daughter of Ḥajji Ismail; he has been village headman of Dareh for sixteen years, and although he has blue-green eyes, he is too shy to play Shemr.)

Fig. 1.7. An old woman and two sages in a garden. Bukhara, ca. 1520–1530, typical of Uzbek court style miniatures. 22.1 × 14.2 cm. S86.0216. Courtesy of Arthur M. Sackler Gallery, Smithsonian Institution, Washington, D.C.

Of my father's village occupations and religious roles, I have already spoken in the preceding section.

If the date of my birth certificate is to be believed, I was born on the tenth of Shahrivar 1331 Shamsi (August 31, 1952). I know I was born during the month of the ḥajj because people always said I was a *ḥājjī*, a *ḥajjī shekamī* (a "womb ḥājjī"). You know, the Ḥājji Āghā of Sadeq Hedayat's novella is a *ḥājjī shekamī;* he had never been to Mecca. I was the sixth surviving child. My oldest sister, Safa, had already married two years earlier and had a son; she married the eldest son of my father's only sister. My brother Ahmad was the second child, and there were three other sisters: Ezzat, Fatemeh, and Robab. My mother was to have, all told, fourteen pregnancies, of which seven survived. (I have a younger brother.) She was sick with me and was advised to abort on the grounds that the baby was taking all her nutrition, but she refused. She said that she was baking bread in the basement kitchen when she felt the labor pains. Everyone had gone to the fields to pick fruit. The old midwife, Robābeh, was a neighbor and could be called in emergency, but my mother thought she had time to finish the breads. When she realized there was no time, it was too late, and she could hardly move. She called out a few times, but no one heard. She began reciting prayers, hoping someone would stop by. So I was born. She cut the cord, wrapped me in some clothes, put me under a basket with a stone on top, so no animal could get at me, and went to call Robābeh. When everyone returned, there was joy that I was a boy, that is, on everyone's part except my elder brother, who felt his special status threatened. A teaspoon of water with some sacred earth of Karbala (*torbat*) was poured into my mouth, and the credo of Islam whispered into my ear.

My father named me Mehdi, but since my eighteen-year-old cousin (mother's sister's son), also Mehdi, had just died, my family decided to address me as Gholām-Husain, or Gholi for short, the name of both my grandfathers. The name Mehdi was used only on the birth certificate, and I was seven before I learned my real name. That happened because when I was registered for school in Yazd, my legal name was given; and when the teacher called out "Mehdi Abedi," at first I did not respond, though I had a vague feeling it might be me. I had never liked the name Gholi, which I associated both with the word for ghouls (*ghūl*) and the word for a small bell (*ghol*) which had been tied around my neck as a toddler. So I went home and said I wanted to be called Mehdi. The custom of changing an infant's name, if there was a death or illness in the family, or even to "sell" the child to another set of parents, was a kind of evil eye avoidance, to confuse the forces of harm so they could not find or identify the child. In Dareh, children were usually "sold" to the nomads who camped near the village for two months every year; almost every child had a nomad parent. The real parents would give the nomad parent money "to feed the child." It is of historical interest that the name Mehdi was not particularly popular earlier in the century, but became very popular for children of my age cohort. This was no arbitrary flux of fashion but a kind of campaign launched by Muslim believers to thumb their noses at the Bahā'īs (who claimed that the Mahdi had already come in the person of Baha'ullah).

Similarly, at the same time, it became popular to call the Mahdi or Imām-e Zaman by the title *A'lā Hazrat* ("his majesty") to deny the use of that title by the shāh. Pro-Khomeini activists, however, soon called for a ban on this practice, as well as on all monarchical titles for the Imāms: thus they asked that one no longer refer to the eighth Imām, Imām Reza, as al-Ṣulṭān or Shāh-e Khorasan; nor should one call Ali by the title Shāh-e Velayat, nor call Husain, Shāh-e Maẓlūmān, Shāh-e Dīn, or Shāh-e Karbalā. Instead, the Imāms ought to be called 'Abd-e Ṣāleh-e Khodā ("righteous servant of God"). The struggle between religious sources of legitimacy and royal ones were symbolized in cities like Yazd by the *azān* (*adhān*), the call to prayer, which served as a public timekeeping device, and by the drum and trumpet sounds (*naqqāreh khāneh* and *surnā*) at dawn and dusk issuing from atop the governor's place. My mother used to say she could always tell from the vigor of especially the latter how stable the government was: when loud and martial, the governor was in full control, when the sound was more playful it was a harbinger that the musicians could feel the governor on the defensive and liable to be deposed. When Reza Shah was deposed, she reported, people said the trumpets' sound bursts seemed to be saying, "*Kos-e zan-e shāh*" ("up the shah's wife's . . .").

Learning to Read: Qur'anic Literacy

At age five, one was sent to a female *mullā* who would have up to ten students. In the Yazd area, *mullā* is the proper term for one who teaches the rudiments of literacy. (Hence Jews were often addressed by the title mullā, because they were almost universally literate.) When I was five, we spent the winter in the city (Yazd), and I was sent to a pious woman mullā to learn the Qur'an. Her name was Monavvar, and she had a number of students, each at a different level. While teaching, she also made bags for a henna company, and we sometimes helped. She taught me the alphabet, and the reading of the first *sūra* of the Qur'an. I already knew much of the Qur'an by heart because my mother was a *ḥāfiẓ* and often recited parts of it. It was a tradition to have a celebration (*noql kardan*) when students finished the first *sūra;* the first, second, and eighth *joz'* (thirtieths) of the Qur'an, and of course when they finished the whole Qur'an. Round sugar balls (*noql*) mixed with nuts and coins would be sprinkled over the scholar's head as for a bride,[19] and the other children could scramble to collect them. There would be a gift for the scholar. The teacher also would be given gifts relative to the family status of the child.

Of the beginning three books, the first was *Qur'an-e Yek Joz'.* This opens in Arabic with three sentences: "He is the opener and He is the One who knows. O God, make it easy, don't make it difficult. Make it easy for us all, God of the world." This is memorized. Next is the alphabet, then the alphabet with vowels. Then comes the first *sūra* of the Qur'an, which is also one of the shortest. Then the last *joz'* (thirtieth) of the Qur'an, ending with *Sūra Naba* (or *'Amma*). (This last *joz'* is done in reverse order, because the shorter *sūra* are at the end. In normal sequence, *Sūra Naba* is the first of the last *joz'.*) The second book was *Qur'an-e Do Joz'.* This is from *Sūra Tabārak* (or *Mulk*) to *Sūra Dahr* (*Insan*). The third book was *Qur'an-e Hasht Joz'.* This begins with *Sūra Yasin.*[20] The rest of the Qur'an was felt to be easy, and would be done at one swoop or at most two.

This constituted the introduction of Arabic literacy. One then went on to the poet Ḥāfeẓ as the introduction to Persian literacy. Various things might follow Ḥāfeẓ: the *Masnavi* of Rumi and the *Golestān* of Sa'di were particularly popular. All of this was just reading, not writing. My older sisters learned the Qur'an and Ḥāfeẓ this way. They can no longer really read, but they can open Ḥāfeẓ and "read" the familiar verses they have half memorized. Such literacy was referred to as "knowing black from white" (*siāhi bā sefīdī farq gozāshtan*), i.e., the print from the page. This is the reference of the term for literacy, *savād,* from the Arabic word for black (*sūd*).[21]

I did not get to Ḥāfeẓ with Mullā Monavver. I got through the first three books listed above, at which point I celebrated my first *noql kardan.* I remember with some embarrassment that my mother wanted to do the ceremony, but we were so poor that she could only afford the *noql* and not a gift. I knew the situation, and so I also scrambled for the *noql* and coins, probably to the dismay of my mother.

Following the celebration, we went back to the village where I was sent to another mullā, an old shroud weaver. Despite the high infant mortality rate, there was barely enough work for her to make a living making shrouds, so she also taught the Qur'an. Each student had a little carpet or goatskin on which to sit which we kept at her house. Going to this mullā could be terrifying, for she would threaten to send us to the *sūrākh-e mār-o-mūsh dūn* (the "snake-mouse hole," i.e., the dark basement, particularly scary in a village mud house perpetually falling into ruins), or she might use her knitting needle to draw blood from the back of our hands, or she might bastinado the bottoms of our feet, if we did not do our lessons properly. I did not like her and soon quit. So I was placed with another mullā, a young widow, a weaver with long dark hair. Her husband had died during a hunting trip from a fall in the mountains. She had a lovely voice, and would sing with the rhythm of her loom. She taught us the rules of ritual cleanliness, and the daily prayers. We were mischievous kids, and there were opportunities for mischievousness when we were sent to the river to do the ablutions for prayer. There were trees that provided cover from being watched too closely. Our leader was a girl of about eight or nine. She liked to take her pants off, and we liked to watch. In the villages, children who are around animals learn about sex earlier perhaps than children in the city, even if they do not connect sex with pregnancy. We would play at sex, comparing penis sizes, having erections, and performing fellatio. One day of course someone saw us, and raised a fuss. The big girl never came back to learn the Qur'an. [Compare the opening scene in A. R. Sharkawi's *Egyptian Earth,* 1962.] We were told that watching sexual intercourse or looking at genitals would cause blindness. There were several blind people in the village, and I thought they must have looked at things they were not supposed to. (It was not until I was in third grade that I understood about procreation. After hearing my report of a classmate's account, my mother first said that children were created by the will of God, then that they came out of the belly button, and finally that tiny babies come from the father's back through his penis into the mother's stomach. I recall Oedipal anger at my father, and resisted the idea that my parents had actually engaged in intercourse.)

We were taught the principles of religion (*osūl-e dīn*) in a kind of catechismic form, "God is one, He is not two," as if preparing us for the argument against the dualism of our ancient Zoroastrian heritage, and of the Zoroastrian minority among us. (Similarly, my secondary school teacher, Nayeb Kabir, would stress that Muhammad was the last Prophet, against the belief of the Bahā'īs.) My father promised me a rial coin when I could name all twelve Imāms, and he would set me on his knee, to ask, "Who is your first Imām?" "Ali, Commander of the Believers." "Who is your third Imām?" "Imām Husain, the martyr" (and I would think of Shemr in the passion play killing Husain). "Who is your fourth Imām?" "Zayn al-'Ābidīn, the invalid," and I would think of Akbar Ramazan, the sickly old man who played the fourth Imām in the passion plays. Another one rial coin was promised when I could recite my ten *forū'-e dīn:* prayer, fasting, *khums, zakāt, ḥajj, jihād,* enjoining the good, preventing evil, loving the allies of Ali, hating the opponents of Ali. *Jihād* brought to mind the image of Ali with his doubled-edged sword, and I thought of him as constantly riding his horse killing enemies of God. Of the *ḥajj,* I only knew it had something to do with the wealthy; and of *khums,* I knew it was money the wealthy were to pay to *sayyid*s, who were descendants of the Prophet and his daughter Fatima and who thus were of an essence different from non-*sayyids.*

Purity rules were something inculcated in the process of life. As a child I had to eat from a separate bowl, while the older members of the family shared a large bowl. Only when I had just come from the bathhouse was I permitted to share in the big bowl. So I learned that children were impure (*najes*) because they are in contact with urine, feces, and other polluting agents, and they cannot be expected to know to wash their hands. Especially with wet hands, children were not to touch many things. The female mullās would not allow their students to touch the Qur'an: to point at verses, pupils had to make paper arrows. (Everyone, of course, makes minor ablutions, *wuḍū,* for daily prayers and touching the Qur'an.) I must have been nearly seven when I refused to eat from a separate bowl, and my mother agreed to let me eat from the large bowl if I washed my hands and face first. Thus I became a *bacha-e mumayyez* (child with discriminating sense).

I had learned just over half the Qur'an when I quit my studies with the mullā. My mother decided it was enough for the time being. It was a bad year of drought. Many villagers had left to work as construction workers in the city. There was nothing to eat except bread made of American wheat. For some reason it was uncleaned, and one day a piece of bread baked with this wheat got stuck in my mouth. When my mother pulled it out, it was found to contain a large thorn. She angrily threw away the rest of the bread and declared that she would no longer live this miserable life in the village and subsist on charity. She would go to the city and work as a maid for her mother's brother, and she would take me: I was old enough to earn a little money. My father got very angry. But a few days later we packed for the city, and left. Thereafter we spent only summers in the village to escape the heat in the city.

Scenes of an Urban Childhood: Class Distinctions

[Schools are fascinating arenas of class differentiation, as well as, for some, routes of mobility into different classes. Mehdi came from the poorest level of rural migrants to the city, and consequently the advisability of his continuing education rather than earning money was repeatedly open to question. A second, very Middle Eastern, theme is that of selfless patronage by better-off individuals of gifted poor students. Schools were partly stratified by class, and were sharply affected by the changing pedagogical and disciplinary ideologies associated with modernization. Mehdi stood out in the public primary school because he already knew how to read; children of the more secular middle classes had not been sent to a mullā, partly because the middle classes were rejecting the tradition of harsh schools. Harsh discipline in certain schools, however, seemed to contribute to excellence, and the semi-Islamic schools were often among those with reputations for both harshness and excellence. Part of the not always healthy dynamic was the competition among teachers and schools for recognition and rewards for producing the best students. Discipline and rote learning were the subject of much debate and despair among American Peace Corps teachers in Iran during the 1960s and 1970s as well as among foreign university professors. But perhaps most interesting is the contribution of cadre provided by the semi-Islamic school system (mentioned briefly in this section and more fully in the next) to the leadership of the Iranian revolution of 1979, and also to the leadership of marxist factions of the early stages of the revolution.]

We settled in a small mud-brick house: two small rooms, a small, dark basement kitchen, and an even darker storage room, plus a well with nonpotable water. It had belonged to my father's father, and was part of my mother's bridewealth. It is still there, in Mahalleh Pirborj: Sarhang Towfiq Alley (called Paknejad Alley today), Farjad Cul-de-Sac. (Dr. Pakn̆ejad, a physician, was the head of the local anti-Bahā'ī crusade, and an associate of Āyatullāh Shaykh Muhammad Ṣadūqi. After the revolution, he became a member of Parliament, and then was killed with the "seventy-two" leaders of the Islamic Republican Party by the Mojahedin-e Khalq; Āyatullāh Ṣadūqi was also assassinated by the Mojahedin. Both will appear again as important figures in my story.) The cul-de-sac had five houses: two belonged to villagers from our neighbor village, Gowsha; one belonged to a widow from our village who had lost her husband and who worked in the local public bathhouse. The fifth belonged to a businessman, and was rented to my first educational savior, Ali Akbar Afsar Yaghmai'i, a retired mayor of Shahrbabak [a small town between Yazd and Kirman, famed for being the seat of the Isma'ili Imām until the nineteenth century when he moved to India and took the title Agha Khan; it is still a center for Isma'ilis].

For several days after we arrived in Yazd, my father tried to find me a job, but everyone he tried said I was too young and too unhealthy looking. The last place we tried was a small *zīlū* factory (*zīlū*s are a flat-weave floor covering, cheaper and usually larger than *gelīms* or, as the latter are better known in the West, kelims, the Turkish name). I remember my father was frustrated and angry, and as we arrived back at our cul-de-sac at sunset, we saw Ali Akbar Afsar Yaghmai'i standing under a street light, dressed in a three-piece suit, tie, shined shoes, playing with his worry beads. He was about sixty. We knew who he was, and my father salaamed and bowed as villagers do to well-dressed urban men. Mr. Yaghmai'i responded warmly and I remember distinctly approximately the following exchange:

> "You must be our new neighbor?"
> "Yes, sir!" my father replied humbly.
> "Is this your son?"
> "Yes, sir. He is your servant if you need one."
> "You are sending him to school, I suppose."
> "School? No. We are from the village. None of my children have gone to school."
> "Times have changed. You must send this one to school. He looks bright. Who knows, perhaps he will have a bright future."

My father laughed and did not take him seriously. At six a child should earn his bread. In the village a child would work in the fields or herd sheep and goats. Mr. Yaghmai'i knew this and continued: "Public schools are free and I will pay for his paper and pencils. He can also eat in our house. It won't cost you anything."

My father was delighted. Like a seller of goats, he pushed me toward the man, saying, "He is yours."

"Then, tomorrow morning you will register him for school. I will write a recommendation."

This encounter shaped my destiny. Many years later I learned that Ali Akbar was a grandson of the famous satirical poet Yaghma. (Yaghma, the story goes, was a shepherd boy when a prince passed and asked who he was. He answered in verse, "We're the little people of Khūr [near Shahrbabak]; we're far from manners and learning [*mā mardomak-e khūrīm; az elm-o-adab dūrīm*]," and was rewarded by being taken to the court of Nāṣiruddin Shāh.) Ali Akbar was educated, a poet, a lover of music and of books. The door to his house was open, and every day he had guests. He smoked: both cigarettes and opium. His wife was unlettered but his children, three sons and three daughters, all were being educated. Manuchehr was already a teacher; Amir was in high school; Morteza was in fourth grade; the eldest daughter had completed primary school and had just married a cousin, Mirza Mehdi, a health agent in the campaign against smallpox; Neisan was in high school; and Nasrin was my age. Mirza Mehdi lived with his father-in-law and eventually had a son and two daughters.

I was registered in the Adab elementary school, the nearest to our house. Adab turned out to be the school to which all the elite sent their children, and I was made to feel my inferiority along with the other poorer kids in the class. The first thing that happened, on the very first day, was that I was slapped by the principal, Mr. Qummi, for coming to school without shoes. As far as I had been concerned until then, shoes were to protect the feet from the rough earth and mountain terrain; but it was fine to go barefoot on the soft sandy soil of the city. I soon learned that there was a different purpose to shoes in school. So my father had to buy me a pair of shoes, made with soles cut from old tires. Other things also set us poorer kids apart: the upper-class kids had full heads of hair, while we had shaved heads. The upper-class kids were well dressed, and a number of them were fat. They had book bags, we tied our books together with pyjama elastic waistbands.

Every morning at eight thirty—sometimes at eight—Mirza Muhammad, the janitor, rang the bell. The bell with its hammer was a contraption put together from two metal pieces of an old car. At the bell, we were to stand in line according to grade. Verses of the Qur'an were recited, a prayer, salutations to the Prophet and his family, good wishes for the shah, and a request to God to preserve the country. A student then read slogans and everyone repeated after him. I enjoyed the thunderous united voice. Then everyone held up the back of their hands for the principal to inspect our cleanliness. Hair had to be short, except for the sons of the governor, chief of police, and other elite families. Violators of the standards of cleanliness were punished. God forbid somebody's hand should be dirty. The principal, Mr. Qummi, carried a leather whip and was feared. He was tall and skinny, about forty, with dark eyes, gold teeth, curly hair, bad tempered and nervous, but always well dressed. There were stories that he had whipped delinquent and lazy students one hundred lashes. Many kids wet their pants at just a severe look or slap from him, but I was a village boy and used to such treatment from my father and older brother. After inspection we filed into our classes.

The first grade teacher was Mr. Aminian, a stocky man with greying hair. He had an accent. Some kids thought he was a new Muslim, a convert from Zoroastrianism; others said he was a Muslim from Ardakan. Who dared ask him? Everything about our teachers was a mystery. There were too many students in the first grade; kids fought over the seats. Everyone wanted to sit with a friend; no one wanted to sit with me. On the second day, the principal appeared without his whip and asked the kids who were poor and dirty like me to come outside and stand in line. I thought we were going to be beaten, but we were led to another school, the newly established Dr. Khan Ali school in the Posht-e Khan Ali neighborhood [the Zoroastrian quarter of Yazd], only a hundred feet from what would be my future father-in-law's house.

I felt even more lost at the new school, and when the last bell rang, I had no idea how to get home. I began to cry. A group gathered round and asked my father's name, but no one knew him. A passing mule cart with construction material stopped; the driver recognized my father's name as a fellow employee and gave me a lift. And so I found my father who was covered in mud. I told the story of my day's travail, and that evening my father met with Mr. Yaghmai'i. The latter promised to help bring me back to the Adab school. He wrote a letter, and the next morning, my father took it to the principal. There was an argument: Mr. Qummi shouted at my father and said he would do nothing. My father angrily threatened to complain to the director of the Office of Education. So, I continued to attend the second school.

We began to learn the alphabet, which I already knew except for the letters which do not exist in Arabic. I was the only one who knew this much, and so I became a kind of teacher's assistant. I would read out the letters loudly, and the others would repeat, while the teacher made sure they were looking at the board. The teacher liked me, and I began to like the school. Two weeks later, the principal came and called me out of the class. He and the teacher then got into an argument, and it took a while for me to realize that I was being transferred back to the Adab school. The teacher shouted, "They've sent me the dumbest, poorest, and most unwanted children. This is the only different one and I'm not going to let him go. If distance is the problem, I'll give him a ride on my bicycle back and forth every day." So the principal phoned Principal Qummi at Adab school telling him I was happy here and they would persuade my father to let me stay. Half an hour later, however, Mirza Muhammad, the janitor of the Adab school, arrived to fetch me.

I was mortified at the trouble I had caused. As soon as we arrived at Adab, I was asked to read the alphabet, which I did. "What a mistake we made," the principal said to Mr. Aminian. I was taken to the classroom and put at the blackboard, and I experienced the admiration of the other kids. I knew the things others did not, all thanks to the Qur'an.

Mr. Aminian was rough in his punishment: his technique was to put a pencil between the victim's fingers and squeeze his hand. He never did this to me, but I tried it a few times on myself and it was very painful. In second grade, with Mr. Varasteh, I have few memories: he was calm and seldom beat the children. When he did, he used a wooden ruler which was not so painful. The third grade teacher, Mr. Mahrami, was older than the other teachers, also calm, and never beat the kids, even when they played tricks on him. He was respected by the other teachers for his fine calligraphy.

In fourth grade, there was a new teacher, Mr. Pedarzadeh, young, handsome, witty, talkative, charismatic. Looking back, I now think he must have had communist leanings. Having come from a poor family, he was particularly sympathetic to the poorer students, and he often told stories of poor children who became famous, such as the son of a furrier who became Nadir Shah, king of Iran, as well as, of course, the case of Reza Shah Pahlavi. He used me too as a kind of example, thereby also intending to encourage me. I'll never forget that one day, he brought me a set of notebooks and presented them to me in class as a sign to the other students that despite my poverty, I was doing well and he expected me to continue doing so. In return, I tried to please him by improving my handwriting. He used to make speeches at public events, such as the annual gathering of the Anjoman-e Khāneh va Madaraseh (a club of richer parents who aided poorer students), and he began to teach me to deliver his speeches in his stead, saying he thought it would make the pitch more effective.

My worst memories are of the sixth grade: a mixture of unjust humiliation and childish religious terror, precipitated by weekly report cards that had been introduced the preceding year. Each week, teachers were supposed to write progress reports to the parents, and the parents were supposed to write replies. In the fifth grade I used to help the teacher, Mr. Reyhani, write these reports, even learning to replicate his signature. That year a city-wide education contest was introduced as well, and I won first prize for the fifth grade. The prize was a box of colored pencils for me and a handsome volume of Sa'di's poetry for my teacher. But in sixth grade my luck turned sour. One day the weekly reports were found scattered about, some torn up. The teacher, Mr. Kebritian, suspected the poorer kids, and for some reason after questioning everyone, he decided I was the culprit. He accused me in class and kicked me out to the jeers of the rest of the class. I was humiliated and enraged, hoping God would strike him dead. There were rumors that he was not really sure and that he was planning to bring a *Tigh-e Hazrat-e Abbās* ("blade of Abbās," the half brother of Imām Husain and martyr of Karbala). [This was a divining technique used with servants and children. Four sticks are held by two persons seated face to face, so the sticks form two rows end to end. The accused places his arm between the sticks and, while someone reads the Qur'an, one watches to see if the sticks move inward to pinch the accused (guilty) or move apart (innocent). I was ready to submit to this test to prove my innocence, though I was haunted by it in my dreams. I would wake up screaming, having dreamt that the device actually cut through my arm. My mother would say prayers and try to put me back to sleep. Next I tried writing a letter to put in the largest shrine in town. I had heard that helpless women often did this, that the "son of the Imām" (*imāmzādeh,* saint) who was asleep, rather than being dead, inside the grave of the shrine would read the letters and then would appear in the dreams of, say, an accuser to defend the innocent victim. I delivered the letter, and begged the saint with tears to convince Mr. Kebritian that I had not done it. As this did not work, I began to lose faith in the shrine, but then I remembered that saints do not answer sinners. And so I not only began to increase my prayers and Qur'an recitations, but all the memories of sins of my childhood began to plague me, the sexual playing in the village, the stealing of the melon from Ḥajji, and so many other things. I repented of all my sins and vowed never to repeat them. None of this helped. Indeed one day, Mr. Kebritian caught me making a print on paper with some soot: I had made a pattern of small needle holes and was teaching myself a primitive sort of silkscreening, thrilled by my success. Kebritian took me to the principal, Mr. Fakhraddini, complaining of my troublesomeness. I tried to voice my own grievances, but to no avail: Fakhraddini shouted insults at me and threatened to kick me out of school. Fortunately, the sixth grade final exams were not given in class but were held on a city-wide level at another school under the proctoring of other teachers. I scored third or fourth in the city, first in the class from my school. I was not satisfied, but our school was not ranked the best in town. That honor was held by the Islami school, where children of rich and religious families went: it was supposed to have the best teachers. At the awards ceremony, Principal Fakhraddini hypocritically presented me as an outstanding student. I don't think I have ever hated anyone as much as I hated Kebritian and Fakhraddini.

During these primary school years, my father came to the school thrice, each time to remind my teachers that a child should be beaten periodically. Now he did not want me to go to school any longer. It was time to work and earn some money. My brother, a copper wholesaler, needed a clerk and was jealous of my schooling. My father decided that for the summer months I could first work with him as a construction worker. I kept careful track of how much I worked and should be paid, but at the end of the summer when I went to the contractor's shop to get my pay, I found my father had already taken it. I came home in tears, and my mother and father had a big argument about my money. Many people told me to continue my education, and so I went to Afshar High School to ask about the possibilities. Because of my grades I was admitted free of charge, and books were provided from a charity fund.

Secondary School, Sexual Purity, and Marriage

[At the time of the revolution of 1979 the international press professed shock at the degree to which the religious rules disseminated by the Shi'ite clergy seemed to have to do with the purity code. These rules are dealt with in our introduction to Khomeini's *Risaleh towzih al-masa'il* (Fischer and Abedi 1984). The texture of fear and desire that is manipulated by the religious code during childhood, and especially at adolescence, is not unfamiliar to the religious traditions of Europe. There is an openness and immediacy about these manipulations in a society that is still close to a face-to-face society of restricted literacy, where religious codes operate as basic mechanisms of psychic as well as public control. These codes are registered not only in language and behavior, but also in dreams.]

Afshar High School was one of the three Ta'līmāt-e Islāmi schools in Yazd. The Ta'līmāt-e Islāmi schools were a compromise between the old style seminary system and the modern schools. They were under government supervision, but included religious programs supervised by Ta'līmāt-e Islāmi headquarters in Tehran. All students were Muslim. Noon and afternoon prayers were done at school. The system had been established first in Tehran by a cleric named Shaykh Abbas Ali Islami. In Yazd, it was the cleric Sayyid Ali Muhammad Vaziri, who was to become my second educational savior, who introduced the program. Afshar was the name of a businessman who provided a private house for the secondary school. Another businessman from Kirman, Ḥajj Ramazani endowed a house for the primary school. A third school was established in the Kheirabad suburb. (All the Ta'līmāt-e Islāmi schools were in former private houses.) The primary school, Dabestān-e Ta'līmāt-e Islāmi Ramazāni, maintained an unrivaled excellence. Initially, the students wore long cloaks on the collar of which appeared the student's name, class, and school emblem so that if they did something in the streets they could be identified. The principal, Mr. Ra'uf (Mr. Kind or Merciful), was famed for his strictness and much feared for his harsh physical punishments, but he collected the best teachers. The school, however, was expensive and served primarily the rich and the well-to-do religious families.

The secondary school, Dabirestān-e Ta'līmāt-e Islāmi Afshār, was not quite so good, but it was not bad. Our geometry and religion teacher, Mr. Qanbar Ali Nayeb Kabir (the last name means "great deputy," the first name is that of Imām Ali's servant), was active in the anti-Baha'i movement, and often spoke about the anticipated Mahdi (see below). He was blunt and open about all matters. I remember the day he spoke about puberty and sexual impurity: he began with the formula "*lā ḥayā'a fi al-dīn*" ("there should be no shame in religion") which allows one to discuss matters in public that otherwise are private. When he started to discuss masturbation and illicit sexual intercourse not merely as a sin and cause of impurity to the self, requiring full ritual ablutions in cold water, but also as a contaminating source of pollution to anything touched, thereby voiding the prayers of others who thought they were praying in a pure place, faces turned white. The following day many of the class went together for a ritual bath. There was a rumor that Nayeb Kabir, a bachelor, was homosexual and liked young boys. I never had any evidence of this, but he did have a maternal uncle with a shop near the school who was well known for such activities. While maintaining a pious facade, this uncle sold cheap calligraphy pens to the boys and subtly would proposition them. (Later, Vaziri told me that Nayeb Kabir's remaining a bachelor had something to do with caring for two elder sisters who never married because their father refused all suitors.)

The algebra instructor, Mr. Abqari ("genius"), a former school superintendent, was both entertaining and feared, and with this combination was able to cajole his students to real excellence. He had all sorts of mathematical tricks to display; and at the same time never feared punishing students, even those bigger than he. I have a memory of him jumping like a basketball player to slap the face of a tall student. Other teachers were less successful. The science teacher, Mr. Dehqan, a former high school principal in Taft (the town just south of Yazd famed for its pomegranates), tried to browbeat us with his temper, and styled himself an expert *kharcharān* ("donkey herder"), we being the donkeys. I used to draw caricatures of him, and was caught, and slapped deservedly. Least liked of all was a Mr. Ayatullahi, a religious scholar who wore the turban and cloak of the theologians, and led us in prayer. We would keep him bowed down during prayers always asking for more time to catch up, until once, impatient, he turned and cursed us (thereby nullifying the prayer), so he had to start all over.

To make money, I tutored a fifth grader at the Ramazāni School in math. I tutored every night for half a toman a night; and I often also ate at the house of this family. There were seven children in Muhammad Majdzadeh's family, he being the eldest. I taught Muhammad and his incredibly beautiful, green-eyed, brown-haired sister, Nasrin, aged ten, who took my heart away with her astonishing charm. Muhammad, at least, became an outstanding student.

It was during this first year at Afshar that I met Mr. Vaziri. On the anniversary of the death of Imām Ali, I was one of several who gave a speech to a large crowd in an exercise to train students in public speaking. After the speech, I was introduced to Vaziri. He shook my hand warmly, kissed my forehead, and gave me a book, which I still have, inscribed, "In the name of God, on Friday, the twenty-first of the blessed month of Ramaḍān, 1385, in the grand mosque of Yazd, Mr. Abedi, freshman student of the Ta'līmāt-e Islāmi, made a wonderful speech. This book is given for his studies. May he reach the highest stages of perfection. Sayyid Ali Muhammad Vaziri. 24 Dey '44." He also gave me a summer job at his library attached to the Yazd Congregational Mosque, paying me one hundred tomans a month ($13). This was both fun, and far better than working for my brother, who did not like me or I him, or with my father, whom I did not trust to let me have access to my wages. I continued to work at the library during the next school year.

The second year of high school was one of rebellion. A group of us established a secret society to rule the class and teachers. We wrote a wall newspaper in which we ridiculed the teachers. It would be put up on the wall of the school at 7:30 A.M. by a student named Husain Makki. He was on good terms with Hashem, the office boy and servant of Vaziri, who also ran a tea shop in the school for the teachers and for those students who had the money to pay. Husain Makki was one of his regular customers. At 8:30, long after almost everyone had read the newspaper, the principal would angrily take it off the wall. We also organized strikes, and created disturbances during prayer. Finally, we were uncovered, lashed and given poor conduct grades.

That year I tutored a fellow classmate, Muhammad Akhavan Tabatabai'i. His parents adopted me almost as a son. The father owned a gas station, and the mother was a beautician. They bought me my first bicycle, and gave me some shirts and pants. They had three sons, and when the mother became pregnant she joked that if the baby were a daughter, I could marry her. I took her seriously and was disappointed when the child proved to be a fourth son. I used to eat dinner with them, and felt at home there. (The second son, Mahmud, later became a teacher in Tehran and father of two daughters. He was martyred in the Iran-Iraq war after a strange kind of mental breakdown. He had a vision in the Shrine of Imām Riḍā, in Mashhad, and screamed, until he was arrested. He insisted he wanted to go to the war front, and made an inspirational video for the regime saying he wanted to sacrifice his soul for Islam. His mother wrote me a letter after his death about the showing of the video in Yazd, saying that it encouraged many to go and fight. The third brother now lives in Washington, D.C., where he works as an electrician. He used to be a Hezbullahi, but now claims to be apolitical.)

That must have been the year—I was about fourteen—when one night I had a striking dream. I dreamt that I lived alone on a tiny island, barren but for a palm tree under which I sat and watched the waves. It was sunny, warm, and nice. Suddenly, a beautiful girl, my age, emerged from the sea, a bit plump, very white, with long dark tresses over her shoulders, and bare breasts with brown nipples. Her lips were pursed, her eyes—no words can describe them. To say they were dark, large, and penetrating, decorated with long eyelashes and thick eyebrows that nearly met, would be to compare them with the usual, stereotypic, beautiful eyes of pubescent Iranian girls. These were special, perfect, all I could ever want in a pair of eyes. She spoke, in which language and what I do not know. I felt myself melting. All at once, she said she had to leave. I begged her to stay, but she disappeared as quickly as she had come. I began to sing in an effort to bring her back. I was singing "I wish I could see my beloved again," when I heard my mother calling my name as she gently shook my shoulders saying, "Mehdi, you are dreaming." She looked like an older version of the girl in the dream, with the same large eyes.

She began to pray and recite verses of the Qur'an. Under the dim light of the oil lamp, she resembled the girl in the dream. She asked me about the dream, but I refused to speak. The next day I kept seeing the face in the dream, appearing and disappearing. My mother was curious and concerned, and did not want me to keep the secret of the dream from her. I thought of concocting a story to get by her inquisitions, but I did not, first, because those who lie about their dreams, we were taught, soon die (see chapter 2, commentary on the Joseph story). Second, my mother was too intelligent to believe a story her own child had fabricated. When I came back from school, she was sewing. Behind her glasses she suddenly burst into tears, and begged me to tell her my dream. Nothing, she said, is more embarrassing than sex, but dreams are dreams. Strange things happen in dreams. Bad dreams often have good meanings. "Tell me, I am worried about your health." So she persuaded me. She said it was a wonderful dream, not to be ashamed, in fact I had become a man. Then she began to instruct me about puberty and ritual purity, that one should take a ritual bath after a wet dream. (I think now that my dream was not of that sort, but that it was a premonition of my life: the bitter story of my homelessness, an unquenchable thirst for a lost love, the exile [*āvāregi, ghorbat*][22] of a village boy on his way to Tehran, Europe, and the United States. When two years later I read Sadeq Hedayat's *The Blind Owl,* I experienced a powerful sense of recognition.)

During the summer I again worked at Vaziri library. I was tired of school, and decided not to return. Vaziri agreed to let me stay on at the library at a somewhat higher salary of 150 tomans a month. I found I still wanted to study, and at the end of the school year I took the final exam for the ninth grade, and did reasonably well. Now that I was allegedly working full time, my father wanted more contributions from me. He was too proud to say so, and instead would make his will known indirectly: he always was angry at me and cursing at me. Finally, I decided to move out and live by myself: a new phenomenon in our world for a teen-ager. I was fifteen. My father was happy to let me go, thinking I would find out how hard it was to do without him. No one would rent a room to me, a young man not under the control of his family. I went to Mr. Vaziri for help, and wonder of wonders, it turned out that Afshar High School was moving to a new location and needed someone to watch the building. He recommended I live in a room in the school, which I did.

I also began studying Arabic grammar under Shaykh Murtaḍa, the *mas'aleh-gū* of the Congregational Mosque. (A *mas'aleh-gū* is someone who explains problems in ritual law; it is a form of didactic entertainment done after prayers from the *minbar,* the stairs on which a preacher sits.)[23] My study companion was Mehdi Quraishi, the grandson of Vaziri. That was the period when we wrote to Āyatullāh Khomeini saying that we had money from the government to do restoration work on the mosque, and asking what to do about such tainted money. Khomeini sent back a message empowering Shaykh Murtaḍā to close the now tainted mosque and to reopen it with a formula of purification (*taṣarruf-e shar'i*) in the name of the Imām-e Zamān by authority of his deputy Khomeini.[24]

That year I barely passed my final exams: I no longer wanted to study, and was thinking about getting married. If I was able to live alone, there was no reason I should not have a wife. This posed problems: I was embarrassed to ask my parents and friends. Yet I had been taught it was a religious duty to get married as soon as sexual desire became uncontrollable. Masturbation was forbidden and said to be harmful to one's health; I was too pious to seek out prostitutes; and women who were available for temporary marriages were too costly, probably older, not so attractive, and, again, embarrassing were I to be found out. While I was studying for the exams, I met Abbas, a carpet seller's assistant, also studying for the exams. We studied together at night under the street lamps on Soraya Street. He knew of a beautiful widow, about thirty-five, supporting several children, with whom a number of his friends had sexual experiences. So one midnight we knocked at her door. Abbas knew how to knock, loud enough for her to wake up, and soft enough not to wake her children. She came out and immediately understood what we wanted. Some nights later we invited her for the whole night, and Abbas brought her to my grandfather's vacant house after midnight, so neighbors sleeping on the rooftops would not notice. At her recommendation we read the temporary marriage formula. For some reason we did not see her again after this. A few months later Sayyid Ahmad Ishkavari, a cleric in his forties, arrived from Iraq and facilitated my marriage.

There was, however, an interesting political sequel to this story, in which she served unwittingly as a cover. Abbas and I continued to study together under the street lamps of Soraya Street, and a mutual friend, Hasan Montazer, persuaded us to distribute, late at night when the streets were deserted, copies of Khomeini's *Ḥokūmat-e Islami* ("Islamic government"–see chapter 2). He got the copies from his brother, an activist, in Tehran, Muhammad Montazer. We hid the books in the alley, and began to study. We had prepared for the eventuality of dealing with the policeman whose beat included Soraya Street by purchasing some foreign filter cigarettes, Winstons. We knew he loved these cigarettes, but Abbas did something particularly stupid: when the policeman came around, he said, if you go "seven steps away from the king's palace" (i.e., if you leave us alone), you can have the whole pack. This was really tempting fate, but it worked. The policeman smiled and said, "Sure,

I know what you fellows want to do." And he took off. We hurriedly slipped the copies of Khomeini's little book under doors in the neighborhood, giving priority, as Hasan had directed, to those in whose house we knew there were literate people and ones likely to be sympathetic. When the policeman returned some three hours later, we were again engaged in our studying. He asked, "Well, how was she?" And we replied, laughing under our breath at the double-entendre, "Great," meaning of course that we were tickled to be screwing and exposing the government. (Such was the ribald idiom that was popularly used for antigovernment activities.) We got away with our lark, but three weeks later Hasan was arrested, and then another friend, Mehdi Mehrizi. Hasan went to jail for eighteen months. I ran into him again a few years later in Tehran. After the revolution he became a writer and journalist, working for *Keyhan-e Farhangi;* he was killed in a car accident with his children. His brother, Muhammad, the head of the Mojahedin-e Enqelab-e Islami (not to be confused with the Mojahedin-e Khalq) was killed during the American rescue mission in the desert outside Tabas. Muhammad was blond and blue-eyed. One story is that the government forces mistook him for an American and shot him; the other version is that he seized documents with the names of collaborators from the disabled helicopter and was shot by the Americans; either way, both he and the alleged documents "turned to ash in Tabas."

Marriage

Sayyid Ahmad Ishkavari, a cleric in his forties, who had served as the librarian at Āyatullāh S. Muḥsin al-Hakīm's library in Najaf for many years, had moved in with me. When he arrived in Yazd, he went to Vaziri. Vaziri, being too old and too ill to give him hospitality in his own house, sent him to "my house" with a male servant who proved to be a good cook. Ishkavari was a tall skinny man, with black turban, and thick glasses. He of course spoke both Arabic and Persian, and had beautiful handwriting. He rarely laughed, but a smile constantly played on his face; he had a good sense of humor and was fond of talking about sex. He was married to an Iraqi woman, Batul, and had several children; he especially spoke often of his son, Muhammad. He had come to Iran to find a job before bringing his family. He had gone first to Qum, and had been directed to Yazd. He was not really an *'ālim,* not having studied *fiqh,* but he wore clerical garb. He had started not unlike myself, as a bookbinder and manuscript cataloger, becoming quite expert at identifying manuscripts. Vaziri was delighted to have him work on the manuscripts in the library, and for six months he was happy to help out. He then returned to Iraq to sell his house, fetch his family, and then he returned to Iran, albeit to Qum, rather than to Yazd. He was offered a job in the larger library of Āyatullāh Mar'ashi, which was also able to pay him more than Vaziri. Our paths would cross again briefly in 1975 in Qum. My relationship with Michael Fischer would invariably draw his comment upon his friend Muhsin Mahdi, who would find him a job in the United States if he wanted to go. He still works today in the Mar'ashi Library in Qum.

He was one of those who were beginning to feel the pressure of the Ba'thist government in Iraq, increasingly hostile to its Iranian residents. Shi'ites of Iranian descent had felt discomfited ever since the fall of King Faisal. Faisal's minister of culture had been Sayyid Hebat-al-din Shahrestani, a blind Iranian Shi'ite *mujtahid.*[25] Since the fall of Faisal, Shi'ites had not again gained exalted positions, and under the Ba'th, religious Shi'ites felt oppressed by the secularism of the regime. Though settled in Iraq, these Iranians refused to behave as Iraqi nationals, e.g., they refused to serve in the military. As friction between the shah's imperial policies and Iraq intensified, the Iranians became even less welcome to the Iraqi authorities. Ishkavari's family was from northern Iran, but he considered himself Iraqi. He was a follower of Āyatullāh Ḥakīm, while I was a youthful enthusiast for Āyatullāh Khomeini. I asked him if he had seen Khomeini.

"Yes, indeed," he said. "He is a very handsome man with much ambition. But he is very dangerous because he is controlled by the so-called revolutionaries in his entourage. They show him a map of Iran with red dots marking oil and mineral locations, and he asks, 'Why don't we control those?' I'll never forget his clash with Imām Ḥakīm. Three days after Khomeini arrived in Najaf [in 1964 after being expelled from Iran to Turkey the previous year], some students of Ḥakīm asked him to pay a visit to Khomeini. Ḥakīm replied that Khomeini was younger and had the duty to pay his elder a visit first. A few days later, Ḥakīm was told there was a rumor that unless he paid a visit to Khomeini, someone would pull off his turban in public. The peaceful Ḥakīm decided to submit to the demand. When the two finally met, Khomeini said to him, 'If I had as many followers as you, I would rise up against the tyrants.' Ḥakīm replied, 'Imām Ali had two sons, Hasan and Husain, each with a different strategy. Hasan's strategy was that of patience and of allowing the oppressive caliph Mu'awiyya to expose his illegitimacy to the people through his evil acts; Husain's strategy was that of rising against Yazd [the son and successor of Mu'awiyya].' Khomeini responded, 'If

Hasan had had as many followers as you, he too would have risen up.' Ḥakīm sagely replied, 'Only on the day of battle can one determine how many followers one has.' They parted neither having convinced the other." (In those days I agreed with Khomeini. The youths of my generation thought of compromise and quietism as cowardice and treason.)

During the month of Ramaḍān, Ishkavari and I spent more time together, and more time talking about sex. I confessed that I wanted to get married to protect my morals and religion. But, I lamented, people said I was too young, I still did not have a beard, and I was too poor: prospective grooms always are asked whether they have a house and good salary. Ishkavari replied that I was old enough, that I had become a man the day prayers became obligatory for me, and that it is God who supplies house and daily bread: I might find a rich father-in-law. When he himself had married, he had had nothing. In any case, he proposed to speak to Mr. Vaziri.

A few days later, early in the morning, when I went to write a few letters for Mr. Vaziri (who was losing his vision), Vaziri asked me how old I was. "Seventeen," I replied. "You look older," he said, and then: "You are my son. I am too old. I am afraid I will die before you marry." "May you live many more years," I fervently replied. Indeed, I really loved Vaziri, so much so, that one night after he had become ill and told me he knew the date of his death, I took a ritual bath and prayed to God that He take half my life and give it to Vaziri. Some nights later I dreamt that Vaziri had died, and that among the mourners assembled in the Congregational Mosque for the funeral was Khomeini. I went up to him and said, "My master, do you see, God took Vaziri away from us." "Not at all," replied Khomeini, "because of your prayer, God has granted him a few more years." I told Vaziri about the dream. He cried and embraced me and kissed me on the forehead.

In any case, regarding my marriage, Vaziri assured me that we need not wait. I said I had not seriously thought of marriage, but only recently had been talking to Ishkavari. "Yes, I know," he replied, "but who is the girl who writes you love letters?" "No one writes me love letters." "But Mr. Ishkavari has seen them." With a shock, I realized that Ishkavari had been going through my things and had read letters from my cousin, Rakhshandah. I told Vaziri it was a misunderstanding, this was an older cousin, and it was not love in that sense. So he asked who among the girls I liked. I said I did not know anyone. "None of the girls you tutored in math and geometry?" he asked. "I never thought of them as potential wives," I replied. What a lie! There was Nasrin Majdzadeh, whom I worshipped, but she was from a high status family. There was also Tāhereh Talsaz, the daughter of the janitor at the Office of Culture, whose brother I had tutored, and she had brought us tea. I never had actually seen her, since she came veiled, and only knocked at the door with the tea, at which Ali would go to take the tray from her. I only could guess that she must look like Ali. In other words, my love for her was an Islamic one. There was also Sūsan Mashrūteh, the girl next door, and a distant relative, whom I had tutored: she was beautiful, but much too liberal for me; her veil was too thin, and she allowed part of her hair to show.

Vaziri asked me to ask my father to come see him. My older brother was sent instead. My mother then questioned me, and I gave her a list of girls. I began telling people I was getting married, and they tried to dissuade me, saying I should finish my education, and that for sex I should go to Qum and get a *ṣīgheh* (temporary marriage). A few days later, when I went to tutor Ali, I saw Tāhereh without a veil: she was washing tea glasses, and when I entered the compound, she jumped up, asking God for forgiveness and ran behind a tree. Was it a set up, to let me see her? One look at a girl one will marry is considered admissible by Islamic convention, and such looks are often arranged. Although in one ḥadīth the Prophet of Islam says "Looking [at a woman] is an arrow from the quiver of Satan" (*al-naẓratu sahmun min sihām al-shaytān*), another ḥadīth has it that, "The first look is *for* you and the second one counts *against* you" (*al-naẓrat al-ūlā laka wa al-naẓrat al-thāniyatu 'alayka*). That day Ali and I did more talking about my marriage plans than math, and after our session, I went straight to my mother and told her I definitely wanted Tāhereh. She was beautiful with long dark brown hair, lovely eyes and eyebrows, well proportioned. My mother agreed with me: she had seen her in the public baths. That night I dreamed of Tāhereh. But the next day my mother, giving me a compassionate look from behind her sewing machine, said she could find someone better. She told me that my older brother was adamantly opposed to Tāhereh, saying we might be poor, but we were the descendants of Ḥajji Muhammad Karīm Isfahāni, and could not have the daughter of a janitor in the family. I became angry but she said to be patient: destiny is always made by God. My brother proposed a distant relative, but her father rejected the idea on the grounds that I had not yet done my military service. Then my brother remembered that his friend and client, Sha'bān, the coppersmith, had a daughter, whom he had seen ten years earlier as a cute four or five year old. My mother went to see her, and forty-eight hours later, just after the end of the month of Ramaḍān, I was married.

Fig. 1.8. Humay and Humayun on the Day after their Wedding, diwan of Khwajū Kirmāni, Baghdad, 1396. Courtesy of The British Library, Add. 18113.

Vaziri presided at the marriage, and in his benedictory speech, he recounted the marriages of the prophets and of the Imāms one by one, concluding, "And now is the time of the marriage of one whose name is the same as the twelfth Imām's." Then he announced that the groom had no house, and thank God, the father-in-law had a big one, and so the groom would live there. So I lived with my father-in-law for four years, when I left in a dispute over a piece of land. I had been paying my father-in-law for this land, but instead of paying the owner, he gave the owner IOUs and used the money himself in the meantime. When I went to collect the deed to the land, the owner showed me the IOUs. Shortly after, the owner went bankrupt and the land was lost. Later my father-in-law tried to give me another piece of land as a substitute, but I refused. More than a dozen years later he is still insisting, often with the threat that if I do not take it, the Islamic government will.

Anjoman-e Zedd-e Bahā'īyat (The Anti-Baha'i Society)

[The Anti-Baha'i organization was started with the permission of Āyatullāh S. Husain Borujerdi by Shaykh Maḥmūd Ḥalabi of Mashhad who became what in contemporary idiom might be called a "Mahdi freak." He started an annual celebration of the Mahdi's birthday in Mashhad, in which everyone who owned canaries would bring them in their cages to decorate a large ḥusainiyeh in which the celebration was held. He also started an organization to stop the spread of Baha'ism which claimed that Muhammad was not the last and final prophet, but that a new dispensation had begun with Baha'ullah. The organization was called *Anjoman-e Imām-e Zamān* to deny any claim that the Bab or Baha'ullah could be considered the Mahdi or messiah: *Imām-e Zamān* ("Imām of the age") is a title of the twelfth Imām who will return as the Mahdi. After the 1979 revolution, the organization Arabicized its name to *Hojjatiyya* after another title of the Imām-e Zamān: *Hujjat Allah 'Alā Khalqih* ("God's proof over his creation"). Ḥalabi moreover hinted that he was in daily contact with the Imām-e Zamān; and eventually he came out against Khomeini, denying that he was a legitimate representative of the Imām-e Zamān. The name *Hojjatiyya* thus now performed two denials: first, it denied the Babi-Bahā'ī claim that the Imām-e Zamān had come or that there was a new dispensation; second, it denied Khomeini's title *Nāyeb-e Imām* ("aide to the Imām") or *Imām.* Ḥalabi invoked the slogan "Should any flag be raised before the coming of the Mahdi, its carrier is an idolator [*ṭāghūt*] and is guilty of the heresy of *shirk* [worshipping something other than God]." Halabi advocated peaceful means of fighting the Baha'is, including harassment, but not direct insult or violence. However, violence against the Baha'is has broken out on several occasions during this century: 1903 in Yazd, 1955–56 in nearby Abarghū, and the 1979 revolution are times of martyrdom for Baha'i history (on the former two, see Fischer [1973, appendix on religious riots]; on the latter, see Fischer [1980]; on Babis and Baha'is, see chapter 4).

In Yazd the Anti-Baha'i Society was headed by Dr. Paknejad, a physician on government salary, who also owned a weaving factory. His office was devoted more to the Anti-Baha'i Society than to healing patients, although he often wrote out free prescriptions for the poor. He wrote a University of Tehran dissertation, and published from it a series of some fifteen volumes on Islam and medicine, called *Avvalīn Dāneshgāh va Akherīn Peyāmbar* (The first university and the last prophet), which is a badly written and confused outpouring of verbiage with little value or coherence. After the revolution he was elected to Parliament from Yazd. He was assassinated, and was succeeded as member of Parliament by Āyatullāh Ṣadūqi's son, Muhammad-Ali Ṣadūqi. (When Muhammad-Ali ran for reelection to Parliament, he was rejected by the Yazd electorate in favor of a mullā from Mehriz, but was nonetheless appointed by Khomeini to be a deputy minister of justice in Tehran. Subsequently, he ran for the Majlis again and was elected, and has now succeeded his father and father-in-law as the main āyatullāh in Yazd.)

A number of Baha'is of Yazd were killed during the revolution. The most dramatic of these stains on the revolution was the execution of Nūrullah Akhtar-Khāvari (see chapter 4), the gentle, cosmopolitan leader of the Yazdi Baha'is, who handled international correspondence for the Derakhshān Textile Mill. He had given Paknejad private tutorials in English. Paknejad not only repaid this with diligent harassment of the Baha'is, but made no move to avert the execution of his teacher. That execution was filmed for television by the zealots of the revolution only to discover that audiences were repulsed: the broadcast was suppressed. Paknejad now has a small street named after him, as if he were a worthy martyr.]

It was Mr. Nayeb Kabir, the geometry and religion teacher mentioned above, who prepared us for ideological combat against the Baha'is, whom he referred to as "the political party." He stressed the verse in the Qur'an (33:40) which refers to Muhammad as *Khātam al-Nabiyīn* ("the seal of the Prophets"), and he prepped us for the Baha'i argument that while *khātim* means "the last," *khātam,* the form here, means "signet ring"; from this, the Baha'is drew the conclusion that there were other "seals" of prophecy, while Mr. Nayeb Kabir insisted that the Qur'an means that

Muhammad was the seal that closes prophethood. He also prepared us for the Baha'i argument that *nabī* is only one of several kinds of prophets, and that *rasūl* and *ulu al-'azm* are other kinds. But one cannot be a *rasūl* without being a *nabī,* and one cannot be an *ulu al-'azm* without being both *nabī* and *rasūl.* And he dealt with the problem of the supernaturally long life of the Mahdi: born in 255/868 he had already lived eleven centuries, and would live to the end of time. Here he would tell us about others who had lived long lives, e.g., Noah; he told us there were contemporaries who had seen the Mahdi; and he said that modern biology had demonstrated that cells could live forever if properly nourished. The last fit nicely with the dogma that all the Imāms had been assassinated, for had their lives not been precipitously ended, they would have lived forever. He taught us the signs of the Mahdi's reappearance, and he had ready answers to objections such as, Why would the Mahdi return with a sword and only 313 followers; would not a few atomic bombs be more efficient? The answer was that in a sword there is discrimination, while atomic bombs kill guilty and innocent alike, leaving no opportunity for verbal persuasion, for people to recant and join the forces of the Mahdi. His forces will not be limited to 313, but many will join: may we all be his soldiers.

I did not know much about Baha'is before this time. Children in the alleys would sometimes chant, *Tū pīr-e bābi ridam* ("I shit on the Babi saint"), and my father had told me that "Babis" (he did not distinguish Babis and Baha'is) did not say their prayers, and were *najes* (impure). In the village, the first *Sepāh-e Dānesh* (literacy corpsman) had been taunted and run out with accusations that he was Baha'i (though that may have had to do mainly with his obvious disinterest in the village, and his always running off to town).

My father had already often spoken to me about the Mahdi. One of his few books, which he seemed never to tire of reading, was a volume called *Nūr al-Anwār* (The light of the lights). It described the Mahdi, gave vivid accounts of false messiahs, the signs of the true Mahdi's reappearance, the names, number, and place of origin of those destined to be among his special 313 soldiers. My father would sigh, "Alas, I am not one of those soldiers, since none of them come from Yazd." He also had a small book by a mullā named Khalisi, called *Crime in Abarghū,* the story of a Baha'i who had killed some Muslims with an ax. The book called on Muslims to rise up for justice. It inflamed people like my father and youths like myself to think of Baha'is as merciless killers; and I remember that after having read it, I had nightmares of a Baha'i trying to kill me with an ax. My father liked to tell me the stories of the year of Baha'i killing (*sāl-e bābi koshi*) [presumably 1905, but perhaps 1955–56; see Fischer (1973, appendix on religious riots)], as if he singlehandedly had killed Baha'is like so many flies or mosquitoes. The verb he used was *saqqat kardan,* the term for beating animals to death. Of course, I knew this was all vicarious bravado: he had never killed anyone in his life.

Nayeb Kabir's approach was different. He did not share the pride of the earlier generations in having physically killed Baha'is. Instead he thought the spread of Baha'ism could be halted, bringing the misguided back to Islam, by training Muslim youths to challenge the Baha'i missionaries (*muballighs*). He had a network of spies who had penetrated Baha'i circles by pretending to be believers. Part of their job was to find people in the process of being attracted to Baha'ism, or merely curious, and reconvert them back to Islam. I was recruited and attended weekly meetings of the Anjoman-e Zedd-e Bahā'ī in a room attached to the Congregational Mosque just across from the old Vaziri Library, belonging to the *Heyat-e Ḥāmiyān-e Masjid-e Jāmi'* (Gathering of Protectors of the Congregational Mosque). I seemed to be the only student in these meetings; everyone else was from the bazaar, except two teachers, Nayeb Kabir from the secondary school of the Ta'līmāt-e Islāmi, and Mir Ali from the primary school of the Ta'līmāt-e Islāmi. There were several such groups of ten or fifteen persons each under the general leadership of Dr. Paknejad. Among ourselves the organization was called Anjoman-e Zedd-e Bahā'ī, but to outsiders we called it Anjoman-e Imām-e Zamān (Society of the Imām of the Age).

These meetings consisted in part of dictations by Nayeb Kabir, which we would copy into notebooks, of arguments to use with the Baha'is, and quotations from their own writings complete with page and line reference. But the exciting part was practice debates in which one of us would play the role of the Baha'i. Soon I was completely preoccupied with Baha'ism. I read all the refutations of Baha'ism I could find. Nayeb Kabir and these books told me about the connection between Baha'ism and colonial politics, that the Russians had invented the Shaykhi sect and its offshoot, Babism; that Baha'ism was an offshoot of Babism supported by the British, and more recently by the Zionists. (Khāliṣi, the author of the pamphlet about Abarghū, had also published the memoirs of Prince Dalgorgi, the Russian who was supposed to have started Babism, by going to Sayyid Kazem Rashti, the head of the Shaykhis, and suggesting to him that the Mahdi might be among us, and pointing out the Bab. Khalisi was exiled to Yazd by the shah, and many old folks still remember his activities aimed at establishing Islamic unity.)

Once, in Dr. Paknejad's presence, I played the Baha'i, and defeated all my fellow Muslims. This ranged from glib adolescent nonsense to much more dangerous areas. To the slur, "Baha'ullah is your God," instead of insisting that he was a prophet of God, I counterattacked: "Suppose it is so, what then?" My opponents took the bait: "It says in your books that he had a hernia, how could God be so powerless as not to be able to cure his own hernia?" To this I glibly responded, "At the beginning of your Muslim prayer you say 'Allah o Akbar' ['God is the greatest']; if God is the greatest, then his testicles must be the greatest." Everyone laughed good-humoredly. But when I began to argue the case for pantheism and metaphor, and cited the Qur'anic verse where God says, "It was not you who shot the arrow, but Allah," things became tense, and Paknejad stopped the proceedings, saying, "Thank God, you are Muslim; were you really a Baha'i, not even Muhammad himself could convince you." Another said, "If someone were as hardheaded as you, it could never be the word of Muhammad that could change your mind, but only the sword of the Mahdi." Everyone laughed.

In these debates we were taught to be polite, to differentiate ourselves from the rabble who cursed the Baha'is. Baha'is were pacifist, so we had no fear of being beaten, and we wanted to show we also had a mission to be as peaceful as they, and to demonstrate that we had a higher logic. Our goal was not so much to win verbal duels, but to intervene with Muslims who were toying with Baha'i propaganda and bring them back into the fold of Islam. We infiltrated into Baha'i meetings under the guise of ourselves being potential converts. Often, of course, Baha'is we engaged in conversation would ask, "Do you know Dr. Paknejad?" We would say, "No, I have nothing to do with him." We were also taught to snatch rare Baha'i books where we could. Two or three incidents in which I participated will illustrate the tactics.

I befriended Kamran, a young Baha'i. We said to each other, "If I can show you the truth, will you accept it," and each of us said yes. He brought me a mimeographed book, which impressed me. I took it to the Anjoman-e Zedd-e Bahā'ī, where as soon as I began describing its arguments, it was identified and the counterarguments laid out. Nayeb Kabir told me it was not an important book and I should return it. Kamran then gave me a rare edition of the *Iqān* (Certitude), published in Cairo. Paknejad recognized it as the original unedited version, and appropriated it. Kamran tried mightily to persuade me to give it back, arguing that were he to have done the same to me, I would never accept his religion; that I was clearly not acting on my own conscience but was being manipulated by others; and that he had borrowed it to show me only with great difficulty, arguing that I was an educated and sincere friend. I remained unmoved, and pointed out that the book was no longer in my hands, but that it now belonged to the library of the Imām-e Zamān.

Kamran also took me to the one Baha'i meeting I ever infiltrated. I remember that there was a Baha'i missionary from Tehran who answered questions of the local Baha'i, and there was one local very agitated man who asked how to respond to questions about the Baha'i calendar having an illogical nineteen months, while all other religions had twelve months aligned with the solar or lunar calendars. The missionary responded that were the questioner Muslim, one could cite the Qur'anic *bismillāh-i rraḥman-i rraḥīm,* which has nineteen letters, and several other phrases which were multiples of nineteen, i.e., to show that nineteen is a divine number.[26] The man in a crude Yazdi idiom retorted, *Kos cheh rabṭi be shaghigheh dareh?* ("what connection does the vagina have with the temples?"; the Tehran idiom is *Guz che rabti* . . . , "What connection does a fart have . . ."). So the missionary replied, "Nineteen times nineteen is 351 days, plus four days we celebrate the New Year, what's so bad about that?" Another item of discussion was that the Baha'i library in the village of Manshad did not have a copy of the Dehkhoda encyclopedia, and money should be raised to supply one. This impressed me because at the time, the Vaziri Library was trying to find someone to donate volumes to complete its set of this encyclopedia, and I thought to myself this village library must be large to have things our library did not. Later I realized Baha'is had a special interest in this encyclopedia because it had a long entry on the Bab. The entries on the Imāms were short, understandably, since every Iranian knows about them, but it angered Muslim zealots like Dr. Paknejad.

The only other evil thing I did against individual Baha'is was when I was transferred to a second group of the Anjoman under Ahmad Fattahi. Fattahi was a registrar of births and deaths. It was he who registered most Baha'i marriages, births, and deaths, so he was a tremendous source of information in keeping tabs on Baha'is. (Baha'i marriages were not legally recognized in Iran; marriages could be registered only under the four recognized religions: Islam, Christianity, Judaism, and Zoroastrianism.) One day Fattahi called me. I had a beard and a black suit, and he gave me a black attache case. He took me to an alley in the Zoroastrian quarter, and told me to knock on a particular door and ask for Abbas. Abbas would not be there. I was to pretend I was an anti-Baha'i activist from Tehran asked by Abbas to come and answer questions he was not capable of answering. Whether or not I was admitted into the house, I was to deliver the message that they should not think what they were doing was secret, but that we knew everything that went on. When I knocked, a woman's voice with a Zoroastrian accent answered without opening the door, "Who is it?" "Engineer Imami," I said. Members of SAVAK were said to use the titles Engineer or Doctor. "What do you want (*che farmāyeshī dārīd?*)," she asked in polite formal language, adding "Our man is not here (*mardemūn khūneh nīst*)", i.e., please go away. "I'm looking for Abbas." "What Abbas? No Abbas lives here." "Abbas, you know, the painter." Silence. I repeated, "Abbas, the painter who comes here to learn from your husband." "He is not here." "He must be here; he sent for me to come all the way from Tehran to answer a few questions. Where shall I go? When will your husband or Abbas be here?" Surprisingly, at this point, the woman opened the door a little, and spoke loudly as if invoking the ears of neighbors, "I already told you, Abbas is not here, my husband is not here." I said, "Tell Abbas if he sends for someone from Tehran, he must be polite enough to meet them." And I turned and walked away. Fattahi was waiting around the corner with his bicycle and took me on it back to his office. There I reported the conversation and asked him what it was all about. Abbas, he said, was a poor painter who had been seen repeatedly in the shop of this Zoroastrian-Baha'i tailor. The ruse worked: when Abbas next went to the house, he was turned away despite his protestation that he did not know any Engineer Imami. A few days later Fattahi sent someone else to Abbas to hire him to paint a house. As the contract was being made, this emissary asked, "You are not a Baha'i or a Jew are you; paint after all is a liquid and conveys impurity, we cannot use a *najes* painter." "No, no," Abbas assured him. Then later while painting, the emissary said, "Sorry I asked you, but you know these Baha'is are such hypocrites and liars." And with such preparation, often an Abbas would spill his own story out of bitterness. So, Fattahi said, we turn potential enemies of the Mahdi into soldiers of the Mahdi.

That is what we called ourselves, *Sarbāz-e Imām-e Zamān* (soldiers of the Imām of the age). It was a kind of war. Perhaps that is why many of the leaders of the Anjoman were not married: Nayeb Kabir, Mir Ali, Fattahi. No one in the organization was a mullā, because clerical dress would warn off any Baha'is. The only one who wore a turban was Shaykh Mahmud Halabi of Mashhad who started the whole thing.

The Sage in the Library: Vaziri

Vaziri was like a second father to me: he gave me my first job in his library, attached to the Congregational Mosque; he helped arrange my marriage; and he provided a model of public service to me. He not only built up a modern library, with one of the finest manuscript collections in Iran, but he renovated the decaying Congregational Mosque, and was instrumental in reviving the Friday communal prayers in Yazd. Although in some respects he was as enmeshed in the conservative religious ideology of Yazd as the other leading cleric, Ṣadūqi, he was more tolerant and open-minded. His life story, which I got to know well over the years, is not only inherently interesting, but a central part of Yazd's development in the past half century.

Vaziri was a serious theological student in Yazd as a youth, but as it happened, he never progressed further in the theological curriculum than Arabic grammar; he never even got to jurisprudence. He was very poor, and to make a living, he started doing *pā-menbari,* i.e., he was the warm-up act before the main sermon (*khuṭba*) in the mosque or at a *rowzeh.*[27] The pā-menbari, usually someone with a good voice, would stand or sit on the first or second step of the minbar and recite religious poetry. Vaziri was good looking, tall, thin, with blue eyes, and he had a silver tongue. One day the daughter and wife of Afsah al-Mulk (a court poet and noble associated with Muzaffarddin Shah) were in the audience; the daughter fell in love with him. The family, after some debate, decided that although he was poor, he was talented, a *sayyid,* with a noble genealogy going back to a vazir of Shah Yahya. (Vaziri's ancestors came from 'Urayḍ, a village near Medina in Saudi Arabia; they were *sayyid*s, descendants of the prophet; and they had served as vazirs to the rulers of Yazd, hence the family name.) They sent a woman go-between to Madrasa Khan where Vaziri was living. As he tells the story, an amusing exchange occurred.

There is a knock on his room door late one night, and when he opens it, he sees an old woman who asks if he would like to marry. Naturally, he thought she was proposing a *ṣīgheh* (temporary) marriage. He says, "no, thank you," and starts to close the door. She hastily says, "Wait, sometimes there is a fortune at your door; don't be so quick to let it go." Vaziri becomes angry: "You call yourself a fortune?" "No, no, you have misunderstood me: I'm not offering myself; I am here to encourage you to ask for the hand of the daughter of Afṣaḥ al-Mulk." Vaziri becomes even angrier; he thinks he is being mocked: "Me a poor *ṭalabeh* (theological student) marrying the daughter of Afsah al-Mulk! *Del-e marā sūzūndī*" ("you've seared my heart, may God burn your heart"). "What can I do to convince you?" she says. "Go to hell," he replies. She leaves, but is sent back the following evening with some bags of gold, and says to him, "If you think poverty is the barrier, here take these and ask for her hand; they will give her to you." And so, Vaziri sends one of his teachers to Afsah al-Mulk, and receives the answer, "Why not."

On the one hand the story resembles that of the Prophet who married Khadija, a rich woman, and of the philosopher Mir Damad, son-in-law of Shah Abbas;[28] on the other hand it is like the ditty that warns *ṭalabehs* that if they marry, their studies will suffer (*dhubiḥa al-'ilm fī furūj al-nisā,* "knowledge is slaughtered in the vagina"). So it was with Vaziri: his studies came to a halt, but with his new wealth and name, he was popular and turned his energies to public service. This was a time when the Baha'is were very active, taunting the Muslims that their decaying mosques were signs of the decay of their religion, that a new dispensation was coming to replace Islam. Vaziri happened to lose his voice, and it was rumored that this was due to poisoning by the Baha'is who feared his silver tongue would help revive Islam. When he regained his voice, he went on the minbar, and began to preach: "The Baha'is say Islam is dying, that its death is symbolized in our decaying mosques. Let's show them." Every Friday he would go on the minbar and make an appeal for money; women would throw their jewelry at him. (Very much the same mode of donation happened during the 1979 revolution.) As soon as he began the project, of course, the government bureau of archeology and public works showed up to supervise. The original mosque had been completed in 777/1375, allegedly on the site of an old Zoroastrian fire temple, so it was an archeological monument. I was present when Engineer Nazarian, a government engineer from the Antiquities Office of the Ministry of Culture, approached the Imām Jom'a and in his distinctive Kermani accent, asked him to help raise money for the project. The Imām Jom'a said, "No problem, I need not raise money, it is available: just tell the government I said they should spend the *khums* on this good act" (i.e., he was sarcastically referring to the Islamic tax on surplus income that should be collected by Islamic governments for public projects).

Vaziri also arranged to have electricity put into the mosque. It was operated by a Zoroastrian in a room attached to the outside of the mosque. He spoke English (probably he had been to Bombay) and was an employee of the Zoroastrian who brought electricity to Yazd, a man we called *gowr-e cherāgh-e barqi* (*gowr* was a derogatory term for Zoroastrians), i.e., "the electricity *gowr.*"

Vaziri was also the one who revived the practice of Friday prayers in Yazd. (On the debate among Shi'ites whether *namāz-e jom'a* is prohibited during times of illegitimate government or until the return of the Mahdi, whether it is required as the Qur'an originally intended, or whether it is a meritorious act in a predominantly Shi'ite community, see chapter 2.) There was little point in restoring the Congregational Mosque, if one did not also revive Friday prayers. At first it was difficult to get people to come. A produce seller used to station himself at the gate and tell people, "We are going to have Friday prayers, we need a quorum of five, please join us." This was in the 1920s.

Most importantly, Vaziri began a modern library. This caused some resistance at first among some of the clerics. They did not like the fact that he was introducing Western style tables and chairs, nor that he was taking away "for preservation" theological manuscripts endowed for the active use of theological students. Vaziri brushed aside the objections, pointing out that now there were printed editions of these fragile manuscripts. Vaziri was so persistent and sucessful in getting people to donate furniture, books, and manuscripts, that people began jokingly to call him *shāh-e gadāha,* king of the beggars. The first library was established with eleven hundred books in 1334/1955 in a room adjacent to the mosque; the room originally was a mausoleum where Vaziri's father was buried, as well as where the previous imām of the mosque was buried. Ten years later when the next imām died, there was pressure to bury him in the same place, and to redignify the place as a mausoleum. Fortunately, by this time, Vaziri had already arranged for a new library building, on a site outside one of the mosque gates, on land that had primarily been used as a public toilet. There were by now some twenty thousand books. The new building was donated by a Yazdi industrialist, Muhammad Herati (later executed in the Islamic revolution). When I began working in the library, it was still being moved into its new quarters, and I and the newly retired head librarian were in charge of ordering the books on the shelves. There were four staff members: the head librarian was a former schoolteacher, who read little, and depended for his knowledge on what people told him the books were about; Shaykh Ali was a theology student and regarded all books on subjects other than Islam as worthless;[29] Sayyid Mustafa was a manuscript expert who was good at letting us know whether an author was Sunni or Shi'ite.

My official title was bookbinder, although I was a jack-of-all-trades, and served as a secretary to Mr. Vaziri. The bookbinding room gave me some privacy to read books that were otherwise forbidden. These were three categories of books: those banned by the government (these I felt obligated to read since I thought they contained things the government was trying to hide from the public); those forbidden on what I thought were justifiable religious grounds, books we thought were written to destroy Islam (in this category were the books of Gobineau, of

Fig. 1.9. Schooling and bookmaking, a miniature attributed to Mir Sayyid Ali, ca. 1540, Tabriz, Iran. Scenes depict a teacher bastinadoing a student, students copying texts, craftsmen making paper, etc. A School Scene. 27.0 × 15.1 cm. S86.0221. Courtesy of the Vever Collection, Arthur M. Sackler Gallery, Smithsonian Institution, Washington, D.C.

Fig. 1.10. Artisans from the library: clockwise from top right: burnishing (smoothing and polishing) of paper, stamping of designs into leather cover, sizing of folios, sawing of a bookstand, preparation of goldleaf, calligrapher. Border from an Indian painting, c. 1600–1610. Mughal, from the Jahangir album. Page is 42.5 × 26.6 cm. 54.116 verso. Courtesy of the Heeramant Collection, Freer Gallery of Art, Smithsonian Institution, Washington, D.C.

Kasravi, and the introduction to *Nuqṭat al-Kāf* by E. G. Browne); those that were forbidden to the masses, but which I thought intelligent people like myself could handle (Hedayat's books were in this category). If people asked for these books, we said, "*Mamnū' ast, nemīdīm*" ("it is forbidden, we do not lend it"). I remember saying this to someone when he asked for Hedayat's story "Spring of Immortality," and then curious, beginning to read the book myself, and getting caught by the head librarian, who seized it, saying, "the books of Hedayat make people commit suicide." I was sixteen when I read Hedayat's *The Blind Owl* for the first time: it was indeed a shattering experience, and I saw that Vaziri had written in his own hand on the cover the warning that it was not to be given out. Not only was *The Blind Owl* shattering because the sufferings of the narrator were so moving, nor only because the imagery powerfully recalled my dream of the girl on the island, but also because it opened my eyes to the numbing repetitions of everyday life, and left me in despair of the absurdity and meaninglessness of my life.

Vaziri collected books indiscriminately. I remember his son, a physician, used to donate old drug catalogs. I sometimes thought I should be given permission to weed out the junk. Once I asked Vaziri why if some books were so dangerous we did not burn them. The idea of burning books was abhorrent to Vaziri: it was the single most heinous crime he held against Ahmad Kasravi, much more than his criticism of Shi'ism and its clerics. I asked him whether books that misguided people had any positive use. First, he said, they are useful for the scholars who refute them. But when I replied, "No misguiding books, no need for refutation," he answered, "Books are like men; you hang a man without a proper trial, and he will become a martyr forever. You burn a book, and its fame becomes greater."

Vaziri was always delighted when foreigners came to visit: it was a way of validating his pride in having distinguished himself beyond other local clergymen, in having accomplished something which was admired by non-Muslims as well as Muslims, foreigners as well as Iranians. In fact, local Yazdis had relatively little interest in the library: they were craftsmen, factory workers, and merchants. Most of the users of the library were high school students interested mainly in the math primers. So, foreigners provided a kind of legitimacy, and he was especially proud of visits of such celebrated scholars as the art historian Arthur Pope. It was through his concern to be hospitable to all foreign visitors that I met the third critical patron of my education.

Clerical Rivalry and Āyatullāh Ṣadūqi

[Āyatullāh Muhammad Ṣadūqi had been an aide to Āyatullāh S. Husain Borujerdi before returning to Yazd to succeed Faqih Khorasani as the local *marja' taqlīd.* He became Khomeini's representative in Yazd, and after the revolution was Khomeini's representative for the southeastern region of Iran. His was the most authoritative voice to be raised in defense of the killing, jailing, and excluding from public service of Baha'is and members of the Mojahedin-e Khalq. After the revolution he changed the site of where he led prayers from the Hazireh Mosque he had built, to the Masjid-e Mullā Isma'il, the largest mosque in Yazd. He preferred this mosque to the Congregational Mosque partly because it was larger, partly because he did not directly wish to displace the Imām Jom'a of Yazd although he was doing so indirectly, partly because the latter mosque had been repaired with "unclean" money of the shah's government, and partly because he did not wish to add any luster to a mosque associated in the popular mind with Vaziri. It was in the Mullā Isma'il Mosque that Ṣadūqi was assassinated, an event captured fully on video tape by a crew that happened to be filming his activities. The Mojahedin-e Khalq claimed credit for the assassination, and said it was in revenge for the killing of the Meṣbāḥ family through the incitement by Ṣadūqi. The Mujahedin had proposed a young former public bath attendant as a candidate for Parliament; Ṣadūqi had called on the public to destroy the Mujahedin. The Revolutionary Guards took him literally, and attacked and killed Meṣbāḥ, his wife, and children.

Ṣadūqi was succeeded by the father-in-law of his son, Āyatullāh S. Abbas Khātami, a man with considerably less charisma but also less brutality than Ṣadūqi. As one Yazdi put it, Ṣadūqi was feared, Khātami was respected. Khātami was an opium smoker, and a story is told that a woman came to him to intercede for her husband who had been jailed for a small amount of opium possession by the Islamic government; Khātami summoned the chief of police, ostentatiously smoked an opium pipe in front of him and asked him to either jail him or release the other man for this minor crime. The man was released, Khātami said that opium is not prohibited by the Qur'an, and only smugglers should be jailed. Another Khātami story is that two men accused of a capital crime but not convicted sent a lawyer to intercede with him. He directed that the two dig their own graves, lie in them, and before a crowd of witnesses repent of their sins. The crowd was moved, and after this moral

Fig. 1.11. Āyatullāh Ṣadūqi, shown on a stamp issued by the Islamic Republic of Iran.

lesson, Khātami released the two men. Khātami died in 1988 and was succeeded by Ṣadūqi's son.

Note that the narrative pattern of Vaziri's conversation with Empress Farah (and the similar story of Bohlul and Empress Farah in chapter 3) fits the pattern of the frame tale to the *Thousand and One Nights,* and of the tale told before a disliked marxist subgovernor in Afghanistan recorded by Margaret Mills in 1975. These are tales told to despotic rulers, tales about despotic rule and the rehabilitation of despots. In the latter two cases they are also "talking cures" like the Joseph story in the Qur'an and Bible: a troubled ruler who cannot sleep is entertained with a narration that must succeed in saving the narrator's life by moving the ruler to pity as well as amusing him, and also must enlighten him about the causes of his affliction which lie in his own behavior. His personal affliction is interconnected with the causes of poverty, tyranny, and misrule in government. What is of particular note is the way in which such tales can be told to superiors by people vulnerable to their arbitrary power. (See Mills forthcoming, p. 146.)

Let me contrast Āyatullāh Ṣadūqi—nobody referred to him as āyatullāh; he was called Hojat-ul-Islam; we did not have many āyatullāhs in those days—with Mr. Vaziri, and also with his predecessor, Shaykh Gholām Rezā Faqih Khorasani, and with the Modarressis. Vaziri was a man of service, Ṣadūqi a man of learning, trained in Qum. I knew Ṣadūqi from childhood: I said my prayers behind him from age eight, and I remember at first when I stood directly behind him, he asked me to stand further back, since he thought I might not know the rules of purity. Later I served both as a *muezzin* (caller to prayer) and as a *mokabber* (who tells the assembly when to bow, when to rise) at his mosque, the Ḥaẓīreh Mosque.

Part of the story of Ṣadūqi I must tell from what my mother narrated to me: Ṣadūqi as a child helped his paternal uncle in Yazd in a place called Ḥaẓīreh, where the Ḥaẓīreh Mosque is today, on the main street of Yazd just up from the clock tower at the end of the street leading to the Congregational Mosque and the Vaziri Library. But in those days it was a *gharīb-khāneh,* a place where poor visitors to Yazd could be given a room and food for a few days or weeks. It had been established as a charitable endowment many, many years ago. It contained a small mosque, where Ṣadūqi's uncle led prayers, and Ṣadūqi as a child would help out by calling people to prayer, and by reading *du'ā* prayers before the *namāz* prayers. This uncle had, as my mother put it, an ugly daughter, who was older than Ṣadūqi, and they gave her to Ṣadūqi. Soon thereafter he left to study in Qum. There he proceeded through the ranks, and ended up becoming the treasurer to Āyatullāh S. Husain Borujerdi (the head of the Qum theological center, and the leading āyatullāh of Iranian Shi'ites).[30] Ṣadūqi had a nigh miraculous memory. He claimed, both to me and to news reporters, that his memory was so good that he was able to pay fourteen thousand theological students their monthly stipends without missing one and without giving one twice, all without any record keeping.

This went on until it was decided to run a son of Shaykh Abdul-Karim Ha'eri-Yazdi, the former leader of the Qum theological center, Mehdi Ha'eri-Yazdi, for Parliament from Yazd. There were a few complications: e.g., Mehdi Ha'eri was not old enough to be a member of Parliament, but that seemed not to matter. Ṣadūqi was sent to Yazd to campaign for Mehdi Ha'eri-Yazdi. This is the period when Ahmad Kasravi mocked the mullās, and this campaign was a perfect target: for years, noted Kasravi, the mullās insisted that the Iranian government was illegitimate and one must not cooperate with it; now when they saw some room for them in it, they attempted to send one of their sons to Parliament.[31] Mehdi Ha'eri-Yazdi lost the election. But something else happened.

The leading cleric of Yazd, Shaykh Gholām Rezā "Faqih Khorasani," died in a village some twelve farsakhs (seventy-two kilometers) from Yazd. People carried the body on their shoulders back to the city. There was perhaps some encouragement given to Ṣadūqi that he should stay and succeed Khorasani, but Ṣadūqi needed no encouragement. In Qum he was merely a treasurer to Borujerdi. Here was an opportunity to govern a town. So Ṣadūqi stayed in Yazd. To comprehend his standing in Yazd, we need to compare him with Khorasani.

Faqih Khorasani is one of those names which will be remembered for a long time in Yazd, particularly for his piety. He is the one we used as an example in the introduction to Khomeini's *Risāleh Towzih al-Masā'il* (Fischer and Abedi 1984: xv): he discovered his mother was not doing her prayer ablutions correctly, and fearing she had never done them right, he undertook to repeat her *namāz* prayers for her entire eighty years' worth lest, on account of ritual failure, she go to hell. People remember him for such piety, and in fact he really was free of love for worldly ambitions. Three or four times he sold his house, and spent the proceeds for theological students and the poor. Finally, a rich man tricked him into a house. The story is that the rich man, after one of these episodes of selling the house, offered him a house to live in. After Faqih Khorasani had moved in, he said, "I give this house to you, you own it, but there is one condition, you may not sell it for as long as you live, and you must live in it." There is another story that a man came to him and said he needed some means to work. Faqih Khorasani asked what he did. "I have been a porter, but I am too old now to carry things." So Faqih Khorasani gave him his personal donkey, saying, "Take this, I do not need it, I can walk." Faqih Khorasani was also a stoic: when his son died, he did all the funeral preparations and ceremonies himself. That day happened to be the date someone was supposed to get from him a sum of money; the man, of course, did not come for the money out of respect for the funeral and Faqih Khorasani's bereavement; Faqih Khorasani chastized the man for not keeping their date.

Faqih Khorasani is also fondly remembered for his outwitting of Reza Shah's decree that the clergy were forbidden to wear turbans. Faqih Khorasani dressed in the garb of a shepherd, with a felt cap, a big staff in hand, and *gīveh* on his feet, with the backs of the *gīveh* pulled up and a *pā-pich* wrapped around his legs. (*Gīveh* are cotton slippers, usually worn with the back turned down so one can slip them on and off easily when entering a room; the backs might be pulled up if one intends some serious walking. *Pā-pich* are wide ribbons of cloth wrapped around the legs as support stockings.) The symbolism was quite apt since prophets were always shepherds in Islamic tradition. People still enjoy talking about how Faqih Khorasani looked like a shepherd ruling over so many lambs in Yazd.

Ṣadūqi, of course, was never able to take the place of Faqih Khorasani. He may have been more knowledgeable than Faqih Khorasani, but not as pious. Why not? The most important thing Ṣadūqi did in Yazd, at least in the early part of his career, was to convert the Ḥaẓīreh from being a hostel for strangers (*gharīb-khāneh*) into a mosque. Many people objected and refused to say their prayers there on the grounds that the endowment and land had been illegitimately usurped. Ṣadūqi argued that it was a *tabdīl be aḥsan* (replacing something with something better). He argued that the place had become an opium den and a place of prostitution, and that anyone could agree a house of God was better than a place of ill repute. But many thought that a proper *tabdīl be aḥsan* would have been to rebuild the *gharīb-khāneh* in a modern attractive way, not eliminate the function for which it was endowed (on the legalities and politics of endowments, see Fischer [1980*a:* 114–20]). It was not as if Yazd lacked enough mosques.

The issue of the conversion of the Ḥaẓīreh into a mosque was a useful tool in the hands of both the circle around Vaziri and also the well-established clerical family called Modarressi. The Modarressis, as their name indicates, were *modarress* (teachers) of theology. They controlled, and still control, some of the theological schools of Yazd. The Modarressis always thought themselves superior to everyone else: they were called *āghāzādeh* ("sons of great men"), they always sat at the highest place wherever they went, and they cultivated a look of disdain at ordinary folk as if they were wise men amid crowds of fools. They never accepted Ṣadūqi as a religious authority in town. Financially, they were quite well off: they had some land, even a few very small villages, I think. So they needed nothing from the town and were content with what they had: their role as teachers, and the endowments they controlled. They looked down upon both Vaziri and Ṣadūqi, but there was a difference: Ṣadūqi responded in kind, but Vaziri accepted that he was not on the same level of scholarship, and overlooked an occasional slight, preferring to maintain relations with the Modarressis. There also was an issue of tolerance. The Modarressis had little truck with the liberals who supported Vaziri, and again Vaziri took no offense.

Vaziri was tolerant in the sense that if he knew that your daughters did not veil, or that you were working for the government, or that you spent your money in questionable ways, he cared, but he did not let it stand between you and himself as human beings. He still dealt with you, he would still allow you to use the library. Ṣadūqi, by contrast, would not do that: he was very strict with those with whom he would deal.

Vaziri did not mind that he did not control any theological schools, a source of clerical prestige. He knew that he was not cut out for such a role; he was not trained and did not know how to teach. He was not interested in that sort of thing. But Ṣadūqi was. And so Ṣadūqi revived the Madraseh Khan, an old theological school in the bazaar, to rival the Madraseh Muṣalla, run by the Modarressis. Eventually he also established a library, Kitabkhāneh Saryazdi, named after a cleric from the village of Saryazd, probably with the intention of rivaling Vaziri's library. He even tried to hire away staff from the Vaziri Library. But Ṣadūqi's library never achieved the standing of Vaziri's, perhaps because the latter was not so "pious" about where it derived its support and clientele.

Let me tell you a story that can serve as a symbol of the situation. One day the Empress Farah came to Yazd. It would have been impossible to get Ṣadūqi to go and welcome her, but Vaziri met her. He even said things that caused her to smile. But he was also extremely courageous. The meeting was to last fifteen minutes; it went on for forty-five, and it was mainly Vaziri speaking, not the empress asking questions. Then, I will never forget, Vaziri pointed to a grave which had just been discovered by the archeologists, and he said, "Here is the grave of a queen who ruled Yazd about a thousand years ago. From her there remains nothing except the good deeds she did for the people. If you want to live forever, you must emulate her." That took guts to say to the empress. Earlier, at the beginning of their conversation, Vaziri said, "Your Majesty, you and I are cousins, so let me speak to you cousin to cousin." They were cousins because both were sayyids. I saw a smile on the face of the empress: she did not mind. But Vaziri was saying, if you are a queen, you are a queen for yourself; but to me you are the daughter of my uncle. (Compare the story of Bohlul in chapter 3.)

I remember the early morning before Vaziri was to meet the empress. He was wondering what to do if she tried to shake his hand. A man is not supposed to shake hands with a female stranger. Some years earlier, when the queen of Denmark visited Yazd, someone suggested he bandage his right hand and pretend to have a serious problem with it. He did so and the ruse worked: when the queen stretched out her hand, Vaziri showed his bandaged hand and excused himself. A local poet memorialized the event: "He did not want his hand stretched toward unbelief / Therefore / The honor of Islam (i.e., Vaziri] bound his own

Fig. 1.12. Empress Farah Pahlavi, *left,* Āyatullāh Vaziri, *right,* Mehdi Abedi, *center.*

hand." This time too, Vaziri thought of doing the same, but was assured by someone that he need not worry, since the empress knew the religious law.

As long as Vaziri lived (he died shortly before the revolution), the liberals, the intellectuals, those who had some higher education, did not pay too much attention to Ṣadūqi. Every government agency head—the police chief, the governor, the mayor, and so on—when they arrived in Yazd would pay a visit to Vaziri, because of his popularity, to create a kind of alliance. One day as I came out of the Congregational Mosque, I saw an old man being helped out of a jeep by a young driver in military uniform. He asked me the way to Vaziri's house, and I led him there. Even before entering, outside the house, he removed his shoes, or rather, because he could not bend over, asked his aide to help remove them, and as if he were entering a shrine, he recited, "O Moses, take off your shoes" (Qur'an 20:12). He turned out to be General Aqevli. He had been a confidant of Reza Shah, was now the head of the Sepah Bank and head of the Society for National Monuments (*Anjoman-e Āsār-e Mellī*), come to pay his respects to the ill Vaziri. The Anjoman-e Āsār-e Mellī helped repair monuments and subsidized many books like the two-volume *Yadegarha-ye Yazdi* (Monuments of Yazd) edited by Iraj Afshar.

Officials and visitors treated Ṣadūqi differently. Even the head of SAVAK, and the police, seemed a bit afraid of Ṣadūqi, considering him a troublemaking mullā. That is, they felt they had to pay tribute to him, lest he make trouble. For instance, once when I was sitting with him, a man came, and as was usual, whispered something in his ear. Ṣadūqi's face turned red, and he said, "I'll take care of him." He picked up the phone and called the chief of police, and said, "You! You'll exile me! Do you think I'm afraid of exile? All I have in this world is a few things I know. I'm an *'ālim,* a *rūḥāni.* No matter where I go, I am worth the bread I eat." It was obvious the man on the other end was saying, "I did not say such a thing." And Ṣadūqi continued, "Suppose that you did say it, I want you to know that I am not afraid. Go ahead and do it." No doubt the police chief responded, "By God, I swear I said no such thing." Ṣadūqi replied, "Well, I'm not saying that you did, but suppose that you did, say it if you want to say it, I am not afraid." And sure enough, while I was still sitting there, the police chief arrived, and kissed Ṣadūqi's hand.

Does this story illustrate something? Such things would never happen with Vaziri. When people came to Yazd, they went straight to see Vaziri because he was an interesting fellow and had a library to show off, and Vaziri would make them feel welcome. With Ṣadūqi there were difficulties, say if a person did not have a head cover, but Vaziri did not mind. In this sense, Vaziri was known for his tolerance, and Ṣadūqi for his fanaticism.

Both Ṣadūqi and Vaziri were excellent preachers, but with quite different styles. Ṣadūqi preached only during the month of Ramaḍān, and he would draw the largest audiences in Yazd. The Ḥaẓīreh Mosque would be packed, especially when Ramaḍān fell in the summer and it became too hot for the shopkeepers to sit in their shops, preferring the fans of the mosque. Ṣadūqi could preach in the most vigorous way for hours, partly because he did not fast. I think he was a diabetic, and so excused from fasting. One year, I remember vividly, he did not preach, and sent the young Rāshed-e Yazdi on the *minbar* in his stead. Rāshed began with an incredible faux pas, trying to explain that Ṣadūqi in previous years had been able to preach because he did not fast, and this year he was not preaching. Ṣadūqi, sitting in the audience, enraged, began shouting, "Tell them why I did not fast. I was ill. Tell them why I did not fast: they will spread stories and rumors. The Qur'an says sick persons are exempted."

Ṣadūqi's style of preaching was a mixture of allusions to contemporary social ills, evoking his audience's guilt and fear of hell, and final vesting of hope for redemption in the intercession of Ali and Husain whose supporters and partisans we Shi'ites are. He would speak seriously for a few minutes, then crack a joke to wake up his audience. Every few moments he would ask the audience to chant a *salavāt* (blessings upon the Prophet and his family), which would have the effect of startling awake those nodding off. He was skilled at alluding to persons without mentioning their names, in such a way that everyone knew who he was talking about. He could thus talk about politics, but more trenchantly he could also talk about those things in society he despised such as the cinema and usury, and invoke the guilt of persons in the local society. Thus, the front rows of the prayer assembly were filled with *nuzūl-khor*s (usurers, shopkeepers, and merchants who made money on loans, futures, short selling, etc.). He loved to scare them with visions of hell, if they did not come to him for the formula converting the forbidden (*ḥarām*) into the permitted (*ḥalāl*), through the devices of "legal deceits" (*ḥiyal* or *kulāh shar'ī;* see Fischer [1980*a:* 158, 278]). He was superb in vividly describing the days of final judgment. I remember having dreams for nights of the Sirat Bridge at which the soul is judged on the third day after death, and of the serpent that will arrive on the desert of resurrection on the day of judgment. Ṣadūqi would give the exact measurements of the serpent, the width of its mouth, its length. The serpent is asked, "What do you eat?" And in a fearsome voice, Ṣadūqi would intone the snake's responses: *al-tārikūn al-ṣalāt wa law bi rak'atin* (those who neglected to say their prayers, even one *rakat*); *wa l-sha'ribūn al-khamr wa law bi qaṭratin* (those who drink alcohol, even one drop); and so on, a long list, till everyone in the audience was cognizant of being a candidate for the serpent's gullet. At the end, Ṣadūqi would release the audience with the thought, "We are the partisans of Husain and Ali. We need to reform ourselves. But for past sins, perhaps Husain and Ali will intercede on our behalfs."

Or he would utilize a vivid form of the story of Karbala, e.g., on the day of judgment, everyone's head is turned back over their shoulders. Why? Because of their sins? No. Because someone says Fatima is entering the Plain of Qiāmat. The people do not see her. Why? Are they blind? Indeed, the kind of eyes that look lustfully at women are not worthy to see Fatima. But that is not the reason. Indeed, the people must close their eyes, lower their gaze. Is that because they are *nāmaḥram* (eligible to marry, hence must obey the rules of modest behavior) to Fatima? But at least the *sayyid*s are her children, and even the *mirzā*s (descendants of the Prophet only through their mothers) are her children, and many more of us have ancestors who were *sayyids*. (Relatives need not veil or circumscribe their gaze before one another.) No, the reason is that Fatima's face is so radiant, brighter than any sun, that ordinary people cannot look upon her. Why has she come? To intercede for you, for your crimes, you gamblers, you usurers, you adulterers, you cinema-goers, you thieves. . . . To intercede on your behalf? No. She carries beneath her chādor, . . . and slowly she takes it out . . . shall I tell you? . . . can you bear it? . . . the finger tip of Husain (lost in the Battle of Karbala; alternatively, the head of Husain, separated from the body and carried off to Damascus as a trophy)! She brings it to God that he should punish the killers of Husain. People would cry, and occasionally even faint.

A favorite story about the anxieties of answering correctly the angels' questions in one's grave was told about the difficulties even of so august and pious a figure as Āyatullāh Abdul-Karim Ha'eri-Yazdi. He had come to someone in a dream and reported that he had been struck dumb when asked who his Prophet was and what his scripture was. He was terrified that his paralysis at each of the three times the question was posed would condemn him to hell. Finally, his tongue loosened and he managed to cry, "I am a servant of Husain," at which the angels cried and said no harm should come to him.

Most of Ṣadūqi's *va'z* ("sermon," in Yazd usually specifically the sermons of Ramaḍān; more generally, what a *vā'ez,* "preacher," delivers, sometimes contrasted with the specific forms of preachment built around the Karbala story, *rowzeh-khāni*) occurred at noon prayers. But he also preached on the nights of *eḥyā,* the three or four nights on one of which the Qur'an was revealed in its entirety: the nineteenth when Ali was mortally wounded; the twenty-first when he died; the twenty-third, his *sevvom* ("third day") when his soul passed to the next world; and the twenty-seventh when his assassin, Ibn Muljam, was executed. Particularly the first two of these nights, the mosque was jammed. These were the nights when one did one hundred *rak'at* of prayer to make up for any missed prayers during the year. At one point, the lights are turned off, and people put the Qur'an on their head, and pray that the fourteen pure souls (Muhammad, Fatima, Ali, Hasan, Husain, and the other nine Imāms) intercede with God to forgive their sins. I remember once that some joker put black ink in a rose water container, so when he sprinkled the "rose water" into their palms and they wiped the "rose water" over their faces during the blackout, and the lights came on, they got a shock, thinking for a moment that God had painted their faces black as a mark of their sin.[32]

Vaziri's preaching was quite different from Ṣadūqi's. He did not dwell on the ills in society, but rather on the glories of Islam and on the history and culture of Islamic civilization. He was fond, especially if he saw an educated person in the audience, of citing names of European scholars who had acknowledged Islam's greatness, names like Gustav LeBon or Arthur Christiansen. (Ṣadūqi would never invoke the authority of a foreigner.) The most moving parts of Vaziri's preaching were his singing: the invocation, and the verse of the Qur'an which he would take as his text, and then again at the end the *gorīz* or "turning" to the story of Karbala. (Ṣadūqi never sang, not even the *gorīz*.)

Each in his own way knew the skills of working his audience, a skill that depends upon knowing the audience. There is an apocryphal story about the mullā who went to Rasht on the Caspian Sea, and did a *rowzeh* for three nights, getting no reaction: no one cried. So he went to a local mullā to ask what was wrong with these Rashtis. "I told them about the thirst at Karbala and no one cried. I told them about the thirst of Sakineh, the daughter of Husain, and no one cried, and I told them about the thirst of the six-month-old baby of Husain. Still no one cried." The local mullā replied: "You don't know your audience. Rashtis have so much water, they have no conception of real thirst. You should tell them about Fadak, the way Fatima's garden was illegitimately confiscated, because recently Reza Shah confiscated many lands of these people." And so the mullā took this advice, and was gratified that many people fainted in sympathetic reaction.

Many of the great preachers of Iran came to Yazd. I perhaps got to know them better than most young men since I was in the entourage of both Ṣadūqi and Vaziri. But youngsters in those days enjoyed imitating their styles; it was a form of public entertainment.

Patronage: The Route out of Yazd

One day as I was binding books, Vaziri came in and asked me to go out and offer my help to a foreign lady inspecting the tiles and inscriptions of the mosque. I too was eager to use such opportunities to practice my English. This lady was different from others I had met: she was accompanied by an Iranian chauffeur and a second Iranian man, both of whom bowed whenever she said anything. After guiding her about the mosque, I invited her to visit our library and our collection of old manuscripts. She seemed to enjoy the visit and especially viewing several miniature paintings. She then asked where I had learned my English. I replied, "In Yazd. Without the help of any teacher. If only someone would send me to England or the United States for a few months."

It was not the first time I had expressed such a wish, and I was already used to the smile of the foreigners after I would so petition. She however did not smile, and seemed to be lost in thought. Then she asked how much I was being paid. Four hundred ninety tomans a month (about seventy dollars). "Not much," she said, "and what do you do for them?" I answered with a list: bookbinding, calligraphy, translation, cleaning, whatever is needed. She said nothing more.

As we were about to exit, Vaziri stopped us and asked if I had told her about the founder of the library, and whether I had asked her to send some books. "Yes, sir," I replied, and I introduced him. "This is Mr. Vaziri, the founder of the library and the one responsible for repairing and reviving the Grand Mosque." I was pleased to see that she already knew better than to try to shake hands with a pious Muslim man. She expressed her admiration, and Vaziri asked me to translate one of his favorite poems, "People see only a bit of [sesame] oil in the bottle/They know not what became of the sesame itself." He meant to say how much hardship he had suffered to accomplish all this, and that these accomplishments were the essence of his existence. My English was not very good, but since he frequently asked me to translate this poem, I had worked hard to memorize a good translation. The lady shook my hand warmly, and said, "See you later." I would learn later that she was Monica Fateh, wife of the road construction engineer, Hasan Fateh, who was paving the road between Na'in and Ardakan (some fifty kilometers from Yazd). At the time I knew enough English to know that "see you later" is another way of saying goodbye, and thought it merely the end to a brief encounter.

One afternoon, two young men approached me outside the library. I knew I had seen them somewhere but could not place them. They said I had met them with Monica Fateh. Since I had not asked her name, this only perplexed me. "We are charged to take you to her," they said, and motioned to a landrover. My heard stopped: my God, I thought, these must be SAVAK agents. Only a few days earlier, SAVAK had arrested three boys who had been regulars at the library. I knew that any resistance or effort to escape would result in my blood being spilled on the street. So I asked if I was permitted to say goodbye to my family. "It's not necessary. You will be back in two or three hours," they said. But I had heard this was the usual answer given by SAVAK agents, and that would be the end of him. So I insisted. The driver said, "Fine, but don't take too long. We will wait outside the house."

I do not know how I said goodbye to my wife and child, but it took no more than a moment. I ran out and got in the landrover. Another man, whom I had not seen, was in the back; his eyes were red; he either had just woken up or was drunk. I was offered the front seat. As we drove to "Monica's place" (which turned out to be on the far side of Ardakan) we hardly talked. Only the driver offered me some pistachios and asked me about my English. I replied I had learned my English by working with two Americans who were writing books about Yazd. We passed through the city of Ardakan, and then into the desert again. "Are we going to Tehran?" I asked. "No," said the driver, "only outside the city to the camp." In my heart I repeated, "Camp, SAVAK headquarters."

We came to a piece of land surrounded by barbed wire. At the guard booth, two men who looked like construction workers made a crude sexual joke to the driver. We drove on and the driver said to me, "Sons of bitches, that's all they think about. And why not? They get to see their wives or pay a visit to the whorehouses in Tehran once or twice a year." I did not know what to say. We drove toward a temporary building, with a loud generator. We got out and I was told to go inside and wait for Mr. Fateh. "Mrs. Fateh?" I asked. "No, Mrs. Fateh is in Tehran." What difference could it make, who knows if these are their real names. I went inside and sat on a chair at a dining table. A man came and asked if I had eaten. "No, but do not trouble yourself," I replied, although I was dying of hunger. A few moments later a heaping plate of rice and a bowl of stew were placed before me. "I am making fresh tea; it will be ready as soon as you finish eating," the cook said, and then with an inquisitive smile, "Are you going to work for the company?" Interpreting this to mean was I going to cooperate with SAVAK, I said I believed in my country, I would never commit treason against it, and I did not know why I was here. He did not say anything further, but left the room as he heard another man enter.

Mr. Fateh shook hands with me as he introduced himself. He thanked me for my hospitality to his wife in Yazd. "Tell me about yourself," he said, as if in a hurry to have the short version of a long story. I did my best. "How about military service?" I said I was about to receive an exemption because of my aging father, my wife, and child. "You are married?" "Yes." "That will make it difficult," he said staring into my eyes. I thanked God it was going to be difficult. "O.K.," he then decided, "if you are really interested in continuing your studies, we will pay the expenses. You must get an exemption from the military so we can get a passport for you. Get a dozen photos, some copies of your birth certificate, and be in Tehran as soon as you can. Here is our address." I was speechless, and before I could say anything, he called the driver: "Qasem, take him back to Yazd, and hurry, his family must be waiting."

Moments later in the landrover, I was interrogating Qasem about Mrs. Fateh and her visit to Yazd, and about Mr. Fateh and what he does for a living. He told me Fateh was the owner of a large construction company. Qasem asked me, "What did Mr. Fateh say? Are you going to work for the company?" "No, he wants to send me abroad." "Yes, to become an engineer and work for his company. He is the best man I have ever known: he has helped so many people." We were at the door of my house. "Good luck," he said, "I will see you in Tehran."[33]

A few weeks later, I resigned from Vaziri library to go to Tehran, with leave-taking scenes appropriate to the characters of my immediate boss, Mr. Vaziri, and Āyatullāh Ṣadūqi. I had had a running dispute with Mr. Entezari, the head of the library, over salary. I wanted fifty tomans more a month. He resisted, and said he would refer the matter to the parent organization of the library, the Office of the Shrine of Imām Riḍā (*Āstān-e Qods*) in Mashhad. They, of course, would back him in not raising my salary. For one reason, as he insisted, I did not have a high school diploma. (He had one, and had been a teacher.) He did not know about the arrangement with Mr. Fateh. I said, "If it is the diploma, I'll get one." "Too late," he replied. "Why? You are married and already have a child." Angry, I retorted, "I'll be a *ḥarāmzādeh* (bastard) if I come back to live in Yazd without a Ph.D., you will see." I wrote out a letter of resignation. Bureaucratically, he wrote across the top, "*Movāfeqat nemīshavad*" ("not approved"). So I took it, tore it up, and said, "I'm leaving, call the police on me if you wish." Entezari went to my father-in-law. My father-in-law, although knowing about Fateh, merely said to Entezari, "It is his own decision."

So next Vaziri called me, and promised me anything, and told me that he planned to make me a member of the governing board of the library in his will. So, I told him that in truth I was resigning to continue my education: *bā yek dast nemitūnam do hendevāneh bar dāram* ("I cannot carry two watermelons with one hand"). He inquired where I was going, and I said England. He approved but admonished me, "If you come back like Mehdi Bāzargan, my blessings upon you; but if you go with religion, and return without religion, may you never get there" (*agar mīrī ferang ke mesle Mehdi-yi Bāzargan bar gardi, pedar va mādaram be fadāyat; valī agar ba dīn miravi va bī din bar migardi omidvāram narasi*).

I then went to say goodbye to Āyatullāh Ṣadūqi. He asked what I was going to study. I said I did not know: political science, or sociology, or languages. He said, "If you could forgo England, I will send you to Japan as a missionary; the Japanese are thirsty for Islam." I replied that I still needed to learn English. He acquiesced, and then concluded, "If you study abroad, study sociology, because I want you to come back and break the teeth of the hypocrite, that no good Shari'ati." (I was a bit taken aback, because I rather liked what I had read and heard of Shari'ati.)

Tehran: Ideological Crucible

I took a TBT bus to Tehran. TBT was supposed to be the best of the bus lines: it had new Mercedes buses; the cheaper bus lines would buy used buses from TBT. Buses left Yazd in the evening and arrived in Tehran early the next morning. My seatmate was a Yazdi whom I vaguely knew, a certain Sabetolqowl (literally, "one who keeps his word"), two years older than I, and a skilled reciter of poetry. (His father was a registrar of birth certificates and identification cards, known allegedly for overcharging and pocketing the difference.) It was from him on the bus that I first learned the word "ideologue." He asked where I was going. I said I was going to study. He replied, "I hope you come back an ideologue." I asked what the word meant. He said, "One who has original ideas."

In the morning we arrived at the Būzarjomehri bus station in south Tehran. It was like the arrival scene in the movie, *Āghā-ye Hālū* ("Mr. Gullible"; see M. Fischer [1984]): I got off the bus, and asked someone for directions to Abbasabad, where my friend Muhammad Tabataba'i, whom I had tutored in Yazd, lived. A man pointed north, and like the greenhorn I was, I picked up my bags and started walking. Instead of asking, at each street I assumed it might only be a street or two farther. It was not until 5:00 P.M. that I arrived in north Tehran at Muhammad's door. When he opened it, his face registered shock, and he said, "Oh my God, what is wrong?" "Nothing, I'm just tired," I said. "What brings you to Tehran? You must be sick. Do you have cancer, you look so pale?" "No, I've come to study." "You will die in this city: it is not for you. You like warm, friendly, cooperative people. Here no one talks to anyone." "I hope you will not treat me like that." "No, no. You are welcome. Stay a few days, even a week, even fifteen days." "Do not worry, I'll only spend the night. I have arranged everything."

The next day he took me to Paradise, the Fateh company. Ahmad Ragerdi, the guard, stopped me with questions: where are you going, who are you, what is your name. But the driver Qasem Reza'i saw me and said, "He's a friend of Fateh, let him in." The secretary, a British woman, Mrs. Akbari, welcomed me and called Fateh. Fateh offered me a room in the building, five hundred tomans a month (slightly more than I had been getting at Vaziri Library), and then told me: "I want you to go to the British Council at Firdausi Circle and register for English classes; I also want you to register for high school; and if you have time, it would not be bad to learn some French at the Institut Français de Tehran." I was a bit surprised. I thought I was to be sent to England. Fateh had already gotten me a passport. But I did not say anything. Mrs. Fateh then arrived and explained they thought it best for me not to go directly to England. I assumed I was being tested. A year later, in a conversation Fateh had with Michael Fischer in my presence, I learned that it had been S. Husain Nasr (then chancellor of the Aryamehr Technical University, and now a professor at George Washington University) who had convinced them not to send me directly to England: this provincial lad, first see if he can survive and flourish in Tehran.

So I registered in three schools. In the mornings I went to the British Council. In the afternoons to the Institut Français. And in the evenings to the Elmiyeh High School, near the Majlis (Parliament). It had been difficult to find a high school that offered the Persian literature program; it seemed Elmiyeh was the only such school. Clearly, everyone in Tehran wanted the science track that would prepare them for jobs. The Elmiyeh High School prided itself that Sadeq Hedayat had gone there.

The night school class was full of characters, almost a grotesquerie. The principal was a foul-mouthed alcoholic who sprayed saliva as he spoke or shouted. The philosophy teacher was Baqer Chubak, a cousin of the novelist, Sadeq Chubak. He was extremely funny, but also outspokenly sarcastic about the shah and his White Revolution, so that we feared the soldiers might burst in at any time. The Arabic teacher was a Kurd, Naserzadeh. I tutored his younger daughter in math, and he regularly gave me a lift to class. We became good friends, and he was the first to tell me about the Kurdish sense of oppression under the Iranian state. He invited me once to a picnic in a village north of Tehran where everyone was in Kurdish dress, spoke Kurdish, drank arak, and danced. His elder daughter on that occasion translated for me, and began to tell me about cultural differences. One of her examples was poetry: in Persian poetry, you speak of the beloved as being like a flower or a cypress; in Kurdish poetry, you speak of the beloved as being like a gun, or walking like a horse.

There were some thirty-five of us students in the class, all trying to get a high school diploma. There was Daoud Hadadi, the young brother-in-law of General Bahram Aryana. He was a playboy in his twenties who had gotten a position in the Plan Organization thanks to the general, but now that the general had fallen from favor, he feared some personnel officer might notice he had no diploma and he would lose his job. I tutored him for a while. Then there was Ḥajji Nekunam, in his forties, who always spoke about Tayyeb, the former strongman of the Tehran bazaar. It seems Tayyeb had gotten him his position as head of the telephone office for the Ecbatana district of Tehran. Again, since Tayyeb's departure, he feared someone would notice his lack of a diploma and he would lose his job. I tutored him as well, and in partial payment he allowed me to telephone anywhere free. I took advantage of this to call Yazd, and once even England. Others in the class included a gendarme who wanted a diploma so he could be promoted to a military rank, a carpenter who wanted a government job, and three others who began my Tehran political education. Saqafi, a clerk in his twenties, was a relative of Khomeini's wife. I tutored him as well, and he spoke often of Khomeini, but especially of Taleqani, who was in jail. He talked of Taleqani as a trainer of guerillas. Another student, a shirt maker from Mashhad, talked to me about the Mojahedin-e Khalq, saying his brother was in jail. He spoke against private property and against the superficial Islam we were taught. Why he sought me out, I'm not sure, but I was a bit afraid of him, and uncomfortable since I was grateful to one capitalist (Fateh) for helping me. I tested him by asking if he could make me a shirt, and how much he would charge. He said of course he would, we could go together and buy the cloth, and he would only charge me a nominal five tomans to make it. I still have that shirt, but I feared to develop the friendship with him.

Finally, there was a student who worked in the pharmacy of the gendarmerie, a zealous fan of Dr. Ali Shari'ati. He was the one who really introduced me to Shari'ati. This man felt personally indebted to Shari'ati. He was born illegitimately, and felt the stigma powerfully. In a heavily religious society, there are various social functions that are prescribed by various qualifications, often beginning with "of legitimate birth." Moreover, he felt the sin of illegitimacy meant he was almost certainly destined for hell, and he kept changing jobs, first to avoid discovery, but also in search of a job which would gain him merit which might counter the sin of his birth. So when he joined the gendarmes, he volunteered to work in the hospital and pharmacy. He never went to the mosque but piously said his prayers at home alone. His great desire was to make a pilgrimage to the shrine of the eighth Imām, Imām Riḍā, in Mashhad. But it was widely believed that anyone of illegitimate birth who entered the shrine would have a nosebleed and be exposed. One day, in the Husainiyeh Ershad, he met Shari'ati and asked to confide in him for advice. Shari'ati heard his story and responded that it was all nonsense, that a good person needed to fear neither the shrine nor hell. "How can I be sure?" the man wanted to know. "I guarantee it," Shari'ati assured him. "Go test it." And the man did so, and was forever grateful. He was to become part of my conscience when I took up the following year with a communist. "With the Islam of Shari'ati," he would chide me, "why do you want to dabble with communism?"

Around that time I went to hear Shari'ati deliver two of his famous lectures: "*Shahādat*" (Witnessing/martyrdom), delivered in the Husainiyeh Ershad on Tāsu'a, the ninth of Muḥarram; and "After *Shahādat,*" delivered in the Congregational Mosque of Narmak on the night closing the day of 'Āshūrā, the tenth of Muḥarram. The former was a long speech, the latter short and electric. I vividly remember how Shari'ati shouted and raised his hands with such power that I thought at any moment the shah's troops would burst in to wreak vengeance. Indeed, there were rumors that Mojahedin pamphlets had been circulated and a few people had been arrested. (It was said that the regime often would arrest a few people and leave, so there would be no witnesses or confrontation, but so that terror would be maximized.) The shah had just killed ten Mojahedin, and Shari'ati spoke in the present tense referring more to the present-day martyrs than to Husain and the martyrs of Karbala. He began with the riveting phrases: "My brothers, my sisters, now the martyrs are dead, and we the dead are alive. Those who had the courage to die chose death, and we the cowards continue to live. The martyrs left us a message, us, the deaf and blind of history. . . ."

I tutored a number of these characters from the Elmiyeh High School. I also put up a notice at the British Council that I was available to tutor elementary math, Persian, and Arabic. A Mrs. Hajizadeh, an English lady married to an Iranian, called and hired me to teach her children Persian for five hundred tomans a month. Both she and her husband were very nice to me, and sometimes gave me extra money with the admonition not to tell the other. Fateh, who proved to be a friend of theirs, found out, and said, "Why don't you teach my children, I'll pay you." I of course replied that I would gladly teach his sons for free. So, I was doing well those days, with free room, often meals at the Hajizadeh or Fateh house, and money in my pocket. I lived in the Paradise Company compound, which once had been the Fateh home, a lovely large house not far from the university. Two of the servants became my companions. 'Amū Reza (Uncle Reza), the gardener, a Yazdi, hired originally by Hasan Fateh's father, came early in the morning and always began cooking soup. He was constantly going back and forth between his gardening and his soup. He had deformed legs and was quite a character. In the evenings he took the bus back to his family.

Ahmad Ragerdi, the guard, was on duty twenty-four hours a day, every day. He complained he got to see his wife, back in the village of Ragerd, near Khomein, only three times a year. He was very lonely, but had a temper, so many people avoided him. He always wanted to invite me to share food, and especially to sing religious dirges (*nowḥeh*) for him, so he could cry, since as he put it he could not go out to *rowzeh*s (the preachments that end with weeping for Husain). Once we shared 'Āshūrā together, and he begged me to sing the dirges for Husain. He began to beat his chest so hard, I feared he would cause himself real harm, so I stopped. He begged me to continue. I said I would, but only if he would moderate his chest beating. We began again. He continued to pound his chest. I stopped, but he continued wailing, "Husain, Husain," interspersing his invocations of and to Husain with laments about his family and hard life, until he collapsed.

The summer after this first year in Tehran, I was sent to England, to Crosby House (or Crazy House as the students styled it) in Bournemouth, an English language school mainly attended by French students. Before I went, I was taken to see 'Allāmeh Nūri. People going to England were often taken to him to strengthen their faith. He was famed for having converted many Christians to Islam. In reality, hippies would be picked up in the streets and taken to him; he would talk to them about Islam, give them books, have their photo taken, and claim to have converted them. He was a rich mullā from Mazandaran, with a large library, and had founded the World Organization for Islamic Services to translate texts into English and to propagate Islam. He also had a Ph.D. from the University of Tehran and taught there, although a recognized member of the opposition to the shah. He had been told my English was good, so he did not try to say anything to me in English, but talked about the untranslatability of idioms.

I was afraid to fly, so I asked Fateh if I could take the bus: TBT to Istanbul, then a German bus to Munich, then another bus to Ostend. I was surprised in London and again in Bournemouth that no one seemed curious about this stranger in their midst: no one stopped to stare or talk, as we did whenever a European appeared in Yazd. When I finally got to Bournemouth and tried to ask directions to my lodgings with a Mrs. Stephenson on Wimborne Road, either people would not stop to answer or I could not follow their rapid speech. One sweet little old lady stopped and asked, "Where are you from?" "Iran." "Never heard of it." "Persia." "Oh. Do you know the shah?" "Yes." "That's nice." And she walked off. Finally, someone put me on a bus, and the conductor said, "When I say cemetery, you get off." Having heard all sorts of stories about racism in England, I took this as an insult, and did not want to get off when the bus stopped and he said, "Cemetery." (I thought he was telling me to go to hell.) But I got off and then saw a street sign for Wimborne Road. Mrs. Stephenson had several rooms to let: there was an Iraqi and a Portuguese student. The Iraqi was an obnoxious twit who claimed to be a communist, but had a new car every month, and a bevy of girlfriends, and was the son of a capitalist. Mrs. Stephenson, a striking woman in her forties, a gymnast, liked to say this Iraqi and I had the eyes of Omar Sharif. The stay in England was good for my language skill, and expanding my horizons—I would return to Europe the next summer as a guide to a rich Iranian family—but to relate most of the incidents that happened would only sound like the travelogue of Amin-ud-Dowleh who visited Europe in the nineteenth century and tells how he fell in love with European girls seventeen times. One incident, however, was significant, and shook my faith.

I had met an Anglican priest in Yazd. So one day I called him and he invited me to spend a weekend with him in Winchester. He took me on his rounds to visit the sick, he showed me the cathedral, and pointed out the graves of several Crusaders as well as that of a bishop who had debated Charles Darwin. I asked who won the debate, fully expecting him to say the bishop. To my surprise, he answered that he thought they had not really understood one another and that each was talking about different aspects of man, the one about biological man, the other about spiritual man. Asked a similar question, at the time, I never would have admitted a Muslim could have not won a debate. I was impressed. I was also impressed with his simple life style and his life of service. I began to think to myself, how could such a man be condemned to hell. (There is a saying of the Prophet, "My religion will divide into seventy-two sects; all of them will go to hell but one." I began to think of Bishop Dehqani-Tafti, the convert to Christianity from Taft near Yazd, and for the first time felt a glimmer of understanding of how someone might come to convert to Christianity. And I thought of Shaykh Gholām Rezā Faqih Khorasani, the late pious āyatullāh of Yazd: he once had visited

Kurdistan and witnessed the rituals of the Aliullahi. Impressed, he had said, "Let us leave lest we stay and lose our faith." So, too, I was relieved that I was able to leave at the end of the weekend.

My second year in Tehran, I discovered that one need not register at a high school to get a diploma, but could just take an exam, and so I registered for the free preparation classes at Hashtrudi High School near the Paradise Company. It was here that I met Shamlu, a relative, I think, of the poet. In the English conversation class, one day we were asked to tell our father's occupation. Everyone answered straightforwardly, except Shamlu, who said, "My father is a proletarian." The teacher responded, "If you say such things, you'll go to the *sūrakh*" ("hole," i.e., jail). "Which hole?" he belligerently responded. "The hole in which they offer you Pepsi" (i.e., torture with a bottle). That was the day I learned the word *proletarian.* I asked him after class what it meant. "A worker; one with nothing but his arm to sell." "Nothing?" I was now being belligerent: "No house, nothing? You chain smoke cigarettes, you must have money." "Don't be so literal." A few days later in composition class, an essay was set on books. Mine ended with the sentence, "Every book is worth reading at least once." Shamlu shouted from the back, "Bullshit." The teacher ostentatiously gave me a 20, the highest grade. Shamlu heckled: "Yes, it is this kind of false praise that gives people false pride, so that even Shemr cannot stop them." After class, he came up to me and said, "Do you know why I said what I did?" "Because you dislike me." "No, just the contrary. I know you read a lot, but you have to analyze things. Your logic is Aristotelian, static, not dynamic, dialectical. You are like the donkey who carries books but does not know their real content" (a transference of the Qur'anic slur against the rabbis [Qur'an 2:101, 62:5]). And so over the next few weeks he introduced me to the vocabulary and argumentation of marxism. I vaguely knew about communists before this, but barely knew the name of Marx: in our childhood folk etymology, *communist* had been, only half jokingly, derived from *Commu* (a putative name of God) and *nist* ("is not"). Shamlu gave me a book (with the cover carefully removed) on dialectical logic; which he warned me was dangerous to talk about, could lead to being condemned to death. It was secret knowledge, knowledge that had been suppressed throughout history. He spoke of the ancient heroes Mazdak and Babak as dialecticians whom history had suppressed. He read me a passage one day, full of exploits of a great man, without revealing the name of the man. I knew enough of the argument against the "great man in history" now to reject the passage. He gleefully pointed out that the passage was about Muhammad, and then turned the tables once more by saying that for his time Muhammad was progressive. Nothing is static: what is progressive in one era is reactionary in another; there is no eternal essence, but things continually are in a process of becoming (something else).

The month of Ramaḍān came, and I vowed not to talk to him unless he fasted. He agreed, but broke his fast each evening with a bottle of beer. One day, he said, "Come to my house and we'll make some kebabs." He had difficulty starting the fire, and he brought out an old Qur'an and used it as tinder. I was aghast: my hair literally stood up on my skin, and I started trembling. I thought death would surely strike us. I had been claiming to be a communist, and he grinned and grabbed my trembling hand, saying: "So you are a communist, no, you aren't." I argued with him that revolution was unrealistic, that people were doing fine, through my tutoring I got to see many kinds of people. "Where do you tutor?" he asked. "Niavaran (north Tehran)," I said. "You don't see south Tehran," he said. "Yes, I do." In fact I was tutoring a Lur from Malayer, and would go to the room he shared in south Tehran with his parents and sister, and a carpet loom. It was after the conversation with Shamlu that this Lur invited me to share a meal: terrible greasy rice with almost nothing in it. Suddenly, Shamlu's words had their effect: I saw sharply the poverty of the room, the poor clothes, and the contrast between the rich serving their dogs meat, and these people having no meat at all. For days thereafter I went about classifying everyone into exploiter and exploited, but I could never persuade myself that the revolution should liquidate all the exploiters without exception. Fateh could not be in that category.

I, of course, did not become a communist, but it was Shamlu who prepared me for the ideological battles I was to find in Lawrence, Kansas. It was a year of confusion, and at one point I thought I would commit suicide. Ironically, it was Ahmad Ragerdi, the sixty-year-old lonely gatekeeper, who prevented me from trying. One Friday, I tried to write out all my confusions, in an effort to judge myself. I had studied enough philosophy to be thoroughly confused by all the conflicting theories; my faith had been eroded; I felt I had not achieved anything in life, and that my life had no direction. I concluded that a confused and worthless life contributes negatively to society, and that such a person should kill himself. Moreover, if such a person's faith continued to erode, he would go to hell anyway, and perhaps this could be prevented by ending the life. I cleaned up my room and determined to throw myself under a large truck in such a way that no blame could attach to the driver. This manner of suicide would avoid having a decaying body be found in the establishment of people who had been good to me. As I left the house, the old gatekeeper grabbed me by the arm and said I could not leave until I read a letter for him. He was depressed again and desperate for company, and forced me to listen again to the sad story of his life: how he had accomplished nothing in his life, how he could not even read. (*Dard-e del* is not only a genre of telling one's sorrows, but in folk theory it is an important mental health release.) He demanded that I recite some religious laments (*nowḥeh*) to help him cry, beat his chest, and relieve his heart. Impatiently, I compiled, but gradually as we mourned together, I decided my suicide could wait.

At the end of this second year in Tehran, I took the university entrance exam, and scored highest among the thirteen thousand literature stream applicants. This entitled me to a scholarship from the shah's government. I had gone to the office of Habib Dashti, a Yazdi in the Ministry of Science and Higher Education, whom I had once met in the Vaziri Library, on the advice of Mrs. Fateh to find out about schools in the United States. He offered me the scholarship, with the condition only that I return to Iran. I said I had to consult Ṣadūqi, which I did. Ṣadūqi told me to reject the offer, the Imām (i.e., Khomeini) had forbidden any cooperation with the government. I rebutted, "It is not cooperation, they are giving me money I deserve." He replied sharply, "You wanted the truth. I gave it to you." When I returned to Tehran, I told Mr. Fateh about the scholarship, and as soon as I started to say, "But," he said, "You don't want it." Again he promised to help me financially, but only myself: he would not support a whole family. That summer I took some rich Iranians on a trip to Europe as their "guide." And when I returned, I began filling out university applications for the United States with the help of Michael Fischer, who had returned to Iran to do a study of the theological schools in Qum. I remember taking advantage of Michael's presence in our very first reunion meeting, to test some of my confusions in what I hoped was a not too revealing manner: he sneezed, and I said, "God bless you, if He exists," and then I immediately asked, "Does He exist?" Michael laughed and said he did not know, what did I mean by the question. I quickly changed the subject and asked if he had ever heard of Karl Marx. He laughed again, and said, "Of course." I asked if what Marx said was correct. Michael replied that some of it was and some was not, which was not much comfort to me at the time, since I was looking for simple, definitive answers to believe in. But Michael's easy confidence at least reassured me that with some more study these things could be resolved.

Although we filled out six U.S. college applications, that from Kan-

Fig. 1.13. Michael Fischer in the Mir Chaqmaq Mosque, Yazd. Photo by Elaine Akhavi.

sas came back first with an acceptance: no SATs were required, the tuition was relatively cheap, and it was a regular pipeline for Iranian students. Indeed, it was called *qafas-e rejīm* (the cage of the regime), since it had some three to four hundred Iranian students each year. For three months, I worked with Michael in Qum: for me, it was an interesting, if sometimes somewhat disillusioning experience to see the workings of the clerical center up close. I brought my wife and three-year-old son, and the four of us lived in a house just behind the Qum shrine between the establishments of Āyatullāh Mar'ashi and Āyatullāh Shari'atmādari.

Lawrence, Kansas

[The United States and Europe have been major breeding grounds for Islamic fundamentalism as well as for other political activisms. It is here that with freedom of expression wider than at home, students and others are able to debate and organize. The alien openness of Euro-American society functions like the relatively fast-paced life in Tehran or Cairo, in causing some youth from traditional families to defensively seek the security of fundamentalist rules and discipline, and to obsessively focus

Fig. 1.14. The skyline of the seminary town of Qum. The smaller dome on the left is the Shrine of Hazrat-e Ma'suma, sister of the eighth Imām (whose shrine is in Mashhad), and the larger dome on the right is the great teaching mosque, Masjid-e Borujirdi. Photo by M. Fischer.

Fig. 1.15. The courtyard of the Faiziya Seminary, the largest theological college in Qum. Khomeini taught here, and immediately returned here after his triumphant return to Iran in February, 1979, after 16 years of exile. The domes are those of the shrine and of the Borujirdi Mosque. Photo by M. Fischer.

on the corruptions of the political elites of their home countries. Iranians divided by political loyalties were often suspicious of one another; not only was there constant fear of SAVAK, but Muslim activists and leftist activists disagreed strongly. In some cities like Boston, leftists clustered at one university while Muslims clustered at another, and quietist de facto loyalists to the shah's regime clustered at yet a third. In other cities like Lawrence, all factions were strong presences on the same campus. After the revolution the divisions continued, and sometimes bloody fights broke out between militant pro-Khomeini Hezbullahis and anti-Khomeini Mojahedin. Baton Rouge, Louisiana, was a stronghold of Hezbullahis; Houston for a time had small but active groups of both Mojahedin and Liberation Movement (*Nahzat-e Āzādī*) people. Houston, the home of Ibrahim Yazdi, the first foreign minister of the Islamic Republic and founder of the Liberation Movement in Houston, also became home to a growing population of non-Iranian Muslims: the growing pains of the wider Muslim community are explored in chapter 4.]

I arrived in Lawrence, Kansas, on 19 January 1976, by bus from Kansas City after a long flight from Tehran. As I got off the bus, I noticed two Iranians quarreling and calling each other names, like cab drivers fighting for the same passenger. I was surprised to discover the quarrel was over me. One had a big "communist" mustache, the other an Islamic beard. They represented the two Iranian anti-shah activist groups in Lawrence. As I soon found out, they were regularly assigned by their groups to find the new students and bring them in for political education.

The communist, "Bahram," who was eventually hanged with his wife Nasrin by the Islamic Republic some years later,[34] grabbed my suitcase out of the hands of the Muslim and put it in the trunk of his big American car. He opened the door for me and asked where I was going. I gave him the name of the dormitory. He lit a fresh cigarette with the butt of the one he was just finishing and filled the car with smoke. Three other passengers were already in the car. He began talking about "these Muslims" who do nothing but fill their stomachs with *ḥalāl* meat, learn to kiss ass with Dr. Ibrahim Yazdi, pursue girls, and pray to God that the shah should fall like an apple from the tree. He went on about the shah as the most brutal and corrupt man on earth, not even merely a running dog of imperialism. By the time I arrived at the dorm, I was already half way to being a convinced communist. I had heard already in Yazd of "revolutionary students" scattered through Europe and the United States, but I did not know there were different feuding groups.

Bahram helped me check in to the dormitory and find my room on the tenth floor. He continued to chain smoke. I was very tired, but too polite to ask him to leave, and had to sit up to listen to him talk and talk. Finally, he said he had an appointment, but would return the next evening to take me to a banquet.

Life in the dormitory required some adjustment. I had privacy in my room, but it was very difficult to share the showers with Americans who did nothing to cover themselves. Three other Iranians were on my floor, two from Isfahan, and one from Shiraz. The one Isfahani, Husain Sarmadi (later a representative of the Islamic Republic in Washington), was chubby, hirsute, talkative, and naive. He had a beard not because he was especially religious, but because his beard grew so fast. He took a shower once a week, just as I had been accustomed to doing back in Yazd. He was from a Sufi family, and I struck an immediate bond with him by reciting some verses of the *Masnavi* of Rumi. The other Isfahani, "Ali," was a thin, "pretty boy," who would never have been allowed to return if he had gone to Qazvin. He was very proud of his mathematical skills, but beyond math and science he had no interests. Both Isfahanis were penny pinchers. Jamshid, by contrast, was just as stereotypically Shirazi: generous with his money, pleasure seeking, compassionate, good-looking, and well dressed.

The next evening, Bahram came. I had told Husain, Ali, and Jamshid about the banquet, and they asked if they could come. Bahram already knew them and called them "our children." The five of us went to McCullum, another dormitory. In the basement a hundred or so Iranian students were gathered in front of a movie screen. An Isfahani, Farhad Amidi, in his mid-thirties was giving a lecture, which I found hard to follow, filled as it was with unfamiliar jargon: "bourgeoisie comprador," "superstructure," "infrastructure," and so on. The lecture ended and the film began. It was about Vietnam and the American crimes. In the dark, pamphlets were distributed. Husain whispered in my ear in a trembling voice, "I am afraid . . . SAVAK." I told him to keep quiet. After the movie we were not allowed to leave. The comrades needed to enlighten us, and so they did for two hours.

When we finally left, Husain gave me his pamphlet and beseeched, "Please, do not report me if you are from the security organization." I assured him I had nothing to do with politics, and not to be ridiculous. But I understood: in Iran we had always been told to dissimulate, even your brother might be a SAVAK agent, and if he is, it is his duty to report on you. The four of us decided after fifteen days to move out of Templin Hall and rent an apartment. With Bahram's help, we found a two-bedroom apartment for two hundred fifty dollars a month, next to a grocery, and on the bus line to the University. The Isfahanis roomed together, and Jamshid and I. Bahram visited regularly to see me—the others quickly lost interest, fearing anti-shah politics to be dangerous—until one evening we had an argument and I threw him out.

Bahram had been discoursing about the reactionary nature of religion in general, and Islam in particular. All of us were angered. We four still said our prayers regularly. I began angrily shouting at Bahram that we would not let him insult our religion, that he spoke of workers without any respect for the religion of the workers, that if he gave an Iranian worker a gun and told him God did not exist, the worker would shoot him before thinking about shooting the soldiers of the shah. Bahram left slamming the door, and shouting that my head was still filled with Islamic bullshit. Bahram later apologized to me, and we continued our talks.

Meanwhile my roommates joined the Muslim Students Association, and asked me to join too. One night we went to an MSA meeting. They said pretty much the same things the communists did, except that they referred to the shah as pharaoh or Yezid, and to Khomeini as Moses or Husain. They criticized Marx for failing to distinguish Islam from other religions which were opiates of the masses. They said Lenin was a despot, and that communism was less egalitarian than Islam. Moreover, communism had no popular support in Islamic Iran, and so anyone who preached communism was some fifty years behind the times. This was a new kind of Islamic gathering for me. It was not the first time I had heard that Ali, Husain, Zainab, and other Islamic heroes were really leftists fighting for the liberation of the poor against the capitalists of their day. I had read Shari'ati. But I also remembered Ṣadūqi's charge to me: "May you study sociology in America, so that you can come back and break the teeth of the hypocrite Shari'ati and so help Islam to triumph." How different were these students from the clerics in whose name they said they were fighting. They seemed to have little idea about the divisions among the clergy. They themselves were divided into those who followed the Liberation Movement of Mehdi Bazargan and Ibrahim Yazdi; and those who followed the Mojahedin-e Khalq and emphasized the writings of S. Mahmud Taleqani. But all agreed that Khomeini was their "Imām." I remained somewhat disaffected from them because of their ignorance of Islam.

After the first term, my three roommates moved to a smaller college. They had come to Lawrence only for English language training. So that summer, I moved in with some Saudis. This was a quite different crowd:

they had money to spend, constantly partied, smoked marijuana, drank alcohol, listened to music, gambled, and were surrounded by women. None of them said their prayers, nor did they have any political interests. "Hamid," said to be of the royal family, drove a red Monte Carlo. "Uthman," a Bedouin by any standard, had a Trans Am. Uthman knew no English except the names of drinks. In the fall, Hamid and I shared an apartment. The arrangement was that I would clean and cook, and he would pay the rent. He also claimed to want a studious roommate to help him get serious about his own studies. But the parties continued, and the apartment was full of Arabs and their American girlfriends every evening.

One night, I was saying my prayers behind closed doors in my room, while a party was in progress. I had just finished when the door opened, and Ibrahim came in. He sat on the bed and began asking questions about my religion. "I am a Muslim, just like you," I said. "No, you are from the party of Ali." "So, what do you mean?" "You are a *rāfiḍī.* You prostrate on the dust of Karbala: that is idolatry." "No, it is not." "Yes, it is." "But I do not drink, gamble, or smoke grass." "That is irrelevant. Wrong is wrong." "But you do not say your prayers. This is the only way I have learned to worship my God." "Your way of worshipping is wrong."

Soon others took his side. I never understood this contradictory fanaticism. But it was an important lesson: one did not have to be a practicing Muslim to be a Muslim zealot. Much of the zealotry is based on ignorance. I remember when Hamid had first introduced me to Uthman, he had joked, "Watch out for this Shi'ite." Unexpectedly, Uthman's face had turned serious, "You are not a Muslim?" He said he had read about Shi'ites, most of them lived in Russia. It took us a moment to realize that Uthman had been told that "Shi'a" and "shuyu'ī" (communism) were philologically connected. Hamid, with apologies to me, corrected him, saying, "We call Shi'ites *rāfiḍī,* which they do not like." This caused Uthman to recall that his shaykh had said the Rafidi religion had been invented by some Jewish fellow. We had to help him remember the name of this person, Abdullah ibn Saba, and tried to tell him that this was a purely mythical figure. "But," Uthman countered, "is it not true that you believe Gabriel made a mistake when he brought the revelation to Muhammad, that he should have brought it to Ali?"

Hamid eventually got a phone call from Saudi Arabia that his father was very ill. He left the States, and his education, apparently for good. So I had to look for a job. I first found one as a dishwasher in the Country Kitchen Restaurant, taking the place of a Shirazi who was to become my roommate. Several Iranians worked there on and off, and I graduated to becoming a cook, cashier, and assistant manager. One of the waitresses was an Iranian girl who styled herself a marxist. She would talk about how we were being exploited by our capitalist boss. One day, I sat down with her and asked how much food she had sold that day, and how much she was taking home in wages and tips; the latter amount proved to be almost as much as the former. The restaurant was in severe financial straits, and the boss hardly much of a capitalist. We had many Iranian customers, including Husain Mahallati, until 1988 head of the Foundation of the Oppressed in New York (Mustazafan Foundation, the former Pahlavi Foundation), and brother of Muhammad Ja'far Mahallati, until 1989 the Iranian Ambassador to the United Nations. He would come in late at night with a stack of Islamic literature, and usually would only order coffee. Another regular was Muhammad the marxist, who was the first to predict to me that the coming revolution would see Muslims gaining the upper hand, and that they would massacre marxists in the name of God. Then there was "Ja'far Mafia," a playboy and alleged drug dealer, who once pulled a gun on another customer. Most of the Iranians who came to the restaurant late Saturday nights were playboys coming from a night at the discothèque.

Later, through a Greek chemistry student who was one of our waiters for a while, I landed a job first as a waiter and then as a cook in a Greek restaurant in Kansas City. If my Muslim scruples were challenged in the Country Kitchen by having to cook bacon and ham, here I had to serve alcohol, and learn the sexual repartee; but the pay was very good. A good waiter could make over a hundred dollars each weekend night in tips (the wages were minimal: five dollars a night).

In the meantime my wife Marziyeh and son Reza came to join me. They stayed for almost two years, then Marziyeh could not stand being in the land of the infidel, and returned to Iran. After working in the Greek restaurant, I too felt a need to renew my faith, and I purchased a ticket to return to Iran. This was shortly before the first Iraqi attack on Iranian territory. My boss urged me not to go, and the Iraqi attack helped change my mind. I stayed.

Eventually, after I moved to Rice University, five years and three months after they had left, Marziyeh and Reza returned. Reza was now just becoming old enough to be eligible to be drafted for the war with Iraq, and it was important that we get him out of the country.

Those were often psychologically difficult years, but that saga of the pain, as well as the triumphs, of a provincial family from Yazd adjusting to America must be left for another time. One dream I had in December 1981, a few months after moving to Houston, may serve as a token. It occurred a few days after receiving a letter from Marziyeh with a photo of Reza who had lost some of his baby teeth, and so his cheeks looked a bit thin to me, but otherwise he looked fine. I dreamt that my wife and son were in the States, along with a composite person who was both my father and my father-in-law. I went with my friend Majid to visit them. Majid was barefoot, and my father/father-in-law tried to be funny, pretending to tie Majid's invisible shoes. I said this was impolite and not amusing, particularly since he did not even know Majid. Then my father/father-in-law asked if I wanted (*pasand*) to see my son. I said, of course. They were huddled under a blanket on the bed as if both were ill and cold. My father/father-in-law grabbed the boy and held him up for me to see. The lad was very pale, his head was shaved, and his cheeks were sunken. The boy began to accuse me: "Why did you stay here in America? You do not even have any *shelter*" (for some reason the word "shelter" was in English). At this point I awoke, shaking, and could not go back to sleep. I had insomnia for the next four nights. I thought I was going crazy. I avoided my friends; if they called on the phone, I would give brief answers and hang up. I went to Half-Price Books and obsessively bought a huge number of books on sale. Finally, my friend Homayun asked what was wrong, and I confided in him. He said, "If my mother were here, she could give you a full interpretation, but it is very clear that the dream is saying you are a concerned father, worried about your wife and child. It is a good dream." And so slowly he helped calm me down. The dream, of course, is more complicated, fraught with insecurities (shelter, lack of shoes, books), guilt (about separation, parenting, illness), cultural imagery (shaved head, accusations about the land of the infidel, maybe the family under the blanket, patriarchal authority) and conflicts of a family caught in the purgatory between cultural worlds.

[The cultural psychology of Iranian adjustment to the United States is a complicated and largely unexplored domain. A study of depression and grief among Iranian immigrants in California has been done by Good, Good, and Moradi (1985). A study of culturally constrained misunderstandings of communication between Iranians and Israeli psychiatrists and physicians has been done by Pliskin (1987). And some further suggestions about Iranian cultural forms of affect have been made by

Beeman (1988), Fischer (1984, 1988), Good and Good (1988). This is, of course, a challenging domain not only for research on Iranian culture, but more generally for psychology, psychiatry, and therapeutic methods that are culturally sensitive: for a recent volume on dreaming in cultural context, see Tedlock (1987).]

Part 2
Texts, Con-Texts, and Pre-Texts

. . . all East Asia was printing, from Nara to Turfan—Japanese, Chinese, and Uigur Turks. . . . But between the Far East that printed, and Europe where printing was unknown, lay the Moslem world that refused to put its literature in printed form . . . all Buddhist and Confucian literature was being spread abroad in printed form. . . . Whatever the reason may be, up to to-day the Koran has never been printed in any Mohammedan country except by lithography.

. . . Rashid-eddin, who was grand vizier of Persia during the Mongol period at just the time when Tabriz was the great bridge between the East and the West, and who wrote a clear account of Chinese printing in his world history, seems never to have contemplated having his history printed. Instead, he provided in his will, and left funds for the purpose, that each year two full copies of all his works should be made by hand, one in Arabic and one in Persian, until gradually there should be a complete copy in the mosque of every large city of the Moslem world.

—Thomas F. Carter, "Islam as a Barrier to Printing"*

The historian al-Jabarti's reaction to the *printed* proclamations to the Egyptian people issued in Arabic by Napoleon was to detail their grammatical errors, colloquialisms, ellipses, misspellings—a sign, as it were, not only of the corruption, deception, misunderstandings of the French, but a forewarning of a new culturally hegemonic world order that would remove control of the rules of ethical communication from oral face-to-face locales to obscure centers elsewhere.

—[paraphrased from] Timothy Mitchell, *Colonizing Egypt*†

*Perhaps the simplest explanation for the resistance to printing in the Islamic bureaucratic empires may be the strength of the guilds of scribes protecting their jobs. Such, at least, is the hypothesis proposed by Ottomanist historian Donald Quataert (personal communication). Miraslav Krek points out that there was block printing of amulets in tenth- and eleventh-century Cairo, and that mistakes in the citation of Qur'anic verses may have bolstered resistance to allowing the Qur'an to be printed (personal communication). Chinese style printed money was introduced in Iran in the second half of the thirteenth century, but was subsequently abandoned in favor of specie, the resistance here being presumably on the part of merchants, although they utilized their own forms of script, drafts, and checks. Non-Muslims were the first to introduce movable type presses in the Islamic world, long before Muslims allowed themselves this technology. Jewish refugees from Spain set up printing presses in Constantinople in 1493 and in Salonika in 1512, printing not only Bibles and prayer books, but secular books and multilingual concordances (Hill 1989). Among the most interesting are an eight-language pentateuch, including Arabic, and Ibn Masadai's "Prince and the Sage," a version of the Balaam and Josephat story, an Arabicized romance based on the Buddha story. (Among the patrons of the Jewish presses in Constantinople was a Marrano diamond merchant dealing in Indian diamonds.) Christians had printed the Qur'an in Arabic in Italy in the fifteenth century; Syrian Christians had a press in the sixteenth century; Armenians and Carmelites set up presses in the Julfa suburb of Isfahan, in Iran, also in the sixteenth century. But the first Muslim presses were not established until the 1720s and then only tentatively: in 1727 a Hungarian Muslim was allowed to establish a press in Constantinople on condition that he not print the Qur'an; the first Turkish book was published in 1728; in 1729 a history of Egypt was printed but aroused such opposition that no more books were printed until the 1820s. In Iran, a printing press was eventually established in 1812 or 1815 under the protection of Crown Prince Abbas Mirza (Albin 1986). On printing in the Muslim world, see further Babinger (1909), Duda (1935), Jahn (1941), Krek (1976), Pedersen (1946/1984).

†Mitchell chronicles the checkered early career of printing in Egypt: "After the departure of the French soldiers the Egyptian government did manage to set up its own press. . . . The bulk of what was printed in the first half of the century was for . . . military instruction. The few individuals who tried to extend the use of the press outside the military project subsequently found themselves removed from office and in some cases exiled. By the 1850s, when Egypt had been forced to abandon its military ambitions, the press had fallen into disrepair, and in 1861 it was formally shut down. Printing was started up again by the government under Isma'il, and by the time of the nationalist uprising [1881] there was an active periodical press. But the government attempted to suppress whatever publication it did not control, and establishment scholars like Marsafi spoke out against the press, blaming the political crisis in part on the wanton spread of printing" (Mitchell 1988:134).

2

Qur'anic Dialogics

Islamic Poetics and Politics for Muslims and for Us

Con-texts to Dialogue

> In the buginning is the woid, in the muddle is the sounddance and thereinofter you're in the unbewised again.
>
> —James Joyce, *Finnegans Wake,* 378.29–30

> The trace left by the Infinite is not the residue of a presence; its very glow is ambiguous.
>
> —Emanuel Levinas, *Otherwise Than Being*

> [A wake: a town mollah read the Qur'an] as a sermon . . . in plainsong . . . a lesson in piety . . . as a teacher, a guardian, he preached the holy poetry with a tinge of the townsman's ubiquitous self-consciousness, *showing* the Koran's beauty, *urging* devotion to it. . . .
>
> [Next a villager read with] such a muted, mellow expression that one could not understand any words, but the listener sensed a oneness, a pouring out of sorrow and faith like liquid over the bent heads . . . unaware at all of where he himself stopped and the community around him began. . . .
>
> When the [literacy corpsman], deputy of the State, took the holy book in hand and clasped it resolutely . . . a vast piazza lay before him . . . filled with the masses awaiting his word . . . his chant reviewed the troops . . . the Arabic poetry now barked out in perfectly measured military cadences. . . . Only Mehrabani of the three readers ever stopped to ask for the correct pronunciation of a word (. . . from the mollah . . . then he would go back and repeat [the passage] as though we had hung on some important details of his command—as though the words . . . had to be spelled out for meticulous, letter-of-the-law fulfillment!). On he goose-stepped through the Koran, lifting aloft, brilliantly ordering, putting everything precisely in its place.
>
> —Grace Goodell, *The Elementary Structures of Political Life*

Fig. 2.1. Noah's ark, cloth painting, Udaipur 1985, personal collection of M. Fischer. After the famous miniature, ca. 1590, attributed to Mughal court painter, Miskin. The word *lawh* means both the "tablets" in the seventh heaven on which the primordial Qur'an is inscribed, and the "planks" of Noah's ark, implying both that the Qur'an is an ark of salvation, and that the trials which God sets man to train his moral judgment are among the signs (*ayat*) God provides so man may decipher His revelations. Photo by M. Fischer.

Three sorts of dialogue are central to the reading of the Qur'an: dialogue in the colloquial sense of oral communication between two face-to-face persons; dia-logue in the Greek etymological sense of cross-play between arguments; and dialogue in the sense of juxtaposition of points of view in a political struggle for hegemonic control of interpretation of how the world should be seen (be it, today, between fundamentalist Islam and liberal Islam, or between Islamic nationalisms and cosmopolitan secularism).

These also translate into three ethical registers: the ethnographic effort to understand other people(s) in their own terms, the political effort to establish a public world where the rights and interests of all can be protected and negotiated, and the self-evaluative or self-reflective effort to break out of ethnocentrism and to place one's own perspectives in historical and dialogical relation to others. This chapter is written in all three registers. (1) It sketches how Muslims historically have read the Qur'an: how there has been a constant tension between the sound of sense and the sense of sound; between the vocal melodic, emotional pragmatics of presence and the textual, debatable graphics of absence; between the sounddance and the woid; thus, how the Qur'an is recognized to be poetic and enigmatic, composed of dialogues and other genres, requiring both an ear and interpretive skills, both for reciting and for reading. (2) It argues that only by knowing at least the structure of this hermeneutic and debate tradition can we effectively deal with or understand the powerful contemporary political movements in the Islamic world, both Shi'ite and Sunni (see Fischer 1980*a,* 1980*b,* 1982*b*). (3) It argues that reviving this tradition can provide an ethical poetics and a tool of critical self-awareness, a mirror into our own half-forgotten ethical dialogic and scriptural traditions.

The Qur'an is a profoundly enigmatic text. For Muslims, it is the word of God, divine in both its meanings and its language, infinite, beyond human capacity for definitive exegesis.[1] To teach its exegesis (*tafsīr*) is inevitably to tread on dangerous theological grounds, to court the hubris and heresy of claiming to know God's intent. Thus it is not a required course in the traditional theological colleges (see Fischer 1980*a:* 247–51). But it is learned on the side, and every Muslim must engage in it. The moral struggle is similar, albeit the accent quite different, to Jewish relationships to the Torah.[2] But the Qur'an is profoundly enigmatic on more than just mythic or dogmatic grounds. Though it is a text generative of a scholastic tradition, the Qur'an insists on its own orality and musicality, and warns against writing: it is a *qur'an* (oral recitation), not merely a *muṣ-ḥaf* (written text). Memorization/preser-

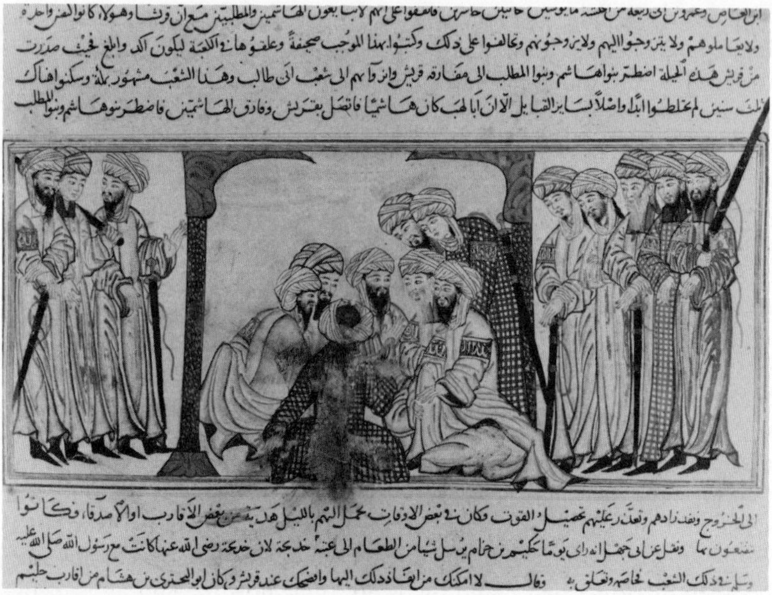

Fig. 2.2. Quraish tribesmen debate the expelling from Mecca of supporters of Muhammad, the Banu Hashem and the Banu 'Abd al-Muttalib. From the manuscript of Rashid al-Din's *Jāmi' al-Tawārīkh* (Collection of Chronicles), commissioned by the Il-Khan Uljaytu. Rashid al-Din, born in 1247 in Hamadan, was the son of a Jewish apothecary. He was court historian and vizier to the Il-Khanids, who ruled Iran from the city of Tabriz, where Rashid al-Din built palaces, mosques, and a scriptorium in which two copies of his *Jāmi' al-Tawārīkh* were to be made each year, one in Arabic and one in Persian. Courtesy of the Edinburgh University Library, Arab 20.

vation (*ḥifẓ* is the word for both) are obligatory for each Muslim community (*wājib al-kifā'ī*) and may not be left to pen and ink. Muslims pride themselves that their "book" resides not on paper but in their chests. The Qur'an, after all, is enigmatically allusive, constantly calling upon knowledge that must be brought to the text. It is allusive to stories from the Torah (and secondarily from the New Testament and pre-Islamic Arab lore).[3] It is also allusive to the historical circumstances of its own production. This allusiveness generates a discourse about references and meanings, a generativeness that produced increasingly analytic disciplines of grammar, history, phonetics, poetics, law, theology, and hermeneutics—disciplines that variously interacted with, or were distinguished from, both Greek-influenced philosophy and logic and the talmudic discourses of Mesopotamia.[4]

Early Muslims seem to have been as ambivalent about writing as was

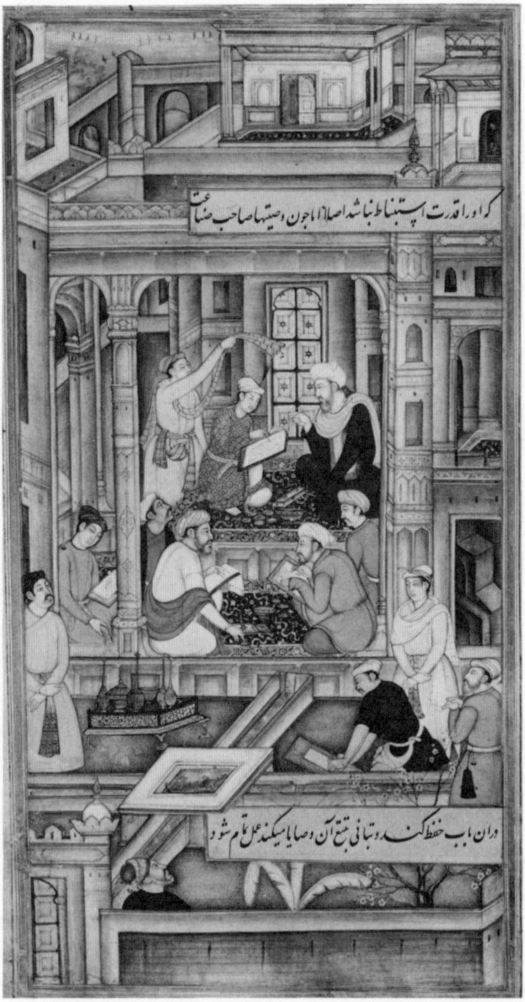

Fig. 2.3. Manuscript atelier, a scriptorum: a master dictates to a scribe; two painters; a paper-maker; a second scribe. From the *Akhlaq-i Nasiri* ("Nasirean Ethics") of Nasir al-Din Tusi (1201–1274), copied for Akbar ca. 1590. This was one of the books Akbar would periodically have read out loud to him. Courtesy of the Collection of Prince Sadruddin Aqa Khan, Ms. 39, f. 196a.

Plato (especially in the *Phaedrus*), and Islamic tradition has always emphasized the oral over the written. In the *Phaedrus,* Plato warns that the technology of writing can destroy the arts of memory and the disciplines of educating the soul; texts all too often are dead, not open to cross-examination or further question. Only the world of dialogue—argument and counterargument, and (perhaps) the actual presence of the debaters so as to monitor the communicative pragmatics as well as the referential sense of the arguments—provides the space for ethical communication. In *The Republic* Plato attempts to find a way of writing that calls attention to its own devices, that constantly subverts any one reading, that sustains a critical attitude of dia-logue ("across arguments") between text and reader, so as to undermine that uncritical attitude of simple mimesis or repetition into which the modes of Homeric epic, the tragedians, and comedians can slide. Plato relies upon a layered or polyphonic structure of irony (not only the irony of Socrates, the arch eiron, but also his own authorial irony in his presentations of Socrates' dialogues) to make his text provocatively enigmatic or poetic in the profoundest sense (Berger 1987; Griswold 1986; Rosen 1987; Seery 1985).

If Plato relies upon irony to keep his texts dialogically supple, the Qur'an relies upon midrashic narrations generated by keywords, letters, incidents, sayings, parabolic stories, and dialogues. The *ḥadīth* ("sayings" of God, the Prophet, his Companions, and the Imāms), *sunna* ("precedents" of the Prophet), and *asbāb al-nuzūl* ("occasions or reasons of revelation"), which serve to provide the con-texts and elaborations of Qur'anic fragments, themselves require authentication and interpretation. The entire structure of Qur'an and ḥadīth is a fun house of mirrors playing upon appearances and resemblances (*mutashābih*) that may or may not be grounded (*muḥkam*), depending upon the perspective and knowledge of the interpreter. It is a structure necessitating a critical sense, but one ambivalently also permissive of uncritical belief and false leads.

It is thus a profoundly ethical structure insistent upon debate (*baḥth, mubaḥatha*) and dialogue (*jadal*), adjustable to the level of knowledge of each person, and open to the educative process of those more knowledgeable. Irony too exists in the Qur'an, e.g., when Umm Salama complained to Muhammad that the Qur'an seemed to be only about men and their rewards in heaven, Muhammad received the revelation (just listen to the irritation): *al-muslimīn wa al-muslimāt, wa al-mu'minīn wa al-mu'mināt* . . . ("male Muslims and female Muslims, male believers and female believers . . .") (33:35)—which as any feminist can tell, only accents the complaint. Ironic readings, like ethics, depend upon the reader/interlocutor, as do dogmatic ones, be they dogmas about the uniqueness of Greek/Western ethical consciousness or dogmas about the meaning of the Qur'an.

Juxtaposing cultural traditions, each taken seriously in its own right, thus can serve as an educative ethics, another form of dialogue. Khomeini, for instance, part of whose authority derives from the regulative ideal of the Platonic philosopher-ruler,[5] serves to remind us of the play in Plato's *The Republic* upon paideia, justice, individual soul, and collective governance, terms that have also become slogans in the Islamic revolution. *The Republic* flirts with moral transcendence (utopia/totalitarianism), but returns to debate, dialogue, dialectics, and politics as defenses against totalitarianism, against monologic fixity, against authoritative textualism. Similarly, key contemporary texts of "Islamic fundamentalism," such as Khomeini's effort (in his 1971 lectures) to argue for a political activist role for the clergy, are internally hampered by a tradition of dialectical debate that restrains utopian enthusiasms.

This essay is divided into three main parts for the three forms of dialogue. First, we discuss the performative, oral Qur'an: the dialogue of the I-Thou relation with God, of the historical God-Muhammad relation, and the staged narrative dialogues between God and Satan, God and Moses, Moses and Khiḍr, Abraham and Nimrod, etc. Second, we discuss the exegesis of the textual Qur'an: the dia-logue of hermeneutical understanding that grows with engagement of the text through dialectical disputation. Third, we discuss how this latter inhibits Khomeini's arguments for the involvement of clerics in governance. We conclude—and frame throughout with epigraphs—with the contemporary dialogic context of rabbinic-Islamic-Catholic mirroring; of nationalist versus global shadowboxing ("East versus West" as the perverse cliché puts it); and of scholastic roots versus postscholastic ethics.

Dialogue and Presence

Iqra! ("Recite!"): The Sounddance, the Oral, Performative Qur'an

> Recite: In the Name of thy Lord who created; created man of a blood clot.
> Recite: And thy Lord is the most generous, who taught by the pen; taught man, that he knew not.
>
> —Qur'an 96:1–5 [the first revelation]

> The divine utterance is silenced as soon as it is pronounced. But we cling to its resonant ring, our inspired words.
>
> —Jabès, *The Book of Questions,* p. 85

Listen to a recitation of Sūra 96, considered the earliest revelation in the Qur'an: it is clear that it is made up of different fragments. The rhythm or music changes, and the content indicates differences between the times the fragments could have occurred. "Recite!" occurred while Muhammad was in the cave, withdrawn from society. In the second fragment, reference is made (albeit without naming him) to Abu Lahab's refusal to submit to Islam, which happened after Muhammad returned to Mecca from the cave.

In these two fragments, we already have several distinctive features of the Qur'an: (1) there is a dual order: the first revelation chronologically does not come first sequentially (the sūras or "chapters of verses" are ordered roughly by length, the shortest coming last); (2) the narrative unit is the fragment, not the sura; (3) meaning is conveyed by the sound, and would be much more difficult to establish by the text alone ("taught by the pen; taught man, that he knew not"); (4) meaning is further established by a knowledge of the occasions or allusions of the fragments, without which the text is inscrutable: legible, but unintelligible; (5) the fragments are of various genres, including (a) dialogues with stages voices (e.g., between God and Abraham, or Moses and Khiḍr, or God and Satan, or Moses and Pharaoh), requiring dramatic recitation; (b) implicit dialogues where Muhammad has been asked a question by Jews or by unbelievers, and must ask God for the answer, and the Qur'an provides the answer, "Say to them (*qul!*) . . ."; (c) the address of God to both Muhammad and through him to Muslims: "Recite! (*iqra!*) . . ."; (6) only by recapturing the divine sound, as best one can, is one able to approach the presence of God, and apprehend His divine word: as human speech is inadequate to the divine, so is the written text a poor transcription of the divine tablet (*lawḥ maḥfūẓ, Umm al-Kitāb*) of the seventh heaven.

More generally, the stress on the oral, performative, dialogic Qur'an is encoded in (1) the dogmas of Muhammad's illiteracy (protecting the Qur'anic divinity: it is not the product of a crafty man, the Prophet could not write) and the Qur'an's inimitability (resting in part on its onomatopoetic aptness of word choice: no poet could have created such resonance); (2) the story of its dual revelation, with interpretation dependent upon the sequence *not* recorded in the written text; (3) the debates about the desirability of writing the Qur'an down and about the way in which an official transcript was produced, including the Ḥadīth of Seven Recitations or Dialects (*Ḥadīth Sab'at Aḥruf*), which provides a charter myth for cantillation variability with consequent variants in understanding; (4) the technical demands (a) of a *scriptio defectiva* (as long as the Arabic script lacked diacritical marks for vowelization, punctuation, intonation, and pitch, an authoritative reciter, rather than the written text, was the *ḥāfiẓ*—preserver, memorizer, guardian—of the text),[6] and (b) of interpretive skills to keep the text supple and poetically densely layered with meanings; (5) the centrality of the dialogues in the Qur'an about uncertain knowledge and the fallibility of unguided reason; (6) the pedagogy of never studying alone or with a text alone.

The story of the revelation is that the primal Qur'an, called the *Umm al-Kitāb* ("mother book"), which resides in the seventh heaven, descended to the heavenly sphere on the twenty-seventh, nineteenth, twenty-first, or twenty third[7] day of Ramaḍān, and thence via the angel Gabriel into the heart of Muhammad. Muhammad first heard the sound of bells, and was set the task of reproducing the heavenly voice of Gabriel reciting from the Umm al-Kitāb. Muhammad instructed his followers to reproduce this sound: "Embellish the Qur'an with your voice"; "he who does not recite the Qur'an melodiously is not one of us."[8] The art of *tajwīd* (cantillation) is aimed at preserving the original celestial music of the Qur'an, that sound which encodes senses beyond human language. Etymologically, *tajwīd* is said to be aṇ Arabicization of Avestan "gatha,"[9] the form of inspired/inspirational poetry chanted or sung by the prophet Zoroaster, a form whose efficacy is said by some to reside as much in the cosmic vibrations of the sound as in the poetic vision. Cantillation styles range from the more "ornamental" (*mujawwad,* from the same root as *tajwīd*) to the "plain" (*murattal,* from the same root as *tartīl* in the verse 73:4: "recite in measured clear chant," *wa-rattil al-qur'āna tartīlan*). *Qur'ān, qirā'at* ("recitation"), *iqra* ("recite"), all from the same root (and like the Persian word *khōndan*), mean both singing and reading,[10] in contrast to words for various sorts of pure texts, such as *ḥadīth* (the sayings of the Prophet), which are never sung, or *muṣ-ḥaf* (the *transcript* of the Qur'an).

The Qur'an was revealed to Muhammad twice (just as, he said, the two sets of tablets of Moses had been):[11] first in complete form, in the order of the present text; and a second time in fragments during the course of his twenty-three-year prophetic career (610–32 C.E.). The latter has been the object of interest for historical, literary, and jurisprudential purposes, but it is the former which is the divine order of the Umm al-Kitāb, and suggestions to publish a Qur'an that reconstructs as best as possible the latter historical sequence have been resisted, although Shi'ites believe that the *transcript* compiled by Ali was arranged in the chronological order of revelation. Ali's transcript, no longer extant, is said to have been preserved by the Imāms, and will be made public upon

Fig. 2.4. Muhammad receives revelation through the angel Gabriel, winged with Seljuk crown. *Jāmi' al-Tawārīkh* of Rashid al-Din. Courtesy of Edinburgh University Library, Arab 20.

the return of the Mahdi at the end of time—a neat charter myth for the efforts of Muslims to reconstruct the Qur'an's plenitude of contexts and meanings.[12]

The debates about how the transcript (*muṣ-ḥaf*) was compiled provide rich material for contemporary discussions about the differences and continua between oral and literate cultures, and for the continuing privileging of the oral over the written in judicial matters. Traditional Islamic accounts credit only "seventeen" persons (like forty, a stereotypic number) in Mecca with literacy—more in Medina, a center of Jewish literacy—and speak of Islam as a vehicle for the spread of literacy. The metaphoricity of the Qur'anic vocabulary referring to literacy is itself interesting both in marking intercultural relations and in giving hints about attitudes toward the technologies of literacies.[13] *Qirṭās,* "paper," is from Greek *chartes;* Sūra 68, "The Pen," begins with the letter *nūn,* meaning "fish" in Hebrew, explained by Muslim exegetes as referring to a fish whose flesh was used in making ink; that Muhammad in the story attached to Luqman's rival scripture asks that it be read out perhaps reflects, if not his own illiteracy, an era of unstandardized shorthand notations, or simply unvoweled and unpunctuated scripts giving texts a private, *aide-memoire* character, so one might not easily have been able to read another's notes.[14] Companions of the Prophet, who had private transcripts of the Qur'an, are thus said to have destroyed their notes before they died, lest the notes mislead others.[15] Similarly, after the Caliph 'Uthmān had an official transcript compiled, he destroyed all other variants (whence his title *Ḥarrāq al-Maṣaḥif,* Burner of Mus-hafs),[16] and he sent a reciter with each copy of the official transcript to the provinces.[17] Still today, reciters of the Qur'an learn their recitations from oral masters, not from the written text; scribes write down the text from recitations, not from other texts;[18] and students study with a teacher, never alone with a text. The oral remains authoritative for the written, not the other way around.

The efforts to protect the oral Qur'an from deformation due to tampering with the written text only begin with the *scriptio defectiva* and the ambiguities that remain even after diacriticals were introduced (vowels, punctuation, cantillation marks): they involved vigilance, as well, against perennial efforts to "improve" the transcript, including "straightening out" the grammar, replacing words with the better ones (*shādhdh,* "odd" changes),[19] or making the text conform to reason. As late as 1958, two shaykhs were tried, forced to recant, and expelled from Cairo's al-Azhar University for issuing a decree allowing *shādhdh* recitations. In the third century of Islam, the grammarian al-Mubarrad opined that were he a reciter, he would say *barr* (charitable) rather than *birr* (charity) in order to make verse 2:177 grammatical. In the following century, Ibn Shanbud and his student Abū Bakr Aṭṭār al-Naḥwi were tried before Ibn Muqla for attempting to make the recitations of the Qur'an subservient to the discipline of grammar instead of relying upon the oral transmission from master reciter to student reciter. Mu'tazilite *kalām* philosophers argued that God could not have recommended suicide (2:54), perhaps not recognizing the passage to be a citation of Exodus 32:27, or accepting the argument that the Torah, corrupted by the Jews, cannot mean what it says. Zamakhshari, in the sixth century of Islam, notorious for his efforts to correct the Qur'an, suggested verse 5:112 should read "ask your God to send" rather than "can your God send," on the grounds that Jesus' disciples would not question God's nature or His capacities. Orthodoxy refused all such corrections: oral recitation (*naql*), not reason (*'aql*), is authoritative.

Disputes over such matters illuminate and mark the history not only of literacy, or of theology, poetics, grammar, logic, and hermeneutics, but also of resistance to taking authority out of the dialogic face-to-face context. Considerable lore recounts misreadings (*taṣ-ḥīf*) caused by the different ways in which the script alone could be interpreted, and hence the stress on always studying with a teacher. (*Taṣ-ḥīf* are the misreadings due to both writing down a dictation incorrectly and reading the text incorrectly.) Imām Ali is credited with the well-known lines: "He who obtains knowledge orally from a master, he is safe from being misled and from misreadings. But he who obtains knowledge from books, his knowledge is nil according to those who know." Perfection in teaching for Shi'ites lies with the Imāms, who are in fact called "the speaking Qur'an." At the Battle of Ṣiffayn (657 C.E.) when his men hesitated to fight because the enemy had placed Qur'ans on their lances, Ali cried: "What you see on the lances is but paper and ink; I am the living Qur'an, the speaking Qur'an." Distrust of the text is not limited to Shi'ites: Imām al-Shafi'i also admonished that it is a mistake to take the written page as your mentor, that he who learns jurisprudence from the book alone loses sight of the law (as-Said 1975: 54).

If the dominant strain in Muslim tradition has been to distrust the text, there has been a minor counterstrain of those who mistrusted memory, and who felt compelled to make a case for the existence of a written Qur'an from almost the very beginning. The names of early Muslims who acted as scribes for the recitations of Muhammad are cited. More fanciful are the traditions that the *kuttāb al-wahy* (scribes of revelation) recorded the Qur'an on branches of palm trees, on white stones, on skin, and on shoulder bones (Ramyar 1967:71; *Quanūn-e Tafsīr,* pp. 116–17).

The decision to preserve the Qur'an by collecting a definitive transcript is said to have been taken after hundreds of reciters were killed in the Battle of Yamāma (12/633).[20] A question arose about a certain verse, and it was feared that all who knew that verse had been killed. Still the Caliph Abu Bakr hesitated, saying if Muhammad had not collected the Qur'an, perhaps it should not be done. It was recalled that a Companion of the Prophet, Abu Sa'id al-Khudri, had asked the Prophet for permission to write down revelation, and permission had been refused.[21] 'Abdullāh ibn 'Abbās, the father of Qur'anic exegesis, later would report a ḥadīth of the Prophet that the cause of the ancients' downfall was partly due to writing.[22] The Qur'an itself says: "If we had sent you writings on paper so that they could teach it, the unbelievers would surely say, it is nothing but magic" (6:7), and "Who then sent down the book that Moses brought? A light and a guidance to man. But you make it into paper for show, while you conceal much" (6:91).

Zayd ibn Thābit was asked to oversee the compilation of the definitive transcript, completing it under 'Uthmān, the third caliph, and using the dialect of the Quraish tribe (that of Muhammad, but also, like thespian Hannoverian German, said to be the most clearly enunciated of the dialects).[23] When 'Uthmān saw/heard the final version, traditions relate that he commented, "I notice some *laḥn* (inconsistencies in "dialect" or "melody"), but the Arabs will straighten it out with their tongues." A variant says, "Had the men of Hudhayl [best in elocution] dictated it and men of Thaqīf [best in transcription] written it down, such *laḥn* would not have occurred."[24] To compile the single edition, Zayd utilized both reciters and *muṣ-ḥaf*s. For each verse admitted, he required two trustworthy witnesses. Ibn Ḥajar interpreted this to mean an oral witness and a written one, but if our argument is correct, the scribes of revelation (*kuttāb al-wahy*) did not hand over their notes to be transcribed (*istinsākh,* copying from text to text), but recited them to Zayd. Abu Khuzaymah was the one person to claim to have the last *āya* of Sūra 9, "Repentance," in his memory. Since he had been recognized by Muhammad as *dhū-shahādatayn* (one whose testimony is worth that of two persons), this verse was admitted by Zayd. In contrast, Umar claimed to know an *āya* that had no other support (the verse mandating stoning for adultery), and Zayd refused to accept it, since there was only one witness. Given the uncertainty of texts without reciters, texts could not witness for themselves.

Establishing a single transcript, of course, was no guarantee of uniform recitations. Muhammad, in a ḥadīth universally recognized to be a fabricated mythic charter (the Ḥadīth *Sab'atu Ahruf*), says that the Qur'an was revealed in seven permissible dialects or styles of recitation (cf. also Qur'an 43:3: "Verily we have made it an Arabic Qur'an," i.e., not just a Quraishi one). So collectors of recitations gradually categorized all variants into seven (or ten; see below). These collectors, as opposed to collectors of the transcript, were teachers of cantillation, knowing where to pause, how to place emphases, what tonalities to use to bring out emotions, and so on. The first such collector is said to have been the Jewish convert from Basra, Hārūn ibn Mūsa (d. 170–80 A.H.), or the Shi'ite, Aban ibn Taghlib (d. 141/759), an associate of the fourth Imam.

The differences among recitations are not just stylistic, but different articulations which can lead to quite different meanings: e.g., *salāmun 'alā iliyāsin* ("blessings upon the followers of Elias/Elijah") versus a slight pause amid the last syllables, *salāmun 'alā āli yāsīn* ("blessings upon the children of Yasin"), Yasin being an epithet of Muhammad. The latter is the preferred reading by Shi'ites, for whom the children of Muhammad are the Imāms. Clearly, then, an effort must be made to limit the ways in which the Qur'an can be articulated. One guards against modes of recitation that lack reliable chains of teachers, that contain inventions by scholars, or that add parenthetical exegeses. Ten ways are recognized as legitimate: the seven *mutawātir* ones which have more than one independent and fully trustworthy chain of teachers back to the early days of Islam, plus three *mashhūr* ones, famous variants based on a particular reciter. They are quite distinctive even to the uneducated listener, e.g., Warsh has long durations of syllables, dropping of glottal stops (*muminūn,* instead of *mu'minūn*), and *imāla* (shifts from /a/ to /e/); Ḥamza by contrast accents glottal stops with pauses before them. Different recitations became fashionable by region and era, e.g., in Egypt since Ottoman times, the style of Ḥafṣ replaced that of Warsh.[25]

In the 1950s, the Egyptian Labib as-Said began an effort to tape all "eighty" ways (*ṭuruq*) of recitation, to document them, to preserve them from modern musical contamination, because he feared the art of recitation was in danger of dying.[26] If it died, the Qur'an itself would no longer be *mutawātir* (certified by multiple chains of trustworthy reciters). There proved to be considerable opposition to the project: many Egyptian Muslims preferred to promote the recitation of Ḥafṣ as the only acceptable one, lest scoffers at Islam be able to claim that Muslims could not even agree on the words of what they claim as divine revelation. There is now an effort throughout the Muslim world to make Ḥafṣ the accepted way of reciting.

What finally is important about the oral recitations of the Qur'an is the way they articulate, transmit, and evoke the mother book in the seventh heaven, the preserved tablet (*lawḥ maḥfūẓ*). Cantillation manuals include explanations of phonology: the points of articulation in the vocal tract, allophones, rules of assimilation, nasality, duration.[27] They include rules of sectioning of the text, of constructing rhythms, and of recognizing repetitive phrases (*mutashābihāt*) in the text that act as refrains and as echoes throughout.[28] Just as a single narrative may be scattered through the text in different fragments, so too in the performance structure, melodic patterns can be used to refer to other parts of the text, other recitations, and other reciters. The beauty and inimitability of the Qur'an resides primarily in the use of the sound of the language, in its frequent onomatopoetics, in the way melodic modes are correlated with emotional moods to picture and color meaning.

Sūra 105, The Elephant, for instance, tells of the Abyssinian invasion to destroy the Ka'ba of Mecca in the year of Muhammad's birth, and how God sent flocks of birds with stones that so bombarded the elephants and men of the invading army that they were like masticated leaves. The word for "leaves" (*'aṣf*) is both ugly and impossible to say quickly; it sounds like a violent clearing of the throat. It is in onomatopoetic ways like this that the Qur'an is said to be inimitable and precise. The phonetic structure of the Qur'an—the alternating rhyme and parallel rhythms; the use of rhyme to unify long verse lines; the use of short lines for special emphasis; the use of longer and longer lines in a verse to delay and intensify final resolution—is distinctive. So too is the way a reciter may repeat a word, or present first short clear phrases and then repeat them in single long units. Thus the first word in verse 24:35, *'Allāh,* meaning "God," but also an expression of wonder and delight, may be isolated, before being put together with the rest of the line: "God is the light of heaven and earth." Using such repetitions, with different intonations, the reciter can bring out different meanings. The two voices in dialogue can be set off musically. Verses about hell are colored in full heavy voice, while those about heaven sparkle with bright, light voice. When the infant Jesus speaks in the sūra "Maryam," the reciter moves from a low voice register to a higher pitch and volume. While various emotions—joy, awe, yearning, grief—are invoked, the master tones are those of *khushū'* (humility, awe, submission), *ḥuzn* (sorrow, grief), and *shaja'* (choked up emotion). Ibn Khaldun says, "The Qur'an is a place of *khushū'* as it is a reminder of death and what comes after it; it is not an occasion to give pleasure in the perception of beautiful sounds" (Nelson 1985: 97). Al-Ghazali agrees: "The reciter contemplates what is in it of threat and intimidation and covenant and contract, then he considers his own shortcomings . . . so that without a doubt it affects him with *ḥuzn* and he weeps" (ibid., p. 98).

Among the most dramatic, and theologically central, passages of the Qur'an are the dialogues between God and the angels (2:30–33), God and Iblis (15: 32–41; 7: 12ff.; 38: 75–84), God and Abraham (2: 260), God and Moses (7:143), and Moses and Khiḍr (18: 66–78). In the first, the angels question why God should want to create human beings who will corrupt the earth and shed blood.[29] God retorts, "If you are so wise, reveal the "names of things." They cannot, but Adam, His new creation, can. Involved in this "naming" are not just words and things (knowledge, language), but hidden qualities, inner feelings, essences as opposed to appearances. Adam, of course, is not as adept as God; only He truly knows what is concealed, but the angels being pure reason without animal passion do not have Adam's capacities for moral struggle, for approaching God through interiority, love, or faith, modalities of intention hidden beneath the surface. Iblis refuses to bow to Adam, perhaps out of a kind of pride: he was made of fire, Adam merely of mud. God reminds him: it was "dry, sounding clay" (therefore resonant, capable of speech) and into it he breathed His spirit. Mud, wet (animate life) contrasts with fire, scorching winds from which Iblis and the jinn were made. Muslims often comment that Satan's sin was not just pride, but monomaniacal insistence on reason, a warning to fanatics, self-righteous egoists, and rigid legalists: God commanded that one bow to no one but God, and so Iblis insists he is being true to this command and to monotheism. Again, it is through misuse of reason that Satan deceives Adam and Eve: they have been told not to touch the tree;[30] if Iblis hands the fruit to them, so Iblis argues, they technically would not have touched the tree.

Abraham's dialogue also turns on the problems of reason and appearances. Abraham asks God to show him how He revives the dead. God remonstrates, "Do you not believe?" (After all, this is the man who is willing to sacrifice his son.) Abraham says, "Of course, but I want an explanation or demonstration that my heart reach certitude." God complies by telling him to cut up four birds, put them on four mountains, and call to them; they will come flying. In a variation, Moses (whose epithet is "he who talks directly with God," Kalīm 'Allāh) asks God to show Himself, and God replies, "You cannot see Me directly, but look at the mountain." The mountain disintegrates into bits; Moses faints. When he recovers his senses, God says, "I chose you, gave you a mission and words; take the revelation." The story of the tablets and the golden calf follow. (Muhammad rejects such miracles as signs of his mission, saying that previous prophets had used them, but to little lasting effect.)

Moses' famous dialogue with Khiḍr, the saint who moves between this world and the heavenly realms (retold in various folktales with other characters, and in a Jewish midrash of Joshua and Elijah),[31] also turns on these same themes of the limitations of reason in a world of appearances. Moses asks if any man is wiser than he (a riddle form also used in stories about Ali), and is told to follow Khiḍr ("one of Our servants"). Khiḍr agrees to let Moses accompany him but only on condition that Moses not question his actions unless he speak of it first. Khiḍr is skeptical that Moses, a mere mortal, will be able to do this: "Verily thou wilt not be able to have patience with me. And how canst thou have patience about things about which thy understanding is not complete?" (Qur'an 18:67). Khiḍr proves correct: Moses cannot restrain himself, and they part. But Khiḍr explains the riddles of why he scuttled the boat in which they were traveling, why he killed a young man, why he took no recompense for setting up aright a wall which was falling down in an inhospitable town. The boat would have been conscripted by an evil king down river, and the boatmen would have lost their livelihood; this way they would recover the boat when danger had passed; the boy would have become a parricide; the wall would have exposed a treasure intended to support orphans, and would have been looted by the evil people of town. What appears to be the case is not always the underlying reality.

The richness of these dialogues is elaborated through the repetitions, modifications, parallels, and cross-references that reverberate through the Qur'an. The play with similarities and simulacra runs throughout the Qur'an on both the thematic and the performative levels. Christians were misled about the crucifixion of Jesus: "They killed him not, nor crucified him, but *shubbiha lahum* [it was so made to appear to them]" (4:157). In the story of the golden calf, the people ask Moses to "ask the Lord to make plain to us what she is: to us all heifers are alike [*tashābaha*]; we wish guidance" (2:70). "Do they assign partners to God who have created as He has created so that the creations seemed similar [*tashābaha*]?" (13:16). The richness of the dialogues is also heightened through dramatic recitation, staging the different voices, and invoking conventional emotional musical modes (*maqām*).[32]

One can, of course, recite the Qur'an in a low inaudible voice to oneself, as well as with full voice to an audience, and each manner has ḥadīth to support its virtues. Thus, Abu-Bakr, asked why he was reciting so inaudibly, replied, "Verily, He in whom I confide hears me"; while Umar, asked why he recited so loudly, replied, "I awaken the sleepy and drive away Satan." The point is to recite with sincere desire to draw near to God. For this reason, al-Ghazali says that recitation from a transcript is better than recitation only from memory, for it is an additional action of viewing and thinking about the Qur'an, and thus it is an additional act of devotion (Abul-Qassem 1982: 56). In fact, there are textual conventions that add not only beauty of calligraphy but also other reminders: in Sūra 2, "The Cow," for example, the first five verses are usually on a page by themselves, so that they are separated from the unbelievers mentioned beginning in verse 6.

These five verses (cited below, Qur'an 2:1–6) are interesting, for they say the Qur'an is not self-explanatory, one cannot just read it and be guided; nor is it a guide for everyone; it can mislead those who are not pious and who do not have five additional characteristics. One needs guidance so as not to be misled. Such guidance comes in various dialogic forms: in the teacher-student, Imam-follower, or student-student debating of dialectical argument-counterargument to clarify the basis for decision making. One may not study alone, with the text alone. The *sic et non* disputational method of Peter Abelard, and the dialogue forms of Renaissance philosophy, historically, are borrowings from Muslim Spain of this Islamic (and Jewish) style of unveiling the arenas of truth (Menocal 1987).

The Graphics of Absence
Guides through the Woid: Plain Meaning, Prolepsis, the Knowledgeable, the Ḥadīth Game

> Every person, place and thing in the chaosmos of Alle anyway connected with the gobblydumped turkery was moving and changing every part of the time.
>
> —James Joyce, *Finnegans Wake* 118.21–23

> The heart of dialogue beats with questions.
>
> —Edmond Jabès, *The Book of Dialogue*

> Writing is one of the representatives of the trace in general; it is not the trace itself. The trace itself does not exist.
>
> —Jacques Derrida, *Of Grammatology*

> That book [the mother book in the seventh heaven] is sure guidance, without doubt, [only] for those of the God-fearing who (a) believe in the unseen, (b) pray, (c) spend [share and distribute] what We give them, (d) believe in the revelations sent to thee and those before, (e) are convinced there is a Hereafter. . . . As for the unbelievers, God has set a seal on their hearts and on their hearing, and on their eyes is a veil. . . .
>
> —Qur'an 2:1–6

Consider verse 3:7, the verse that serves as a kind of litmus test among exegetes:

> He it is who sent down to thee the Book, wherein are verses/signs [*āyāt*] of plain, firm, basic or established meaning [*muḥkamāt*] that are the essence/foundation of the Book; and others that are ambiguous or allegorical [*mutashābihāt*]. Those whose hearts are perverse [*zaygh,* "inclining toward falsity"] follow the ambiguous part, desiring dissension and desiring its hidden meaning or interpretation [*ta'wīl*]. But no one knows its hidden meanings or interpretation *except God And* those firmly

> grounded in knowledge [*al-rāsikhūn fī al-'ilm*] say, "We believe in it; all is from our Lord"; and none grasps the message except men of understanding. (Qur'an 3:7)

It is deceptively simple, indeed the labyrinth gateway, warning against losing oneself in the funferal mazeways of resemblances, appearances, metaphors, allegories, resonances, interpretations, re-presentations, and symbolizations, yet all the while using these very a-maze-ments and a-muse-ments to praise plain sense. God is "He," Muhammad is "thee," and "sent down the Book" is (already) figurative: Muhammad did not receive a book, but a series of revelations over twenty-three years, which were memorized or jotted down by the "scribes of revelation" and were subsequently recollected into a book after the death of the Prophet. The first real "sign" of trouble is *āya* (pl. *āyāt*): "sign," "miracle," "fragment of the Qur'an," "verse." "Wherein are the signs of established meaning" is quite different from the possible gloss "verses of plain meaning": divine signs may signify more than they say. For Shi'ites, for instance, it is quite established that "the Qur'an is a *khaṭṭ* ["inscription"] occulted between two covers; it does not speak with a tongue; it must have an interpreter [*tarjumān*]; it is men who speak on its behalf" (*Nahj al-Balagha* 182); the speaking Qur'an (*al-Qur'an al-nāṭiq*) is the twelve Imams. "This Qur'an, make it speak! It shall not speak, but I inform you of it" (*Nahj al-Balāgha* 223). "Beware! The Qur'an, its *ẓāhir* [exoteric sense] is elegant, its *bāṭin* [esoteric meaning] is deep, its wonders never end, and the darkness is not broken except through it" (*Nahj al-Balagha* 18).

But exegesis requires controls on interpretation, and the first major methodological puzzle comes with the terms *muḥkam* (plain meaning) and *mutashābih* (allegorical meaning). Philologically, *muḥkam* is a cognate of *ḥukm* (judgment, verdict) and *ḥikmat* (wisdom); its root (ḥ-k-m) connotes "restraint." *Muḥkam* would seem to be a verse with limited and unquestioned meaning. In contrast, *mutashābih* is a cognate of *shibh* ("likeness") and *shubhah* ("obscurity," "vagueness," "uncertainty," "doubt," "specious argument," "sophism," "judicial error"), and of *ishtibāh* ("to mistake one thing for another due to an apparent similarity"). *Mutashābih* contrasts with *mushābih* ("similar"): the latter refers to "real" similarity; the former to "apparent" similarity. *Muḥkam* verses thus might be expected to contain a *ḥukm* or *ḥikmat,* while *mutashābih* verses might be figurative or allegorical, if not chimeras of similarity, mis-takes, and misinterpretations.

In fact, the definitions of *muḥkam* versus *mutashābih* in the exegetical literature contain a fan of meanings:[33]

muḥkam	*mutashābih*
regulations, prescriptions, rules[34]	objects of faith, opinion, meditation insight[35]
apparent, clear, one interpretation, plain meaning	figurative, allegorical, multiple interpretations requiring *ta'wil* (interpretation)[36]
independent to itself:[37] direct understanding rationally comprehensible[40]	must be referred to something else[38] (a similar *āya,*[39] relevant *sunna* or *ḥadīth*[41] (interpretable through research)
words not repeated in other parts of the Qur'an[42]	
abrogating verses (*nāsikh*)	abrogated verses (*mansūkh*)[43]
present in all scriptures, and thus in the Mother Book[44]	esoteric signs such as the sigla (letters that stand independently before some verses)
knowable	unknowable: things no one can know (e.g., the time of resurrection); things knowable only by the *rāsikhūn;* things knowable to scholars[45]
human language	sublime language[46]

All the ambiguities opened up by verse 3:7, interestingly, do not make Muslim exegetes classify it as *mutashābih.* It is classified as *muḥkam.* The Qur'an describes itself in 11:1 as "a book whose verses are made *muḥkam* and further explained in details"; but in 39:23, it admits, "God has revealed a book which is *mutashābih.*" A classical solution to this apparent contradiction is to say that *muḥkam* and *mutashābih* refer to the form of the verses rather than their content: the Qur'an is well founded (*muḥkam*) throughout, as the various techniques of exegesis elucidate, with each of its words and phrases aptly selected. Since some verses resemble others, it is *mutashābih.* Obviously, also, what is *muḥkam* to a more learned exegete may seem *mutashābih* to a less learned one. But there are other answers as well.

Al-Raghib al-Isfahani, a twelfth-century exegete, provides a typology of *mutashābihat* by human capacity for understanding: some *muta-*

shābihat verses he says are about things no one can actually know (e.g., the time of resurrection, and other metaphysical matters); some are things that can only be known by those the Qur'an calls "those firmly grounded in knowledge"; and some verses can be known by ordinary scholars of the Qur'an. A similar formulation is given by contemporary Shi'ite theologians: man's language is made for daily life, not for sublime meanings; sublime meanings require figurative language, especially when attempting to communicate with common folks. The Qur'an intends to provoke thought, not lay everything out for passive reception, and (a particularly Shi'ite insistence) the *mutashābihat* are a way of indicating that the book cannot be read without guides, the infallible Imāms.

Where this leads, of course, is to (a) the ultimate unknowability of much of the Qur'an, and thus to (b) an openness of interpretation that requires (c) moral struggle, as well as (d) access to the disciplines and traditions of interpreting the Qur'an. Four important guides are available: (1) the disciplines for laying bare the plain meaning of the Qur'an (including most importantly the identification of which verses abrogate other ones, the historical circumstances of revelation, and grammatical analysis); (2) interpretive means of *tafsīr* and *taw'īl* (exegesis, prolepsis) and dialectical disputation (*baḥth*); (3) "those firmly grounded in knowledge" (*rāsikhūn fi al-'ilm*); (4) and the politics of the ḥadīth game also played through dialectical disputation with *taw'īl* and grammatical analysis.

Abrogation causes some verses to be considered *mutashābih:* if a verse commands something, but that command is no longer in force, an unskilled exegete might be misled. Theoretically, there are three types of abrogated verses: verses continuing as part of the Qur'an although they contain outdated commands (*ḥukm*) which at some point in the life of the Prophet were replaced by other *ḥukm;* verses whose wording has been abrogated but whose *ḥukm* remains in force (e.g., the alleged verse about stoning for adultery, mentioned above); verses whose wording and *ḥukm,* both, have been abrogated. Only the first of these is accepted by most Muslim scholars. The other two are most often rejected on the grounds that they imply imperfection in the "perfect word of God," and open the sensitive debate about the incompleteness of the Qur'an.[47] An example of the first type of abrogation is the three verses about drinking: 4:46 says, "O believers, do not pray when you are drunk until you know what you are saying." The story is that some drunks attempted to recite Sūra 109, a verse of negations, but forgot the negations. A stricter rule came next: "There is both good and evil in alcohol, but the evil outweighs the good" (2:219). Finally, the absolute prohibition was revealed: "Intoxicants are of Satan" (5:90).

Obviously, one needs to know the historical contexts of revelation to know which abrogrates which. These are recorded in books of ḥadīth, *sīra* (biographies of the prophet), and *maghāzi* ("raids", especially those in which Muhammad took part), as well as in separate collections.[48] Two occasions of revelation are given for verse 3:7, each tagged to a phrase. First, tagged to the warning against hidden meanings (*ibtighā' ta'wīlihi*) is the story of Christians who asked whether Jesus was not God's spirit (*rūḥ*) and logos (*kalima*), as is said in 4:171. Muhammad had to agree, but denied the implication that this confirms the trinity of God, for 3:59 explicitly says, "Jesus is to God as is Adam: He created him from dust, then said, 'Be!' and he was." Again, 43:59: "Jesus was no more than a servant [of God]: We granted Our favor to him, and We made him an example to the children of Israel."

The other, tagged to the warning against interpretations made with the intent of seeking dissension or testing (*ibtighā' al-fitnah*), is a story about the sigla or letters with which a number of chapters of the Qur'an begin: Hayy ibn Yakhtab, his brother, and some other Jews tell Muhammad that numerology provides the interpretation of these mysterious letters. Those of Sūra 3 add up to 71, the number of years Islam will last. (*Alif* = 1, *lam* = 30, *mim* = 40.) This is but one of the Qur'an's examples of Jewish mischievous, illegitimate play, which Muhammad rejects, noting that other chapters begin with other letters that add up to larger totals.

Grammatical analysis of the *wāw* ("and") in āya 3:7 is perhaps the most controversial part of its exegesis: is the *wāw* a connective or a disjunctive, does one pause before it ("no one knows its hidden meanings except God") or does one not pause ("except God and those firmly grounded in knowledge")? Two other ambiguities: to what does "its" refer—to the Qur'an in its entirety, or only to its *mutashābihat?* And who are "those firmly grounded in knowledge"? For most Shi'ites, they are the Imāms, and in this case, the *wāw* would serve as a connective, not a disjunction. However, the Shi'ite philosopher and exegete, Allameh Sayyid Muhammad Husayn Tabataba'i is among those who stop at "'Allah": God alone knows.

Those who take the word *wāw* ("and") to mean inclusion can cite verse 3:18 ("There is no God but He: that is the witness of God, His angels, and those endowed with knowledge") and can argue that the Companions of the Prophet and the exegetes have discussed the *muta-*

shābihat, so there is nothing in the Qur'an known only to God; or, more cogently (as Ibn Taymiyah says): God commanded the believers to meditate on the Qur'an and to try to understand it. How could He ask his servants to do the impossible? Ḥadīth in Sunni collections, not only Shi'ite ones, are read by Shi'ites to support the idea that the Imāms are the "firmly grounded in knowledge" who know the *ta'wīl* ("interpretations," but see below) of the Qur'an. The prayer of the Prophet for Ibn Abbas says, "God, make him knowledgeable in religion and teach him *ta'wil*". Verses 10:38 and 27:82 condemn those who are not knowledgeable about the Qur'an and its interpretation. The Prophet had a mission to clarify the revelation; how could he be ignorant of parts of it? Imām al-Sadiq bitterly condemned those who regarded any portion of the Qur'an as ambiguous, since the Imāms know God's meaning.

On the other side, those who read the *wāw* as meaning exclusion can cite the traditional recitations. The nontraditional recitations of Abdullah ibn Abbas and Ubyy ibn Ka'b (first century A.H.) even change the word order, putting the verb before the subject, making the exclusion yet clearer: *wa yaqūl al-rāsikhūn. . . .* Those who stop at "Allah," meaning that God alone knows the interpretation, range from those who refuse any but the most minimal figurative interpretation of any verse of the Qur'an to those who think of *ta'wīl* and *tafsīr,* two words for "interpretation," as essentially different.

Ta'wīl, understood to mean prolepsis, prefiguration of events that come to pass, is an extremely interesting control on interpretive freedom. The word occurs twice in āyā 3:7, and seventeen times in the Qur'an. It is a key term. The story of Joseph, where it occurs seven times, uses it in the context of dreams; the story of Moses and Khidr applies it to the humanly unknowable; āyā 4:58 and 17:35 use it to mean a decision in a dispute; āyā 7:53 and 17:35 use it to indicate a kind of fulfillment.

There are four dreams requiring interpretation in the Joseph story of the Qur'an. First, Joseph dreams that eleven stars and the sun and moon bow to him. Jacob interprets the dream, suggesting that God has chosen Joseph as a prophet, like Abraham and Isaac, and will teach him the *ta'wīl* of *aḥadīth* (dreams, stories, events). Here, the sun and the moon appear as Abraham and Isaac. But later events reveal the real meaning of the dream, when Joseph is ensconced like a king, and his father and mother (sun and moon) as well as his eleven brothers bow to him. "O, my father, this is the *ta'wīl* of my dream of old; God has made it come true" (12:100). In prison, Joseph is told two dreams by fellow inmates. The first, of pressing wine, Joseph interprets literally:

Fig. 2.5. Scenes from the story of Joseph. Joseph receives his brothers in Egypt without revealing his identity. A gold cup is planted in Benjamin's baggage, he is accused of theft, and detained. When the brothers return again from Palestine, and tell Joseph of their father's blindness, Joseph reveals his identity and gives them his shirt so that when Jacob touches it, he will regain his sight. Figurations of sight and insight. The miniature is from a *Falnama* ("Book of Divinations") ascribed to Ja'far al-Sadiq, the sixth Imām, c. 1550, Tabriz or Qazvin, Iran. Joseph Enthroned. 59.4 × 44.5 cm. S86.0255. Courtesy of the Vever Collection, Arthur M. Sackler Gallery, Smithsonian Institution, Washington, D.C.

the dreamer will become a presser and server of wine to the king. The second, of birds eating bread off the head of the dreamer, Joseph interprets with only slightly less literalism: the man will be crucified and the birds will eat off his head. Perhaps bread and flesh are symbolic substitutions here. According to some ḥadīth, this second dream was a fabrication to test Joseph, both to see whether he can interpret it and to see how far from plain meaning he might stray, into dangerous, unconfirmable *ra'y* ("personal opinions"): events substantiate Joseph's interpretations as literal meaning. There is a further literal meaning and moral lesson: folklore has it that one who fabricates dreams will die. Finally, there is Pharaoh's dream of seven fat cows and seven lean cows, seven full ears of grain and seven withered ones. Pharaoh calls for an interpretation of his *ru'yā* (visions), but his sages find them to be merely *aḍghāthu aḥlām* (meaningless dreams), the same words used by the unbelievers to describe Muhammad's revelations in verse 21:5. Joseph finds mildly symbolic keys: there will be seven years of plentiful food (meat and grain), and seven years of poverty. The proof of the *ta'wīl* in all these cases comes through subsequent events. (Prescience of events which will actually occur is the restricted definition of the miraculousness of the Qur'an according to Ibrahim al-Naẓẓām and his Mutazilite defenders; al-Naẓẓam was condemned by 'Abd al-Baghdādi [d. 429/1037] for contradicting a broader definition of the Qur'an's miraculousness, suggested in verse 17:90, that it is forever inimitable.) Note that even in dream interpretation, symbolism is used with great restraint. This is characteristic of orthodox *ta'wīl,* and is used to distinguish the orthodox from the mystics and sufis (the *Bāṭinī*); Shi'ites are systematically relatively more *bāṭinī* than Sunnis, but they too recognize a gradation between orthodox plain meaning, or interpretations provided by the Imāms, and dangerous mystical or personal flights of fancy.

The story of Moses and Khiḍr (18:66–78; related above) poses the problem of *ta'wīl* as one of knowledge of the unseen. When they part, Khidr reveals the *ta'wīl* of his riddlelike actions. Verses 7:53 and 10:39 use *ta'wīl* for the final fulfillment, the end of the world; and those who seek *ta'wīl* are sarcastically asked to await that time when it is too late. This sense of the final interpretation is posed slightly differently in verse 4:58 where disputes are referred to God and His messenger for *ta'wīlan.* Also in verse 17:35, *ta'wīl* means "decision" or "settlement of a dispute."

And so, since *ta'wīl* has the sense of something that ultimately will be settled only by God or by the course of events, it is *tafsīr* that Muslims use instead to refer to exegesis. Interpretation (*ta'wīl*) can lead astray, but *tafsīr* is rather a disciplined explication (including pointing out the sources of ambiguity). For instance, while Tabari (d. 310/923) seems to use *ta'wīl* and *tafsīr* interchangeably, Tha'ālabi (d. 428/1038) distinguishes *taw'īl* as the reality or truth of the meaning (*ḥaqīqat al murād*), from *tafsīr* as the means of reaching *ta'wīl.* Thus, he says that in the verse, "The Lord is on a watch tower" (89:14), *tafsīr* explores the meanings of the word *mirṣād* ("watch tower"), while the *ta'wīl* is that God is not literally in a watch tower, but is all-knowing.

To return then to our verse 3:7 in its usual Shi'ite recitation, "but none knows its *ta'wīl* except God and those well-grounded in knowledge," who are those well-grounded in knowledge? At issue here is a larger difference between Shi'ite and Sunni exegesis than merely that Shi'ites identify the well-grounded as first of all the Imāms while Sunnis do not. It is that Sunnis rely upon the *sunna,* the precedents of the Prophet and his Companions, for interpreting the Qur'an. Shi'ites rely on these and on the interpretations of their Imāms. Two variants of the Ḥadīth al-Thiqlayn codify the difference: according to Sunnis the Prophet said, "I leave among you two weighty ones, the book of God and my *sunna.*" The Shi'ite version is: "I leave among you two weighty ones, the book of God and my family, the two shall not be separated." So while for Sunnis, the *sunna* act as the standard of meanings in the Qur'an, for Shi'ites it is the Imāms who provide the standard. For instance, the Qur'an mandates fasting, and how one is to fast is determined by the practice of the Prophet. Here, the sunna are the standard of interpretation: deeds interpret words.

But verse 62:9 mandates Friday communal prayer. For Sunnis this is an obligatory practice mandated in the Qur'an, and practiced by the Prophet. But the Shi'ite Imāms forbade it because control of the communal prayers and sermons had fallen into the hands of usurpers, and these occasions were tools of propaganda and mobilization. For Shi'ites, what an Imām does is a *ḥujjat* (authoritative precedent). Through the ages Shi'ite jurists have taken differing stands on the obligation of Friday communal prayer: A minority regarded it always as obligatory, on the grounds that the reasons for the ban by the Imāms was historically limited and no longer in force. (Ḥajji Āghā Raḥīm Arbab of Isfahan held such prayers in his own house with the minimum quorum of five, since he did not recognize the legitimacy of the state-appointed *imām jom'a* [communal Friday prayer leader].) Another minority regarded it as forbidden, either because there is still a living Imām (albeit occulted) and he would have to remove the ban first; or more usually, because unjust government still existed and so the reason for the original ban still existed. Many of those who took this position abandoned it with the establishment of the Islamic Republic of Iran: now at last, there was a true Islamic government, and not only was the Friday noon communal prayer again obligatory, but the sermons were also an obligatory organizational device for the polity. And so we have the now familiar picture of the leaders of the Friday prayer holding the sword or gun of authority in one hand as they deliver their sermons. The majority through the years took a politically flexible stance, regarding Friday communal prayer, even led by state-appointed *imām jom'a,* as either allowable or recommended for the general solidarity of the community. The point here is that the word of the Imām acts for Shi'ites as an abrogator of the Qur'an: the Imām is the standard of meaning.

Or again, take the verse 9:36: "the number of months, with God, is twelve in the book of God, the day that He created the heavens and the earth; four of them are sacred. That is the right religion. So wrong not each other during them. And fight the unbelievers totally. . . ." What could be clearer, say the Sunnis, no verse is as *muḥkam* as this. But, says Imām al-Sādiq, Muhammad would not be so simple minded as to merely tell us that there are twelve months in a year.[49] Rather, here is a reference to the twelve Imāms, four of whom are sacred, that is, four of whom have the name of God, Ali (the first, fourth, eighth, and tenth Imāms). "Religion" refers to the imamate; and the day that God created the heaven and the earth refers to the *nūr* doctrine, the doctrine that at the beginning the Prophets and the Imāms were created from a ray of divine light (*nūr*), and that these divine sparks were breathed into human form at appropriate points in the unfolding of history, often making for a miraculous birth (see Fischer 1980*a:* 26).

Another example is the verse inscribed on the gates of mosques and shrines: "A voice cried, 'Moses, I am thy Lord, put off thy shoes, thou are in the holy valley, Ṭuwā'" (20:12). The orthodox interpretation is that one takes off one's shoes as a token of respect (or, alternatively, perhaps the leather of Moses's sandals was not ritually pure). But Shi'ite tradition has it that the five-year-old twelfth Imām explained to Ali ibn 'Isā that shoes represent attachment to worldly comfort: if one wishes to approach divinity, one must leave such attachments behind. Again, the standard of interpretation is the Imām.

There is, however, a difficulty for Shi'ites regarding the Imāms: they failed to provide their followers with the kind of *ta'wīl* that would clarify all the ambiguities of the Qur'an. Those said to be "firmly grounded in knowledge," aside from the Imāms, must be persons who know the discipline of *tafsīr,* and who are pious in the sense of not allowing their personal opinions to distort the application of the methodology of *taf-*

sīr. Little wonder, then, that when an exegete ends his comments, he humbly says, "God knows best" (*wa Allāhu a'lam*). One may well wonder how many legitimate ways of interpreting *āya* 3:7 and the Qur'an there are. 'Abdullāh ibn 'Abbas, the founder of Qur'anic exegesis, recognized four: the most accessible way is open to everyone and no one is excused from knowing the Qur'an; a more nuanced way is known primarily to the Arabs because they know the cultural linguistics of the Arabic of the Qur'an; a deeper way is known to the learned who are schooled in hermeneutical skills and complementary knowledge bases; but the most complete and correct way is known to no one except 'Allāh.

The existence of esoteric meanings known to the Imāms and transmitted orally to their disciples opens up a continuing possibility of conflict between the scholars who are merely literate (however good their critical skills) and those who claim to have access to this protected chain of interpretive understanding. We will see a hint of this conflict in the next section, when we turn to a key political text of the present day, Khomeini's *Islamic Government.*

The Politics of Interpretation

Exposing the Unbewised: The Ḥadīth Game, [Blind] Followership, Rule by Faqih/Amir, and Islamic Economics

> *Khalq-rā taqlīd-eshan bar bād dād*
> *Ay do ṣad la'nat bar īn taqlīd bād*
> It was *taqlīd* that blew the people with the wind [destroyed them]
> Two hundred curses upon this *taqlīd* [followership]!
> —Jalāl al-Dīn Rūmi, *Masnavi*

> Kafka's writings . . . had to become more than parables. They do not modestly lie at the feet of doctrine, as the hagaddah lies at the feet of halakhah. Though apparently reduced to submission, they unexpectedly raise a mighty paw against it.
> —Walter Benjamin

The Ḥadīth Game

The Qur'an calls itself "the best of the ḥadīth" (39:23). Most ḥadīth are sayings of the Prophet: some explicitly, like the Qur'an, are regarded as divine sayings (*aḥādīth qudsi*), and the rest are divinely inspired.[50] Verses 53:3–4 say the Prophet speaks not on his own account, but via revelation. Shafi'i, founder of the Shafi'i legal school, used this verse to justify the *ḥadīth* (sayings) and *sunna* (practices) of the Prophet as bases for Muslim law (while still attempting as far as possible to use the Qur'an alone; hence the insistence that the stoning verse once existed). Muhammad in a famous ḥadīth promised great rewards to those who narrated forty of his sayings, and so there are a number of collections in later centuries entitled *Araba'ūn Ḥadīthan* or simply *Arba'īn* ("Forty ḥadīth"), e.g., by Muhammad Baqir Majlisi, Shaykh Baha'i, and Ruhullah Khomeini. At the same time there was fear that later generations might mistake such ḥadīth for parts of the Qur'an; for this reason, the caliph 'Umar banned the writing down of ḥadīth (on the assumption that oral transmission preserves as well the knowledge of the status of what is being recited). The ban was removed by 'Umar II, who encouraged ḥadīth collections. The earliest ḥadīth collections, called *musnad* ("documented"), were arranged by alphabetical order of the earliest narrator.[51] In the second/eighth century there emerged regional competing schools of ḥadīth collection.[52] Later ḥadīth collections, called *muṣannaf* ("collections") were arranged by subject matter; six of these, all composed by Iranians, survive and are the main sources of Sunni jurisprudence.[53] Shi'ites, particularly Iranian Shi'ites, have indulged in using these collections to prove that Ali rather than Abu Bakr should have succeeded Muhammad.[54] Shi'ites have their own collections of ḥadīth.[55]

Analysis of the genres (ḥadīth, story, genealogizing, battle narrative) invoked in early Muslim compositions may help in distinguishing distinctive regional schools. It was in Medina, 'Abd al-'Aziz al-Duri (1960) suggests, that the study of ḥadīth and sunna were worked into a critical discipline focused on the evaluation of the trustworthiness of the narrators,[56] the independent confirmation of accounts by multiple sources, and the analysis of internal coherence of accounts. Such work began with two men: 'Urwa ibn al-Zubayr (d. 94/712), the author of the first book on the battle narratives of the Prophet's time (*maghāzi*), a work that survives only as quotations in later works; and al-Zuhri (Muḥammad ibn Muslim ibn Shihāb al-Zuhri, d. 124/741), who began to combine the accounts of individual narrators (*ruwāt*) into continuous narratives, and whose writings, partly inspired by queries from the Umayyid court, were kept in the court library, perhaps as part of an emerging need for a cultural or ideological defense of the regime and Islamic community against regional, factional, tribal, and Persian cultural resurgences. Al-Zuhri's student, Ibn Isḥāq (d. 151/768) produced the first biography (*sīra*) of Muḥammad that has survived, and Duri points out that a genre analysis of its composition shows a portion comes from a culling of ḥadīth, a portion comes from popular stories (*qaṣaṣ*), and a portion comes from Isra'illiyat legends from Wahab ibn Munabbih (Duri 1960). (Wah'b ibn Munabbih, a Yemini of Jewish or Persian descent, son of a convert to Islam, and himself a judge, knew Hebrew and Syriac, and compiled from various sources what constituted essentially a prose Yemeni epic to refute the claims of northern Arabs to preeminence.) Ibn Hishām (d. 213/828) redid Ibn Isḥāq's *sīra,* weeding out much of the latter two genres and making it more acceptable to the emerging critical use of ḥadīth. Similarly, al-Wāqidi (130–207/747–822), compiler of the earliest extant book of battle narratives (*maghāzi*), was more rigorous in his culling of ḥadīth than was Ibn Isḥāq. When European Orientalists such as de Geojein (1864) began to struggle with the problems of critique of the ḥadīth literature, they recognized al-Waqidi as a probably reliable source, as opposed to such sources as Sayf ibn 'Umar, whom Wellhausen in 1899 cited as a particularly unreliable source since almost all the hundred and fifty Companions of the Prophet he names are (most improbably) members of his own tribe (the Tamīm).

By contrast with Medina and the emerging critical use of ḥadīth there, Duri suggests that Kufa and Basra were tribal garrison towns in which social status and financial reward was bolstered by genres of *ayyām* (stories of valor) and the renewed importance of genealogies. Early historians from these towns tended to rely on accounts and accomplishments of their own tribes (e.g., Abū Mikhnaf relies on his own tribe, al-Azd; Sayf ibn 'Umar favors his tribe, the Tamīm; Nasr ibn Muzaḥim is the first partisan Shi'ite *akhābrī* (collector of narrations).

Duri describes the second century of Islam as a time of regional collections of ḥadīth, as well as a period of Persian cultural resurgence (the Shu'ūbiyya movement, involving the translation of Persian books, and the infiltration of Persian materials and perspectives into Islamic historical accounts). Thus there was a need for the Islamic state to counter such regional perspectives with a unified universal history, and by the third century, al-Balādhuri, al-Ya'qūbi, al-Danawari, and al-Ṭabari were producing these. The evolution of law, recently surveyed by Burton (1977), provides a similar account (albeit Burton belongs to the faction of European scholars—Albrecht North, Michael Cook, Patricia Crone, John Wansbrough—who regard Duri as overly optimistic in claiming to be able to distinguish sociologically grounded regional schools). Islamic law recognized local custom as a legitimate source of law except in cases explicitly violating Islam. Schools of law based on the critique of the Qur'an and sunna evolved in the second century of Islam in Basra, Kufa, Mecca, and Medina (and briefly in Syria). Through the critique of the trustworthiness of narrators and chains of narration, and the soundness of ḥadīth, three categories of abrogation were generated, as noted above. Burton suggests that the stoning verse is one of those local legal procedures for which jurists attempted to find Qur'anic or sunna legitimation. He suggests further that this kind of seeking of Qur'anic and sunna legitimation is the background to the myth of variant *muṣ-ḥaf,* the idea that the extant Qur'an may not be complete, and the imposition of a single canonic *muṣ-ḥaf* by the caliph 'Uthmān. In any case, the interplay between local law and critical use of the sunna, ḥadīth, and Qur'an is an important feature of Islamic law. Quite to the contrary of nineteenth-century European stereotypes of arbitrary or rigid "qadi law," judges (*qāḍī*) and jurisconsults (*faqīh, mujtahid*) worked in a dialogic setting between local circumstance and Islamic precedent, more like common law procedure than like Roman administrative law.

What is of compelling interest to those who still today play the game of invoking ḥadīth are the challenges of the ideological, legal, or political outcomes, of gaining a consensus and thereby formulating history among those skilled enough to point out weaknesses in chains (*isnād*) of narration, contradictions or anachronisms in the texts of the alleged narrations, etc. If experts agree that all links in the chains are reliable, the ḥadīth is graded *ṣaḥīḥ* ("correct"); several independent reliable chains make it *mutawātir* ("confirmed"), the highest grade. Below these two grades, ḥadīth may be evaluated as *maqbūl* ("acceptable" only because a faqīh has issued a *fatwā* based upon it), *ḥasan* ("good," but not fully reliable), *mursal* (lacking connected chains), *ḍa'if* ("weak"), or *maj'ūl* ("fabricated"). The culling of fabrications reflects the development both of critical judgments and of sectarian canons. Take, for example, the Sunni allegation that the Shi'ite sect was founded by one 'Abdullah ibn Sabā, a Yemeni Jew who converted to Islam during the reign of 'Umar ibn al-Khaṭṭāb. This tradition, which makes Shi'ites livid, is narrated by Ṭabari through a chain that goes back to Sayf ibn 'Umar al-Tamimi al-Barjami al-Kūfi (d. 197 A.H.). Two other historians are said to provide independent chains, but they can be shown to also go back to Sayf ibn 'Umar al-Tamīmi. So what the Shi'ite ḥadīth expert (*muḥaddith*) must do is to show that Sayf ibn 'Umar al-Tamīmi is unreliable, a task which in this case is not difficult.

Two central political issues will illustrate the ḥadīth game with more serious import: followership (*taqlīd*) and rule by the cleric or amir.[57]

[Political] Followership (*Taqlīd*)

Taqlīd, the duty of ordinary Shi'ites to follow the *fatwā* ("opinion" reasoned through the disciplines of exegesis) of the leading jurist of the day, became a key political issue during the past century as various *mujtahids* were called upon to rally Muslims against imperialism. Until the late nineteenth century, Shi'ites followed regional *marja' taqlīd* ("sources of imitation"), but from the time of Shaykh Murtaḍā Anṣāri (d. 1864), single supreme *marja* were periodically recognized: Mirza Hasan Shirazi in 1891–92 when he rallied Iranians with a *ḥukm* ("judgment," not merely a *fatwā* or "opinion") against giving a tobacco monopoly to the British; Mirza Muhammad Taqi Shirazi in 1919–20 when he rallied Shi'ites in Iraq in a *jihād* against the British manipulation of Iraqi politics; Shaykh Abdul-Karīm Ha'eri-Yazdi from 1920 to 1935 when he revitalized the theological colleges of Qum; and Ayatullah S. Husain Borujerdi from 1944 to 1961. (On the history of the debate over the role of the *marja' taqlīd* and its projection backwards into history, see Fischer [1980*a:* 86ff., 252–53, 275 n. 11].)

The debate over *taqlīd* divides the two "schools" of Shi'ite jurisprudence—the Akhbāris and the currently ascendant Uṣūlis—and lays the groundwork for Khomeini's argument that the supreme *marja' taqlīd* should exercise political rule. The Uṣūlis initially advocated *taqlīd* as a means of rebuilding the institutional structure and activism of the clergy after the fall of the Safavid dynasty in 1732. To do *taqlīd* meant in part to give to the *marja' taqlīd* that half of the *khums* tax called *sahm-e Imām* ("share of the Imām") which helped provide the Shi'ite clergy an independent financial base, allowing them periodically to chastise or organize protests against secular governments.[58] The Akhbārīs rejected *taqlīd,* placing a heavier duty of religious caution and responsibility on individual Muslims. Murtaḍā Muṭahhari (1962:46), an Uṣūli and leading figure in the Iranian revolution, points out that the Akhbāris are also thus more tolerant than Uṣūlis, since reliance on weighing the evidence of one position versus another for oneself tends to teach one humility.[59]

The debate over *taqlīd* illustrates the tactics of argumentation that Khomeini later also used, which place on the defensive not only common folk, but also the merely literate who depend upon texts (such as the authors and readers of this chapter), asserting special privilege for jurists with superior oral chains of authority and permission. Both Shaykh Murtaḍā Anṣāri in the nineteenth century, and Khomeini in the twentieth century, admit that the key ḥadīths supporting *taqlīd* and Khomeini's idea of *velāyat-e faqīh* (guidance by the jurists) are very weak. Yet, they say, these ḥadīth have the "scent of truth." In effect, they claim access to the truth independent of the ḥadīth text. Khomeini might challenge our analysis of his use of ḥadīth by saying, "Where do you get your information?" And when we reply, "From *al-Kāfi,* from *Wasa'il al-Shi'a,*" he could reply in the manner of Plato's *Phaedrus* and in the manner of the early Muslims, "Ah, only from books; but you have no permission (*ijāza*) or access to the interpretive intent as I do through the oral chains of ḥadīth narration, being both a master narrator and a *faqīh* [one who can evaluate and distinguish among ḥadīth]."

One of the fascinating contemporary sociological dramas is to watch to what extent this kind of argument can continue to carry any weight: Dr. Ali Shari'ati prematurely thought its time was finished, telling young Iranians that being literate they no longer needed the clerics. One can, after all, respond to such invocations of special privilege with the traditional retort: "I suspect you of fabrication; are you the only one to have heard what you say? Either others can be cited to support your position or you are, at best, on weak, non-*mutawātir* grounds." Hence the importance of multiple narrators. But fabrication is not always deceitful falsification: it often is done relatively openly to provide mythic charters for contemporary events, much as an advertiser creates a jingle to lodge a product in one's mind. For instance, when Khomeini returned to Iran, a calendar was published, ornamented with several newly minted ḥadīth saying a leader would come from Qum, would be beset by the world powers, but they would be unable to defeat him.

Although several ḥadīth may be invoked in support of *taqlīd,* the key one is narrated by Ahmad ibn Ali ibn Abī-Ṭālib al-Tabarsi from the eleventh Imām, in which in the midst of a passage condemning *taqlīd* in favor of each Muslim assuming full responsibility for his own actions, the following occurs. "But among the jurisprudents, whoever is pious, keeper of his faith, pursues reason independent of his own desire, and is obedient to God—it is the duty of common folk to follow him." Defenders of *taqlīd* to enforce unified political action cite only this part of the ḥadīth. Moreover, this ḥadīth is not found in any of the four basic Shi'ite collections of ḥadīth. It comes instead from the seventeenth-century Shaykh Ḥurr al-'Āmili's *Wasa'il al-Shi'ia.* 'Āmili unequivocably rejects *taqlīd,* challenging both the chains and the interpretation of the text by advocates of *taqlīd.* He cites thirty-four other ḥadīth which also condemn *taqlīd.* The story behind the ḥadīth is said to be Imām al-Ṣādiq's reply to queries about Qur'anic verse 19:31, condemning Jews and Christians who took their rabbis and monks as lords: it meant not that rabbis or priests asked people to worship them, but that blind obedience is wrong. Because people indulged in uncritical obedience, unscrupulous rabbis and priests were able to falsify the law making what is proscribed permitted and vice versa. All that is permitted by the full ḥadīth, 'Āmili points out, is clarification of technical matters by a *faqīh,* e.g., the validity of a narration or a judgment about the technicalities of law. It excludes personal opinion (*ra'y*); it excludes decisions having to do either with basic principles of jurisprudence (*'uṣūl*) or with religious duties (*furu'*); and it has nothing to do with politics. One problem (or strength from a political institutional point of view) with the doctrine of *taqlīd* as it has evolved is that it is not divisible: one cannot decide that one will follow a particular *marja'* in all matters except a few where one feels oneself better informed than he. One must follow in all things; however, one can switch *marja'*. Among the thirty-four ḥadīth condemning *taqlīd* cited by 'Hurr al-'Āmili is this: "Beware of leaders who seek leadership. No sandals followed a man, save that he perished and made others perish."

'Hurr al-'Āmili is not alone in his rejection of *taqlīd:* this was the common position before the reassertion of a vigorous Uṣūli point of view in the eighteenth century by Waḥīd Behbehāni. Opponents of *taqlīd* invariably invoke the couplet from Rumi's *Masnavi* placed as an epigram to this section. More orthodox, perhaps, is the riddle attributed to Mulla Ṣadrā on the impossibility of *taqlīd:* you must be a *mujtahid* (i.e., be educated enough to exercise the disciplines of knowledge and interpretation) to have the ability to pick someone to follow, and *mujtahid*s are not permitted to follow others, they are obligated to exercise their own interpretive abilities. Another frequent hostile saying is that the *marja' taqlīd* are not only *muqallad* (one who is imitated), but they are also *muqallid* (one who imitates), because they are swayed by the financial support they get from bazaar merchants.[60] Most recently, Dr. Ali Shari'ati, asked if he practiced *taqlīd,* is said to have curtly replied, "I am not a monkey." Shari'ati did attempt to reinterpret the notion of *taqlīd,* claiming that its original application was for an underground resistance organization against the tyranny of unjust governments, built on four principles: leadership (imamate), secrecy or dissimulation (*taqiya*), readiness to die (martyrdom), and unquestioning obedience (*taqlīd*).[61] In a free society, however, he argued, there is no place for *taqlīd.* Shari'ati's argument is implicitly reflected in the popular punning response to the question, Do you practice *taqlīd?*: Do I want a [dog] collar (*qallāda*) around my neck?

From debate over *taqlīd* in the last century, and over a supreme *marja' taqlīd* in this century, Khomeini shifted debate in the 1970s and 1980s to political leadership and rule by the jurist.

Islamic Government: Khomeini's Dialogic Use of the Ḥadīth Game

A key text, which is not a text, but a faulty textual record of a "Socratic" dialogue, serves not only as the legitimating argument behind the constitution of the Islamic Republic of Iran, but also as a model of the dialogic method of the *faqīh* or jurist in interpreting the Qur'an and Islamic revelation. This is Khomeini's *Ḥukumat-e Islāmi: wilāyat-e faqīh* (Islamic government: guardianship by the clerical jurisconsult) in which he attempts to show with the help of a series of ḥadīth that the highest ranks of the clergy are the successors to the Prophet and the Imāms, and that they were intended to provide governmental leadership: that they and not merely the Imāms are the referent of the Qur'anic verse (4:59): "O you who believe, obey God, His messenger, and the issuers of orders among you (*ulu al-amr*)." Eventually, these lectures served as support for the new constitution, for elevating Khomeini in his role as supreme *faqīh* to head of state, and for justifying that a majority of the Parliament be composed of clerics.

Hukumat-e Islami originated as a series of lectures in 1970–71 to clerical students in Najaf. Some students previously had asked Āyatullāh Abu'l Qāsem Mūsavi Khoi if the clergy were entitled by Islamic law or the ḥadīth to take active government posts such as head of state, legislator, or governor. Khoi took a traditional quietist position and said no. Khomeini, in response to this opinion of a leading *mujtahid* and *marja' taqlīd,* attempted to stake out the activist position that Islamic jurists were to "exercise all the worldly functions of the Prophet" (1981: 124).

Interestingly, this debate between Khoi and Khomeini is a kind of replay of an earlier dispute between Āyatullāh Shaykh Muḥsin Ḥakīm and Khomeini, in which the issues of both personal precedence and leadership of the political struggle were underscored. In 1964 on the third day after Khomeini arrived in Iraq,[62] some of his followers threatened to publicly rip off Ḥakīm's turban if he did not visit and pay his respects to Khomeini. (Shades of Khomeini's behavior in 1979 when he returned to Iran and went first to Qum: there was jockeying to see who would pay the first visit to whom among the *marja' taqlīd;* eventually, Khomeini did have Āyatullāh Shariatmadari stripped of his turban.)[63] Ḥakīm, generally acknowledged as the *primus inter pares* among the *marja' taqlīd* during the late 1960s and 1970s, came to Khomeini, and was challenged (see pp. 44–45):

Khomeini: "With all your vast followership, why do you not rise up against the oppressors?"

Ḥakīm: "Imām Ali had two sons: Hasan embodied the path of patience and allowing the oppressive caliph Mu'awiyya to expose his illegitimacy through his evil acts; Husain demonstrated the path of revolt."

Khomeini: "If Hasan had had as many followers as you have, he too would have risen up."

Ḥakīm: "Only in Karbala may one know how many true followers one has."
(Ḥakīm did demonstrate his following: periodically he would move from Najaf to another southern Iraqi city, and enormous crowds would turn out to send him off and receive him. Saddam Husain dared not touch him, but when he died, Saddam had ten of Ḥakīm's sons killed. Two sons survive, one of whom, Muhammad-Baqir Ḥakīm, became head of a government in exile in Tehran.)

The 1970 lectures were circulated on cassette tapes and in written mimeographed form from student notes, then later edited, added to at the beginning and the end, and published both in Persian and in Arabic translation. The first edition was a third the size of the third edition used by Hamid Algar for his English translation. One can recognize in places where the textual discontinuity seems to imply objections and questions by listeners. Dual page numbers in the following discussion refer to the Persian edition reprinted in 1357 Sh./1978 and, following the slash, to Algar's 1981 translation, the most available English version; single page numbers refer to Algar.

In reading the text, one must exercise one's imagination to listen to an oral dialogue, much as Hans-Georg Gadamer has recently taught us to listen to Plato, asking always what questions the recorded comments are answering? The Persian text marks breaks in continuity with spacing, headings, and graphic separators between oral segments. Algar's translation suppresses these (as well as several of Khomeini's parenthetical asides), and often does not provide the full *isnād* (chains of narrators) or texts of the ḥadīth which introduce oral segments, skipping to Khomeini's glosses, losing thereby some of the interplay between the text and the reinterpretation. The Persian text, interestingly, provides the ḥadīth in their Arabic original, and then a Persian translation, a fingerprint of the fact that the printed text is amended for laymen: the clerical students to whom Khomeini was speaking would not have needed translations.[64]

Imagine, then, that we sit with Khomeini's students in Najaf as he delivers these lectures. Khomeini's style is not to answer questions or objections that are normally tossed out during the flow of such talks. Rather, he receives these oral interruptions silently; and begins with them at the beginning of the following day's session, or works them in at breaks in the flow of his thought. A dramatic dialectic form guides his lectures, as it does the lectures of other teachers in the seminary system. This form is called *ishkāl* ("criticism," "question"), and is triggered in three ways. The lecturer uses traditional or common opinions as foils, or he anticipates questions and objections from his audience, or his audience actually interjects questions and objections.

Khomeini is quite clear that he is testing the limits of an argument, and that the game of ḥadīth on which as a *faqīh* he must base himself provides shaky grounds: "If the only proof I had were one of the traditions I've been citing, I would be unable to substantiate my claim" (p. 99). Four sources of authority are in fact invoked: reason, the practices (sunna) of the Prophet and of Ali, the Qur'an, and the ḥadīth of the Prophet and the Imāms. Although a score of Qur'anic verses are cited at various points—some to illustrate functions of an Islamic government such as taxation (8:41, 9:03) or implementing the penal code (24:2); some to illustrate the command to rise up against tyranny of kings and pharaohs, against idolators (*ṭāghūt*) and corrupters of the earth (28:4); some to illustrate the condemnation of religious leaders who fail to guide their followers (5:63; 5:75–78; 9:71)—one verse in particular and the one preceding it are central: "O you who believe, obey God and obey the Messenger and the holders of authority (*ulu al-amr*) from among you" (4:59). For Shi'ites, the holders of authority are the Imāms, the twelfth and last of whom remains alive albeit in occultation.

Khomeini wants to show that "holders of authority" must also refer to the highest rank of the clergy—the *fuqahā* or *mujtahidīn*—those who have attained the level of knowledge in which they are not only permitted, but enjoined, to wield the interpretive rules for coming to independent decisions on novel questions (*ijtihād*). The preceding verse is, "God commands you to return trusts to their owners, and to act with justice when you rule/judge among men." Khomeini wants to show that the "trusts" are not merely, as traditional interpretations have it, (1) worldly property to be returned to rightful owners and (2) divine trusts (i.e., Islamic law, the *sharī'a*), which to Shi'ites means the return of political and religious leadership to the Imāms, usurped by the first three Sunni caliphs, the Umayyids, and subsequent monarchies. In addition, he wants to show that the "trustees" here are the *fuqahā*, the word for "rule/judge" means "rule," not just "judging," and "God commands you" refers not only to Muhammad, but to both the Imāms and the jurists. The Prophet exercised rule, not merely judicial functions: he appointed governors and ambassadors, he taxed, he enforced the penal code, he commanded battles and campaigns, as well as arbitrated, guided, and interpreted the law. Imām Ali, when he was caliph, did the same. The Shi'ite dogma of the imamate credits all twelve of the Imāms with this function. Khomeini's exercise is to show that the Qur'anic command has continuing addressees, and that the current addressee is not the twelfth Imām but that the first clause of verse 4:58 is addressed to all believers, and the second to the clerics (*fuqahā*).

Khomeini begins by dismissing three quietist arguments. (1) For almost two centuries Islam was instituted politically under the Prophet, under Imām Ali, and as best as could be done in adverse circumstances, under the Imāms; but just because the twelfth Imām has occulted himself, that does not mean Islam should no longer be instituted. (2) Should the *khums* tax—half of which goes to support indigent sayyids, and half for the Imāms—really be thrown into the sea or buried where the Imām could find it (p. 36/45)?[65] No, obviously, the taxes mandated by Islam are so great that they were intended to provide state revenues. (3) If Islam is meant to provide government institutions, who should guide them, who should rule? Surely not those uneducated in Islam.

Khomeini marshalls sixteen ḥadīth—three major ones (nos. 1, 2, and 9 below) and thirteen lesser ones—of varying reliability and applicability. What he accomplishes is not a proof, but only a plausibility that an Islamic society should be guided or ruled by jurisconsults (of Islamic law). We will take up these sixteen ḥadīth sequentially, not so much for their argument, but for an illustration both of the dialogic structure and of the ḥadīth game. As in Plato's Socratic dialogues, the partners in dialogue are not equals: here they are teacher and students, albeit students of the highest stage in the theological system; in Plato's dialogues, Socrates' superiority is used to guide his partner and the reader through false positions toward more correct ones, and in the process acquire the skills of dialectics. Here the dialogue is an oral, actual one, only slightly deformed by subsequent transcription and editing; Plato's dialogues, of course, are written forms in which Socrates is a staged character whose opinions are often not those of Plato. Plato's dialogues wield mistaken opinions as mirrors for the reader, and work as phantasms that lead the seeker onward, rather than as icons of truth; they seek to prevent the logos from becoming autonomous. Here, Khomeini's dialogue also wields mistaken opinions as mirrors, and seeks to prevent the ideals of Islam from being merely utopian ideas. What is perhaps most interesting is that the play of dialogue, dialectic, and hermeneutic prevents the closure that Khomeini seeks. Just as the Socratic dialogues explore an arena of argumentation but do not assert final conclusions, so too Khomeini's dialogue provides at best only the possibility of the position he wants to assert, and provides as much ammunition against his position as for it. The ḥadīth game works in similar fashion, as a way of exploring possible meanings in the texts, both exposing the constructivist rather than the definitive meanings of tradition and placing constraints on the free play of contemporary constructions, tempering them via the experiences of past generations.

First ḥadīth:

The first ḥadīth that Khomeini cites introduces us to the disputation between teacher and learned students. It is a ḥadīth of Imām Riḍā, the eighth Imām, used to support Khomeini's argument from reason that it is "self-evident" and "necessary" that the obedience in the Qur'anic verse 4:59 refers to the functions of government and not just ritual duties (p. 45/51). The ḥadīth says (1) that without a "trustee" (*amīn*) people would not stay within the bounds of the licit, (2) that no group has ever existed without a ruler and it "would not be compatible with divine wisdom to leave mankind to its own device," i.e., to send Muhammad but not provide for successors to execute the laws he brought, and (3) that without trustees, "innovators would increase and deniers would erode religion," e.g., through fabricating ḥadīth and through undisciplined, misguided interpretation. Khomeini does not bother to analyze the chains of narration (*isnād*) or to present the full text (*matn*) of the ḥadīth. He merely wishes to shore up with a ḥadīth his admission that his argument—that Islam is neither just a private ethics nor merely a ritual system—depends upon "self-evident" reason as much as upon the Qur'an, sunna, or ḥadīth. He claims that only one percent of the Qur'an has to do with ritual duties, while the rest has to do with social rules proper to government enforcement; and that the ratio in the ḥadīth literature likewise is 3:47, ritual to social rules. But Khomeini does not escape so easily.

The qualities of a legitimate ruler are "self-evidently" *'ilm* (knowledge of the law) and *'adālat* (justice). The former implies, minimally, submission by rulers to guidance by *fuqahā* who know the law. The discussion here seems long-winded and banal, unless one assumes that the students have already raised two questions. A first student says, "You have contradicted yourself: first, you claim that Islam does not recognize kings; now, you claim a supervisory role for the *fuqahā* over kings, thereby implicitly recognizing their legitimacy." There is a play here with the ambiguity of the cognates from root *ḥ-k-m,* depending on the exact location of a long "a": "the *fuqahā* are the wise men [*ḥukamā*] or advisers of the kings" versus "the *fuqahā* are the rulers [*ḥukkām*] over kings." The two versions of the ḥadīth record the long "a" differently. This is a richly charged ambiguity that was left to play upon the imaginations of the political alliances within the revolutionary forces of 1979:

liberals chose to believe Khomeini meant *ḥukamā* (advisers); radicals chose to believe *ḥukkām* (rulers). Either way, Khomeini meant to place authority, if not power, in the hands of the *fuqahā*. A second student objects, "You are saying that the *fuqahā* are on the same level as Imāms and the Prophet, but there is a critical difference. Imāms and Prophets have independent authority, whereas *fuqahā* have no such independent authority." The reference here is to the rich imagery and dogmas of *wilāyat-e takwīni* (played up and used as a heading in the Persian text, but dropped by Algar) and the *nūr* doctrine.

The latter says that the Imāms and Prophets were created from a divine ray of light (*nūr*) at the beginning of creation; they command the material particles of the universe, even if, unlike God, they cannot create ex nihilo. *Takwīn* ("creation," "genesis," from the same root as *kun*!, "be!") is creation through *logos:* God says, "Be!" and it is so. An Imām may say to a tree, "Move!" and it will, but the Imāms are but guardians (*wulāt, wilāyat*) of creation, not the creators. Khomeini replies that *fuqahā* do not have the same qualities of being or virtues as do the Imāms or the Prophets, but they have the same responsibilities (*mas'uliyat*): if the law says a hundred lashes for fornication, the *faqīh* will not inflict fewer because his rank is lower. *Wilāyat-e takwīni* (creative or independent guardianship) is contrasted with *wilāyat-e i'tibāri* (dependent guardianship), dependent on the guidance of higher authorities. The reasoning here constitutes an interesting admission: *wilāyat-e faqīh* (guardianship by the clergy) then is dependent, not a tyranny of independent judgment; it is entangled precisely in the web of evaluations, and ultimate indeterminacy that makes the *tafsīr* of the Qur'an so dangerous.

Second ḥadīth:

If the first ḥadīth introduces us to the dialectics of disputation between teacher and student, the next ḥadīth introduces more clearly the evaluative play of the validity of *isnād* (chain of authority) and *matn* (text):

> Shaykh Ṣadūq (may God's mercy be upon him) has related this tradition with five chains of transmission (actually four, since two of them are similar in certain respects) in the following books: *Jāmi' al-Akhbār, 'Uyūn Akhbār ar-Riḍā,* and *al-Majālis.* Among the cases where this tradition has been designated as *musnad* [i.e., the *isnād* goes back to a Companion of the Prophet], in one instance we find the words . . . and in the other instance we find. . . . Wherever the tradition is designated as *mursal* [the

> *isnād* goes back only to a second generation follower, with no Companion named, or is a broken *isnād*], we find only the beginning of the sentence. . . . (p. 74/68)

Note the admission that this ḥadīth is not of the greatest degree of reliability, being neither *mutawātir* nor *ṣaḥīḥ,* but at best *musnad* and perhaps even *mursal* (see p. 125 above). Nor is it to be found in the four basic Shi'ite collections of ḥadīth. In Ḥurr al-'Āmili's *Al-Wasa'il al-Shi'a* it is counted as merely *mursal:* there are missing links in its chain. As to the four of five mutally confirming *isnād,* Khomeini is shading things: *Ma'āni al-Akhbār* and Shaykh Ṣadūq's *Al-Majālis* both give two *isnād,* but they are merely branching variants of the same basic one; Shaykh Ṣadūq's *'Uyūn Akhbār al-Riḍā* has three *isnād*s, and Khomeini claims that the narrators of these lived so far apart that they constitute independent confirmations, but they lived in Marv, Nishapur, and Balkh, all towns of Khorasan which were on the circuit of scholars collecting knowledge (*raḥla fī ṭalab al-'ilm*).

There are two slight variants of the text (*matn*):

> The Commander of the Faithful [Imām Ali] (upon whom be peace) relates that the Most Noble Messenger [Muhammad] (upon whom be blessings and peace) said, "O God have mercy on those that succeed me/are *khulafā'i* ('my caliphs, assistants')." He repeated this twice and was then asked: "O Messenger of God, who are those that succeed you/are your *khulafā'i?* He replied: "They are those that come after me, narrating [*yarwūna*] my traditions and practices (and teach them to the people after me)." (p. 74/68)

One can almost hear the lively student object: "There is no word *fuqahā* in this ḥadīth. All it mentions is narrators. Furthermore, if we cannot establish the reliability of the chain of authority, how do we know that some narrator might not have interjected some of his own opinions, only to have later generations think these part of the ḥadīth itself?" (Indeed there is a discussion of the relative competences, and their use of personal reason [*naẓar*], of Shaykh Mufid and Shaykh Ṣaduq, that seems to be a response to such a question; otherwise, the passage seems disjointed from the preceding thought [p. 69].) Khomeini argues that those who teach ḥadīth and sunna are those who can distinguish (1) authentic from fabricated ḥadīth; (2) ḥadīth with only limited application versus those with general application; (3) ḥadīth involving plural forms but singular meanings and vice versa (*jam'ha-ye 'uqala'i;* Algar translates this implausibly as "rational categories"); and (4) ḥadīth issued under conditions of dissimulation (*taqiyah*) – i.e., *fuqahā* who not only narrate reliably but are capable of exercising *ijtihād.* Khomeini used the ḥadīth against two weak ḥadīth "fabricated by court preachers" that advise Muslims to make peace with kings, in contradiction to the Qur'anic injunction to rise up against Pharaoh. A knowledgeable transmitter of ḥadīth knows better than to repeat false ḥadīth that contravene explicit injunctions or the logical intent of the Qur'an.

The two "weak" ḥadīth of "court preachers" are not identified, but probably they are the one in which Muhammad says he was born during the reign of the just King Anushiravan, a ḥadīth popular among apologists for Iranian nationalism and the Pahlavi monarchy, who wanted to bolster Iranian traditions of justice independent of Islam; and even more likely, "the king is the Shadow of God on earth" (*al-sulṭān ẓill allāh fi arḍih*), used as a title (*Ẓill-allāh*) of the Safavid and Qajar kings of Iran.

Third ḥadīth:

If in this second ḥadīth Khomeini argues that context and implication make it clear that *fuqahā* are the kind of narrators meant, even if the word *fuqahā* does not appear, the third ḥadīth provides a clear didactic example in which he can show that that word can be dropped and the meaning still be established by context. (One can almost hear our lively students having triggered this example by objecting: "If it is so common to have a word or phrase dropped – as the dropping of the concluding clause from the variant of the second ḥadīth – how can we trust the ḥadīth?") The third ḥadīth (p. 83/73), from the seventh Imām, is found in two versions in *al-Kāfi.* It is useful to Khomeini because it refers to the *fuqahā* as the "fortresses of Islam"; Khomeini takes this to mean that the *fuqahā* must take active protective roles in Islamic society. He sarcastically observes: "For example, we recite the verse, 'Administer to the adulterer and the adultress a hundred lashes each' [24:2], but we do not know what to do when confronted with a case of adultery. We merely recite the verse in order to improve the sound of our recitation and to give each sound its full value" (p. 85/75). One variant says, "Whenever a believer who is a *faqīh* dies, the angels weep. . . . A crack will appear in the fortress of Islam, that naught can repair because (*li'anna*) believers who are *fuqahā* are the fortresses of Islam. . . ." The other version does not have the clause "who is a *faqīh*" in the first sentence. This is a case where not only is there a second fuller version, but the second version confirms the contexualization made by the conjunction *li'anna,* which specifies that the believers being spoken of are *fuqahā.*

Fourth and fifth ḥadīths:

So far, we have no "proof texts" or ḥadīth of any great reliability or clarity, only a concatenation of possible supports for the thesis. It seems the students now begin citing ḥadīth against the thesis. This may be indicated by the break in the Persian text marked graphically with three asterisks before the next paragraph which begins with a ḥadīth from the sixth Imām, as if a new session on a new day were beginning with Khomeini taking up a ḥadīth passed to him to comment on by a student:

The ḥadīth says, "The *fuqahā* are the trustees of the prophets, as long as they do not concern themselves with this world (*fi al-dunyā*)." It is as if Khomeini says, "You are right, this ḥadīth seems to go against my thesis of having the clergy politically active in the world; but if we reinterpret *fi al-dunyā* as concerning themselves with illicit things in the world, then my thesis can still hold." (Algar skips the citation of the ḥadīth proper and only provides Khomeini's reinterpretation, thus destroying the dialectical structure of the passage.) Indeed, Khomeini continues, let us not examine this ḥadīth in detail, but only consider the phrase "trustees of the prophet" (*umanā al-rusul*), "because of its relevance to the topic of the governance of the *faqīh*" (p. 76). He quickly goes on to consider what duties and powers the prophets had, which might be what their trustees will also have: "The *fuqahā* are the trustees who implement the divine ordinances in levying taxes, guarding the frontiers, and executing the penal provisions of the law" (p. 79), and they "execute as a trust all the affairs for which Islam has legislated—not that they simply offer legal judgments" (p. 80). He then cites very briefly another ḥadīth from the eighth Imām, Rida, which also speaks of the *fuqahā* as trustees of the prophets, and which speaks of the need of communities for leaders (*imām*); these two assertions, he says, can be combined to support his thesis: the *fuqahā* are the imāms of the community.

Sixth to eighth ḥadīths:

The next three ḥadīth again seem to be cited against Khomeini's thesis. Again, all three times, the ḥadīth are set off graphically in the Persian edition (not in Algar's) with asterisks and a break in the text as if a new day's session is beginning. Again, all three times, Algar gives only Khomeini's reinterpretation, not the initially hostile ḥadīth followed by Khomeini's domestication of it. And again Algar translates some of Khomeini's words in an effort to help Khomeini, but thereby loses the punch of the original.

The sixth ḥadīth, from Imām Ali addressed to Shurayḥ, the judge of Kufah, appointed by the caliph 'Umar, says, "The position you occupy is filled by a prophet [*nabī*], the successor [*waṣī*] of a prophet, or a sinful wretch [*shaqī*]. . . ." Ali of course, was charging Shurayh with not being a legitimate judge; with being a *shaqī;* with, as Khomeini puts it, being "one of those *ākhūnd*s [preachers] who associated with the usurper Mu'awiya." (Algar drops the politically potent contemporary sarcasm, "one of those *ākhūnd*s," perhaps out of a misguided desire to clean up Khomeini's anachronistic use of *ākhūnd,* or out of an inappropriate desire to defend all clerics before an English-speaking audience. Algar also translates *waṣī* as legatee, perhaps in an effort to make this ḥadīth seem to follow naturally upon the preceding ones where *fuqahā* are called "trustees of the prophet" and "fortress of Islam." *Waṣī,* however, normally in Shi'ism refers to Ali and the Imāms. Khomeini freely admits this, but wants to link the term with the *fuqahā.* He does so by first dismissing the issue of appointment. He says the issue of governance by the *faqīh* is not the issue here, and is disputed by scholars, but that judges must be *fuqahā* is something everyone agrees upon (p. 82). The functions of judging continue after the Imāms, and so one may expand the meaning of *waṣī* to those who have the qualifications to carry on the responsibilities with which the Imāms initially, but not exclusively, were entrusted.

The seventh ḥadīth, from the sixth Imām, handed down both through a weak chain of authority and through a reliable one, says, "Refrain from *ḥukūma* ("governing," "judging") because *ḥukūma* is reserved for an imām . . ." who is knowledgeable and just. Our lively student shouts out: "See, it says he must be an Imām" (one of the twelve); and Khomeini replies, "What is meant here by *imām* is the common lexical meaning of the word, 'leader,' or 'guide,' not its specific technical sense" (of *Imām*): the Persian, of course, does not graphically differentiate with capitalization between *imām* and *Imām.* Since only *fuqahā* are knowledgeable in the sense required to be a judge, and since the second qualification of "justice" theologically means adherence to the ordinances (*aḥkām*) of Islam, says Khomeini, the *faqīh* should be the leader of the nation (*ra'īs-e millat*). Although the use of the singular can be a collective noun, in historical retrospect the shift from plural *fuqahā* to singular *faqīh* takes on a significance it did not originally have. (This is the issue of meaningful singulars and plurals, *jam'ha-ye 'uqala'i,* mentioned before in discussing the second ḥadīth. Khomeini clearly indicates that a single *faqīh* is not necessary [p. 54/64], and he speaks of *wājib 'ainī* [obligations of an individual] versus *wājib al-kifā'i* [communal obligations that an individual undertakes only so that the community's obligations are fulfilled] though again, in retrospect, he shades it in favor of the former: "If this task falls within the capabilities of a single person, he has personally incumbent upon him the duty to fulfil it [*wājib 'ainī*]; otherwise it is a duty that devolves upon the *fuqahā* as a whole [*wājib al-kifā'i*]" [p. 64].)

The eighth ḥadīth comes as a letter from the twelfth Imām, delivered via the deputy of the Imām, given in Shaykh Ṣadūq's *Ikmāl al-Dīn wa Itmām al-Ni'ma.* It says, "In case of newly occurring circumstances (*al-ḥawādith al-wāqi'ah*), you should turn for guidance to those who relate our traditions (*ruwāt aḥādīthina*), for they are my proof (*ḥujjat*) to you, as I am God's proof to them." Our lively student objects: "new circumstances" means new issues of jurisprudence for which there is no explicit law (*al-masā'il al-mustaḥdatha*); but Khomeini expansively interprets the phrase to mean "not legal issues without precedent" but "social problems" (pp. 84–85). Our student objects: what is *ḥujjat,* "God's proof," or source of authority (p. 85)? This cannot be a *mutawātir* ḥadīth, it cannot be more than a singly attested ḥadīth (*ḥadīth-e wāḥid*), because it is a secret letter; the authority is merely a text, not even the witnessed word of the Imām. Khomeini argues that "proof of God [*ḥujjat,* source of authority] is one whom God has designated to conduct affairs; all his deeds, actions, and sayings constitute a proof [source of authority] for Muslims"; but Khomeini laconically admits, "it is possible to have certain reservations about its chain of transmission." A major challenge is building here: none of the ḥadīth cited so far are much better than *ḥadīth-e wāḥid.*

Ninth and tenth ḥadīths:

The pivotal ḥadīth cited by Khomeini is the *maqbūla* of 'Umar ibn Ḥanẓala. Neither *ṣaḥiḥ* (correct, strong) nor *mutawātir* (confirmed), it is merely *maqbūla* (accepted) because some previous jurisconsults have based *fatwā*s upon it, despite the fact that 'Umar ibn Ḥanẓala is not in the category of *thuqāt* (trustworthy). Still, says Khomeini, it helps clarify the key Qur'anic verses 4:58–59: the latter warns against taking disputes for adjudication to illegitimate rulers (*ṭaghūt*), and the former advises returning trusts to their owners, which Shi'ite exegetes interpret as referring to the imamate, and Khomeini now to the *fuqahā*. The question of trusts Khomeini refers to the concept of *wilāyat,* and notes that some authorities speak of *wilāyat-e faqīh* as referring only to trusts for orphans, when he would argue for it to apply to all of society. The *maqbūla* of 'Umar ibn Ḥanẓala is a direct commentary on verse 4:59. 'Umar ibn Ḥanẓala says:

> I asked Abu Abdullah [Imām Ṣādiq] about two men among our friends [*aṣ-ḥabina*] between whom there was a dispute [*munāza'a*] over debt [*dayn*] or inheritance [*mīrāth*], and who sought adjudication from the sultan and the judges [*fataḥākamā ila al-sulṭān wa ila al-qudat*]. Is this permissible? He said: "Anyone who takes judgment to them in matters of rights [*ḥaqq*] and false claims [*bāṭil*] has sought out false authority [*ṭaghūt*]. The judgment is void and the man is forbidden to repossess [the object] even though it be his demonstrable right. God says, 'They wish to seek judgment from *ṭaghūt,* even though they have been commanded to reject the *ṭaghūt*' [4:60]." I asked, "What should they do?" He said, "One must look for one among you who narrates our ḥadīth and has looked into our permissions [*ḥalāl*] and our proscriptions [*ḥarām*], and who knows our ordinances [*aḥkām*] . . . content himself with such a person as *ḥakam* [mediator], for I have made him a *ḥakīm* [judge, ruler] over you.

Now, traditionally, this ḥadīth has been thought to do with arbitration in such things as debt and inheritance; thus, Ḥurr al-'Āmili places it in his chapter on *Ṣifāt al-Qāḍī* ("qualifications of the judge"). Khomeini wants to extend the meaning more broadly, and does so by playing on the words *ḥukm* (decree, judgment, rule), *ḥakam* (mediator), ḥākim (ruler), *ḥakamiyat* (mediation, arbitration), *ḥukūma* (government), *ḥikmat* (philosophy, wisdom), *aḥkām* (laws), and other cognates. The ambiguity is abetted by an orthographic one: in scripts without diacriticals, that thus do not distinquish long and short a, *ḥakam* (arbiter, حكم) looks the same as *ḥākim* (ruler حكم); the only difference is a small mark above the first letter, but in the old Kufic script not even this diacritical existed. (In the Algar version, although the word *ḥākim* has both meanings, Khomeini insists that Imām al-Ṣādiq first appoints such narrators (who by the arguments already cited must obviously be *fuqahā*) as judges (p. 93), but separately then also appoints them as rulers (p. 95). Such a distinction is hard to maintain in the original. A second word play also obviously has attracted Khomeini to this ḥadīth: *ṭāghūt,* he says, is a cognate of *ṭughyān* (rebellion), a somewhat dubious etymology, but one that caught on with great popularity, as people began to call the shah and his officials *ṭāghūti,* rebels against God.

Our lively students object by citing a ḥadīth of the sixth Imām, narrated by his companion Abū Khadīja, which says, "When enmity and dispute arise . . . [do not go to the *ṭāghūt,* but] designate as judge [*qāḍī*]. . . ." The point of the citation is that in the *maqbūla* of 'Umar ibn Ḥanẓala, the sixth Imām says, "*Fa innī qad ja'altuhu 'alaykum ḥakama,*" whereas here he changes one word in the sentence (*fa inni qad ja'altuhu 'alaykum qāḍiyan*), thereby specifying that he means judge (*qāḍi*) when he says *ḥakam.* Khomeini responds by arguing that the two sentences mean just the reverse: he says not to go to *ṭāghūti* judges, nor to the illegitimate authorities which appoint such judges. (All this is somewhat lost in Algar's translation, since he does not provide the by-play between the words *qāḍī* and *ḥākim.*)

It is here that Khomeini admits, "If the only proof I had were one of the traditions I have been citing, I would be unable to substantiate my claim," although with a sleight of rhetoric, in the next breath he says, "Its essence, however, has been proved by the traditions already cited" (p. 99). He is responding to the objection that individually none of the ḥadīth he has discussed are either very reliable or provide much support in their content. His argument is that nonetheless, collectively, they overlap one another in such a way as to provide support for what is the logically obvious intent of Islam.

Eleventh to fourteenth ḥadīths:

Our learned students decide to try to help him, and suggest a *ṣaḥiḥ* ḥadīth of the sixth Imām in which the scholars are referred to as "heirs of the Prophet" (*warathat al-anbiā*), and what is inherited is not dinars or dirhams, but knowledge. This would be the first *ṣaḥīh* ḥadīth cited. But Khomeini, the teacher, now switches roles, and shows that this ḥadīth, known as Ṣaḥiḥa of Qaddāḥ, may not be so reliable after all, or at least must be handled with care: there are a number of versions, and the Sunni ones add a phrase for political reasons suggesting that the legacy is only the ḥadīth and knowledge, and not property, thereby attempting to deny the daughter of the Prophet's claim to the garden of Fadak, which became a symbol of Shi'ite claims to legitimate rulership over the lands of Islam. Khomeini does, however, accept this ḥadīth, and discusses five objections to it, including several possible misreadings of the *ṣaḥīh* version. He dispenses with the idea that "scholars" here should mean only the Imāms, or that heirs must have the same quality of being, status, or virtue as those from whom they inherit responsibilities. Here he cites Sūra 33:6, and the ḥadīth of Imām Baqir that this verse was revealed concerning governance and command: the responsibilities of the Prophet regarding the functions of governance must apply to his "heirs." This is used against the possible misreading of the *ṣaḥīh* text that the prophet only left as a legacy traditions and knowledge, and not the functions of governance, nor property.

Two weak ḥadīth follow, one from *Fiqh-e Radawi,* which says, "The rank of the *faqīh* in the present age is like that of the prophets of the Children of Israel," and thus Khomeini argues "the same function of rulership and governance that Moses exercised exists also for the *fuqahā*" (p. 108); and another from the *Jāmi' al-Akhbār* in which the Prophet says, "The scholars of my community are like the prophets preceding me." About the *isnād* of the latter, Khomeini says nothing, and admits that the *isnād* of the former cannot bear scrutiny.

Fifteenth ḥadīth:

Next, Khomeini very briefly refers to two variants of a ḥadīth to the effect that "the scholars are rulers over the people" in which the nineteenth century recording uses the word *ḥukamā* (wise men), but the earlier source from which it is taken has the word *ḥukkām* (rulers). Clearly, he thinks the latter version correct, and says, "If its chain of transmission is valid, it may also serve to support my thesis"—not a terribly optimistic comment.

Sixteenth ḥadīth:

Finally, from the *Tuḥaf al-'Uqūl,* Khomeini cites a ḥadīth of Ali narrated by Imām Husain, together with an account of Husain's speech at Mina, in which the *fuqahā* are charged with using *jihād* to overthrow tyrannical rulers and establishing Islamic governance. Unfortunately, Khomeini laments, the *isnād* is weak. Here he echoes Ansari: even so, "the content of the ḥadīth being veracious, bears witness that it was uttered by one of the *ma'ṣūmīn*" (pure ones, i.e., infallible Imāms) (p. 124).

What Khomeini has established through this exercise is not a proof, but rather a plausibility that an Islamic society is to be guided and ruled by jurisconsults, and/or by Islamic law. Whether this is to be through a single *faqīh* or a college of *fuqahā* (the debate over a supreme *marja' taqlīd*), or even through a combination of *fuqahā* and laymen, is not explored (although it is raised, p. 64); indeed, the principle that one *faqīh* cannot override another is affirmed (p. 54). The constitution of the Islamic Republic enshrines all three possibilities: Khomeini as head of state represents a singular Guardian; this is to be continued if possible after him, but provision is also made for a collegial leadership; and a Council of Guardians composed of both *fuqahā* and secular members was instituted to veto parliamentary legislation contravening Islamic law.

What, finally, is most interesting here is the degree to which this structure reflects Islamic restraint about knowing what God really wants: it is remarkable, given Khomeini's iron will and drive against compromise with the shah or with *fuqahā* who provided cover for oppositional factions to Khomeini's role as supreme *faqīh* (especially Āyatullāh Muḥammad-Kaẓem Shari'atmadari and Sayyid Maḥmūd Ṭāleqani), that Khomeini's style of leadership over government and policy formation systematically was one of arbitrating among factions rather than either dictating policy or backing one faction against another. Nowhere is this clearer than in the remarkable history of factional stalemate about economic policy represented most symbolically by land reform. Hashemi-Rafsinjani, then Speaker of the Parliament, repeatedly (1981, 1983, 1984) asked Khomeini to intervene and direct Parliament, the Council of Guardians, or the executive branch to follow what he designated as correct policy: Khomeini refused. One grounding of this restraint lies in the degree to which there is an Islamic economics encoded in the Qur'an and ḥadīth. Contrary to the strident apologetics of lay Muslims, professional *fuqahā* move very carefully in this territory because to fulfill the program of a political economy such as envisioned in Khomeini's *Hukūmat-e Islami,* considerable *ta'wīl* is required. It is an interesting exercise, and it is quite astounding how little patience for it have even such *fuqahā* as the late Āyatullāh Muḥammad-Bāqir Ṣadr, who wrote the fullest contemporary Shi'ite statement on the subject, but whose *Iqtesaduna* (Our economics) is amazingly poor in locating proof texts in the Qur'an, ḥadīth, historical *fatwās* or *ḥukms*.[66]

Anfāl (Public Goods) and Islamic Economics

The idea of an Islamic economics which is a "third path" between communism and capitalism is a standard slogan of modernist Islam over the past century. It rests upon the dual observation that while all transactions—as in laissez-faire capitalism—are calculated as contracts between willing and knowledgeable partners, unlike the situation in pure private property capitalism, property under Islam does not ultimately belong to individuals but to God or the community. Individual rights are protected as usufruct rights, and so strongly protected as to often merit the claim that "private property is sacred in Islam," but only so long as the property is productively used and taxes paid. Not only is there a taxation system to redistribute to the public domain and to the poor what is not being used and what, through inevitable inequalities, builds up in the hands of the fortunate; there are rules of commercial practice—including the rules of fair price and the prohibition on usury—principles of the public good which may be invoked to limit individual rights, and principles of substituting "something better" (*tabdīl*) used to modify endowment contracts. (On *tabdīl,* see Fischer [1980: 118ff.]; on the literature on Islamic economics in Iran during the 1970s, see ibid. [pp. 156–59].) Most of the literature on Islamic economics remains in a speculative and apologetic mode projected into the future (as opposed to a historical analysis of how Islamic reasoning was used to think about or challenge innovations in the political economy over the last thirteen centuries).[67] Khomeini (1970: 44–45) thus talks of the taxes of Islam as easily being able to provide the revenues for a modern state—*khums* (one fifth of surplus income after customary expenses), *zakāt* (alms, which he notes would not represent an appreciable amount), *jizya* (the tax on non-Muslim protected minorities, i.e., Jews, Christians, and Zoroastrians), and *kharāj* (tax on land given free for development, once it is productive). And he too mouths the slogan that Islam provides for every detail of life (ibid., pp. 30, 43). Various versions of specific Islamic policies such as Islamic banks, which do not charge interest, have now been instituted in different parts of the Islamic world (see the bibliography compiled by Abedi and Mirakhor (1988).

In Iran, the Islamic revolution nationalized banks, insurance, large industries, undeveloped land, and some trade. This all was done in the name of the public good, of the defense of the revolution or of the Muslim community, of rooting out unjust corrupt practices (banking interest, excessive profiteering by large companies controlling large shares of a market), and of ensuring equitable circulation of God's wealth. Trouble comes with land reform, where redistribution of wealth is pursued not by expropriating to the state or community, but by taking from one individual and giving to another. We will take only one small example of the kind of argumentation such debates take. At issue here is not the application of such local laws as inheritance or personal rules for taxation, but the large-scale issues of the role of the state in economic affairs.

In 1341/1962 as part of the discussions about the future of the Shi'ite clerical institution, including the discussions about the role and possible reorganization of the *marja' taqlīd,*[68] Ali Gholzādeh Ghafūri delivered a lecture on "*Anfāl* or the Public Good," later expanded and published as a small book. Ghafūri was one of the clerics, like Murtaḍa Muṭahhari, who was willing to engage with Islamic modernist intellectuals such as Mehdi Bazargan, in a set of monthly discussions (published in a journal, *Goftār-e Māh*). He later was a supporter of Khomeini, and was elected to both the Assembly of Experts, which drafted the constitution for the Islamic Republic of Iran, and to the Parliament of the Republic. (Subsequently, he fell afoul of Khomeini's wrath.)

The burden of his lecture is to demonstrate that *anfāl,* the title of Sūra 8 of the Qur'an, is not just about the "spoils of war," to which its association has become restricted over time because no true Islamic society has existed and, Ghafūri suggests, because eaters of public property (such as kings and capitalists) have a vested interest in promoting an interpretation that sees this as merely an archaic verse to be recited as a matter of merit, not a verse with any contemporary practical application. Western Orientalists (and translators of the Qur'an) have been misled, he says, by Sunni exegetes, who take literally the circumstances of revelation (*sabab al-nuzūl*) of the verse: at the Battle of Badr, the enemy ran away leaving behind a vast amount of booty, and the Prophet was asked what to do with it; he replied it belonged to God and His Messenger, and he then divided it among all Muslims, not just those who had taken part in the battle. Now, clearly, Ghafūri says, echoing arguments of S. Maḥmūd Tāleqani, one does not give anything material to God, but rather the meaning must be that one must spend or use material things in a manner pleasing to God; and similarly, the Prophet did not register this booty as his private property, but took it on behalf of the community. In Shi'ite books of jurisprudence, *anfāl* is defined as that which belongs to the Imāms. Lexically, as well, *anfāl* is a cognate of *nafl,* meaning something given to God, also "something extra" beyond what is required. Thus in the Qur'an the term *ṣalāt al-nāfila* is additional prayers beyond the required number; so *nāfila* property would be that surplus above one's basic needs or basic standard of living.

In support, Ghafūri turns to Ḥurr al-'Āmili's *al-Wasa'il al-Shī'a,* where seventy-three ḥadīth are listed in four chapters of the section on *anfāl.* He cites three of these, one each from three different Imāms, all of which provide a list of things that fall under *anfāl:* mines, forests, abandoned land, dead land or unreclaimed land, property of kings (unless illegally taken from others, in which case such property should be returned), property which has fallen heirless, all land which has fallen to Muslims without military effort, mountain tops (i.e., mountain pasturage), valley bottoms, all booty taken without permission of the Imāms, and all fiefs (*iqtā'*) given by kings (unless illegitimately taken from others, in which case it should be returned).

Ghafūri then recites the story of how the caliph Umar instituted a policy of giving out land free to those who would develop it, only as much as one could work oneself, and charging a *kharāj* tax upon the produce of this land when it became productive; how Ali even lightened the taxation load and further encouraged productivity; and how the Umayyids reversed this policy, by giving land out to political allies rather than to those who would work it, and by increasing taxation, so that the state revenues fell dramatically.[69] Finally, Ghafūri rhetorically asks who should control this public land, and he cites the numerous verses against the *safīh* ("stupid," "ignorant ones"), citing additional ḥadīth of the Imāms, that *safīh* are wine drinkers, sinners (*fūssāq*), and corrupters of the earth. In so doing, he is playing rhetorical games with terms used to identify the shah and his supporters, as well as hinting through implicit rhyme that *safīh* contrasts with the unmentionable, in this context, proper guidance by *faqīh.*

Despite the apologetics of Khomeini, Ghafūri, and others that Islam provides a blueprint for all aspects of life, there is no economic doctrine encoded here. One can as easily argue from the doctrine that land can be owned only by those who work it, that Islam favors peasant agriculture and opposes landlord-tenant or large-scale industrial agriculture using hired labor, as the opposite. Sayyid Raḍī, the compiler of Imām Ali's sayings as *Nahjul al-Balāgha,* was only one of many early model Shi'ites who were landowners with vast spreads.

The point, here, is not that the ḥadīth literature is such a mass of contradictions and fabrications as to make it unusable for serious history, but on the contrary that the use of ḥadīth can provide access to ideological, sectarian, social, and political history. This is a history that must be approached dialectically (i.e., aware of the range of counterarguments in a given historical period), hermeneutically (i.e., aware of the allusions and contexts, nuances and changes in word usage), and dialogically (i.e., aware of the political others against whom assertions are made). It is an ethical discourse in the sense that it is always conducted in a communicative environment that assumes persuasive dialogue with others, that attempts to persuade those others to join one's own moral and political community.

Conclusion: Dialogue, Ethics, Politics

> A wake! Come a wake! . . . Every old skin in the leather world, infect the whole stock company of the old house of the Leaking Barrel, was thomistically drunk. . . . But twill cling hellish like engels opened to noneuropeans, if you've sensed, whole the sum. So be vigil.
>
> —James Joyce, *Finnegans Wake*

Western audiences, out of ignorance, yield too easily to fundamentalist Muslim claims that Islam is prescriptive in simple ways. To argue otherwise requires knowledge of Islamic hermeneutics, dialectics, and dialogics. This knowledge is difficult for those who have lost contact with their own Christian and Jewish traditions of hermeneutics, dialectics, and dialogics, or with those of ancient Greece which too often are nostalgically idealized and hypostasized into paragons of virtue no longer viable.

We have argued not only that such dialogic traditions are neither obscure nor distant, but also that they are fundamental to ethical discourse, whether written or oral. The constitute a family of resemblances with overlapping origins and many commonalities,[70] but it is only through the play of their differences, and their acknowledgment of cultural interreferences, that the fullness of the dialogic emerges from its parochial veilings and monologic chauvinisms. Consider only the metaphoric differentials of stress in Greek *biblos* (from the Phoenician city that exported papyrus), Christian *scripture;* the Jewish oral and written *torah* (from *ohr,* "light"); Islamic *qur'an.* Christian tradition seems to privilege the archetype relation: the world as realization of the logos, language as representation, New Testament as realization of the Old, writing as secondary to an originary word, scripture as codification (hence, perhaps, the Christian self-projective image[71] of Judaism and Islam as "legalistic" rather than hermeneutic). Jewish tradition privileges the "trace," "divine sparks," or play of meaning (Israel, "he who wrestles with God"), claiming that both written and oral forms require disputational, hermeneutic explorations to pursue the plenitude that through language creates the human, moral world.[72] (In the language of Levinas and Derrida, there is no presence "behind," only a creative absence: Issac Luria's *tsimtsum;*[73] the universe contained in the dot of the *b* of "*bismillāh*".)[74] It is this play that seems to draw the frustrated wrath of the Qur'an upon the Jews,[75] this embrace of the ambiguities of the text with which Muslims also struggle. Muslim tradition privileges the oral, the Qur'an, viewing the written book as but an imperfect transcript,[76] seeing the Torah and Evangels as corrupted texts that illustrate the dangers of writing. It plays up context, intent, face-to-face event, and distrusts both archetype *ta'wīl* (Christians mistook the crucifixion) and hermeneutic play, although adept at both: the search is for plain meaning in a world of appearances.

It is perhaps James Joyce who most fully provides a cosmopolitan text that explicitly acknowledges the interplay of these traditions and places them in the postmodern context of centers and peripheries (Europe-Ireland, America-Iran) that generate "third world" political moral dilemmas. And it is perhaps Edmond Jabès who is the poet of the contemporary world where dialogue and its discontents are the (w)hole condition of meaning. Can the tradition of disputation (*baḥth;* Gadamer's hermeneutics, Habermas's communicative ethics) provide an image of a democratic public ethos, particularly given the role of *taqiya* (dissimulation) as a concrete element symbolizing both (1) the necessity to incorporate the realities of power/interests into the model of communicative ethics and (2) strategies of feigning temporary communicative agreement for long-term advantage? Can one protect against the old Platonic and modern Hegelian tendencies of etatism (Khomeini's *wilāyat-e faqīh*)? In the contemporary Muslim world, can the tradition of disputation (*baḥth*) overcome the unitarian ideologies (*tawḥīd*) that deny and suppress all conflict, be it class conflict or other principled divisions within the *umma* (community of believers)? Can the polysemic and nomadic meanings of a text such as the Qur'an overcome the unbewised efforts to reduce it to monologic decree? At issue methodologically is the distinction between a dialectics that assimilates some arguments, refuting others which cannot be digested, and a dialectics that provides synoptic visions of the entire range of argumentation. Given the unknowability of the Qur'an (there is no single correct interpretation, either because of the infinity of God's writing and speech or because of the limitations of human hermeneutics in the absence of an infallible interpreter or Imām); and given the labyrinths of ḥadīth and other interpretive con-texts, is it possible for such an enigmatic text as the Qur'an to function as a poetic touchstone for a universalistic ethics?

The political dialogues of the contemporary Islamic world, grounded in traditional scriptural-based dialectical disputation and in dialogically performative experience, provide an interesting mirror (1) to our Western roots (e.g., the *sic et non* Catholic disputational methods borrowed from Muslim Spain; the shimmering similarities of Muslim and Jewish hermeneutics); (2) to our global present in which Islam presents a paradigmatic dialectic of a third world constructed against and within a world system; and (3) to the effort to construct a democratic pluralism that protects cultural differences without yielding to cultural positions that claim unique access to truth.

3

Fear of *Différance*

The Ḥajj "Rodeo"[1]

Ḥajj Pretexts and Re(rites): Ethics and Politics in the Play of Nationalism, Class, and Gender

> Apep and Uachet! Holy Snakes, chase me charley, Eva's got barley[2] under her fluencies! [494.15–16] . . . my stavekirks . . . arked for covennanters and shinners' rifuge: . . . Hams, circuitize! Shemites, retrace! . . . hereround is't holied! [552.3–10]
>
> —James Joyce, *Finnegans Wake*

> Man's relationship with the other is better as difference than as unity: sociality is better than fusion. . . . From an ethical perspective, two have a better time than one (on s'amuse mieux a deux)!
>
> —Emanuel Levinas, "Interview"

> Collective identities are funny fictions . . . semiotic contradictions . . . simultaneously descriptive and prescriptive, presupposing and creative.
>
> —Virginia Domínguez, *People as Subject, People as Object*

One of the primal scenes of Islam is the ḥajj. It is the womb of return, of "hystorical"[3] rebirth, of reorientation in the collective unconscious,[4] of reawakening from the oblivion of ordinary life,[5] of retautening the productive tension between individual moral responsibility (*ādam, ensān,*[6] Abraham, and Hagar) and submission (*islām*) to the spiritual collective (*umma*).[7] Adam and Cain are unthinking agents for whom repentance (*tawba*) and God's mercy[8] bring another chance; Abraham is the figure of true moral individualism and steadfastness; while Muhammad and Isma'il (and Abu-Dharr for some)[9] are repetitions of Ab-

Fig. 3.1. Stoning the idols at Mecca. Pilgrim in ḥajj garb stones the devils of imperialist soldiers wearing gas masks. Courtesy of the Hoover Institution Archives.

raham's self-discovery and commitment. It is Hagar, however, who is the central figure, albeit marginalized, almost repressed, and "deferred" onto the menfolk; it is in reenacting her role, during the ḥajj ritual, that Muslims replay the "hystorical" running back and forth between faith and reason that is the moral center of Islam.

Fig. 3.2. A stamp issued to commemorate the breaking of idols by Muhammad.

Ethics of *Différance*

Différance, Derrida's pun, playing on *difference* and *deferring,* is a key term in his analysis of the way language and writing operate: language depends upon oppositions or differences to make meaningful sounds (phonemes) and utterances, yet each utterance or writing can be altered by subsequent contexts, so that final meaning is always deferred. This is most obvious in puns like *différance,* where meaning disseminates in multiple directions, and where an attempt to freeze one meaning through an initial writing or context can be undone by reviving alternative meanings. Much of language operates similarly.

Tobin Siebers (1988) provides a useful survey of the ethical project not only of Derrida, but also of Lacan and French feminist theorists such as Luce Irigaray, representing three interrelated strands of thought: linguistic, psychoanalytic, feminist. The linguistic project, going back to Rousseau (and including Lévi-Strauss), suggests that the oppositions of language freeze the flux of reality into artibrary, "unnatural," thus "cultural" discriminations, hierarchies, essentializings, and hypostases. These latter are the operations of ethnocentrism and sexism (as well as of what Derrida calls logocentrism). Only by seeing through this arbitrariness, by neutralizing the oppositions, can one achieve an ethics of moral pluralism, which Tobin usefully defines not as reducing the other to the same, but as the "hypothetical sameness that allows us to conceive of different people as being equal to ourselves" (p. 202). (Skeptics note: this need not imply absolute relativism, only a sensitivity to the grounds of difference, so those grounds can be evaluated.) The psychoanalytic project sees the unconscious as a space to reorient aggressive impulses detrimental to human relations, and to defer them as long as possible, rerouting them in more life-giving ("erotic") directions; this too, then, is an ethics of deferral (in Lacan's formula: the unconscious is structured like language). Irigaray and other French feminist theorists utilize a similar notion metaphorized as the inherent plurality and multiplicity of the female sexual body as opposed to the singular sexual organ of the male, centralizing and hierarchizing his desire. The metaphor provides a political allegory: a decentered form of generous and omnipresent communication nurturing all parts (an economy of affluence rather than of scarcity), that to more centralized forms appears "hysterical" and "uncontrolled" and thus threatening. Although some feminists merely wish to reverse the power relations in which men have dominated women, this metaphor might rather suggest a "neutralization" of oppositions for purposes of reflection and consideration, critique à la Derrida.

The point here, in any case, is that the rhetorics of contemporary politicized Islam both simply fear difference and block access to the ethics of *différance*. They are defensively anxious about manhood and insistent on subordinating women.[10] They exhibit an anxious pattern of denial about the rights of minorities and are insistent on the eventual erasure of cultural, religious, class, and national differences in the name of Islamic universalism.[11] They are indifferent to the rights of individual conscience, due process of law, and civil and human rights, and are insistent that social discipline and the imposition of Islam, as they see it, override all such rights.[12]

The strategy of this chapter, in vaguely Derridian fashion, is to point out the alternative female body at the core of Islamic ethics, by invoking Hagar's centrality in the ḥajj, to point out the inherent contradictions in the (pan)nationalist discourses of Shi'ism that keep all such discourses decentered and unconsolidated ["female"] as well as challengingly tense and potent ["male"], and to point out the play of national and class differences in the ḥajj, in the Ramaḍān ritual of chapter 5, and in provincial street life where the Rabelaisian or Diogenesian cynics prosper.[13]

Fig. 3.3. The *mi'raj* of the Prophet, showing the Ka'ba and the Prophet ascending on the winged Buraq. From a fifteenth century *Khamsa* of Nizami, done in Herat. Courtesy of The British Library, Or. 6810.

Four Ḥajj Seasons

Four ḥajj seasons provide the historical contexts for this chapter: 1964, 1968, 1971, and 1987. Nineteen sixty-four was the year that Khomeini was exiled from Iran after helping to lead the 1963 uprising against the shah's White Revolution; it was the year in which he began his annual sending of messages to the pilgrims, using the ḥajj both as an occasion when sizable numbers of Iranian believers were away from the control of the secret police and as a potential international Muslim forum to spread his message also among non-Iranian Muslims.

Nineteen sixty-eight was the year of the ḥajj immediately following upon the 1967 Arab-Israeli war, felt by Arabs and Muslims as a devastating blow to Nasserist and pan-Arabist hopes. At that ḥajj the slogans were first raised that "Islam had not been defeated upon the battlefield; Islam had not even entered the battlefield"; it was rather the false ideology of (Arab pan)nationalism that had been defeated. A bitter lesson had to be learned from the Jews, whom some Muslim commentators represented as having fought under the banner of their religion: one must construct a revolutionary ideology true to Islam. The 1968 ḥajj marks an important impetus to contemporary Muslim fundamentalist ideologies. Two of those present at the Islamic Conference of Scholars where these discussions took place, a conference that occurs in tandem with the ḥajj, were Sayyid Maḥmūd Ṭāleqāni, who upon his return to Iran sermonized upon the embarrassment Iranians felt before other Muslims because the shah had given aid to Israel (and who would become the patron of the Islamic left during the revolution), and Murtaḍā Muṭahhari, who upon his return delivered a series of lectures (later published) on *Mutual Services of Islam and Iran* which helped formulate the civilizational vision underpinning the Shi'ite fundamentalist ideology leading to the revolution of 1977–79 that created an Islamic Republic of Iran. A third personage present at the ḥajj of 1968, but excluded from the Islamic Conference of Scholars, was Ali Shari'ati, who attempted to provide Iranians with a less fundamentalist revolutionary ideology, and who provided a detailed counterbrief to Muṭahhari, entitled *Return to Self.* Shari'ati's ideas were important in helping create the 1977–79 revolution, but the debate between him and Muṭahhari also reflects some of the important dynamics that led to the defeat of Shari'ati's "modernism" at the hands of Muṭahhari and Khomeini's "fundamentalism." This debate will provide a central focus to this chapter.

Nineteen seventy-one was the year that the shah celebrated 2500 years of continuous monarchy, attempting to consolidate a national identity that reached back to the ancient Zoroastrian empire and its subsequent cultural lineages (in epic, poetry, music, carpets, miniature painting, and other visual, craft and performance arts) for a sense of world importance, for a heritage of tolerant cosmopolitanism (multiethnic, multilinguistic, multireligious), for emotional release from an Islam grown puritanical, full of *ressentiment,* and tied too closely to the destinies of an Arab world seen by Iranians as less cultured, less energetic, and less modern than itself. But when the shah went to inaugurate his celebration at the tomb of Cyrus the Great, mullās across Iran sermonized to the masses: "Cyrus has nothing to do with us; Islam came to replace hereditary monarchy, occupational castes, pagan Gods, Zoroastrian dualism, and dealing with the Jews." Khomeini sent a message to the 1971 ḥajj declaring the celebrations a Zionist-produced, anti-Islamic event, and declaring it the religious duty of Muslims "to refrain from participation . . . to engage in passive struggle against it . . . and to express by any means possible their disgust".[14] Nineteen seventy to seventy-one was also the year that Khomeini was delivering his lectures on Islamic government, analyzed in chapter 2. Although these lectures were rapidly disseminated among religious folk (see chapter 1) in mimeograph, cassette, and printed form (the title page discreetly torn off), upper-class and secularized middle-class Iranians, to this day, insist that most Iranians did not know who Khomeini was before the revolution.

After the revolution of 1977–79, the Islamic Republic of Iran called for the ḥajj to become the international macrocosm of the weekly Friday sermons of an Islamic government: a communal gathering to discuss the dissemination of the Islamic revolution. Each year at the ḥajj, the Iranian pilgrims became more provocative toward the Saudi Arabian guardians of Mecca who attempted to keep the ritual apolitical. Nineteen eighty-seven was the year that violence finally broke out: over four hundred pilgrims were killed, nearly three hundred of them Iranians.

From an Iranian point of view, then, 1964 and 1971 are markers of the successful national struggle to overthrow hereditary monarchy and establish an Islamic government; 1968 and 1987 are markers of the international struggle. All four pilgrimage seasons witness to the argument that an apolitical ḥajj is meaningless: the ḥajj itself is a call to institute Islam as a reality: personally, socially, religiously, and politically. The four ḥajj seasons display class lines (Pahlavi-Islam), lines of nationalism (Shi'ism-Islam), and lines of position within the world political economy (Islam–the West): three relations of self-definition central to Iranian—perhaps all third world—positioning.

In this chapter, we wish to look not only at the ḥajj itself (both the "primal scene" and its inflected meanings[15] in both its class and its historical-political contexts), but also at the debate between Muṭahhari and Shari'ati over the nature of Islam, Shi'ism, and Iranian Muslim identity, triggered by the 1968 ḥajj (both the debate and the debaters being tokens of two sociological types).

Ḥajj as Primal Scene

> And remember that Abraham was tried by his Lord with certain words [*kalimāt*] which he fulfilled: He said, "I will make you an Imām to the nations." . . . Remember We made the house [Ka'ba] a place of assembly for men and a place of refuge; and take ye the station [*maqām*] of Abraham as a place of prayer; and We covenanted with Abraham and Isma'il that they should purify my house for those who circumambulate it, or use it as a retreat, or bow, or prostrate themselves.
>
> —Qur'an 2:124–25

> "Going towards God" is not . . . a return to, or reunification with, God. . . . "Going towards God" is meaningless unless seen in terms of my primary going towards the other person. . . .
>
> it is only in the infinite relation with the other that God passes [*se passe*], that traces of God are to be found. God thus reveals himself as a trace, not as an ontological presence. . . .
>
> To be in time is to be for God [*être à Dieu*], a perpetual leavetaking [*adieu*].
>
> —Emmanuel Levinas, "Interview"

Imagine the crowds of Muslims from all over the world during the annual ḥajj pilgrimage to Mecca: (1) Fellow Muslims present, actually visible, number in the millions: what more impressive sense of spiritual community (*umma*) overriding status, national, or other mundane distinctions?[16] (2) The crowds are separated into national units, and smaller units led by ḥajj guides. "Iranians carry *aftābeh*s; Turks have long tubes with bulbous ends . . . Lebanese and Syrians have plastic *aftābeh*s that are smaller than ours—and the Indians and Africans carry kettles. These are the most meaningful national emblems."[17] Iranian mullās lead their flocks in distinctive prayers, such as the *du'ā Komeil,*[18] and the prayers (*du'a*) that include curses of the first three Sunni caliphs. What more impressive *mise en scène* of Islamic diversity, and of the perceptible, but not visible, alternative interpretations of Islam and the ḥajj rite, indexed by this diversity? (3) What more open forum for political theater, like a Friday communal prayer assembly writ large? What more obvious arena for revolutionary Shi'ite interpretations to be advanced: not merely expressed in some reflective commentary, but enacted as obligatory duty? "Thus have We made of you an *umma* justly balanced, that ye might be witnesses (*shuhadā*) over the nations" (Qur'an 2:143).[19] (4) Under modern conditions of international bureaucracies, transportation, food and sacrificial animal supply, medical and surveillance personnel, and media capacities (microphones, tapes, hand-carried video cameras, as well as international media), what constraints on dissident or even unregimented expression,[20] what peer pressure exercised by the *umma*'s collective sensibilities, and what opportunities for disruption and dissemination of dissident messages?

Ritual often works both like a play and like chains of metaphors, or like what the Qur'an calls *mutashābih* (figuration, similitudes, appearances). Like a play, it has characters, plot, process, or character development, and emotional work, cathexis, or catharsis. Like a metaphor, it has a surface story, and allegorical meanings that resonate one with another, reinforcing, expanding, reworking initial understanding. "Normal"[21] ritual works to reaffirm norms, status, social structure, emotional bonding, commitment, sense of moral and communal duty, and the *conscience collective* (the Durkheimian *différance:* conscience and consciousness). It does so by bringing into the open and venting tensions, contradictions, and aggressions;[22] by redefining individuals in new or old statuses;[23] and by con-fusing and condensing biological-emotional matter with moral-cognitive norms.[24] Such ritual is "read" by identifying the multiple levels of meaning register, and by referring the more localized, politicized, or historically specific meanings to more basic moral, libidinal, transcendent, or eternal sets of meanings.[25] Histories of religion are often "exemplary," screening out the grounded meanings, abstracting only the Platonic ideal forms thought to exist immanently in them as "worthy," transcendent contributions to moral persuasion. Rituals, however, are subject to contestation over their allegorical meanings (as well as their forms), are often constructed with cultural interreferences to and interferences from the larger world outside their own cultures,[26] and are always, like language, inflected with contemporary meanings.

Four inflected meaning registers should be acknowledged regarding the ḥajj: the moral philosophical; a Judaicizing anxiety that easily is transformed into contemporary anti-Israel or anti-Jewish readings; a Shi'ite frame that provides both general meaning and contemporary politicized meaning; and the modern conditions of the ḥajj, which both give it an administered, package tour feel and provide the opportunity for political theater with a global scale audience.

Performing the ḥajj is enjoined in the Qur'an, and much of its form is mandated there (2:124ff.). It is, says Ali Shari'ati, a *ḥukm mutashābih* (a command fulfilled through appearances, similitudes, figurations). Its language is not one of words (*lafẓ*), but one of *ḥarakat-e ṣāmit* (silent movements). "As the Qur'an is Islam in words, and the Imām is Islam embodied in a human figure, so the *ḥajj* is Islam in *ḥarakat* (setting out, movement)." *Ḥarakat* is a resonant word: ritual drama employs a language of gesture and movement, it teaches by having the initiand enact its message, one learns kinesthetically. But more precisely, *ḥarakat* means "setting out," movement toward a goal, as in the original name of the Lebanese Shi'ite political movement, Amal, founded by Imām Mūsā Ṣadr: *Ḥarakat al-Maḥrūmīn.*[27] (Ḥarakat resonates with the Qur'anic description for the timing of the sacrifice-trial imposed upon Abraham and Isma'il: Isma'il, the first son of the aged Abraham, had just reached the age of running [e.g., *ya bunayy,* "my little son," Qur'an 37:102].) The ḥajj is a theater of creation (with its references to paradise, Adam, Cain and Abel), of history (with its references to Muhammad, struggles between classes, sects, and religions), of monothesim (with its references to Abraham and Isma'il, the covenant between human beings and God), and of *ummat* (society of faith); its main characters are Adam, Abraham, Hagar, and Isma'il; and a single actor plays all the parts: "You! whoever you might be, woman, man, old, young, black, white . . . you play the lead in the agon of God and Satan" (Shari'ati 19 pp. 21–22). Shari'ati draws explicitly on the trope of oblivious repetition: the ḥajj is an awakening from the ordinary life of emptiness, stagnation, and repetition; it is a time of revolutionary resolution (*niyat-e enqelabi*), of hijra (withdrawal to renew one's strength for a push to victory after temporary defeat). Some connect the word *ḥajj* with Hagar,[28] the paradigm is the *hijra* Muhammad made from Mecca to Medina until he could gather the forces to subdue Mecca,[29] and the word *hijra* was used, for instance, by Egyptian fundamentalists in the 1970s for their strategy of withdrawing from corrupt secular society until such time as the state could be overthrown). It begins at home with farewell visits to kin, neighbors, and friends: to prepare to meet God, one must pay off one's debts, reestablish broken friendships, settle affairs in which the rights of others are involved, and prepare one's will. In Mecca, the rite itself begins with the shedding of street clothes, of social distinctions, of the masques and coverings of daily life—"like the shedding by a snake of its old skin"[30]—and the putting on of a shroud (*iḥrām*). *En masse,* people move down toward the bottom of the valley of Mecca, toward the sacred enclosure (*ḥaram*) of the great mosque, chanting *labbayk! labbayk!* ("God, I am coming"). As the masses enter the *ḥaram,* they fall silent. The Ka'ba is at the very lowest point: a black stone encased in a house of stone, itself nothing but a sign on the path of God. It is a rite of death and rebirth, both tomb and womb.

The ḥajj is literally and figuratively the touchstone for Muslims: a central gesture of the rite is to touch or kiss the black stone of the Ka'ba, symbolizing the hand of God in a gesture of renewed allegiance (*bay'at, mithāq*). The black stone is said to be a meteorite (*sang-e asmāni,* "heavenly stone") and/or to have been brought from paradise by Adam, and its housing, the Ka'ba, to have been built around it by Abraham and Ishma'il to mark their covenant with God,[31] affirmed through their respective trials by ordeal. Abraham had survived the fires of Nimrod after breaking the idols; Isma'il had been willing to allow his father to sacrifice him. According to both Muslim and Jewish legend,[32] Sarah allowed Abraham to visit Hagar only on condition that he remain seated on his camel. The first daughter-in-law, Aissa,[33] refused to give Abraham a drink or to look at him, cursing both Isma'il and his children. Abraham left the message, "An old man from the land of Canaan was here, and asked you to remove the main pillar of your tent and to replace it by a good one." Isma'il divorced the first wife and remarried.[34] When Abraham again visited, this daughter-in-law, Fatima, insisted that he partake of food and drink, and (in the Islamic version) that he let her wash his head. Abraham explained he had taken a vow to remain on his camel until he returned home, but allowed her to wash his head by keeping one foot on the camel, and placing the other on the stone, now known as the footstep (*maqām*) of Abraham. It was after this that Abraham received the call to build the "House of God" together with Isma'il. Muhammad renewed Abraham's prophetic mission, purifying the shrine of idols, even before his Prophetic call replacing the black stone which had fallen, and instituting the ḥajj ritual mandated in the Qur'an. Various tribes wanted the honor of replacing the black stone, and Muhammad arbitrated the issue by having it placed on a cloth so that all could hold an edge; however, the stone turned black because it had confronted so many sinful faces. Among the key elements of this ritual are the sevenfold circumambulation (*ṭawāf*) around the Ka'ba and the attached crescent-shaped tomb of Hagar, the standing for prayer on the footstep or footprint (*maqām*) of Abraham, the sevenfold ordeal (*sa'y*) of running between Ṣafā and Marwa as Hagar did in search

Fig. 3.4. Imām Zayn al-Abidin visits the Ka'ba. From a *Silsilat al-dhahab* ("Chain of Gold") of Mawlana Nuruddin Abdul-Rahman Jami, 1550, Tabriz, Iran. Jami, the famed Timurid poet, tells the story of the Abbasid caliph Hisham who vainly attempted to reach the Ka'ba through the pilgrimage crowd, and then watched as the crowd parted to allow the fourth Imām to touch and kiss the Ka'ba. The caliph did not recognize the Imām, so the poet Farazdaq recited a *qasida* (eulogistic poem). Infuriated, the caliph had the poet jailed. The Imām rewarded the poet, sending him twelve thousand silver coins. Iran Miniature. Folio 66. 17.8 × 13.5 cm. S86.0044. Courtesy of the Vever Collection, Arthur M. Sackler Gallery, Smithsonian Institution, Washington, D.C.

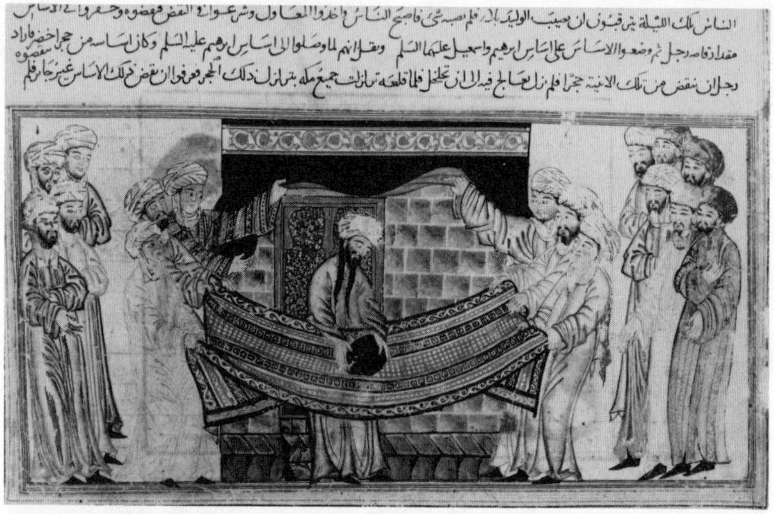

Fig. 3.5. Muhammad solves the dispute among the four tribes over the honor of lifting the black stone into position at the Ka'ba. *Jāmi' al-Tawārīkh* of Rashid al-Din. Courtesy of Edinburgh University Library, Arab 20.

of water for the infant Isma'il, the stoning of the three idols of Satan, and an animal sacrifice.

Each of these elements can open into dense associations of meaning and interpretation, and are intended to do so, recalling to Muslims the core values of Islam and its mission. Shari'ati draws particular attention to the dialectical tension between the circumambulation as a rite of submission—in which Muslims, "like moths to a candle," attempt to seek relief and extinction in illumination and the salvation of the hereafter—versus the *sa'y* (ordeal) as a rite celebrating reason and effort, "like an eagle in search of bait." In both the structure of the rites and the character of Abraham and Hagar, Muslim exegetes insist, neither faith nor reason alone is sufficient. Hagar set the thirsty, crying infant Isma'il down, and desperately went in search of water; when she returned, she found that the kicking heels of the infant had created enough of a depression to reveal some water (the Zamzam well). (God helps those who help themselves.) Likewise, the circumambulation is not merely submission "like moths to a flame," but is participation in a communal experience, and the return of a spiritually purposeful individual to ordinary life. The shroudlike garb of the pilgrim is the dress of the hereafter, of spiritual resurrection. One moves, says Shari'ati, from alienation to consciousness, from racial, national, and class distinctions

Fig. 3.6. Crows show the Arab tribe Jurhum where to dig to discover the Zamzam well, linking the story of Isma'il and that of an Arab tribe which raised him, see f. 34. The textiles are Central Asian; the faces and landscape show Chinese characteristics. *Jāmi' al-Tawārīkh* of Rashid al-Din. Courtesy of Edinburgh University Library, Arab 201.

to equality, from self-centeredness to God, from slavery to freedom. The circumambulation en masse is the primal experience of the *umma,* the maternal spiritual community. *Ummat* is one of the terms Shari'ati tries to invest with philological play, connecting it with the dynamic, goal directed words *amm* ("decision to go") and *imamat* (leadership), and with *umm* ("mother"). In the Qur'an, *umma* is used only once for an individual, Abraham ("Abraham was indeed an *umma,* devoutly obedient to God" [16:120]); it occurs in the verse used as the slogan of the Husainiyeh Irshad, the teaching center of Shari'ati in which Muṭahhari also participated for a time ("Let there arise out of you a band of people [*umma*] enjoining the good and prohibiting the evil" [2:104]); and it occurs in the verse taken up in the Colonel Mu'ammar Qadafi's national anthem for Libya ("you are the best of peoples [*ummatin*]"). Abraham, like Hagar, presents an image of both reason (breaking the idols of his father) and faith (his ordeal by fire, his willingness to sacrifice his son). The pilgrim stands on the footstep (*maqām*) of Abraham to pray (2:125), to take on this dual attitude of reason and faith, of discernment and obedience to God's will, of readiness to sacrifice what one most loves for God, of repeating Abraham's journey from being an idol carver to being a builder of monotheism.

After the circumambulation and the *sa'y,* one goes to 'Arafāt at high noon, representing for Shari'ati the light of knowledge: he says the word *'arafa* means "to know and understand," and that this was the site where Adam and Eve met and knew each other the first time after being thrown out of paradise.[35] One makes a halt (*wuqūf*) on the plain of 'Arafāt to listen to sermons, to reflect upon one's intention, and upon the meaning of the ḥajj. (Burton [1853] observed that Egyptian and other women paid people to call out their names here to ensure their coming the next year.) At sunset one proceeds to Mash'ar al-Ḥarām (sunset, a time for planning; *mash'ar,* a place of consciousness) where one selects seventy pebbles ("smaller than walnuts, but larger than pistachios") in preparation for the next day's *jihād.* Shari'ati insists that the pistachio-sized pebbles mean in fact "bullets." At Minā (cognate, says Shari'ati, of *muna,* "love") the next three days, three idols are stoned. It is, of course, a dual repetition: commemorating both Abraham's breaking of his father's idols and Muhammad's breaking of the idols of the Ka'ba, cleansing the house of God built by Abraham and Ishma'il. The three main idols of the Ka'ba were Lāt, Manāt, and 'Uzzā; but there were some three hundred and sixty idols in total. Another interpretation has it that the three idols represent the three times Satan whispered to Abraham that it was only a bad dream, that God had not ordered him to sacrifice Isma'il. Shari'ati names these idols as representatives of tyranny (Pharaoh, Cain, wolf), exploitation (Croesus, capitalism, sly rat), and hypocrisy (Balam, clerics, fox), resonating with his slogan, taken up by the revolution, against *zūr, zar,* and *tazwīr* (force, gold, deceit; or also *malik, mala', mulla,* i.e., king, landowner, cleric). He finds trinities of evil in each religion, and also speaks of the three idols as the superseded religions of Christianity, Zoroastrianism, and Judaism. In an amusing comparison, the popular preacher Shaykh Muhammad Taqi Falsafi sermonized that when the shah went to Austria, dissident students could see the devil they were throwing rotten eggs and tomatoes at, but when you go on the ḥajj you unfortunately don't actually get to see Satan.

Cain is an interesting figure here.[36] For Shari'ati, Cain is the figure who by killing his brother introduces class relations (subordinating pastoralists to landowners, peasants to landowners) and power relations of tyranny, exploitation, and inequality. But in more traditional accounts, although Cain sinned through lust for his brother's wife or his own sister when his brother wished to marry her, he did not mean to kill his brother, and is a figure of deep repentance. Cain and Abel were innocents. The brothers took their dispute over the woman to their father who told them to let God decide by making offerings. Abel in sincere devotion and love of his wife offered his best camel or his best flock of sheep; Cain in the same casual spirit as his desire, thinking himself entitled because he was the elder brother, offered a handful of wheat. The judgment is overdetermined, God accepting both devotional sincerity and regulation of marriage. Cain again in casual anger kills his brother, and is appalled at what he has done. He repents and knows not what to do until God sends two ravens; one kills the other and then scratches at the earth showing Cain how to perform a burial (5:31).[37] Thus Cain might be a figure of repentance, as pilgrims are enjoined to repentance (*tawba*) and rededication to the rules of Islam.[38] (Many a ḥājji will joke that he used to drink alcohol or engage in other vices until he went on the ḥajj!) Adam, of course, is the primal figure in the Qur'an of repentance (2:35), Cain being a repetition in the next generation of further sin and repentance. A more aggressive interpretation, that provided by the Yusuf Ali translation of the Qur'an, is that Cain stands for the Jews, the "elder brother" Semitic religion,[39] who "tried to kill Jesus and exterminate the Christian . . . to kill Muhammad and put down his people."[40] Yusuf Ali does not grant that Cain was really repentant, but had to be reminded by the raven to have the decency even to bury his brother. One stones Cain in retribution, then sacrifices an animal as did Abel. Yusuf Ali allegorizes the younger brother: he is Islam, and God's favor passed to him when it was forfeited by the elder brother. Yusuf Ali further reads the first line of this set of verses ("Recite to them the truth" [5:27]) as revealing the truth that was cryptically suppressed in the "bare narrative" of Genesis 4:1–15.

After the stoning of the idols, one sacrifices, says Shari'ati, as a sign of temporary victory and continuing commitment. It is of course a re-enacting by each person of the sacrifice of Abraham and Isma'il (or Isaac)[41]. In the Qur'anic version, Abraham has a vision, and consults Isma'il, who tells Abraham to do as he is commanded, and he, Isma'il will be patient and persevering (*ṣābir, ṣabr,* a key virtue) in his faith and covenant with God (37:102). One sacrifices a camel, sheep, or other horned domestic animal (22:34–37) on the tenth of Dhū al-Ḥajja. This day, 'Id al-Aḍḥā, is celebrated by Muslims everywhere with a sacrifice and sharing of the meat with the poor. It comemorates the day of the covenant between human beings and God and, later, between the children of Israel and God (when God asked who would take the responsibility for his law, all refused but human beings/the children of Israel).

In some ḥadīth the ram or goat presented by God to be sacrificed by Abraham in place of Isma'il is the same animal offered by Abel, and "for forty years" is kept in the Garden of Eden. (Jewish tradition has the ram created specially during the days of Creation.) After the sacrifice, one shaves one's head, discards the *iḥrām* garb, and returns to the ordinary state (*iḥlāl*).[42]

The description of the movements of the ḥajj and its associated stories allows comment on the first two registers of meaning. The first is the moral philosophical. Despite the difference between the Qur'anic stress that all prophets are the same in their message and in their covenantal relation to God and the Jewish didactic uses of an evolution of the covenants from the angels and Adam, to Noah, to Abraham, to Moses and the children of Israel at Sinai,[43] fundamentally both traditions incorporate a tension between active moral self-assertion and unquestioning submission (to God, to the covenant with God, to a covenantal idea of moral obligation, first to members of the community and then to the world at large). Islam tends to stress the former, at times to the point of overstressing fusion, unity with God, and the limitations of human reason. Thus, *tawḥīd,* unity, theological oneness, in contemporary fundamentalist discourses often is used to project a utopian vision of society without class divisions, without feelings of inequality or injustice, and without differences of opinion. Judaism often stresses the latter, reveling in disputation with God, holding God to His promises, to His side of the covenant. The sacrifice of Abraham and Isaac/Isma'il provides a convenient and central exemplum: Isma'il says he will exercise faith, trust in God, patience/perseverance (*ṣabr*). Jewish explanations often suggest that Abraham was calling God's bluff: a covenant was in effect, sealed by Abraham's circumcision, and included a divine promise about Abraham's progeny for generations to come.[44] Still, if there is less direct wrestling or arguing with God in Islamic imagery, the figure of Hagar is stressed by Muslim exegetes to carry the message that one may not simply rely on God alone, but one must exercise one's own reason, skill, and moral judgment. Instead of categorizing the two traditions as necessarily or essentially having different moral structures, juxtaposing the variations of the stories associated with these biblical and Qur'anic figures helps clarify their possibilities for moral discourse.

The second register of meaning has to do with the way in which Judaicizing anxiety may easily be transformed into systematic anti-Jewish readings, exemplified in Yusuf Ali's reading of the Cain and Abel story as an allegory of Jewish unrighteousness and Muslim victimization, a reading that is pressed further by contemporary fundamentalisms, both Sunni and Shi'a.

Two further meaning registers need brief exploration before turning to the debate between Shari'ati and Muṭahhari about Islam and Iranian identity: the modern conditions of the ḥajj and the Shi'ite inflection or reading of the ḥajj; its increasingly administered, package tourlike nature, on the one hand, and its potential for political theater with an instantaneous global audience, on the other. These two registers of meaning have become more significant over the past two and a half decades: from 1964, when Āyatullāh Khomeini first began issuing annual messages (*e'lāmiyeh*) to the pilgrims, to 1987, when some four hundred Iranian demonstrators provoked, and were killed by, Saudi security forces. Speakers at the rally before the latter demonstration included Shi'ite fundamentalist leaders from Lebanon (Muhammad Husain Fadlallah of the Hezbullah and Abbas Musawi of the Islamic Amal), and Iranians reading from Khomeini's call to all Muslims to join in solidarity with Iran and to form cells of Hizbullah ("party of God") throughout the world.

The Shi'ite inflections for the ḥajj incorporate it into the meaning structure of "the Karbala paradigm," the story of the martyrdom of the third Imām, Husain, grandson of the Prophet at the hands of Yazid, the Umayyid caliph, who for Shi'ites is the archtyrant, usurper of legitimate leadership for the Islamic *umma,* and destroyer of its promise of social justice. It is the paradigmatic story of existential tragedy, of evil in this world triumphing over good, and of the duty of a true Muslim nonetheless to sacrifice himself, to witness for truth and good, to shock others into returning to the cause of Islamic social justice; the emotional work is to channel grief, rage, and anger at loss or injustice into stoicism and quiet determination. It is this story that is the moral measure and comparative frame for all others. Thus, Adam, when first put on earth, wandered across the future site of the battle of Karbala and cut his toe, a prefiguration, God told him, of the more serious blood that would be shed there by the martyr Husain. Isma'il, too, is told his ordeals are but lesser prefigurations of Husain's: the infant Isma'il suffered thirst but found water, Husain and his children suffered greater thirst and were denied water. God substituted a ram for Isma'il, but the great sacrifice (37:107) was Husain, who was in fact slain. It is no accident, as Shari'ati noted in the epigraph below that Husain's ordeal began during the ḥajj. Pressed by the Umayyid forces to render an oath of allegiance to the tyrannical usurper Yazid, Husain bought time by going on the ḥajj, to a place of peace and refuge, a month in which no fighting is allowed. Yazid showed his true nature by sending assassins to kill Husain during the ḥajj. Understanding the threat, Husain left his ḥajj unfinished so that the central shrine and rite of Islam would not be polluted with the blood of murder. Knowing he would be martyred, he released all those who had sworn allegiance to him: no one should feel obligated. With "seventy-two" followers, he responded to the call of the people of Kufa to lead them in a revolt against Yazid. Before he could reach that town in southern Iraq, the Kufans abandoned him, bought off by Yazid. He and his followers were surrounded on the dusty desert plain of Karbala, and one by one they heroically went to their martyrdoms. In the annual Muharram reenactments (passion plays, processions), Ali-Akbar and some of the supporting characters are dressed in shrouds, bloodied at the hands of the Syrian soldiers of Yazid. Throughout the 1960s and 1970s, Yazid stood for the shah, and Khomeini or other willing religious figures stood for Husain; people flagellated themselves in repentance for being like the people of Kufa, failing to fight for Husain and thus allowing tyranny to exist. In the revolution of 1977–79, young men wearing shrouds placed themselves between the mass of marchers and the army tanks: no longer was one failing to fight for Husain; now one was witnessing actively, struggling actively in his cause. This is a powerful inflection of the garb of the ḥajj, the *iḥrām,* shroud, signifying willingness to sacrifice all for God and the righteous path. In the 1980s the struggle continued in the war against Iraq and at the annual ḥajj. Banners read, "We are not the people of Kufa" (i.e., we will not allow Husain to be defeated), and "Labbayk ya Khomeini."[45] Each year after the revolution, the Iranians became a bit more provocative, insisting that the Saudi efforts to depoliticize the ḥajj were anti-Islamic, usurpations of the very meaning of the ḥajj: the rededication to the goals of Islam, the oath of allegiance renewed at the black stone of the Ka'ba, the stoning of the idols, the sacrifice.

But if there are old Shi'ite inflections available for contemporary political use, there are also conditions, scales, and meanings of modernity that are new. The Iranians planned their provocative demonstration at the 1987 ḥajj with modern care: the two-kilometer route was supplied with loudspeakers complete with generators, and ice-cold water for demonstrators and spectators; video cameras caught much of the action. Today, in general, the staging of the ḥajj is a vast international enterprise, processed by bureaucracies both in home countries and in Saudi Arabia.[46] Iranians going on the ḥajj have increased from 12,000 in 1961 to 57,000 in 1972 to 150,000 in 1987. By the mid 1970s all Iranian ḥājjīs were flown to Saudi Arabia by Iran Air; prospective ḥajjis had to register with the Endowments Office, pay their money into a bank, and get medical clearance from a government doctor. Such bureaucratic procedures, not only in Iran, allowed a fair amount of corruption.[47] In 1987 the Saudi Livestock Transport and Trading Company secured a three-year contract to supply half a million head of sheep for each annual ḥajj, much of which in turn was subcontracted from the Australian Meat and Livestock Corporation, and 3,420 Turkish butchers were recruited. The Islamic Development Bank built two modern slaughterhouses, each capable of processing a thousand head per hour. Through Al Rajhi Company for Currency Exchange and Commerce, the Islamic Development Bank sold pilgrims $9.6 million worth of coupons to support an $11 million program to slaughter in their name some 350,000 head of sheep, freeze them with liquid nitrogen, and distribute the meat to refugees and the poor in the Sahel, Somalia, Sudan, Egypt, Burkina Faso, and Bangladesh, and to Afghan refugees.[48] The Saudi Arabian Transport Company operated 1,200 ordinary buses and 500 air-conditioned ones round the clock on the Mecca to Medina road, transporting over four million passengers. In addition, special Japanese Hino buses were being tested by Jamjoom Vehicles and Equipment Company. In 1983 Kawasaki Heavy Industries subcontracted with the American company Dynalectron to supply helicopter pilots to monitor the crowds and provide emergency medical or firefighting aid: pilots were sent to Tokyo for courses in Islam ending with a certificate of conversion.[49] These figures and items are but indications of both the scale and the rapid deployment of modern technological services in the areas of transportation,[50] meat for the sacrifice ritual, and crowd control.[51] Similar indicators might be cited for medical services,[52] food kiosks, water (King Fahd Bottling Plant distributed 21 million free liter bottles of drinking water), communications, sewage, maintenance, and cleanup (the 1987 cleanup contract for Mecca was for nearly $180 million, and employed a labor force of 5,765).[53] Interesting modern institutions have also developed around the ḥajj in home countries, such as the Tabung Ḥajji banking and investing system in Malaysia, including wholly owned subsidiaries that own plantations, apartment buildings, etc. (Asaria 1985).

Only a few years ago things were quite different: for instance people complained that an enormous tonnage of slaughtered meat was simply plowed under the earth, because there was no way to make use of, preserve, or transport it. Traditionally, the meat was dried and salted and eaten throughout the year, but in recent times the amount of meat slaughtered became more than could be dealt with. Jalal Al-e Ahmad (1985), who went in 1964, was appalled by the plowing of meat into the earth. The popular Egyptian preacher Shaykh Kishk admonished the Saudis for wasting meat, reciting the Qur'anic verse that the meat was to be preserved and distributed, and observing that modern means of preservation should be introduced (cassette tape, distributed by Islamic Society of Greater Houston, n.d.). The Ghanaian Ibrahim Abdulai, a recent ḥajji, was duly impressed by the modern, lighted highway from Jedda to Medina, and the eighty-four-person, air-conditioned bus;[54] while Jalal Al-e Ahmad in 1964 wrote that the same road was too narrow for more than one bus to pass at a time lacked telephone lines, and he described the buses as decrepit American Fords, Chevrolets, and Dodges, unable to travel in the daytime for fear of overheating.[55] In 1964, most animals for slaughter seemed to Al-e Ahmad to be from Ethiopia, driven on foot by drovers mobilized six months prior to the ḥajj. Ḥajj Ibrahim is impressed by the electricity in the tents at 'Arafāt, although he is amusingly candid about the overwhelming of the toilet facilities.[56] In 1964 there were half a million kerosene lamps, and the toilet facilities were worse, although at Mina in 1964 the tents already had electricity. Both Ḥajj Ibrahim and Al-e Ahmad provide terrifying portraits of the massive slaughtering of animals. Al-e Ahmad (1985:90) is outraged at the waste of meat, arguing that it should be distributed around the world to the poor. He reflects on the urges at play: "Kill animals in order to refrain from killing human beings. . . . Several times I saw people cutting up carcasses just for fun, and such a gleam of delight in their eyes. You'd think they were all studying anatomy, or exulting in victory after some heroic deed." Both accounts detail the age old extortions by ḥajj guides and agents, the marketing of food and commodities,[57] the local landlords who make their year's rent in a few days or weeks, the beggars and the poor porters who live off the ḥajj. (There are porters to carry luggage, but also porters to carry the old in the circumambulations.) Al-e Ahmad's account is good in detailing a moment of transition in technology, scale (40 thousand in 1850, 200,000 in 1902, a million ḥājjīs in 1964, two and a half million in 1983), and architecture (the use of functional concrete to widen and replace the Ottoman colonnades).[58] He also mentions in passing two political issues: (1) the destruction of tombs in Medina and the damaging of shrines and tombs in Karbala and Najaf by the Wahhabis, and the posting of Saudi guards who refuse to let pilgrims touch the tomb of the Prophet in Medina;[59] (2) the 15 Khordad 1963 uprisings in Iran, after which Khomeini had been exiled from Iran: this was known and asked about by a Shi'ite employee of Aramco (there is a sizable Shi'ite population in the eastern province of Saudi Arabia, and a sizable proportion of Aramco local labor is Shi'ite).

There is in all this a richness of texture, of Rabelaisian humor, and of prehistories of old conflicts, which should not be forgotten. Ḥajj

Ibrahim Abdulai (Chernoff 1984:84) provides a lovely nonchalant account of an ordinary ḥājjī, just going along with the flow, observing all with humor: "Yorubas always like to be climbing up on the hill [of Mount Arafat] because it is said that if you climb up on the mountain and shit there and come back, you will be getting money. And so any time you go there and you see a lot of black people on top of the mountain, then you should know that they are all Yorubas." About the circumambulations at the Ka'ba:

> If you don't fear death, if you take it that it doesn't matter if you die there, you can continue running it throughout the time you are in Mecca. I've told you that if you die there, you will be just like a child before God. And I told you that death is nothing at Mecca. It is nothing strange: it is just a joke. If it is the running, people can just walk on you and kill you. Nobody can fall there and get up again. And truly, at times we were running and we saw some people running naked. Naked! If you ask why, maybe that person didn't put a belt on his cloth or else his belt loosened, and the cloth was dragging on the ground; if somebody steps on it, the cloth will fall. And he can't bend down to take it. And so at that place there is no shyness. This is what is happening there. As for Mecca, there is nothing to compare to it, unless the day the world will end. And the Kaaba too, there is something inside the Kaaba just like a hole, and there is something inside the hole like a breast. You put your hand inside and touch the breast and pray to God, and then put your mouth by your hand and suck from your hand and be praying. And at that place too, there is death. At times, someone can reach there and his head will get into the hole, and someone else will also be struggling to put his own head there. And at that point they will remain there. . . .
>
> This throwing stones is another dangerous thing at Mecca. On that day, whether you will be dead or you won't be dead, you won't know unless you finish throwing the stones. . . . And so these thousands of people are throwing stones and knocking each others' heads.[60] (Chernoff 1985:81, 85)

The many perspectives, accounts, and interpretations of the ḥajj should be set one upon another like palimpsest, not so that it may become dense with all-encompassing, unified meanings, but on the contrary, so that it may be seen in its historical and phenomenological variety, one interpretation critiquing another, reminding us of the philosophical, theatrical, and historical variety and depth of Islam.[61] In this context, the political violence of the 1980s can also be seen as not unique albeit unusual: earlier in the century, an Iranian, Abu Taleb Yazdi, was executed by the Saudis for having vomited into his shroudlike ḥajj garb while circumambulating the Ka'ba. He was merely sick, but the Saudi guards thought him a troublemaker intentionally meaning to pollute the sacred shrine. Diplomatic relations between Saudi Arabia and Iran were strained as a result.[62] More importantly, in terms of history, symbolic resonance, and ideological interpretation, the famous mystic, Manṣūr al-Ḥallaj was constantly in trouble and was eventually executed; among his heresies was the idea that one need not physically go on the ḥajj; not only was the true ḥajj a matter internal to the heart (an interpretation used by many mystics, including entire sects such as the Isma'ilis), but also, local enactments of the ḥajj were permissible, an idea dethroning the uniqueness of the ḥajj in Mecca and the political status of the dynasties which ruled Mecca. The mystic Bayazid similarly told people setting out on the ḥajj to put the money they planned to spend next to him, and to circumambulate him instead, for the spirit of God was in his heart. Equally to the point are the satires of the poets Nāser Khosrow and Sa'di that if one went on the ḥajj but did not see Abraham and Hagar, it was as if one had not gone, or rather perhaps as if one's camel rather than oneself should be accorded the title ḥājjī.

We turn now to the 1968 ḥajj, the context for Muṭahhari's *Mutual Services of Islam and Iran,* the debate with Shari'ati over Islam and Iranian identity, and the formulation of a revolutionary Shi'ite ideology. We want to pay attention to the texture of popular discourse, to the audiences for the lectures of Muṭahhari and Shari'ati, to the play of difference, the humor, the interaction among the several discourses of social strata as well as of particular lecturers, thinkers, or authors. At issue are Iran's relations with the global political economy ("the West," "the Christians," "Zionist imperialism," "the Jews"), with the Islamic commonwealth (*ummat,* the relations between Shi'ites and Sunnis, nationalism), and internal class and social strata relations ("Muṭahhari versus Shari'ati").

The 1968 Ḥajj, the Rise of Islamic Ideology, and Renewable Shi'ism

> Just as one day you Arabs will fight the Iranians to bring them to Islam, so will they one day fight you to bring you back to the path of God.
> —Ḥadīth of the Prophet, *Safīnat al-Biḥār*[63]

> Husayn has taught us another lesson more important than his *shahādat* [martyrdom/witnessing]. . . . He leaves half-finished the revival of the

pilgrimage for which all his ancestors, his grandfather, and father struggled. From the half-finished ḥajj, he proceeds to *shahādat* in order to teach all pilgrims in history . . . that if there is no imamate and leadership, if there is no goal, if there is no Husayn, and if instead there is Yazid, circumambulating the house of God is the same as circumambulating the house of idols. Those who continue their circumambulation in the absense of Husayn are equal to those who circumambulate the Green Palace of Mu'awiya.

—Ali Shari'ati, "After Shahādat"

The defeat of the Arabs by the Israelis in the 1967 war was one of the turning points of recent Middle Eastern history. Journalists often elicit statements from Arabs that it was one of those central generational experiences, a life-changing experience of deep humiliation. For many it was a devastating bursting of the bubble of hope and pride that Nasserism had inflated: the end of pan-Arabism whether led by Iraq, Syria, or Egypt; of "Islamic socialism"; or of simple charismatic mobilization around a hero figure like Nasser. For Islamic fundamentalists in Egypt (and Syria) who had refused to be recruited into the war against Israel because they felt it more important to defeat the secularizing Nasserist and Baathist states, the defeat caused renewed debate over priorities. (Although the leadership, veterans of Nasser's prisons, continued to maintain that true *jihād* must be against Nasser and Sadat, rather than against Israel, the younger generation began to revive anti-Jewish lore and emphasize anti-Zionism.[64]) For Iranians such as Muṭahhari, it exposed once more the falseness of Arab nationalism, pan-Arabism, and Arab misunderstandings and misuses of Islam.

This Iranian perspective on Arab politics was played out in the theater of street politics as well as in the lecturings of preachers and politicians. Combined with the international arena of Muslim politics epitomized in the 1968 Islamic Conference of Scholars (held each year in Mecca along with the ḥajj), this Iranian perspective provides the shape of aroused passions against the Jews, against the Arabs, and against the shah (who had aided Israel in the 1967 war), amidst which Muṭahhari delivered his influential lectures on the *Mutual Services of Islam and Iran.*

During the ḥajj of 1968, following the Arab-Israeli War of 1967, a delegate to the annual Islamic Conference of Scholars is said to have formulated the slogan of the next two decades: "Islam was not defeated by the Jews. Islam never even entered the battlefield." Muṭahhari reports that a Pakistani commented further: "[Arab] nationalism was

Fig. 3.7. Stamp showing Dr. Ali Shari'ati.

defeated by religion: Jews stayed true to their religion while the Arabs abandoned theirs." Muṭahhari himself says this is not quite fair: Judaism is not a pure religion, but Jews mix religion and race.

Muṭahhari became one of the key figures who articulated the themes: that religion had defeated nationalism; that the Arabs had fought under the banner of nationalism while the Israelis had used the far more potent mobilization of religion; that nationalism at best was a force once powerful in Europe but now universally in decay; that nationalism was a tool of imperialism's divide and rule, privileging one racial group over others and dividing the subordinates against one another; that Nasser and the Baathists were but nationalists attempting to revive the ancient Arab imperialism over non-Arab Muslims; and that Muslims had to learn a bitter lesson from the Jews: they had to recover their Islam and fight under it, abandoning nationalist perversions, be they Arab perversions, or be they the pre-Islamic, Zoroastrian pretensions being promoted by the Pahlavi monarchy.

Muṭahhari delivered nine lectures on these themes upon his return from the ḥajj. Three, entitled "Islam and Nationalism," were delivered to the Society of Islamic Engineers, the society organized by future

Fig. 3.8. Stamp showing Murtaḍā Muṭahhari.

prime minister and leader of the Iran Liberation Movement (*Nahzat-e Āzādī*), Engineer Mehdi Bazargan. Six more lectures, entitled "Mutual Services of Islam and Iran," were delivered to the Husainiyeh Irshad, the leading center of discussions of modernist Islam, soon to be dominated by, and identified with, Dr. Ali Shari'ati. The nine lectures were transcribed, added to, and collected under the title *Mutual Services of Islam and Iran.* They were reprinted year after year with additions by "Otaredi" and a long introduction by an anonymous member of the Society of Islamic Engineers ending with Muhammad Ali Iqbal's rousing poem "Wake Up." The eighth edition appended listings by generation of Islamic jurists, exegetes, philosophers, and mystics (after the tenth century, Muṭahhari suggests, mystics became charlatans) to demonstrate both the unbroken line of authoritative Islamic scholarship, and to illustrate the preponderance of Iranians and Shi'ites among them. An ironic, but perhaps not unwelcome, effect of these additions was to reverse the relative size of the two halves of the text, making the sections on Iranian contributions to Islam much longer than those on Islam's contributions to Iran.

The result was to reinforce the old Iranian nationalist theme, going back to the *shu'ūbiyya* movement of the ninth century, that it was primarily Iranians who historically have carried the responsibilities of Islam. Only one philosopher, it is claimed, was ever produced by the Arabs, and even his ethnicity is unclear: al-Kindi (Yaqub ibn Ishaq, Jacob son of Isaac). Traditionally, this contempt for Arabs is phrased in readings of the Qur'an and a series of ḥadīth. For example, the Qur'an (9:97) says, "Arabs are the worst disbelievers and hypocrites" (*al-a'rābu ashaddu kufran wa nifāqan*). (Commentaries often try to explain that *a'rābu* here means "bedouin," or historically pin the revelation to the circumstances of Muhammad's troubles with his own Qureysh tribe.) Again, the Qur'an (26:198) says, "If the Qur'an had been revealed to non-Arabs, the Arabs would not have accepted it." The implication, explained Imām al-Ṣādiq, the sixth Shi'ite Imām, is clearly that the Iranians could recognize its worth from its content, while the Arabs could not. Asked who were more virtuous, the Arabs or the Ajam (Iranians), Imām al-Ṣādiq replied, "Arab hypocrites accepted Islam only out of fear, while Iranians accepted it willingly." Indeed, when the Arabs say, "We believe", the Qur'an (49:14) retorts, "Say rather, we submitted."

If there is a deep underlying tension here between Iranian nationalism and Islamic universalism, one which is played upon in different ways by almost every Iranian thinker, the political struggle was to define an Islamic ideology which at the same time could ward off Arabism and the form of Iranian nationalism promoted by the Pahlavi monarchy. It is rare in modern times for Iranian Muslim polemicists to take the trouble to refute Zoroastrianism: the Zoroastrians are a tiny, inoffensive minority. Mutahhari's text takes on both Zoroastrianism itself and the modernist ideology promoted by such scholars as Pur-e Davoud and Muhammad Mo'īn, which rooted not only Iranian identity but also Shi'ism in the pre-Islamic heritage of Zoroastrian Iran. Mo'īn's doctoral dissertation, "Mazdayasna and Persian Literature," done under Pūr Davoud, was a tracing of pre-Islamic locutions in post-Islamic literature, especially in the gnostic or mystic metaphors for locating wisdom in the wine of the Magi, the *zunnār* or *kostī* (Zoroastrian sacred thread tied around the waist) of purity, Pir-e Moghan (the saint of the Magi), and so on. There was also the thesis, picked up by the French scholar, Henri Corbin, that Shi'ism was a relatively transparent translation of Zoroastrianism into Islamic idiom: the divine light of the Imāms was but the *farrah-e Izadī* (the divine grace of legitimate sovereignty); the Mahdi or Islamic "messiah" was but the Soushyant or Zoroastrian "messiah"; the seventeen rakat of prayer come from the seventeen times of tying the *kostī*, the *jiziya* tax on non-Muslim protected minorities is merely the Arabicized name of the Sassanian *gazya* or "poll tax"; hereditary succession of the Imāms is from the hereditary transmission of the charisma of kingship, and there is the legend of the marriage of the royal house of Iran and the house of the Imāms (Shahrbanu, daughter of Yazdegird III, the last Sassanian shah, and Imām Husain).

Diogenes in Yazd: Agha-ye Bughlaneh ("Bullhorn") and Bahlul

> His existence is absorbed in the anecdotes he provoked. . . . Witty and instructive stories buzz around [Diogenes], as they do around his colleague, Mullah Nasrudin. . . . Greek kynicism discovers the animal body in the human and its gestures as arguments; it develops a pantomimic materialism. Diogenes refutes the language of philosophers with that of the clown.
>
> —P. Sloterdijk, *Critique of Cynical Reason*

This struggle over national heritage was one enacted, not merely in the verbiage of ideologues, but also in the streets. In the months before the 1967 war, the radio waves and newspapers were filled with verbal duels between the Israelis and Nasser's pan-Arabism. The Iranian media were filled with warnings that Nasser also had designs on Iran's southern province of Khuzistan, which the Arabs (in Baghdad especially, but also in Cairo) insisted on calling Arabistan. Books printed in Beirut or Lebanon that referred to the Arabian Gulf were banned or reprinted in pirate editions that corrected the name to the Persian Gulf. In Yazd, the government organized a large demonstration at the open square of Mīr Chaqmāq. Students were brought to sing the national anthem. The governor recited a poem in the epic style of Firdausi: "If Iran is not to exist, may my body not exist / May not a soul exist on this land / God forbid the day Iran become the dueling ground of wolf and lion / Better we submit to death than yield to the enemy." One by one, representatives of all the guilds and organizations took the microphone set up on the roof of Ḥājjī Khalifeh's Sweets Shop to condemn Nasser. The head of the coppersmith guild recited the poem by the Freemason Adīb al-Mamālek, "We are those who received tribute from kings/We are those who stay the ocean waves" (the reference of this well-known poem first to Darius who received tribute from the kings of the known world, and then to Xerxes whipping the Bosphorus into submissive calm so that his soldiers could cross over into Greece). Aghdas Bagha'i, the representative of the Women's Organization, in her turn, shouted, "We the women of Yazd, with iron fists, will smash the jaw of the Copt, Nasser" (*ma jama'eh-ye zanān-e Yazd ba moshtha-ye-ahanīn gardan-e Abdu Nasser qebtirā mishekanim*). A sayyid and local character, Agha-ye Bughlaneh, standing below, carried away by her enthusiasm, memorably responded in rich street language to great laughter, much repeated for days thereafter, "*kir-e to bokhoram*" ("I eat your penis," i.e., I love you). Then some prankster dropped an empty water barrel from a roof into a nearby alley, which resounded so loudly that people thought Nasser's bombs had started to fall, and the crowd scattered, running for fear. The next day, children were chanting, "*Mā mellat-e Irānīm/ Az dalleh gorizānīm*" ("We are the Iranian nation/ We run from water barrels"). The prank was a historical quotation, a repetition: once before there had been a public demonstration in the same place, at the time of Mosaddegh, and the same prank had been played, with the same result.

This was shortly before the 1967 war. During the war itself, the newspaper seller at the kiosk in Mīr Chaqmāq spent hours listening to his radio for each detail. As the disaster became clear, in fury he threw the radio into the street, crying that he had not bought it to bring him such bad news. A few days later there was a nasty incident in the bazaar, at the top of Bazaar Khan. A stocky, bearded Jew was leaning on his bicycle, kibitzing with a shopkeeper, saying that the war had been between Arabs and Israelis, not between Muslims and Jews, and that if the Arabs had not been preoccupied with Israel, they would have found an excuse to try to invade Iran again. Suddenly, a sixteen-year-old youth ran up to the Jew and slapped him hard in the face, screaming curses at him, and shouting, "How dare you crow over a Jewish victory in a Muslim bazaar, I'll kill you." The Jew cried, "Police!" A policeman did respond. He collared the boy, who was still shouting and cursing, "Yes, I slapped him, and I'll kill him too. As if we Muslims had no *gheirat*" (honor, that form of honor that restrains men from spoiling the honor of other men). The policeman began leading him away, but the boy turned and taunted the bazaaris: "All of you are Jews, Zionists. Is there not a single Muslim among you to ask why I'm being taken away? Is this not a Muslim country? Is this not a Muslim bazaar? Now I know how Husain felt at Karbala." Shop shutters began to slam shut, and a few bazaaris began to surround the policeman, and then the crowd grew. The Jew, realizing that a real tinder point was imminent, cried out, "I forgive him; let him go." The boy spat: "You forgive me? I will not stand for such humiliation. A Jew forgive me!" The unfortunate Jew shouted in desperation, "He never hit me." The boy was let go.

Meanwhile the ulama had called a boycott of Jewish shops. Such boycotts were called in various towns, and in response the government attempted to ban various preachers from public preaching and incitement, which only increased the sense among Muslims of struggle against the shah's regime. A clerk in the Saderat Bank spread the rumor that Jews of Yazd had been sending money to Israel, and that even a poor street sweeper was not as poor as he seemed, for he had sent a hundred thousand tomans to Israel. (This same clerk was to be involved twenty years later in the postrevolution killing of Nurullah Akhtar Khavari, the leader of the Yazdi Baha'is.) All the windows of the new synagogue were smashed. It had been noticed that during the war the Jews had spent all day in the synagogue praying. Muslims posed the question, Why had God answered the Jews' prayers and not those of Muslims? There was a traditional theological answer for such questions: the angels typically ask God to quickly grant the request of foul human beings so the angels would not have to look on their ugly heaven-turned beseeching faces; the angels typically ask God to delay granting the request of blessed human beings so the angels can look longer on their beatific faces.

But if there was anger at the Jews, there was also anger at and contempt for the Arabs. Bahlul, one of the most interesting preachers of the twentieth century, the trickster preacher par excellence, who had triggered the 1936 riots in Mashhad over Reza Shah's attempt to unveil women, and who during the Nasser period was the head of Radio Cairo's

Persian broadcast service, transmitting antishah propaganda to Iran (see Fischer 1980: 98–101), returned to Iran after the 1967 war. He came to Yazd and related both his means of entering Iran, having been sentenced to death in absentia on several occasions, and his experience with the Arabs.[65] First he wrote a forty-five page letter of apology to the shah. When he arrived at Tehran's Mehrabad Airport, he asked to see the shah. Told the shah was unavailable, Bahlul asked in his folk Persian to see the shah's "great lady" (*olia mokhaddara*), using the term for Fatima, daughter of the Prophet. The queen agreed to see him. He told her, "I have relatives in both worlds: in this world and in the next world. I want to visit them both, but I have come here to visit the former first, I have not come to create trouble. Let me visit my living relatives. But if you want to kill me, I'll go and visit my dead relatives directly." Queen Farah laughed, and asked him, "What will you do after you visit your relatives?" He replied, "I want to farm my land in Gonabad." (Bahlul always claimed to have supported himself by farming, being among those clergy who thought it illegitimate to support themselves by preaching or teaching. Preaching and teaching ought to be selfless contributions to the community of Islam.) In fact, Bahlul became a government preacher, never accepting invitations without getting clearance, and being used to rouse the people against Saddam Husain in the disputes over the Shatt al-Arab (called the Arvand Rud by the shah and by the Islamic Republic), Khuzistan, and the small islands in the Gulf of Abu Musa and the Tumbs.

Bahlul spoke from his personal experience of Arabs, "Do not be afraid of them: they are as courageous as mice." The children in the streets chanted, "*In Arab-e sag naneh/ Rafteh bālāy-e gardaneh/ Hey dāreh dād mīzaneh/ Shatt ul Arab māl-e maneh*" ("This Arab, whose mother is a dog/ Has gone on the hill [like a bandit surveying the route of a caravan]/ Hey, he's making such a noise/ Saying that the Shatt al-Arab belongs to him"). Another ditty that the children chanted was in mock epic meter and rhyme: "*Arab dar biyabun malakh mikhorad/ Sag-e Isfahān āb-e yakh mīkhorad*" ("Arabs eat locusts in the desert/ While even the dogs of Isfahan have ice cubes for their water"). (Iranians often say, "*Arab nistam*" (I am not an Arab), meaning, "I am not stupid"; or also, "*Az bikh Arab budam*" ("I was thoroughly Arab"), meaning "I was thoroughly ignorant" about something.)

Such was the anti-Arab feeling that even some of the mullās could be heard to say, "So who are these Palestinians anyway, but descendants of Yazid, the slayer of Husain?" And, "The Jews gave the gardens of Fadak to Fatima, and Umar took it away." (Actually, the Jews of Medina were massacred long before Muhammad bequeathed the garden to Fatima; but Fadak became a symbol for Shi'ites of the moral legacy of a just society usurped and perverted by the Sunni caliphs.) And finally, of course: "The Jews' return to Palestine is a welcome sign of the last days, heralding the return of the Mahdi."

These aroused passions against the Jews, against the Arabs, and against the shah (who had aided Israel in the 1967 war) provide one reception or audience context for the impact created by Muṭahhari's *Mutual Services of Islam and Iran.* A second context is to be found in his biography, seen as a figuration of the anxieties of a sizable number of his generation, especially of those within the clerical hierarchy who were to become the activists in the revolution of 1977–79, anxieties about marxism and modernism.

Neither Materialist nor Modernist: Muṭahhari's Bioglyph (1919–79)

> "our *mullā nuqatis*" [nitpicking mullās]
>
> —Ali Shari'ati, *Return to Self*

Murtaḍā Muṭahhari was assassinated on May Day 1979 by the Furqān, an anticlerical guerilla organization inspired by Shari'ati and taking its name from the Qur'anic term meaning knowing the "difference" between right and wrong. The Furqān issued a declaration that Muṭahhari was guilty of treason for having diverted the course of the revolution of the masses, and so in compliance with a verdict of a people's revolutionary court, he had been executed. Khomeini is reported to have shed tears, calling Muṭahhari "the fruit of my life." Muṭahhari had been Khomeini's student in Qum, one of the close circle of students of those days that played a key role in the revolution. Muṭahhari was, at the time of his death, the chairman of the secret Revolutionary Council, the guiding power of the new revolutionary government operating behind the public government led by Engineer Mehdi Bazargan, often to the dismay of the latter, in a classic dual sovereignty phase of revolution.[66] Khomeini had not cried when his own elder son Mustafa mysteriously died in the fall of 1977, an event which had helped trigger the revolution (see Fischer 1980*a*), saying stoically at the time that it was a "hidden blessing of God."

Beyond his connections, and his role in the revolution, Muṭahhari had been a powerful intellectual force for almost a quarter of a century, challenging simultaneously the stagnant clergy, secular nationalists, secular marxists, and pseudoreligious left for whom Islam served as no more than a borrowed language or masque. Interestingly, his public fame came through a debate in a women's magazine, a reflex of a simple writing style used also by Khomeini in his *Kash-e asrār* (Revealing the secrets; 1363 Q./1943). Khomeini's students are distinctive in being fully trained *mujtahid*s who write and speak simply with a direct political slant, instead of asserting authority through a mystifying scholastic style, or restricting themselves to discourses on morality.

The story of Muṭahhari's involvement in the magazine *Zan-e rūz* (Today's woman) debate, which eventuated in his book *Nezām-e ḥuqūq-e zan dar Islam* (The system of women's rights in Islam), captures in miniature much of the dynamics of the success of the mullās in their argument with the secularists of the Pahlavi establishment. Shaykh Muḥammad-Taqī Falsafi, a popular preacher, famed for his role in stirring up the anti-Baha'i disturbances in the 1950s, called Muṭahhari on the phone one day to tell him that the magazine was planning a serialization of Ashley Montague's *The Natural Superiority of Women,* together with a series of articles by women writers, and by a judge arguing for the expansion of women's legal rights in Iran. The judge, Ibrāhim Mahdavi Zanjāni, had previously published a draft for a new law on women's rights, and the magazine had asked for reader responses. Falsafi had talked to the editor who agreed to invite Muṭahhari to write responses to the judge in an ongoing series of exchanges in *Zan-e rūz.* Muṭahhari's responses (the first in issue 87, 7 Aban 1345/1966) were enormously successful: he had obviously prepared by reading his opponent's writings, while the judge mistook Muṭahhari for an ignorant mullā. Muṭahhari, after all, was not only a *mujtahid* trained in Qum, he was also a Ph.D. and professor at Tehran's Faculty of Theology, a figure who participated in the deliberations of the leading Islamic intellectuals on both the orthodox clerical and liberal lay sides. After six weeks, the judge suddenly died, but the editor invited Muṭahhari to continue his contributions, and he did so for thirty-three weeks. Collected, these became the book which in the 1970s was regarded as the fullest and most reasoned clerical statement on the subject.

Muṭahhari was not only a scholar trained both in the traditional scholastic system and in the modern university system, but from his autobiographical sketches it seems he was also a man driven by an intense anxiety caused by finding marxism and modernism so seductive. His arguments seem thus not simply sparrings with political opponents, but ones waged for his own soul, an internal tension like that of an American country singer caught between the devil's music and God's.

Like Shari'ati, Muṭahhari was from Khorasan. He was born on 13

Jamādi al-Awwal 1338 Q (or 13 Bahman 1298 Sh., 2 February 1919) in the small town of Fariman, sixty kilometers from Mashhad, the fourth of five sons of a local mullā, Shaykh Muḥammad Husain Muṭahhari. He began his education in his father's *maktab,* at age twelve he went to Mashhad's theological seminaries, and then at age seventeen to Qum. He says he was attracted to the philosophers and mystics, and aspired to study with Mirza Mehdi Shahīdi Razavi, the theologian-philosopher. However, the latter died in 1355/1936, the year Muṭahhari arrived in Qum, and as a substitute he found himself powerfully attracted to the classes in gnostic ethics taught by "Ruh-e Qudsi-e Ilāhi" ("the heavenly divine spirit", i.e., Sayyid Ruhullah ["spirit of Allah"] Khomeini). He describes an atmosphere of ecstasy created in those classes, with much crying and wailing, always concluded with the teacher raising his hands and giving a long and moving prayer which again would bring tears to the eyes. Muṭahhari went to these sessions with his roommate, Shaykh Husain Ali Montazeri (after the revolution named by the Council of Guardians to succeed Khomeini, serving for eight years as heir apparent until Khomeini asked him to resign in 1989 shortly before Khomeini died).

During this period, Muṭahhari says he was wracked by questions about the existence of God, questions he could not openly discuss in Qum, and so he spent much time isolating himself in meditation, and in serious study of his lessons in Arabic and principles of jurisprudence so as to be able to pursue these issues in the writings of the great philosophers. In 1320/1941 he finished the *suṭūḥ* level of preparation for the higher levels of jurisprudential study.

The following two summers (times of intense heat in Qum, when the theological schools close and students disperse to cooler cities) he went to Isfahan and sought out Ḥajji Mirza 'Alī Āqā Shirāzi Isfahāni in Madrasa Ṣadr. Ḥajji Mirzā 'Alī Āqā was, apart from being a jurisconsult, a mystical philosopher, a traditional physician, and also a teacher of the *Nahj al-Balāgha* (the sermons, letters, wills, and aphorisms attributed to Imām Ali, collected by Sharīf al-Raḍi). Shi'ites call the *Nahj al-Balāgha* "the brother of the Qur'an," and it too, like the Qur'an, is not a regular, required text in the seminary system (see chapter 2). Before meeting Ḥajji Mirzā 'Alī Āqa, Muṭahhari had thought of the book as a straightforward collection, perfectly understandable without a master; with Ḥajji Mirzā 'Alī Aqā's help he was introduced into levels of meaning he could not have found alone. Eventually, Muṭahhari produced his own selective exegesis, *Sayri dar Nahj al-Balagha* (Passage through the *Nahj al-Balāgha*).

In 1322/1943 Muṭahhari went to Borujerd to study *khārij-e fiqh* (the highest level of jurisprudence) with Ḥajji Aqa Husain Borujerdi. The next year Borujerdi moved to Qum and became the acknowledged leader of the Iranian Shi'ite community. Muṭahhari studied *manqūl* (narrational knowledge, including jurisprudence) with the luminaries of the day: Sayyid Ṣadr al-Dīn Ṣadr, Sayyid Muḥammad Muḥaqqiq, Sayyid Muhammad Khwansāri, Sayyid Muhammad Hujjat, Sayyid Husain Borujerdi, and Sayyid Ruhullah Khomeini. He studied *ma'qūl* (rational knowledge, including philosophy) with Aqa Mirza Mehdi Āshtiyāni, Āyatullāh Mazandarani, Sayyid Ruhullah Khomeini (with the latter two, the *Manzūma* of Ḥajj Mullā Hadi Sabazavari), and Sayyid Muhammad Husain Tabataba'i (the theological section of Ibn Sina's *Shafā*). His classmates under Tabataba'i included both Shaykh Husain Ali Montazeri and Mūsa Ṣadr (the missing Imām of Lebanon).

Around 1944 he began to read modern philosophy with a particular interest in materialist philosophies, and in 1945 he began systematically to read the literature produced by the Iranian communist party, the Tudeh, as well as the radical literature of Egypt. He took extensive notes on Dr. Taqi Arāni's *Dialectical Materialism,* and wrote a precis of George Politzer's *Elementary Principles of Philosophy.* In 1949–51, it seems Muṭahhari cooperated closely with the Feda'iyan-e Islam, a fundamentalist group founded by Nawwab Safawi inspired by Egypt's Muslim Brotherhood, and responsible for a number of political assassinations, including those of Prime Minister Razmara and the anticlerical historian Ahmad Kasravi.

In 1952 he moved to Tehran, married the daughter of a Khorasani mullā, began work on a Ph.D. in Islamic philosophy, established the Islamic Council of University Students, delivered Islamic messages each week on Iranian National Radio, and delivered a series of public lectures. By this time he had received the degree of *ijtihād.* With Sayyid Maḥmūd Taleqāni and others, he helped organize the Congress of Islamic Societies. In 1955 he became an instructor at the University of Tehran's Theology Faculty, a position he held until 1977. When Āyatullāh Borujerdi died (13 Shawwal 1381/ 1961), Muṭahhari was one of the prominent religious leaders who lectured on the need to reorganize and change the direction of Shi'ite clerical leadership: three of these lectures appeared in the important volume *Baḥthī dar Barah-e Marja'iyat va Rūḥāniyat,* edited by 'Allāmeh Tabataba'i et al. (see Fischer 1980*a*: 164–65, 183).

Following the 15 Khordad 1342/1963 uprising against the shah's White Revolution, like many others, Muṭahhari was arrested and imprisoned for a few days. After his release, he joined the ranks of the so-called *'ulamā-ye Mubārez* (the combatant clergy), which maintained a low profile on antishah politics and kept close contact with Khomeini who had been exiled first to Turkey and then in 1964 to Iraq where he was to remain until 1977. It was in the aftermath of the 15 Khordad events that Dr. Ali Shari'ati returned to Iran from studying and organizing Iranian dissidents in France, and Muṭahhari wrote to him to see if they could cooperate.

In this period, Muṭahhari's popular reputation began to grow. There are a number of reasons. First, in 1333/1954 he began editing, with an extensive commentary, the lectures of Sayyid Muhammad Husain Tabataba'i entitled *'Uṣūl-e falsafa va ravesh-e realism* (The principles of philosophy and the method of realism). This originally had been a series of lectures given twice a week by Tabataba'i to a small philosophical circle in Qum. It was in a form accessible only to the initiated. Muṭahhari convinced Tabataba'i of the urgency of popularizing an Islamic philosophical response to the increasingly popular marxist literature, and with Tabataba'i's blessing he prepared a text simplifying whatever he thought difficult for the general public, and launching a counterattack on the work of the Iranian marxist, Dr. Taqi Arāni (assassinated fifteen years earlier).

Second, he began to write for the journal *Maktab-e Islam* (founded in 1378/1958 under the guidance of Āyatullāh Muḥammad-Kāzem Shari'atmadāri). Third, he also published a series of his own public lectures, *Bist guffar* (Twenty lectures). Fourth, he became one of the founders of the Husainiyeh Irshad, a center for discussion of modern Islam, endowed by a businessman named Muhammad Humayun. Eventually, the Husainiyeh came to be dominated by Dr. Ali Shari'ati, and Muṭahhari quit. But this institution played a role in rousing an Islamic ideological fervor among the educated youth of Iran that cannot be underestimated.

In 1966–67, as already narrated, Muṭahhari attracted attention for his writings in *Zan-e rūz*. The following year he delivered the nine lectures on "Mutual Services of Islam and Iran," and then collected them into a volume which was widely read. In 1969–70 he gave two lectures at a Tehran junior college (*daneshsarā-ye 'āli*) on the "Causes of Inclination toward Materialism" (*llal-e gerayesh be maddigari*). The published version was double the length of the original lectures, and by the eighth edition (1978) yet another hundred pages had been added. The eighth edition was published in a run of ten thousand copies. In a long introduction, Muṭahhari attacked the poet Ahmad Shamlu (without naming him) for having put out a new edition of the odes of Ḥāfeẓ with a preface describing Ḥāfeẓ as an atheist; he attacked the leftist Ali Mirfatrus (also without explicitly naming him) for his biographical reading of al-Hallaj depicting the great mystic as a leader in the class struggle who had used the allegorical language of mysticism as a veiled way of denying the existence of God (Mirfatrus had in turn been responding to the magisterial biography of al-Hallaj by Louis Massignon); and he attacked the Mojahedin Khalq and Furqān (who would eventually assassinate him) for being hypocritical materialists (*materialism-e munāfiq*), reinterpreting God's words with unjustified materialist meanings.

Muṭahhari's politics kept him under SAVAK surveillance, and eventually he was prohibited from public lecturing. SAVAK surveillance had begun at least as early as the 1963 uprisings, when he had first been arrested. A SAVAK report says:

> . . . Since [13]42 [1963], [Muṭahhari] has frequently uttered agitational, misleading and contemptuous words in different religious gatherings both in Tehran and other cities under the cloak of "religious issues" and "the history of Islam." One of his activities is initiating vast efforts in [13]49 [1960] which include opening a bank account for collecting funds for the Palestinians from the religiously zealous people through public lecturing. (The account was reported to your Excellency earlier.) While issuing warrants to prevent the collection of such funds and taking this person under surveillance, the director of the internal security of Savak then determined that [this person] was "not fit to be professor of the university and [his incompetence] must be reported to the university." (*Ettelaat,* 12 Ordibehesht 1363/April 1984)

In 1972, both the Husainiyeh Irshad and the Masjid al-Jawād, where he lectured (though he had recently quit the Husainiyeh Irshad) were closed by SAVAK. Muṭahhari was again briefly arrested and released after promising to refrain from public lecturing. SAVAK, in an internal report, complained that he continued to lecture to students at the university mosque, and that he should be dismissed from the university. This, however, did not happen.

As was said before, Muṭahhari is a key figure of his generation not only for illuminating the dimensions of traditionalist Shi'ite thought, but also for illuminating the antimarxist motivational anxiety, and the powerful propaganda techniques of wielding the popular rhetoric of Islam. In contrast to both Shari'ati and Sayyid Maḥmūd Ṭaleqāni, he wished to purify, not reconstruct, Islam. And in contrast to them, he was driven by a fear of losing his faith and the entire structure of Islamic learning and accomplishment, should the atheist arguments of marxism or modernism hold. It is perhaps for this reason that Muṭahhari was so adamantly opposed to Islamic reformers like Shari'ati and the Mojahedin for mixing Islam, marxism, and modernism and thereby inevitably, he thought, weakening Islam.

Muṭahhari's *Mutual Services of Islam and Iran* and the Paradoxes of Nationalism

> There is no substance to Christianity; it consists of no more than a few moral teachings . . . Islam came to reform society and to form a nation. Its mandate is the reform of the whole world. . . .
>
> —Professor "Āyatullāh" Murtaḍā Muṭahhari, "Jihad in the Qur'an"[67]

> . . . the philosopher-kings of the "underdeveloped world" all act as Westernizers and all talk like narodniks.
>
> —Partha Chatterjee, *Nationalist Thought in the Colonial World*[68]

> [Nationalism's] myths invert reality: it claims to defend folk culture while in fact it is forging a high culture, it claims to protect an old folk society while in fact helping to build an anonymous mass society. . . . It preaches and defends continuity, but owes everything to a decisive and unutterably profound break in human history. It preaches and defends cultural diversity when in fact it imposes homogeneity both inside, and to a lesser degree between political units. . . .
>
> —Ernest Gellner, *Nations and Nationalisms*[69]

Muṭahhari's vision of Islam is set against notions of nationalism, and yet turns out to be so heavily indebted to Iranian contributions that it is hard to distinguish from traditional Iranian Shi'ite efforts to convert the majority Sunni world, which in the current period of the Islamic Republic also goes under the name of the "export of the revolution." Nonetheless, it is an effort to construct a discursive system that can protect its users from the ravages of imperialism, by deconstructing colonialist discourses as often grounded in racist conceptions and by offering a culturally constructed alternative. Shari'ati sought a similar discursive shield, but constructed it in a strikingly different way. What makes Muṭahhari's argument valuable for us to consider is its display of (1) the paradoxes in which Iranian idioms of identity perennially seem caught, paradoxes illustrative more generally of nationalist discourses as analyzed by Benedict Anderson (1983), Partha Chatterjee (1986), Virginia Domínguez (1989), Ernest Gellner (1983), and other writers on modernizing ideologies; (2) the power of the vision that motivates and underpins the Islamic Republic, that partly depends on maintaining the tension in the paradoxes of identity, and that partly depends upon a particular style of hermeneutical detail and invocation of historical richness. History, of course, is the battleground for cultural definition in the present.

Indeed, this is what makes Muṭahhari's argument so important for us to consider: Politicians, academics, and journalists badly misunderstand the vision that powers the Islamic Republic when they locate it simply in the martyr complex or minority-underdog determination of Shi'ism. It is better seen as one of the contemporary expressions of third-world resistance to underdevelopment and imperialism. Muṭahhari himself lays considerable stress on the difference between ideologies that can engender love and those that operate primarily on hatred or fear. He, like Eli Kedourie (1960, 1971), sees nationalism as driven by the latter passions, as a racist-tending set of ideas that emerged in recent European history and was exported to the Middle East where it had only invidious, divisive, and oppressive effects. The racist tendencies, Muṭahhari argues, are obvious not only in Nazism, but also in colonialism, both European colonialism and earlier Arab colonialism. Muṭahhari contrasts the invidiousness of nationalism with the encompassing positive vision of Islam, noting that Islam provided the fertile context for an extraordinary flowering of Iranian genius. Iranians were major developers of jurisprudence, ḥadīth collections, philosophy, science, logic, and statecraft throughout the Islamic world. He argues that this can be so again, that Islam provides a transnational framework of potentially global, and certainly universal, reach.

Non-Muslims will find little comfort in his understanding of their aspirations or perspectives: Muṭahhari's Islam is open and supportive if and only if you are Muslim, although it is supportive of Jews and Christians, as People of the Book, but only as long as they are content to be subordinate, nonpolitical elements within a Muslim polity. There is no sympathy for Zoroastrianism or other religions, nor for the civil rights that postreligious secularists think basic to modern society. The profoundness of Muṭahhari's defense of the legal structure of Islam, understood in its traditional, fundamentalist sense, must not be forgotten, and is explicit in his lecture on *jihād* and his work on the rights and duties of women under Islam.

Yet one also must not be mesmerized by the surface content of what he says, but must probe first at functionalist analyses of how ideologies work, what structural interests they advance. Only then may one, and must one, return to the cultural and hermeneutic level, to explore how social power is rhetorically mobilized, how history and identity are culturally reconstructed. Muṭahhari, himself, is not averse to a functionalist analysis when he argues that religion has to do with mentality, instilling courage, charity, knowledge, introducing vigorous customs, and doing away with decayed traditions. There is a refrain here that attentive readers of Khomeini's lectures on Islamic government may recognize. Khomeini thought in 1970 that it might take two centuries to overthrow the Iranian monarchy, that fundamentally at issue was not a particular government but changing the mentality of the Iranian people, something that is slow and that takes concerted effort. Muṭahhari argues that it is by the ability to promote a proper mentality that governments or nations must be judged. He dismisses definitions of nationalism based on race or ethnicity: nationhood, he says in good functionalist fashion, is a myth constructed by governments. All nations are composed of intermingling peoples; all attempts to trace back to a common ancestor is mythic. Nor does ethnicity guarantee acceptance by one's fellow nationals: Buddhism eventually took hold in China more than in India, Christianity in Europe more than in Palestine, marxism in Russia more than in Germany.

An appreciation of the paradoxes of nationalism helps pose the functionalist questions. Benedict Anderson (1983:14) summarizes three basic ones: nationalisms are objectively modern, but subjectively constructed around antiquity; they are formally universal, but irremediably particular in their concrete manifestations; they are politically powerful, yet philosophically impoverished if not incoherent. Ernest Gellner initiated a new round of functionalist analyses in 1983, arguing, one step further than Muṭahhari, not merely that nationalisms are myths created by governments, but specifically that nationalism is the creation of the industrial state. Industrial and technological society requires persons who are operationally literate, a mobile labor force adaptable to interdependent industrial, bureaucratic, and technological operations. The standardized literacy and education required is what Gellner here calls "high culture." Anderson took this line of argument two steps further: he stressed the importance of print technology in standardizing and fixing languages and in creating new unified fields of communication, and he sketched out the evolution of nationalisms from nineteenth-century European ideologies in defense of the state that depended upon promoting a vernacular print language to post–World War II nationalisms that can more flexibly build upon differentiated technologies (radio, mass parties) and models of generating "imagined communities." Partha Chatterjee explores further the stages of nationalisms, using India as his prime example: the first reaction, stressing Eastern spirituality and Western technological superiority, involves an elitist program of cultural synthesis, mobilizing the masses in anticolonialism while distancing them from the control structure of the state; there then follows a moment when the "national" can be consolidated, à la Mohandas Karamchand Gandhi, by decrying the "modern," preparing for expanded capitalist relations of production by using an anticapitalist ideology; this is succeeded by a Jawaharlal Nehru style use of nationalism as a discourse of order. All three writers take pains to warn that nationalism is not quite what it seems. Its rhetoric feeds off reification (Marx) and positivity (Foucault): despite its origins in human invention, it veils itself in an aura of organic authenticity.

Such functionalist paradoxes, grounded in social complexities that ideological discourses help to mediate through, help focus on the sociological structure of society and the kinds of ideological "projective screens" or "compromise formations" that are needed to keep that structure supple. An industrial modern society does place a premium on at least basic literacy, and for countries such as Iran this is a major transformation of the past generation, one that Shari'ati invoked more fully than Muṭahhari. Gellner (1983:123, 124) says of nationalist thinkers, "Their precise doctrines are hardly worth analyzing," and hence "a conspicuous feature of our treatment of nationalism has been a lack of interest in the history of nationalist ideas and the contributions and nuances of individual nationalist thinkers." In one sense Gellner is surely correct, as anyone knows who has tried to read the turgid, special pleading arguments of nationalist polemicists, Muṭahhari and Shari'ati included. However, in another sense one needs to read these polemics as discursive systems (rather than "precise doctrines") for their positioning vis-à-vis other discourses, and for the functional effects of their recommendations: in Muṭahhari's case, the appeal is to a clearing away of parochialisms, a cleansing of Islam, so that it might once again function as the overarching frame for the coordinated international expansion of knowledge. The image is of past golden ages of Islamic learning and achievement, but the functional thrust is a contemporary opening to learning. The paradoxical tension between the coding of universalism in terms that are resolutely ethnocentric and religiously parochial is what both gives Muṭahhari's lectures their power and makes them problematic. This paradoxical tension is rhetorically maintained by phrasing his reasoning in a series of negations of alternative arguments about Iranian identity and Islamic attachment. The rhetorical technique creates for his listeners a powerful illusion that the positive argument being made through the negations is a correction of historical mistakes, of logic, and of parochialism, rather than an alternative construction of similar historical, logical, or particularistic validity. Muṭahhari's discourse, moreover, rehearses Iranian history with a chronological depth that makes it a useful access to many elements of Iranian self-perception.

He makes three pairs or six sets of interlinked arguments. First, he argues against the sociological validity of trying to mobilize Iranians on the basis of a Persian nationalism that sees itself distinct from Islam and, correlatively, against notions that suggest any special connection between Islam and Arabs. Further, Muṭahhari argues, Islam was not imposed upon Iran, nor can Iranian Shi'ism be seen as an Islamically recoded Zoroastrianism. Finally, he argues that Iranians did not become Muslim reluctantly, but on the contrary that the generations of Iranian scholarship created what we know as Islamic civilization.

Against the Pahlavi state's ideology of an Iranian national identity:

Muṭahhari begins by invoking the existence of an umma that includes today over seven hundred million Muslims, a solidarity that transcends nationalisms. He rejects the attempt by the Pahlavi shahs to invoke the pre-Islamic Zoroastrian heritage of Iran as a nationalist basis of mobilization, saying that it is sociologically, linguistically, and logically misconceived. Sociologically, the depth of attachment that Iranians have always felt for Islam, even when they were resisting misguided Islamic caliphs and kings, will never allow the replacement of Islamic heroes such as Ali and Husain, around whom emotional life is structured, by newly rediscovered nationalist heroes such as Babak, Maziar, or Sinbad. Nor can there be a return to the prophet Zoroaster after so many years of broken connection. Linguistically, the usage of *millat,* the Persian term for "nation," is a philological mistake symptomatic of the artificiality of efforts to construct a Persian nationalism. *Millat* is a Qur'anic word; it appears in the Qur'an seventeen times, always meaning a way or path that a prophet offers a people. It comes from the root [*m-l-l*], "to dictate"; for example, God dictates a path to a prophet. The term functions much like the word *dīn,* "religion," with the exception that one can say *dīn-e Allāh,* the religion of God, whereas *millat* can be attached only to the name of prophets, e.g., *millat-e abīkum Ibrāhīm* ("the way of your father Abraham"; 22:78) or to the religion of a people. The modern Persian use of the term *millat* to mean "nation" dates only from the constitutional period, and probably came from dropping the word *payravan* from the idiom *payravan-e millat-e Muhammad* ("followers of the way of Muhammad") which then became generalized to *millat-e Iran, millat-e Turk,* and so on. Logically, the idea that nationalism is based upon notions of race or place is incoherent: there is no such thing as unmixed nations; there are only the myths and ideologies imposed by having a government, flag, or law. (Though Muṭahhari recognizes the critical role of the state in creating nationalism, he treats it as a perversion rather than as a tool. This, of course, would change radically when the revolution occurred, and the state was used as a powerful tool for the imposition of the ideology promoted by Muṭahhari. Even then, however, ideologically, the state was spoken of by Khomeini as a mere administrative mechanism, not as itself a structural determinant.)

Against any particular connection between Islam and Arabs:

Next Muṭahhari demonstrates that Islam has nothing specifically to do with Arabs. Islam from the beginning was a universal message (Qur'an 81:27, 34:28, 21:105, 7:158). The Qur'an (6:89) says of the Arabs, "If they reject [the words of the Qur'an], behold We shall entrust their charge to a new people." The fifth and sixth Imāms suggested that Iranians were that other people. Imām Ja'far al-Sadiq, the sixth Imām, said it was Iranians who accepted Islam wholeheartedly, while Arabs bickered over it in the earliest days, and perverted it under the Umayyids. The Umayyids attempted to institute a privileged position for Arabs, and Iranians resisted, citing the Qur'an (49:13), "We created you from a single pair . . . the most honored among you is the most righteous." The resistance movement took on the name *shu'ūbiyya* from the usage in the same verse of *al-shu'ub:* "We made you into nations and tribes that you may know each other." It was, Muṭahhari argues, not always an Iranian nationalist resistance movement against Islam as represented by modern Iranian nationalists, but frequently a movement in the name of Islam against its usurpation and perversion by the Arab racist and monarchist Umayyids. (Muṭahhari downplays the fact that the Behafarid movement did want to revive Zoroastrianism and intended to destroy the Ka'ba, and that Babak had no love for Islam and must have had grassroots support since he resisted the caliphal armies for more than two decades.) Muṭahhari bolsters his argument with six ḥadīth of the Prophet: (1) "People, you all are from Adam, Adam is from the dust, and there is no superiority of Arab over non-Arab, except through piety." (2) The Companions of the Prophet were proudly comparing their ancestries, and asked Salman Farsi ("the Persian") about his. He responded, "I am Salman, son of a servant of God. I was lost but God guided me through Muhammad. I was poor but God made me rich through Muhammad. I was a slave but God liberated me through Muhammad." Just then Muhammad entered, and approved of Salman's response. (3) "Pride in one's ancestors is like stinking dung beetles who transport filth with their noses." (4) "He whose actions do not gain him anything, his bloodline cannot gain him anything either." (5) Salman Farsi was called by Muhammad *minna ahl al-bayt* (a member of our family). (6) At the Battle of Uḥud, an Iranian youth let out a battle cry as he slew an enemy of the Muslims: "Take that from an Iranian lad!" Muhammad admonished him, "Say rather you are an *Anṣār* ("helper"; one who joined Muhammad's cause in Medina).

Against the idea that Iran was conquered and oppressed by Islam:

Iran was one of the two superpowers at the time Islam arose. Islam was victorious not by force of arms, but because of the internal decay of the Zoroastrian Sassanian Empire and because of Muslim religious passion, clear goals, and faith in their historical mission. Moreover, Muṭahhari points out, it was Islam that suddenly allowed a spectacular flowering of Iranian genius throughout the Islamic world as it rapidly expanded as far as Spain in the West and China and Southeast Asia in the East.

There is a historical parable in the biographies (*sīra*) of the Prophet that represents the way Iranians converted to Islam. It has to do with the first Iranian converts, the Iranian Yemenis. Sayf ibn Dhi-Yazan, ruler of the Yemen, sent a messenger to Khosrow Anushiravan, the Iranian emperor, asking for help in expelling an Abyssinian invasion. The story, as Otaredi tells it, is that Anushirvan was so arrogant that he made the messenger wait seven years before an audience was granted. Then he said he would not sent an army of his men to aid non-fellow believers, but he would send an army of prisoners who had been sentenced to death. The army of one thousand men slew thirty thousand Abyssinians. The leader of this army, Vahraz or Kharzad, succeeded Sayf when the latter died, and his troops formed the nucleus of an Iranian colony. At the time Muhammad began to preach, Badhan ibn Sasan was the Iranian governor of Yemen and the Hijaz. He sent reports back to the Sassanian shah Khosrow Parviz about the new faith. In 6 A.H., Muhammad sent a letter to Khosrow Parviz calling him to the new faith. Khosrow Parviz tore up the letter, and ordered Badhan to send Muhammad to Ctesiphon. ("Their intention is to extinguish God's light"; Qur'an 61:8.) When Badhan's men came to Muhammad, the Prophet told them that Khosrow Parviz had just been stabbed to death by his son, his stomach torn just as he had torn up the Prophet's missive, and that the real significance of Khosrow Parviz's filling the Prophet's messenger's boots with dirt and hanging them round his neck was that the land of Iran would fall to the Muslims. Muhammad further said that if Badhan accepted Islam he would keep his throne. When confirmation of the assassination arrived, Badhan converted to Islam. Badhan's son Shahr became one of the first Muslim martyrs in the battle against Aswad 'Anasi, an apostate from Islam, who upon hearing Muhammad was ill after his final pilgrimage to Mecca, declared himself prophet, attacked San'a, killing Shahr, marrying his widow, and declaring himself ruler of the Yemen from the Hadramaut to Nejd, Taif, and Bahrain. He lasted three months: the resistance came from the Iranian Yemenis led by Firuz, Dadawayh, and Jashish Daylami, aided by Shahr's widow, Azad. Again, when Muhammad died, another apostate, Qays ibn 'Abd Yaghuth attempted to seize power; and again he was foiled by Iranian-Yemeni resistance led by Firuz and Jashish. Dadawayh having been martyred.

It is a parable of the corruption of Sassanian Iran and the loyalty of Iranians to Islam. The oppressive caste system, lack of social mobility, inegalitarian access to education and religious activity, the arrogance and self-indulgent pride of the rulers, and the decadence of the court and nobility made Sassanian Iran a structure to which Iranians felt little loyalty. Muṭahhari does not add, as many authors do, the ruinous wars fought with Rome that may have drained the economic well-being of the empire, and increased the sense of oppression. For his purposes, the argument is strong enough by contrasting the egalitarianism of Islam and its insistence on equal rights to access to education and religious activity. He notes that Christianity was spreading rapidly in the Zoroastrian Empire, that it was the Christians who were the educated and enlightened intelligentsia. And in the east, Buddhism was making similar inroads. The Zoroastrian Empire was thus culturally a dead shell. Islam came and released the intellectual capacities of Iranians in a way that had not been available to them under the Zoroastrian Sassanians, and in the process stopped and supplanted the advance of Christianity and Buddhism.

That Islam was not felt to be an imposition, but rather an empowering release, for Iranians is validated by Muṭahhari in the history of Iranian revolts against the Umayyids and the Abbasids. It was an Iranian-based revolution starting in Khorasan that overthrew the Umayyids, yet there was no thought of reviving Zoroastrianism or abandoning Islam. This revolution was in the name of Islam. Similarly, when the Abbasids abandoned the Islamic ideals of the revolution that brought them to power, Iranians rose up against them, again in the name of Islam. There were many Zoroastrians, Sabeans, Christians, Jews, and Buddhists in Iran for several centuries, even a number of regional dynasties that traced themselves to the Sassanians. But when the Tahirids and Buywids created independent dynasties, there was no move to revive the Avesta. (This is a bit disingenuous: in the Buywid case, this would not have been possible, operating as they were in Baghdad in the heart of the Islamic world: though themselves Shi'ite, they maintained allegiance to the Sunni caliph.) Moreover, says Muṭahhari, the revolts led by Babak, Maziyar, Sinbad, and Behafarid which were touted by twentieth-century Iranian nationalists were put down by Iranian troops loyal to Islam. (Again, this is a bit disingenuous: Babak, for instance, resisted repeated campaigns from Baghdad for twenty-five years: it would seem he must have had loyal troops as well as a loyal peasantry and artisanry to supply his army.)

Against the idea that Shi'ism is but Islamically coded Zoroastrianism:

Zealous Sunnis, such as the Egyptian Ahmad Amin, have from time to time attempted to portray Shi'ism as essentially a political party, only using Islam as a cover. Shaykh Muhammad Husain Kāshif al-Ghita, in his *Aṣl al-Shi'a wa Uṣūluha,* refuted such charges at length. Iranian nationalists—Parviz Sani'i, Pur Davoud, Muhammad Mo'in—as well as some Europeans—Gobineau, E. G. Browne—have from time to time suggested that Shi'ism has preserved Iranian culture, merely translating Zoroastrian concepts into Islamic form. They note such things as the hereditary and divinely inspired succession of the Imāms matching the old Iranian idea of the divine charisma of the kings (*farrah izadi*), the use in Persian poetry of images of the master of the Magi (*pir-e moghān*) or wine drinking as an image of wisdom, and the legend of the marriage of Shahrbanu, the daughter of the last Sassanian king, to Husain, the third Imām, thereby ideologically fusing for Iranians the charisma of the royal house of Iran with that of the divine line of Muhammad.

Muṭahhari pours scorn on these suggestions. First, the poetic imagery indicates nothing about nostalgia for Zoroastrianism: even Imām Ali's *Najh al-Balagha,* an unquestionably and thoroughly Islamic book, uses the metaphor of the wine of wisdom. Moreover, these nationalist authors never bother to count up the number of images that might derive from Judaism or Christianity to see if they do not outnumber and outweigh those from Zoroastrianism. As to the legend of Shahrbanu, if Iranians had been interested in the Sassanian royal house, why did they refuse to give Yazdigird III shelter as he was chased across Iran by the Muslim forces? Second, Shi'ism gives his daughter Shahrbanu no special status, certainly no more than any other wife or mother of an Imām. Such women came from all ranks: Nargis, the mother of the twelfth Imām, was a Roman slave. Third, the legend itself is of a most doubtful status: it can be found in Ya'qubi's history and in the ḥadīth collection of al-Kafi, but there are two unreliable links in the chain of narrators. It would seem the legend is a pure fabrication.

That Iranians might be concerned to preserve elements of their Zoroastrian past seems incredible to Muṭahhari. Here he allows his prejudice free reign, scorning not only the caste system of Sassanian Iran, but the religious symbols, theological metaphors, and rituals of Zoroastrianism. He ridicules as idolatry the allegorical symbols of God, as if God were conceived as having horns and wings, crown and walking stick. He denies vehemently that Satan in Islam is anything like Ahriman in Zoroastrianism, because the latter has a role in creation, while the former is merely a fallen angel. The Zoroastrian book of purity rules, the Vendidad, he dismisses as being a collection of superstitions about demons, with about the same sympathy as Shi'ite rules of purity were derisively received by American readers during the Islamic revolution of 1979. Of Zoroastrian rituals he asks, "Is there anything more superstitious?" He claims that Zoroaster had outlawed the use of the elixir hom, but that its use had been revived illegitimately by the Sassanian priesthood, and that similarly the Avesta was full of superstitious corruptions and additions to the original Gathas. Zoroastrianism became under the Sassanians such a corrupt state creed that there were widespread conversions to Christianity among the elite. The system was thus corrupt from top to bottom. At the bottom there was oppression; for example, he cites from Firdausi a story of blocked social mobility: a shoemaker saved the royal treasury, but was refused permission to allow his son to study to be a scribe. At the top, princes like the son of Khosrow Parviz slew their siblings and parents. While it is true that two women became Sassanian rulers, Purandokht and Azarmidokht, daughters of Khosrow Parviz, this was only because they were of royal seed and their brother had killed off all their male siblings. According to Muṭahhari, in the Zoroastrian system of unlimited polygamy and harems, women had no choice in marriage, had no property rights, and married their closest kin. He cites Imām al-Sadiq, who apparently gently admonished a Muslim for calling Zoroastrians bastards, because after all Zoroastrianism permitted incestuous marriages.[70] Indeed, he cites a ḥadīth from Sadūq's *al-Tawḥīd* that when the soldier Ash'ath ibn Qays al-Kindi asked Imām Ali why Zoroastrians were ever counted as People of the Book, Ali replied that once they had had a heavenly book, and a prophet, and next-of-kin marriage had been forbidden. But one night the king became drunk and lay with his daughter. The people turned from him, but he argued that Adam and Eve had been brother and sister, and so obviously God must have allowed such unions. Muṭahhari goes on to claim that discussions of such stories by jurists like Abu Hanifa who themselves were second-generation converts from Zoroastrianism lend credence to the existence of such practices. Islam, he says,

> took dualism, fire worshipping, hom worshipping, Sun worshipping, and man worshipping away from Iran, replacing them with monotheism and God worshipping. . . . Islam replaced the notion of a horned, winged, bearded and moustached god, who had a walking stick and a cloak on his shoulder, and had curly hair and crown, with the idea of one God beyond any imagination and analogy. . . . Islam abolished wife lending [*istilḥāq* marriage],[71] next-of-kin marriage, marriage by proxy, and the authority of man over women. (p. 470)

Not only did Islam oppose the debauchery (*lahw*), music (*ghina*), and voluptous living (*'ayyāshi*) of the Iranian nobility,[72] but it was Iranian Muslims who opposed such depravities when Iranian court styles were picked up by the easily seduced provincial Arabs. Muṭahhari suggests that this was one of the first bones of contention that the Shi'ite Imāms had against the Arab court life of early Islam.

In any case, even were there something worth preserving in pre-Islamic Iranian culture, the continuity between Zoroastrian Iran and Shi'ite Iran is not immediate or direct: until the Safavid Dynasty (sixteenth century A.H.), most Iranians were not Shi'ite, but Sunni. The appeal of Shi'ism for Iranians was essentially the same as that of Islam itself: the appeal of equality and justice. At each attempt of Sunni caliphs to impose Arab racial superiority or other inequities, Shi'ism became a banner of revolt in the name of true Islam. (Amusingly, Muṭahhari elsewhere, in *Jihād in the Qur'an,* even attempts to deny the continuity between the *jizya* tax and the Sassanian *gaziya,* insisting that the former derives linguistically from the Arabic *jaza,* "reward," and is God's reward for the services of protection that the Islamic polity performs for the minorities forced to pay the tax.)

Against the idea that Iranians became Muslims reluctantly:

The strongest part of Muṭahhari's brief is his vision of the creative synergy between Islam and Iranians. Islam, he says, gave Iran (1) unity of belief, where previously there had been a state religion and numerous different local religious units (including Christians, Sabeans, Jews, Mazdakites, Buddhists, Manicheans, etc.); (2) escape from becoming Christian and thereby escape from the dark ages of the Christian world; instead there was the brilliance of building the Islamic civilization which among other things preserved knowledge for the Christian world when it reemerged from its dark ages; (3) a world stage for release of Iranian energies and talents. Iranians became the leading jurists, administrators, and scholars throughout the Islamic world from Andalusia to India. The history is quite the reverse of that assumed by those who would see the first two centuries of Islamic Iran as a period of stagnation, until nationalism revived, and New Persian came into being as a vehicle for that nationalism. Persian became a major vehicle of Islam; Iranians created most of their artistic and scholarly masterpieces in the service of Islam. Muṭahhari cites the famous story that Hisham ibn Abd al-Malik (r. 724–43 C.E.) asked who the leading scholar was in each of the following places, and if he was Arab or *mawla* (attached client, in this context "Iranian"): Medina, Mecca, Yemen, Yamama, Damascus, Jazira, Khorasan, Basra, and Kufa. In each case, except the last, the answer was an Iranian.[73] All ten basic collections of ḥadīth, the six of the Sunnis as well as the four of the Shi'ites, were compiled by Iranians: six from Khorasan, one from Qum, and one from Qazvin.[74] Two of the founders of the four extant Sunni schools of law were Iranians from Khorasan.[75] Four of the seven "original" reciters of the Qur'an (*al-Qurrā al-Sab'a*) are Iranian; two of these are Shi'ite, and two of the three non-Iranians are Shi'ite.[76]

Region by region, Muṭahhari recounts how Iranians were central to the spread of Islam and the administration of Muslim states. (He draws here upon the volume edited by Kenneth Morgan.)[77] The Abbasids came to power in Baghdad thanks to a movement from Khorasan, and they appointed Khorasanis to govern North Africa and Spain.[78] They were accompanied by Khorasani judges, scholars, and army officers. Ghenghiz Khan sent Iranian craftsmen and scholars to China so that Persian became the lingua franca of Islam there. In Southeast Asia and East Africa, Islam was spread by sailors and merchants from Fars in southern Iran. Kashmir was converted by the Iranian Shah Mirza in the eighth century A.H. In India, the Ghaznavids, who first brought Islam to India, are usually said to be Turks, but in some accounts they are said to descend from the Sassanians;[79] the founder of the largest Sufi order in India was an Iranian,[80] and was one of a number of Iranians at the Ghuri court in Delhi;[81] the Teymurid dynasty founded by Babir, grandson of Tamerlane, employed many Iranians at court, including I'timād al-Dawla Mirza Ghiyāth Beg, a former governor of Marv under the Safavid Shah Tahmasp, who came to serve Akbar, whose daughter married Jehangir, and whose granddaughter married Shah Jehan;[82] the Taj Mahal is the grave of the Iranian Shi'ite Mumtaz Mahal. Shi'ism was promoted in India by Iranians: the kings of Oudh were Shi'ites descended from S. Muhammad Nishapuri, and their court in Lucknow attracted an influx of Khorasanis; the Shi'ite king of Bijapur in the south, Yusuf 'Ādilshah (r. 1489–1511) came from Saveh; and so on.

That the generations and genius of Iranian scholarship created Islamic civilization:

At the end of Muṭahhari's brief, he provides lists of Iranian and Shi'ite writers of *tafsīr,* compilers of ḥadīth, jurisconsults (*fuqahā*), theologians (*mutakallimūn*), philosophers, and mystics. These lists are intended to demonstrate not only the overwhelming contributions of Iranians to the development of Islam, but more importantly to demonstrate the unbroken chains of authority in each of these fields. The lists of writers of *tafsīr,* compilers of ḥadīth, and theologians are unsystematic and incomplete, meant merely to illustrate some of the significant figures. The list of *fuqahā* is both more complete and more important: it relates directly to the debates over the leadership of the Shi'ite community, which became a practical political issue at the time of the Islamic revolution (see chapter 2). Muṭahhari's list may be compared with the list compiled by S. Aḥmad Ishkavari (the librarian mentioned in chapter 1).[83] Ishkavari's list belongs to those attempts that credit one *faqīh* with being the supreme interpretative authority at any given time: the notion of a single *marja' taqlīd* (source of imitation). Muṭahhari lists overlapping leaderships, giving credence to the idea that there are several *marja' taqlīd* at any given time. The notion of formalizing a collective leadership, or a division of tasks among the leading *fuqahā,* was debated after the death of Āyatullāh Borujerdi in 1961, a debate to which Muṭahhari contributed.[84] After the Islamic revolution, Āyatullāh Khomeini ruthlessly suppressed all dissent and opposition from other religious leaders and *marja' taqlīd,*[85] despite the fact that his own *Risāla towzīḥ al-masa'il* says that no *faqīh* is superior to another.

The lists of philosophers and mystics are even more interesting. He says that the contribution of Iranians to Islamic philosophy is greater than to any other subject, that the majority of Muslim philosophers are both Iranian and Shi'ite, and even the non-Shi'ite philosophers have Shi'ite tendencies. Especially northern Iran (Gilān, Māzandarān, and Gorgān) has produced philosophers, and since the Safavids, Islamic philosophy has been almost exclusively Iranian and Shi'ite. He systematically lists the major figures in thirty-three generations, and thereby provides an outline of the development of Islamic philosophy from his perspective. Islamic philosophy begins with a period of translation from the Greek in the third and fourth centuries A.H.: the translators he says were mainly Jewish, Christian, and Sabean. Practically no Muslims nor Zoroastrians were translators. But those with independent thoughts of their own were Muslim. Shades of Judaicizing anxiety (see chapter 1) appear here.

The first Muslim philosopher is Abū Ya'qūb ibn Isḥāq al-Kindi (177–260/796–873). Now, many have thought because of his name that this father of Jacob son of Isaac al-Kindi must be of Jewish descent, and there are even some traditions that claim he intended to write a refutation of the Qur'an. But these traditions, says Muṭahhari, are fabricated ones, and the attribution of Jewish descent and intent to refute Islam are slurs due to jealousy. He was a pure Arab, and probably a Shi'ite. He attempted to harmonize philosophy and Islam, but where they were contradictory, he always sided with Islam, as in his support for the dogma of resurrection.

From the fourth to seventh centuries, most philosophers were also physicians. They included Muslims, Jews, and Christians, but by this time Sabeans have dropped out, and none of the Jews or Christians can be ranked as great philosophers. (Muṭahhari does list in his fourth generation the Christian logician Yaḥyā ibn 'Adī Manṭiqī Naṣrānī [d. 364]; perhaps he considers him merely a logician and not a creative philosopher.) For instance, Muṭahhari says, the Christian, Abu al-Faraj ibn al-Ṭayyib, in the sixth generation, is much admired by his contemporary Ibn Sinā as a physician, but not as a philosopher. Abu al-Barakat Baghdadi, an independent minded Jew, and Hasan ibn Suwār, a Christian, might be counted as exceptions, but they both became Muslim. There are no Zoroastrian philosophers, physicians, or mathematicians, with two or three possible partial exceptions: Abu al-Hasan Bahmanyār ibn Marzubān (d. 458/1065) of Azarbaijan was a philosopher and Ibn Sina's best student, but he converted to Islam; Ibn Miskawayh (or his father) was a convert from Zoroastrianism; and Ali ibn Abbas Ahwāzi, "Ibn al-Majūsi," a physician of great repute, may possibly originally have been Zoroastrian or his ancestors were, but he also was a Muslim. (There is also in the fifth generation Abu Sulayman Muhammad ibn Tāhir ibn Bahrām Sajistani, from the name at least, a grandson or son of a convert from Zoroastrianism.)

This delicate sifting out of Muslims, and among them Iranians and Shi'ites, and among these the more creative versus those who merely are links in the chain of transmission, is systematically pursued. For all its tendentiousness in terms of Gellner's "precise doctrines," Muṭahhari superbly displays the discourse structure of a vision of Islam that appeals powerfully to Shi'ite Iranians. It is a discursive system that makes Iran central to Islam, transcending the sectarian claims of Shi'ism, while at the same time supporting those claims, and displacing efforts to separate out an Iranian historical identity apart from Islam. It is a discursive system that attempts to block the seduction of hegemonic ideologies of the superpowers (American modernism, Soviet marxism) that would devalue Iran and Islam as backward, as needing tutelage (educational, political, economic) in order to emerge as (perennially dependent) actors in the modern world. And it provides a context in which the Pahlavi elites' Persian nationalist ideology seems not merely tawdry and artificial, but coherent only as a form of yielding to the idea of subaltern nations that need to be coordinated by the global industrial economy of the West or the marxist empire of the North: defender of oil resources, regional garrison state to keep the peace on behalf of the oil economy. As a compromise formation between conflicting elements in Iranian historical identities, it grounds its Islamic accent not on a vision of victimization, but on one of achievement and accomplishment; it appeals to pride and self-dignity. In terms of nation-building functionality, this ideology has had the effect of marginalizing or forcing abroad the middle and upper classes who supported a more Persian nationalist interpretation of Iranian history, and it has provided ideological grounds for the Iran-Iraq war beyond defense of territorial integrity or defense against the Baathist gesture at destroying the revolution. It is too soon to be able to evaluate such functionality: the reorganization of the labor force, stratification system, and distribution of wealth, and the political economy in general, are all still very much open to question both in parliamentary legislation and in actual social reality, even if it appears that it is the petit bourgeois classes that seem to have gained the most by the revolution so far.

Shari'ati's *Return to Self:* Alienation and Authenticity as Work on Myth

> . . . in my opinion, this is not Islamics. At best we might call it poeticizing Islam (*Islām-sorāii, Islam-shāéri*) . . . it is beautifully composed, but it is fermented more from socialism, communism, historical materialism, and existentialism than from Islam.
>
> —Murtada Muṭahhari on Shari'ati's "*Jehanbīnī tawḥidī*"[86]

> [Contemporary threats of alienation through Westoxification] are not like those of the past, from savage ethnic groups lacking culture, such as the Macedonians, the Arabs, the Mongols, the Ghuzz, the Turks, and the Tartars. The enemy-digesting power of our nation . . . turned these floods into nothing in the midst of its own ocean; first it got rid of their polluting colors and odors, and then it annihilated them.
>
> —Ali Shari'ati, *Return to Self*

If Muṭahhari built his argument around a principled rejection of nationalism so as to be able to build a case for political mobilization around Islam, Shari'ati builds his argument around the more neutral notion of alienation so as to be able to evaluate and reconstruct both nationalism and Islam. Both Muṭahhari and Shari'ati are concerned to construct a discursive system that can protect their compatriots against the ravages of colonialism and imperialism. Muṭahhari deconstructs colonialist forms of nationalism, as ideologies that work through attribution of virtue to colonialists (sometimes racially, sometimes culturally, but usually in a way that stresses such an essentiality of difference it might as well be genetic) and through the divide and rule attribution of difference among the subalterns (again often posed in tribal, racial, or essentialist cultural terms). Muṭahhari's vision of Islam as a discursive system that can counter this sort of imperialist ideology stresses, in contrast, the cultural constructiveness of identity, and the powerful role that Iranians have played in the past and can play again. However, it is still bounded by traditional scholasticism, grounded upon traditional metaphysics of unquestionable faith, and it calls for a return to Islam in which might be called a romantic or nostalgic conception of authenticity.

Shari'ati dismisses Muṭahhari's understanding of the threats of imperialism as archaic. The challenges of modern global technological and information-based society, powered by a market capitalism that uses advertising and manipulation of psychological desire, are on a scale and of a subtlety that require a major rethinking of Iranian cultural resources so as to respond creatively to the new civilization and become an active participant and not a self-isolating enclave. Shari'ati sketches an oscillating model of periods of relative cultural alienation succeeded by periods of reintegration, "return to self," and reconstruction of an authenticity that incorporates what has been received or learned from others. Shari'ati also calls for a return to Islam, but not the Islam of Muṭahhari: by contrasting original Islam, corrupt traditional Shi'ism, and modern religion, Shari'ati provides grounds for a critique and reconstruction of Islam and Shi'ism. Shari'ati was tremendously impressed with the Algerian revolution and with the degree to which Islam generally has provided the cultural resources for relative protection against the kind of colonial penetration that Africa south of the Sahel had suffered. Such cultural resources, however, were not simply a clinging to traditional Islam, but the use of Islam to recreate contemporary ideologies. Modern religion for Shari'ati is a metascientific vision of the sort invoked by Radhakrishnan, Albert Einstein, Karl Jaspers, and Max Planck. It is to be sharply distinguished from the dogmas and intersectarian rivalries of traditional religion. Shari'ati repeatedly attacked the traditionalist clergy and called upon the young generation, a new literate generation that could read the old texts for themselves and think for themselves, to help him reconstruct Shi'ism.

The attack on Muṭahhari's *Mutual Services of Islam and Iran* is subtle, but entirely within character. As befits an era when Shari'ati and Muṭahhari were competing for overlapping constituencies, particularly among the youth, yet were tactical allies against the shah, Shari'ati does not name Muṭahhari. Instead, his *Return to Self* begins with almost identical sentences as Muṭahhari's *Mutual Services,* and follows the argument of the latter closely, as if presenting a corrected version, taking Muṭahhari's sentences, theses, and examples, and rewriting them. This intertextuality works powerfully in Persian, and is well attuned to the circulation of oral arguments, not stigmatizing a text or author by name so it/he will not be read, but placing the arguments in a new light, so that the names and stories from the past are reinforced but their meanings are differently inflected.

Both Muṭahhari and Shari'ati begin with sentences acknowledging that the history of every nation contains strands of creative growth as well as negative moments and directions. For Muṭahhari, such negative moments and directions are those of nationalism: both Arab racism pretending to be Islam and anti-Islamic, Iranian nationalism. Shari'ati, in contrast, lists a series of seven sources of alienation that have historically affected Iran, in order to introduce both different valuations of the past and a very different conception of alienation, one that is less absolute and that poses instead questions of gaining mastery over new ideas. In passing, he also ridicules and inverts Muṭahhari's philological-diagnostic observations about the Persian word *millat* ("nation"): the use of *millat* is not, as our *mullā nuqaṭis* ("nitpicking mullās") suggest, an etymological mistake or an imprecise translation. On the contrary, Iranian intellectuals knew exactly what they were doing when they emphasized the cultural foundations of nationalism rather than racial or ethnic ones. True, the Western term *nation* has a root meaning *birth,* and so perhaps can mislead in racist directions; but the Arabic *sha'b* ("branch") means merely formal division, and the Persian *millat,* borrowed from the Qur'an, means common culture, not blood, kinship, or birth. *Millat* is neither just a derivative of a Qur'anic usage nor just a translation of a Western idea, but refers to a cultural spirit, esprit de corps, which if kept properly authentic can respond to and control sources of potential alienation.

The initial sources of alienation that periodically affected Iran are that (1) Iran is a geographical crossroads so that repeated invasions could tear apart the cultural fabric; (2) Iran is surrounded by world religions and civilizations so that outside influences at times could be overwhelming; (3) extreme class divisions grew periodically, e.g., in the Sassanian period and in the medieval Islamic period, and this growth led to social discord; (4) Iran was governed repeatedly by alien rulers in whose interest it was to weaken national sentiment (Seleucids, Arabs, Ghuzzes, Ghaznavids, Seljuks, Mongols); (5) Islam was used ideologically to cut off Iranians from their pre-Islamic heritage and to effect submission to others (Umayyids, Abbasids, Ghaznavids); (6) marxist, communist, class universalist ideologies attempted, less successfully, to subordinate Iran and the Islamic world in favor of the Soviet Union; and (7) the cultural imperialism of Europe and America, which poses as the bearer of universal rationality, devalued Iranian culture as being merely traditional and historical. Note, with respect to the fourth of these, that while Muṭahhari claimed the Ghaznavids were both Iranian (descended from the Sassanians) and proper Muslims (having taken Islam to India), Shari'ati invokes the more usual Iranian sentiments about the Turkic Ghaznavids. He cites Mahmud of Ghazni's scorn for Firdausi's *Shāhnāmeh,* the national epic of Iran, and Firdausi's famous reply. Mahmud refused to pay Firdausi for the epic, saying, "There is nothing in the poem but stories of warriors like Rustam, and there are many such warriors in my own army." Firdausi replied, "No mother ever gave birth to anyone like Rustam," meaning, of course, not only that Mahmud was affronting the national dignity of his Iranian subjects, but that he was an uncultured lout who could not distinguish between the literal vehicle and the allegorical meaning of a metaphor; Rustam is a mythos, a figuration of heroism, not just a champion (*pahlavān*).

Alienation, Shari'ati explains to his Iranian audience, is rather like what in folk belief is called the madness or possession by a *jinn* or *dīv* (Arabic *majnūn,* "being possessed by a *jinn*"; Persian *divānegi* "craziness" due to a *dīv* or demon); i.e., something invades the body or mind and usurps control. Shari'ati reviews the various kinds of alienation that European theorists have described: Hegel's alienation of conscious reason from absolute ideas recovered through the dialectical movement of history; Feuerbach's alienation of human beings from human responsibility by attributing to God all power and knowledge; the socialists' alienation of people from community through subordination of their other motives to the increasing need for money; Marx's alienation of workers from the product of their labor by subordination to machine production; Heidegger's alienation of men from nature through an ever expanding technological mentality, turning all of nature into merely calculable standing reserves; Sartre's alienation of people's desires through words. Shari'ati domesticates some of this for his audience, comparing Feuerbach's ideas with the notions of Sufis like Mansur al-Hallaj (merging of the self with the divine), the *ḥulūliya* (God or a hero figure has taken the place of the "I"), and Majnun possessed by love for Layla ("if you apply bloodletting to me, I fear you may slice into Layla's jugular"). Shari'ati elaborates by reminding the reader of the polar kinds of alienation Islam has always tried to avoid: mortifiying the flesh or desire; and forgetting man's origin in the divine spark. Mortification is the sin of changing one's creation; Islam permits enjoyment of life: "Who has forbidden the beautiful gifts of God?" (Qur'an 7:32). Equally sinful, however, is permitting only the material side of man to flourish, forgetting the divine essence from which man has fallen and to which he will return. This is the meaning of the Islamic notions of *raj'at* (return), the idiom of *dhikr* (remembrance, reminding), the use of *ḥikmat* (wisdom, Indian *vidya,* ancient Iranian *sepantā mainū*), and the discipline of *taqwā* ("piety" in the sense of self-discipline). Cultural or national alienation in the modern world, then, is due to those ideologies that attempted to be substitutes for religion: capitalism and communism both err on the side of giving attention only to the worldly, of therefore promising what are but mirages of salvation. Indeed, although promising the lifting of oppression, capitalism is built upon the exploitation of labor, of industrial reserve labor, and of the colonized. Communism similarly is built upon the concentration of power in the hands of dictators.

What is needed is a return, on the one hand, to religion, not à la Muṭahhari, to the old, but to a new, metascientific vision that builds upon and provides transcendent speculative and moral grounds for scientific knowledge. In the same way, what is needed, on the other hand, is a return to authentic nationalism, not à la Muṭahhari in the sense of racial or ethnocentric chauvinism, but in the sense of an evolving, synthesizing, integrative culture. And here Shari'ati defines Iranian culture as a particular historical formation that has always combined elements of East and West: Eastern inspiration, anxiety toward the unseen (*ghayb*), and Western analytic, rational, calculative logic. Islam is closer to Hellenism than to India, for example, in its disciplines of *uṣūl* (principles of jurisprudence), *kalām* (theology), and *ḥikmat* (philosophy); and it is no accident that the Iranian Ibn Sina (Avicenna) and the Andalusian Ibn Rushd (Averroës) were vehicles of Greek thought for Renaissance Europe. Yet Rumi, the author of the "Persian Qur'an" (*Qur'ān-e 'Ajam*), the *Masnavī*, teaches illuminationist (*ishrāqi*) philosophy, a kind of philosophy that draws equally upon rationalism and mysticism. Iranian culture at all levels strengthens itself with such transcendent bonds: martial and athletic champions or heroes (*pahlavān*) are associated with purity of virtue and faith; guilds are associated with sufism; neighborhood strongmen and Robin Hood bandits are associated with mysticism. Rustam is the figure par excellence of such bonds and associations, and it is precisely the incomprehension of such spiritual meaning that makes Mahmud of Ghazni external to, and an oppressive ruler for, the Iranian nation.

Shari'ati goes on to argue—it is his turn to be a bit tendentious—that it is this sense of nationality that not only prevents such nominalizing idiocies as insisting that the French actor Robert Husain must be counted as an Iranian, or Rumi an Arab because descended from Abu Bakr, but also accounts for the fact that Jews have always lived peacefully in Islamic lands and produced no Zionists there. Zionism is a reaction to the anti-Semitism which began among the Romans, was developed by Christianity, and reached its apotheosis in fascism. Thus, contrast Caesar, who caused the diaspora of Jews from Palestine, with Cyrus the Great who is praised both in the Book of Daniel ("a ram with two horns will arise from the east and save the Israelite captives from the claws of Babylon") and in the Qur'an as *Dhu al-Qarnayn* ("the two-horned"; see Qur'an 18:83, 86, 94).

This passage was guaranteed to enrage the Shi'ite clergy by praising

Cyrus, a non-Muslim and, worse, the ancient emperor claimed by the shah as the founder of the imperial tradition to which he was heir. Moreover, it introduces an argument in favor of nationalism as opposed to the internationalism that Muṭahhari claimed for Islam. Internationalisms, historically, says Shari'ati, have come in three forms, all disastrous: religious, humanist, and class internationalisms. Christianity is the most egregious example of religious internationalism: no power, he says, has shed more blood than Christianity, a religion claiming Latin as the language of God, inauthentic to either the language of Jesus or the language of the Bible. It was national movements in Europe that finally halted the religious wars, and that worked together with the Renaissance recovery of science to establish European civilization. Islamic internationalism has had similar problems, although Islam itself has never been opposed to nationalisms within it. Muhammad made contracts with tribes who joined the *umma:* to each tribe he sent two representatives, one a Companion of the Prophet to represent the correct interpretations of the new faith, the other a leader of the tribe itself. The idea, says Shari'ati, was to invite groups to share in the *umma,* not to repress nationality.

If religious internationalisms have been disastrous, so have humanist and class internationalisms. Humanists such as Bertrand Russell have argued that natural resources should belong to the human species at large; in practice this would mean that oil should not belong to those who happen to live on the land containing petroleum deposits. Class internationalism effectively has meant support of imperialism: the working classes both in Europe and in the colonies have supported the empire because it meant jobs. Marxism has been no better, viewing nationalist revolutions as pseudorevolutions because they generate unity across classes, blocking proletarian internationalism, and because they do not necessarily generate a change in internal class relations.

But, in fact, nationalist movements proved to be the only mechanism for opposing colonialism and imperialism, e.g., in Algeria and Vietnam. Moreover, if one looks at history, one can see an oscillation between periods of alienation and periods of nationalist authenticity. The latter are healthy periods of borrowing, whereas periods of turning inward and isolation are periods of decline. For Shari'ati, then, the sixteenth-century Safavid Empire is not, as it is for Muṭahhari, a period of glory and of the triumph of Shi'ism, but rather it is one of decline into dogmatism, sectarianism, stifling of scholarship into mere commentary writing, and inauthenticity. Hence, Shari'ati's categorical distinction between Safavid Shi'ism, the label he uses for dogmatic, sectarian, corrupt Islam, and Alavi Shi'ism.[87] Until the Safavids, Iran was the heart of the Islamic world and Persian spread as the language of cultivation: Persian poetry was recited in the Ottoman court, Persian was the official court language of India, and Persian street names were applied in Zanzibar. Shari'ati draws an analogy with Muslims in British India: priding themselves as the former rulers of India, Muslims refused to send their children to British schools, and so Hindus positioned themselves to become the new rulers of India.

Shari'ati's vision of Iranian history looks quite different from Muṭahhari's. Muṭahhari dismisses all of pre-Islamic Iranian history as caste ridden and idolatrous, a divisive conglomeration of confessional groups, and therefore spiritually weak, open to inroads by Christianity and Buddhism. Shari'ati, by contrast, sees the Sassanian Empire as a positive return to Iranian authenticity after a period of Hellenization and inauthenticity under the Parthian Ashkanian dynasty. The Parthians, says Shari'ati, did not rely on Zoroastrianism, but imitated Greek culture. The Sassanians rallied the three elite strata of Iranian society, claiming descent from a chief priest of the Istakhr fire temple, and reestablished Zoroastrianism and Iranian self-confidence. The Abbasids similarly, says Shari'ati, were Hellenized and devalued the scholarship of the Family of the Prophet, thus fostering an underground opposition under Shi'ite auspices.

Shari'ati classifies the series of oscillations between cultural alienation and return to authenticity in three movements: Hellenization (*yūnān-zadegi*), Arabization (*'arab-zadegi*), and Westernization or Wextoxification (*gharb-zadegī*).[88] Pursuing Muṭahhari's concern with disentangling Islam and Arabization, Shari'ati elaborates on Muṭahhari's example of Abū-Ḥanīfa, the founder of the Hanafi school of Sunni jurisprudence, and the *shu'ūbiyya* movement as a correction of the kind of alienation represented by Abū-Ḥanīfa. Abū-Ḥanīfa was an Iranian, yet he issued a legal opinion interpreting the rules of *kufuw* (social equality) in marriage, that Arabs are more noble than *'ajam* (Iranians), and thus while Arab men may marry Iranian women, Persian men may not marry Arab women. Muṭahhari cites this as a conundrum, claiming Abū-Ḥanīfa as an example of the genius and leadership Iranians gave to Islam, but also an example of one fallen into the errors of Arab racist nationalism.[89] Muṭahhari is concerned only to present the *shu'ubiyya* movement of Persian literary and political-religious resistance to Arabization as itself Islamic: its name comes from the Qur'anic (49:13) assertion of equality of all nations under Islam, and rejection of Arab superiority (*faḍīlat*). Shari'ati, however, insists on preserving a more differentiated view and recognizing the Persian cultural component being defended. The *shu'ūbiyya* prepared the ground for the revolts of Abu-Muslim, the Ustādhis, Bābak, and later the dynasties of the Saminids, Tahirids, and Safarids, and for the literary movement of Rūdaki, Daqīqī, and Firdausi that created New Persian. Shari'ati thus argues that a characteristic defense mechanism against alienation was established, consisting of external accommodation and an interior authenticity. He illustrates this both in his account of cultural politics and in his account of the importance of the linguistic development of New Persian.

The Abbasids were brought to power on the backs of an Iranian movement, making their capital, Baghdad (a Persian name), on the site of the Sassanian capital, Ctsesiphon. Their dynastic name came from the Bani-Abbas branch of the Prophet's family, in whose name they chose to mobilize against the Umayyids after they were unable to gain the support of Imām Ja'far al-Sādiq.[90] Once in power, fearing the influence of the Iranians who brought them to power, they killed Abu-Muslim, the military architect of their victory. But even at the height of their influence under the caliph Harun ar-Rashid, real power lay in the hands of Iranian families like the Nowbakhti, Baramki, and Al-e Sarakhs, who while working for the Abbasids also opened the way for the influence of Iranian culture.[91] Revolts against the Abbasids, often in the name of revenge for Abu-Muslim, led to regional dynasties who dealt externally with the Arab caliphs, but internally represented an Iranian response. A similar pattern also characterized the stratification system: sufism was the vehicle of elite, intellectual, and urban resistance; Shi'ism became the vehicle of peasant resistance. Here, again, Shari'ati challenges Muṭahhari's interpretation of the accusations of *zindīq,*[92] *majūs* (Magi, Zoroastrian), and *mazdaki* (Mazdakite) that were used as political weapons against pious Muslim Iranians who disagreed with the political or clerical authorities, especially mystics and those engaged in the rational sciences. Abū-Ḥanīfa, Muṭahhari notes, was one of those jurists who refused to accept the repentance (*tawba*) of *zindīq*s, while other jurists treated their repentance in the same way as they would the repentance of an apostate (*murtadd*). Muṭahhari is only concerned to insist that these accusatory labels do not mean that Iranians were reverting to the pre-Islamic religions of Zoroastrianism, Manicheanism, or Mazdakism. Shari'ati, by contrast, sees them as indices of the authentic national spirit of Iranian culture, and notes that Shi'ites later were sometimes called Mazdakites by Khwāja Niẓām ul-Mulk (d. 485/1092) and Shahristāni (d. 548/1153) because Mazdakite (Khorramdin) and Surkh-'Alam (Babaki) resistance had been based in rural areas just as were the Shi'ite resistances in their day. Such movements of resistance are important reminders to Shari'ati not only of healthy undercurrents of Persian national spirit, even in times of apparent hegemony by external political forces, but also of class-linked egalitarian consciousness. Zaydite, Qaramathian, Isma'ili, Sarbedar, and Safavid movements were all initially rural based. The Sarbedar revolt was the first major resistance to the Mongols, and the Safavids who were to establish Shi'ism as the state religion of Iran also began as a rurally based Sufi order.

The story of the role of the Persian language parallels and reinforces this differentiated political-cultural picture. Muṭahhari, again, is concerned only to show that revival of New Persian cannot be seen as anti-Islamic, since it became a major vehicle for the dissemination and elaboration of Islam. But Shari'ati insists, first, on the role New Persian played in protecting against alienation both to the Turkic speaking courts of Mahmud of Ghazni and later Turkic rulers of Iran and to the Arab caliphates. Firdausi's *Shāhnāmeh,* written in this New Persian, was a poetic codification of the national legends preserved by the gentry from pre-Islamic times. Firdausi ends with a rousing affirmation of Shi'ism;[93] but more importantly, the power of the language of New Persian was so strong that Mahmud of Ghazni sent poets ahead of his army to the ancient city of Rayy to recite in Persian, to assure the people that he was not a barbarian, to attempt to reassure them about his rule. This power of the literary energy released by New Persian leads Shari'ati to a second argument: that had the translations into Persian, sponsored by the Samanids, which began with the Qur'an, the Tafsir of Tabari, and the history of Tabari, continued, there might never have developed the hierarchical structure of Islam in Iran that allowed the clerics to claim exclusive control over authoritative knowledge and allowed another class of *mas'aleh-gū* (explainers)[94] to mediate between the clerics and the people.

In sum, Shari'ati made a three-pronged attack: First, he attacked the Shi'ite clergy as obscurantist, parallel to the mobeds or priests of the Sassanian period, an attack that was a continuing source of anger to the clergy. Second, he asserted that contemporary conditions of literacy among the Iranian youth provided the grounds for by-passing the clergy and making Islam a modern faith. Third, he argued that contemporary threats of alienation were of a scale and subtlety that made arguments like Muṭahhari's at best irrelevant and at worst dangerously close to encouraging self-defeating separatism. The translation of *gharb-zadegī,* Westoxification, plays up the metaphors of poisoning used by Iranians from religious folk like Khomeini to secular leftists like Jalal Al-e

Ahmad. Shari'ati prefers to use the language of "assimilation," "alienation," and "authenticity" derived from Sartre, especially from Sartre's vivid introduction of Frantz Fanon's *The Wretched of the Earth,* where the assimilé is described as being the brightest student taken to the métropole, there emptied of all indigenous ideas, and refilled with French ones, then posted back to the colonies as a seed for the demands and desires needed for the expansion of the metropole's market. Shari'ati in a number of places talks about the role of cosmetics to hook women into the market, the use of sex in advertising, and the manipulation of desire as key mechanisms of contemporary alienation. Shari'ati, in striking contrast to Muṭahhari and most other writers of this period, filled his discourse with French terms and references to European theorists. In part, this may have been self-aggrandizing claims to universal erudition, or a hook to dazzle and seduce young students, but it also had a more serious function of domesticating, mastering, and turning to local use the reigning vocabularies and discourses of the "first world." Shari'ati, while never apologizing for his usage of these foreign terms, did point out that they had perfectly good Persian equivalents, e.g., *jenzadegi* or *az khod bigānegi* for "alienation," and *tashabbuh*[95] for "assimilation."

Rethinking Islamic (Post)Modernism: Shari'ati's Bioglyph (1933–77)

> I do not mean to say . . . that a revolution must devour its children. But . . . [the] struggle with the external foe resulted in victory, whereas the struggle with the internal foe ended in defeat. These foes, described in Islamic terminology, in the language of the Qur'an, as "hypocrites" [*munāfiqīn*] are considered more base and dangerous than the kāfir or even the polytheist. The Prophet is thus the manifestation of victory on the foreign front, over *kufr* and polytheism, while Ali is the manifestation of Islamic defeat within the ranks at the hands of hypocrisy.
>
> —Ali Shari'ati, "Shahādat"[96]

By 1972, Dr. Ali Shari'ati had become by far the most popular of the intellectuals in the opposition to the shah. The hostility between him and the traditional clergy had served the purposes of the monarchy, dividing the opposition; but now the hostility had become so marked that activist clerics appealed to Shari'ati's father to ask him to moderate his tone, lest there be an explosion or open conflict that would invite the security forces to intervene more directly. Shaykh Muhammad Taqi Shari'ati, himself a well-known religious activist, wrote his son an open letter, and Ali Shari'ati replied, saying that a movement was emerging that could not be stemmed. In 1973 the state closed the Husainiyyeh Irshad, Shari'ati's institutional base, and arrested a number of its associates, including Shari'ati's father. Ali Shari'ati himself escaped into hiding, but when he realized that his hiding place had been discovered, and moreover that there was a plot against his life, he offered to give himself up in exchange for the release of his father. This was done, and Shari'ati spent eighteen months in jail. After his release, in March 1975, Shari'ati's movements were constrained, and though he continued to write and speak, it was now mainly to small groups, and his lectures were often taped for later dissemination. In 1976 he was still able to appear at a public panel discussion on 11 Muharram with Murtaḍā Muṭahhari, Fakhroddin Hejāzi, and Ali Khameneii. In May 1977 he left Iran for London, saying in a letter to his son, in which he asked him to inquire about the possibility of getting a U.S. visa, that his life seemed to have divided itself into five-year periods, and that a new period was now beginning. Presumably, this would have been a period of organizing and propagandizing from the West. But on 19 June 1977, he was found dead. The British autopsy report states it was a heart attack; many Iranians suspect foul play on the part of SAVAK, the Iranian secret police, or at least suspect that the death stemmed from a weakened condition incurred during his imprisonment.

When the revolution of 1977–79 came, Shari'ati's portrait was prominent in the demonstrations of those tumultuous fourteen months. Graves of those killed in the demonstrations were often inscribed with one of his slogans: *shahīd qalb-e tārīkh ast* (martyrdom/ witnessing is the heart of history).[97] During the revolution, his followers tended to connect him and Khomeini; their portraits were carried together, and often adorned political meetings. It was not unusual, for instance, that when Shahriyar Rowhani, a son-in-law of Dr. Ibrahim Yazdi, spoke to the 1977 Convention of Muslim Associations in Oklahoma City, he pointed to the two portraits and shouted Shari'ati's slogan: *har enqelāb do chehreh dārad, khūn va payām* ("every revolution has two components: blood and message"),[98] Khomeini representing the latter since Shari'ati had been martyred. Yazdi represents a significant nexus here: he was an associate of Mehdi Bazargan, a founder of Iranian Muslim student associations in North America, a founder of the Houston Mosque (see chapter 4), and would shortly become, first, a key translator and organizer for Khomeini in Paris (sitting at his side in most interviews with Western journalists) and, then, the foreign minister of the provisional government under Mehdi Bazargan when the revolution succeeded. When Shari'ati died in 1977, Yazdi sent a telegram of condolence in the name of the Muslim students of North America to Khomeini, then still in Najaf, Iraq. Khomeini acknowledged receiving the telegram, sent back regards to the students, but pointedly omitted any reference to Shari'ati or his death.

Yazdi understood the necessity of Shari'ati to the revolutionary movement. Without Shari'ati, the appeal of Khomeini would be blunted. For many students to whom Shari'ati was a teacher and inspiration, Khomeini was just a traditional mullā, slightly better than most only because he was willing to be politically active against the shah. Yazdi and the students assumed that Khomeini could be used to mobilize the masses, but that they, the heirs of Shari'ati and the generation of the future, would be able to put Khomeini back in his place once the revolution succeeded. The calculation on the part of Khomeini's former students—Muṭahhari, Montazeri, Beheshti, Khameneii, Bahonar, et al.—was just the reverse, and they proved to be correct. After the revolution, a series of *fatwā*s by various *mujtahid*s, including Khomeini, were issued condemning Shari'ati.

Shari'ati represents a very different sociological phenomenon than Muṭahhari. Although both came from clerical families of Khorasan, and although Muṭahhari received some modern education at the University of Tehran and educated himself by reading widely in Western sources, his primary ideological formation came from experiences within the traditional scholastic system, while Shari'ati represented the new generation fully raised in modern schools, albeit from traditional families, and was painfully aware that such schooling might lead only to a subordinate place in a global economy and cultural system centered in Europe and America. Shari'ati saw himself forging a path between two dead ends: traditionalism on the one hand, and modernism on the other hand. To simply become "modernized" in the sense of accepting values from the outside was to accept subordination. The task was to forge a new position which would be modern in all the capacities needed for handling modern technologies, without losing one's own culture and sense of identity.

To do this, Shari'ati not only called for a reworking of his generation's understanding of Islam, and for a modern religion based upon, and transcending, science in the manner of the religious feelings expressed by Einstein (or indeed Durkheim, who articulated very similar descriptions of the religion of the future), but also, and much more impressively, created a vocabulary with which to think, with which to critique the past, and with which to reconceptualize Islam for the future. Muṭahhari is correct: part of Shari'ati's appeal is poetic.

Shari'ati's life can be divided into three periods: the formative period before he left for education in Europe; the Paris years; and the return to Iran when he galvanized the youth. In the first period, three themes are most important: the activist and religious background of his family; the use of the romantic genre of *keviriyat* (desert purity) to think about what is worthwhile and what is corrupt in modern life; and the involvement with the *Khodā-parastān-e socialist* (God-worshipping socialist) underground movement in the World War II and Mosaddeq periods.

Shari'ati rarely mentioned his maternal family, a landowning family, except to dedicate to his mother his lecture/essay "Fātima is Fātima," in which he spoke of the young educated women of Iran who were rejecting not only the role of the old-fashioned illiterate mother-wife supposed to produce children at home and tears in the *rowzeh*s (religious mourning sessions), but also the modernized role of a shopping animal, programmed by consumerism only to alleviate the overproduction of the first world, to buy cosmetics and clothes and thereby to keep the market going. His paternal family, on the other hand, provided him with a proud lineage of local religious leaders, about whom villagers loved to tell stories of piety, and who refused the publicity seeking of being a *marja'taqlīd.* A grandfather's mother's brother was Allamah Bahmanabadi, who was invited by Naseraddin Shah in the mid nineteenth century to teach Islamic philosophy at the Sepahsalar Seminary in Tehran. He stayed in Tehran for a while and then returned to the village of Mazinan outside Sabzavar eschewing the public life of Tehran. The conflict between piety and the pressures of worldly pragmatism is encoded in the famous story told about Mullā Hadi Sabzevari. The shah came to his house and asked for something to drink. The philosopher offered him some *dūgh,* a yogurt drink. The king asked for wine. Now, there are two possible interpretations of this ambiguous request: either the king was asserting his absolute power and liberty to demand what is forbidden by Islam even in the presence, and from the hand of, a Muslim divine; or wine here is the traditional symbol of wisdom. The philosopher's reply covers both possibilities: "Yes, I know, were you able to drink wine, I would have offered you wine instead of *dūgh.*"

Shari'ati's grandfather, Mullā Qurban Ali, "Akhund-e Ḥakīm," was also well educated, having studied in Bukhara, Najaf, Sabzavar, and

Mashhad. But he too returned to Mazinan. Only with Shari'ati's own father's generation did the menfolk leave and settle permanently in Mashhad, the shrine town of the only Imām buried in Iran. Khorasan is dense with historical symbolism: not only is Mashhad the shrine of Imām Riḍa, but also the nearby town of Tus contains the grave of Firdausi, the poet of the national epic, the *Shāhnāmeh*. Moreover, Sabzavar to the west was the seat of the Sarbedarans, who led a glorious revolt against the Mongols in the fourteenth century, establishing a brief independent state. And Khorasan as a whole was the seat of the revolt that overthrew the Umayyid dynasty and established the Abbasids. Shari'ati drew on this symbolism in his various early pen names: Khorasani, Sarbedari, Mazinani.

Mazinanis loved to tell deprecatory stories about townies, seeing them as corrupt and effete: swindling beggars, and bearded women. Shari'ati identified Mazinanis and himself and his vision of Islam with Abu-Dharr as desert figures of integrity. Abu-Dharr for Shari'ati was an early socialist, who campaigned against economic injustice, and for his pains was banished back to the desert by the caliph Uthman. (In 1944, Shari'ati translated the radical Egyptian 'Abd al-Ḥamīd Jawdat al-Saḥḥār's biography of Abu-Dharr, portraying him as a socialist, and retitled it, "*Abū-Dharr, Khodā-parastān-e Socialist*" ["Abu-Dharr, the God-worshipping socialist"].) But for Shari'ati, Abu-Dharr is also an early existentialist and, like Abraham, tested the idols of his family religion, found them impotent, and came to Islam on his own before the mission of Muhammad. Shari'ati spent summers in Mazinan and learned much local lore from the family servant.

He was actually born in Mashhad and went through the secular schools system there: primary, secondary, teacher training, and the newly opened University of Mashhad. He speaks not only of disliking the school system, and its advocacy of sterile history (*tārikh*) and kowtowing to Western modernity represented by Taqizadeh (he would later joke about evil *t*-words), but also of a severe adolescent crisis, caused by reading some European skeptical works and some mysticism, and perhaps most important, by experiencing the turmoil of the war years in which communists and Western forces seemed to have the run of the country. At one point he contemplated suicide, and was only dissuaded by perusing and finding strength in Rumi's *Masnavī*. The *Masnavī*, called by Muslims "the Qur'an of the Iranians," would serve him again later as a young man in despair in Paris. With the founding of the Muslim organizations to renew Islam for the modern world in a progressive way, he found new direction. Three of these were central: in 1940 his father founded the Center for the Propagation of Islamic Truths (*Kanūn-e Nashr-e Ḥaqāyeq-e Islāmi*), holding its first meetings in the home of Taher Ahmadzadeh, who would become the governor of Khorasan in the postrevolution provisional government of Mehdi Bazargan. The center was established to counter the communists then ideologically active; similar centers were established in other cities. It remained active until 1954 when it was closed by the government. Shari'ati writes of the difficulties they had in the earliest days getting funds from the tight-fisted bazaaris on whom Islam seemed to be dependent, and he bitterly remembers that they gave much more freely to a more popularly oriented religious organization that had no ideological ambitions, progressive ideas, or political consciousness. The second important group was the *Khodā-parastān-e socialist* ("God-worshipping socialist"), to which his translation and reshaping of the biography of Abu-Dharr were keyed. This was an underground movement that intended to bring Islam and socialism together. It split over tactics, those opting for overt politics evolving into the Mardom Party, and those opting for more covert educational activities being led by Mehdi Bazargan. The third group was the *Nahzat-e Āzādi-ye Iran* (Liberation movement of Iran), led by Bazargan, which would provide important leadership for the progressive Islamic forces for the next decade and a half.

Aside from the biography of Abu-Dharr, Shari'ati published two other important pieces in this period. First was the translation in 1953 of the grand ayatullah, Shaykh Muhammad Husain Kāshif al-Ghiṭā's letter to the vice president of the American Friends of the Middle East (Garland Ivan Hopkins), in which Kāshif al-Ghiṭā declined an invitation to a Christian-Muslim anticommunist congress to be held in Lebanon in April 1954, citing the grievances of the Muslim world against Western colonialism, and going so far as to say communism was the lesser evil, and a weapon to be used by the Arabs against Western imperialism. The next year, Shari'ati published the first part of his *Middle Way School of Thought* (*Maktab-e vāseṭeh*), in which he posed Islam as a third path between idealism and materialism, communism and capitalism, East and West. It used *salafi* rhetoric: the real battle was not Islam against the West, but decadent traditionalists against the emergent new reformed Islam.

In 1955 Shari'ati was arrested with thirteen others, including his father, in a government roundup of those still supporting Mosaddeq's policies of negative balance (*movāzeneh-e manfī*). After he was released, he first thought of going to Beirut for study, but was then given a government scholarship to the Sorbonne in Paris.

In Paris, Shari'ati became the editor of *Iran-e Āzād* (Free Iran), the organ of the Confederation of Iranian Students, helped found a chapter of the Nahzat-e Āzādi-ye Iran, proposed establishing revolutionary cadres, and became involved in the politics of other third-world movements. He was hospitalized for three days after a police beating during a demonstration in support of the Algerian revolution, and he was jailed during a pro–Patrice Lumumba demonstration that set the Belgian Embassy afire. He translated Che Guevara's *Guerilla Warfare,* Fanon's *Wretched of the Earth,* and *A Dying Colonialism.* He exchanged letters with Fanon disputing Fanon's belief that religion was divisive for third-world alliances, and arguing that for Iran at least, Islam would be an important unifying force as well as a crucial armor against the seductions of commercial imperialism. He suggested that students drop out and that some should get military training, while others should stay in Europe and the United States as liaisons and money raisers.

He claimed to have studied with many famous Sorbonne professors including George Gurvitch and Louis Massignon. His later writings borrow eclectically and superficially from many European theorists including Max Weber, Karl Marx, and Jean-Paul Sartre. These were names with which to conjure the youth of Iran with his challenge to combine the best of European sociological science with a renewed Islam purged of its superstitions and dependencies upon reactionary mullās. His dissertation, however, actually was done under G. Lazard: he edited, translated, and wrote an introduction to *Fazael-e Balkh,* a classical Persian text.

In 1964 Shari'ati returned to Iran, in the aftermath of the uprising against the shah's White Revolution, which had led to the exile of Ayatullah Khomeini. He was arrested for six months for transporting illegal books. After his release, he first taught high school for a year, and then in 1966 became an instructor of sociology and history of religion at the University of Mashhad. His public lectures began to attract crowds, and he delivered important lectures in Abadan, Ahwaz, and Tehran. Some of these were collected in the volumes of his *Islāmshenāsi* (Knowing Islam).

Forced out of the university in 1970, he eventually moved to Tehran in 1972, and became the moving force of the Husainiyeh Irshad, a teaching center established in 1965 by the philanthropist Muhammad Humayun. By this time his lectures were becoming famous and were passed around in written form from youth to youth, as well as circulating on cassettes. In his 1968 *Tashayyu': Mī'adgah-e rūḥ-e sāmi va rūh-e āriyāi'i* (Shi'ism: Rendezvous of Semitic and Aryan spirit), he speaks of a turn in his ideas that makes his previous *Islāmshenāsi* seem archaic, and he talks of the sharp differences between Semitic temperament and religion (impatient; exoteric; quick to anger; dichotomizing everything into right and wrong, good and bad; rebellious against any impositions from outside, witness the constant rebellion against the thirty-five years of British colonial rule in Iraq) and Aryan (more serene; inwardly; seeing that everything has good as well as bad sides; able to endure colonialism, witness the century-long British rule in India), Iranian Islam being a unique transcendent fusion of the two. In his 1969 *Tamaddon va tajaddod* (Civilization vs. modernization), he draws on Herbert Marcuse among others to speak of cultural alienation, and the way the market makes people into robots of consumption, turning third-world folk into *shotor-gāv-palang* ("giraffes"), that is, a queer creature made of camel-cow-leopard without being any of them. Modernized man (*motajadded*) is not civilized; the truly civilized is progress without loss of identity. In "A Look at the History of Tomorrow," Shari'ati suggests that religion of the future must be based on science, and invokes the example of Einstein. In "Alavi and Safavi Shi'ism," Shari'ati sharply attacks the clergy for promoting a religion of superstition, and calls for a return to original Alavi Shi'ism. And in a will he draws up before going on the 1969 ḥajj, he writes that he hopes his son, Ehsan, will grow up to be independent minded, will travel and see the world, and will reject all the *t*-words: *tikrār* (repetition), *tarjumān* ("translation" of European ideas), and *taqlīd* (imitation). In "Religion against Religion," Shari'ati speaks of the possessors of *zar* (gold), *zūr* (power), and *tazwīr* (deceit)—i.e., the wealthy, the kings, and the clergy—as repeatedly suppressing true religion. *Zar, zur, tazwir* was to become an important slogan of the revolution. In the 1971 *Ḥajj,* Shari'ati gives a powerful analysis of the polyvocal symbolism of the ḥajj. In "Yes, So it Was, Brother," he delivers a sharp, if indirect, attack on the shah's 2500 Years of Monarchy celebration, in the form of a letter to the workers who built the pyramids for the pharaohs of ancient Egypt. In 1972, *Ummat va Imāmat* (Community and leadership) provides a philologically speculative connection between the two title words, key symbols of Shi'ite Islam, thereby making the point that Islam is intended to be dynamic, that the Imām is one who prepares the umma for self-government. The lecture was an important contribution to the theorizing about the political form of revolutionary Islam that would legitimize Khomeini's leadership. The same year, Shari'ati staged two political plays: one about Abu-Dharr, another about the Sarbedar followers of Shaykh Kalifa who revolted successfully against the Mongols to establish a Shi'ite state in

Sabzevar. (The theme of fighting the Mongols is an important one in contemporary Sunni fundamentalism as well, deriving from Ibn Taymiya, who sanctioned the taking up of arms against so-called Muslims in the struggles against the Mongols who after seizing Baghdad had become Muslim; in the contemporary world, this justifies armed struggle against so-called Muslim elites and corrupt governments. See Sivan [1985:21].) In "Shi'ism as a Total Party," Shari'ati reworks traditional theological terms as equivalents of contemporary underground revolutionary ones: *taqlīd* (obedience), *taqiyya* (secrecy), *shahādat* (willingness to die for the cause); and in "External Enemies, Stupid Zealots, and Traitors" (*Qāsetin, mareqīn, nakesin*), delivered on the anniversary of Ali's death, Shari'ati argues that Islam is usually victorious against external enemies, but defenseless against internal ones: thus was Ali defeated, and so is he Shari'ati being attacked. In two powerful lectures, "Shahādat" and "After Shahādat," delivered during Muḥarram, just after the government had executed ten young Mojahedin, including two students of Shari'ati, he spoke of using one's own death tactically to disgrace an enemy when an honorable life had become impossible: one should make one's death count. "After Shahādat" begins with the powerful words:

> Sisters and brothers! The *shuhadā* are now dead, and we—the dead—are alive. The *shuhadā* have conveyed their message and we—the deaf—are their audience. Those who were bold enough to choose death, when they could no longer live, have left; we—the shameless—have remained. We have remained for hundreds of years. It is quite appropriate for the whole world to laugh at us, because we, the symbols of abjection and humility, are weeping for Husayn and Zaynab, the manifestations of life and honor. This is another injustice of history: that we—the despicable—should be the mourners of these mighty ones. Today the *shuhadā* delivered their message with their blood and sat opposite us in order to invite the seated ones of history to rise.[99]

By this time in late 1972/ early 1973, it was clear that Shari'ati was unrivaled in his appeal to the youth: the clergy sent a letter to his father asking for restraint, but Shari'ati replied that no one could stop the movement. The government responded by closing the Husainiyeh Irshad.

Shari'ati's power lay in his ability to wield and weld together progressive/modern ideas and Islamic terminology. This is a game Islamic modernists have often played. Shari'ati not only played it particularly well—with a richness that went beyond reinterpretation of legal terms into political ones, into mythology and generalized symbolism—but also occupied a sociologically resonant position and moment. That moment has now passed, and much of his rhetorical flourish now seems unconvincing and overly florid. But the legacy is there. He had the wit to suggest that like Ali and Husain he, if defeated, would be defeated by internal foes, not external ones.

Conclusion: Giving Hagar Voice

There is no point in speculating what role Shari'ati would have played in the revolution had he lived, nor Muṭahhari had he lived longer. The issue is rather to assess the way their discursive systems operate, and to assess the degree to which the juxtaposition of their discursive systems (with each other and with other competing discourses, such as Iranian nationalism or other pan-Islamisms) create a critical purchase on them all. Muṭahhari represented an articulate voice for an existing constituency; Shari'ati created a new audience by being a "strong poet" in a discourse that (1) drew on multiple languages (Arabic, Persian, French, German), thereby involving Iranians in both Islamic and European styles of thought; (2) invoked an existentialist philosophy of language (derived from Sartre) stressing both recovery of hidden linguistic resources and freedom to take one's own destiny and discourse in hand; and (3) used a generalized class analysis through reinterpretation of such words as *mostazafan* (the oppressed), *zūr-zar-tazwīr* (force, gold, deceit), *ṭāghūt* (idolatry/false rulers), as well as through reinterpreting such suppressed images as those of Cain and Hagar. Hagar, perhaps, is of particular import as a sign not only of the slow but insistent growth of a feminist consciousness in the Muslim world (for which the Iranian Tahira Qurat al-'Ayn,[100] the Turk Edibe Halide,[101] and the Egyptian Nawal al-Sadawi[102] may serve as landmark figures), but more generally of the form of alternating submission/self-assertion of alternative discourses from the street, from the lower classes, from oral life worlds, from the world of women heard and felt as vigorous in life albeit little represented in textual worlds.

Shari'ati and Muṭahhari's lives are themselves hieroglyphs that can stand as condensed forms of social types or groups much as Hagar and Abraham stand for ethical parables that "unfold" like paper boats, or that like prisms carry the traces, and reveal the sources, of their illumination. These are the methodological terms proposed by Walter Benjamin in his attempt to recapture Baudelaire's evocations of the origins of modernity in nineteenth-century Paris. Benjamin proposed juxtaposing ethnographically rich portraits with historical descriptions of taxation, economy, and other social features. He insisted (against Theodor Adorno) on not making the ethnographic portraits mere illustrations of pre-posed theory, but rather on keeping the ethnography close to descriptive reality, only embedding it with traces of theoretical interest, so that in a culminating decisive context, there would come a sudden illumination. Theory should be like a sudden ray of light, but one that prismatically deconstructs so that one sees its sources and structure. The method of this "philological attitude" ("unfolding" meanings) is a way of bringing the resources immanent in social history to bear on readers.

The emotional work and anxiety structures staged in the ḥajj, alluded to periodically in this chapter, are part of these immanent structures and resources. Blocked or mischanneled, they can become isolating cells of frustrated energy, but brought into play (*différance*) they can be sublimated and cultivated (encultured) into positive creativities. Three sets of these "voices of Hagar" are worth listing again: (1) the availability of bodily "gut" emotional substances, acts, and settings—blood, nakedness, aggression/stoning, immersion in a crowd—for ideological attachments; (2) the channeling of grief, rage, anger at loss/injustice into stoicism and determination;[103] (3) the decentered *jouissance* of multiple voices of ideological interpretation, and its counteranxieties of loss of control involving Judaicizing anxieties (about the purity of Islam), Zoroastrian and Iranian national anxieties (about the Islamic purity of Iranian Shi'ism), Arabicizing anxieties (about the Iranian authenticity of Islam), class, gender, and minority anxieties (about the authoritativeness of any given interpretation), and especially anxieties about modern secular ideologies (marxism, modernism).

In the present chapter, we have tried to use the ḥajj as well as the discourses and lives of Shari'ati and Muṭahhari (and those of several Diogenesian figures) as such Benjaminian ethnographic portraits. In so doing, we have tried to raise questions not only of relevance to Iran, but more generally questions of (1) interpretation and representation as posed through alternative discourses and their relations to each other; (2) paradoxes of collective identity that affect the nationalisms, state legitimacies, and polities of us all; and (3) the role of deconstructive and reconstructive poetics as social praxis. Fear of *différance* is an anxiety attending not only Muslim fundamentalists; more troublesome is that it is an anxiety attending cultural conservatives in the American academy who fear both the need to learn about other cultural traditions, and to learn from them the alternative interpretations available within our own "Western" culture.

4

Social Change and the Mirrors of Tradition

Baha'is of Yazd

In Memoriam: Nurullah Akhtar Khavari (1919–80)

Introduction

Al-mu'min mirat-ul mu'min [The believer is the mirror of the believer].
— Islamic ḥadīth

The strength of anthropological accounts often derives from a dual focus: a rootedness in concrete historical and ethnographic contexts and a comparative perspective.* The Baha'i faith (or Baha'ism)[1] is a worldwide religion, and like other such religions it operates differently in different contexts.

When I first knew I was going to Iran in 1969, I visited the Baha'i temple in Wilmette, Illinois, to get a foretaste of one of the Iranian religions I would encounter. My surprise could not have been greater. Instead of finding mainly dark-haired Iranians conversing in Persian, I found a predominance of blond, blue-eyed Midwesterners, who handled Persian words as mystical, Oriental fetishes, and who conducted a prayer meeting reading texts from many religions. This was, perhaps, the syncretism[2] that the Baha'i faith claims to foster: when one becomes a Baha'i one does not reject one's previous faith, but adds to it; one learns to distinguish what is eternal morality, and what are historically conditioned instruments of that morality. As an anthropologist, however, I was somewhat disappointed: what was read from each text destroyed the particularity of the tradition from which it was drawn, leaving, seemingly, but banal platitudes. What I found in Wilmette, I decided, was but another American Protestant sect, a latter-day Unitarianism, inter-

Fig. 4.1. Baha'i villagers of Moriabad (Mariamabad), Yazd, in 1936. One can tell by their dress which are Zoroastrian-Baha'i women and which are Muslim-Baha'i women. Photo courtesy of Nurullah Akhtar-Khavari.

esting no doubt in its own right, but having relatively little to do with the agonizing social strife in Iran from which Baha'ism grew and drew its original strength.

I was surprised again—two times—when I visited the world headquarters of the Baha'i faith in Haifa, having spent several years living in Iran. For again, here was an organization which seemed to have relatively little to do with things Persian, an organization dominated by Englishmen and Americans, who behaved toward me less like Unitarians, and more like Jehovah's Witnesses. On my first visit, I slowly worked my way up the hierarchy, beginning with a young black American clerk, and ending with a late-fiftyish English former engineer. I kept inquiring about possible archival materials on Yazd, the town in which I had lived in Iran. At each level a game had to be played: I had to demonstrate that I knew more about Iranian Baha'i history than my interlocutor before I was passed up the hierarchy. At each level I was proselytized. The Englishman, after half an hour of cross-purpose conversation—

I vainly asking about historical materials; he insistently probing in search of my spiritual needs—reluctantly introduced me to Habib Taherzadeh (son of the author of the *Tārīkh-e shuhadā-ye Yazd* [History of the Martyrs of Yazd]), who happened to be visiting from Brazil. What a change: as the two of us happily became lost in a conversation about places and people in Yazd, the poor Englishman withdrew.

A couple of years later, finding myself again in Haifa, I went to visit the shrine set magnificently on the slopes of Mount Carmel, and quite innocently asked about Baha'ullah's family and what might be left in Haifa or Accre of a Persian Baha'i community. I was told there was nothing of either. Since I had set up an interview the following day with a Persian Baha'i and had heard of descendants of Baha'ullah still resident nearby, I was nonplussed and reformulated my question, thinking I had been misunderstood. I was thereupon, in agitated tones, directed to leave the premises. On my way out, I did stop by the pilgrim house and found a "higher up" who spoke to me pleasantly and explained that there were indeed a few descendants of Baha'ullah in the area, but that there had been an unfortunate split and they were no longer part of the community. My innocent question had turned out to be a quite sore point with a somewhat unpleasant history, stemming from the disputes at the time of Shoghi Effendi's succession and the subsequent orders for most of the Persians to return to Iran.

I relate these three encounters as tokens of a religious movement that is no longer a small unified sect, but has become a global organization with a richly differentiated history, growing from an Irano-centric orientation to a Euro-American one, and today increasingly looking toward the third world. These changes in orientation have involved changes in theological formulations, as well as administrative and missionary procedures. This rich diversity has been little mapped. In its general outlines, Baha'i history is well known, repeated both by Baha'i writers and outside observers. But in its details, the sociological dynamics and diversity have been all but ignored, and I hope to stimulate serious inquiry into this richness. To those who fear dealing with internal disputes, one can only reply that no human history is immaculate; and that honest faith and morality is not endangered by worldly struggles: quite the contrary. To those who fear that this is not the time because of the dangers to Iranian Baha'is from the government of Āyatullāh Ruhullah Musavi Khomeini, one can only reply that secrecy feeds paranoia. Indeed, I hope my efforts here—iconoclastic and critical though they may appear to some—will contribute to new ways of resisting and stopping the declared genocidal call of Khomeini's government and entourage to consider Baha'is *murtadd-e fitri* (renegades or apostates by nature) and *mahdūr al-dam* (who may be killed without legal process).

Yazd: Mirrors of Diversity

> Prophets are like a doctor who takes the pulse of a patient and changes the prescription as the condition of the patient changes.
>
> – Baha'ullah, *Tablet for Maneckji*

Let me begin this mapping by turning to the ethnographic and historical context I know best: the town of Yazd, not only centrally located in Iran, but in many ways a microcosm of Iran. Until the growth of Tehran in this century, Yazd was the largest refuge of Zoroastrianism, the pre-Islamic religion of ancient Persia. Yazd has a reputation as one of the most conservative of Muslim cities in Iran, second only to Qum and the shrine area of Mashhad. Yazd served briefly as a seat of the Isma'ili Imām; and for twelve years Yazd was the home of Shaykh Ahmad Ahsa'i, leader of the Shaykhis. Yazd supported a sizable and old Jewish community with twelve synagogues. Not only religiously, but economically as well, Yazd is a microcosm. It has a reputation for industriousness. In the nineteenth century it was an important trade entrepôt with a network of Yazdi traders from Bombay to the Caucasus. In this century it became Iran's second modern industrial textile town, hosting in the 1940s even a vigorous branch of the Tudeh (communist) party. During the current revolution, Yazd has been active on all sides of the political spectrum. If Yazd may be considered a kind of microcosm of Iran, the development of Baha'ism there may be seen as a set of mirrors to the social development of Iran over the past century and a half.

Yazd was central to Babi and Baha'i history as well. It was here that the massacre of eighty-four Baha'is occurred in 1903, recorded in the *Tārikh-e shuhadā-ye Yazd* by Muhammad Ṭāher-Malamiri, read at least in Baha'i groups in India as a kind of *rowzeh* (a lamentation form, constructed around the Shi'ite story of the martyrdom of Imām Husain at Karbala, which is supposed to elicit tears but also renewed stoical dedication to the fight against injustice, no matter how overwhelming the odds); there are also accounts of these massacres in the Church Missionary Society archives and the British Public Records Office from Europeans in Yazd at the time. But long before 1903, in Yazd in the spring of 1845, Mullā Sadiq ("Muqaddas"), after being expelled from Shiraz for including the Bab's name in the Muslim call to prayer, came and preached, stirring up the crowds so that he had to be rescued from physical harm by the mujtahid Husain Asghari. Later that same year, 1845, Sayyid Yahya Darabi (son of the famous Muslim scholar Ja'far Darabi "Kashfi") came through Yazd, where he had a house, on his way to Shiraz, sent by members of the royal court of Muhammad Shah, to investigate the alleged heresy of the Bab. He announced his mission from the *minbar,* promising to return and report his findings. He returned a convert. He and Mirza Muhammad Ali Barfurushi ("Quddus") engaged the local 'ulamā in public debate until expelled by an angry mob. Darabi and Barfurushi continued on to Kirman with a letter from the Bab to the Shaykhi leader, Karim Khan, proposing an alliance. Karim Khan rejected the proposal, defeated Darabi in public debate, and had Darabi and Barfurushi expelled from Kirman.

Five years later, in 1850, Sayyid Yahya Darabi led a brief insurrection in Yazd before fleeing (and leaving the local Babis to be arrested and tortured to death) to Nayriz, where from an old Sassanian fort outside the town he led raids on Nayriz until troops captured and executed him. Darabi's martyrdom and those of his Nayriz followers are among the more frequently retold of Babi martyrdoms, dramatic in their gruesome details, and resonant in their parallels with the Shi'ite stories of Karbala. In 1852 there were three more martyrdoms in Yazd during the disturbances following the attempt on the life of Nāsiruddin Shah.

It was in Yazd again in 1891 during the struggles over the Tobacco Regie (the monopoly given an English company to collect and market the Iranian tobacco crops) that seven Baha'is were martyred in a dramatic fashion, making this also among the more frequently retold of Baha'i martyrdoms, and again resonant in its parallels with Karbala. Most stunning and dramatic, of course, were the massacres of 1903 in Yazd. In 1955, during the political struggles in the aftermath of the overthrow of Mosaddeq, the hamlet of Hormuzak-e Sakhvid, was the site of seven more martytdoms.[3]

Finally, during the current revolution, it is Yazd which was the seat of Ayatullah Muhammad Ṣadūqi, the former aide to Khomeini, who early in the revolution (April 1980) first publicly declared Baha'is *murtadd-e fitri* and *mahdūr al-dam,* who in a Friday sermon in June 1980 called on the public to turn in all Baha'is to the revolutionary prosecutor, who in September 1980 allowed the execution of seven Baha'is, including my friend Akhtar-Khavari, and then invited people to sign a statement approving the execution. This set of executions occurred on the anniversary of Black Friday (17 Sharivar 1978), a turning point in the revolution when the shah's troops had fired upon a crowd in Zhaleh Square in Tehran; and the revolutionary court of Yazd issued a statement saying the executions were a salute to the martyrs of that day and of the revolution in general. Both Ṣadūqi and Dr. Reza Paknejad, head of the local anti-Baha'i monitoring group,[4] have themselves been devoured by the revolution they attempted to monopolize.[5] They, more than the desecration of the Baha'i cemetery in 1979, or the damage against Baha'i communal and private property, represent the deliberateness of the campaign against the Baha'is, a campaign that continued after them.

These are, of course, but the political and most violent markers of Baha'i history in Yazd. I lived in Yazd in the early 1970s. There were at the time roughly one hundred Baha'i families. The Pahlavi state protected their physical safety, but gatherings were prohibited, marriages allegedly were unrecognized, and technically Baha'is could not hold state jobs (although they did, usually by leaving blank the question about religion on the application forms, and allowing some friendly bureaucrat to later fill in the name of one of the four recognized religions—Islam, Judaism, Christianity, or Zoroastrianism). Petty and not so petty harassment was a sport among the more fanatic Muslims. A Baha'i teacher in the town of Meybod, nearby, was not allowed to use the common tea glasses in the faculty room: he was *najes* (impure, polluting). A Muslim lad remembers that the first Literacy Corpsman (*Sepāh-e Dānesh*) sent to his Yazdi village was cursed by the children as a Baha'i and so tormented that he spent most of his tour of duty away from the village. The children would wash his pens before handling them as if they were *najes,* and they shouted: *tū pīr-e Bābi!* ("up the Babi saint"). They baited: *pīr-et gāidam* ("I screwed your saint"); *pīr-eshūn nakon, javūn-eshun bekon* ("don't screw his old ones, screw his young ones"; *pīr* = old man, also saint). Or they chanted: *'Abbās Effendi koshtanesh / Be ab-e sende shostanesh. . . .* (Abbas Effendi, they killed him / they washed [his corpse] with excrement).[6] Nor was this tactic limited to children. A mullā, Vā'ez Sayyid Hedayat Ja'fari, proposed putting up a neon sign on the Ṣāḥib al-Zamān Mosque across the street from the Baha'i center, the *Ḥaẓirat al-Quds,* taken from a poem by the Sufi poet Baba Taher 'Uryān: *Mata-e kofr-o din bi moshtari nist / Gorūhi ān, gorūhi īn pasandarand.* (neither the wares of unbelief nor of belief lack clients; / some are attracted to the one, some to the other). Ayatullah Ṣadūqi, ironically, objected only on the grounds that this would acknowledge Baha'is: Baha'is were not even *kāfirs* (unbelievers), they were to be regarded as nothing. In fact, the Ṣāḥib al-Zamān Mosque was built amid Baha'i properties to serve as an irritant, a place for chanting anti-Baha'i slogans, making anti-Baha'i sermons, projected over loudspeakers so the Baha'is too would hear.

The organization operating out of the Ṣāhib al-Zamān Mosque called itself the Anjoman-e Imām-e Zamān, thereby intending by its name to deny the claim that either the Bab or Baha'ullah could in any sense be considered the Imām-e Zamān.[7] It was a national organization led by a Mashhadi named Shaykh Mahmud Halabi, who had originally gotten approval from Āyatullāh Sayyid Husain Borujerdi, the leading ayatullah of the 1950s. The local Yazdi leader was Dr. Sayyid Reza Paknejad. The latter claimed that he had some fifty double agents who had infiltrated the Baha'is, kept tabs on them and harassed them when feasible. (He claimed there were some two thousand local Baha'is.) One of his most active assistants allegedly was the head of the local office of registration, which is perhaps how Baha'is in that period obtained necessary documents: despite the allegations that marriage, births, and deaths could not be legally registered, Baha'is did have passports and identity cards (identifying births and marriages), the latter being necessary for registering children in school, etc.

After the revolution, the Anjoman-e Imām-e Zamān Arabicized its name and became known as Ḥujjatiyeh (one of the Mahdi's titles is Ḥujjat Allah). Halabi hinted that he was in daily contact with the Imām-e Zamān, and eventually came out against Khomeini, denying that Khomeini was a legitimate representative of the Imām-e Zamān. The name Ḥujjatiyeh, thus, played a dual function: to deny the Babi-Baha'i claims that the Imām-e Zamān had come or that a new dispensation had come, and also to deny Khomeini's title Nāyeb-e (or aide to the) Imām. The slogan of the Ḥujjatiyeh was: "Any flag raised before the coming of the Mahdi, its carrier is *ṭāghūt* [an idolator] and worships something other than God [i.e., is a heretic]." The dispute between Halabi and Khomeini (between the Ḥujjatiyeh and the Maktabi factions of the revolution) is an extraordinary replay of some of the disputes between the conservative 'ulamā of the nineteenth century and the Babis, Khomeini taking up the Babi slogans. Halabi took the old Uṣūli view, endorsed by Āyatullāh Borujerdi, that the Imām-e Zamān would come when the world was filled with injustice (the world must decay completely before it can be renewed), that believers must simply await his return. The Shaykhis, the Babis, and Khomeini all argue to the contrary that one cannot merely await but must prepare the way, for the Mahdi will need soldiers in the final battle, and there is a dialectical relationship: the Mahdi will not appear among the unawakened. The sentiment is clearly expressed by Muhammad Reza Hakimi in the motto he placed at the head of his pro-Khomeini 1963 pamphlet *Khorshid-e Magheb* (The sun rising in the West," one of the signs of the return of the Mahdi), reissued in an expanded 488-page edition after the revolution of 1979:

Khalqie ke dar entezār-e ẕuhūr-e moṣleḥ be sar mibarad bayad khod ṣāleh bāshad (a people awaiting a reformer must itself be reformed).[8]

In short, the treatment of Baha'is in Iran has become a mirror of conscience. As is true elsewhere, the treatment afforded minorities often becomes the index of morality by which a society may be judged. Iran and Yazd, at the moment, are not doing well by this scale. Any citizen of the world has a duty to point out and protest such matters of conscience. Anthropology, however, has a further duty, which is to try to explore the dynamics of belief patterns and social conflicts. I want to use the Baha'ism of Yazd to trace out changing patterns of rhetoric and social positioning over the past century, and to suggest that while Baha'i rhetoric has always been on the progressive side of general Iranian rhetorics, Iranian Baha'ism has remained very close to the patterns of Iranian society in general: a kind of progressive mirror, if you will.

I will divide Baha'i history into three broad phases and will pay the most attention to two cases within the second phase, and to five rhetorics: political millenarianism, syncretism, rationalism, tragedy, and irony or a more distanced and nuanced rhetoric not yet in evidence.

The Babi Period

> The difference between Babism and Baha'ism is quite profound, different approaches for different times. Babism arose within the expectant messianism of Islam, and the early Babis behaved as would any strong Muslim who believed the Mahdi had come: they preached in public and fought. Baha'ullah, however, stressed like Christianity that it is better to give one's life for what one believes than to take someone else's life. Fighting was made unacceptable and the emphasis was placed on teaching: if someone does not accept your teaching you pray for him. In the early days of Babism there was a gap between the leaders and followers. . . . Even the Bab stressed his transitional leadership not simply by using the rhetorical terms of "I am the gate to the greater manifestation of God," but by insisting that his writings should not be published but left as they were until the next manifestation could approve or dismiss what was said in them.
>
> —N. Akhtar-Khavari, 1970[9]

The first phase is that of the prehistory of Baha'ism, the history, that is, of Babism, the predecessor to Baha'ism (1844–63). The rhetoric of this phase was a qualified egalitarian, politicized, and even revolutionary, millenarianism. This was a period of considerable religiopolitical debate, and also one of economic and intellectual engagement with two colonial powers (Russia from the north and Great Britain from the south). Only four years before the Bab declared his mission, Agha Khan I, based in Kirman and Shahrbabak, not far to the southeast of Yazd, had led an insurrection, had been defeated, and had taken the Isma'ili imamate to India. The Shaykhis were active, and promoted both a messianic expectation and an activist attitude toward politics: the Mahdi's return would always be indeterminate unless people began to prepare the way. Much of today's Islamic debate about Islamic government (Khomeini), purification of Islamic terminology of literalist and excessively other-worldly meaning (Shari'ati, the Mojahedin-e Khalq), and social reform is simply the continuation of a fund of traditional arguments developed in the nineteenth century by Isma'ilis, Shaykhis, sufis, and Babis, as well as within the bounds of more mainstream twelver Shi'ism.

From Isma'ili, sufi, and mystic traditions, Babis took the notion of purifying popular Shi'ite concepts of gross, literal meanings: all Prophets reveal the same truth, but there is either a progressive unveiling of esoteric truth so that subsequent revelation is more complete, or ordinary understanding falls into decay and ancient perfect wisdom needs to be recovered through the guidance of the few (or the unique) perfect souls granted each generation or age. Resurrection does not refer to some literal other-worldly rising of the dead for a final judgment, but to the acceptance of a revelation which brings spiritual renewal and thus paradise. Hell, conversely, is the rejection of spiritual truths, and thereby condemns people to stagnate in unnecessary suffering. From the Shaykhi and Akhbari traditions, Babis took the expectation of an imminent return of the Mahdi, together with the need to prepare the way. The return of the Mahdi implied the institution of a just society, and thus Babis brought property rights, the taxation system, and the political hierarchy into question.

In 1845 the Babi missionaries Mullā Sādiq and Mirza Muhammad-Ali Barforushi asserted to the governor of Shiraz that all property belonged to the Bab, and all legitimate political appointments also belonged to the Bab. The Bab's *Qayyūm al-āsmā* (1844) called for a holy war to prepare for the Mahdi. In 1848 at Badasht, the abrogation of the Qur'an and of Muslim law was announced—laying one foundation for the Muslim charges of apostasy and of the crime of creating dissension among Muslims thereby causing "corruption of the earth"—and a holy war was initiated. In the insurrections of the following two years, rallies of the dispossessed were variably included: in Zanjan, for instance, the prison was stormed and tax debtors released.

The Babi movement was a mixture of progressive ideas and initiatives and reactionary theocratic ones. On the one hand, there were the demands for equality of men and women, symbolized by the unveiling of Qurrat al-'Ayn at Badasht; for the laicization of the clergy (abolishing their role in leading prayers, in making legal decisions, or in handling the finances of the community); and for more equitable distribution of land and wealth. On the other hand, there were notions of theosophically graded beings culminating in the "Point" or "Bab," the supreme authority and access to divine wisdom; of a holy war intended to create a pure Babi land (five provinces—Fars, the two Iraqs, Azarbaijan, Khorasan, and Mazandaran—were to allow no non-Babi residents except for temporary visits by Christian traders); of permission to expropriate the land of unbelievers and to divide it as booty among the believers (as in the older Islamic law). The calls for aiding the poor, moreover, were ambiguous: not really calls for redistribution of wealth, but rather, again following Islamic law, simply an emphasis on the rich helping the poor. Qurrat al-'Ayn herself exemplifies this mixture of progressive and regressive elements: however radical in her demands for equality of men and women and for treating land as communal property, she also insisted on her special divine powers (including the powers of her gaze to purify whatever was put before it).

Two elements in the Babi appeal seemed particularly potent: the rhetoric of self-help and the rhetoric of martyrdom drawn from the Shi'ite stories of Karbala. Some Babis banned all talk about God: whatever one says is blasphemous (*kufr*); the attributes and imaging of human language are not adequate; even to say that God is all powerful is blasphemy since it justifies the evil in the world. The focal concern should be on what man can do to create a just world. In the strong words of Qurrat al-'Ayn: *Ay mardom, rastākhīz nakhāhad būd, magar ān rastākhīzī ke shomā dār rāh-e iḥqāq-e ḥaqq bar pā dārid. Behesht va jahannam-e shomā hamīn dunyāst.* (O people, there will be no resurrection except that resurrection which you institute in the way of truth [or regaining rights, or administering justice]. Paradise and hell for you are in this world.) The Babi slogans were resonant with sentiments such as "the Mahdi is among you; the Mahdi is he who rises and starts the holy war," or, *Kāri ke bā khodast moyassar nemīshavad. Mā khod khodā shavīm o barārīm kār-e khīsh.* (Work left to God never materializes. We ourselves become God and fulfill our destiny.) Combined with this heady activist interpretation of Islamic terms was the emotionally powerful rhetoric of Karbala and martyrdom. Mullā Husain Bushru'i rallied his forces in Khorasan in 1848–49 with calls to enter into martyrdom in the path of God as had Imām Husain at Karbala. The rallying cry of the Babi forces was *ya Ṣāḥib al-Zamān* ("Lord of the Age"). Coins were issued in Zanjan in the name of the Qā'im ("savior") and the *Ṣāḥib al-Zamān*". Most impressive are the accounts of martyrdoms which explicitly draw on the Karbala story. Taheri-Malamiri retells the martyrdom of Sayyid Yahya Darabi with the following details:

> Sayyid Yahya was skinned and the skin stuffed with straw and dispatched to Nāsiruddin Shah. Some four hundred men were decapitated. Their women's heads were shaved, and the women placed on unsaddled camels and given each a head on a pike to carry. The procession went to Shiraz first. The town was decorated and the governor, Prince Firuz, together with the Kalantar, Qavam, presided. "Only one thing is missing: were the town illuminated, the procession *would be just like the procession when Imām Husain was killed* and the women taken to Damascus." This shocked the governor, who reacted by visiting the prisoners in the caravanserais. There he saw an old man and asked him to recant and he could go free. The old man replied, my name is Mullā Abdullah. I was the Imām Jom'a of Nayriz. I am ninety years old. You see those three heads over there? They are my newly wedded sons. You see those three women over there? They are my daughters-in-law. The governor of Nayriz also wanted me to recant: he called me into his office and told me that unless I did, I would be sorry. I told him I would not. He had my three sons sit in my lap while he decapitated them. And you ask me to recant!" From Shiraz the procession went to Abadeh by which time the heads were so putrified they had to be buried.

In the mid nineteenth century all this was a powerful mixture. It attracted the well educated, the well-to-do, and the approbation of Western observers such as E. G. Browne and Lord Curzon. The Babis of Yazd, for instance, included the wealthy merchant family of the Afnans with trade connections from Hong Kong to Istanbul; members of scholarly families like Yahya Darabi; as well as more humble folk. In the circumstances of nineteenth-century Iran, this rhetoric and the violent political practice it encouraged provoked a bloody near civil war, and a bloody repression.

The Baha'i Period

> Abdul Baha is full of problems for someone with a modern education. He insisted, contradicting Baha'ullah who had maintained there was no connection between Zoroaster and Abraham, that the former was a descendant of the latter. He further insisted that Palestine was a meeting place for all the prophets including Zoroaster, Krishna, and

> Buddha. In his conversations with Laura Barney, he explicitly rejected evolutionary theory [see Barney 1908:205–14]. He was quite taken with theosophy, and talked of vibration theory, the metaphysics of ether, correspondences between the five spiritual portions of man and of the universe.
>
> —N. Akhtar-Khavari, 1970

Baha'ism under Baha'ullah (1863–92), Abdul Baha (1892–1921), and Shoghi Effendi (1921–57) developed a more quietistic, syncretistic rhetoric. The effort to encompass and incorporate all of the religious rhetorics that Baha'ism came into contact with provides a series of interesting cases. Two of the key cases can be explored with material from Yazd: Zoroastrianism, which is perhaps the first religion outside the Islamic rhetorical framework that Baha'ism encountered; and, of course, Shi'ite Islam, Baha'ism's parent religion, and one which continues to exert extremely strong influences on Baha'i rhetoric. (Christianity and Judaism do not provide rhetorically as much of a challenge as Zoroastrianism, since they were deeply involved in the formation and development of Islamic rhetorics from the beginning. It is interesting to note that almost no Yazdi Jews converted to Baha'ism, a sociological circumstance quite different from that of western Iran, where quite a few Jews converted.) Of the seven Baha'i leaders executed in Yazd by the Khomeini government on 8 September 1980, two were of Zoroastrian background, five of Muslim background.

Zoroastrianism and Baha'ism:

> We do not know who God is, nor where He is; we only know the prophets.
>
> —Baha'ullah, *Tablet for Maneckji*

Although Zoroastrians were aware of Babis, witnessing beatings and martyrdoms of Babis in 1850 in Yazd, and in 1852 in Yazd, Kashan, and Tehran, it is not until well into the Baha'i period that there are converts from the Zoroastrian community. From the 1880s on, there were a considerable number of Zoroastrian converts, so that today it seems that almost every Yazdi Zoroastrian family has at least a few Baha'i members: the process caused considerable bitterness and conflict within the Zoroastrian community. On the positive side, it helped encourage a process of liberalizing and rethinking a Zoroastrian tradition that had stagnated and rigidified; this latter process was also fostered by the increased engagement of the Yazdi community with their Parsi (Indian) coreligionists, particularly through the efforts of Maneckji Limji Hataria who came to Iran in 1854, recruiting students for modern schooling, helping reconstruct religious institutions, intervening with the government to alleviate oppressive taxation and discriminatory ordinances, and establishing relations with other religious communities, including the Babis and Baha'is.[10] Maneckji visited Baḥa'ullah in Baghdad, and in 1976 hired Mirza Abdul Fazl Golpayegani as a Persian teacher, when the latter lost his job in a Tehran Muslim school for being Baha'i. Golpayegani became an important influence on his Zoroastrian students, particularly through Ostad Javānmard ("Shirmard"), a student who later became the principal of the Zoroastrian school in Yazd.

The first Zoroastrian convert to Baha'ism was Kei Khosrow Khodādād, who had a cloth shop in Kashan: I have not yet found an account of his conversion process. More important was his apprentice, Mullā Bahrām ("Akhtar Khavari"), who converted in 1882–83 after several encounters, including discussions with Kei Khosrow Khodādād, inquiries at the time of the 1879 slaying in Isfahan of Sayyid Muhammad-Hasan and Sayyid Muhammad-Husain, and finally, discussions with Ḥajji Muhammad Taheri-Mālamiri. Mullā Bahrām became an active figure in the conversion of other Zoroastrians to Baha'ism, and I know of two different accounts of his conversion process: a theological one from the memoirs of Siyavush Sefīdvash and a pragmatic one from his grandson, Nurullah Akhtar-Khavari.

Siyavush Sefīdvash, another Yazdi textile merchant, converted in 1895 in Qum with three other Zoroastrians, and became an active missionary to the Zoroastrian community. His memoirs provide one rich perspective on how the Baha'i-Zoroastrian syncretic rhetoric was stitched together. Sefīdvash emerges from his memoirs as a likable, if naive and gullible, personality, one who was very much interested from his early days in the signs of the end of time and the return of the Zoroastrian *soushiants* (saviors), particularly Shah Bahrām Varjāvand. Sefīdvash claims that Mullā Bahrām had a similar passion, but it is impossible to tell from the memoir how much of this is Sefīdvash and how much Mullā Bahrām, who seems to have been a more sophisticated person. The Babi movement, of course, had raised general consciousness and interest in questions of the return of the saviors, and Sefīdvash was interested in looking at Baha'i books; but when he tried to read Baha'ullah's *Iqān* (*Certitude*), he was repelled, since it quotes exclusively from the Qur'an to demonstrate within Islamic rhetoric that the Bab's mission was foretold there. Sefīdvash is more impressed by the letters or tablets of Baha'ullah to Maneckji and particularly by the one to Ostad Javānmard in which Baha'ullah claims to be Shāh Bahrām Varjāvand, and in which he confirms Mirza Abdul Fazl Golpayegani's genealogical tracing of Baha'ullah's ancestry to Yazdegird III, the last Zoroastrian emperor of Iran. (The Bab also can be connected to the Zoroastrian royal family via the legend that Imām Husain's wife, Bibi Shahrbanu, was the daughter of Yazdegird III.[11] The Bab's primary affiliation, however, is as a *sayyid,* a descendant of the Prophet Muhammad. Golpayegani's genealogical suggestion for Baha'ullah was far more attractive to Zoroastrians like Sefīdvash: the Nuri family of Baha'ullah was said to be an old family of Mazandaran which had refused for some time, after the Islamic conquest of Iran, to convert to Islam and had helped maintain the independence or semiautonomy of Tabaristan.)

Sefīdvash also began corresponding with Abdul Baha. The letters he received again display the open process of Baha'i efforts to appropriate Zoroastrian sensibilities and draw them into a syncretic web. The first letter is written in pure Persian without a single Arabic loan word: the content is minimal; the point lies in the linguistic seduction. The second letter plays on the legend of Siyāvush (killed in the way of truth), thus preparing the latter-day Siyāvush as well for possible martyrdom. Gradually, the letters from Abdul Baha become more and more Arabicized.

If Sefīdvash's conversion illustrates the linguistic play of the syncretic effort, Mullā Bahrām's story as recounted by his grandson stresses the breaking with the rigidity of the Zoroastrian priests. Sefīdvash is later also part of these struggles, in which the Baha'i faction of the community was allied with the liberalizing, Parsi-supported faction that remained Zoroastrian.

Mullā Bahrām became a member of the large merchant firm Iranian, based in Shiraz and Yazd. Together with a cousin of the Bab, he founded the village of Mehdiabad (locally also called Ghulabad),[12] just outside Yazd. His activities on behalf of Baha'ism did not please the Zoroastrian *dastūr*s (priests), and when his fourteen-year-old daughter died of diphtheria, permission was refused to place her in the *dakhma* (tower of silence):

> It was a hot summer and the body began to putrefy. The priests collected a handful of men to guard the *dakhma* and ensure that the corpse was not placed there. Three leaders of the Zoroastrian community – Kei Khosrow (the merchant who built the Kei Khosrovi school), his brother Goodarz, and the *kalāntar* Dinyar – interceded. The *dastūr*s Namdar and Tirandaz were obstinate, charging that not only was the corpse the daugh-

> ter of a Baha'i but she probably was not even a virgin. Incensed, Goodarz is said to have drawn out his mule whip, shouting that they might have doubts about the virginity of the corpse but he knew for certain about the lack of chastity of their (the *dastūrs*') daughters, and he rode to the *dakhma* challenging anyone to oppose his order to place the girl in the *dakhma*. He prevailed and even forced the *dastūrs* to perform the funeral service. It is further said, incidentally, as an indication of the split between the educated elite and the *dastūrs*, that as they began to recite, Goodarz challenged them to explain what they were reading, but they [as they are not supposed to talk while reciting] merely kept reading. (N. Akhtar-Khavari, 1970)

The relation between the Zoroastrian educated elite—the fruit of Maneckji's educational reforms—and Baha'ism is still the subject of bitter controversy. Some, like the family of Akhtar-Khavari and part of the Aidun family (cofounders of Yazd's second textile mill), were openly Baha'is. Others were sympathizers, seeing Baha'ism as an Islamic reformation to be encouraged as part of Iran's modernization, although not particularly among Zoroastrians where modernization ought also to be encouraged but indigenously as started by Maneckji. In the 1890s the Zoroastrian community, under the guidance of Maneckji's successor, Kei Khosrowji, established an elective twenty-three-member self-governing society (the Anjoman-e Nāseri) composed of laymen, half at least of whom were Baha'i or sympathetic to Baha'ism. (In fact, Abdul Baha sent a letter of congratulations at the time of the initiation of the Anjoman.)

The struggle within the Zoroastrian community was not merely one of liberals versus conservatives, but was complicated by the fears of stirring up the ire of the Muslims against the tiny Zoroastrian community. An incident involving Mullā Bahrām and the great Zoroastrian financier, Arbab Jamshid, may illustrate. Mullā Bahrām intervened to save the life of a Muslim Baha'i (Ghulām Husain Banadiki) by getting a message to the prime minister, Amin us-Sultan. The latter had Shaykh Sabzavari, the mullā who had ordered the death of Banadki, expelled from Yazd, and sent a copy of his order to Arbab Jamshid, thinking thereby to please the latter. Arbab Jamshid's reaction was one of fear for the Zoroastrian community: defending a Muslim heretic could endanger them all. Arbab Jamshid's complaint to the Anjoman in Yazd forced Mullā Bahrām's resignation and departure for Bombay for a year. However, when in 1903 Mullā Bahrām managed to escape the great massacre of Baha'is in Yazd, Arbab Jamshid took him in and gave him a job.

Arbab Jamshid's fears are dramatically illustrated in an incident at the beginning of that massacre. The mob marched out to the village of Abbasabad, owned by the governor, Jalal ud-Dowla, and leased to Mullā Bahrām and other Baha'is. Mullā Bahrām ordered all the villagers inside their houses while he and a few other Zoroastrian Baha'is faced the mob. A mullā who had handled legal affairs for Mullā Bahrām was present and stood forth, saying that no one had a right to harass Zoroastrians; did anyone have a specific complaint against these Zoroastrians? Another mullā joined in, testifying that Mullā Bahrām had often given food and water to poor Muslims. The crowd dispersed. The following day a Muslim Baha'i was spotted, dragged out of the village, and killed. In other words, as Zoroastrian, one was safer; as Baha'i, one was a Muslim apostate, subject to the death penalty.

Siyavush Sefīdvash returned to Yazd in 1915, after fleeing Qum and working in Tehran for Arbab Jamshid (who was forced into bankruptcy in 1915). An ardent missionary, Siyavush helped precipitate the process of the gradual separation of the Zoroastrian Baha'is from the Zoroastrian communal institutions, and the creation of Baha'i institutions. The *dastūr*s refused to perform at a *gahambār* (a memorial feast) for Siyavush's father; so Siyavush performed the service himself. When he wished to marry his daughter to his brother's son, the *dastūr*s refused to perform the ceremony or issue a marriage certificate. For a monetary consideration, a Muslim *mujtahid* issued a legal opinion (*fatwā*) that laymen could perform marriages; and this was confirmed by the Anjoman-e Naseri. (The *mujtahid*'s opinion was necessary so that the marriage would be seen as legal by the state.) The *dastūr*s, incensed, attempted to get the *mujtahid* to allow them to impose the death penalty on apostates to Baha'ism. Confronted at the next Anjoman meeting by Ostad Master Khodabakhsh, the *dastūr*s hired an assassin and had this liberal educator and leader killed. At issue in this assassination were also the elections for the Zoroastrian parliamentary representative, for which Khodabakhsh was the liberal candidate.

The establishment of a separate Baha'i cemetery also required the approval of a Muslim *mujtahid.* The legal document of endowment for the cemetery was written by Mujtahid Labkhandagi: he could not resist inserting that finally Zoroastrians were thinking better of the barbarous custom of the *dakhma* and were following Muslim procedure. Abdul Baha wrote in much the same tone, applauding the efforts to end the "noxious" practice of the *dakhma.* The opinion of a liberal Zoroastrian priest from Kirman was also obtained: he said that in ancient times the Zoroastrian elite had buried their dead, so there was no objection to burial; the *dakhma* was probably a custom of the commoners, which after the Islamic conquest had become community wide.

Siyavush Sefīdvash was instrumental in establishing Baha'i cemeteries all over Iran. His company, the *Sherkat-e Pārsiān,* for some sixty years also served as a financial and administrative link between the Baha'i world headquarters in Haifa and the National Spiritual Assembly of Iran. Baha'is began to issue their own birth and marriage certificates. They established their own schools, which lasted until 1935 when Reza Shah began closing all missionary schools as part of his campaign to secularize Iran (including putting pressure on Muslim institutions such as *ta'ziyeh* mourning for Imām Husain, the veil for women, the turban and cloak for men, and the traditional Islamic *madrasa* or school system).

Gradually, then, Zoroastrian Baha'is separated from the Zoroastrian community and joined with Muslim Baha'is in a new community with its own institutions. Many kinship ties, of course, remain, and a 1933 picture of 42 women of Mariamabad (Moriabad), a Yazdi village with many Baha'is, provides an interesting sociological document, illustrating differential marriage and residence patterns. Five of these women were of Muslim background, easily distinguished by their dress: all 5 of them remained in Yazd as of 1970; of their 18 children, 13 remained in Yazd, 2 migrated to Pakistan, and 3 to Tehran. But of the 37 Zoroastrian Baha'i women, only 9 were still in Yazd in 1970, 14 had moved to Pakistan, 3 to India, 6 to Tehran, and 4 to elsewhere in Iran; and of their 114 children, only 12 were still in Yazd, 40 were in Pakistan, 11 in India, 21 in Tehran, 15 elsewhere in Iran, and 15 elsewhere abroad (including one I later met in Surinam). The marriage pattern reveals a similar dynamic: only 14 of the 114 had married a non-Zoroastrian or non-Zoroastrian Baha'i; and of the 37 Zoroastrian Baha'i women themselves, only 4 did not marry Zoroastrian Baha'is. These latter figures reflect two normal patterns in conversion communities: one of the last things to change is marriage within the old communities of origin, despite the ideological encouragement of Baha'ism to marry out so as to gain new converts; and second, "intermarriage" is much harder to sustain in a conservative community like Yazd, and can occur much more easily once people have moved to Tehran or abroad.

In sum, Baha'ism played an important part in the liberalization movements that swept through all Iranian confessional communities in the late nineteenth century. It was particularly forceful within the Zoroastrian community, but was only one of several parallel forces at work. Three key processes are illustrated in the engagement between Baha'is and Zoroastrians: the rhetorical effort by Baha'is to appropriate and reinterpret Zoroastrian symbolism and language; the challenge to follow tradition only when it could be intellectually defended, which initially brought Zoroastrians into Baha'ism, but which also helped Zoroastrianism itself to become intellectually richer; and the sociological gradual separation of Baha'ism into its own institutional community but one having lingering ambivalent relations with Zoroastrians in part forced by the denial of legal rights by the Iranian state.

Shi'ism and Baha'ism:

Of the seven Baha'is executed in Yazd in 1980, five had Muslim names; the vast majority of Iranian Baha'is are of twelver Shi'ite background; and the rhetoric of Iranian Baha'ism still reflects this very strongly. I have already spoken of the rhetorics of syncretism, rationalism, and tragedy or martyrdom. One might add here the symbolic construction of Baha'ullah as a prophet figure, and the proofs of Baha'ism built around the prophetic formulation: proof by dream or vision, by divine retribution against Baha'i oppressors, and by the willingness and even joy in suffering and martyrdom. All these have an almost axiomatic or at least anchor centrality for Baha'i rhetoric in Iran; all reflect the Shi'ite matrix out of which and against which Baha'ism has defined itself.

Take the prophet figure itself: neither Zoroastrianism nor Judaism left to themselves display much interest in their prophet figures. Legendry exists, but it exists with only anecdotal, or at most ad hoc didactic weight, not with any theological weight; it is only within a Muslim environment that each of these traditions has been forced to elaborate a single and central prophet.[13] To a secular Westerner, Iranian Baha'ism seems very much a halfway house: a rhetoric containing many progressive ideas, but one designed for traditional folk who cannot do without prophets, hierarchical authority, dreams, signs and wonders. Prophetic status in such a rhetoric is a primary guarantee of a divine message; as a Yazdi Baha'i put it (echoing Baha'ullah):

> Men cannot perceive God, but know of him, his laws, angels, spirits, etc., only through his messenger. How do we know a prophet? There are five indicators,[14] but primarily we recognize a prophet by . . . contrasts. There are many who claim to be prophets and by comparison we recognize who is true and who is false.

There are at least two elements in the construction of the Baha'i prophet figure: the old gnostic notion that all prophets carry the same spiritual message and that in each age there is a perfect soul who can serve as a link to divine knowledge; and the specific construction of the legendry around Baha'ullah. Jelal Azal, grandson of Subh-e Azal, has compiled an extremely interesting account of how this construction occurred: how the dates of the call of Baha'ullah were fitted to the predictions in the writings of Shaykh Ahsa'i and the Bab; how titles were taken on and created; as well as how the family disputes took place (including poisonings and deaths in both the families of Baha'ullah and Subh-e Azal) over the consolidation both of leadership and of the legitimating symbolic structure. From a Baha'i point of view, Jelal Azal's work may have had the intent of questioning the veracity of Baha'ullah's claim to prophecy by showing a play with the facts; but to a student of comparative religion, what it shows rather is the extraordinarily interesting process of symbolic legitimization, a process central to any tradition.

Syncretism, as was noted above, is an outsider's term, but there is much to be learned from Baha'i play with symbolic poetic as well as rationalist debating technique which from the inside is less easily distinguishable in analytic terms. Two quick anecdotal examples from the same Yazdi Baha'i:

> "Baha'ullah is Christ returned, the fifth Buddha, the twelfth Imam, Shah Bahram Varjavand, Krishna incarnate, and for Israel the everlasting Lord of Hosts." When I pointed out that the last lacks parallel status, being the name of God himself, he replied—instead of correcting it—with the mirror analogy, logically a more encompassing solution: "A mirror reflecting the light of the sun can simultaneously say, 'I am the sun' and 'I am not the sun, but merely glass.'"

Then there is the famous story about Mirza Abul Fazl Golpayegani.

> His horse threw a shoe in the town of Reyy near the shrine of Shah Abdul Azim. The blacksmith, while shoeing the horse began: "I see from your turban that you are a learned man. Tell me, I have heard there is a ḥadīth that every drop of rain is brought to the ground by an angel; is that true?" Golpayegani: "Yes." The man worked for a while, and then said: "Another ḥadīth I have heard is that in a house where there are dogs [considered *najes* or polluting by Shi'ism], angels are not found, is that true?" Golpayegani: "Yes." Said the blacksmith: "Well, put the two ḥadīth together: how can that be?" Golpayegani was surprised and angered at having been bested by a simple blacksmith, but he accepted a copy of the *Iqan.* It took another ten years of reading and debate before he converted to Baha'ism, but so it began.

Dreaming—as a vehicle of divine communication and foreknowledge—is another important category of symbolic play, one critical to many conversion stories as well as to the construction of martyr stories.[15] But of key importance is suffering and martyrdom, the assertion that not merely is witnessing for the truth a powerful persuasive beacon to others, but that only those who hold the truth can muster the strength to suffer the most horrible of tortures. Both Shi'ites and Iranian Baha'is play upon these themes, and Baha'i accounts of their martyrs resonate with those of Shi'ite accounts of Karbala. Siyavush Sefidvash was prepared by Abdul Baha for martyrdom and asked for it, though at this point Abdul Baha interposed a key lesson: not to seek out martyrdom, only to accept it with dignity should it be forced upon one. Abdul Baha wrote Siyavush and gave him the name Sefidvash to distinguish him from the ancient martyr, as different as black (*siāh*) and white (*sefīd*): it is witnessing (*shahīd*) to God's truth, not martyrdom (*shahīd*) itself which is of value. Not all, as Baha'ullah earlier had pointed out, who are *shahīd* die, nor of course are all who die on account of their religious affiliation necessarily martyrs.

The spirit of Sefidvash's desire is conveyed as well in the savoring of stories of martyrdom by a Yazdi watchmaker in 1970; he told me about an uncle who rejoiced at the time of the 1903 massacres that he would be allowed to witness to death, and related in loving detail the famous story of Mullā Ali Sabzevari's martyrdom in 1892, described in the *Tārīkh-e Shuhadā-ye Yazd.* I have mentioned the use of the *Tārīkh-e Shuhadā-ye Yazd* as a *rowzeh*-like text and the references in its account of Sayyid Yahya Darabi to the martyrdom of Imām Husain at Karbala. Again, in that text's account of the seven who were slain in Yazd in 1892, Mullā Ali, the third to die, asked his executioner to cut the muscles on either side of his wind pipe, but to allow him a final word before the wind pipe was cut. As the blood flowed, he caught it in his cupped hands and showed it to the crowd crying, "Look at this blood by which I swear to the truth of my faith." *Hazrat-e Shahīd* [Husain ibn Ali] *farmūdeh, 'Hal min nāṣirin yansur-uni; man nemigūyam hal min nāṣirin yansuruni; man migūyam hal min nazirin yanzuruni.*'" The line plays on the words *nāṣirin* (helper) and *nāẓirin* (observer): i.e., Husain at Karbala cried, "Is there no one to help me!" Mullā Ali contrasts his own situation: "I don't say, is there no one to help me; I say, is there no one even who will observe and recognize what is happening?" Taheri-Malamiri's comment is the Baha'i comparative refrain: and the Shi'ites think that the person in the universe who suffered most (was most *maẓlūm*) was Husain!

This savoring—both of martyrdom, and of the resonances and comparisons with Karbala—can be seen in the new 1980 publication of the *Lawḥ-e ibn-e Dhi'b* (Tablet to the son of the wolf), and in the account by Muhammad Labib of the seven martyrs in 1955 in the village of Hormozak-e Sakhvid (southwest of Yazd). Labib, patterning his narrative style on Taheri-Malamiri and on *Nabil's Narrative,* has Aqa Ghulam-'Ali say, "To be killed for the sake of our Faith is now, and has always been our greatest and most cherished aspiration. We will not hinder you" (Labib 1980:13); again of Aqa 'Abdu'r-Razzaq, Labib says, "He even developed an intense longing for martyrdom in the path of the Faith of God . . . and praise be to God, he eventually attained his heart's desire" (ibid., p. 17). These and other passages should not be construed to mean that the martyrs of this village did not take whatever practical steps they could to avoid their deaths, but that when it became clear that their neighbors were intent on harming them, they made themselves ready and refused to lift a hand to physically fight their attackers. Labib, as do the authors of many Baha'i accounts of persecution, major and trivial, ends by cataloguing divine retributions in the form of mortal illnesses and accidents and flood visited upon the persecutors.[16] Muhammad-Ali Fayzi's introduction to the new publication of the *Lawḥ-e ibn-e Dhi'b* is far more erudite in its references to the Karbala story, calling Jalal ud-Dowla (the governor of Yazd) *Ẓālim-e Ard-e Yazd* (despoiler of Yazd), just as Shi'ites called Yezid's general Shemr "*Ẓālim-e Arḍ-e Karbala*"; and calling Ẓilus-Sulṭan (the governor of Isfahan) *Shajara-e Jaḥīm* (tree of hell), just as Shi'ites interpret the cursed tree of the Qur'anic verse 17:60 as the family of the Umayyids.[17]

Two positive processes are illustrated in the above examples: first, the engagement with Shi'ite rhetorics, just as (and more intensely than) illustrated with Zoroastrain rhetorics in the previous section; second, the provision of models of courage for an embattled minority. One cannot help but be impressed by the strength that the martyrdom frame gives people in the face of death and torture. This is revealed most recently in the letters from people today just before their execution or by their family survivors.

And yet, there are two dangers, one academic and one practical. The academic danger is that of taking Baha'i martyrdoms out of their political and sociological contexts, thereby heightening their emotional appeal, but denying their intelligibility (and thereby perhaps blunting efforts to stop the causes of persecution). Simply historically, Babi and Baha'i martyrdoms occurred in Yazd in 1850, 1852, 1891, 1903, 1955, and 1980. All of these dates, to any student of Iranian history, are significant dates, indices of larger political processes. The years 1850 and 1852 are, of course, the dates of the Babi efforts at armed insurrection, and at the assassination of Nasiruddin Shah (on Qajar modes of public punishment, see Fischer [1980*a*]). Both 1891 and 1903 are dates of agitations against Qajar government efforts to raise revenues through economic concessions to foreigners: the Tobacco Regie, and the Russian loans of 1903. In both cases, the government, in severe financial straits, became dependent on Europeans who attempted to rationalize state revenues, thereby squeezing Iranian merchants and landowners who, in time-worn style, translated their displeasure into religious idiom voiced by clerics in Isfahan, Shiraz, and the *'Atabāt* (the shrine towns of southern Iraq: Najaf, Karbala, Samarra). Anti-Western agitations often turned against Christians and other minorities seen as proxies and agents of Europeans: Armenian liquor stores were destroyed in Tabriz, English missionaries were harassed in Isfahan, and so on. Demands were issued repeatedly against employment of Europeans in the government, against European economic concessions, against reorganizing taxes and tariffs under Europeans, against Belgian customs officials, and against foreign loans. These demands were often complicated by private political manipulations; the British as well were not above supporting the agitations in 1903 so as to prevent a third Russian loan.

What is most interesting in these agitations is that the mujtahids were very clear that when their messages were allowed to reach the shah and he responded favorably, they could and did counsel patience, even to the point of saying that fighting public sale of alcohol or Baha'ism should be left to the government, that it should not be pressed by the people. But when blocked, the mujtahids and their merchant supporters were quite capable of flexing their muscles with attacks on minorities, of whom the Baha'is were the most vulnerable. Take the 1903 massacre in Yazd. This occurred in the aftermath of demonstrations during Ramaḍān in Isfahan, and in the aftermath of open Baha'i missionizing in Yazd. It was triggered on the birthday of the Prophet Muhammad. What is interesting is that Aqa Najafi who orchestrated the agitations in Isfahan attempted to foment riots similar to those in Yazd in the towns of Sultanabad, Qazvin, Shiraz, and Tehran, but was unsuccessful. Two years later, in 1905, again there was an effort to stir up the people of Yazd against Baha'is, and it fell on deaf ears. There were in 1903 disturbances in a number of places against Christians: the four great mujtahids of the *'Atabāt* sent a telegram disavowing those disturbances, but approving the Baha'i killings in Isfahan and Yazd. In other words, religious riots were a political strategy in struggles against the subordination of the state to outside economic and political forces: Baha'is were a pawn.

This point can be made in another way as well: one of the most striking facts about the 1891 murder of Baha'is in Yazd is that it took the form of a public ritual, quite in the fashion that Michel Foucault (1979), following the work of Georg Rusche and Otto Kirchheimer (1939), describes for premodern France. Public torture and execution involved an effort at confession, at a public demonstration of power, in which socially defined truth was inscribed on the bodies of the executed. In Yazd, each of the key seven martyrs was tortured and executed in a key public space; a symbolic procession from the citadel to the bazaar was effected. A similar ritualized set of executions occurred in Yazd in 1852.

These sociopolitical dynamics, and penal customary forms, do not in any way lessen the moral opprobrium falling on the perpetrators of these murders; rather, their analysis exposes the social pressures the perpetrators were able to exploit, and those who would counter similar events today and in the future would do well to understand them. The current campaign against Baha'is in Iran is not merely the function of a few fanatic clerics. It draws upon a deep and widespread antagonism no longer held in check by the state, but encouraged by it. Among the reasons for this antagonism is of course the insistent proselytism of Baha'ism which not only openly denies popular interpretations of Islamic doctrine (e.g., that Muhammad is the final Prophet), but which also reinterprets standard Islamic rhetoric: while the majority-minority and predecessor-successor relationships are inverted, the antagonism of Muslims toward Baha'is parallels that of medieval Christians toward the Jews who refused to accept Christian reinterpretations of the Old Testament.

The competition between Baha'is and Muslims as to who can suffer more and thereby demonstrate possession of divine truth seems today archaic and self-defeating for Baha'is. No doubt some Muslim Iranians will be impressed by the heroic witnessing of Baha'i martyrs. But it is not an auspicious time for such contestation: the tragedy that Shi'ite Iranians feel themselves to be suffering is likely to outweigh that of a few hundred Baha'i martyrs. After all, they see themselves facing the entire world, and they have lost many more martyrs in the Iran-Iraq war (that Baha'is do not count brainwashed children and youths as martyrs does not make them any less martyrs in Shi'ite eyes). In terms of world audiences, rather than Iranian ones, martyrdom is likely to have become a dated rhetoric. There are too many horrors in the twentieth century for any given one to carry rhetorical force merely on the basis of suffering: it has become an increasingly dehumanizing and mechanical condition of large parts of the third world: one need only invoke the tragic litany of Cambodia, Vietnam, Nicaragua, Guatemala, Afghanistan, Argentina, Lebanon, the Gulag of the USSR, and the Iran-Iraq border war.

My point here is a simple one. Jews who suffered the Nazi holocaust want us to remember so that it never be allowed to happen again; but they do not want themselves defined by the holocaust. I do not agree with the suggestion of the National Spiritual Assembly of the United States that Baha'is not be taught about the martyrdoms of their faith; but I also think that if Baha'ism is to mature in Iran, perhaps, Baha'is need to develop new rhetorical defenses against Shi'ite fundamentalism, rhetorics perhaps of satire, of serious comedy, of the hair-raising laughter that comes to haunt cultural criminals (as Sadeq Hedayat suggests in *The Blind Owl*). One of those uncanny mirrorings that Hedayat loved is that Khomeini was more than a little a Babi in his rhetoric and slogans (a rhetoric that yesterday was a progressive stance, today a reactionary one).

I, of course, do not exactly know what such a new rhetoric might look like, but the challenge to produce one is strikingly apt for Iranian Baha'is. Baha'is claim Iran as a sacred land, Persian is a language of revelation for Baha'is, and Baha'is are among the leading scholars of Persian letters. And yet—let me cite here a complaint from within Baha'i ranks—where is the creative writing of Baha'is: the novels, the plays, the films, the poetry not about religion but about contemporary life? There seems to be a curious timidity: scholarship and commentary is safe; own-account creativity is more dangerous. The complaint is no doubt unfair—universalizing and reinterpreting are creative and clearly not without danger—but the challenge nonetheless is a worthy one. As Baha'ism matures within Iran, it must increasingly escape the "gravitational pull" of Shi'ism, and of commentary upon both Shi'ism and the writing of the past.

Nurullah Akhtar-Khavari

Let me conclude by paying tribute to one of the contemporary martyrs of Yazd: Nurullah Akhtar-Khavari, executed by the Khomeini government in 1980. I remember him best sitting in his office at the Derakhshan factory, a wool spinning and weaving mill, the second oldest in Yazd; he handled all the foreign correspondence. He introduced me to the personnel manager who helped me do a survey of the work force. I have amusing memories of workers who in this manager's office told me to list their religion as Muslim, but who quietly later told me to correct the listing to Baha'i. Akhtar-Khavari had no need of such masking: he, after all, was indispensable to the factory. He wore his Baha'i ring prominently on his hand. After the revolution, when there was agitation to have him removed, the factory requested him to work out of his house: satisfy the fanatics in public but still get the factory's work accomplished. Akhtar-Khavari also had no need to dissimulate, because he was secure in his knowledge: widely traveled, he knew a great deal more about Islam than most of the Muslim workers. It is said that Muslims of various sorts, ranging from young student provocateurs to mullās, would come to his house to debate him; they always left disappointed, defeated. He also knew a great deal about Zoroastrianism: his family came from the Zoroastrian community, and still lived in one of the largely Zoroastrian villages, Mariamabad (or locally, Moriabad). He tutored many of the Yazdis in English, another skill which made him in demand: it is said that he had even tutored daughters of Ṣadūqi, and Dr. Paknejad himself.

My fondest memories of Akhtar-Khavari are of sitting with him in his factory office, discussing the history of Baha'i-Zoroastrian relations. As the quotations from my field notes indicate, his faith was not blind, but was processed through his own reason, experience, and learning. There is an interesting story about his excommunication from Baha'ism. He lived for a number of years in India (among other services to the community there, he purchased the land in New Delhi on which the mother temple for India is being built). One day, suddenly, he was asked by Shoghi Effendi to return immediately to Yazd. He asked for an extension of time to finish some business; the request was denied, but he stayed a bit longer any way, before returning to Yazd. There are two variants, not necessarily contradictory, to the story. The one relates that there was a dispute between Akhtar-Khavari and other members of the National Spiritual Assembly of India: Akhtar-Khavari thought that these officers of the faith should not draw salaries, but should hold other jobs and serve the faith voluntarily; they not only disagreed but felt threatened and complained to Shoghi Effendi. This variant of the story relates that Shoghi Effendi ordered his return to Yazd out of respect for the general will of the Indian community, and after a brief time, readmitted Akhtar-Khavari to the faith. Indeed, it is said that Shoghi Effendi held Akhtar-Khavari in special regard, keeping a photo of him in his office, where it may still be seen today. The second variant of the story is a much more interesting and powerful one. It relates that

Shoghi Effendi asked a number of successful Yazdis living abroad to return to Yazd to serve in that conservative society as exemplars of how modern, liberated individuals acquit themselves with self-confidence and initiative. Of these, Akhtar-Khavari was the only one to remain into the 1970s, and indeed returned to Yazd after the revolution, having visited both Europe and America, where his sons reside.

So why, I asked myself when I heard of his execution, had he not taken the way out exercised by his grandfather, Mullā Bahrām. This is not the Middle Ages; people don't go to their deaths these days for some literalist or ritualistic nonsense. All he had to do was say yes, he was a Zoroastrian. Another day when passions were different, he could then be present to engage again. To die was to choose, in a sense, not to fight. These first reactions, obviously, are not those of a Baha'i. Honesty, said some of my Baha'i friends, is a fundamental principle: we refuse to play the Shi'ite game of *taqiya.* To a non-Baha'i this is not very persuasive: if a crazy man puts a gun to your head and says if you do not curse your brother he will kill you, you would not die for that. Of course, things were not quite so easy for Akhtar-Khavari: he was a leader of a community; were he to take his grandfather's way out, he would be forced to behave in certain ways by the watchful Muslims, he would be open to further coercion. But it was not only I who had such questions: his sons too pleaded with him when he was out of Iran not to return (Kamran Akhtar-Khavari [1983]). He replied (with, I like to think, his infectious and slightly mischievous smile) that Shoghi Effendi had ordered him to stay in Yazd. Besides, how could he let down the others left behind in Yazd?

He must have known he was courting death. Here the story becomes a challenge for the narrator. As I see it, two kinds of story can be told. The more powerful one is of the exemplary figure, the modern man who had decided to operate in a very conservative society, not to badger or embarrass it, but to show a new and open mode of behavior. The challenge here is to show how one operates in such a society: it is almost an ethnographic challenge, the kind of challenge that requires the eye of a novelist for local color and knowledge of local detail. It is a challenge to describe how a society changes, sometimes moving in reactionary self-destructive directions, but nonetheless irrevocably changes, in ways involving considerable internal conflict. The exemplary individual as well as all other individuals have to make choices, have to negotiate pragmatic as well as moral decisions.

The other narrative that can be told – by far the weaker story, I think – is to turn Akhtar-Khavari into a standard Baha'i martyr. It is this that I fear will be his fate. I fear it not only because I will no longer recognize my friend, but also because he was larger than such stereotyping allows. His personality (like every human being's) was unique; it was also graceful, informed, and forceful, and thus worth preserving. The leaden mail coat of the martyrdom topos is being forged with the following links of prophecies, extraordinary childhood, dreams, and desires for martyrdom. His grandfather, Mullā Bahrām, is said to have asked Abdul Baha for the gift of divine wisdom; Abdul Baha said Mullā Bahrām was too old, but the gift would accrue to his offspring; this offspring would be Nurullah Akhtar-Khavari. Nurullah as a child was given only six years of education before being sent to work, yet he turned out to be a well-educated man, educated far beyond most of his contemporaries, fluent in several languages. (Unstressed here is that as a boy he worked during the day and went to school or taught himself at night, the pattern of many a successful man.) It is said that during the early days of the revolution, he and his wife were detained by Revolutionary Guards in Taft, a large village near Yazd, having been found carrying copies of a Baha'i newsletter; when they were released, his reaction was that they did not receive the bounty of being imprisoned or martyred in the path of divine witnessing. Again when he had his two heart attacks (one in Florida, and one after returning to Iran), he worried that he would die, as it were, a meaningless death; he fought for his life. In Yazd, he actively fought to protect his community, sending telegrams to President Bani-Sadr, Ayatullah Khomeini, and Ayatullah Ṣaduqi to stop the harassment of innocent people. Revolutionary Guards wrote on the walls of his house, "Death to Akhtar-Khavari; Nurullah Akhtar-Khavari must be executed." When Paknejad was elected to Parliament, he immediately had Akhtar-Khavari arrested. It is said that when he was arrested, he gave sweets to those who came to seize him, and that he did the same again for his executioner. Both his wife and he had premonitionary dreams about the arrest and its aftermath. His wife's dream was of being disallowed to follow him and being told to pioneer in America; his own dream was of being executed with three bullets in his chest and one in his temple, exactly as was to be the case. At the trial, Akhtar-Khavari was the spokesman for the seven; apparently, he did so well that the authorities took the tape off the television, lest it stir up the population. Asked to choose between denying faith in Baha'ullah and the firing squad, Akhtar-Khavari replied that the latter would be a great bounty to achieve. At the execution in the Bagh-e Samandar Khan, each man was given a chance to recant; they were killed one by one so that pressure would mount on those remaining.

Akhtar-Khavari was the fifth or seventh[18] to choose death: it is said he placed a piece of *nabāt* (crystallized sugar) in the mouth of his executioner and thanked him for what he was about to do. He is said to have told the executioners that the seven were being martyred by the will of God and that they did not wish to live without faith; moreover he urged them to do their task quickly so that the executioners could go home and the martyrs could also be made comfortable. His corpse, it is said, not only had bullets where he had dreamt they would be, but there was a radiant smile on his face. A Muslim woman spectator is said to have blurted out that it was a repetition of Karbala. The place where the seven corpses were dumped (near the Zoroastrian graveyard in the desert off the Kirman road) is said to be the place where many years earlier Mullā Bahrām's daughter had been dumped before she was finally placed in the *dakhma.*

Now, all these things may be true. But they are only part of the story. Martyrdom stories function in several ways. They are often used as didactic devices: stories to tell children and other novices. Perhaps much more importantly, they serve those who have to face martyrdom as a source of strength. Fereshteh Taheri-Bethel (1984) has begun the task of collecting and analyzing the writings of those martyred between 1979 and 1982; in several cases she can trace the gradual shift from shock and complaint about what was happening to them to preparation and welcoming acceptance. Under extreme stress, human beings often do not become depressed or disorganized, but instead transcend the conditions around them. The Baha'i martyrs have demonstrated a remarkable strength and willingness to witness for their faith.

As didactic devices, the martyrdom topos, for me at least, and I think for many nonbelievers, are much less powerful, because they are so stereotypic. One can see the baneful effects of the martyrdom ideology even in as sophisticated a work as Taheri-Bethel's thesis, where her accounts of martyrdom in other, non-Baha'i traditions would be unrecognizable to members of those traditions; they have become completely assimilated to Baha'ism. Moreover, where Muslim Iranians have begun to defend Baha'is as innocent victims of the Khomeini regime—e.g., a figure like Mansour Farhang,[19] who in the early days of the revolution on nationwide American television defended the right of the revolution to discriminate against Baha'is—it is not because they are impressed by the heroism of Baha'i martyrs, but because they recognize that a revolution which provides no impartial protection devours also Muslims like themselves.

I wish in no way to denigrate the suffering or the heroism of Baha'i martyrs. In drawing attention to the rhetoric(s) of Baha'ism, I wish rather to raise for discussion the possibilities for more effective ways of countering the genocidal atrocities of the Khomeini regime. For me, the legacy of Nurullah Akhtar-Khavari is not a dialogue of martyrdom with Shi'ism, though obviously in part it is that too: that is the gravitational pull. For me, the legacy of Nurullah Akhtar-Khavari is the possibility of living in Yazd as if it were the twentieth century, as if one could live without fear of religious fanaticism, as if people could live and let live each by his or her own lights.

Part 3
Shifting Ritual Grounds (to Houston)

. . . Agni araflammed and Mithra monished and Shiva slew as mayamutras the obluvial waters of our noarchic memory withdrew. . . .

Between me rassociations in the postleadeny past and me disconnections with aplompervious futules I've a boodle full of maimeries in me buzzim and medears runs sloze, bleime, as I now with platoonic leave recoil in (how the thickens they come back to one to rust!) me misenary post for all them old boyars that's now boomaringing in waulholler, me alma marthyrs.

He beached the bark of his tale; and set to husband and vine: and the harpermaster told all the living conservancy, know Meschiameschianah how that win a gain was in again. Flying the Perseoroyal. Withal aboarder, padar and madar, hal and sal, the sens of Ere with the duchtars of Iran. Amick amack amock in a mucktub.

—James Joyce, *Finnegans Wake,* 80.24–25, 348.5–11, 358.17–21

5

Diasporas: Re-membering and Re-creating

Exiles and Immigrants, Authenticity and Identity

> Aztecs, Toltecs, mestizos . . . and a lot of Texans. I'll learn the ropes. . . . My first American wife said, in the dog-eat-dog world, Alfred, you're a beagle. My name is Alfie Judah, of the once-illustrious Smyrna, Aleppo, Baghdad—and now Flushing, Queens—Judahs. . . . We spoke a form of Spanish in my old Baghdad home. . . . I, an Arab to some, an Indian to others. . . . From His perch, Jesus stares at me out of his huge, sad, Levantine eyes. In this alien jungle, we're fellow Arabs. You should see what's happened to the old stomping grounds, compadre.
>
> —Bharati Mukherjee, *The Middleman and Other Stories*

> The *turath* (heritage) is the guide to self-understanding for most of those who are concerned with Arab or Muslim identity or authenticity. There is, however, an important difference in the range of connotation between the notions of identity and authenticity. . . . Authenticity is to accept, or even embrace, a fate, and it is linked to a self-knowledge which is derived from an "archeological" investigation. . . . Identity may also mean the negation of one's past, overcoming the particularities of kinship, culture, community, and even personal experience.
>
> —Leonard Binder, *Islamic Liberalism*

Iranian culture increasingly is woven on a geographically situated loom, one beam end set in Iran and one set abroad in America and Europe. Each end is itself a generative locus of *différance,* of identity, contributing new bits of warp or woof. (The result perhaps is not so much replicated carpet pairs like those woven on a traditional loom, but rather a carpet of subtly changing variated pattern, perhaps like a Shalamzar Bakhtiari carpet in which each square is different, or those Qashqa'i-Shirazi carpets in which new figures—radios, airplanes, cameras, trucks,

Fig. 5.1 *a.* Fused image of Bilal, the first muezzin of Islam, and Malcolm X, the American convert from the Black Muslim movement to Islam, who issued a call to other American blacks to join the Islamic community (stamp issued by the Islamic Republic of Iran in a propaganda campaign to urge Americans of African descent to rise up against the United States government and to join a world-wide Islamic revolution). *b.* skyline of Yazd; *c.* skyline of Houston.

televisions—are constantly being introduced onto the field.) In Iran the polarities and juxtapositions of East and West, past and future, Iran and Islam, nationalism and cosmopolitanism generate one sort of cultural and sociopolitical space, arena or interweaving;[1] in Europe and America, there is, in addition, a psychocultural space generated by the copresent, yet opposed, attitudes of exile and immigration. Exiles (*āvāreh*), says the psychiatrist-writer Gholam Hosein Sa'edi, are different from migrants (*muhājir*) who move voluntarily and assimilate happily. *Āvāreh* feel themselves paralyzed or suspended in an unreal limbo or purgatory (*barzakh*) unable to move forward into a new life, unable to return to their roots. The feeling is not a freezing of time, but a slow dying from gradual gangrene. Thus *āvāreh* live in a world of memory, idle talk, jokes, folkloristic references, and parables. Sa'edi himself was such an *āvāreh;* he died of a despair quickened by alcohol abuse. But others have found inspiration and renewal in the liminal spaces where cultures meet and cross-fertilize. Iran and Iranian habitations abroad are both "crazy" hybridized spaces: at times fertile and comic, at times sterile and painful; in either case, hard to image, hard to project into a future that gives the present significance. The two settings, Iran and Iranian habitations abroad, mirror each other at acute or oblique angles, mutually affecting each other's representations, setting off mutating variations. We will be concerned in this chapter primarily with immigrants, with those who intend to live in America, but who do not wish to, or cannot, give up core elements of their past, especially their sense of being Muslim Iranians.

Both settings, Iran and Iranian habitations abroad, turn upon the notions of authenticity and identity. Authenticity, notes Leonard Binder, "stands for the freedom to be what one, in some sense, already *is,* while identity may also be referred to the freedom to be what one wants to be" (ibid., p. 320); these Heideggerian and Ericksonian definitions are but poles in a dialectical field, as the Moroccan social historian Abdullah Laroui points out with regard to Arab identity: "For Laroui, it is no longer possible to realize a pure Arab authenticity. The Arab identity has been so tied to that of Europe that it is no longer possible to engage in a cultural monologue. There can be no Arab self-understanding which is not also an understanding of the European other, and it is gradually becoming clear to the European intelligentsia that the same is true for them" (Binder 1988:322). Moreover, as the Egyptian liberal, Zaki Nagib Mahmud, argued, "contemporary borrowing of alien or *wafid* cultural elements merely repeats the practice of the *turāth* (heritage), for one origin of Islamic rationalism was Greek, while many of the mystical and gnostic influences in Islam were borrowed from India and Iran" (ibid., p. 306).

Hybridized cultural spaces call for imaginative frames for description, narration, self-recognition, and sense of (alternative) perspectives. America and the idea of modernity are both themselves such hybridized notions. "Plotting the West," "imagined communities" of "cities on the hill" in the "New World," "death and rebirth" (in revitalization and revival cults, in the crucible of "the frontier"), "experiments in democracy," "Americanizing" without becoming "lonely in the crowd" of individuals, dealing with city slickers and confidence men—these are the perennial tropes both of America and of modernity.[2] The themes are those of picaresque maintenance of virtue in a corrupt world (individual ethics); arranging marriages with strangers, the theme of immigrant novels, but also of traditional fairy tales with their comic-monstrous pairings and results (family and community); and negotiating harmonious governance (civil society, pluralist "melting pot"). These themes have found classic expressions in Iranian films: *Aghā-ye-Hālū* (Mr. Gullible) is a comic film about modernity in Iran, based on a television play by Sa'edi, that traces the misadventures of a rural bumpkin who comes to town and is taken advantage of by a series of city slickers, and only barely manages to leave the urban Babylon with his virtue intact.[3] *Aghā-ye Avāreh* (Mr. Exile) is a parallel, if considerably less polished, comic video about immigration to California, composed of a series of skits that follow an Iranian Charlie Chaplin-like Everyman in suit coat, loosened tie, and canvas shoes carrying a green flight bag as he tries to find a house to rent, to get a job, etc. Events in Iran intervene not only in his nightmares of Khomeini, revolutionary demonstrations, and sounds of the Iran-Iraq warfare, but also in his rejection by Pakistani or Indian and Mexican employers, and even by redneck winos, because he is Iranian.

Ghassem Ebrahamian's film, *The Suitors,* is a polished weaving of such situation comedy skits into a deadpan black humor story about a working-class ḥajji who returns from Iran to New York with a young bride. Four young male friends throw a party for him, slaughtering a sheep in their apartment bathtub: blood drips into the apartment below causing the superintendent to fear an Iranian terrorist cell. A police SWAT team clears the building, storms the apartment, and kills Ḥajji, leaving Ḥajji's widow to the marital attentions of his four young friends. One of these, together with Ḥajji's business partner, essentially kidnaps the young woman in an effort to marry her and thereby claim the insurance. She escapes with the aid of another of the young men and attempts to fly to Europe in a suitcase, but on the runway with the other baggage, thinks better of flying in the hold, unzips the suitcase from inside and climbs out, only to face New York again without language, without friends, without passport or papers.

The appeal of the film is in the emotional tone of the set pieces: the U.S. immigration official who insists on seeing the face (all the way to the ear) of Ḥajji's wife covered in her chādor; the elaborate meal (*sofreh*) spread when Ḥajji arrives with his bride; the five-acres of farm land that one of the young men buys to raise sheep, the taking of live sheep back in their station wagon so they can taste fresh kebab, and a subsequent reminiscence scene about the gourmet delights of breakfasting on sheep's head soup; the slaughter of the sheep, complete with disputes about which way to face the animal toward Mecca, feeding it a last drink, and total incompetence with the knife; the SWAT team and subsequent police station scene, with the hapless Iranians trying to maintain their innocence, dignity, and rights in the face of the New York police; Ḥajji's funeral (*porseh*) where the four young men make eyes at the widow, and their individual visits to her each with a different line; the effort of the young woman to go out, to shed her chādor, and to avoid the moralizing insistence of the men that she remain modestly veiled and sequestered in the apartment, depending on them for all contacts with the world; her encounter on the street with two youths, her effort to ask directions, and their effort to pick her up; the fancy house of Ḥajji's partner, complete with a library that "came with the house," site of a marriage proposal via the would-be-groom's sister, familial language of caring for the bereaved widow (not reciprocated), and a sewing scene where the sister and the partner's wife discuss the would-be bridal gown (that the young widow manages to steal and tear apart); the gas station where her rescuer and other bachelor immigrants work, complete with television tuned to "The Dating Game"; the effort to buy an airline ticket and leave the country without a passport (Ḥajji's partner has appropriated her passport), eventually trying the desperate ruse of hiding in a huge suitcase and being sent in it down the conveyor belt. The scenes are neatly stitched together with a kind of symbolic logic, done in neither slapstick comedy nor full melodrama. There are playful Freudian clichés (the street lads who try to pick her up taunt her with a huge snake; in the final airport scene, the camera focuses for a second on a cat carrier, a pussy in a cage). And there are deft uses of American counterpoint background details: the initial airport scene focuses ever so briefly on passing Hassids, surely as weird-looking as Ḥajji in his three-day growth, wool cap, and collarless worker's shirt, laden with suitcases and samovar, followed by a young chādored woman; there is a scene of Miryam, the widow, lounging in the apartment in her slip, reading fashion magazines, while the radio spews out adult dating ads (in a language she does not understand); the scene of the blood dripping into the apartment of Lou, the building supervisor, brilliantly has Lou listening to a Christian fundamentalist preacher, fully as wackily paranoid as Lou and the New York policemens' fantasies about Iranians as terrorists; and the television show watched by the gas station attendants is an apt counterpoint to the deadly dating game being played at the same time with the widow by Ḥajji's partner and the young man he has selected to marry her. Miryam is not exactly an *āvāreh* in Sa'edi's sense: she more or less voluntarily married Ḥajji as a way of coming to America and of continuing her education, she has fantasies of bringing her mother to America, and in the end she is determined to stay. But she is an *āvāreh* in the sense of being an exile, caught in a new land, with little language, with no resources except her wits, struggling to break free of the cages imposed by Iranian males, who themselves are struggling to create new lives.

The *āvāreh* is caught betwixt and between not only because of his or her own psychology, but also by external events: the revolution and the Iran-Iraq war have transformed Iranian consciousness in ways that still have not yet found their Henri Balzac nor Naquib Mahfuz, nor their Jaroslav Hasek, Joseph Heller, Thomas Pynchon, or Günter Grass.[4] However, a remarkable series of films has been made in Iran since the revolution, of which the most important is Mohsen Makhmalbaf's "Marriage of the Blessed" (*Arusi-ye Khuban,* 1988), in which a shell-shocked photographer documents the war, the hospitals for its victims, and the poverty of society. This film was among 16 post-revolutionary films screened at U.C.L.A. in April 1990. (Mohsen Makhmalbaf, the maker of eight films, is also the founder of the Art Bureau of the Organization for the Propagation of Islamic Thought.) Among exiles, Gholam Hossein Sa'edi did make a preliminary gesture in the television/video play, *Othello in Wonderland,* a satirical portrayal of how producing a Shakespeare play under the Islamic Republic would lead not merely to censorship by the mullās, but also to their playing all the major roles themselves and in the end turning the action into a passion play of martyrdom. Parviz Sayyad's film, *The Mission,* portrays the human, ethical, and ideological negotiations of royalists and revolutionaries in New York, where again the attraction of the film is in the emotional tone of the set-piece scenes and in the moral human interactions of the lead characters within the story of an idealistic young man sent by the Khomeini regime to assassinate a former SAVAK colonel. Finally, Hamid Naficy has begun analyzing the war imagery used in Iranian television shows produced in the exile community in Los Angeles (see below).

One should not, however, downplay the optimistic cultural fusions which, after all, may be the leading edge of the New World and world expansion of Persian culture, not unlike the exuberant Perso-Islamic release that occurred when the formation of New Persian in the tenth and eleventh centuries freed Islam from the constraints of Arabic. For example, a Noruz 1989 (the Persian New Year) concert in Washington, D.C., which attracted several thousand middle class Iranians, featured not merely classical Persian music, poetry recitation, some terrible kitschy folk dances, but also a stunningly well performed set of small orchestra pieces fusing Persian classical and Western symphonic styles. Even the kitsch dances attempted bicultural fusion: a ballet to taped Persian music with piano accompaniment; fake Levantine belly dancing to the tambak drum; a cossack style dance with ballet spins and jumps; but also a precision, tour-de-force kerchief dance, modernized yet true to the original form. The orchestral pieces achieved true fusion and counterpoint of high cultures, and was conducted by Khanom-e Khaligi, herself the daughter of a well-known Persian musician-conductor, Golnush Khaligi. Similarly, the poetry recitations featured new works by such leading poets as Mehdi Akhavan-e Sales, read with professionally clear enunciation by a well-known radio personality, Parviz Bahadur.

Perhaps the most impressive art form represented that evening was a kind of *khaṭṭāshī* graphics display in the lobby by satirical cartoonist and calligrapher Bidjan Assadipour. *Khaṭṭāshī,* coined by the poet Isma'il Shahroodi, is a Joycean contraction of *khaṭṭnaqqāshī* ("line drawing") that sounds like *khaddāshī* ("scratching"). Bidjan Assadipour's version is a calligraphic-cartooning fusion: e.g., a cartoon titled "the living martyr" shows a young man in T-shirt and ironed trousers (i.e., modern dress) seated on a chair whose head (brain) is replaced by a classic calligraphic bird shaped from the letters of *bismillāh* ("in the name of God"). Another, less clearly legible, calligraphic chicken balances precariously on the barrel of two guns pointed toward each other held by two kneeling men, one in army helmet, and other in civilian hat; the drawing is titled "civil war" and has verses from Sa'di's *Golestān* warning that the talebearer who stirs up enmity between friends will be destroyed by the fire of enmity he creates. Other cartoons have calligraphic tattoos on arms and bodies with displaced mouths and faces to create figures entitled "contemplation," "too much to say"; or calligraphic birds and flowers replacing heads such as "the living martyr" and "calm under pressure"; intertwined figures of "civil war," "cold war," "class conflict"; animal transformations, and elaborately wrapped figures in intricate designs reminiscent of block-printed textiles or mosque faience designs. "War Handicapped" is a man dressed like a hero/athlete (*pahlavān*) in traditional gymnasium (*zūrkhāneh*) shorts styled like an ornate faience mosque archway, the pillars/legs of which end in peglegs, one with a castor made of rounded letters. The cover of a collection of Bidjan's drawings has a man (poet, storyteller, reciter) in colorful embroidered robe and cap (a similarly decorated butterfly flits nearby) standing over three reclining men (listeners); calligraphic inscriptions float on either side like butter(gad)flies from Sa'di invoking the dionysian or golden ass humor of critique: "Transporting cows and asses are better than heartbreaking people". "The Epic of Holy Defense" is a witch-like figure on a horse on wheels (Trojan horse?); an ornately embroidered banner such as are hung for passion plays is labeled "war" five times in place of the names of the five pure souls (Muhammad, Ali, Fatima, Hasan, and Husain); the face of the flag carrier is a calligraphic composition (appropriately?) hard to decipher with words such as *enemy, thousand,* and *goal* (for another prominent, now American resident, khaṭṭāshi master see Mohassess 1989).

Immigrants from different places bring with them different perspectives and genres of narration. This has been given some attention in reverse: modern literary genres being adapted for use in the Persian and Arab worlds. For instance, Laroui casts a critical eye on the use of folklore, the *roman,* and the *nouvelle* in modern Arab writing. Use of folklore in creative writing (as well as in nation-building rituals such as folk dance displays), he suggests, is often inauthentic: romantic, parochial, nostalgic, regressive, and a distorted image of the past. The *roman* or novel, he suggests, is a European bourgeois form not well adapted to Arab experience: the Arab bourgeoisie, he suggests, did not slowly evolve through individual experimentation as did the Europeans in the eighteenth- and nineteenth-century; rather the Arab bourgeoisie took over Ottoman and European positions. But it is the *nouvelle* that Laroui finds the most dangerous. It is, he suggests, "the conclusion of an unwritten *roman,* the description of a situation and its impact on an isolated human being without pretending to explain how the world works," a dark, pessimistic, film noir-like evocation of a society dominated from afar by foreign capitalism, dangerous because it can "perpetuate the image of a fixed and completed past, which will impede the grasping of a new reality." Ideological forms are subject to similar dangers: Laroui provides an incisive account of the attractions of marxism in the third world, and how third-world marxism is different from Eurocommunism, closer to that of Marx, the first third-world intellectual to go to the metropole to understand how the engine of capitalism cast an iron grip from afar on his own third-world country, a career many a third-world intellectual has since repeated. The danger, as the 1980s have made even clearer, is that marxism is the language of the elites, not of the masses, and it can easily alienate the elite intellectuals from the masses, whose discourses are those of Islam.[5]

But relatively little attention as yet has been paid to the discourses that ethnographically immigrants actually use in making sense of their own lives, in comparing their own value systems with their new settings, or in forging philosophically resonant frames that draw on the genres, tropes, metaphors, imagery of both old and new cultural settings. (Parviz Kima'i's film *Moghūl-hā* did begin to dramatize the question of how television was beginning to replace traditional epic parable forms in Iran.) These of course require mapping against different class and social strata, different geographic and urban ecologies. What exists among monarchists in a reconstructed North Tehran now resituated in Beverly Hills–Westwood, Los Angeles, will be quite different from what exists among Muslim activists who see themselves as a network of cells distributed across the United States, which in turn will be different from what exists among essentially secular individuals in dispersed cities like Houston who on occasions of ritual events require Islamic anchorages. In a study of the Chicago Iranian community's oral public communication patterns, an enclave community on the Near North Side, Katirayi (1987) mentions settings such as "open houses" where Persians are welcome to drop in at any time, and female *sofreh*s in parks with children in tow, and analogizes the questioning of sources and validity of rumors and oral information to the procedures of evaluating the *isnād* of ḥadīth in traditional Islamic hermeneutics. *Sofreh*s literally are "table cloths" spread with votive offerings to the angels (*pari*) who are invoked in ritualized, communal, work stories, and asked to aid with tasks, troubles, and crises.[6] In Chicago, presumably, it is only the form and the idea that is invoked, not the actual rituals.

Iranian television and videos being produced in Los Angeles provide another distinctive genre and access to a particular segment of Iranian-American life. These are being currently surveyed and analyzed in a fascinating series of studies by Hamid Naficy. In 1988, there were seventeen hours per week of Persian TV programming in Los Angeles, more than for any other ethnic group, except Hispanics. All of these programs were anti-Khomeini, predominantly secular and promonarchy. They drew their program logos and opening/closing framing clips from ancient pre-Islamic motifs, from Pahlavi era motifs, or from Albert Lamorisee's visually stunning celebratory film, *The Lover's Wind.* These and other techniques, says Naficy, fetishized Iran as "a ruined land in the throes of death." Among these techniques were the constant "depiction of the body in crisis: bodies maimed by torture and bodies wounded and destroyed in the war with Iraq," not only in news clips, but more important, in interviews with Mujahedin and others who had been tortured and who showed their scars; in verbal accounts of assassinations, hangings, stonings, raping of women, shortages, disruptions of utilities; and in hyperbolic descriptions of Iran as "a total ruin and a vast cemetery." Naficy notes that it is the destruction which is foregrounded, and a tragic sense of helplessness which is promoted:

> Even when action and resistance is shown, it is injected with tragedy. For example, in the same program we see demonstrations by Iranians in Los Angeles (which lasted several days) against the so-called "war of the cities." We see demonstrators marching and making impassioned speeches, but we also see them crying for what has befallen Iran, accompanied by an extradiegetic song on the soundtrack (revealing the programmer's own commentary) whose refrain is, "lonely homeland, indigent homeland." Sometimes, such visual or verbal invocations of home as a ruin [are] inappropriate. . . . If Islamic Iran is designated as a signified for "ruin," then any picture of ruins will do. . . . (Naficy 1988:8)

The psychology of this tragic mode, Naficy suggests, promotes solidarity, justifying and reducing the guilt of having chosen exile. The tragic modality fits with other accounts of the tragic and mourning frames in Persian culture, particularly the exploration of depression among Iranians in California,[7] as well as the use of tragic idioms in both popular religious mobilization and secular avant garde literary forms.[8] It also fits with the split between the inner (*bāṭin*), private, real, melancholic sense of gravitas as opposed to the exuberant public (*ẓāhir*) masques necessary in a corrupt, superficially pleasurable world of appearances.[9] Compare also the tragic tones of the Qur'an underlying the jouissance of the play of appearances in the discussion of the *muḥkam/mutashābih* distinction in chapter 2.

Thus, Naficy brilliantly suggests, while the tragic mode dominates the programming, the interstitial commercials are celebrations of consumer capitalism, masking "the inner pain and displacing it with pleasure of consumption" in quite literal ways:

> As a whole, commercials on Iranian tv programs depict a vibrant culture of consumerism which is capable of providing in exile all types of products that displace the pain of loss and confusion, from the most esoteric herbs to BMW cars. In addition, all forms of construction, or rather, reconstruction and renewal of the self are advertised, from cosmetic plastic surgery to transformation of one's legal status. (Naficy 1988:9)

An orgy of this sort of displacement grew to a peak in 1987, when some programs were as much as three-quarters commercials. Two other formal features underline the "split imago" of these psychological processes: the frequency with which singers on music videos, logos, and other visuals are split into superimposed dopplegänger figures, and the pastiche magazine format which is constantly juxtaposing "self-other, home-exile, here-there, and present-past" (ibid, p. 10). Sensory overload and repetition (increased through the use of video cassettes) turn these features into "a form of closing the self off from the threatening outside." It is, says Naficy, "tantamount to whistling in the dark when alone or carrying a boom box" (ibid, p. 12).

Another axis on which to paint Iranian-American life is to think through the occupational translations in America. Among the culturally more interesting are restaurateurs and shopkeepers because they often recreate nostalgic cultural settings in their public spaces. Houston has had a succession of unsuccessful Iranian restaurants, with varying degrees of public offering. Pizza Town served quite good chelo-kebab and khoreshts for awhile, and even offered Persian music on the weekends, but one had to be in the know, because the signs were all in English and those signs only offered pizza. An equally split personality was the Swiss Deli, run by an Iranian Zoroastrian. More successful, eventually, were two real Persian cafes, one run by promonarchists and one by leftists, both attempting to recreate the sense of a Tehran working-class cafe, the one a bit more aestheticized with a fountain and tiled floors, the other a bit more "authentic" with plastic tables, booths, and a continuously running little TV (showing Los Angeles–made videos). Authenticity was added by the clientele, ranging from Iranian mechanics to middle-class folk nostalgic for a sense of home; these behaved with the warmth of polite recognition or real friendship that created a familial ambiance quite different from the anonymity of an ordinary restaurant. The names of restaurants and groceries are those of Tehran: Super Villa, Darband, Shomineh, Super Vanak.

Persian carpet shops are perhaps the quintessential Persian locale. There were about twenty carpet dealers in Houston in the 1980s, four of whom were Pakistani, one Lebanese, one Armenian, and the rest Iranian. The Iranians ranged in style (like the cafes), business strategy, and savvy, from the frugal *bāzārī* or *kāsebi* style to the flashy big-spender, from aggressive *gheychi kardan* (pincer tactics of killing off competitors by opening shops on either side of them) and perennial auctions and closing sales to the more sedate use of carpet shops as only one kind of investment in a wide spread of businesses across investment sectors, across the country and internationally.

The frugal *bāzārī* style is represented by a ḥājjī and his three sons, who are from an old merchant and industrialist family of Kashan, intermarried with an important and famous family of mullās, as well as related to the owners of the largest industrial empire of Iran under the Pahlavis. The carpet business is a family business: each member of the family (including in-laws) has shares; each has his own inventory of carpets, just like shepherds who may herd sheep belonging to many people but who know exactly which animal belongs to whom. Ḥajji is an *ostokhwāndār* (literally, "holder of bones"), i.e., solid: he owns his own capital, is not dependent upon borrowing, does not pay interest, has a stock of merchandise that is growing in value, and so does not care if customers buy or not (in sharp contrast to merchants who use borrowed capital and are under the gun to have steady sales and liquidity so loans can be repaid, and interest payments minimized).[10] When a customer walks in, Ḥajji looks to see if she or he is serious; if not, he's not interesting in talking, wasting time, and may even say, "Sorry, we do not carry what you are looking for." Ḥajji wryly comments on the changing carpet market, saying that Persian carpets used to be luxury items and one dealt with connoisseurs, however defined, but increasingly now one is dealing merely with design commodities, where color and design are the only considerations, not quality:

> Last week I got a call from a man who said he needed a five by seven foot rust-orange carpet. So I took a carpet to the address he gave. When I drove up, I recognized two trucks and a car of other dealers: "Asghạrian" was taking two five by seven carpets out of his truck, the car was unloading a carpet, and three carpets were being taken from the other truck. I ran to be first at the door, but when I was let in, I found two more dealers inside, and the man was negotiating with both at the same time. I exploded and said: "Did you really have to do it like this, calling all of us at 4:00 P.M. on a Saturday? Couldn't you have staggered the times, one at 2:00, one at 3:00, and so on?" The man just looked at me as if to say, I am the buyer, you are at my mercy. So I took my carpet and left, thinking it is time to get out of this business.

Ḥajji buys bundles of carpets from wholesalers in Tehran or in New York. This is a slight gamble since you do not know what will be in the bundle. A bundle of ten carpets sold to Ḥajji for, say, $10,000 might contain one exquisite carpet which can be sold for a large amount, three carpets that might be sold for 40–70 percent above the average $1,000 price, four carpets that cannot bring more than $1,000, and two that will sell at "under cost" of the average $1,000. Ḥajji also has agents who bring carpets from Tehran, but this tends to be a more expensive way of acquiring stock since one is buying carpets individually.

"Asgharian" (a pseudonym) presents the contrasting style. Four brothers and a sister own a chain of stores in New York, Washington, New Orleans, Atlanta, San Antonio, Austin, Dallas, and Houston. This is a business run aggressively with borrowed capital, ostentatious big spending (not merely do the owners drive fancy cars, but they pay for tables of potential customers at Persian concerts and nightclubs), cultivation of an aristocratic style (the owners order peons to do all the work in their stores, in contrast to Ḥajji who does everything, including washing the carpets, with his employees), and aggressive *gheychi kardan* (pincer/cutting of competitors by opening shops on either side) and "auction," "clearance," or "closing" sale tactics. By 1988, Asgharian had bought up the Lebanese shop and an Iranian competitor, and was moving in on one of the Pakistanis. He had located his main store in a prime location owned by a Yazdi real estate magnate. The auction tactic is to advertise in the Sunday papers: "FBI case: Hundreds of Persian Carpets, Values from $100–1000 at Auction, No Minimum, Auctioneer: Colonel X." These are not items seized by customs, being auctioned off, but space rented at the custom house, Colonel X being a retired customs officer hired by the carpet dealer. It is, among other things, a way of saving the costs of having to transport the carpets into the shop in town. One of the Pakistani dealers is notorious for having perennial closing sales: finally, legally, he is being forced to close, but the shop will reopen under a new name run by his Iranian partner.

A third style is represented by Mr. "Yazdi," whose carpet shop is but one piece of a diversified set of investments. Mr. Yazdi, like Ḥajji, is an old style Iranian small business entrepreneur (*kāseb*):[11] he dresses in baggy pants, sports a Yazdi accent and Yazdi walk, and speaks no English. He spends his time traveling between his investments in several cities, letting his sons run the local business. Bitter about the Islamic revolution, he says he suffered two revolutions, the one in Iran and then the economic depression in Houston. He made his first money in Iran drilling deep wells and selling pumps and irrigation pipes. At the time of the revolution the company was, like so many "capitalists," accused in the public Friday prayers of Tehran University of marking up prices exorbitantly. A brother was jailed and he was sentenced in absentia. In Houston, the family built a new shopping center on the west side, but with the economic downturn they have almost been bankrupted: only a Chinese restaurant has done well, a fast food store failed, a bakery failed, a computer store never opened, and a black entrepreneur accepted a year's free rent contract and then left after the year. But investments in other cities are doing well, and the carpet business essentially began a mechanism for transferring funds out of Iran, with outlets in several cities, the Houston store being primarily the central headquarters from which telephone directions around the country are conducted, rather than being necessarily the best retail outlet. Mr. Yazdi is disaffected from the Islamic Republic not merely because of being scapegoated, but also because he has stories of corruption of the mullās. Once he used to be a pious business man who paid his religious taxes (the *khums* and *zakāt*), and who went to the mullā to cleanse his money (*mālesh sāf o pāk konad*).[12] He used to pay his religious tithes (*khums* and *sahm-e Imām*) to Āyatullāh Ṣadūqi until one day Ṣadūqi, who had a farm near the Abdul Malek coffeehouse,[13] asked him to install a water pump and then told him to take the payment out of his *khums*. "I did not pay *khums* for Ṣadūqi's personal benefit!" Mr. Yazdi still fumes, each time he tells the story, "and so I wrote the pump off as a loss." Then he is likely to launch into accounts of monies he borrowed from various mullās at exorbitant interest rates, and the hypocritical rationales these clerics gave for why interest could be charged (*kolāh shar'ī*),[14] although usury is condemned by the Qur'an. Teased by outsiders for being *af'i rū-ye ganj* (serpents sitting on treasure),[15] entrepreneurs like Mr. Yazdi and his sons are likely to reply by invoking the virtues and hard realities of *kāseb* entrepreneurship.

Of these three styles of dealer, Asgharian in Tehran might or might not have been religiously active, except as a patron when solicited on ceremonial occasions. The other two would traditionally have been one of the basic sources of support both for religion as a social and moral code and for the clergy as an institution. None are supporters of the Islamic institution in Houston. Their only contact might be at times of ritual need: weddings, funerals, maybe Ramaḍān or Muharram.

Mehdi Abedi and I have shared experiences of Iran and of life for Iranians in America, but we also have distinctive experiences. For me the "crazy space" between exile and immigration exists in part in the wry tales of my father, vignettes that are emblematic of differential points of view and value systems. There is the tale of my father sitting at his card table on the deck of the *Zamzam,* an aging steamer named for the Meccan well that succored Isma'il and whose redemptive/curative waters ḥajj pilgrims still bottle. Originally a British freighter on the Burma run, when she became unfit for the high seas, she was sold to Egypt, renamed the *Zamzam,* outfitted with a small mosque, and used as a ferry on the Red Sea to Jidda, the port for Mecca. Now she had been refitted to take cotton to New York, and on the upper deck and cabins she took Jewish refugees from Palestine to the New World, zigzagging to avoid Nazi submarines. (On the return trip she was in fact sunk.) There he sat, in 1941, literally between the Old World and the New, and temporally between the prewar and postwar civilizations, the young European professor writing his first English language book, entitled *The Passing of the European Age: A Study of the Transfer of Western Civilization and Its Renewal in Other Continents.* Another equally emblematic tale is one of spending the first summer in America in Alpine, Tennessee, where the Baptist pastor told his flock: "Glory be. Many of you sitting here will see the coming of the Lord. For it is written that the Jews will be scattered into the four corners of the world. That will be a sign. And now the first Jews have arrived in our county." And he stretched out his hand to welcome my father, saying, "I thank the Lord that He permitted me to shake hands with a blood relative of His son." (He would also write a letter of recommendation for a teaching job phrased in that same quaint rhetoric: "When Dr. Fischer enters a room, it is as if Father Abraham himself were entering.") Another, more historical emblem of differential perspectives was the tale of committing a faux pas at Alpine, part of the TVA project area, when a farmer asked which American president was most highly regarded in Europe, and my father without hesitation blurted out "Herbert Hoover," remembering his help as the head of the League of Nations Commission that saved millions from hunger and starvation after World War I. The farmers were upset: to them Hoover was the source of all evil, the one who had caused the great depression. A more serious, if still emblematic, tale is that of being one of only two persons in his Office of Strategic Services (OSS) office who were depressed and sat apart from the general celebratory atmosphere at the announcement of the dropping of the bomb on Hiroshima and Nagasaki. A lighter tale is that of voting for the vegetarian candidate for president in 1948 and discovering afterwards that two other members of the geographical research institute at the University of Virginia had done the same, accounting for three of the seven protest votes in Charlottesville for that candidate. Behind these tales is a Central European vision—moral, humanist, liberal, and cosmopolitan—a vision that Milos Kundera has called the perspective of the small nations.

For Mehdi Abedi, the crazy space between exile and immigration exists in experiences of student life (chapter 1 above), of politically factionated Iranian exiles, of emotional Islam displaced and often nostalgically rather than knowledgeably remembered, of entrepreneurship on small, middling, and large scales, of dealing with non-Iranian Muslim brethren, of newly important immigrant groups from the Middle East, Africa, South Asia, and Central America who reimage the immigrant experience in ways new to America and to Europe.[16] This is an imaging that has only begun to be explored in the short stories of Bharati Mukherjee, the plays of Farokh Dhondy, the films of Jahmil Dehlavi and Hanif Kureishi, and the novels of Salman Rushdie, an imaging that has a stronger South Asian than Middle Eastern slant, but still one that includes strong Persian and Muslim tonalities, and one that problematizes the roles of Islam.[17] Behind these tales is also a humanistic vision, one that, with both humor and sometimes with a stark grimness not seen in Europe since the 1930s and 1940s, points up areas of blindness both in Western complacencies and in Islamic and patriarchal fundamentalisms.

In this chapter we wish to explore four small pieces of the space between exile and immigration, and how they might be retold, and how those tellings might project a future identity and authenticity: (1) negotiating funerals, (2) negotiating marriages, (3) celebrating Ramaḍān, (4) negotiating the counterdiscourses of black, feminist, American Muslims. There are affinities in the ethnographic form of these four set pieces with the folktale, the novel, and the journal montage of a film noir. The folktale here, however, is not the commodified folkloristic search for a past, but rather a philosophical form of narration. The novel, here, is a process of individuals seeking out how they can weave the fragments of their pasts and presents into a meaningful basis for a future. And the film noir is a metaphorical set of vaguely threatening cultural and social contexts that surround the controllable interactions and searchings for community, fellowship, and moral renewal.

The communities of Muslim Iranians in Houston, and those secularized Muslims who have a need for Islamic ritual at crisis points, life cycle changes, annual reaffirmations of communal solidarity (e.g., at the fast of Ramaḍān), or occasional individual reaffirmations of spiritual strength, present a quite different slice of life than does what Naficy calls "fetishized Iranian TV." There are various kinds of accommodations with religion among Iranians as with those of any other religious background, and many Iranians can be outwardly involved with the displacements of commodified indulgence (the *zāhir*) while still feeling themselves inwardly to be fundamentally Muslim (the *bāṭin*). Even among those who give a high priority to being Muslim, and to living an externally marked Muslim life-style, the manner of engaging in communal Islamic activities ranges from participating in discussion and/or political circles or organizing or attending formal ritual occasions.

Houston's major mosque is the Islamic Society of Greater Houston (ISGH). It has several branches. Iranian Shi'ites use it mainly for marriages, funerals, and other occasional needs. Most Iranians in Houston are not religious. A small group associated with the *Nahzat -e Āzādī Iran* (Liberation Movement of Iran), the party of Mehdi Bazargan and Ibrahim Yazdi (prime minister and foreign minister, respectively, in the first government after the revolution), used a private home (belonging to relatives of Yazdi) for religious gatherings. A *khānaqāh* (Sufi lodge) has been established and follows the California-based *pīr* Sadeq Anqa. Sadeq Anqa himself is said to be in the computer business, and his Houston followers are mainly well-to-do folk. In 1988, Sayyid Zaki, with funds allegedly from the Mustazafan Foundation (the former Pahlavi Foundation, turned into the Foundation for the Dispossessed after the revolution), bought the bankrupt Gandhi Center to refurbish as a Shi'ite mosque. This ends the period in Houston of lip service to Islamic unity represented by the ISGH. Sayyid Zaki, a native of Basra, Iraq, with a B.A. from the College of Fiqh in Najaf, claims to be a *mujtahid* and to be in touch with the *marja* of the Age (Khomeini). He holds public services on Thursday night for reciting the Shi'ite prayer, Du'ā Komeil, and performs *rowzeh*s (sermons framed in the Shi'ite stories of the martyrdom of Imām Husain). The constitution for his organization reflects the format of the constitution of the Islamic Republic: he as imām can dismiss all elected officials, but he himself is appointed by and can be dismissed only by the Imām of the Age (Khomeini). Women may vote, but may not be elected to office. The tensions described below in the Ramaḍān 1984 period at ISGH thus may now find a more open expression in the rivalry between the new mosque and ISGH.

This chapter is a very preliminary ethnographic exploration of some of the negotiations of Islamic life in a new land (see also Williams 1988). It is only part of a larger ethnographic canvas that needs to be painted in. It is, for instance, a very different segment of Iranian-American life than that currently being surveyed by Hamid Naficy's studies of Iranian television and video use in Los Angeles.

How are these things narrated, imaged, plotted by Iranian Muslims? Are there *afsāneh*—moral parables, folktales like those that power *The Thousand and One Nights, Kalileh and Dimneh, The Book of Kings,* and other such collections—that provide wombs of imaginative growth?

A tale told by a village storyteller near Herat may serve us allegorically. Told in 1975 at an evening's storytelling session arranged for folklorist Margaret Mills in the home of a young marxist subgovernor by a storyteller who had been jailed briefly but, he thought, unjustly by this subgovernor, the tale is a classic multilayered talking cure. Allegorically, it may serve us as a kind of genre type for all those Iranian mutterings about America as the land of lack of (Islamic) morality, for all those *dard-e del*s (the genre of telling one's troubles) of life in America. The tale has a frame story, very much like that of *The Thousand and One Nights:* a king subliminally troubled by his tyranny has a dream which will not allow him to sleep but which he cannot remember; the king tells his vizier to find someone who can tell a story that will bring him to both tears and laughter; a storyteller is found, whose tale not only diverts the king, but illuminates the unrighteousness of the king in such a way that he can correct the underlying causes of the dreams that afflict him. The 1975 message, of course, was meant for the marxist subgovernor: a tale the young marxists, would-be reformers of Afghanistan, did not appreciate (understand or like if they understood), and the nightmares thus induced by tyranny increased for the society as a whole. The tale itself begins with the deathbed scene of Salim the Jeweler's father: the deathbed advice given of how to live a proper life of course was violated by the young man, thus motivating the story. Salim journeys abroad and engaged in marriages to beasts and fairies with inhuman results until he returns to his wife, reestablishing marital harmony, and by his tale also causing the king to institute restitutive acts that reestablish harmony in the polity (see Mills forthcoming).

Our tales below might be seen as following this triangular structure: we begin with the attempts to establish proper funerals, and the difficulties thereof; we then recount efforts to contract marriages outside the familiar structures of information gathering that would facilitate matters in Iran; and finally, we consider the effort to establish communal worship. The stories in the first two sections are unlike fairy tales in being ethnographically true, but like fairy tales, they take place in a culturally displaced space. The third, and longest section, is told in diary form: daily vignettes. In a parallel effort to image the reality of a new kind of space, albeit far more brutally decultured, Ghada al-Samman's "Beirut Nightmares" adapts the journal form to chronicle 206 nightmares of a seven-day reality. In the Houston journal there is no fantasy, no similar violence; only conflicting desires, remembrances, and controlled agonistics. Perhaps the three sections, like the tale of Salim the Jeweler, can work as a folktale of America, exploring boundaries, limits, proper fences within which Islamic life can be reworked in a new environment, where Muslims not only are a minority, but also come from differing traditions themselves.

But note: it is a folktale, rather than a fairy tale, the literary form of the folktale: these ethnographic fragments are the parables of ordinary folk, their lives, their follies, their hard-earned wisdom. They are fragments in the rough, still being polished, only at the beginnings of their retellings. Descendants in the future may retell these stories differently and in more seamless, less discordant form, but for the moment they serve as birth pangs of something new.

Prologue: Negotiating Death and Marriage in a Loose Social Structure

> Iranians are masters of their own communication magic. . . . In knowing how to use the resources of their own language in conjunction with their knowledge of society and its dynamics, they are able to negotiate and even transform an uncertain world with skill and grace. Though all men are able to do the same in their own tongues, it may be a particular Iranian skill to be able to carry out this magic with an elevated sense that raises the enterprise above mere pedestrian conversation and into the realm of art.
>
> —William O. Beeman, *Language, Status, and Power in Iran*[18]

Shortly after Mehdi Abedi arrived in Houston, he began to be drawn into helping immigrants and exiles give their marriage ceremonies a more Iranian and Islamic setting. The legal side of marriages is generally done before the American court system (in cases where at least one of the two parties is a citizen or permanent resident) and/or registered with the Iranian interests section of the Algerian Embassy in Washington. The religious side of marriages is done either at the Islamic Society of Greater Houston (ISGH) or very often in a traditional ceremony supervised and performed by Mehdi Abedi. He has over the past seven years performed several hundred such ceremonies. A large proportion of Iranians in Houston are not particularly religious, and most are openly opposed to the clerical regime established by Khomeini. Still, at times of major rites of passage, even many of these would like to have the familiar traditional trappings. Performing such ceremonies almost inevitably draws one into the complicated lives of the immigrants, and Mehdi has found himself occasionally providing counseling to keep marriages together, as well as being consulted about divorce procedures. Initially, as he became identified with marriage ceremonies, the community explicitly wanted to keep him separate from funerals: weddings and funerals, rites of fecundity and death, should be kept apart. He was consulted on procedures, supervised a few funerals from a distance, and of course was involved as a mourner—in one particularly tragic case, the wife of a couple he had married barely a year earlier was brutally murdered, and he had to play a central role in calming, consoling, and coaching the bereaved husband by providing traditional words and frames for the expression of grief. He reminded the young husband of Imām Ali's grief when he lost his beloved eighteen-year-old wife, Fatima, through complications of a miscarriage caused by Umar kicking her door open against her belly; and by slowly channeling the husband's grief, he was able to prompt him into being able to ask the assembled mourners to help him pray both for his wife's soul and for his own sanity and peace of mind.[19] Funerary functions were not as intimate for him as were marital functions. Indeed, even more generally, Iranians in Houston seemed not to want to be associated with death: this created problems, since, despite the religious duty and merit in washing corpses, they did not wash their own corpses; instead, they hired Pakistani Muslims and others, again an occasion for minor conflicts over procedures. This estrangement from funerary functions began to change in 1989 after the establishment of a Shi'ite mosque.

Funerals: Shi'ites and Sunnis in a Non-Muslim Land

> My father got sick and called me and said, O son . . . after you have buried me . . . sit down with people of wisdom, sit down with those who govern, sit down with the Muslim man, the seeker of God.
>
> —"Salim the Jeweler," in Mills forthcoming

> "To be born again," Gibreel Farishta said to Saladin Chamcha much later, "first you have to die. Me, I only half-expired, but I did it on two occasions, hospital and plane, so it adds up, it counts. And now, Spoono my friend, here I stand before you in Proper London, Vilayet, regenerated, a new man with a new life. Spoono, is this not a bloody fine thing?"
>
> —Salman Rushdie, *Satanic Verses*

Some of these conflicts can be sketched with the help of a Pakistani Shi'ite case. The family were regulars at the ISGH mosque, and they also sponsored flagellation ceremonies each year on 'Āshūrā in their home. Iranians were invited to their 'Āshūrā sessions, but that generated mutual irritation too: the Iranians found the Urdu recitations of the Karbala story outlandish and funny, rather than tragic. The deep emotional tones of mourning simply could not be produced for them in the up and down cadence of the Urdu language. And so in the midst of one of these sessions, when the Iranians retired to another room to do one of the *namāz* prayers, they were accused of being disrespectful to the martyr Husain.

In any case, the old mother of the family died on a Thursday night. The ISGH has a contract with the Hyde Park Funeral Home, where the body is prepared by Muslim volunteers—an Egyptian engineer, often working with a Pakistani accountant and a Pakistani insurance agent. The next day, immediately after Friday prayers, before people had time to disperse, the casket was wheeled into the ISGH mosque from the hearse, and everyone was invited to join the *ṣalāt a-mayyit* (prayer for the dead). Some two hundred people stayed.

Problems began immediately. Sunnis say four *takbīrāt* (glorifications of God), Shi'ites say five. The deceased was Shi'ite, but the mosque was a Sunni majority institution. Shi'ites are allowed to follow Sunni custom in such circumstances, but families want to make sure that everything is done correctly to ensure the deceased easy passage to the next world. The family had designated a Shi'ite to lead the prayer, and he insisted on doing it in the Shi'ite manner, not deferring to Sunni style as is usual in the ISGH. There was some whispering among the Sunnis, but they all went along with the five *takbīrāt.* There are two versions of the *ṣalāt a-mayyit,* and the Shi'ite imām chose to do the longer one, causing more whispering. The funeral procession of forty or fifty cars proceeded to Forest Lawn cemetery, where amidst the Christian graves there is a small area reserved for Muslims. Burying a Muslim in the graveyard of infidels, or burying an infidel in a Muslim graveyard, is prohibited.[20] The area for Muslims was already nearly full. It includes the wife of the former director of Prime Minister Hoveyda's office; a poor Iranian painter who had died a few months earlier; a young Iranian boy; several Pakistanis; several Arabs; a couple who must have died in an accident because their dates of death are the same. Many of those who can afford to do so are buried in their homelands.

The grave was too deep, and it was facing in the wrong direction: the deceased should face Mecca. A dispute with the gravediggers ensued, and finally a small bulldozer was brought up and the grave modified. The next problem was the casket: cemetery regulations required burial in a casket; Islamic law requires the right cheek of the corpse to touch the soil. There was a long, angry dispute with the cemetery director. Finally, they hit upon a compromise. The corpse was lifted out, and the bottom of the casket was filled with soil, then the corpse placed again in the casket on the soil. The next problem was that the imām jumped into the grave to whisper in the ear of the deceased the Arabic words of confession she should repeat to the angels, Nakir and Munkir, who would come to interrogate her about her faith and her prophet; the cemetery officials began shouting and threatening to call the police. The imām had to climb out and squat by the opening to read the instructions, followed by prayers for her soul. The Sunnis seemed embarrassed as they listened to the Shi'ite rhetoric, but no one said anything. It went approximately like this:

> Listen well, Bibi Khanom, daughter of. . . . Do you still witness that there is no God but God who is one and without partner, and that Muhammad is His servant and messenger, master of the prophets and last of His messengers? And that Ali is king of the believers and master of the successors, and he is the Imām to whom obedience is made incumbent by God upon all who live in this world? And that Hasan, Husain, Ali son of Husain, Muhammad son of Ali, Ja'far son of Muhammad, Musa son of Ja'far, Ali son of Musa, Muhammad son of Ali, and "the still living one," the Mahdi our Imām, salutations of God upon them all, are Imāms of the believers and the proofs of God for all men, and they are your Imāms who guided you to become a pious person? O Bibi Khanom, daughter of . . . , when the two angels of God come and ask you about your God and your prophet, your religion and your book, your *qibla* and your Imāms, you must not fear nor be sad; in response say to them: Allah is my God; Muhammad, salutations of God upon him and his relatives, is my Prophet; Islam is my religion, the Qur'an is my book, the Ka'ba is my *qibla* . . . Ali is . . . [the names of the Imāms are repeated with some of their attributes]. And you should know that Allah . . . is the best God, Muhammad is the best Prophet, Ali . . . [again the names of the Imāms]. Death is truth, resurrection is truth, the bridge [to the next world] is truth. . . . Have you understood, Bibi Khanom, daughter of. . . .

For Shi'ite believers, the first night after death is fraught with fear, for if one answers incorrectly, one goes to hell. There is a rich amusing anecdotal literature and jokes about these beliefs. There are jokes about Iranians not being able to understand the Arabic of the angels,[21] and jokes about secular substitutes for the traditional formulas of belief.[22] But believers are terrified by stories that even after having lived a pious Muslim life, some souls suddenly right after death slip back into Judaism or Christianity or worse, and are condemned to hell. Most poignant is the oft told story of Āyatullāh Abdul-Karim Yazdi-Ha'eri who became tongue-tied when the angels came to him, and nearly was consigned to hell, till at last he was able to cry out, "I am a servant of Husain," at which point the angels cried and promised him protection.

Shi'ites call themselves "the saved group" (*firqah-e nājiyah*), feeling that on the basis of their sinful lives everyone would be consigned to hell, except those who on the first night after death are interceded for by Ali, Fatima, or one of the other fourteen Pure Souls (the family of the Prophet: the Prophet, his daughter Fatima, and the twelve Imāms).

Marriage

> "Only move, I mean like a woman. . . ." She shrieked in horror. "My God, what have I married? I know you Europe-returned men. . . ."
>
> . . . the wedding went off well enough. Parvati's formal conversion to Islam (which irritated Picture Singh, but on which I found myself insisting, in another throwback to an earlier life) was performed by a red-bearded Haji who looked ill-at-ease in the presence of so many teasing, provocative members of the ungodly. . . . She took a name which I chose for her out of the repository of my dreams, becoming Laylah, night, so that she too was caught up in the repetitive cycles of my history. . . .
>
> —Salman Rushdie, *Midnight's Children*

Marriages, in an immigrant Iranian community, come in various categories and with varying motivations. Shi'ism recognizes temporary or fixed-term marriage (*mut'a, ṣīgheh*) as well as permanent marriage ended only by divorce or death (*'aqd, nikāḥ*). In both cases, children enjoy full rights of legitimacy and inheritance, but a *mut'a* wife has no right of inheritance from the husband. Both cases have explicit contractual forms: a verbal formula must be recited by one or both parties or their proxies, preferably in Arabic and in the past tense, and a settlement of money or property is given to the woman. In the case of permanent marriage, there is a written contract, and the settlement of money (*mahr, ṣadāq*) is intended as support for the woman should she be divorced or widowed. In Iran, the *mahr* was often set very high and was to be fully paid only in case of divorce; it was set high both to symbolize value and to discourage the husband from even thinking he could financially bear to divorce. Among middle-class Iranians, however, the *mahr* in recent times has become purely symbolic—a coin, a Qur'an—in conformity with modern ideas that marriage should be a bond of love rather than a material one, and in visceral rejection of any connotation of "selling" daughters.

Traditionally, *mut'a* or temporary marriage was not only used by men on long trips away from their families on business trips or pilgrimages.

Shrine towns are known for their supply of women who provide *mut'a* services. These were acknowledged as being a form of quasi-prostitution, albeit strongly defended by mullās and other men as socially useful means of channeling loose male lust, and thus protecting respectable society. But *mut'a* marriage was also traditionally used as a legal fiction so that men and women or girls not related to them could be in the same room together. For instance, if a man were engaged as a tutor to a married woman, he might contract a *mut'a* marriage with her daughter, thus making his student his technical mother-in-law. Or if a man had to accompany an unrelated woman and infant on a trip, a similar use of the *mut'a* might be employed in which he married the infant for the length of the trip. Some *mut'a* relationships of this sort in the past have had written contracts, although most are only verbal. Mehdi discovered in the Vaziri Library tucked inside an old manuscript one such old contract, complete with names, dates, length of the marriage term, amount of the *mahr,* and on the back the date of termination with the testimony of the husband that the woman was still *ghayr madkhūla* (literally, "not penetrated"). More recently, *mut'a* has been revived under the Islamic Republic (technically, it was banned by the Pahlavi government, but it was nonetheless quietly practiced), used among other ways as a mechanism for dating by young people. It is also, more exploitatively, a form in which poorer women who have been ostracized from family social support networks by divorce, urban migration, or other circumstances, try to attract husbands; they are looking for love and support, and are vulnerable to men merely looking for temporary liaisons, or unofficial second wives.[23] In the United States, *mut'a* marriage may also be used, by persons of varying religious scruples or sense of guilt and propriety, for "dating," for temporary liaisons, or as mechanisms for couples intending to marry before they can organize family for a public wedding. However, a stigma is attached to *mut'a,* and most Iranian women attempt to avoid such relationships. The *mut'a* form came in handy as a benign legal mechanism, circumventing an inegalitarian technicality in Shi'ite marriage law as it relates to intermarriage, in the first case below.

Mut'a is not the only legal form subject to potential abuse. Immigrants, not only Iranians, often engage in green card marriages, in which the object is to obtain permanent residence in the United States. Iranians jokingly refer to it as "American marriage" (*izdiwāj-e amrikā'ī*). The Immigration and Naturalization Service has attempted to crack down on blatant marriage for pay arrangements, by imposing a two-year wait on green cards, combined with visitations and questioning whether the couple actually lives together, whether there is a real marital relationship, whether the partners can identify details of their alleged residences, and so on. But immigrants may contract real marriages, intending to divorce after gaining their green card and then remarry their original husbands or wives from their countries of origin and thereby gain green cards for them as well.

The most complicated cases, however, have nothing to do with legal form or customary practices. Rather they have to do with the delicate negotiations of relationships outside the close social networks of control, support, information, traditional expectations, and resources for meeting those expectations, available in Iran, but not in Houston. The following notes are again written in the autobiographical form of chapter 1, as sondages into cultural issues of transferring Shi'ite sensibilities into a new environment, and of slowly coming to terms with being a minority community in a non-Muslim world.

Since a few months after arriving in Houston in 1981, I have been performing marriage ceremonies for the local Shi'ite Iranians and occasionally for those in other cities of Texas and elsewhere. Although I have not kept statistics, I must have performed several hundred by now. This unexpected career began in a weekly Islamic gathering when a friend asked me about the laws of marriage, and followed up a few weeks later by asking if I would perform a ceremony for two friends of his. I was reluctant, but he insisted. It turned out that the groom was an Iranian, the bride a South American Catholic who did not wish to convert to Islam. By Shi'ite jurisprudence, she could not be married in a permanent union, but only in *mut'a* marriage. Shi'ite men may marry in *mut'a* a woman of the People of the Book (i.e., Jews and Christians, and according to most, but not all jurists, Zoroastrians). When we met for the ceremony, before I could ask her anything about the matter, she whispered to me that she wanted to keep her religion. I had to agree. I had not been asked to perform a temporary marriage ceremony. But I decided to use it as a clever way to save embarrassment and keep the occasion a very happy one. When everyone was ready, and the couple was sitting before the traditional bridal display, I asked them, as is the necessary technical preliminary, whether they accepted me as their proxy. They answered yes. I asked the groom what he would give the bride as *mahr*. He answered softly, "A volume of the Qur'an and an ounce of gold." I asked the bride if she consented to the amount. Smiling, she said yes. Then I told the bride and groom that I only had the authority to pronounce them man and wife for the fixed period of ninety years.

Fig. 5.2. Mehdi Abedi writes out a marriage contract.

After this period, I said, you can call me to perform another ceremony for another ninety years. Unaware of the technical difficulty that obliged me to fix the term, they interpreted it as a good omen. Everyone was happy, and a small but lovely celebration of dancing and dinner followed.

Otherwise, with a few modifications, it was a classic Iranian marriage ceremony. It was held in the bride's house. The bridal display was laid out on a silk cloth on the floor near the wall. A large mirror was set up, its back toward Mecca. On the cloth was bread (symbolizing life and blessings), cheese, green vegetables (symbolizing growth and happiness), nuts and eggs (symbols of fertility), sweets, a jar of honey so bride and groom could each dip a little finger in and put in it each other's mouth (symbolizing a sweet shared life), a prayer cloth (*jā namāz*) and *muhr* (clay from Karbala or other martyr's shrine used in prayer), and a Qur'an. Bride and groom sat on two pillows facing the mirror. As I recited the formula, four married women (symbolizing auspiciousness) held a white cloth like a canopy over the heads of the bridal couple, while a fifth married woman ground two sugar cones over the cloth. Each time I uttered the names of the couple, the woman with the sugar cones would grind them against each other, wishing them good luck. A sixth married woman had a threaded needle and pretended to be sewing the canopy, ritually sewing the bride and groom together, as well as sewing up the tongue of the "jealous mother-in-law." The few modifications from tradition were that men and women were together in the same room, the bride and groom sat together, and alcohol was served in the celebration afterwards.

Gradually, the idea of using me to perform such ceremonies spread by word of mouth. Occasionally, I was criticized by anti-Khomeini types for using Arabic at all: Persian is our language, the ceremony should be in Persian. I would reply that I do the ceremony in three languages, Persian, Arabic, and English. Arabic is the language of our religion, Persian our mother tongue, and English so that American guests would not be left out. No one ever suggested dropping the English, only the Arabic, muttering such things as, "We are not Arabs and don't understand Arabic," or "The Arabs devastated our culture in the name of Islam." Sometimes I had to take the initiative in inserting a traditional Persian joie de vivre in assemblies made overly dour by the pro-Khomeini religious consciousness.

One such case was that of a couple who were attached to the Ḥizbullah (Party of God) fundamentalist supporters of Khomeini. They actually had two ceremonies in an interestingly awkward attempt to negotiate the form of the marriage. The first ceremony was held at the ISGH mosque. A large color picture of Khomeini was displayed, despite Sunni objections that no image should appear in the house of God. Men and women, modestly attired, sat separately, the bride hidden among the women, and the groom surrounded by his male friends and relatives. A few slogans of "death to America" and "death to Israel" were chanted in Persian. A Pakistani Shi'ite read the marriage formula. Since the house of God is not a place of *lahw* (music, singing, dance, games, or other vices of idleness), there was no music or dancing, there were only cookies and sweets.

Afterwards, we all went to the house of the bride, where the marriage ceremony was repeated, this time by an Iranian couple. Despite being Ḥizbullah, the couple were also Iranian, and wanted the traditional Iranian ceremony done before the traditional bridal display, described above. Such a display was not possible in the Sunni-dominated, non-Iranian mosque of the ISGH, despite the fact that no Sunnis had been present.

Following the second brief ceremony, people sat and chatted mainly about politics and Islam. Men and women sat in the same room, although modestly apart. Suddenly, a cassette tape recorder began to play Persian music. The child who had pushed the button was chastised, but almost everyone wanted the music, and no one shut it off. A Turkish song followed: the bride's mother was from the Turkish-speaking province of Azarbaijan. The zealous Muslims slowly relaxed to the music, forbidden by Islamic jurisprudence. A male friend and I began to dance. Using the excuse that a female friend was outside and wanted to enter, I borrowed the veil of Dr. Y.'s wife, and put it on, pretending to be a traditional Muslim woman. My friend and I then enacted a bawdy musical dialogue, traditional at weddings, though usually done in the women's quarter by women for women, and sometimes by male performers dressed as females for menfolk. The bawdy double entendres are to entertain, but also to advise grooms and brides of proper behavior toward each other, warning against the vices satirized in the wedding songs. Occasionally, the objects of satire may be specific individuals present, or new social roles and their potentials for abuse as in the case of the verse about Revolutionary Guards (*pasdaran*).

"I shall not marry a mullā."

"Why not?"

"Mullās make you bend down."

A threefold pun is involved here: the bending down refers to the bowing (*rukūʿ*) and prostrations (*sajda*) of the namāz prayer; to the bowing of respect conventionally due a mullā; and to anal intercourse (including homosexual).

"I shall not marry a colonel."

"Why not?"

"They do it with cannon and gun. . . ."

The pun here is not merely the sexual double entendre, but also the pain and suffering they bring through their roughness and warfare.

"I shall not marry a general."

"Why not?"

"They do it in a jeep."

The pun here involves the idea both that they never come home and that they issue commands from afar, never descending into real life.

"I shall not marry a butcher."

"Why not?"

"They make you tired."

Here the reference is to the butcher's reputation for making women, especially young women, wait while they slowly cut up the meat, engaging the customer in flirtatious talk. A similar sentiment is used about grocers. About Revolutionary Guards it is said only that they make you pregnant (while illegitimately exercising their authority to conduct searches and investigations). About *ākhūnd*s (another, disparaging term for mullās) it is said they do it with their fingers, referring to the habit of preachers to shake their fingers for emphasis.

A few faces turned red at first, but eventually everyone gave in to laughter. A photographer even took pictures. A few shoulders began to shake with the music. And the women began to move into a separate room where dancing and clapping started up. We men were excluded, but the groom went in to dance. At the end of the party, we were thanked for enlivening the party. But later on, we were bitterly criticized by the Ḥizbullahi participants including the groom and his bride.[24]

Some marriages are badly arranged and do not work out. One of the more egregious of these that I unfortunately got involved in concerned the son of a landowner in Iran, call him Reza, and the daughter of a wealthy bazaar merchant, call her Giti. Reza owned part of a hamburger stand in a small Texas town and, despite his well-to-do background in Iran, was just getting by in America. He had been married to an American woman, had a child by her, but was divorced. Giti had been married to an Englishman, and was a woman of expensive tastes. They met at a party: Reza came to her table, lighted her cigarette and asked for a dance; she refused. Her father, concerned to get her settled again, was attracted to the handsome Reza, and began to ask about him, even calling Iran to determine that he was of a good family. He began to encourage Reza, and to put pressure on his daughter. Eventually, she gave in. A negotiation session was held between the men to work out the details of *mahr,* and other matters. As Reza later told the story, he was advised to talk about his part ownership of the hamburger stand as owning a restaurant, and he was supposed to have three months to sell his small apartment and find a house. Instead, the marriage was rushed. In fact, I was called on very short notice, and was somewhat offended by that fact. When I arrived, Giti's father took me aside and began to dictate how I should write the contract; again I felt his interfering bossiness. The ceremony went well, and a party was held at a large club in the evening. Three days later, I got a telephone call from the father: they wanted to see me. Giti was with him, and it turned out that they wanted the marriage annulled. Reza had been pressed to take her immediately to her new home. Although he had scrubbed and decorated his apartment, she was outraged at being brought to such a small place, shouted at him, and left. I told them, I could not just annul a marriage, that I would have to talk to Reza, and to get him to accept me as a proxy. I also asked about the *mahr,* and they assured me it was unimportant. I met with Reza and he told me his sad story, how he had been manipulated, and how he was now in great debt. I negotiated with Giti's father to help Reza financially. He first refused saying: "We do not pay tribute," but then was persuaded. Giti, however, insisted that Reza should not be helped: "It is a lesson to him." It took several weeks of talking to Reza to get him to give up the idea of getting damages from Giti's family, and agreeing to a divorce. In the end, Giti's family did not even wait for any divorce procedure. Perhaps they did not care, because the marriage had never been registered.

Meddling by kin who claim rights or responsibilities in arranging marriages can sometimes be helpful and sometimes destructive. There was a case recently in which a twenty-year-old girl fell in love with a man twenty-five years her senior, a liaison abetted by her mother. Her father's brother, however, adamantly opposed it and summoned her father from Iran who tried to dissuade her. But the marriage was held. It was a bit strange: the ceremony proper was done in a closed room with only the closest family, excluding the uncle. There was a large party afterwards, and the uncle took part. My sense is that the marriage is quite likely to work, the groom being eager to demonstrate to the uncle that the match is a good one, and the uncle providing a safety valve for disputes. In another case, however, an uncle broke up an engagement. The couple, a young engineer and a student, had met through the friendship of their respective mothers who were visiting their children in the United States. The prospective groom asked the girl's mother for her hand. The mother in turn had to consult the father back in Iran, and in the meantime suggested a traditional *mahr* of 1500 gold coins (the so-called *bahār-e āzādī,* "spring of freedom"). The father proposed four conditions to be reserved to the bride in the contract: the right to finish her education, to choose her location of residence, to have an occupation outside the house, and to divorce. In the negotiations the *mahr* came down to 600 gold coins. But in the meantime the groom's father's brother, claiming to be the proxy for the groom's father, began to make trouble, saying he had not been sufficiently consulted, making demands both on property arrangements and on the bride-to-be's behavior. He thereby caused the bride to cancel the engagement.

Sometimes marriages that do not work can be given a second chance. I got involved in a faltering marriage while performing a marriage ceremony for a friend who himself had been through some complicated negotiations. My friend, the younger of two brothers who came to the States for education, call him Said, is an assistant professor at a Texas college. He met an Iranian girl, call her Zahra. He also had an American girl friend. At first his problem was only whether he could string both of these along, but he eventually ended the relationship with the American, and promised to marry Zahra, but not until he could accumulate a bit of money and not until their respective parents could come from Iran. Zahra's brother who lived with her began to become impatient, pressing her to get a commitment or to stop seeing Said. To stall for time, Said convinced her to come with him to me, so that I could perform a "formula" (i.e., a *mut'a*) so they could be legally married to each other, until they could do the real wedding. Zahra reluctantly agreed. In the meantime, however, Said's mother had started arranging a marriage for him in Iran. This was during the period when phone connections with Iran were cut off for several months. Gifts between the families had been exchanged. I insisted that Said call his elder brother, Ali, both to consult him and to prepare him to come to the future wedding; one could not just arrange matters and expect an elder brother to appear; elder brothers expect to play a key role in the arrangement of family affairs. Ali was upset: he thought Said was obligated to the girl in Iran. Said wanted simply to call their mother and have her cancel the engagement, but Ali objected, not only because of the money and obligations already incurred, but also because it would damage the girl's reputation. A girl whose engagement has been canceled may have a hard time finding other respectable suitors. Said was not sympathetic. The case was complicated by the fact that the girl in Iran wanted very much to come to the United States; but this also provided an escape. The brothers decided that they could back out of the engagement by saying that Said's application for a green card was not proceeding quickly, that he felt guilty in postponing the arrangements indefinitely, and that he could not come to Iran to fetch the girl because of his pending application and the bad relations between Iran and the United States. This saved face, and Said was freed from that entanglement. Said then, under pressure from Zahra's brother, set a date for the wedding.

It was a small, but nice, affair. Among the people present was the couple who had introduced Said and Zahra: Mustafa and Fatima. The bridal display was simple with only almonds and walnuts sprayed with gold, and wild rue (against the evil eye). So I filled in some of the rest of the display verbally, saying that this was a special wedding. Said was like a younger brother to me, and I wanted to explain what marriage is. Thus, for instance, the word for spouse, *hamsar,* means "same head," and the idea is made visible through the mirror of the traditional bridal display. Whenever *hamsar*s look into the mirror of their life, they see their spouse as well as themselves. (This was received with appreciative murmurs.) I recited a little poetry about marriage, and delivered a short sermon in all three languages about the tradition of marriage in Iran and the role I would play as their representative, formally asking them to appoint me to such a role that I might conduct the contract of marriage. Then, to break the formality of the occasion, I used my standard joke of offering them the keys to my car to escape now before the ceremony was finalized if they were unsure. As always it brought a giggle or laugh. Mustafa and Fatima squeezed each other's hand and looked at each other with smiles. (I thought of pointing them out as an exemplary couple for the about to be newlyweds, but fortunately restrained myself.) Then I raised the issue of the *mahr.* Islam requires a *mahr,* but what is it really? "Dowry and bridewealth is love, oh friend/love is the meat, the rest but the shell" (*Jehāz o mahr-e zanmehr ast ay dūst/ Mohabbat maghz o bāghihā hame pūst*). Again this got appreciative responses: "*Bah, bah.*" With this introduction, I said I was not the authority in this matter, and I turned to the brother of the bride: "I am sure you represent your parents. If there is anything you want to add, any messages from the family, now is the time." What else could he say: "No, you said it all in that poem. All we want is that Said love my sister." I turned to Ali: "As Said's elder brother, do you have anything to add?" "No, you said it all." So, I could then sum up the *mahr* relationship by saying Zahra was so wonderful that, after all, there could be no adequate *mahr* for her, and that since I did not know her well, to speak much about her virtues might be taken as mere words, but I did know about the good taste of the groom and congratulated him on his choice. (People again murmured appreciatively at the verbal finesse: "*Bah, bah.*") I said I would pronounce them *hamsar* under conditions of mutual love and respect, for better and worse, richer and poorer, in sickness and health (but omitting any mention of death). I then asked if they each would accept me as their representative: Said said yes; Zahra, as tradition dictates, said yes only after the third time she was asked. I gave a short Arabic sermon, prayed for them (to murmurs of "amen"), and pronounced them man and wife. We then celebrated until midnight.

Mustafa and Fatima complemented me warmly on the ceremony before they left. They had in fact seemed particularly loving toward each other during the ceremony as if I were reminding them of their marriage vow, holding hands and looking at each other. Mustafa insisted with special intensity that I visit them the next morning, saying that if he had it to do all over he would have me preside, his own wedding had not been like this, that I knew the right things to say. After they left, Said told me more about them, and that they were separated and planning a divorce. It turned out that Fatima was Mustafa's second wife. He had been married to an American, and had a son by her, who lived with him. After the divorce he had gone to Iran and met Fatima. Fatima very much wanted to live in America. They married, but as soon as she got her green card, she began to want to be independent, to go off to California, to complain that she could not handle someone else's child. She even beat the child, and it came out in school, so that Mustafa had to appear before an embarrassing inquiry about child abuse. It was now four months since they had separated. It was one of those cases, someone said, where the woman thinks she comes from a good family and need not work, while the husband came to America to work hard to create a new life.

The next day, Mustafa received me warmly. He repeated, "We were impressed by the things you said during the ceremony." I replied that saying such things at such moments can have efficacy; and that I thought it better than, as so often in Iran, merely focusing on talk about the money involved in the *mahr.* Mustafa found an excuse to leave me alone with Fatima. At first she was silent, so I said that I was grateful for her help in introducing my friend Said to Zahra, and that I liked to see couples like her and Mustafa that set such good examples. She replied with tears that they were in the midst of divorce. I pretended not to have known, expressed my sympathy, apologized for speaking so much about marriage, and offered any help I could. I said, "You're my sister, let me ask a few questions, and see if I can help you cope with this difficult situation." She agreed and we talked about their separation of four months, the fact that they nonetheless still saw each other and made love, occasionally initiated by him, occasionally by her. She admitted that Mustafa loved her, and she liked him but felt uncomfortable in the relationship, that they were just too different, and that she felt uncomfortable with being a stepmother (*mādar-khandeh,* literally one "called mother"), the very word she felt was hateful. I elicited the fact that no one called her stepmother, that it was a projection she placed upon the relationship. I suggested if she had a child of her own, maybe it would teach her to have mercy on a child that did not have a mother or was under the custody of another. (She was unimpressed.) I asked if she believed in God, and she said yes. So I suggested, without anyone knowing, she open an account with God for this child, wishing that your own child never be under the custody of a stepmother. (This seemed to move her.) I talked about problems all marriages face, and how one can choose to be like fragile glass that shatters when it is but tapped, or like gold that becomes purer with the more fire it endures. I talked about difficulties in my life and how one always had the choice of running away or facing problems. We talked about the things I said during the wedding ceremony, and she contrasted them with what had been said at her wedding, which was only strange Arabic words about money, contracts, and religious fear. Indeed, when Mustafa returned, after she had cried a lot and I had discovered her vulnerabilities, we watched a video of their wedding: there was an angry-sounding Arabic intonation of Qur'anic verses about marrying girl slaves, and about God making believers rich, and about marriage being only partial insurance, that one should worry about the rest of one's faith. The longest part of the ceremony was about the *mahr.* I sympathized with them, saying I thought the ceremony terrible, and that they should do it over again. Again I talked to Fatima and Mustafa, each alone. I told Mustafa that my wife was in the hospital and I needed to return to her, but I felt I was on a divine mission, and that I would not leave until I was sure his wife would return to him. He was in tears, his chin atremble, saying I was a good man. I called Fatima and put their hands together, saying: "Erase the past. You've both done wrong, but you are both innocent in my eyes because you did not have the experience to deal with the rough spots in life. Wherever there is a rose, there are also thorns. Wipe your tears, and let's go in and watch Said and me clown a bit." Said and Ali had arrived, and we made some bawdy jokes about my having to get back to my wife, and told the old joke about how marriage is like the servant and his old much used *āftābeh* (the water pitcher for toilet ablutions): one day his master heard the maid servant wailing inconsolably; she had just broken the *āftābeh.* So get another, says the master. Not so easy says the maid: this *aftābeh* was *maḥram* to my vagina, it will take long to get used to a new one. (*Maḥram* are the degrees of familiarity under which one need not observe the rules of modesty.) Both Fatima and Mustafa smiled and relaxed.

Said and Ali left, and Mustafa and I went to pick up his son, and on the way back, I had them stop at a florist, and I made the boy present flowers to Fatima and say: "Mummy, I love you very much". (He agreed to do it only for a bribe of money, but he did it, and then ran off to his room.) I told Fatima and Mustafa I had planted a rose tree in their house, but it was up to both of them to water it. I said that mere oral words lose efficacy over time, and so I would write a prayer that they should recite holding hands every night. In elaborate calligraphy, I wrote out, "O God, keep the flames of the fire of love alive, and the mirror of our union shining." They insisted I stay for dinner, but I said I would share a meal only provided no one cooked and no one served. Instead I would take them to a restaurant so that someone else could serve all four of us. At the restaurant I played indecisive over the menu, and allowed Mustafa to take charge, while I entertained the boy. Then Mustafa took the boy to the washroom, giving me another space with Fatima alone. She was still doubtful, and I recited the poem of

Layla and Majnūn: *To-rā 'āsheq shavad peydā valī majnūn nakhāhad shod* ("you may find another lover but he will not be another Majnūn"), assuring her that Mustafa loved her dearly, and if he could not do more for her it was only because he was caught between two loves, the love of his child and the love of his wife, and that was hardly a fault. I told her of how I lost my wife once for five years and three months. Again she was in tears, again I recited the line of Majnūn. Finally, as I left, we set a date: in three months on their anniversary, I would return to perform a new marriage ceremony for them.

It is perhaps a fragile hope, but there was a real kindling of desire between them, sparked by the wedding of Said and Zahra, and fanned by judicious invocations not just of sentiment, or of similar problems others have faced, nor just of therapeutically "talking through" practical issues, but of deeply anchored, association-rich metaphors, poetry, ritual displays like the mirror, physical reminders like calligraphy, and other resonating cultural forms. This, as much as the wedding ceremony itself, is what efficacious ritual process involves, something particularly desperately desired in a strange land where traditional social networks are not densely available. Again, it is not the ceremony, but how the ceremony is done. It is a kind of powerful magic, not just linguistic or rhetorical, but a magic of cultural form.

A Month among the Believers: Ramaḍān in Houston, 1984

> In the name of Annah the Allmaziful, the Everliving, the Bringer of Plurabilities; haloed be her eve, her singtime sung, her rill be run, unhemmed as it is uneven!
>
> —James Joyce, *Finnegans Wake,* 104.1–3

If marriages and funerals represent personal negotiations of ritual, communal rituals present other opportunities, challenges, and forums for competition of interpretation. Houston does not yet have many mosques although Sunnis, Shi'ites, and U.S. Black Muslims tend to meet separately. The largest group, the Islamic Society of Greater Houston, is led primarily by Pakistanis and Egyptians, but has adherents from all over the Islamic world. Ibrahim Yazdi (the first foreign minister of the Islamic Republic of Iran, under Prime Minister Mehdi Bazargan) was one of the founders. During Ramaḍān more people than usual come to the ISGH (an ambitious mosque is planned) for prayer, and to listen to sermons delivered occasionally by illustrious visitors. In 1984 a cleric associated with the assassins of President Sadat of Egypt spoke, as did an older liberal Egyptian cleric saddened by Sadat's death. An Iraqi spoke about how he had converted from Shi'ism to Sunni Islam in Basra. Under superficial expressions of Islamic brotherhood, there was intense competition, wariness, and mutual proselytization. Among the cliques and factions, the most interesting was the handful of young Iranians. Unlike others, they did not sit together or come with families. They dispersed and engaged people in discussion. They set up a table with pamphlets supporting Islamic revolution as spearheaded by the Islamic Republic of Iran.

It has often been noted by journalists that the United States and Europe are major breeding grounds for Islamic fundamentalism. It is here, with a freedom of expression wider than at home, that university students are able to debate and organize. No doubt the alien openness of Euro-U.S. society functions like the relatively fast-paced life in Tehran or Cairo of the 1970s in causing youth from traditional families to defensively seek the security of fundamentalist rules and discipline[25] and to obsessively focus on the corruptions of the political elites of their home countries. The spirit of activist self-sacrifice seems to be a widespread response, not only on the fundamentalist side of the political spectrum. The esprit de corps of pro-Khomeini youth is matched by that of the cadre of the Mojahedin-e Khalq, who were said to work at multiple jobs, donate their salaries, and live as cheaply as possible in communal arrangements to raise money, medical supplies, and material for the causes of overthrowing Khomeini. There have been a number of bloody clashes between pro-Khomeini Hizbullahis and Mojahedin in the southern and midwestern United States.

But beyond the conflict of organized groups and the tactical arguments of young activists are widespread existential dilemmas, personal and social, which activists with their eyes on their countries of origin and, differently, immigrants with their eyes on America are seeking to identify and resolve. The Iranian revolution has created, at minimum, a deep generational experience for Iranians, but also for Muslims worldwide, an experiential moment for many believers of optimism and self-confidence that one can control one's own destiny and society. Like the sixties in the United States and France, that moment did not live up to its initial promises, yet many of those promises continue to live on in the hearts of its carrier generations.

The following diary, kept by Mehdi Abedi, may provide a feel for some of the competing currents—political, existential, and ethnic-cultural—in one immigrant-exile community of the United States.

1 Ramaḍān 1404 A.H. (Friday, 1 June 1984)

It is 10:30 A.M. In the Islamic Society of Greater Houston (ISGH) at 3110 Eastside the doors are still locked with burglar bars, and the parking lot is empty. There are fliers and signs on bulletin boards in three languages: English, Arabic, and Urdu. A sign on the door asks us in English to pray for our Muslim brothers fighting in Lebanon. Another announces in Arabic that there will be a guest lecturer from Egypt, a *mujāhid* (holy warrior). A grocer has placed ads in all three languages, offering items such as Islamically slaughtered meat at reasonable prices. A Muslim jeweler has a picture ad enticing customers to buy jewelry with Muslim designs. There is a short critique in Arabic of a recent book on Islam. There are ads for garage sales, baby-sitters, roommates, and so on.

A man parks his car and approaches. He is a Pakistani with a well-trimmed beard and is well dressed according to the Muslim dress code. It is Abdulrahim Buzdar, a regular member of ISGH, and a friend with whom I have spoken on many occasions. We shake hands. He unlocks the iron gates of the breezeway, and leads us into his office. The phone is ringing. He points to a model of the future Islamic center and mosque, which someday is supposed to replace the present facilities on a site in the center of the city. While he answers the phone, I leaf through an album of diagrams, illustrations, and information about the building plans and the history of ISGH.

Dr. Ibrahim Yazdi, a cancer researcher, long-time Muslim activist, representative of Khomeini in the United States and Canada, interpreter for Khomeini in Paris, minister of foreign affairs in the first provisional government of the Islamic Republic under Prime Minister Mehdi Bazargan, and currently a member of the Iranian parliament, helped organize the society in 1968. It had first met in private homes. In 1971 a former church building on Richmond Avenue near Woodhead was obtained. The mortgage was immediately liquidated through private donations and interest-free loans from members because usury—including, according to most interpretations, all interest-bearing loans—is forbidden in Islam. The Richmond site quickly proved too small, and in 1981 the property on Eastside was purchased, followed by two satellite centers on Bellaire Boulevard and at Greens Road, North Freeway. The Richmond site now serves as a dormitory, and there are plans to establish an Islamic library there. The three mosques offer public prayer five times a day.

Between phone calls, I ask Buzdar about current attendance. He says total membership is over a thousand, two hundred attend regularly on Sundays, and four to five hundred come for Friday prayers. More attend when the Saudi Educational Mission is closed. Roughly fifty percent are Arab and fifty percent are *'Ajam* (non-Arab). There are nine officers: six Pakistanis, two Egyptians, and one Iraqi. Six are engineers, one an accountant, one a businessman, and one a geophysicist. Buzdar is secretary of publications and public relations. The proposed new mosque will have a dome and minarets, classrooms, an apartment for the imām; its total area will be 96,629 square feet, and it will cost an estimated $5,175,000.

Two men and a woman enter. They are a brother and sister from Iran and the American fiancé of the woman. Buzdar is busy answering the phone, repeatedly affirming, "Yes, today is the first of Ramaḍān. *Imsāk* (the time fasting begins) is at 4:54 A.M., *Ifṭār* (the time of breaking fast) at 8:19 P.M." I strike up a conversation: the American wishes to become Muslim so he can marry the woman. I provide some information, and when Buzdar gets off the phone, I summarize the situation and he confirms that the man should first convert before Muslim witnesses, go to an American court for the legal marriage, and then return to the mosque for a Muslim marriage. The Iranian brother is concerned that the marriage may not be recognized by the Islamic Republic of Iran. He wants to consult a member of the Muslim Students Association Persian Speaking Group (MSAPSG), that is, a follower of Khomeini. He asks me in Persian, "Is it all right that they are Sunnis? Does Khomeini recognize this institution as Islamic?" I answer affirmatively. The Sunnis even surpass the Shi'ite requirements for the validity of marriage by requiring two male witnesses. Shi'ites do not require witnesses in this case. In my view, neither brother nor sister appear or behave as "true Muslims." He is chic, well shaved; his shirt is unbuttoned. She seems uncomfortable in head cover, thick hose, and long dress. One can tell she has just washed off her makeup to look proper when confronting Muslim authorities. Mischievously, I quip, "Becoming Muslim is easy, give me a knife and I'll do the circumcision." The American does not hear, but she turns white, her eyes beseechingly asking if this is serious. I recall a year ago, when a Chinese woman married an Iranian friend of mine, her friends teased her that she would have to be circumcised.[26]

A man enters and asks Buzdar to open the mosque. An Iraqi, Tahir A., another active member, enters and greets everyone. He is angry over an editorial cartoon in the *Houston Post* that showed Khomeini and the Iraqis, with an American commenting, "Well, at least they have not so far spilled any oil, just blood." Before I can clarify why he is so furious—is he angry at the "Jewish media," at Khomeini, at Saddam Husain, or at the Iran-Iraq war?—the muezzin calls us to noon prayer.

Friday Prayer, 1 Ramaḍān

[The call *adhān,* for "joining," invites the individual to abandon his individuality and to immerse himself in the public by standing behind the *imām,* the prayer leader, facing the *miḥrāb* (niche that marks the direction of the Ka'ba in Mecca). From the same root as *miḥrāb* comes the word *ḥarb* ("warfare"): Muslims stand in rows the way they would line up in battle; by praying, they battle against the forces of evil. The imām begins each act, and the Muslims follow: should a Muslim precede the imām, his prayer is void. Prayer is a microcosm of social unity and leadership. Like the ḥajj, it is a ritual of the utopian vision of the Muslim spiritual community (*umma*): the ḥajj is like the day of resurrection, in which no one has more than a white shroud; the Friday prayer instills a sense of communal discipline.

There is pressure to keep all disputes unvoiced, but potential lines of dispute are many. Activist newcomers are regarded with suspicion: both Qais al-Kalbi and I are examples. In the middle of Ramaḍān, Qais suddenly appears. He is a vocal advocate of fundamentalist Islam. Only a few members rival him in knowledge of Islam, and none have his eloquence or charisma. He speaks out against Shi'ite beliefs, and threatens Muslim unity in ISGH. In reality, none of the Sunnis approve of Shi'ite beliefs. Each group disapproves of many things that the other does; yet, even if it be superficial, Muslim unity is desired by virtually everyone. Qais is confronted not by the Shi'ites but by his Sunni brothers. Suspicion grows. Some whisper that he may be a spy. My own case was less dramatic, but my questions and curiosity brought suspicion, although I had attended ISGH prayers before and had been a regular attendant the previous Ramaḍān. I had been promised access to records of the ISGH, but I overheard through a closed door board members saying, "Who knows, maybe he is from the C.I.A.," and I was politely refused access to records: "We don't keep records." I did not press the matter.

The Shi'ite doctrine of *taqiya* (dissimulation) helps keep disputes between Shi'ites and Sunnis covert. Shi'ites are permitted to pray behind a Sunni imām, and to behave like Sunnis when among a Sunni majority. Religious reformers from al-Afghani in the last century to Khomeini have stressed the priority of unity, and so Shi'ites who in their hearts detest the first three caliphs and Aisha (the youngest wife of Muhammad) and who have little faith in Abū Ḥanīfa or Aḥmad Ḥanbal (the founders of Sunni schools of jurisprudence) do not verbalize these feelings. Nor does a Shi'ite bring to the mosque his *muhr,* the dry clay from the grave of a martyr (especially clay from Karbala), upon which he touches his forehead when doing the prostrations of the *namāz* prayer. Sunnis regard this as a kind of idolatry. Shi'ites pray only on natural substances—ground, stone, or wood—not on polyester carpets; Sunnis have no such scruple. Shi'ites do not object when Abū Hurayra, whom they consider a fabricator of ḥadīth, is quoted with great frequency by Sunni preachers, nor do they insist upon citing instead Imām Ja'far al-Ṣādiq. What is important is that Sunnis call Shi'ites "brother." What is important is that all rally to Khomeini's call for a unified Muslim world.

A second covert division is that between political and nonpolitical Muslims. The latter still engage in occasional disputes over dogma. The former have stopped disputes over dogma, and are working toward common understandings that Islam is the best system of government, that Islamic governments must be established, and that overthrowing secular regimes in Muslim lands is a religious duty. Although ISGH is a nonpolitical institution, it is a breeding ground for fundamentalist politics. Members included representatives of the Muslim Brotherhood, of Khomeini activists, of the Pakistani *Teḥreek-e Mujahedīn* (*Pakistan Beyrūne Waṭan*) who want to overthrow General Zia and establish a Khomeini-style state, and a few Iraqi fundamentalists. Palestine and Afghanistan are two political subjects on which all are agreed. There is no doubt among the community that Palestine belongs to Muslims, and that the Palestine issue is a Jewish-Muslim dispute. Everyone agrees that the Soviet invasion of Afghanistan is a plot to establish materialism in Muslim lands, and that the Soviet Union and the United States are covertly united in this aim. The Iran-Iraq war is only somewhat less a subject of consensus: everyone agrees that the cause of the war is America. It is a catastrophe imposed upon Muslims by the grand Satan. Saddam Husain has virtually no supporters. The division is only between those who say the war has gone on too long, and has failed to establish a Muslim government in Iraq, and those who counsel patience, hoping week by week for news of Saddam's fall.]

By 1:00 P.M. the crowds begin to arrive, and by 1:30 the mosque is packed. Latecomers must sit outside in the courtyard and parking lots. Along two sides, tables display literature from the Islamic Republic of Iran in three languages: English, Persian, and Arabic. Even if Iran is not a perfect model, the enthusiasm for Islamic revolution is strong, and Muslims from other countries condemn their governments as agents of Satan, Zionism, imperialism, and disbelief (*kufr*). The Iran-Iraq war is a second topic of interest. The cover of the English language magazine *Echo of Iran* shows a young boy, a woman, and a man, burned by Iraqi chemical warfare. The inside cover has a picture of Sayyid Muḥammad Bāqir Ṣadr, a leading cleric and representative of Khomeini in Iraq, who was martyred by Saddam Husain. In the picture, Ṣadr holds the green flag of Islam; and the Qur'anic words are written: "Triumph is from Allah and victory is near." Articles are about Morocco, the International Conference on Islamic Ideology, Muhammad in the Bible, women of Islam, chemical warfare, and cultural revolution. A pamphlet in Arabic, written by the well-known cleric Sayyid Hādi Khosrowshāhī, explains "Why we don't accept the peace plans." A second English language magazine, *Horizons,* warns that Dr. Hossein al-Shahristani, an Iraqi nuclear physicist, is in danger of execution by Saddam Husain. The two English language editions of the major Iranian newspapers are available as is the slick *Sorūsh* magazine. A booklet lists the services the Iranian government supplies its people, and describes Iran's self-sufficiency in building a military bridge.

Pro-Khomeini propagandists stand by the tables, calling their Muslim brothers to come and get the latest news on the Iran-Iraq war. These are men only; perhaps the women are similarly engaged among their non-Iranian sisters. Segregation of the sexes is marked. At the very beginning of Islam, such segregation at times of prayer did not exist; but this was only temporary as long as there was danger of attack from non-Muslims. Such egalitarianism was again temporarily revived by Khomeini in Paris, at the prodding of a prominent Houston Iranian woman. She complained that men were protected inside while women, who needed extra protection in the lands of unbelief, were left outside.

Friday prayer is well known for its political nature. It consists of two units (*rak'at*) which replace the normal four units of noon prayer. Preceding the prayer are two sermons usually on daily problems or moral principles. While these may not themselves have political content, the name of the supreme authority is invoked. For Shi'ites this would be the Imām of the Age. But the attempt of various governments to insert their names has caused Shi'ite clerics to take various stands on whether Friday prayer should be held (see chapter 2). Thus, in the ninth century, Ṭāhir Dhul Yamīnain, the governor of Khorasan under the caliph al-Ma'mūn, declared the independence of Iran by mentioning his own name instead of that of the caliph. In my hometown of Yazd, Sayyid Ali-Muhammad Vaziri revived Friday prayer in this century and made it a popular event through his oratory (see chapter 1). The orator holds a weapon in his hand as a symbol of authority. After the establishment of the Islamic Republic of Iran, Friday prayer became obligatory, and was used as a forum for political announcements. Sayyid Maḥmūd Ṭaleqāni was the first imām jom'a of Tehran, drawing great crowds until his death; his last sermon warned of the encroachment of tyranny by the clerics. In Houston, the preacher does not hold a weapon, and politics is not a usual subject. When Ṣādiq al-Mahdi, grandson of the Mahdi of the Sudan, a Ph.D. and leading politician of the Sudan, preached at ISGH when it was still on Richmond Street, he did not speak of politics; subsequently, he spoke at the University of Houston, discussing the Iranian revolution and pledging his support.

Friday Night, 1 Ramaḍān

After the *maghrib* prayer, the crowd stampedes to the tables of food: rice, beef stew, chicken, cantaloupes, watermelon, and coca-cola. One cannot but be amazed at the quick service. In minutes everyone is served, and in minutes the tables are cleared, chairs folded and stored, the ground is swept, and everyone is ready to say *'ishā* prayers. After *'ishā,* many leave, but many stay for *tarāwiḥ* prayers. (Shi'ites do not practice *tarāwiḥ,* considering it an abrogated tradition and forbidden, reinstated by the second caliph, Umar, on the advice of the unreliable Tamīm al-Dāri.) After *tarāwiḥ* prayers, there is a recitation of the Qur'an. An Egyptian expert, Shaykh Barakat, has been invited. He is dressed in turban and cloak, but oddly is well shaven. He has a beautiful voice, and is much appreciated. There is anticipation because he is to be followed by Shaykh Aḥmad al-Maḥalawi, a "holy warrior" scholar, invited by the Organization of Muslim Youth.

But first a tall American with two smaller men moves forward. One of the latter whispers to the president of the ISGH. The president stands, as if victoriously, and facing the crowd, takes the microphone to announce that the American has after much study decided to embrace Islam. He asks the American to repeat after him the credo, "I witness that there is no God but God; I witness that Muhammad is his Prophet." He repeats this six times, three times in Arabic, three times in English. Thereupon the crowd shouts, "*Allah-o-akbar!*" ("God is great") several times. The president delivers a short homily on the principles of Islam.

Mahalawi now ascends the pulpit and speaks in classical Arabic "so that everyone who knows the language of the Qur'an may understand." His message is the need to revive religion if Muslims desire to enjoy again the glory of the early Muslims. Shakir, an Egyptian and follower of the Muslim Brotherhood, takes notes, and then translates into English. Around midnight the crowd disperses. Nasser, another Egyptian, asks if I know who Mahalawi is, and tells me that he was arrested after Sadat's assassination as the founder of the movement that killed Sadat. People are crowded around Mahalawi, shaking his hand, and Nasser guides my hand toward him, whispering, "Hurry, shake his hand before it is too late." I do and Mahalawi looks straight into my eyes, as if attesting to his sacredness.

I notice that Shaykh Barakat has not yet greeted Mahalawi and several people are encouraging him to do so. Finally there is a formal, somewhat cold handshake. "You blessed us," says Barakat stiffly. Mahalawi utters an equally polite phrase. Curious, I follow Barakat outside, where he sits with several Egyptians, and criticizes Mahalawi indirectly saying, "Blood only brings more blood. We are experts in religion. Politics should be left to the politicians." A minor debate ensues, but Barakat emerges persuasive.

Saturday, 2 Ramaḍān

It is 3:00 P.M. Buzdar is running around taking care of ten jobs at once. The tent for the women has blown down. He must set it back up. A couple has come to register their marriage. The telephone is ringing. The courtyard must be swept before tables and chairs can be set up. Buzdar is running and sweating while murmuring verses of the Qur'an and prayers. I help with the tent. It is made in Pakistan with beautiful elaborate designs. We use blankets and a blackboard to provide walls so the women can be protected from male eyes.

The couple who have come to Islamicize their marriage wait. The man, "Hamid," is an engineer from Isfahan. He is Muslim. The wife, "Mary," is a Christian American. They were married seven years earlier here in Texas in a Christian ceremony. They have no children, perhaps because, with a Christian marriage, their children would be considered illegitimate. Now they want to have their marriage acknowledged by a Muslim institution. Buzdar asks the wife to fill in a formal marriage contract, so that there will be no misspellings, after the shaykh utters the marriage formula. In Islam a Christian or Jewish man may not have a Muslim wife, but a Christian or Jewish woman may have a Muslim husband. This is because children are counted in the patrilineal line. Mary need not convert. I ask how she plans to raise her children, as Christian or Muslim? She says they will teach them the good points of both traditions. They donate fifty dollars to the mosque and leave.

There is another marriage contract on the desk: "Husain" and "Ellie Sue". On average, someone embraces Islam once every three days in this mosque. Most of these conversions are due to marriage.

While working on the tent, someone tells me that Mahalawi has canceled his program because of insufficient attendance. Someone says it is because the time was changed, and people are too lazy to come to a lecture in the afternoon. A Pakistani comments, "It is a pity that such a great scholar comes from so far to guide us on the straight path, but people do not come." His mind takes a leap, and he continues, "Iranians are lucky to have a divine revolution. It is an act of God. It is strictly and only by the will of Allah that it succeeded. We need such a revolution in the entire Islamic world." I question him: "But don't you think there is political repression in Iran, even more than what existed before?" He answers, "I don't know, brother, but I think, for Islam, one is justified to sacrifice everything." I ask about the repressive regime of Zia ul-Haq in Pakistan. He says, "Zia is not perfect, but he is good. Look at the other alternative, the corrupt Bhutto family. Poor Zia, every time he wants to hold an election, they agitate and he must postpone it." Buzdar wipes the sweat from his brow and interjects, "We are Muslims, the worshippers of Allah, praise be unto him. A Muslim should not worship any hero. It is a kind of idolatry. I wish our Iranian brothers would not emphasize so much on Imām Khomeini." Then, closing his eyes, he recites the Qur'anic verse, "O Prophet, fear God" (31:1).

After *maghrib* prayers, Abdurrahman, the former secretary of the ISGH, sells cassettes of Mahalawi's speech; many buy.

Sunday Night, 10 Ramaḍān

Tarāwiḥ prayers have ended. Most people have left. A handful remain in the mosque to receive instruction on how to recite the Qur'an. A black man grabs the microphone and begins to shout in terse, rhythmic phrases resembling a machine gun or a rap singer, criticizing Muslims for wearing Western shirts and trousers and coming into the mosque bareheaded. "Listen, my brothers, let us return to our traditions. Why not wear Islamic garb and put on sacred turbans? The reason I don't wear one is I don't have one to wear. If I had one, I would put it on. You should do that too. There is nothing to be ashamed of in the Muslim dress code. There is nothing shameful about a turban. Let's wear it, brothers. . . ." No one seems to take him seriously.

Two Iranian cab drivers, Abbas and Mehdi, approach and ask me to teach them to read the Qur'an. I agree and we sit in the courtyard.

Imām Kamaluddin sits with us to listen. We exchange compliments. He leaves after a while. Behind me, three Iranians sit and whisper. They all have ill-trimmed beards and "nerdy" clothes, quite the opposite of Iranian playboy style. An air of tension and intimidation is created by their presence. Abbas goes to the bathroom and never returns. When I glance quickly behind me, I realize that he has joined them. Soon, one of the three, who later introduces himself as "Hasan," comes and sits at our table, but a few chairs away. I have seen him several times at ISGH and at several weddings. I open a Qur'an and hand it to him. He indicates that he does not wish to join. He murmurs an excuse; I do not catch the words. Suddenly, he interrupts us, saying to Mehdi, "If you don't mind, I would like to speak with this gentleman alone." Mehdi leaves immediately, and Hasan turns to me: "Perhaps you don't recognize me. I know you from Lawrence, Kansas."

"I sure don't! When . . ."

He interrupts. "Never mind. I have listened several times to your radio program on KPFT. Why do you attack Imām Khomeini?"

In the blink of an eye, I remember how lucky I am to be in the free land of unbelief, rather than a prisoner in the Islamic paradise of Khomeini, where you are not even asked why. I answer, "I support peace."

"That is what the great Satan, America, wants."

"So be it; but I don't think America and I necessarily want the same thing. I simply say a Muslim should not kill a Muslim. We should not support this madness of killing." (We both know we are speaking of the Iran-Iraq war.)

"Who wants war?"

"You tell me; I don't . . ."

He interrupts again. "If you believe in God, which I don't think you do, is it right to speak against Islam, when Muslims are engaged in jihād with the unbelievers?" (The Muslim Iraqi soldiers are constantly called by the Iranian state controlled media *kuffār-e Ṣaddāmī* "unbelievers who follow Saddam"]. In the view of Khomeini and his followers, the Iraqi regime is a Zionist regime. Similarly, the Iraqi authorities accuse Khomeini of having bought arms from Israel.)

"Wait a second! How do you know that I don't believe . . ."

"By your actions. I know you from Lawrence, Kansas."

"What about Lawrence, Kansas?"

"Well, you know! The reason I told the other guy to leave is that I did not wish to embarrass you. My Islamic morality forbids me to embarrass sinners." (I sense what he is getting at, but I want to hear what he has to say.)

"We are all sinners, what specific sins?"

"Music, dance, adultery, and so forth."

"I love music and dance."

"They are *ḥarām.*"

"Not in my opinion. Many great Muslims such as Rumi . . ."

"Never mind! In the book of Aghā [Khomeini] . . ."

"Never mind Khomeini: he has his opinion, I have mine."

"How about other āyatullāhs?"

"They have their opinions, too. Let us get to the issue of adultery. This may be more exciting: have you seen me in action?"

"Well, you see, holding the hand of a girl who is not your *maḥram* is a kind of adultery."

"Do I get stoned to death? How many lashes . . ."

"I am not an Islamic judge. If such should judge that you need some lashes, even I would have to do it to you."

"You see, brother . . ."

"I am not your brother."

"Fine! You see, whatever your name is, here is our difference. I don't consider holding a girl's hand adultery. It may be a sin, but not adultery. It depends upon one's intentions . . ."

"The Qur'an says it is."

"There is nothing about holding hands . . ."

"*Kāfi* [one of four major Shi'ite collections of ḥadīth, compiled by Kulayni, d. 328 A.H.] . . ."

"I have read it; I believe in some of it."

"Then I am right to say you don't believe in God."

"God did not write *Kāfi.*"

"Then if I say the book of Aghā, you will say he, God forbid, is not a *faqīh* [expert in jurisprudence]."

"On the contrary, he is a good *faqīh,* in a sense."

"Then you believe some of what he says and do not believe some."

"Exactly. Right is right."

"What kind of Shi'ite are you? Whom do you follow [*taqlīd*]?"

"I do not have to tell even whether I do *taqlīd* or not. I have one of three choices."[27]

"Even Shariatmadari. . . ."

"You mean that great scholar, *Āyatullāh* . . ."

"He committed mistakes." (Āyatullāh Shariatmadari, a rival of Khomeini, is under house arrest.)

"That is your opinion."

"I am not here tonight to fight you."

"I know, we are having a conversation . . ."

"Yes! As a Muslim, I tolerate your insulting me, but if you insult Islam, I cannot tolerate that."

"We are having a friendly conversation. You should not even mention the word *fight.* It scares me because . . ."

"I know and you should watch out. Once we stabbed a guy eighteen times. I am telling you as my religious duty, do not attack Imām [Khomeini] on the Zionist radio. The only reason why they let you have a program is that you tell them what they want to hear. You are helping them against yourself."

I look back and notice that Abbas and the two other Iranians are listening. For a moment I think there is a plan to stab me. I decide that if I am to die, I should do so bravely, so I say: "Listen! Fortunately, I will die only once. Dying for one's belief is glorious. I have expected this moment all . . ."

"Who wants to kill you? You are nothing."

"I know, but you are threatening me."

"What threat? If you try to stab me, I will defend myself. I am simply reasoning (*bayyina*) with you not to help make Zionists." (The threat is now veiled, but very much still present: first there is *bayyina,* then comes "iron," the sword: Qur'an 57:25; i.e., the time for stabbing may come later, if I do not submit to his *bayyina.*) I am not even asking such a godless person as you to join us. You see all these Muslims? They are all with us. Have respect for our brothers who are fighting Saddam, who has raped the country of Islam. Why do you become happy when Saddam has the upper hand? Why are you sad when we win?"

"I am not happy at any rate. There is no winning. It is all losing."

"Despite people like you, Saddam will fall."

"I hope so. I don't like the guy."

"Why do you have that anti-Islamic radio show?"

"You mean antiwar!"

"You play music there, and that is *ḥarām.*"

"I don't. Others do."

"You participate in it."

"Still I don't . . ."

"Yes, you do. If you sit with those who drink alcohol as if you were drinking yourself . . ."

"Don't you help perform marriages? I have seen you in such events. There is alcohol, music, dancing. So, by your logic, you have committed everything I have."

"That is different."

"Yes, because they pay you money."

He is no longer able to stand me. He joins the others. I light up a cigarette. Mehdi rejoins me. Abbas does as well, but only after he is sure the other Iranians have left. I ask him to ask them if they would do an interview with me for my research. He says they have left, but I insist they are nearby. Abbas reluctantly gets up to ask them. He returns soon with some literature. "They were talking about you; I did not want to interrupt." The literature is *Al-Jihād,* a magazine published by the Islamic Republic of Iran, in Arabic, with an article about the struggle of the clergy against secularism; a weekly newspaper also called *Al-Jihād;* the Arabic version of the magazine *Sorūsh,* with a cover story on chemical warfare and inside a photograph of Khomeini voting; the Arabic version of the state-controlled newspaper *Kayhān,* with headlines about the Iran-Iraq war; and the journal *Al-Da'wa,* said to be put out by a group of warrior scholars (*al-'ulama al-mujahiḍin*) in Iraq, but with a mailing address in Iran, which opens with Khomeini's 22 April 1981 declaration eulogizing his martyred representative in Iraq, Muhammad Bāqir al-Ṣadr, and calling upon the lower rank Iraqi army officers to revolt.

As I go to my car, the pro-Khomeini Iranians are still deep in conversation.

Monday, 11 Ramaḍān

For some reason, the number of people attending has decreased: fatigue of Ramaḍān fasting? The number of pro-Khomeini supporters, however, has increased to ten. I notice that these men do not usually sit together, but disperse throughout a crowd, each engaging in a conversation with someone. They move about quite a bit to assist each other when necessary. As *tarāwiḥ* prayer begins—Shi'ites regard *tarāwiḥ* as an abrogated tradition and forbidden—they convene behind the walls to evaluate their efforts. They are effective users of gossip, telling people to avoid certain individuals, and organizing ostracism.

An hour before sunset, the pots are boiling in the kitchen: rice, beef stew, green beans. Some people bring their own food. One or two people cut up watermelons to quench the thirst of the summer fast. There is also plenty of boiled water and tea bags. A Pakistani drink of sugar and rose water is also available. In the kitchen, men and women work together. Tables and chairs are set up. An Indian man at the door of the mosque hands a date, from a large box, to each person along with a napkin. The professional reciter or an assistant recites the Qur'an. Then there is the *adhān* (call for prayer). At this point, many break their fasts with the date. Dates have a quasi-sacred character: they were a major source of nutrition for early Arabs, a favorite fruit of the Prophet, as well as a staple of his Muslim warriors. People believe that date sugar passes directly from the mouth into the bloodstream to provide energy and strength. The Sunni majority break their fast early according to a tradition they follow.[28] The Shi'ite minority reluctantly hold their dates until after the *maghrib* prayer, for they hold the technical sunset to be a few minutes later than the actual one. After *maghrib* prayer, everyone stands in line for the break-fast dinner.

Shaykh Barakat sings prayers from the Qur'an during dinner. I sense that he is planning to leave soon. Later, as people line up for *'ishā* prayer, Barakat notices a young teenaged boy in the front line. He says: "Well, we know children should not stand in front. Men in front, boys next, then women. Are you a child or a man?" The boy, reluctant to give up his position, says, "A man." Encouragements come from the audience, "Of course, he is a man." Barakat smiles and lets him keep his place. The event can signify that the boy has reached puberty (fifteen lunar years, or the growth of pubic hair, or a wet dream) or just that the boy wanted to be a man before his time.

During *'ishā* prayer, Barakat commits two errors. He is corrected. A follower is rewarded for correcting his imām. One corrects by shouting out the correct verse or raising one's voice to draw attention. Once the imām corrects himself, everyone continues following. Symbolically, this practice can be applied to correcting the imām in social leadership too. After the prayer, Barakat turns to the audience and apologizes for his absentmindedness: "I am leaving tomorrow to attend an international contest of Qur'an reciters in Malaysia. That is why I became absentminded. Thank you for correcting me, may Allah reward you. May I see you soon."

After *maghrib* prayers, I discover that my shoes have been lost. In Iranian shrines and mosques there is often a *kafshadārī,* a shoe check person who gives you a numbered claim check. Else one carries one's shoes or leaves them outside the door. Shoes can be mistaken. Shoe theft is not a frequent crime, although when I was a child in Yazd, a shoe thief was caught and publicly embarrassed with a big bag of shoes that he had to carry on his back. There is also the famous anecdote that if a shoe thief is caught he should be made imām of the prayer: it gives him a profession so he need not steal, and as he stands in front, everyone can keep their eye on him. Theories emerge from all sides: "Are you sure you had your shoes when you came to the mosque?" "They must be here somewhere, you just can't see them." "Someone took them by mistake and will return them." "Shoes are never stolen here, it is the first time. . . ." "Shoes are stolen if they are brand new." "Those who don't like you did it." "It is a way of keeping the unwanted out of the mosque." "It is non-Muslims attempting to ruin our name. They steal so many things from here." "It must be the pro-Khomeinis. I'll talk to them about it." "Search the trash cans." "They just wanted to tease you: in America no one needs to steal shoes; they must be hidden somewhere." At any rate, I drive home barefoot.

Tuesday, 12 Ramaḍān

The number of people attending has again declined. One pro-Khomeini activist is present. For some reason, more liberal Iranians are in attendance. I learn that the substitute for Barakat is a high-ranking Egyptian scholar, Shaykh Zahir al-Zoghbi. We speak briefly and agree to meet for an interview. I mention I have seen him with Mahalawi, and he jumps at the statement as if it were an accusation: "I just happened to be in the same place; I am not with him." The recitation of the Qur'an is done by senior pupils of Barakat and is short.

A Pakistani health professional is arguing with Mr. Y.: "Why don't you act as a missionary and attract non-Muslims to Islam?" Mr. Y. is a high school dropout who served as concierge in the Richmond mosque, and later was attracted to the Saudi Educational Mission. He is also the only Mexican Muslim I have known to come to ISGH. He is dressed in Islamic garb with a white turban, long white coat, and white trousers. He has a peach-fuzz beard and has shaved his mustache. He replies: "There are thousands of Muslims in Houston, and still it is often hard to have the minimum five people to hold Friday prayer. How can I work as a missionary when Muslims themselves do not practice Islam?" The other persists: "We have a revolution to carry out in the land of unbelief. One Muslim life is worth more than those of all the unbelievers. One may not kill a Muslim, but unbelievers, if the authorities command it, should be killed. See how for the sake of Allah Imām Khomeini kills the unbelievers. Nothing should stop us from obeying Allah, we must be inventive and seek new ways of propagating Islam." Y. answers that the best way of propagating Islam is to set a good example. Words do not mean much if they are not practiced. The other man disagrees.

Wednesday Afternoon, 13 Ramaḍān

For the noon prayer, there are only six people, including imām Shaykh Zahir al-Zoghbi. Someone is repairing the air-conditioner and is asked to stop and join the prayer. Afterwards, Al-Zoghbi is told there is a marriage ceremony for him to perform. In the office, he gives the bride, "Sue," and the groom, "Gholam Husain" from Iran, the marriage forms. Sue desires to convert before the actual Islamic marriage ceremony. They have already been married in a Christian ceremony for two years. Al-Zoghbi insists that Muhammad Naseem of India should do the ceremony, calling him professor and pretending Naseem has greater authority. Naseem is equally deferential, and asks me to beg Al-Zoghbi to stay. Naseem puts on his white Indian-style cloak and meets with the couple and a male and female friend. Naseem begins, "There is no priesthood in Islam. Anyone can perform the ceremony, even you yourselves, or a trusted representative of the bride and groom. I don't like the term *conversion.* Sister, you are not converting, you are reforming. Islam is not only the religion of Muhammad, it is also the religion of Moses and Jesus. The term *Christianity* was not used by Jesus but only by later generations, who modified his teachings. Thus, when we say, 'There is only one religion and that is Islam,' we mean that all the prophets carried the same message from the same God. Sister, you are not obliged to convert to Islam. You may keep your religion intact if you wish to do so." Sue indicates her need to "reform." Naseem says, "Then let it be so." He explains the three foundations of Islam: oneness of God, prophethood, and resurrection. "I advise you on behalf of Islamic law to avoid pork and avoid wine and other alcoholic beverages. You should learn to say your prayers and to fast. And remember, covering is very important: you may only show your face and hands to others."

Then come the two testimonies: "Sister, repeat after me, I witness there is no God but God, Muhammad is His servant slave and His messenger." Then prayer: all present raise their hands and pray that she might be a good Muslim and have a happy, prosperous life. Then the marriage ceremony: each agrees to accept the other as legal spouse according to the law of Islam. Gholam Husain and Sue have brought only one man and one woman as witnesses. There must be at least two men or one man and two women. Naseem does not seem to want to disclose at this point that, in the matter of witnessing, a woman is counted as half a man. He looks at me and says, "You and this gentleman sign as witnesses." Mischievous as I am, I say, "I don't know the couple and their actual names; I have just met them, so I cannot witness." Al-Zoghbi volunteers to act as witness. The designated witness woman is a bit annoyed but keeps quiet. "There is no fee for what I have done," Naseem says. "May God be pleased that I did it. Yet it is a tradition that each couple married in the center donate fifty dollars for this institution. You can donate, if you wish, when you pick up your marriage contract."

Friday Prayer, 15 Ramaḍān

My American assistant, N.S., had insisted he wanted to participate in Friday prayer today. He arrived before me. I found him wandering around looking for the ablution room. He has parked his car in front of the kitchen, and I tell him in French that there are several improper items (a *Studio X* magazine, and a cassette of hard-core reggae) on his dashboard he should remove before he raises suspicion. He asks where to make ablution, and I advise him to skip it. Later I explain to him that ritual impurity of non-Muslims is quite serious. Impurity is contagious through wetness. Some say that People of the Book, if they wash in front of you, are ritually pure; but others say that all non-Muslims are always ritually impure. If a non-Muslim makes ablution, he can, in some eyes, pollute the washing room and the mosque. I sit with N.S. and show him how to perform the prayer. Afterwards, I introduce N.S. to a few Iranians. Someone asks if he is Muslim, and I say, "He is learning, and he has been fasting for Ramaḍān." Someone asks his occupation. N.S. says he is a writer, a poet. The Iranian says, "The Qur'an has a chapter about poets. It condemns them." "Not really," I intervene; Muslim poets are excepted, and the Prophet distinguished between proper and improper poetry. The merchandise table of the Pakistanis has been mostly taken over by the pro-Khomeini Iranians. There are posters commemorating Jerusalem Day (*Rūz-e Quds*), and encouraging Muslims of the world to help Iran liberate Jerusalem via liberating Baghdad. I try to take one of the newspapers, but Abdul Hamid Yunosi takes it back, saying, "This is of no use to unbelievers. You don't need it." I retort, "Just looking at the cover, I know what it says." And to tweak him further, I ask someone else if I can borrow the magazine they have just picked up. "Sure, anytime."

Saturday Afternoon, 16 Ramaḍān

It is four o'clock and there is quite a scene in the courtyard. A marriage ceremony has just ended, and it is just like what one might expect at a Christian church: women in long pink and white sleeveless dresses, and the groom in a tuxedo hugging his bride and kissing her. About ten young Muslims are sitting and glaring at them. I suggest to one of them that if he does not like it, he should take it upon himself to inform the merrymakers that they are behaving improperly in a public Muslim place. He replies, "When the pious imām of the mosque approves of such promiscuity, what can we young people say? Do you know, they went inside the mosque just the way you see them? Al-Zoghbi performed the ceremony. They took photos and Al-Zoghbi stood beside the bride, and she put her arms around him. I admonished him, but he said, 'We do it at al-Azhar [university, Cairo]. I don't believe these pious men. And when I became angry, Mr. Buzdar told Al-Zoghbi to ignore this young man." The bride and groom have a long kiss. Then they get into their Mercedes and drive off.

Saturday Evening, 16 Ramaḍān

The number of worshipers is few. After prayer, Tahir Assafi says, "Brothers, I am going to tell you something you won't like, but I must. Last night I collected only $3.50 in the donation box. I'm not asking even for a dollar, but please, fifty cents a piece. That is nothing. And also, please clean your tables and take your plates to the garbage. As you would do in a cafeteria, do the same here."

Saturday Night, 16 Ramaḍān

It is 1:00 A.M. Shafiq Helmi asks all those sitting in the courtyard to help clean the yard and fold the chairs. Someone suggests that while we work I should recite the Qur'an and prayers. I am reminded of Negro songs when they worked as slaves in the fields. I consent. When we finish, I am asked to recite some more. I sing some Arabic poems about confession of sin. Ibrahim, a youth of about twenty with a beautiful voice, alternates singing with me. I first met Ibrahim at the beginning of Ramaḍān: he was wearing a green T-shirt advertising "Hungry International," an Iranian-owned restaurant where he worked, a sandwich and beer place. Two days later he had replaced the T-shirt with a long white dashdash, and when I asked if he still worked at the Hungry International, he said, "I quit. It was not proper. I think it belongs to an Iranian Jew. I am a Palestinian, and I can't work in a restaurant that serves Tel Aviv Reuben sandwiches and Israeli beer." He proved to be an excellent Qur'an reciter, and led prayers a number of times quite professionally. A long discussion breaks out first about the impropriety of men and women mixing in the mosque, then about the Iran-Iraq war, then about marxism. Ibrahim rejects any style of marxism as a "Jewish ideology."

Finally, we are interrupted by a Pakistani man. You can tell he has some mental problems. Before each sentence, he clears his throat and spits, saying, "Excuse me." He stutters every few words. He has red eyes and body odor. "Excuse me, brothers. There is nothing wrong with me. I can do all kinds of work. I am living with two Mexicans. I am not comfortable there. Excuse me, brothers. They bring girl friends, drink beer, and smoke grass. We don't have any shower, there are many mosquitoes, and it is hot. Excuse me. Last night they kicked me out. Excuse me, brothers. I have my permanent residence and a Texas driver's license and social security card. I am a legal alien. Excuse me, here are my papers, check them out. Five months ago I got married in Pakistan. I am fine. Excuse me, I can do all kinds of jobs. I just need a place to stay, and somebody please, excuse me, please help me go back to my wife and country. I have asked everybody to help me, but they ignore me. Excuse me, brothers. I went to Ben Taub hospital. They said I was physically and mentally fine. There is nothing wrong with me. I am a little bit lonesome. No one likes me because I spit. It is my bad habit. Excuse me, brothers. I can do all kinds of jobs. I used to work in construction, but I don't like the Mexicans. They don't like us either."

Abdul Hafiz asks, "Have you talked to the president?"

"Yes, brother," he replies. "They did not help me. Excuse me."

"I will talk to them tomorrow. Everything will be fine. And tonight you can sleep in the back room here," assures Abdul-Hafiz.

"Yes, brother. Thank you, brother. Excuse me, brother. Can somebody give me fifty cents for a coke?"

Sunday Evening, 17 Ramaḍān

The place is packed. There are popular picnics on Sunday evenings in the courtyard. Abdul Hafiz has expressed worry about behavior at these events, especially the laxity about female modesty. There is a great variety of food. Pamphlets are being circulated concerning the feast after Ramaḍān, 'Id al-Fiṭr. There is a flier for Imām Khomeini calling upon all Muslim scholars to revolt against their regimes and fight the superpowers, who plot destruction of Islam. This happens not to be an Iranian-produced flier, but one disseminated by Pakistanis for whom Zia is not Muslim enough. Part of the flier is in Urdu. I was surprised to see Buzdar holding the master copy before xerox copies were made; I had not expected such a mild man to be so involved. Most of the picnickers leave before *'ishā* prayer. After prayer I sit with friends and recite the Qur'an. An Egyptian approaches us and asks Abbas if he knows anyone in Baton

Rouge. Abbas says yes. The Egyptian speaks to me in Arabic, saying he can express himself better. He tells us that his Christian American wife has left him, taking their child, and is hiding in the house of an Iranian in Baton Rouge. He has gone there, but the Iranian chased him off and said he hated Arabs. He wants to find an Iranian who can talk to this man. The Egyptian takes out a whole file of canceled checks of child support, a receipt of a registered letter to his wife, a seven-page letter. Abbas agrees to try to help.

Monday and Wednesday Nights, Eves of 19 and 21 Ramaḍān

There are no Iranians present. The eve of the nineteenth is the night Ali was mortally wounded, and possibly the night the Qur'an was revealed. Ali died on the eve of the twenty-first. Shi'ites prefer to stay among themselves and not mix with Sunnis.

Friday Night, Eve of 23 Ramaḍān

This is the second night, orthodox Sunnis speculate, which might have been the night of Qadr, the night the Qur'an was revealed. It is recommended that Muslims stay awake all night, saying prayers, reciting the Qur'an, and renewing their covenant with God. *Qadr* is one of those multiinterpretable words: power, destiny, measurement, worth, divine decree. It is both the night on which the Qur'an was revealed and the night on which the angels descend to earth, the night on which the destiny of each individual is determined by the Almighty. In my hometown of Yazd, people assemble in the mosques. They stay awake all night, and if they missed a prayer during the year, they say it at this time to clear the debt. There are usually a hundred units of public prayer said. There is a rite of putting the Qur'an as intercessor on one's head and praying to God for all one wishes. After an emotional speech by the imām about the night of Qadr, the martyrdom of Ali, and forgiveness, the atmosphere is ready for divine connection, and the lights are extinguished, so no one can see any worldly object, and so people will not be embarrassed if they start crying and wailing.

The process begins with the prayer, "O Lord, I ask thee by means of your revealed book and what is therein, and therein is your greatest name. . . ." Then God and the fourteen pure souls are invoked as intercessors. "Thou Allah" is recited ten times; "for the sake of Muhammad," ten times; "for the sake of Ali," ten times; "for the sake of Fatima," ten times; . . . and, finally, "for the sake of the Mahdi," ten times. Then the long list of wishes is uttered. Every step is taken first by the imām, and then by the people. The utterance of some of the names is more emotionally charged than those of others: Ali in particular since this is the last night of his life; Husain the martyr of Karbala; and Fatima, the daughter of the Prophet and mother of the Imāms, usually gets a strong reaction from the women. When the ritual ends, people return home to have a meal and prepare for the fast.

Some rose water is given to people in their cupped hands which they rub on their faces. There is a famous story that a practical joker, on the night of Qadr, mixed black ink with the rose water and distributed it while the lights were out. When the lights came on, everyone had a black face. There was panic: people assumed their faces were blackened because of their sins.

In Houston, such devotional rituals are not observed, except perhaps in private gatherings. Only a few people came to the mosque for the all night wishes. But suddenly I notice Qais al-Kalbi is gathering people around him and is giving a speech in Arabic. He is a thirty-five-year-old Iraqi, with untrimmed beard, a small white turban, and a long white dashdash. His speech soon centers on Shi'ite-Sunni differences. "Shi'ites are unbelievers. They believe Ali and Fatima also received revelations. Their leaders have huge turbans but no faith. None of them say their prayers properly. I used to be a Shi'ite myself. Then I read the Shi'ite books and found much stupidity and many mistakes. I became Sunni, and so did my family, except for my father, whom I disowned." The focus then shifted to the Iran-Iraq war. He condemned both Saddam and Khomeini for creating a blood bath. An Egyptian objects: "You are not supposed to talk about such things. Sunnis and Shi'ites are brothers. Minor disputes should not be stirred up and old wounds should be left to heal. We should preserve our unity." An Iraqi Kurd concurs: "This is hypocrisy. It is not right to say these things in the house of God. He is a spy of Saddam." People are disturbed and do not know how to react: Is he a true believer simply arguing that right is right and a true Muslim should not compromise his religion for politics; or is he a hypocrite stirring up trouble? It is puzzling because he has until now always kept to himself.

Sunday, 24 Ramaḍān

Muhammad Barakat has returned from Malaysia. First prize in the Qur'an recitation contest went to a Filipino, second prize to an Iranian. Among women, first prize went to a Malaysian. The Sunday picnic today is similar to that last week.

At 6:00 P.M. I attend a weekly program in which non-Arabs, mostly Pakistanis, participate. It is a session in which rituals of prayer, fasting, etc., are explained. Verses are written on the board and translated word for word. Some people take notes. Today, the program is about the rules for ʿId al-Fʿitr, and instructions are given. It will be Saturday or Sunday depending upon the moon. The prayer will be held in Albert Thomas Hall, the doors will open at 8:00, and prayers will begin at 8:45, *inshāʾAllāh.*

I go into the mosque for *maghrib* and *ʿishā* prayers, and when I come out, I discover that my shoes have again been stolen or lost. I wonder how many more times this will happen.

It is 12:00 midnight: the recitation of the Qur'an has just ended. Qais al-Kalbi delivers his second lecture. He is eager to gather a crowd. Before he begins, an Egyptian asks if he may speak privately to Qais. Later I learn that Qais is warned about me: "He is an Iranian, a Shiʿite, and he speaks Arabic. Be careful so there will be no trouble." In a two-hour speech, Qais covers many topics: propagating Islam; proving the existence of God; refuting Marx and his notion of dialectics; refuting Christianity and the doctrine of the Trinity; describing the scientific contexts of the Qur'an (Qur'an and modern biology, physics, oceanography, and astronomy); proving from "ridiculous" passages in the Bible that it cannot be the word of God nor even of a sane mortal; proving that the land of Palestine no longer belongs to the children of Israel; condemning Yasser Arafat, George Habash, and other non-Muslims whose attempts to liberate Palestine will fail. Qais mentions that all these topics are covered in his book. Immediately after his talk, he asks if anyone has had a dream he needs interpreted. When I try to ask a question, he says he has to pray: "We will do it another time." It is near dawn, and some of us sit to eat with Shaykh Barakat, and discuss the Qur'anic recitation.

Tuesday Night, Eve of 27 Ramaḍān

Tonight is again a possible night of Qadr, a stronger possibility than the eve of the twenty-first, twenty-third, or twenty-fifth. Many of those who come to break-fast will stay on tonight for the recitation of the Qur'an in its entirety. The Qur'an is divided into thirty parts (*juz'*). Twenty-nine of these are passed out to twenty-nine different people, each of whom recites his allotted portion simultaneously. The mosque sounds like a beehive (an image from an early ḥadīth describing the recitations of early Muslims) or the martyrs of Karbala on the night before their death. The thirtieth *juz'* of the Qur'an (which includes the earliest revelations, but appears at the end of the Qur'an) is recited last and differently. Everyone takes a turn reciting a sūra from it. A great deal of devotional singing occurs between each sūra and the next. Then a prayer is chanted which celebrates the completion of the recitation.

Meanwhile, outside, Qais sits at a table with his followers, and delivers a speech on women and *ḥijāb* (veiling, modesty). It is recorded by Abdul Rahman. I listen while Qais watches me warily.

At 2:30 A.M. there is an excellent meal: stuffed grape leaves, stuffed squash, lamb soup, salad, and coke. After eating, I find Qais sitting alone, and join him. I sense he has wanted to talk to me alone, and now is an opportunity. He opens up: "I am from Basra, from an ex-Shiʿite family. I am a lawyer. In 1976 Saddam put me in jail. One night I had a crucial dream. I was in paradise and I saw four men sitting and there was a woman, whose body was covered in black. She dropped a handkerchief on my lap. I awoke and asked my uncle to interpret it for me. The next day I debated a group of Sunnis and decided to convert. This was the fulfillment of my dream. The four men were the four grand caliphs, Abu Bakr, Umar, Uthman, and Ali, may God be pleased with them; the woman was Aisha, widow of the Prophet. In my Shiʿite life I had to curse the first three and this lady every time I heard their names, and I had to worship only the fourth. Thanks to this dream, I found the truth. Now no one can take my faith away from me. All my family, except my father, converted. You see: *al-manāmu qabl al-kalām* (dreams reveal more than words). By the way, who are these Iranians who sit with you? Don't you sense danger from them?" I tell him, "They are not fanatics, and anyway they do not understand Arabic. I am quite open and willing to learn." Qais suggests we have more private conversations. Someone comes up and wants to sell a plane ticket to Qais.

Wednesday Night, Eve of 28 Ramaḍān

It is 12:00 midnight. I arrive at the mosque, and find Qais and his disciples sitting around a table. Qais is speaking about the rights of the mother in Islam. At almost every sentence, a man interrupts:

"Once upon a time a companion came to the Prophet . . ."

"Which companion was it?"

"It doesn't make any difference."

"Of course, it does; I want to know which companion it is."

"Okay, I will tell you later."

"No, tell me now."

"Please brother, may Allah bless you, let me speak."

The man was obviously drunk. I am amazed at the tolerance Qais and the others show him. I expect Qais to order eighty lashes for this man for his impudence and immorality. The issue suddenly changes to wine, the mother of all sin (*umm al-kabā'ir*). The man interrupts: "I disagree. I drink, but I bother no one. I am a Muslim from Hama in Syria. I belong to the Muslim Brotherhood. But don't mistake me, brother, I am not a Shi'ite. I am a good Sunni." Someone interjects: "A good Muslim does not drink. Intoxication is the root of all big sins." "Not all," he replies, "adultery is worse." Qais says, "How is he going to fast tomorrow, I hope he is sober by then." The man answers, "As a matter of fact, I was fasting today, and broke my fast with some Scotch." Everyone is incensed, but no one does anything. The drunkard is quite calm and confident. "I'm not bothering anybody. I'm sitting here minding my own business, learning. I'm open to any logical argument, but you cannot feed me with just anything you wish." Qais stops trying to lecture.

Friday, 29 Ramaḍān

The last Friday of Ramaḍān is called *Jom'at al-Widā'* (Farewell Friday), perhaps an analogy with the *Ḥajjat al-Widā'* (the farewell pilgrimage of Muhammad before his death), or the saying that "Friday prayer is the ḥajj of the poor".[29] This Ramaḍān encompassed five Fridays; both the beginning and the end of the month were marked by *Jom'a.* Today there are words of farewell in the air, and much talk of the Id prayer which will be held tomorrow. The crowd fills the hall, but is not the overflowing multitude expected. Muhammad Naseem leads the prayer. The first sermon is full of sentiments of farewell: "Farewell Ramaḍān. Farewell! Brothers and sisters, tomorrow is our graduation day. Some will get an 'A'; and some, God forbid will get an 'F'; a bad student knows he is a bad student." Analogy is made to the last judgment. "So, brothers and sisters, let us think about that day." The second sermon compares the Qur'an to moon rocks with strange inscriptions. Were the latter to be displayed, no one would hesitate to go to see such a novelty. One should be equally curious about the word of Allah in the Qur'an.

Prayer ends. Fliers are distributed: Five Star Groceries announces special prices; A & N Automotive and Body Shop, 10 percent off; Visit Shamiana Sweets; Granny's Buffet invites everyone to a complete 'Id program with poetry and music. . . . There is no Iranian newspaper table. Rumor has it, they are at a demonstration today. Today has been declared

Jerusalem Day by Khomeini. There are demonstrations in four major cities: Washington, Detroit, Toronto, and San Franscisco.

Saturday, 1 Shawwal, ʻId al-Fʻitr

It is 7:45 A.M. The door opens at the Albert Thomas Exhibition Hall in downtown Houston, and people begin to file in. Pakistanis, Arabs, and Indians wear the clothes of their traditional cultures, intentionally flaunting their ethnicities. Everyone brings a small carpet, blanket, or sheet. Boxes for the collection of *zakāt* and *zakāt al-fiṭr,* as well as for donations to build the new mosque, are set up in the hallway with big signs. Shaykh Barakat begins the chant of *takbirāt,* and everyone is encouraged to join. People sit in rows facing Mecca. As always, women are relegated to the back. In the middle of the chanting, a member of the ISGH board takes the microphone abruptly and announces, "Brothers and sisters, if you have not paid your *zakāt al-fiṭr,* you should do so before the prayer, three dollars per person. The prayer will begin at 8:45. Please straighten the rows. The brothers distributing pamphlets, please stop doing so now. Distribute them after the prayer. That's it for now." The microphone is handed back to Shaykh Barakat, who seems a bit perturbed by the rude interruption. The chanting recommences. The words to the chant are displayed in both Arabic and English transliteration. The man sitting next to me takes out his checkbook and conspicuously writes out a thirty-dollar check. "Last year," he explains, "I paid twenty-seven dollars, but this year there was a new birth in the family, so *māshā'Allah.*" I ask, "You have eight children?" He answers proudly in the affirmative. The box for *zakāt al-fiṭr* is passed. Once again Barakat is interrupted by another member of the board. "Brothers and sisters, *salam alaikum* and *id mubarak* to all of you. Every year, *alhamdu'lillah,* it is getting better and better. Be it known that ISGH depends only on your generosity and participation. It is independent. It is not subject to the rule of any earthly government. ISGH is trying to provide larger and better programs year after year. . . ."

Someone in the middle of the crowd gets up and shouts, "This is not the time for such announcements, let people chant *takbirāt.*" He is ignored. When the microphone is given back to Barakat, he seems to be getting angrier. Ten minutes later, yet another member of the board takes the microphone, and with a heavy Pakistani accent, deep voice, and serious demeanor, says, "Brothers and sisters, if you have not paid yet, please do so. Three dollars per person for sins. Please. Very soon, Said Jumʻah will lead the prayer. Straighten your lines. Your chanting is not loud enough to shake . . . [he points to the ceiling or sky].” The chanting begins anew. The Pakistani sitting on my other side tells me, “God did you hear that man? He has a frightening face. He reminds me of Zia of Pakistan.” I smile. He continues, “I'm not kidding you. Each of these guys may be a powerful political figure in the future. Now they are merely practicing.”

It is 8:44 A.M. At least four thousand people must be here. Yet this is a small number compared to the total number of Muslims in Houston. Iranians alone are said to number fifteen thousand in Houston.

Said Jum‘ah stands to lead the prayer. A microphone is attached to his collar. He explains, “Brothers and sisters, there will be seven *takbirāt* in the first unit, and five in the second. Then there will follow the *khuṭba* (sermon) which is part of the prayer.” His hands are raised to his ears: *Allah-o-akbar*”. Everyone repeats. After the *takbirāt* there is dead silence. He continues with the second unit. The *khuṭba* is about the fast of Ramaḍān: “When the believer pays the *zakāt al-fiṭr,* the fasting is accepted by God. . . .” The *khuṭba* ends with a list of projects of the community: the new mosque, additional satellite mosques, a radio station to propagate Islam. . . .

Slides are to be shown, but first more announcements. I find an Indian selling “Sikh-kebabs” (*sic*). At three dollars a piece, they are a rip-off and I complain to my friends. One jokes, “Sikhs are difficult to capture; you have to get them out of the Golden Temple; do you expect their flesh to be as cheap as goat meat?” I do not laugh. It is easy to joke about bloodshed at such distance, but it is not the time to be overly serious. It is, after all, a celebration.

Amid much handshaking, hugging, and kissing, people pour out as quickly as they poured in. A few pro-Khomeini pamphleteers show up with magazines and the latest declaration of Imām Khomeini. They have just returned from Washington, D.C., and proudly tell of having succeeded in burning an Israeli flag in public. Lost children are reunited with their parents over the P.A. system. For latecomers, the prayer is repeated with about a hundred participants. It is the beginning of a new month. Yesterday, fasting was required, today it is forbidden.

Saturday night, 1 Shawwal

It is 9:00 P.M. I go to the mosque and find only six people. The Palestinian Ibrahim, comments, “Look how people appear and disappear.” The Iraqi, Qais, says, “Today they can be excused, they are tired.” After the prayer, we gather around Qais and he recounts his feelings of being under suspicion during the last month. I comfort him, reminding him that Jesus was crucified for his beliefs, Muhammad had his teeth broken in Taif, and Jamaluddin al-Afghani was poisoned by his fellow Muslims. This cheers him up somewhat. The others are silent: they are not sure who Qais is. Several days later when I went to keep an interview with him, I was told, "He left for good, *inshāAllah.*"

Tuesday Night, 10 July

It is 10:30 P.M. The doors are locked and barred, the lights are off, and there is not a soul around. "Islam was born lonely, alien; and so it shall return, lonely, alien." Thus spoke Muhammad.

Voices of Hagar: An African-American Muslim Woman Talks to an Iranian Muslim Man

[One of the stamps issued by the Islamic Republic of Iran shows a black *muezzin* calling people to prayer, and to Islam. It is a superb condensation of two potent images. (1) The face is that of Malcolm X, appealing to American blacks to join the Islamic revolution and throw off the oppression of white American capitalist imperialism, and more generally asserting that Islam is the vehicle of third-world revolution, encompassing the struggle of American blacks. (2) The image evokes Bilal, the first Muslim muezzin, a black man, and is an icon of the claim that Islam is color blind. Islam was an important moment for many American blacks in the 1960s. A decade later, at the time of the Iranian revolution, many of these black American Muslims became interested in the Iranian experiment. A few visited Iran, a few married Iranians. The Islamic Republic attempted to appeal to American blacks as a natural constituency. But black American Muslims have their own agendas, their own history of political education.

Their perspective provides an interesting critique, and countervoice, sympathetic yet critical, within the Islamic and "third-world" community, to the discourses of the Islamic Republic. There is little real engagement or dialogue, response-counterresponse, because Iranians do not in general (aside from individual cases such as this interview) see American blacks as real partners or fully acculturated Muslims; they would like them to be followers (see the topic of racism in Islam, below). Nonetheless, for outsiders attempting to gain a feel for how Islamic discourses articulate social experiences, how they operate in the real world (not just in ideal theological dreamings), and where their blind spots, limitations, and contradictions are located, the response to Islamic ideology by black Americans can be illuminating, as well as interesting in its own right as an important part of the development of the American political and cultural fabric.

These perspectives are particularly strong as viewed through black women's eyes, who provide a matter-of-fact, undefensive, and articulate, class-analytic feminism, often quite different from that of white middle-class American feminists, and very different from that of Muslim male ideologues. We think a clarity of critique is achieved by juxtaposing socially grounded discourses that is not achieved by simply subjecting texts or statements individually to logical, philosophical, or other intellectual critique. Juxtaposing socially grounded discourses leads, we think, to sociological and political analysis; while subjecting texts or statements to analysis in isolation tends rather to lead toward rationalization (making arguments more coherent or systematic and then evaluating them), essentializing and idealization (elaborating the ideals, values, or defects of a system, at the expense of showing the way the ideals are "corrupted" and "used" in practice), and the turning away from social reality (the social forces underlying hermeneutic or interpretive contestation).

We invoke the metaphor of Hagar (see chapter 3) as the voice of counterdiscourses – discursive systems created by women, blacks, and Muslims from diverse backgrounds – and as the dialectic between assertiveness in defense of fulfilling important needs versus cooperative submission to collectively undertaken goals and projects. Hagar's voices, in this sense, are powerful and omnipresent. Ignoring them, or treating them as if they are silent, causes social derailment, a frequent occurrence.

The following interview with a young American Muslim black woman seems to us to be an articulate example, rich in the rhythms of black American speech, and a token of the increasing diversity of cultural work occurring in American urban settings between new immigrants of the 1980s and older immigrant, ethnic, black, and working-class cultures.

The interview was conducted by Mehdi Abedi on Thursday evening, 21 Ramaḍān 1984.]

From Black Nationalism to Islam

> "And so I functioned in purda for about ten years. . . ." ". . . and I was saying, 'This is not reality. We cannot sit here and *dhikr* for like three hours and expect to help the community.'"

For a long time, I've been always searching, okay, as far as a God-force. When I was a little girl, I was very Christian, and when I was a teenager I wanted to be a nun, fanatically, a nun. It was something about inner peace that I'd never had, that I was searching. And I knew there were answers and what-not. So I went to various churches and various organizations and there were always Muslims around on the street, on the corners in Pittsburgh, Pennsylvania, where I grew up. And there were a lot of old Muslims there who used to practice Islam in the twenties, and they used to have to have the mosque in a basement for fear of oppression, being Muslim. So I was always around it, but never really knew that much about it, and I grew into being a cultural nationalist in the community, and I was doing a lot of work with alternative school systems, teaching black children and canvassing and registering the vote—the whole thing—feeding kids. I was like in the tenth grade then. And I was pushing for black studies in schools.

One day it was really strange, I was walking down the street, and this brother came out on the corner and started calling the *adhān* for prayer. I didn't know what he was saying, but if I reflect, it must have been *maghrib*—the sun was going down; I can remember the sun right in my face, it was low. I was living in a commune. I was eighteen years old, and I was walking down the street, getting ready to go to a meeting, and he came out of the mosque and called the people of prayer, and something told me to run to the mosque. So I went to my house and put down all my papers, and I ran to the mosque. And they were getting ready to make *ṣalāt* (prayer), they were making *wuḍū* (ablution). The imām was there and I just sat there, I was like scared, really afraid, and then they started explaining Islam to me and at the same time I met a Muslim man who wanted to marry me. Like immediately. I don't know what was happening with that. But anyway, he had a lot of influence on me and Islam, and he taught me how to make *ṣalāt* and explained things and we got married. And then he soon became the imām of that mosque, the first Muslim mosque in Pittsburgh, and from then on it was just learning and reading, studying Maududi from Pakistan, working in the mosque. I had another teacher from Libya. He was a good teacher, and we lived in the Islamic community then. And we started an Islamic school, so I became very active.

But my first real important transition was when I joined the Islamic Party of North America. The imām there was Mustafa Uddin. That was in Washington, D.C. And it was more political. It was more than just praying, more than just reading Qur'an or fasting in Ramaḍān, you know. I had been influenced by the *Tablīghī Jamā'at* from India, too.

But I was not satisfied with the *Tablīghī Jamā'at;* it was too Sufi-type, and I was saying, "This is not reality. We cannot sit here and *dhikr* for like three hours and expect to help the community." So I still miss that part of the nationalist community, and I left all my nationalism behind when I became Muslim, all right, threw everything away. And I was writing and reading poetry then. I stopped writing: I threw all my poetry away. I destroyed it, because I thought and was told that it was not the right thing for a Muslim woman to do.[30] So at the same time I went into seclusion, *purda,* put on the *ḥijāb,* okay, and that was from the influence of Maududi, and *purda* and the laws, the jurisprudent laws on women in dress and women in seclusion, the role of women. It was influenced by the *Tablīghī Jamā'at,* very strict on women. And so I functioned in *purda* for about ten years, and was part of the Islamic Party in North America, and we gave *da'wa* (invitation) and *tablīgh* (propagation), and I taught first grade in our school in Washington, D.C., and we had a very large community—the school, we had our own cab company, health food store, bookstore. We basically laid it out in Washington, D.C. And I liked it because they were starting to mix politics. Muslims and non-Muslims went to our school.

But I always had a hard time fitting in as far as the roles of women and the role of wife and mother. So there was always a conflict. I always asked too many questions. Like when we went to study, I would always take all my ḥadīth—nine volumes of ḥadīth!—and no one else would bring their books because they would just do what imām told them do do. And I would look up and I was saying, "This doesn't make sense," you know, and "answer this." And there was a lot of resentment because I could not be just a blind follower. Even though, as I look back now, I was a blind follower. I would basically do anything the imām told me to do, because I had faith in the imām. This is what the sunna of the Prophet Muhammad said, "Obey your imām." But the Islamic leadership in this country is oftentimes somewhat corrupt. It's more so a dictatorship. And it's more a dictatorship when it comes to women.

M: To which organization was your main connection? Was it Jama'at Islami of Pakistan, Wallace D. Muhammad, or what?

H: Okay, I was never connected to Wallace D. Muhammad. I never belonged to a temple. I never believed in what Elijah Muhammad taught as far as Islam was concerned. I never believed that white people were devils. I was always uncomfortable with that. At that time Wallace D.

Muhammad was just basically a Sunni Muslim. But his father wasn't, and there was always this controversy between him and his father. But after Elijah Muhammad died, Wallace D. Muhammad took his place and changed it up, but that's something else we can cover. I still have disagreements with that. But I was basically always just orthodox Muslim, following Maududi, and being heavily influenced by *Tablīghī Jamā'at* from Pakistan, and India, you know, real strict, but nothing connected with Elijah Muhammad or anything like that.

M: Could you go into some of these questions you mentioned for which there were not satisfying answers?

Islam and Battered, Mentally Abused Wives

> "There's a lot of abuse in Muslim communities in America and, from what I hear, in the world."

H: I guess most of my questions were around what I was supposed to be about as a woman: strict obedience to the husband. There was a lot of weight put on it if you disobeyed your husband, you would not go to paradise. And I could not understand that. And I have yet to get a real logical answer as to why that is true. And I saw a lot of women being mentally abused because of this. It was like women were inferior. You know, all the parts of the ḥadīth, or maybe the way men interpret the ḥadīth, or whatever, meant that we could not intellectually aspire as human beings, because all we were supposed to be doing was having babies, or being the wives of one man. And that was like our occupation. And I would always ask why. Why can't *they* stay home with the babies? Why can't *they* do this or that? And then parts of the Qur'an were taken and used to justify beating women. There is a lot of abuse in Muslim communities in America, and from what I hear, in the world. And I question that. For ten years I was a battered wife. And I questioned that, and I often got beat because of my mouth. And all my Muslim women friends were battered, too. But they weren't brave enough to question it. They would just hide or cry or take it, and I just knew that there was something better than this. I was completely dissatisfied with it.

M: When you approached Islam, what was your expectation, and then what was the reality?

H: My expectations were that I was looking for spiritual peace. When I took *shahāda* I was satisfied with that, the inner self, you know, finding the *tawḥīd,* the oneness of God. I could get up on that, I could understand that, and that made me feel good inside. I still go along with that. I still believe there is a God-force. Everybody has their different name. But the reality was that I was female, and that brought on a whole new level of oppression for me. That was the reality, and that took away from my aspirations of spiritual peace. That took away from that and it was like a nightmare.

M: Let's face the reality. You are a woman, and women bear children. Men cannot even get pregnant. I could give you a long list of objective differences. Men and women have two functions. How can they be equal?

H: I don't have any qualms about the way my body is made. It's okay and I'm very proud of that, very at peace with my body, my femaleness, my periods, breast milk, children, you know, I've had babies, and that's okay. I think that's a blessing, because I'm able to bear the future in my body. That's okay. But because of my physical makeup, because of what I have to do physically, I happen to be weaker than the average man, physically. And so women are taken advantage of on that level. And because of the way the capitalistic system is made up and the way Islamic social laws are written, we have to take the back seat. And that doesn't have anything to do with my body. Because how I'm built should not bring that kind of second-class citizenship within the Islamic community. That's my problem right there. I don't understand that problem. There's no difference between my intellectual ability and your intellectual ability.

M: Do you think women are like second-class citizens in Islam?

H: Yeah, they are.

M: Do you think men as far as women are concerned are somewhat hypocritical?

H: Yeah. But I don't put the whole weight on men, because I see hundreds of women submitting to the submissive role because they blindly follow Islam. They read and they're afraid to question because they think if they are questioning they are going against Allah. But Allah has not said anything about you're not allowed to question anything. You're allowed to ask questions. He made us with the ability to be curious about things, so we should. But that fear—and I had that fear, too—will keep your mouth closed. You'll just do it. And I grew out of that. I started asking questions, because, logically, you know, Allah knows what's in your heart. He knows what's in your mind, so why be a hypocrite. But that took years of getting out of that for me. I was in severe seclusion—during Ramaḍān, I never went out at all. The clothes that we wore were terrible. Some of the women in our community used to faint, they had so many clothes on. Face veils, you know, I wore a whole *purda.* I was very uncomfortable wearing all those clothes in the heat. It was totally ridiculous, and in some of our communities we had to wear gloves. And the social laws of sitting behind curtains all the time. Not being able to hear other people lecture on things, because we had to sit in a small room with fifty million children. So I noticed within the Muslim community that women are conditioned not to aspire for intellectual growth. They don't even listen to the lectures now. See, because they've been trained not to know, so they don't even go for it anymore. They just submit themselves and they're pretty unhappy.

M: Islam is submission to the will of God. Suppose now a grand expert of jurisprudence comes to you and says, "H., I didn't have anything to do with this law. It's not my discrimination against you. It is divine discrimination against you. God has willed that men and women have different functions." What would you say to this?

State of War

> "We are in a state of war in this country. . . . Now when we are in a state of peace, then you can tell me to stay in the house, or . . . wear this or that, and maybe I will reconsider. But not now, because it is very urgent that I be out in the front line. . . ."

H: First of all, I always give people due respect. But it is depending on what he is telling me I can and can't do if I agree or disagree. Now I understand the concept of *tawḥīd* and believe in the oneness of God and all that; I don't disagree with that. But the application is where I disagree. You know, we are in a state of war in this country. Not just African people. Not just Muslim people. But people, the working-class people in the country are under a state of genocide. And so the state of war and the state of peace in Islam is different, you function different. Historically, when women were functioning in a wartime situation, they wore short clothes. In various ḥadīth you can read during wars and stuff, women pulled their dresses up, because you can't fight with long clothes and veils and what not. And it got to the point where women and men fought wars, too. Even though a lot of times women did nursing and things like that, but it got to that point. And not just with Muslim people, but with all poor, working-class people, there was always a time in their revolutionary efforts when women were just as much in the forefront as men. So if he told me that, right now in '84, that is the context I would put it in. I'm in a state of war. Once we're in a state of peace, then let's come back and talk about some other things that we can do.

M: Against whom? Be more specific about this war.

H: The war? I guess basically against the capitalist system. The system is a vampire. Khomeini set an example of what Muslim people are supposed to do as far as the capitalist system is concerned. You are supposed to fight, because oppression is worse than anything in Islam. So that's basically my everyday function. We are in a state of war. African people, poor people, Iranian people, whatever, are under the foot of the capitalistic system, and why should we act as if this is not happening? Now when we are in a state of peace, then you can tell me to stay in the house, or you can tell me to wear this or that, and maybe I will reconsider. But not now; because it is very urgent that I be out in the front line, just like you. So that's the way I would weigh what he would say. Just because he's a shaykh or a great name in Islam does not have any effect on me at all.

M: More specifically, how do you regard Khomeini altogether?

Khomeini

> "I am in a transition stage as far as Imām Khomeini is concerned." "People need to know how to survive . . . and the application of Islam as something that comes out of the mouths of the imams is not doing that. . . . Muslims have failed the people.

H: At one time in my life, Khomeini was a very big hero to me. He did something to inspire Muslims. He told them that you are strong and you can fight these great powers that want to take your land or want to take your culture, or want to disrespect your religion. So Khomeini is real good on that level. But a lot of Muslims have not caught on to that. They should follow that inspiration. But as far as Khomeini and his attitude about non-Muslims, maybe I have a disagreement. You know, I'm in a transition stage as far as Imām Khomeini is concerned. I don't think that they look at people through a class analysis as much as they should. I think that I have a disagreement with Muslims who conglomerate all non-Muslims as bad, the kāfir or the unbelievers, because there are a lot of people who call themselves Muslim who are oppressors, like in Saudi Arabia and various other parts of the world. But as a whole, I think he did a good thing for Muslims. He stood up to America. He showed that he was not afraid. And he did let Muslim women get a step higher than anybody else. You know, those sisters in Iran, they can train; they were martyrs, and I admire that. During the revolution that was going on, they were not afraid. They went out on marches. They gave their life. And he let them do that.

M: That is of course an honor, to become a martyr. We see in almost every revolution, at the beginning, women come out. They confront the cannons and machine guns with their babies and kids and become martyrs. But as soon as the goal is achieved, they are pushed back into their houses to assume passive roles. Don't you think this happened in Iran?

H: See, I don't know yet. I'm still looking at it. Okay, there is a great possibility that women are losing their revolutionary status that got Iran to where it is now. Now if they roll back the time on women, then I will be greatly disappointed. But I'm not sure yet. I have some friends in Iran and I'm trying to get over there so I can see for myself. And then once I see with my own eyes then I can maybe formulate more what's happened to the status of Muslim women in Iran. So right now I'm just observing.

M: How would you describe Western women in comparison with Muslim women? Some see Western women as just tools of consumerism.

H: That's true.

M: Is this degrading for women?

H: It is. Western women basically are prostitutes. You know, we focus on the woman on the corner, like on Westheimer [Street, Houston] that is a prostitute. We're all prostitutes. The Western housewife is a prostitute. Instead of prostituting herself to many men, she just prostitutes herself to one man. You know, she gets his inheritance, she gets his security, she gets his protection . . . and that's a historical fact. That started a long time ago when the mode of production changed. Because at one time in our civilization, women were the top thing. They headed households; they made decisions; they were leaders. Children carried their names. And so this declined as the mode of production changed. So we're all prostitutes here. All of us. Me, everybody. And this is because we've had to sell ourselves to get protection, security, and what not. So maybe the prostitutes that we call prostitutes are some of the most honest people, because they're very out front with the way they have to survive. But we've all had to survive. Our mothers train us to be prostitutes, too. On one level or another, in America. And now we have to connect that with Muslim women, too; because, I believe, at the present time, with the present-day status of Muslim women, that they are prostitutes, too. I mean because of the status of women in marriage.

M: What is this transitional period? You sound inspired by marxism. Are you turning your back on Islam?

H: I don't think I'm turning my back against Islam. I believe in a God-force. I guess my propagation is different. I don't go out and say, "Everybody come to the mosque." I don't do that anymore, because the mosque is not what people need. People need to know how to feed themselves. People need to know how to survive. People need to know their class interests. And the application of Islam as something that comes out of the mouths of the imāms is not doing that. So that's my transitional phase. Yes, I do read a lot of marxism. I've just started to study it. I do look at the way I do my work through a class analysis; and I look at Islam through a class analysis. And that's why I look at it the way I do. I don't think that Islam has failed the people. I think that Muslims have failed the people.

M: You remind me of Malcolm X and he probably, following al-Afghani, would say that we must make a distinction between Muslims and Islam. So you think there is a difference between the real Islam and what comes out of the mouth of the clergy?

H: Yeah, there's a class analysis in Islam. Islam does not have anything about color; and Islam is against interests and the way the capitalistic economic system is set up. Islam is basically a socialistic attitude. But when you start talking about "these people can't do this" or "these people can't do that" because they're not Muslims, I disagree. Shari'ati read and studied Fanon and he wasn't Muslim. But he did a lot of studying under that man and read a lot of his books; and I really admire that in Shari'ati, because he made an example that we can learn the truth from anybody.

M: This surprises me that a woman from the United States has read Shari'ati. Have you read his book *Fāṭima is Fāṭima,* about the daughter of the Prophet?

Racism in the Muslim Community

> "Most foreign Muslims do not look towards blacks for anything."

H: I scanned through it. I haven't read a lot of his things in detail. When I was following what was happening in Iran, day by day, it was a great thing to go to the newspapers and to go to the mosque and discuss what was happening in Iran. That's how I got exposed to Shari'ati, through friends that I had that live in Iran now. And when I read a little bit of what he was saying about Fanon—and this is a black man he was talking about, too. That's another thing, because there is a lot of racism in the Muslim community. And most foreign Muslims do not look towards blacks for anything.

M: You mean you have seen racism among Muslims here?

H: Extreme racism.

M: But I have been there and I haven't seen that.

H: But you aren't black. I'll explain it like this. Blacks who take up Islam have a tendency to imitate foreign Muslims, because they don't have any cultural roots, because of the cultural rape that they've gone through in this country. They have no identity. They're like empty cups. They fill themselves up with foreign Muslim ideologies and ways and concepts and life styles. They dress like foreign Muslims. I know you've seen some blacks do that. And so foreign Muslims come over here, and they take on the characteristics of white people to a certain extent, the way they feel about black people, the stories and stereotypes that they've heard before they came to this country. And they act out according to what they've been told. Everybody in the world sees the status of the European people as the ultimate. America—let's go to America. I've seen foreign Muslims get so excited about coming to America. And so they come to America with the racism that they have been prepared with. And so they treat us just like white people. You know, they're naive about it; they treat us just like white people. They think we're inferior. I've gone to the Saudi Arabian mission for help, and they were saying, "Go to your own people," and that's not Islam.

M: Suppose you were given an all-expense paid, round-trip ticket to Iran. What would you most want to observe?

Blind Followership

> "The problem is not that we are afraid of Allah, we are afraid of people. And that is the biggest contradiction in the mosque . . . the whole world is turning over. And I don't want to miss out on that."

H: The first thing I would look for, I would want to go among the women. I would want to see how their life has changed. I would want to see the support system that mothers have, so that they could still acquire the intellectual growth and education and training. You know, that's a big sign in a progressive country.

. . . I think that the problem is not that we are afraid of Allah, we are afraid of people. And that is the biggest contradiction in the mosque. We do things because of what people think, and not because of what we think Allah is thinking. And that's one thing I have gotten away from: dressing for people, praying for people, going to the mosque for people. There was one point in my life where I didn't wear but four colors—brown, grey, black, and white—because it was immodest to wear prints or pink. I didn't wear jewelry because if your jewelry made noise, that was wrong. They called in the jinns and the devils and what not. I didn't wear anything like that. No perfume. Because in ḥadīth it says that men can wear perfume with scent and women can wear perfume with color. But in America we don't wear henna. . . . In Arabia . . . the whole hand was painted. But that's not our culture. So how's an African woman in America supposed to relate to that. Well, you go to the mosque and everything is smelling like musk. It's the men. You know what I'm saying? They're putting oil in their beards, they're pouring it all over them, and you're trying not to notice this. But we have noses. So you turn where that scent is coming from, and how is that supposed to keep you modest?

You see, there's all these contradictions, and we've gotten Islamic fundamentals mixed up with cultures of various foreign Muslims; and we conglomerate all that and get very mixed up in America. I mean, if we could, some black people would ride camels down Main Street, "because Prophet Muhammad did." Blind following, you understand what I'm saying? So those things, because I understand national minorities must have a concept of their history, their land-space, their culture, their roots . . . I don't have the problem of imitating Pakistani women. I don't want to wear a sari. I don't want to be like Iranian women. Not because these Pakistani or Iranian women are bad, but because Allah created me African, and it's very good to be African. But because of America and the slave trade, the Negro was created and the African killed. And so I've gone through a whole political, cultural, social transition of reclaiming my national minority status, reclaiming my roots, reclaiming my African identity, and saying it's okay to be African and Muslim, and reclaiming the right to affirm my political growth, which is seeing Islam and everything else through a class analysis. But you know, studying marxism or studying Che or socialism doesn't make me uncomfortable, because we're in a progressive war, a cold war, now more so in America, but the whole world is turning over. And I don't want to miss out on that. So you've got to study everything, you know. And this has caused me great problems with the Muslim community, especially men, because they're very uncomfortable with assertive Muslim women, or assertive women in general. They're not used to that.

M: Would you tell me about your marriage?

The System is Getting Worse

> ". . . we've got a fantasy in this land that because you are a Muslim, you can escape. . . . [Battering situations] come from that and it is enhanced by the cultural teachings of Muslim communities."

H: I'm divorced now. That was really strange. I was in a battering situation, and the battering situation did not leave room for proper divorce procedures. We had to flee. And my husband decided he didn't want any part of political struggle or the way that we felt about Islam. He just wanted to be to himself. He didn't want to be a husband, and he didn't want to be a father. So it sort of just annulled the whole relationship, since he wouldn't go through any sort of procedure. So I went through *'idda,* three months of *'idda* [the three-month waiting period, mandated by Qur'an 2:27], and the divorce was finalized; even though in America, you just have to get an American legal divorce to satisfy their laws. But technically I'm divorced. I have three children and I am raising them.

M: Is your husband paying for . . .

H: No. I see him off and on. My husband is a victim of oppression in this country—my ex-husband—okay, and there are a lot of intricate designs that go into divorces in this country. It's not the total fault of one person or both; we're victims of a system that is built against us as African people. . . . And this comes from slavery times, with the breeding system that you go and you breed. You have no responsibilities except to the master. And you still find men with those values. And the sad part about it is they don't even know why they act the way they act. . . . The problem is raising the consciousness of men and women so they can understand that, so they can recycle themselves and counteract this. And until we get to that level, our divorce rate is high; it will get even higher, because the system is getting worse. Repression is getting worse. There are more poor people every day. . . . We've got a fantasy in this land that because you are a Muslim, you can escape. You know, "That's just happening to the nonbelievers." Well, the system don't care whether you are a Muslim nor non-Muslim: if you're poor, working class, then you reap the seeds of oppression. And so when you find men who can't find stable jobs, and they've got kids to support, you find men who because of their color, they're kept out of some opportunities that other men who are white might have. They will take this out on whoever's close to them.

And so that's where battering situations come from. They come from that and it is *enhanced* by the cultural teachings of Muslim communities. "Oh beat your wife lightly." That's all the Muslim man needs to hear. So when he gets fired, he comes home dissatisfied, "Allah has justified this." So one little thing she does, she can get beat, and it's okay. And Muslim men in general support this.

M: I'm sure you know there is a passage in the Qur'an [4:34] that there is a step-by-step progression. The first step is you separate from the bed. Isn't that enough to give them a warning?

H: It's the criteria in which you read that makes a difference. In a normal situation, in a normal, balanced society, after a revolution, okay, where everyone understands where we have come from and that it's collective this and collective that, and women or men go against the group, maybe, for example, want to reestablish the capitalistic system, or like, bringing the shah back, then that woman would be considered a lewd woman because she is going against the group and so she should be punished. But that would be the same for men too.

M: I like to hear it like that, because that makes a lot of sense: that if the woman is a traitor, then separate yourself from her. . . .

H: But not because of his personal feelings. Not because the man is personally upset. That shouldn't be the criterion for that woman being punished. It's if she goes against the collective will of her people.

Individualism and the General Will

"... the will of the husband is flaky."

M: So you attribute this to *nushūz,* which is the Qur'anic word for disobedience of the general will of a class, of the people, rather than the whim of the husband?

H: Yes, because the whim of the husband is flaky. That's a human being that makes mistakes, with defects, and I can never live under that rule, that what mood my husband is in, that means that he'll sleep with me that night. That's totally ridiculous. That doesn't even make sense. It's the collective will of the group, the struggle of the group, that if that individual becomes so individualistic that it hurts the group, then man, woman, or child, that person should be punished. But not on a personal basis, like if you were my husband and you were dissatisfied with me—I burned your toast—so all of a sudden I gotta go to hell because you're displeased with me. You know, that's not right. That's wrong. That's out of context right there. So that's the way I look at that. Now it goes on to "separate your bed" and then mutual consultation, or whatever, and then "beat them lightly." And we have to be real careful about that.

M: Well, "lightly" is not in the verse.

H: Oh, it's just "beat them." Well, we have to be careful.

M: Are you familiar with new interpretations of this verse? For example, we heard, "beat them lightly," and the commentary says, "beat them with a toothbrush". . . .

H: A *miswāk.*

M: Yes, that's the word. But that won't help, except to hurt a little less. But the new interpretation focuses on the plural verb, attributing this right to the community or representative rather than the husband.

H: I hadn't heard that.

M: What did your husband tell you?

H: That he has the right, because I belong to him.

M: But what could you do if you were disssatisfied?

H: Okay, now that's the problem. You see, when women are dissatisfied with men in various Muslim communities, they'll go to the imām or they'll go to their guardian, because some schools of thought say that you should have a guardian.

M: You had a guardian when you were mature?

H: Yes. My guardian's function was to get me married, because my marriage was arranged. It was a man. I've never seen a woman guardian.

M: Was he a relative?

H: No. He wasn't related to me, because most Muslims in America don't have Muslim relatives. So he was just a person in the mosque. The guardian in our community in Washington was a person that arranged the marriage. I talked to him and asked his advice about the man I was going to marry. We had a first-come-first-serve system, where, when it was time for a brother to get married, he'd marry the sister who was next in line. Like if, the seniority, if you had been waiting the longest, then it was your turn to get married more so than the sister who just came into the mosque. It was more verbal than a written list. Everybody knew who was who. . . .

Marriage: Temporary (*Mut'a*), Polygamous, and Monogamous

"... they have a tendency to abuse *mut'a* and marriage and polygamy."

M: Who told you about *mut'a?* What do you know about this?

H: I have Shi'a Muslim friends, and I've been in *mut'a* situations.

M: You mean you were temporarily married to someone?

H: Yes. When I first heard about *mut'a,* I hated it. I considered it slanderous to Islam. "How could they do this?" . . . a lot of the marriages that we were around broke up over *mut'a* situations. . . . I've never been in a *mut'a* situation with an Iranian; blacks practice *mut'a* too. . . . I knew [black] women who were involved in *mut'a* marriages with Iranian men. . . . Most Iranian men who have *mut'a* sitautions are not married. They are students, or they live here temporarily and are going back home, and they can't afford a full-fledged marriage. And they don't want to have any babies. . . . Now I understand it and I don't see anything wrong with it. Because how can a man come all the way over here, poor, trying to get an education, can't afford a marriage or to have children. Is he supposed to be celibate for four to eight years, however long it takes to get an education? That doesn't make sense. That's not practical, so they should have that right. Not just Iranian men, all men and women should have that right to have that type of sexual freedom. But before I didn't understand and I hated it, but more so I hated the application because people were hurting people. Men were being disrespectful. Now I'm not as narrow-minded about the whole thing. I think it makes everything much healthier. *Mut'a* can have a real progressive function, as long as it's not abused. Anything can be abused. You know, with people in this country and the way they have been trained sexually and how to treat women, they have a tendency to abuse *mut'a* and marriage and polygamy. I've been around all sorts of situations.

M: What about polygamy?

H: Most of the polygamist situations that I've seen did not work because the status of the women was an oppressive status, so they couldn't function. They couldn't flourish, they couldn't get along. There was always some type of conflict, jealousy, fighting; and a lot of the men would ego-trip off that, to make them feel powerful. You're talking about poor, working-class Muslims who have no power over the mode of production in this country and the only power they have is over women and children; so that's bound to get somebody abused or misused. So that abuse comes through our marriages, even it's a one-on-one. You know, like I said, we're all on a prostitutional level in this country, until things change. And I think polygamy can work in the right environment.

M: How can women free themselves?

H: If I had it to do all over again, I would just start having babies now. I would maybe just start thinking about getting married now. I would never have gotten married and never have started having babies so young. . . . I would have read thousands of books first, went to thousands of schools, got a job. I never worked except five years ago when I started working, because I was always being taken care of. A person who is being taken care of does not have the opportunity to grow.

M: Do you think you are alone in your ideas, or are there many other women who feel this way who suffer but don't have the guts to talk about this?

Feminist Consciousness

> "The political consciousness of the women tells you where the men are."

H: I think that they suffer. I think that they don't have the guts to speak out or question or inquire. And I think that their consciousness is not raised to the level where they understand what is happening to them. They don't see their class interests in this situation, so they don't understand how to get out of it. . . . At least the women's movement has brought it to the surface as far as women getting complete satisfaction from the sexual relationship and being verbal and telling men about their needs. . . . Women are trained to satisfy men, and all the rest is a big fake. We're trained to fake, and you're unhappy for the rest of your life, because you can't verbalize what you want, you can't say anything, because you'll hurt your husband's ego. And no woman wants to hurt a man's ego in our society, because that's your security, so you lie, if not verbally, physically or whatever, and you got the rest of your life totally unsatisfied, mentally, spiritually, and physically. And it's a horrible feeling. It is a horrible feeling. And women talk about these things somewhat in their circles. You know, we had a workshop when I first came to Houston on sexuality in Islam. And it was like—for any other functions, we couldn't get any of the sisters to come out of their houses; but when we had a workshop on sex, the whole house was filled. Women in veils, women without veils—everybody came. Because they wanted to talk about it. They wanted to ask questions. They wanted to learn. They were dissatisfied; that's why they came. . . . One of the basic topics was orgasm . . . every woman has a right to have an orgasm. But it's how you train your husband. . . . And we talked about the sex act in general. . . . You know, I guess you can deal with your wife like a till (Qur'an 2:23). Wow! What about your husband? . . . So we talked about that a lot, and how to get that different; how to rearrange that. And we talked about masturbation. . . . How do we train our children in sexuality? . . . that's a big thing, that's a problem: in Islam you're not supposed to be an aggressive woman, so that passiveness is in your bed; so your politics and your bed are the same. And it's just like the community. The political consciousness of the women tells you where the men are. . . . Those women are naive and narrow-minded and they don't read and they're not active. Then that's a big defect in the male part of the community. Because our nation, and when I say "our nation," I mean all poor people. Sometimes I say "my people" and I might mean African people, but basically my people are all people. And until women acquire a certain level of political growth and maturity, our people will always be in chains. And that maturity has to be sexual, spiritual, mental, physical, whatever. That's real important. And until the status of mothers and children is high, then our people will never be free. And so if I ever got to go to Iran, I would investigate the status of mothers and children; because mothers are to be treated like expensive glass, because we carry the nation. It should be a big thing to be a mother. In America, to be a mother is not a big thing. You go to find a house: no dogs! no kids! The same with what they think about motherhood. But in a progressive community, mothers and children should have high status, should be supported, should have collective day-care systems. I would look for that in Iran. Women should be able to get away from housework, because that's their oppression. There should be a socialistic attitude toward housework. There should be a collective attitude toward that. . . .

Part 4
Visual Projections

Courtesy of Wally Fawkes and *The Observer.*

6

Concluding Notes

Autographically Changing Iran: Minor Media and Bicultural Graphics

Emergent Ethnographic Subjects

> If not for the invention of photography and motion pictures one could perhaps still think of history in the manner of nineteenth century painting and Soviet Revolutionary posters.
>
> —Charles Simic, *The Uncertain Certainty*

> Part of the aesthetic of Afghan traditional storytelling is that stories of differing genres, scales of complexity, and construction . . . are juxtaposed and caused to reflect upon one another.
>
> —Margaret Mills, *The Mullah and the Mason*

> The Arabian Nights has a polyphonic style of storytelling in which as in a piano piece, the left hand provides a framing accompaniment that fills out the harmonic texture, a basic story, and lets the right hand carry out the melody of a subsidiary tale and then return to the bass and leave it again with another melody.
>
> —Anton Shamas, "The Shroud of [Naguib] Mahfouz"

One of the themes of the Iranian revolution, as well as of cultural conflicts generally in the Islamic world over the past century, has been the struggle over the terms of global integration: over the means and forms of local autonomy and of global connectedness. Traditional ethnographic frames—community, kinship systems, rituals, power structures, local economies and ecologies—remain important, but are clearly insufficient for describing and explaining the variated nature of emergent local and transnational forms. Contemporary ethnography perforce must prob-

Fig. 6.1. Bat over Washington, D.C. Courtesy of Hoover Library Archives.

lematize traditional constructions of the spatial, the temporal, and its own textual voice. Spatially, neither bounded locality nor nation-state is sufficient, but rather ways must be found to grasp cultural formations that occur in many different kinds of places (Dareh, Yazd, Tehran, Lawrence, Houston, for example) whose differences mutually define the cultural formations. Temporally as well, the contemporary condition is one of awareness of provisionally dominant, residual, and emergent conditions; tradition, memory, identity, ideals, values, morality, and multiplex forms of *conscience collective* are no longer conveyed primarily or simply through communal rituals or shared stories, but are reworked in multiple hybridized, individualized, or factionalized re-creations, by utilizing a wide array of communicative channels. Finally, the ethnographic voice itself has become pluralized, aware that subjects described may dispute accounts, and also that the writer's own worlds are implicated and interactively structured by the active interventions of the subjects described. A dialogic trope replaces the descriptively definitive one by displaying the range of argumentation, of alternative possibilities present in political contests, and of competing moral impulses available both to subjects described and in the ethnographic project itself. These revisions of traditional styles of presentation have emerged also in this volume through the challenges of its ethnographic subject.

The structure of this volume has been chronological as well as thematic: we have moved from prerevolutionary Iran; through the generic structures of Islamic reasoning, debate, rite, and ideological disputation; to the diaspora of postrevolutionary Islam in America. We have also moved from childhood socialization, through national mobilization, to global cultural interaction. In these final pages we take note of some of the minor media and the "bi" (multi)-cultural[1] graphic virtuosity of the Iranian revolution as clear registers of the hybrid, (post) modern character of the emergent new cultural formations of Shi'ism and of Iran, as well as of the intercultural "language" of our emergent pluralist global society.

An accompanying thematics of this volume and of these emergent forms has been a comparativist and philosophical counterpoint, a play of European and Islamic "harmonic thirds."[2] The stress on the hermeneutic (interpretive, debate, dialogic) dimension of Islam is not only a counter to the stereotypes of Islam as a legalistic or fanatic rigid structure either of simple mechanical rules or of arbitrary *qāḍī* justice. (That some Muslim catechismic slogans seem to argue this,[3] and that some Westerners who claim to be friends of Muslims accept it, is evidence not of its validity, but of a particular ideological discourse that is one of several competing class- or interest-linked discourses. The anthropological challenge is to map this competition and its sociological carriers.) The stress on the hermeneutic dimension of Islam is also a mirror to the hermeneutic dimensions of Jewish and Christian discourses, and particularly of the modern, post-theological renewal of interest in hermeneutics as an analytic tool into the ways in which language operates and meaning and truth are mediated and controlled linguistically. An inquiry into the visual may provide one further sensory channel to review the themes of the preceding chapters.

The visual has long been posed as the dialectical foil to the linguistic. Where words seem slippery, the visual often seems direct and clear. Yet, at the extreme, as in modernist art which attempted to rid itself of narrative, of words, of the material world of reference, and to find through direct perception beauty, truth, and spirit, one found that nonobjective, nonreferential art became a machine for verbalization. Without the verbal theories generated by artists and critics, or the "chatter" of gallery and museum goers, one could not "see" this art.[4] Iranian calligraphic art has long played an intermediary role, being both visual and verbal, being also like arabesque one of a number of graphic leavens absorbed over the centuries into Western aesthetics.[5] Theories about the visual have been stimulated by revolution, the French Revolution in particular, when the categories of the sublime, the metamorphic grotesque, and the beautiful underwent elaboration.[6] How does one represent something new? While the Iranian revolution may not have stimulated quite the same aesthetic theory development, its graphic products both may help the contemporary questioning of neo-Kantian orthodoxies about the abstractness, disinterestedness, nonreferentiality, and autonomy of beauty and art[7] (including "Orientalist" essences of an Islam abstracted from all historical or regional contexts)[8] and may help us "see" the hybridized (post) modern character of the changes Iran is undergoing.

Minor Media as Reminders of the Postmodern Condition: Posters, Cartoons, Emblems

> Since the revolution, cigarettes are not sold in kiosks, but in groceries. Beans and rice which used to be found in groceries are now distributed in mosques. Communal prayers used to be held in mosques, now they are at the university. The university used to be for science and

education; now (re) education is done in the jails. Jails used to be for criminals; now the criminals are in the government.

—Iranian joke, circa 1981[9]

Suppose that I write a book, let us say "Plato and telecom.," . . . on the postal agency of the Iranian uprising (the revolutionary role of dis-tancing, the distancing of God or of the ayatollah telekommeiny giving interviews from the Parisian suburbs. . . .

—Jacques Derrida, *The Postcard from Socrates to Freud and Beyond*[10]

Television kills telephony in brothers' broil. Our eyes demand their turn.

—James Joyce, *Finnegans Wake,* 52.18–19

The "small media"[11]—jokes, songs, tapes, leaflets, graffiti, posters, cartoons, insignia, local Diogenes characters, and *matalak-gū* (jive, repartee, aggressive humor)—are revealing indices of consciousness, world historical locus, and sociological positioning. The revolutionary posters of the Iranian revolution, some of which grace the stamps of the Islamic Republic of Iran, not only are artistically well wrought but also vividly articulate the cultural interreferences of modern Iran, bringing together on the one hand traditional graphic traditions of the Persian miniature, of murals used as props by epic storytellers, and of calligraphic and arabesque design, and on the other hand an international third-world revolutionary modernist graphic lineage that dates back via the Cuban revolution to the Russian revolution. Often different posters fit into one or the other tradition. But not infrequently, these two traditions come together in brilliantly powerful condensations, or in equally powerful disseminations (in which two sets of meanings do not fuse but remain in creative tension generating different chains of associations).

Political cartoons have an even longer historical international lineage (and nearly a century-long Iranian one before they fade back into other forms of humorous line drawings): they trace back at least to Protestant graphics during the religious wars of Europe, coming then via Holland and Britain as a middle-class political form, to a battling of wits during the French Revolution of 1789. Cartoons on all political sides of the Iranian revolution provide not only inventories of images, symbols, and visual puns,[12] but perhaps also an access to the increasing politics of signs in the postmodern world, where a semi-independent circuit of signs seems to operate only in indirect relation to underlying social processes and complexly negotiated realities. There would seem to be more happening in this indirection than merely reductionism and stereotypy: the danger of course is that the recirculation of signs obscures, short-circuits, and replaces serious inquiry. Television news broadcasts are a serious site of this transformation from inquiry into genre narrative formats of newsman as hero or detective, or of emotional melodramas, staged in short segments like a comic strip. Cartoons retain the saving grace that they work primarily as oppositional forms, exposing and poking fun at the pretensions of the national or international political order and its claims for legitimacy. Aesthetically, they intrigue (in both senses) through their gestures at abstraction—which might be defined as the gesture toward true insight, truth in sight, optical purity, access to essence, form, or spirit, through suppression of the interest-laden play of language[13]—though this gesturing remains in the realm of the recognizable picture as well as being usually a mixed textual-visual form (through captions, labels, thought or voice balloons, depiction of verbal metaphors, etc.).

Calligraphy, an Islamic art par excellence, mediates between the linguistic and the visual, and is a flexible design device which like the flowing arabesque can integrate and harmonize new elements with the old. Calligraphic emblems of the revolution such as the emblem on the flag of the Islamic Republic not only provide portmanteau ideograms of symbols, but also remind us of the grammar of ornamental, architectural, textile, and graphic design that the Iranian and Islamic world has long provided the world, a reminder as well that intercultural borrowings are deeper and more complex than either political discourse or us/them, self/other essentializing dichotomies allow.

Embedded within the emblem of the Islamic Republic of Iran is a tulip. The tulip is an icon of martyrdom and of revolutionary determination. Ironically, it is also Kant's example of pure beauty, and Hegel too uses "the religion of flowers" as a figure (*Vorstellung*) of the Garden of Eden drama, a first step toward consciousness, self-representation, and moral responsibility.[14] The tulip, of course, comes to Europe both iconographically (on pottery, brass work, and embroidery) and naturally as a flower from the East, from Persia by way of Venice or Turkey, as its names indicate.[15] Tulips were the focus of one of the first great stock market crashes in Amsterdam in the seventeenth century. The tulip, the rhetorical and the iconic use of flowers, playfully, may help trace some of the intercultural traffic and differential reception of aesthetics between the secularist bourgeois revolutions of the nineteenth century, and the need for a more integrative aesthetics in the belated[16] revolutions of the twentieth century.

Truth in Tulips: Emblems, Arabesque Design, Allusive Graphics

> . . . he observed that the learned Ibn Qutaiba describes an excellent variety of the perpetual rose, which is found in the gardens of Hindustan and whose petals, of a blood red, exhibit characters which read: "There is no god, but the God, Mohammad is the Apostle of God."
>
> – Jorge Luis Borges, "Averroës Search"

> "for example [*zum Beispiel*][17] the tulip." . . . A paradigmatics of the flower orients the third *Critique*. . . . In Kant's footnote, the tulip appears to be placed, deposited on a tomb. . . . Only free (independent) beauty gives rise to a pure aesthetic judgment. . . . Free beauty, that of the tulip, is *pulchritudo vaga,* the other is *pulchritudo adhaerens.* Why these Latin words in brackets? Why this recourse to an erudite and dead language? It is a question we must pose if we are to follow the labor of mourning[18] in the discourse on beauty. . . . Each time Kant has recourse to a dead and scholarly language it is in order to maintain the norms in a state of utmost rigidity, to shelter them in a hermetic vault. . . .
>
> . . . it lacks nothing because it lacks an end. . . . A beautiful flower is in this sense an absolutely *coupable* [guilty, cuttable] flower that is absolutely absolved, innocent. . . . A concept always furnishes a supplement of adherence. . . . Attach the flower to its end, efface the beauty of the *sans* by according the flower its place in the seminal cycle. . . . The seed wanders (*s'erre*). . . .
>
> Starting from a signifier, one can account for everything except beauty, that is at least what seems to envelop the Kantian or Saussurean[19] tulip.
>
> – Jacques Derrida, *The Truth in Painting*

> It is necessary . . . to go beyond the self-evident character of the dominant concept of art and lay bare the anthropological foundation upon which the phenomenon of art rests and from the perspective of which we must work out a new legitimation for art.
>
> – Hans-Georg Gadamer, "The Relevance of the Beautiful"

Graphic design is among the most long-standing contributions of Iran and Islamic civilization; it remains vibrant in the arts of the Islamic

Republic. Among such designs, calligraphy has played a central role, mediating the visual and the linguistic, subordinating the pictorial to the graphic, balancing the abstract and the particular, meaning and form. Interlaced arabesque, geometric as well as curvilinear, is another such design feature. Both are integrative, open to incorporation of new elements, simple yet encompassing of intricacy, complexity, and multiple allusions, vehicles for harmonizing the old and the new, modernity and tradition.

The emblem of the Islamic Republic of Iran is an exemplar of such graphic design, and is not only one of the most frequently used components on stamps, posters, official insignia, and other visual documents and propaganda; but also a compendium of graphic design features and symbolic allusions.

The official emblem of Iran before the revolution was a male lion in motion, a sword in its right paw, facing the viewer, its tail toward the left (moving from east to west like the sun), a rising sun in the angle formed by its neck and backbone, above which was the imperial crown. The lion has a long historical lineage in Iran, and is familiar in royal iconography throughout Asia, as are the rising sun and the relation between the powers of nature and the mystical or divine grace of kingship. There was an indirect religious association: "the lion of God" (Asadullah) is the epithet of Ali, the first Shi'ite Imām, always pictured with his sword, the full epithet being an ambivalent pun: Asadullāh al-Ghālib ("lion of the victorious God" or "victorious lion of God"). The Iranian Red Cross was called the Red Lion and Sun (after the revolution it became the Red Crescent). The emblem was used on government documents and in the center of the flag on the white strip between the top green and bottom red stripes.

The Islamic Republic retained the colors of the flag, but added a line of white calligraphy to the green and red stripes: an infinite iteration of the phrase, *Allah-o-akbar* ("God is great"), each of the two words patterned into a squared shape, giving their continuous repetition a form analogous to the "Greek key" motif or a line of Chinese characters (figure 6.2). The emblem of the Islamic Republic on the white stripe in the center is composed of four crescents, a vertical bar, and a short orthographic stroke (the *shadda*) above the latter, a calligraphic form in a script reminiscent of old ornamental Kufic, the mother of Arabic scripts. The emblem has multiple readings and invokes multiple visualizations, many of which are made explicit in different posters, stamps, and other media (e.g., figure 6.3).

First of all, it reads "Allah": read from right to left, the first crescent

Fig. 6.2. Emblem of Islamic Republic formed from the Iranian flag, tulips, doves with blood on their chests, cogwheel. Courtesy of Daftar Tabliqhat Islami, 1986.

Fig. 6.3. Emblem of Islamic Republic formed out of the wings of two doves and a tulip. Courtesy of Daftar Tablighat Islami, 1986.

is an *alif,* the first letter of the alphabet. The second, larger crescent, which crosses the next letter, is a *lām.* The vertical bar in the middle is another *alif,* which can be visualized (and is so realized in many designs) as one or all of the following: an olive tree, a torch, a minaret, a sword or dagger or lance, an arrow, the center post of a tent (*'amūd*). The vertical bar (and these symbols) connects heaven and earth, representing the "straight path" of Islam, revelation, the connection between God and His servants. To the left of the vertical bar is a mirror image of the initial letters: an *alif* and the curved stroke of a final *ha.* Thus one can see this emblem on soldiers' helmets followed by the word *akbar* ("God is great").

Alternatively, the emblem can be read as a *lā* ("no!"). The outer crescents now are frames for the central mirrored image of the two letters *lām* and *alif.* In modern Iran, Dr. Ali Shari'ati drew attention to Islam as a religion of "no"s, not so much as a system of ritual interdictions or taboos, but rather as a system of protest against false gods, false ideologies, false justice. He also institutionalized the logo *lā* by putting a Kufic *lā* (borrowed from the inscription on the tomb of Rumi in Konya) on the cover of all his books and published lectures. This logo has been taken up in different variants by several factions within the revolution including the Pasdaran (Revolutionary Guards), the Mojahedin-e Enqelab-e Islāmi (followers of former president Bani-Sadr), and the Mojahedin-e Khalq (the Islamic leftists), by putting together the stylized Kufic *lā* with a rifle (replacing the traditional double-edged sword of Ali and symbol of Islamic sovereignty), thereby graphically combining elements from Islam, modernity, revolutionary third-world traditions, and claims to the legacy of Shari'ati.

A third reading is suggested by the stage in mysticism following that of *lā* or negation of false gods: the state of *illā* ("except": "there is no god except Allah"). *Illā* and its mirror image again share the middle vertical bar, the *alif,* the "alpha of creation."

Fourth, then, putting these three visualizations together, one can see that the emblem also clearly may be read as the Islamic credo, *lā ilāha illā Allāh* ("there is no deity but Allah"): all the letters and diacriticals necessary are present, forming each word in succession, like a flashing neon sign atop a mosque. The pair of crescents on each side of the vertical bar face inward, their backs turned toward the right and the left, and one can sense the credo's transform in the modern slogan, "neither East nor West, Islam is best." As the *ummatan wasaṭan* ("middle nation"; Qur'an 2:143), Muslims declare their independence from the imperial superpowers. Indeed, if the emblem is taken as an abstraction of the globe (as is realized in posters and stamps), the straight and vertical bar contrasts with the two superpower blocks, neither of which is "straight."

Among the multiple visualizations suggested by the emblem, and frequently realized in different designs, three are most important: the lamp, the tulip, and the hand. The lamp is inspired by the *nūr* ("light") verse in the Qur'an:

> Allah is the *light* of the *heavens and the earth.* A likeness of His light is as a *niche* in which is a *lamp,* the lamp is in a *glass,* [and] the glass is, as it were, a brightly shining *star,* lit from a blessed *olive tree* neither eastern nor western. Its oil almost gives light though untouched by fire. Light to light, Allah guides to His light whom He pleases, and Allah sets forth parables for men, and Allah is cognizant of all things. (Qur'an 24–35; italics are added)

The vertical bar of the emblem is the flame, and the four crescents represent the niche and the glass. The bottom of the emblem, where the second, third, and fourth letters cross, resembles the "star lit from a blessed olive tree." The *shadda* diacritic above the olive tree/flame emphasizes the independence of Islamic vision from the ideologies of communist and capitalist materialisms.

The tulip in Persian is *lāleh,* also the word for a candle lantern with a tulip-shaped glass. In poetry it is associated with the blood of lovers who die in the course of their quest on the battlefields of love; and this is easily transformed into the blood shed in the quest for the ultimate Beloved, martyrdom in the way of God. These are old associations going back to pre-Islamic, central Asian imagery of a tulip growing from the cheek of the martyred Siyavush, an Iranian prince slain for reasons of state by the Turanian enemies of Iran. It is translated into the imagery of the martyrdoms at Karbala. Tears, moreover, water the blood-red tulips of martyrdom: blood and tears provide the nutrient irrigation for making the cause of the martyrs strong in the memory and rededication of the living. The tulip has become *the* icon of martyrdom for the Islamic Republic, and it is one of the most omnipresent symbols in the republic's visual arts. Its iconography has become stylized in the shape of the emblem we are discussing: two of the outer petals are often shown falling, representing the heavy price Muslims pay for protecting the "light of God," the "pure tree," the "straight path" connecting God and His servants; the two inner petals remain in the shape of *lā,* protecting the seeds/light of the tulip, and are illuminated by this inner light.

The emblem is also presented as the five fingers of a hand, again a resonant, multiregister symbol. It is the Qur'anic verse 48:10, "the hand of God is above all hands" the hand of unity (*yad-e wāḥida*), the hand of refusal or *lā* (*dast-e radd bar sina-e kasī gozashtan,* "putting the hand of refusal on someone's chest"), the hand of Fatima (a widespread prophylactic against the evil eye used in amulets and jewelry), the hand of Abbas (the half brother of Imām Husain, the representative of loyalty), the hand of the five pure souls (*panj tan*) of the family of the Prophet (Muhammad, Ali, Fatima, Hasan, and Husain) for whose sake, according to the Ḥadīth of the Cloak, the heavens and the earth were created. The five pure souls, together with the rest of the twelve Imāms descended from Husain, are for Shi'ites the fourteen infallible guides for Muslims, who possess *wilāyat-e takwīnī* (the power to miraculously intervene in the process of creation). They are of God, without being His partners. They are the light of God, and through their intercession (*shafā'at*) God answers the prayers of the believers. The *shadda* above the emblematic *panj tan* hand represents the angel Gabriel who descends from heaven to join the five *panj tan* and to bring/reaffirm the divine message.

Derivative visualizations of the emblem include the onion and the scales of justice. The onion, or perhaps the onion-like bulb of a tulip, represents life and growth, the *shadda* on top like the bud of a new blossom. The vertical bar, the *alif* or alpha of creation, is strong and permanent, while the outer petals may fall away; the vertical bar thus is like the vertical stand to which the balance arm of the scales of justice is attached, while the petals are the weighing pans that might be bent down by corruption and evil, but that in their upright position in the emblem of the Islamic Republic represent justice and order in the universe.

The games of visualization and symbolization are infinite,[20] and the point here is not merely to draw attention to those that are in fact realized in the explicit pictorial elaboration or verbal commentary,[21] but to emphasize the richness of a graphic design tradition that is both venerable and modern, that has yielded contributions to European design particularly since the sixteenth century, that as an inspiration to such modern art movements as Art Nouveau should not be dismissed as grasping Orientalism, but be recognized as a vibrant design grammar, and as a sign of the fact that cultural exchange has always tended to be much deeper and richer than the reductions to political stereotype, or self versus other essentializings, would suggest.

Revolutionary Operatics and Cartoons for Export

> Caricature is a subversive model whereby a political model is dismantled by means of an aesthetic model. The caricaturist perverts the rules of ideal representation in order to create the image of a human figure who is himself a representative of authority. Hence, in caricature there is transgression (of an aesthetic norm) for the purpose of aggression against a social model.
>
> —Michel Melot, "Caricature and the Revolution"[22]

> Innocence is now out of the question of course . . . the most striking thing about "otherness" and "difference" is, as with all general terms, how profoundly conditioned they are by their historical and worldly context. . . .
>
> —Edward Said, "Representing the Colonized: Anthropology's Interlocutors"

> Suddenly, in our century, the world is closing in around us. The decisive event . . . was surely the 1914 war, called (and for the first time in history) a world war. Wrongly, "world". It involved only Europe, and not all of Europe at that [and not called World War I until after World War II]. But the adjective "world" expresses all the more eloquently the sense of horror, the fact that henceforth, nothing that occurs on the planet will be merely a local matter.
>
> —Milan Kundera, "Conversation with Milan Kundera on the Art of the Novel"

The operatics (workings, theatrics, passion-playing,[23] demon-strations,[24] Qur'anic recitations, ritual inflections, repetitions and re-petitions,[25] progressions and [dis]harmonics)[26] of the Iranian revolution compose a complex arabesque that is poorly represented by any single Iranian spokesperson or factional discourse. Operatics is perhaps a provocative term invoking not only Wagnerian synergistic fusion of all the sensual arts—a panoply of features that richly reward investigations beyond their surface politics—but also the melodrama of overstatement, of the exaggerated expressivism used to break through conventional consciousness and normal or hegemonic frames of reference. It is, after all, not only an Edward Said or an Abdel Kebir Khatibi who understands the Foucaultian and Derridian call to analyze and redeploy the power of writing styles and knowledge conventions: a top priority of the Iranian revolution was to gain control over the media—television, cinema, radio, newspapers, books, poster art, stamps, sartorial style, etc. These were powerful vehicles of articulation and manipulation of public opinion during and after the revolution: cassette tapes of sermons,[27] use of BBC broadcasts to coordinate demonstrations,[28] postrevolutionary demonstrations at the American Embassy (and elsewhere) staged for satellite transmission to America, revolutionary posters on walls in public spaces in Iran, secondarily worldwide, and political cartoons in propaganda forums for both internal and external consumption.

Indeed, the fascination (an obsessively consuming one for many Iranians) lies in deciphering and disentangling the processes that lie behind the comic book pronouncements of Khomeini (e.g., calling the United States "the Great Satan," comparing acceptance of the ceasefire with Iraqi President Saddam Husain to swallowing poison; telling Soviet leader Mikhail Gorbachev that communism is dead and he should read the Qur'an; dismissing economics as trivial). A parallel might be drawn with Americans who, after a period of bemusement, became used to viewing former president Ronald Reagan (e.g., describing the Soviet Union as "the Evil Empire," announcing a "Star Wars" Strategic Defense Initiative thought technically unfeasible by most of his leading science and defense advisers; unable to remember the substantive details of policy) as a "genial" character within the mirror play of synoptic television syntax—systematically building arguments from a visual scene; citing photos, films, television, scenes in novels; using lines from films and novels; suppressing verbs in favor of nondiscursive connections.[29] Such synoptic syntax and comic book style are surface chimera of less visible processes. In both cases, one wants to ask both about the power of symbolic politics and about how such politics relate to underlying social processes.

In the Iranian case, as in the American, the politics of signs is often only indirectly connected to other political circuits.[30] Institutional developments and the factional politics within the policy-making bodies of the Iranian government reveal a quite different picture. Parliaments (that take active roles in debating policy, denying ministers votes of confidence, etc.), elections (albeit controlled), parallel institutions, cell structures, parties, ability to fight a modern war (albeit at times with World War I strategies of substituting masses of men and boys for scarcity of tanks, armor, and mine sweepers)—these, while not constituting a liberal democratic regime, are hardly the return to seventh-century social forms caricatured in hostile cartoons. Moreover, the persisent factional disputes within the government, between parliamentary factions, and between the Parliament and the Council of Guardians are those easily recognized as a debate between state centralization (nationalization of central sectors of the economy, land reform, welfare state, labor protection laws) and laissez-faire conservatism (often glossed as a struggle between a petit bourgeois technocracy and the bazaar's commercial bourgeoisie). Khomeini's own role—again not that pictured in Western or emigré hostile cartoons—is not one of dictatorial control, but one of adjudicating between factions, initially to make sure the coalition needed to keep the revolution together did not break apart, and more recently to make sure that the revolution did not slide entirely into the hands of the conservative defenders of traditional law (*fiqh-e sunnati*) at the expense of promoters of progressive Islamic law (*fiqh-e pūya*).[31]

Cartoons obviously are not always the most subtle of forms. The better ones are those that are inventive, that draw on other than the usual stock of imagery, and that fuse together international and Islamic imagery. But perhaps the most important thing to be said about those cartoons directed at international relations and international audiences is that they attempt to insist upon a rhetoric that dramatizes a sense of global interconnections, one that positions Iran as encircled by a network of hostile forces, one therefore that has millenarian overtones in the kinds of persistence that are required to overcome such overwhelming odds, and yet one that stresses the blindnesses, self-destructiveness, and vulnerabilities of the enemies of Islam and Iran. Two sets of cartoons may illustrate.

In a study of the 1253 visual images in twenty-four issues of *Imām,* an English language monthly put out by the Iranian embassy in London, Annabelle Sreberny-Mohammadi and Ali Mohammadi found that nearly half dealt with foreign affairs. Of these 573 images, the largest number by far dealt with the United States (150); the USSR came second with 39 images, and Europe represented almost entirely by England and France had only 12 images. Both superpowers were dealt with as rapacious imperialists. Israel was almost always dealt with as an appendage of U.S. imperialism. The Arabs were alternatively presented as puppets of the United States or as precarious in their Islam (e.g., Arafat and King Hussein of Jordan balanced on the cutting edge of the scimitar of Islam). The Western media were represented as an imperialist evil, literally pounding messages into heads (with a hammer), or as the devil trumpeting. Most of the imagery was readily recognizable to English-speaking audiences: Brezhnev sewing Afghanistan onto the USSR, Andropov plowing up Afghanistan with a tractor pulling a sickle and preparing a grave for Muslim martyrs; Uncle Sam forcing a bottle of nationalism down Muslim throats, or milking the world of its oil; Reagan as an American eagle with a withered olive branch in his talon; Israel as a globe-girdling snake or scorpion. Some of the better ones drew on Islamic associations and imagery: the Russian bear licks up Afghanistan while the U.S. pig swallows Palestine and Lebanon (this is made more trenchant if one realizes that the pig is *najes* [ritually polluting] and the bear is associated with foolish friendship);[32] the hammer and sickle is broken into fragments by an arrow ("the straight path of Islam") or by the Islamic credo in Arabic calligraphy; the devil trumpets his tune, music being a seduction viewed with suspicion by traditional Muslims.

Another sample is provided by the "War in Caricature" set of thirty caricatures produced by the Revolutionary Guards on the occasion of the second anniversary of the Iran-Iraq war. These were intended for export as propaganda: the captions are in English and Arabic (not Persian). Their primary intent is to portray Saddam Husain as a Zionist stooge of U.S. imperialism, and to link together the conflicts in Lebanon, Palestine, and Iraq. "It is *wājib* [religiously obligatory] to destroy Israel," the cover and one of the caricatures quotes Khomeini as decreeing in Arabic (the English, "Israel has to be destroyed," is less potent, if no less militant). But the only way to Jerusalem is through Iraq, liberating the oppressed masses from the Zionist 'Aflaqī government. (Khomeini called Saddam Husain Saddam 'Aflaqi, and insisted that Michel Aflaq, the Christian ideologue of the Baathist party, d. 1989, was a Zionist and a Jew; hence also he calls the Baathist party Ḥizb-e 'Aflaqī.) Thus, Begin lifts his skullcap to reveal a tank driven by Saddam flying a flag with the Star of David; Saddam wearing a beret with the Star of David carries a grenade marked "made in U.S.A."; King Fahd and Menachim Begin hold olive branches in their mouths, the other ends tied together, while a Star of David is sewn onto the flag of Iraq; King Fahd as a toy Arab shaykh is dressed in a U.S. flag with a wind-up key in his back under a peace agreement that gives Palestine to Israel; a Palestinian corpse drips blood into a goblet marked "Nobel" from which Begin drinks; Begin with a vacuum cleaner sucks up the army of Egypt, and dumps them out transformed into Israeli soldiers in Lebanon; Uncle Sam cries while Begin pulls an ox cart with the corpse of Saddam wrapped in a U.S. flag; pilot Saddam crashes his new French Mirage jet and sees stars (of David); the hand of the Islamic Republic holds up Saddam with two disdainful fingers as if holding a polluting mouse (figure 6.6); Saddam with a Star of David on his chest is upside-down inside an hourglass; a boulder inscribed "Revolutionary Government of the Islamic Republic of Iran, Ministry of Foreign Affairs, Declara-

Islam was not insulted during the reign of Reza Shah and Mohammad Reza Shah, but Jebheye Melli (The National Front) has insulted Islam.
استقامت کنید!
لم يسب الاسلام طوال فترتي حكم رضاشاه و محمدرضاشاه ولكن الجبهة الوطنية قدسبت الاسلام.

Fig. 6.4. Transition prime minister, Shapur Bakhtiari, as king.

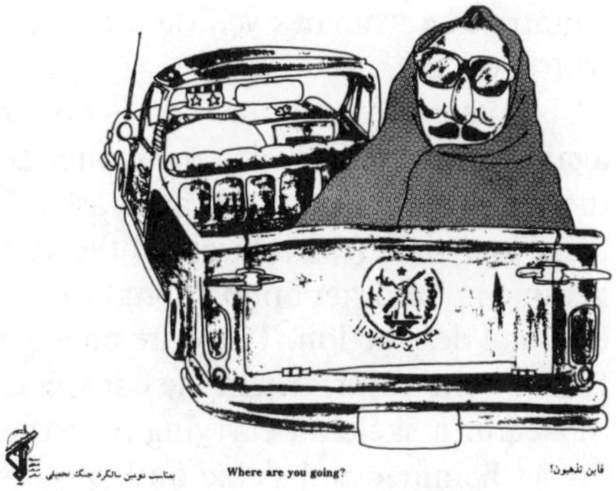
Where are you going?
فاين تذهبون؟

Fig. 6.5. Former President Bani-Sadr flees in a woman's chādor.

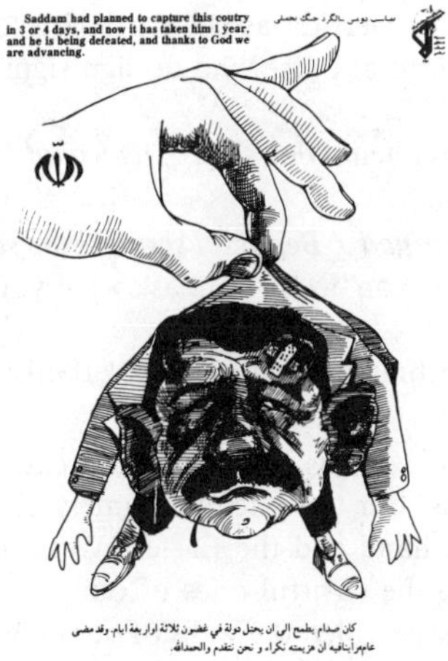
Saddam had planned to capture this coutry in 3 or 4 days, and now it has taken him 1 year, and he is being defeated, and thanks to God we are advancing.

Fig. 6.6 Iraqi Premier Saddam Husain as rodent held by two disdainful fingers.

THE WAR IN CARICATURES
الحرب كما يروي الكاريكاتور
جمهوری اسلامی ایران

Fig. 6.7. Death in American flag.

tion Number One" falls on Uncle Sam. The cartoons of Shapur Bakhtiar's regal style (figure 6.4) and former President Bani-Sadr fleeing the country in a woman's veil (figure 6.5) are defining images the two men will never escape.

The narrative structure here is not only one that depicts a conspiracy against Muslims in which the United States, Israel, Iraq, Saudi Arabia, the USSR, Britain, and France are all partners; but also one that depicts over time (the hourglass) the vulnerability of Iraq, of the Mujahedin, and of other oppositional forces (Bani-Sadr, Bakhtiar) and their eventual destruction. There are millenarian overtones, expressed powerfully on the cover, where the conspiracy is depicted as the grim reaper of death: a skeleton carrying a scythe and wearing the U.S. flag, the Soviet hammer and sickle on his shoulder and the Star of David and flames below (figure 6.7).

Revolutionary Posters and Cultural *Intereférences*

> Postmodernism is a name for the end of writing without a subject . . . of hegemonic ideology, of all that is expressed as consensus. . . . The goal is to read and write by repetitions that make small changes inseminating "pasts" of every word in the way of a smell, or a taste, or a snatch of song or etymology. . . . Derrida as-signs priority to difference and to the signifier, the inverse of those who de-sign signified prior to signifier.
>
> —Stephen Tyler, *The Unspeakable*

> *Na porsid Islam baraye shoma che mikonad / Beporsid shoma baraye Islam che mikonid* [Ask not what Islam can do for you; ask what you can do for Islam.]
>
> —Wall slogan on a Tehran branch of the Central Bank[33]

> . . . the impact of the language of art . . . has frequently and effectively been used in the struggle against our two enemies namely, the Shah's oppressive regime on the one hand and the Eastern-Western blocks on the other. . . . Even before the rightful cries of our "ummat" crumbled the walls of the oppressive ruler, the walls of our cities had gone to war against the walls of the oppressive regime consequently weakening and shaking their very foundation.
>
> —Daftar Tablighat Islami, Preface to *Profiles of the Revolutionary Art*

The most interesting of the graphics of the Iranian Revolution are the quite extraordinary, colorful, artistic, visually and allusively rich posters (and postage stamps).[34] They, even more than the cartoons, demonstrate a confluence of local Iranian and global world-historical traditions and processes, and provide material for speculatively exploring the aesthetic means of different revolutions for representing changes in consciousness. The French Revolution saw itself as something new and as something universal, something that had never occurred before, and it generated a rich elaboration of thinking about aesthetic categories of the sublime (storms of nature, volcanoes, earthquakes),[35] the beautiful (island of calm; meadow after a storm) and the grotesque (metamorphoses) as vehicles for thinking about social change and the future. Most revolutions since then have seen themselves in relation to predecessor revolutions. Revolutions, after all, are not only processes over time in their own national contexts (structurally, the 1977–79 Iranian revolution was the fifth time since 1872 that a coalition of religious leaders and secular reformers forced either a major policy change or a change in form of government), but they borrow internationally from predecessors elsewhere in tactics, organizational forms, strategies, rhetorics, and visual symbols and graphics.

In an insightful short essay, William Hanaway (1985), analyzing twenty-nine posters, distinguishes two graphic traditions they seem to fall into. One is an international style that stems primarily from the Russian Revolution with contributions from the Cuban Revolution: these posters are done in simple red, white, and black colors, with little detail, expressing a single idea or event, depersonalized and symbolic ih form, and humanistic in ideology (i.e., human beings are in control of their own destiny). In an example of an abstract "constructivist" style poster (figure 6.8), a red arrow moving from right to left (like the Arabic script), inscribed "revolution," breaks a black rectangle (a crown falling off its upper surface), and is beginning to destroy the second of three such black rectangles, this one inscribed "internal reactionaries"; the third block awaiting its turn is labeled "imperialism" and is capped with Uncle Sam's hat; on the far side is a red sun/victory. Another poster in this tradition (figure 6.9), which Hanaway recognizes as adapted from a Cuban poster, is also in black and red on a white background: two rifles form a triangle within which is a stylized dove, its body and head formed of pen points; out of the top pen point comes a red flower of martyrdom dripping hearts of red blood; the neck connecting the body and head is a coiled arabesque, looking like the rope of a hubble-bubble;

Fig. 6.8. Constructivist red arrow of revolution breaks crown, internal reactionaries and imperialism. Jim Hitselberger Collection, courtesy of the Hoover Library Archives.

the caption reads, "For a free press" (*āzādī-e qalam,* "freedom of the pen"), and in good modern designer style, the poster has the artists' credits along the sides.

The other graphic tradition is that of Iranian painting of Persian miniatures, of cloth murals used in coffeehouses to prompt epic reciters, and 'Ashūrā banners. Posters derivative of these styles are done with a broader palette, including prominently Islamic green; much more detail and multiple events are portrayed on single posters; individuals are portrayed rather than roles, although some of these such as the family of the Prophet are recognized by standardized, traditional iconography; references to Iranian tradition and to Islam are many and rich; and the ideology is God centered rather than human centered. A classic example of the Persian miniature style is the poster of Khomeini in the role of Moses with a dragon/serpent at his feet ("He [God] said, 'Cast it down,' and, lo, it was a serpent, gliding" [Qur'an 20:19–20]), victorious over Pharaoh ("go thou unto Pharaoh, lo he has transgressed" [Qur'an 20:24]), pointing toward the upper left corner portrayal of tortures in hell that await the shah ("theirs is the curse and theirs is the ill abode" [Qur'an 13:25]), who cowers lower left with broken crown and sword, holding on to the coattails of imperialism in the figure of Uncle Sam with British and Israeli insignia ("in that day their excuses will not profit

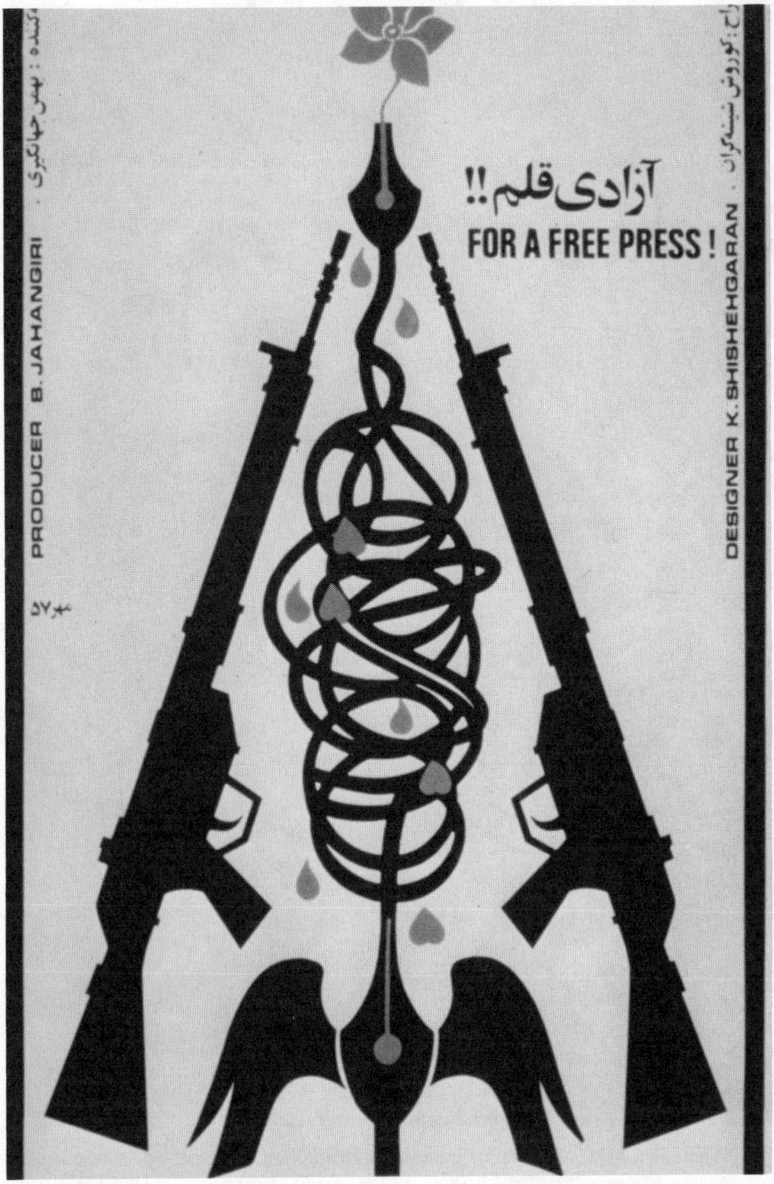

Fig. 6.9. Stylized dove as two pen nibs dripping hearts of blood between rifles ("For a Free Press"). Jim Hitselberger Collection, courtesy of the Hoover Library Archives.

6.10. "There is a Moses for every Pharaoh," with inserted cameos to claim the legacy of S. Mahmud Talegani and Dr. Ali Shari'ati. For original 1979 poster, see Fischer (1980). Jim Hitselberger Collection, courtesy of the Hoover Library Archives.

those who did injustice" [Qur'an 30:57]); a non-Qur'anic line reads: "There is a Moses for every Pharaoh" (figure 6.10). The version of the poster shown here has cameo inserts of S. Mahmud Taleqani and Dr. Ali Shari'ati in an attempt by the Khomeini regime to claim their legacies; for the original poster, see Fischer 1980a. A similar miniature style poster shows the shah fleeing Iran, carrying his overflowing money bags, stepping across the Shatt-al-Arab, while Khomeini presides over the revolution, illustrated in details of demonstrations and incidents within the outline map of Iran.

How far back this sort of use of Persian miniature painting may be traced is an interesting question since some readings of the miniatures that illustrate the epic *Shāhnāmeh* suggest that they were designed to support or comment upon the legitimacy of the royal patrons who commissioned them (Grabar and Blair 1980). Closer to contemporary propaganda uses are the Persian miniature posters designed by British intelligence during World War II: e.g., figure 6.11, Hitler as the mythic demon Zahhak (with serpents from each shoulder demanding to be fed the brains of Iranian youths) being chained to Mount Demavand (Zahhak will break his chains at the end of time for the final apocalyptic battle between good and evil) by the forces of Churchill, Stalin, and Roosevelt (seated on the horses). This is one of a series of six such posters in the Yale University Archives.

Wall murals illustrate another traditional style of painting. In both miniature and mural styles, a wealth of detail fills the entire surface of the poster, with rich allusions to Islam and Iran. Mural style posters or wall paintings may be composites of incidents from the revolution (figure 6.12), or they may portray the people of Iran.[36] Among the latter is a mural of village reconstruction (masons building a house), mobilization for war (peasants with shovels receive a rifle from a mullā), and refugee women carrying their belongings. A huge mural shows farmers and workers, with a mullā among the leaders, armed only with shovels, pitchfork, and pickax, backed by their womenfolk in veils, all under the flag of the Islamic Republic, facing a much more heavily armed crowd under the aegis of Uncle Sam, including a soldier wearing a gas mask, a man in a Hispanic-looking cowboy outfit, and various Western dressed individuals. A less elaborate mural similarly shows men and women holding shovels and pitchforks holding up a white banner with slogans of the revolution. Another mural shows a woman sitting in the courtyard of the ruins of a once elegant urban house, ruined in the war with Iraq; a similar wall painting shows another woman sitting in the rubble in front of a more modest village house under palm trees. A third poster

Fig. 6.11. Hitler-Zahhak poster designed by the British during World War II. Courtesy World War II Collection, Manuscripts and Archives, Yale University Library.

Fig. 6.12. Mural: Events of the revolution.

in this vein shows a boy soldier, arm bandaged, squatting before the ruins of a village out of which rise disembodied arms holding rifles. Another mural shows soldiers seated behind a wall of sandbags listening to a mulla speak, with an inset portrait of Speaker of Parliament Ali Akbar Hasemi-Rafsinjani.

A third major graphic tradition that shows up in Iran's posters after the first few years of the Islamic Republic is what might be called "commercial art" and even psychedelic "heavy metal" art.[37] Of these, many are sentimental, in the style of devotional, wedding, or birthday card art; some are expressionist swirls of blood-red enfolding figures of martyrs or of Gorman-like madonna and child; others are heroic-mythic images of, for instance, doves transforming out of statues of soldiers. A number use collage techniques. There is quite a variety of styles. The most powerful are those like the one reproduced in chapter 3 of the stoning of the three idols during the ḥajj, reimaged as stoning the gas masked soldiers of imperialism. The color scheme, which could not be reproduced for this volume, is particularly vivid, the stone-throwing pilgrim being bathed in saturated indigo, blue, and turquoise light. A second poster in this set is of a purple-black bat, goggle-eyed and big eared as in a comic book, with the U.S. Capitol in white light and a more distant Kremlin above the outstretched wings which rain bombs down on a mosque and village in a green palm oasis, lighted by lurid red-orange flames.

But most interesting are those posters that fuse the two graphic traditions into a kind of condensation, or rather an interferential[38] dissemination structure, a cultural counterpoint that keeps dual sets of reference in play. Thus, for instance, on a poster done essentially in the international style, a worker in overalls holds a rifle aloft, a broken chain flying from his wrist, a mallet in his other hand; he is set against a red background and a white anvil (figure 6.13). Diagonally across the top left of the poster is written the Qur'anic verse of Iron: "We sent Our messengers with revelations, the book, and scales, that the people may rise for justice" (57:25). This is a Mojahedin poster issued for May Day. Another Mojahedin poster (figure 6.14) shows a colossal calloused hand emerging out of a crowd of men, some holding rifles aloft, done in a kind of Expressionist style with rust and brown tones, and inscribed, "the only hand the Prophet kissed was the hand of a worker";[39] it fuses with the traditional iconography of the hand of Abbas, the hand of loyalty. But it is not only the Islamic leftist, Mojahedin, who invoke the international revolutionary tradition. The Islamic Republican Party (IRP) issued a poster with similar working-class imagery, inscribed in Arabic, "He who earns his bread is like a man fighting in the way of God," and in Persian, "The committed laborers (*kārgarān-e mota'ahhed*) are holy warriors": in a kind of socialist realist style it shows working-class men kneeling in prayer, the man in front with a wrench in his pocket and a *muhr* (clay from Karbala) before him, against a background of industrial scales (figure 6.15). Other May Day posters issued by the IRP show two hands holding a wrench and a red tulip, done again in black, white, and red abstract form; and two hands held out over a rake, shovel, gun, and wrench, with the legend, "These are the hands that shall never burn in the fire of hell." Another poster is a simple revolutionary fist inscribed with an iconographic green silhouette of Imām Ali with his Zulfiqar sword inside a red tulip dripping blood (almost as if the hand of Abbas were severed half way down the arm) (figure 6.16). Behind are abstract desertlike bands of orange and yellow, a red flag of vengeance and a green flag of Islam. The flags are on standards with the hand of Fatima or Abbas or the Five Pure Souls, the one with a portrait of Khomeini in the palm, the other with the emblem of the Islamic Republic. The fist and the standards with their hands reiterate and reinforce one another. Along the sides are great stripes with infinitely repeated icons of Ali with Zulfiqar.

Fig. 6.13. Worker breaking his chains with the anvil/Sūra of Iron. From Ali, 1985.

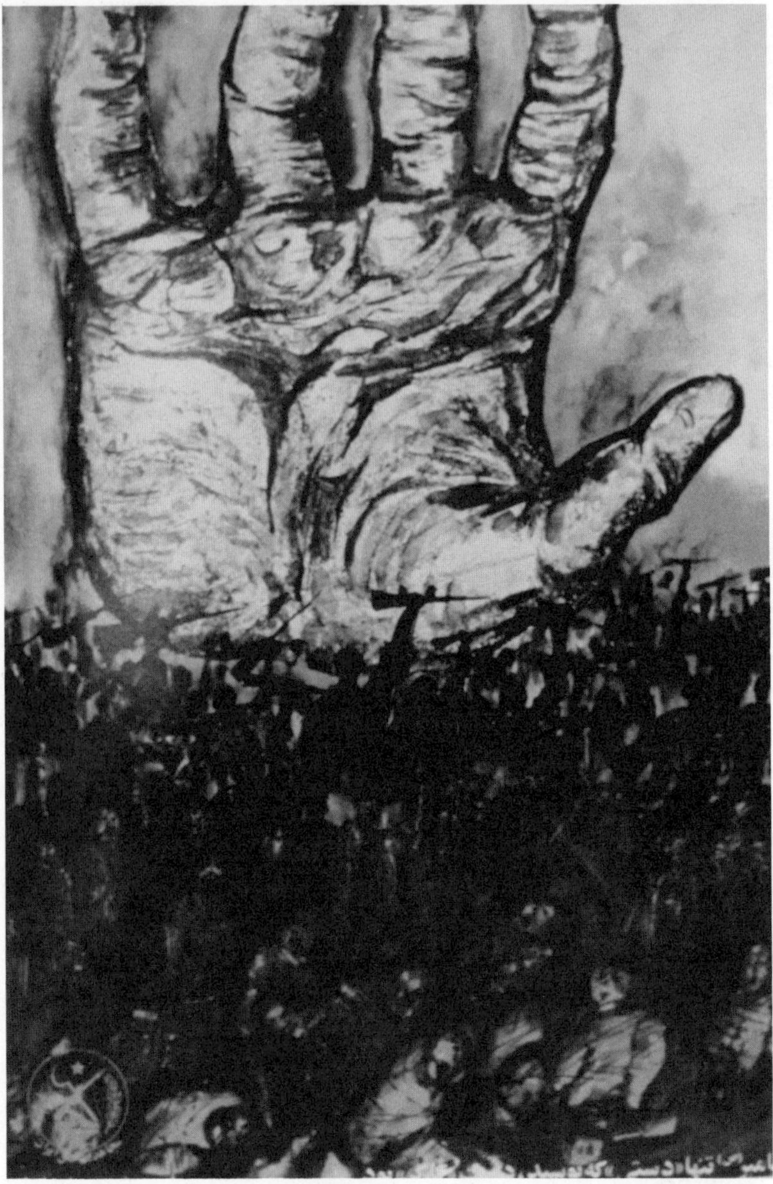

Fig. 6.14. Colossal hand (worker; Abbas) of the masses. Jim Hitselberger Collection, courtesy of the Hoover Library Archives.

Fig. 6.15. Workers kneel in prayer with *mohr* and scales of justice. Jim Hitselberger Collection, courtesy of the Hoover Library Archives.

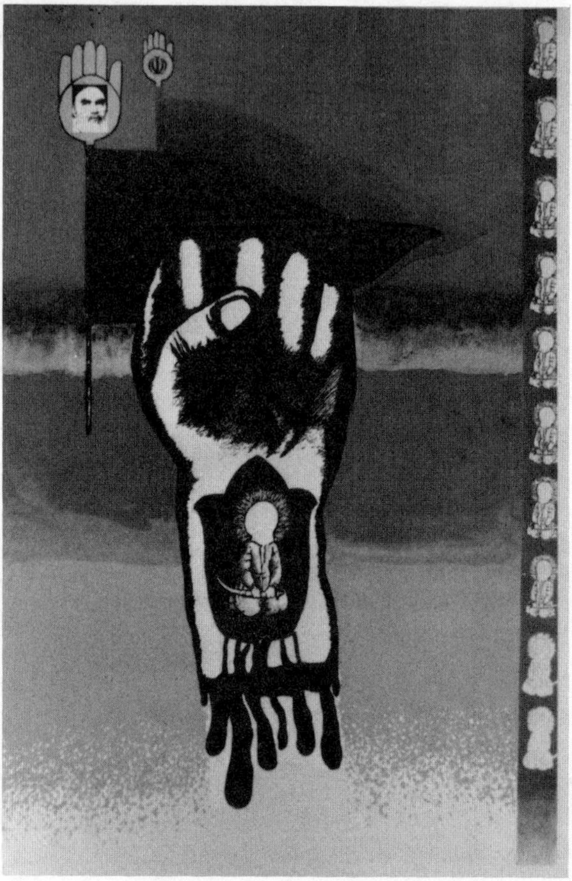

Fig. 6.16. Imām Ali, tulip, blood and fist. From Ali, 1985.

Many images are those of fighting imperialism: in one poster a Star of David shaped barbed wire fence around the Dome of the Rock in Jerusalem is pulled apart (figure 6.17); a series of posters about the oil industry in the Persian Gulf are inscribed with the slogan, "Continuation of the revolution until the termination of looting," e.g., a hand flicking away an American flag beach ball (figure 6.18); a hand choking an American flag serpent above an oil derrick on the beach by the gulf, inscribed with verse 14 from Sura al-Tawba, "Kill/fight them, may God punish them through your hands and humble them, and give you victory over them" (figure 6.19); a set of gasoline pump nozzles marked "U.S.," "USSR," "Israel," and "England," against an abstract background

Fig. 6.17. Star of David barbed wire pulled apart from around the Dome of the Rock. From Ali, 1985.

of oil derrick, refinery cracking tower and pipes, and a flare chimney that ends in a fist. A powerful one put out by the Ministry of Islamic Guidance shows the United Nations as a foot with five toes (the five powers with a veto in the Security Council) stomping on justice (figure 6.20); the big toe is shaped like an ear with a hole in it, a visual allusion to the idiom *gūsh-esh bād gīr-e* ("in one ear, out the other," i.e., whatever it is told, nothing happens). A variant of this poster appears on one of the stamps of the Islamic Republic, but this time instead of a foot, a hand of a demon comes out of the U.N. building in New York, and the sword of Islam comes to cut it off. A similar dark poster issued

Fig. 6.18. Flicking away the beachball of imperialism. Jim Hitselberger Collection, courtesy of the Hoover Library Archives.

by the same ministry (figure 6.21) shows imperialism as a skull draped in the flags of Britain and Israel, with flags of the USSR and United States in its eye sockets, being choked by a strong hand (of Islam). A more colorful and humorous one, done in red, yellow, black, and white, shows a fist inscribed with the Islamic credo coming down on the head of a caricature shah with long nose, lipstick, a dollar sign in one lens of his glasses and a red heart in the other; it is a hint of effeminacy, of the idiom of exposure of the early days of the revolution (figure 6.22).[40]

Fists and victory signs merge with Islamic symbols and also with photos of demonstrating crowds. A colossal fist breaks through barbed wire in a fury of fire that also ignites an American flag in the foreground, a symbolic image of the demonstrating crowds in a blue haze behind (figure 6.23). An orange fist from the sea bends five rows of guns; this poster, commemorating the 15 Khordad 1963 uprising which the Khomeini forces count as the beginning of the revolution, is inscribed interestingly with a pre-Islamic Iranian reference, "Beginning of the struggle between faith and the armed Ahriman."[41] Another poster (figure 6.24) commemorating the 15 Khordad uprising shows a mullā with fist breaking a crown, a sickle, a Star of David, and a British flag, and is inscribed, "Day of the manifestation of the clergy of Madraseh Faiziyeh, and the

Fig. 6.19. Choking the serpent of imperialism. Jim Hitselberger Collection, courtesy of the Hoover Library Archives.

Fig. 6.20. U.N. as foot stamping out justice. From Ali, 1985.

witness of the collapse of the bourgeoisie of the world." A poster commemorating the death of Zeinab (figure 6.25) and honoring revolutionary women, shows Zeinab in white silhouette with raised fist cracking apart an orange crown and green entrance pillars (the "green palace" of the tyrant Yezid in Damascus); the bottom of her chādor (veil) is a picture of demonstrating chādored women with their fists raised; to the right is a line of camels each with mother and child moving toward an arched and pillared building with palms (the tomb of Zeinab?), and the inscription reads, "Zeinab, Oh spokesperson of Ali," a line from Shari'ati). The Mojahedin counter with their own tribute to revolution-

Fig. 6.21. Imperialism-death choked by the hand of Islam. From Ali, 1985.

ary women: a white silhouetted woman with the Mojahedin logo, fist raised, holding a gun, rises out of blue, black, and red waves into a red egg, vagina, flame, or tulip-shaped space with the Mojahedin slogan, "God prefers warriors to those who sit idly" (Qur'an 4:95), and below are portraits of five Mojahedin women martyrs.

Images of martyrdom and the blood of martyrdom abound: the hatchet of the United States cuts down *one* red flower growing from a mosque, inadvertently causing *three* more red spots to spurt forth;

Fig. 6.22. Shah brained by fist of the Islamic credo. From Ali, 1985.

a man in black silhouette on his knees in the *qunūt* prayer position (asking God for personal desires), holding a tulip (praying for *shahādat*), another red tulip on his throat, is the most upright of four red images of him in lower angles of prostration into the blood red ground (celebrating the reopening of the Husainiyeh Irshad) (figure 6.26). A white silhouette of a man holding out his hands has, where his face would be (and where a veil appears on the icons of Muhammad and Ali), a red tulip inscribed with the emblem of the Islamic Republic; its stem pours blood into the hands, which enframe pictures of a crowd holding Khomeini's portrait and a skyline of the seminary town of Qum with a red flag with the Islamic credo (figure 6.27). Above the figure is a white dovelike form, or perhaps manna, since the legend is Khomeini's praise, "Dear nation, you gave all you had sincerely for God, and you obtained this heavenly manna." On another poster, a white dove against a red

Fig. 6.23. Fist breaking through barbed wire ignites the American flag. From Ali, 1985.

background rips a hole through the army green and black bars formed by the letters U.S.A., and the legend reads, "We value the blood of martyrs of the way of truth, and we hurry toward the Islamic Republic." In another image of time or process through revolutionary sacrifice, red footprints march over a broken crown. Calligraphic posters themselves can be very dramatic and give a sense of movement: among the best are a line of revolutionary fists that spell out the Islamic credo in reds and black, and an Olympic style torch, the flame of which again is the Islamic credo.

Among our favorite posters are Khomeini's stern stare melting U.S. guns (figure 6.28); a wounded woman with child, on an asphalt imperial highway (a *shāh-rāh,* built with petroleum literally and with its profits) through desert desolation at the end of which great tulips rise leading

Fig. 6.24. Mullā breaks crown, sickle, Star of David, and British flag. Jim Hitselberger Collection, courtesy of the Hoover Library Archives.

Fig. 6.25. Zeinab cracks apart the crown and green palace of Yezid/Shah. Jim Hitselberger Collection, courtesy of the Hoover Library Archives.

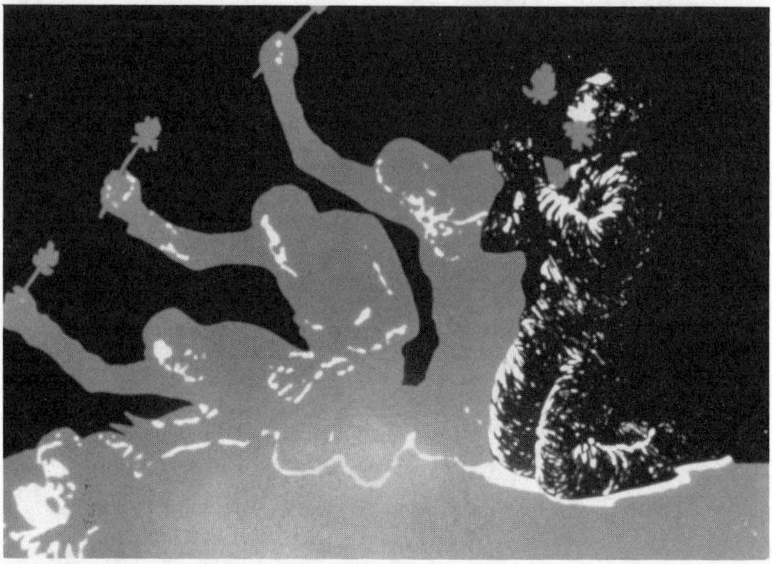

Fig. 6.26. Martyr's prayer

to the image of Khomeini looming over the horizon (figure 6.29); and a stamp portraying the merged images of Bilal (the first Muslim muezzin or caller to prayer, a black Ethiopian) and Malcolm X calling people to the Islamic revolution (see chapter 5). A poster in Persian and English shows a cameraman, his camera pointed toward the viewer, its lens reflecting a demonstration; it is inscribed with a plea to journalists to show the Islamic revolution as it really is (figure 6.30). A modern soldier runs alongside a traditional Muharram image of the Imam on horseback (figure 6.32).

Apart from the contrapuntal play between graphic and symbolic traditions, allusions, and allegories, the posters also dramatize the competition over legitimacy and symbol use by the different factions within the revolution. Within our samples, we have posters from the Islamic Republican Party, the Ministry of Guidance of the Islamic Republic, the Mojahedin-e Khalq (Islamic leftist opponents of the regime), the Mojahedin-e Enqelabi (partisans of former president Bani-Sadr), the Fedai'i (secular leftists), the Nahzat-e Āzādī (Liberation Movement of former prime minister Mehdi Bazargan), and of course a number that cannot be clearly identified.[42] Competition occurs as illustrated above with respect to insignia emblems (invoking the *lā* of the Islamic credo, rifles or swords, phrases from the Qur'an, and so on), claims to the loy-

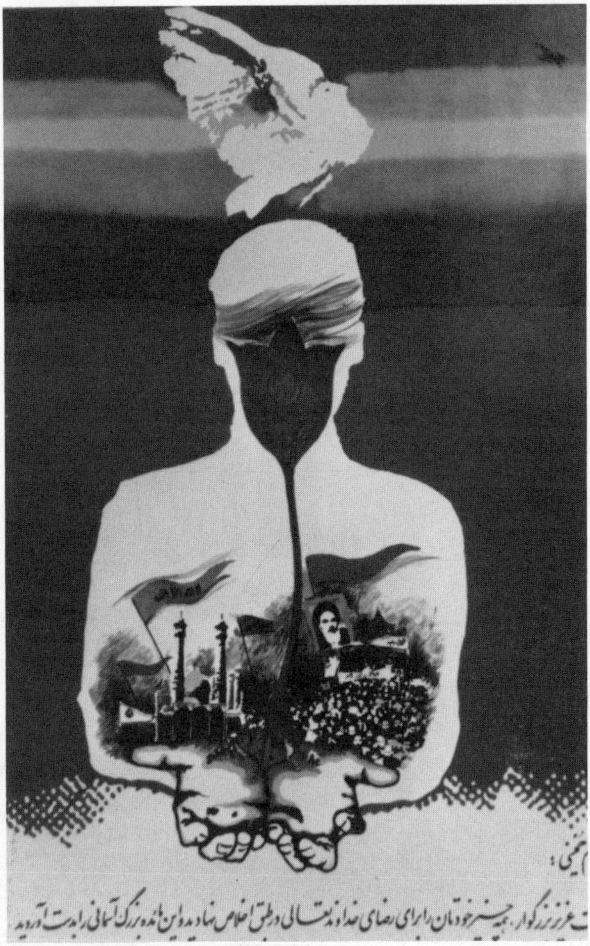

Fig. 6.27. Tulip/man collage with Qum skyline and crowd holding Khomeini's portrait. From Ali, 1985.

alty of workers or of women, claims to the legacy of Shari'ati, and claims to the revolutionary meaning of Islam. A handsome black, red, and white Mojahedin poster illustrates the competition for meaning well: four Mojahedin martyrs are portrayed in black T-shirts, a prison bar behind each, and a red splotch on each chest pouring blood down into a red flood below; the inscriptions translate an Arabic verse of the Qur'an ("and those killed in the way of God, their deeds will not go astray" [Qur'an 47:4]) not only into Persian but into a leftist jargon and nuanc-

Fig. 6.28. Khomeini's stare melts guns of U.S. From Ali, 1985.

Fig. 6.29. Woman and child on desert road of petroleum seek salvation in the tulip and Khomeini. From Ali, 1985.

Fig. 6.30. Camera man. Courtesy of the Hoover Library Archives.

ing: "And those who in the goal possessing context of experience [i.e., not only Muslims but those who die in the way of the "perfection of history," *takāmul-e tārikh*] in the way of God attain martyrdom, their deeds shall never wither away; 31 Farvardin, commemorating the martyrdoms of Ali Mihandust, Nasser Sadeq, Ali Bakeri, Muhammad Bazargani, four of the people's Mojahedin-e Khalq who like little drops join the great ocean of the martyrs of the Muslim masses. . . ."

The Mojahedin in particular, but also other marginalized factions, invoke photographs of martyrs, to remind people of sacrifices and efforts ignored by the government: photography is a localizing, personalizing device. Among the most artistic of these are a series of posters the Mojahedin issued to commemorate the legacy of "Āyatullāh" Sayyid Mahmud Taleqani, who defended the Islamic left and whose last Friday sermon warned of tyranny by the mullas: a poster shows Taleqani characteristically seated, head in hand, on the floor away from the seats of honor claimed by other clerics; another shows Taleqani's head in the sky looking down on portraits of Mojahedin in the jails of the Islamic Republic; and most potently, a poster shows Taleqani's head superimposed on the cover of the famous children's book by Samad Behrangi called *The Little Black Fish,* a protest parable about the oppressiveness of conformity to government rules (figure 6.31).

Hypertextual Feints and Constraints

Auto-graphics in the title of this chapter refers to a dual problematic with which these concluding notes deal as have all the previous chapters: (1) self-representation and interpretation by others; (2) the relation between the tropological and the political, or between the seemingly infinite play of meaning (textualization and its critical reading for aporias and alternative meanings), and the relation between ideologies and their social carriers (the selection of meanings insisted upon by particular social actors in the world). *Hypertexts* is a term taken from contemporary efforts to construct computer programs for education in which the linearity of traditional learning is overcome: a student reading a text about, say, the Iranian revolution, can at any point punch a key and have access to a different set of information: maps, biographies of names mentioned, demographic or economic statistics, explanations of theological or other Iranian terms, etc. A hypertext, then, is a multidimensional text, with multiple horizons, and in some sense is analogous to the multiple horizons of meaning with which hermeneutical and

Fig. 6.31. Taleqani and (Samad Behrangi's) *The Little Black Fish.* Jim Hitselberger Collection, courtesy of the Hoover Library Archives.

deconstructive analyses provide ethnography. The worry about hermeneutics and deconstruction, particularly as practiced by some literary critics rather than others, is that there are no constraints on the play of meaning, that everything becomes internalized to the interpreter's own play, that all becomes apolitical, and removed from the world. But hermeneutics and deconstruction are only tools, and for a critical anthropological practice, they are ways of providing "hypertextual" horizons and maps that help locate, place, and critique from the "inside" as well as from "without" cultural and ideological forms. Hence the stress on discourses, on class or interest or other sociologically based linkages.

Self-representation. The emblems, posters and cartoons, at least, are autogenetically produced products of contemporary Iran, not effects of the present authors' descriptive rhetorics. That they may be infused with, and/or dialectically related to, "Western" influences—including the revolutionary tradition as well as elements of the emerging capitalist information society—is of course part of the real world: one wants to be able to analyze the degree to which local nationalist or religiously phrased ideologies recirculate, adapt, and redeploy ideas, tropes, or discourses from global settings. That they are designed by particular artists who have their own individual training and influences is also a

Fig. 6.32. Soldier and Ali. From Ali, 1985.

matter of interest and investigation: we know the names of some of the artists, and we know the sponsoring institutions for whom they work. These graphics register both such local-global interaction, and debates within Iran. Graphics as-sign the differences at play.

The tropological and the political: autobiographies and autographics. We began with an autobiography, a narrative built around the life of one person, and end here with autographics, signatures composed with collective symbols. Autobiography as a narrative genre, however, mirrors processes larger than the individual life: as Roland Barthes, among others, described, if one looks at photographs of oneself or any other individual over time, one sees that there are changing bodies and selves, and the continuity between them is constructed by a third narrative self. The construction of this third narrative function, itself, can be interrogated so as to open up into ever expanding horizons of knowledge, like a hypertext. The point, however—and here Barthes failed us as a model when he increasingly slipped from a project of critique of bourgeois ideology into mere textual jouissance—is not infinite exploration, but the use of empirically grounded and reconstructed fragments such as individual lives (or posters, or ideological discourse) as vehicles both for exploring the multiple horizons of knowledge and for locating these vehicles one against another. It is important to recognize the hermeneutics of the Qur'an, the paradoxes of nationalism, the dialectical relation of new religions or revolutions vis-à-vis their predecessors, in order to understand their social locus, their cultural form, and their dynamics. Anthropological critique is para-doxical: requiring exploration of the critical apparatuses of local cultural forms and doxas and also the use of comparative juxtapositions to achieve a framework for getting beyond local doxas.

We have attempted to use non-European examples—real world ones, as opposed to artificially constructed ones such as those of Barthes' elegant Japan of the *Empire of Signs*—as interlocutors in contemporary theories of autobiography, heremeneutics, visual imagery, national identity, and moral philosophy. We would like thereby to break the narcissistic repetitions of endless commentaries on the same philosophers and writers and especially to invite new interlocutors that can contribute to the construction of more adequate intercultural concepts, language, and theory for the pluralist global society that is fast becoming a reality.

7

Postscriptural Parergon: Bombay Talkies, the Word and the World

Salman Rushdie's *Satanic Verses*

The film is the art form that is in keeping with the increased threat to his life which modern man has to face. Man's need to expose himself to shock effects . . .

—Walter Benjamin, "The Work of Art in the Mechanical Age of Reproduction"

. . . [Strindberg's plays of the 1890s] are effectively *film* scripts: involving the fission and fusion of identities and characters; the alteration of objects and landscapes by the psychological pressures of the observer; symbolic projections of obsessive states of mind: all, as material processes, beyond the reach of even his experimental theatre, but all, as processes of art, eventually to be realized in film.

—Raymond Williams, "Cinema and Socialism," *The Politics of Modernism*

Numerous affinities exist between the instantaneities of writing and photography, both being inserted in time which is "exposed" rather than simply passing.

—Paul Virilio, *War and Cinema: The Logistics of Perception*

. . . discursive "transparency" is best read in the photographic sense in which a transparency is also always a negative, processed into visibility through the technologies of reversal, enlargement, lighting, editing, projection, not a source but a re-source of light.

—Homi Bhaba, "Signs Taken for Wonder"

. . . a mass industry, basing itself upon psychotropic derangement and chronological disturbance, was directly applying cinematic acceleration to the realism of the world. This new cinema was particularly aimed at the ever wider public which had been torn from its sedentary existence and marked down for military mobilization, exile and emigration, proletarianization in the new industrial metropolises . . . and revolution. War had everyone on the move, even the dead.

—Paul Virilio, *War and Cinema: The Logistics of Perception*

Many people now see and know that they are being misrepresented . . . from the simplest forms of labelling through plot manipulation and selective editing to the deepest forms and problems of self-presentation, self-recognition, self-admission, there are processes of production in which we can intervene. Here the special properties of film . . . can be much further developed.

—Raymond Williams, "Cinema and Socialism,"
The Politics of Modernism

In the brave new world of Elsa County [Baden, Iowa: a basic German community where even the Danes and Swedes are thought to be genetically unpredictable at times: inscrutable Swedes, sneaky Dutch] . . . Bud Ripplemeyer has adopted a Vietnamese and is shacked up with a Punjabi girl. There is a Vietnamese network. There are Hmong, with a church of their own, turning out quilts for Lutheran relief.

When I was a child, born in a mud hut without water or electricity [albeit uprooted by Partition from a big stucco house in Lahore] the Green Revolution had just struck Punjab. Bicycles were giving way to scooters and to cars, radios to television.

Educated people are interested in differences; they assume I'm different from them, but exempted from being one of "them." . . . Even though I was just an *au pair,* professors would ask if I could help them with Sanskrit or Arabic, Devanagari or Gurumukhi script. I can read Urdu, not Arabic. I can't read Sanskrit. [Father refused to speak Hindi, the language of Gandhi who approved Partition; he hated Urdu and Muslims, and tuned into Punjabi radio only.

[Darrel said] "I was hoping you'd come up with a prettier name. Something in Indian." I wanted to say, "You mean in Hindi, not Indian, there's no such thing as Indian," but he'll be crushed, and won't say anything for the rest of the night. He comes from a place where the language you speak is what you are.

—Bharati Mukherjee, *Jasmine*

They Shoot Novelists Don't They?[1]

> . . . the migrant sensibility . . . I believe to be one of the central themes of this century of displaced persons. . . . And for the plural, hybrid metropolitan results of such imaginings, the cinema may well be the ideal location.
>
> —Salman Rushdie, 1985

> All those who henceforth may intend to write such a book or turn it into a film, or display it in movie theaters, or publish it—all of them will now have to contend with the danger of death from Muslims.
>
> —President Ali Khameinei, Friday prayers, 3 March 1989[2]

> Salman Rushdie is in hiding, but in the Muslim world he is everywhere. In the old section of Dhaka, in Bangladesh, he may be seen on posters stuck to moldering walls, with a noose around his neck. A recent march there, provoked and politicized by Islamic fundamentalists, was led, I was told, with the chant, "Salman Rushdie must leave Dhaka!" The sloganeers were informed that Rushdie was not in Dhaka, that he is somewhere in England. They were unfazed. "Salman Rushdie must leave England!" they cried, and marched on.
>
> —Mahnaz Ispahani, *The New Republic,* 3 July 1989

Aside from being a brilliantly funny re-visionary novel, *Satanic Verses* has become a highly charged social text, a lightning rod or projective screen against which contemporary cultural and social conflicts are drawn, enacted, and elaborated. For our purposes, it is a novel that illustrates features of chapter 2, provides a literary counterpoint for chapter 5, and makes vivid the point that the secular intelligentsia and the religious intelligentsia are engaged in cultural class warfare, each using systematic discourses the other only partially understands (Fischer 1984a, 1982b, 1980). This cultural class warfare operates at two non-homologous levels simultaneously: on the domestic level within countries such as Iran, Pakistan, and Egypt for control of the state and of the general collective consciousness of the masses; on the international level to create a space for cultural diversity. The power relations involved are complex: the secular intelligentsia is very much on the defensive in the domestic arenas throughout the Islamic world, including the communal or minority enclaves inside Western nations; yet they appear to be allied with the stronger forces on the international scene. The complexity, of course, is richer than this, and the issue is how to create means of translation and negotiation between the contending ideals and self-protective defenses on the various sides, lest the cultural warfare become merely self-destructive to all. Rushdie's novel is a major achievement because, among other reasons, it opens up vistas both within its text and in its relations with the world outside the text that illuminate the complexities, and at least gesture at the inadequate tools for translation. Humor, when it works, is one of the healthiest tools, because it holds in stereoscopic view alternative perspectives. As Carlos Fuentes puts it, "Humor, certainly cannot be absent, since there is no contemporary language that can utter itself without a sense of the diversification of that same language. . . . Fiction is not a joke . . . [it] is a harbinger of a multipolar and multicultural world. . . . Our future depends on the enlarged freedom for the multiracial and the polycultural to express itself in a world of shifting, decaying, and emerging power centers."[3]

Rushdie's *Satanic Verses,* thus, simultaneously illustrates and illuminates, that is, transcribes and causes others to enact further: (1) national and global cultural class warfare; (2) the struggles over restricted literacy versus hermeneutical critical skills that have used the Qur'an as a battlefield for thirteen centuries; (3) anxiety-laden ambiguities of an increasingly pluralist world in which selves, cultures, and language itself are undergoing reassembly through mass population migrations at the proletarian as well as the middle-class levels—reassembly in radically multiple, composite, humorous, and deconstructing ways, where translation rather than tradition is forever at issue, providing both desired and unwanted unending critiques and non-absolutist revisionary perspectives; (4) new communication forms and media which constitute the crucibles in which these new conditions of life are being worked: the novel, the movies, video, radio, television, magazines, advertising, propaganda, and nightmares generated by the anxieties of constant demands on translation and interaction with cultural others with whom consensual grounds of agreement cannot be taken for granted. The third of these is at the heart of the novel and includes: (i) contributing to the "decolonization of the English language," turning English into an ever more compendious world language that encompasses the cadences, rhythms, allusions, and cultural flexibilities of other languages; (ii) bringing back an appreciation of Persian(-Mughal) cultural sensibility, intended in part to expand European consciousness into a larger Old World cosmopolitanism, but also working to highlight the politics of difference within the Islamic world of Shi'ite versus Sunni interpretations, thereby disturbing the pieties of all Muslims that the Qur'an is a catalogue of simple rules that provide unambiguous guidance for all aspects of life; (iii) having fun with the psychological and emotional dynamics of the *chamcha* (Urdu, "spoon," "toady") figure as a range of intercultural types from the sycophantic servants of colonialism to the immigrant New Man/Woman in the (post)modern world who must operate in and out of multiple cultures; (iv) providing hilariously vital and humanizing portraits of several classes of "hystorical" immigrants spilling into Britain from the Indian subcontinent, intended to dispel racist stereotypes; (v) and together with Rushdie's previous novels, gaily attacking nationalist pretensions, ideologies, corrupting institutions of power (state, family, religion, the media), narratives of the British Raj and its successor states (India, Pakistan, Iran, Britain), and focusing especially on that uneasy overlay of England and the Perso-Indo-Islamic world that is to be found in working-class England (Bradford, Birmingham, Leister, Southall, the East End), Oxbridge England (Rushdie himself), the Anglified upper-class areas of Bombay (Malabar Hill), Karachi, Lahore, or Islamabad, and above all in the movies.

Satanic Verses stands in two sociologically distinct currents of writing, corresponding to the two arenas of cultural class warfare. On the one hand, it stands within the stream of modernist writing that attempts to find a home within Islamic countries for modern sensibilities, the tradition in Iran of Sadeq Hedayat, Bozorg Alavi, Muhammad Ali Jamalzadeh, Gholam Hosain Sa'edi, Sadeq Chubak, Jalal Al-e Ahmad, Simin Daneshvar; in Egypt of Taha Husain, Tawfiq al-Hakim, Nagib Mahfuz, Nadwa al-Sadaawi; and many others in North Africa, the Levant, and Mesopotamia.[4] On the other hand, *Satanic Verses* stands within the stream of the postmodern comic novel—the tradition of James Joyce, Gabriel García Márquez, Thomas Pynchon, and Günter Grass (with roots going back to *Tristram Shandy, Don Quixote,* and *Gulliver's Travels*)—that has done so much to re-envision the contemporary world and revalue the narratives of the past. Although Rushdie is the first major postmodern comic novelist for the Muslim world, he does not stand alone even here in Middle Eastern and South Asian writing. He is part of a gathering stream of writing and filmmaking by Jamil Dehlavi, Amitav Ghosh, Elias Khoury, Hanif Kureishi, Parviz Kimiavi, Rustam Mistry, Bharati Mukherjee, Mira Nair, Anton Shammas, Bapsy Sidwa, Sara Suleri, Adam Zameenzad, and the "Decentrist" poets of Beirut (Ghada al-Samman, Hana al-Shaikh, Emily Nasrallah, Laila Usairan, Daisy al-Amir, Calire Gebeyli, and Etel Adnan).[5] Few of these latter, except Dehlavi and Rushdie, are concerned with Muslim belief structures. But all are concerned with the psychic transformations that living in or with the modern West has wrought for those of non-European background—themes central to *Satanic Verses* more than Islam per se.

Thanks to the death threat issued against Rushdie by the late Ayatullah Khomeini, *Satanic Verses* has become the most heavily publicized novel ever written about Muslims. A black humor joke among Iranian exiles in America speculates that Khomeini must have signed a fifty-fifty percent promotion contract with Rushdie to secure for the Islamic Republic a share in the proceeds of increased sales due to Khomeini's advertising. The book was published in late September 1988, and was given a dismissive review in Tehran without any special notice or concern. Rushdie was well-known: both *Midnight's Children* and *Shame* had been translated into Persian, the latter even winning the state prize, awarded by President Ali Khamenei, for the best translation of a novel. Both these previous novels contain considerable satire about (mis)uses of Islam. It was only four and half months later, on 14 February 1989, that Khomeini issued the *fatwā* declaring Rushdie essentially an apostate, *mahdūr al-dam* (one whose blood may be shed without trial, the term used to facilitate the execution and murder of Bahai's). This *fatwā* was disputed in its legal validity by various Muslim jurisprudents. It is significant that the agitations against the novel began not in Iran, but in two quite different political arenas: India and Britain.

Let us deal with the political arenas first, then the Islamic objections, so that we can clear the ground to actually read the novel. "Let's remember," as Rushdie wrote in October 1988 to India's Prime Minister, Rajiv Gandhi, after India banned the novel, "that the book isn't actually about Islam, but about migration, metamorphosis, divided selves, love, death, London and Bombay."

Beyond the Text

> Even more shocking and saddening . . . is the communication gap between the Muslim community and the so-called intelligentsia. . . . It's unbelievable that what pains one section gives pleasure to the other. . . . Yes, Mr. Rushdie, we are a religious people. . . . Call us primitive, call us fundamentalists, call us superstitious barbarians, call us what you like, but your book only serves to define what has gone wrong with the Western civilisation—it has lost all sense of distinction between

the sacred and the profane. . . . Yes, I have not read it, nor do I intend to. I do not have to wade through a filthy drain to know what filth is.

—Syed Shahabuddin, Indian M.P. (Janata Party), initiator of the ban

The intensity of Muslim reaction can only be understood in the context of the deep suspicion and alienation prevailing between the Asian community as a whole and its intellectuals . . . the large masses of Asians have long felt that those Asians who write, make films and television programmes or engage in instant punditry about them do not understand their innermost hopes and fears, and that they earn a handsome living and white acclaim by selling tired stereotypes and biased stories. Many Asians view their intellectuals as being as racist as the whites. This is broadly how the Hindus felt about Nirad Chaudhury's idiosyncratic writings on India, the Bangladeshis about Farrukh Dhondy's television play *King of the Ghetto* and the Muslims about Hanif Kureishi's film *My Beautiful Laundrette* and recently about Rushdie's *The Satanic Verses.*

—Bhikhu Parekh, *Independent,* 23 February 1989

In most Arab countries Hanan El Sheik's novels, Nawal El-Saadawi's writings and the poetry of [Muẓaffar] El-Nawab and Mahmoud Darwish are banned. . . . The Jordanian novelist Zulickheh Abu-Risheh's *In the Cell,* a novel based on her experience of being married to one of the Muslim Brethren, is being attacked from the pulpit as the most serious threat to Islam. . . . I experienced similar problems when my novel *Nisanit* was published by Penguin earlier this year. . . . A group of men accused Suhair El-Tell, a Jordanian journalist and novelist, of promiscuity for using a phallic image. . . . Most of the sixty-six Arab intellectuals blacklisted recently by a Saudi Islamic group who announced the holy jihād on Modernism live either in London or Paris.

—Fadia Faqir, *Times Literary Supplement,* 6–12 January 1989

This is, for me, the saddest irony of all; that after working for five years to give voice and fictional flesh to the immigrant culture of which I am myself a member, I should see my book burned, largely unread, by the people it's about. . . . I tried to write against stereotypes; the zealot protests serve to confirm, in the Western mind, all the worst stereotypes of the Muslim world.

—Salman Rushdie, *Observer,* 22 January 1989

There are four primary, only loosely interconnected, political arenas ignited by Rushdie's novel: (1) immigrant politics in Britain: Pakistani-led, Saudi-funded Muslim politics, the competition between Saudi and

Iranian fundamentalisms, but above all a politics that turns upon the difficulties of an immigrant working class actively recruited by Britain in a time of labor need, but now being squeezed in a time of economic transition; (2) anti–Benazir Bhutto politics in Pakistan, where fundamentalists wish to destabilize a government that would prefer to be a secularist balance wheel against ethnic, sectarian, and religious forces; (3) communal politics in India and the struggles over the decline of Congress Party hegemonic control of the state; (4) and in Iran, jockeying between those who would normalize relations between Iran and the West and those determined to try to insulate internal Iranian development from the powerful influences of the West. For our purposes here, we need only briefly indicate the shape of these political arenas.

Great Britain

> . . . there is no choice in the matter. Anyone who fails to be offended by Rushdie's book ipso facto ceases to be a Muslim. . . . continual blasphemies against the Christian faith have totally undermined it. Any faith which compromises its internal temper of militant wrath is destined for the dustbin of history. . . . Those Muslims who find it intolerable to live in a United Kingdom contaminated with the Rushdie virus need to seriously consider the Islamic alternatives of emigration (*hijrah*) to the House of Islam or a declaration of holy war (*jihād*) on the House of Rejection. . . . with God on one's side, one is never in the minority. And England, like all else, belongs to God. As for *hijrah* . . . non-Muslims would do well to remember that the last time there was a *hijrah,* a unified Muslim enterprise of faith and power spread with phenomenal speed in the fastest permanent conquest of recorded military history.
>
> —Shabbir Akhtar, Bradford Council of Mosques, *Guardian,* 27 February 1989

> The anti-racists' views on children's books/stereotyping/prejudice fascinate me, as a non-English English-speaker. Most of my waking childhood hours were spent reading . . . what those books reinforced was my stereo-type (since slightly revised) of the arrogant, unimaginative, hypocritical and exploiting Englishman, rampaging around the world with a Bible in one hand, a gun in the other and an accounts ledger in his tin trunk. At no age did I receive an imprint of inferior peoples dependent on Whites for every sort of salvation; spiritual, material, legal, sartorial. . . . Even very young children read critically or sceptically, if books fail to confirm the stereotypes *already* acquired from home, school, and societies.
>
> —Dervla Murphy, *Tales from Two Cities*

Great Britain, in some ways, is the most important of the political arenas for understanding the novel, since after all, the novel is about Muslim migrants from the Indian subcontinent to London. Still, as with the other political arenas, there is a bit of indirection: the constituency of the protest in Bradford where the book was publicly burned on January 14, 1989, seems to be Pakistanis of rural background (primarily Mirpuris from Azad Kashmir), whereas the novel is primarily about people from urban Bombay. One of the best accounts of the dynamics of the situation in Bradford, written long before Rushdie's book was published, is Dervla Murphy's *Tales from Two Cities: Travels of Another Sort.* The Dickensian title, and the play upon travel and ethnographic genres, is appropriate to an Irish writer who spent a year living in two inner-city immigrant enclaves of Bradford and Birmingham, and who identifies the troubles of the Mirpuri, Campbellpuri, and Sylheti Pakistanis with the Irish immigrants who underwent not so different experiences in the same cities during the early days of the industrial revolution. Pakistani migrant labor from Mirpur first came to Bradford during World War II, initially as seamen, and then, directed from the port of Leeds nine miles away, to man the munitions factories. The 1947 Partition of India stimulated the growth of a temporary male migrant labor force, and this it remained through the 1950s: in 1961 there were 3376 male Pakistanis in Bradford, and 81 women. Thousands of women and children arrived during the eighteen months before the 1962 Immigration Act made it more difficult to maintain the pattern of working in Britain for a few years, then returning home, going back and forth. In 1967 a further stimulus to migration was given by the Mangla Dam hydroelectric project which flooded 250 Mirpuri villages, displacing 10,000 people. In the 1950s and 1960s Britain actively recruited labor both in the Caribbean and in the Indian subcontinent for the textile mills and foundries, for London Transport, and for the British Hotel and Restaurant Association. In the 1970s, economic conditions worsened, and Bradford was one of the cities worst hit. Racial tensions increased, and it is a place where unemployed whites don't mince words about their resentments of Browns, and unemployed Brown youths bitterly turn to religion and politics. Nor are fears, hostilities, and stereotyping merely black-white ones:

> In Bradford, Mirpuris deplored the loose living of Gujarati Muslims who allowed their *wives* to drive delivery vans. . . . Blacks deplored Pakistani heroin-dealing and Sikh arrogance. Hindus deplored Muslim faction-fighting and Black laziness. Sikhs deplored the sharp practices of Gujarati merchants, the drug-peddling of Blacks, the Mirpuri ill-treatment of

> women—and the dangerous politics of Sikhs attached to rival Gurdwaras. And so on and on, in apparently infinite permutations and combinations of misunderstanding, dislike, jealousy, contempt, fear, ignorance, resentment. (P. 81)

Still, the Pakistani Muslims are hard-working, highly disciplined, education-seeking, upwardly mobile communities. The Irish did not have, says Murphy, the same tightly knit *biraderi* (kinship groups) and so "no Irish self-servicing network of businesses was at once set up" (p. 71). Statistics are revealing: at High Hill School, there was only one Brown pregnancy, while pregnancies among Whites were commonplace; in Britain generally "the proportion of unwed mothers among Browns is one percent as compared to nine percent among Whites, and thirteen percent among Blacks" (p. 69); "a survey of 500 retail businesses in Bradford, Southall and Leicester discovered that sixty per cent of Asian traders are graduates, as compared to nine per cent of White traders" (p. 63); and a third of Britain's hospital doctors are Browns. Under conditions of deteriorating opportunity, and deteriorating relations between ethnic groups, for many young Muslim men being religiously hardline is also a way of asserting their personal and cultural identity. Frequently, it is the younger generation which is more militantly fundamentalist than their fathers. (For a grim account of Bradford, see Kureishi 1986.)

For nearly two years in 1984 and 1985 Bradford was rocked by disputes over Ray Honeyford, the Drummond Middle School headmaster, who was appalled at having to allow: "the serving of *ḥalāl* meat, permission for Muslim girls to wear track-suits during P.E. lessons; separate-sex P.E. and swimming lessons; tolerance of occasional Brown breaches of the school attendance law; the adoption of a multi-faith syllabus for R.E.; the evasion of sex instruction" (p. 117). Brown breaches of school attendance had to do with sending children on visits back to Pakistan, occasions that other educational authorities suggested broadened their experiences and made them better students. Honeyford was a dedicated teacher who himself had come up the hard way from the slums of Manchester and believed firmly in the old virtues of hard work and Christian values; he was opposed to the faddish introduction of multicultural curricula, and gradually became associated with the *Salisbury Review,* journal of the New Right Conservative Philosophy Group, whose founder, John Casey (a Cambridge University don), called for the repatriation of Browns and Blacks or at least reducing them to a legal category of guest-workers, this in 1982 when nearly half of the Browns and Blacks had been born in Britain. Casey, Roger Scruton (the editor of the *Salisbury Review*), and Honeyford argued that the new immigrants from the Subcontinent, East Africa, and the West Indies were unlike earlier immigrants to Britain who were absorbed into a strong culture; these new immigrants somehow would threaten the stability of British culture. After a two-year campaign, Honeyford was forced out, although many Muslim parents were increasingly uncomfortable with the political leadership that accomplished that end.

Murphy's account of Bradford prepares one easily enough for the furor over Salman Rushdie's book. Within ten days of the book's publication, not only had India banned the book, but Indian Muslim activists had urged their colleagues in Britain to do the same. Offending passages were photocopied and distributed to leading Islamic organizations, embassies, and published in such journals as M. H. Faruqi's *Impact International.* It was these excerpts which became the text for Muslim protesters, insofar as they bothered with the text at all. The Union of Muslim Organizations asked the government to ban the book under the Public Order Act (1986) and the Race Relations Act (1976). It is claimed that initially the protesters would have been satisfied had Penguin/Viking or Rushdie been willing to insert a disclaimer that there was no relation between the contents of the novel and Islam. The demands quickly became by the end of October 1988: (1) withdrawal of the book from the market and pulping all extant copies; (2) public apology; (3) payment of damages to an Islamic charity. The eventual burning of the book in Bradford came after four months of feeling ignored, exacerbated by the exposure of the fact that Britain's blasphemy laws applied only to Christianity. Efforts were made to have the blasphemy laws extended to Islam. But as a solicitor advised, if publicity and attention was what they wanted, they might burn the book, a shocking but nonviolent act. As with so many demonstrations in Bradford, this was done in front of the police station. It had an electrifying effect around the world.

Among the more interesting and disturbing effects was the furor of debate set off about multiculturalism. The Labor Party seemed to be in the worst disarray, with a century of socialist secularism abandoned by Labor MPs attempting to represent Muslim constituents, even going so far as to support the call to revive and extend Britain's blasphemy laws. Other Labor MPs called for a multiculturalism that a number of Brown intellectuals skewered for being a way of preserving conservative, separatist enclaves, in order to strengthen those who traditionally delivered the ethnic vote to Labor. Homi Bhaba, among others, observed that Labor remained impervious to rethinking socialism from a minority point of view, and that the party seemed only engaged in tactical defensive maneuvers (*Statesman,* 28 July 1989). In March, a month after the book burning, a London group organized itself as "Women against Fundamentalism." One of its Pakistani Muslim spokespersons, Hanna Siddiqi, observed:

> When the Rushdie affair blew up many women immediately identified with him. In my family there were lots of fights about how I should live my life. . . . Over the years, my parents have become less orthodox. But my brothers have got more religious. (*Guardian,* 25 July 1989)

These women run a counselling service for immigrant women whose sons are repeatedly arrested by the police, or who themselves are subject to domestic violence, rape, and incest. To them, fundamentalism is about the control of women, and they opposed sex-segregated schools as places where girls are isolated and taught only to be wives and mothers.

Condemnations of Rushdie come to many Muslim lips easily, but sometimes other attitudes emerge underneath. An Indonesian restauranteur became quite agitated at the mention of Rushdie. He had read the novel and felt it clearly insulted Islam. He would not kill Rushdie himself, but he would not care if someone else did. He claimed that Rushdie describes God as a bald-headed man and says Islam condones sodomy. When pressed, he said that Rushdie was only out to make money (though he agreed this was not evil: running a restaurant is also done to make money), that Rushdie knew he would create anger, that Rushdie is part of a Jewish conspiracy (his publishers and most of the writers who sign petitions in his defense are Jewish), and finally (and most importantly) that it is a matter of control: parents must take challenges like this seriously or their children (his own sons) would not take religion seriously. One of his sons came and sat with us after the father left. He too began by condemning Rushdie, but then did a fascinating about-face, recalling with some heat how he had been kicked out of the mosque in northern Sumatra when he was twelve for daring to stand up and condemn the imām for telling risque jokes during the sermon (*khuṭba*), and again being curtly dismissed when he dared challenge his teacher on a ḥadīth interpretation.

Confrontations such as the Honeyford and Rushdie affairs not only clarify divisions within society, they also create new phenomenological subjectivities. There is now a growing Muslim subjectivity in Britain that is replacing earlier political categories (Black, Brown, Asian). As one British-born Muslim intellectual notes, racist graffiti and catcalling has shifted from "you fucking Paki" to "fucking Muslim," and what the racists do not comprehend is that the latter is both less hurtful and more resistance provoking, because it is where one draws the line and makes a stand. If Rushdie fears that fundamentalist book burnings, bombings, death threats, campaigns against publishers, to extend blasphemy laws, and to have separate schools, etc., will confirm the worst stereotypes of non-Muslims about Muslims, Muslims out on the streets retort that the graffiti and catcalling confirms their worst fears that Rushdie's novel has made it legitimate for non-Muslims to openly attack and ridicule their faith. The disagreement makes it increasingly clear that intellectuals such as Rushdie, Hanif Kureishi, Homi Bhaba, and Tariq Ali have no standing to speak for the Muslims. This Muslim observer had particularly harsh observations about Tariq Ali, who after twenty years of trying to create a secular socialist consciousness among Pakistanis, suddenly discovers that he is "ashamed to be a Muslim," and produces a satirical play about Khomeini's death threat, done under tight security at the Royal Court Theater – on elite turf for largely non-Muslim audiences, reinforcing their prejudices, a quite different politics than performing in Bradford for the Muslims directly involved in an effort to create bridges of communication.

In sum, the Rushdie affair in Britain is serious politics that has to do with at least four issues concerning Muslims in which they feel their voices have been systematically ignored: (1) Education: Catholics and Jews have their own schools, why not Muslims? As to content, this may be a moot point, since a national curriculum is being made. (2) The poll tax proposed by Prime Minister Thatcher: the shift from property taxes to a head tax not only is regressive, but also, given family demographics, will fall most heavily on immigrant families who crowd to share space and save expenses. (3) Patriarchy–family control–feminism: suddenly people who never were particularly feminist have discovered this issue, and why do the Women Against Fundamentalism talk mainly about Islam, and not about the beatings of Hindu women whose families fail to come up with the absurdly high dowry prices? To the response that abuses in Hindu families are equally of concern, Muslims point out with some justification that there is a mood of using comparative evils among other communities as a none too subtle false cover for selecting Islam as the most troublesome of the world religions. (A similar argument is made by Muslim fundamentalists in the United States about the American Academy of Arts and Sciences' Fundamentalism Project.) (4) Multiculturalism: the left (Labor) seems to have great difficulty in recognizing that people for whom they wish to speak have ideas at variance with secular socialism. The Tories meanwhile are pushing a strong assimilationist line: multiculturalism is fine as long as it is practiced in private; people who come to Britain must adapt to British ways. Interesting parallels are drawn with the Jews: to the argument that Jews have managed to put up with a low level of casual anti-Semitism and Muslims must learn to do the same, the response of some Muslim observers is first, that Jews in fact paid a very high price in Germany for such willingness; second, that Jews are now accepted as part of the West and today it is Muslims who are the alien excluded and that the next time it will be Muslims and blacks in the ovens (this is not idle fear to anyone who has heard German jokes about Turkish workers in Germany or observed the rise of the New Right in France, England, and even Belgium); and third, that the frequent liberal line about having fought two world wars to establish the right of freedom of speech sounds disingenuous to Muslims who feel they have no access to the media and cannot seem to get their issues listened to, much less attended to.

In other words, the political arena in Britain is a fascinating and serious one, but the relationship of Rushdie's novel to it has more to do with the social relations beyond the text than with the content of the text.

India

> You know, as I know, that Mr. Shahabuddin, Mr. Khurshid Alam Khan, Mr. Suleiman Seit and their allies don't really care about my novel one way or the other. The real issue is, who is to get the Muslim vote?
>
> —Salman Rushdie, letter to Gandhi, October 1988

The political arena in India is even more deadly fraught than that in Britain. The history of communal violence has deep historical roots, exacerbated since independence by cynical manipulation of patronage networks to control or contest electoral politics, complete with both monetary corruption and underworld violence. When Rushdie's book was published, general elections were scheduled to be held within the year, and with Congress Party fortunes failing, Prime Minister Rajiv Gandhi could not afford to alienate Muslim voters. Syed Shahabuddin, the opposition Janata party M.P., who spearheaded the effort to get the novel banned, published an interesting open letter in the *Times of India* (13 October 1988), part eloquent defense of Muslim religiosity ("Call us primitive. . . . Civilization is nothing but voluntary acceptance of restraints"), part clichéd assertion about Western decadence, part aggressive complaint about Rushdie's portrayal of Islamic figures in a novel that Shahabudin proudly admitted he had not read, and part lawyerly invocation of the constitutional laws that protect religious feelings of Indian citizens. The Indian government took an easy way out: it banned the book on the grounds of public safety, but as part of the Ministry of Finance decision (under section 11 of the Indian Customs Act), it explicitly added that "the ban did not detract from the literary and artistic merit of Rushdie's work." Twelve persons were killed during anti-Rushdie demonstrations in Bombay on February 24, 1989 when police opened fire during a struggle between two factions to assert control over Muslim leadership.

Pakistan

Pakistan and South Africa followed the Indian example. In South Africa the tactic worked as well as in India, albeit not before the anti-apartheid *Weekly Mail* was shut down for a month, amid anti-Semitic insinuations by the Muslims who objected to the newspaper's invitation to Rushdie to speak at a book fair it was sponsoring. In Pakistan, things were considerably messier. Fundamentalists could not forego the opportunity to use anti-Rushdie marches to threaten the new government of Benazir Bhutto. Bhutto, leader of Pakistan's first democratic government in a decade, was put in the uncomfortable position of having to ban a book, and to order troops to shoot demonstrators who were using the book to challenge liberal democracy. Moreover she could have had little love for Rushdie who had mercilessly satirized her in *Shame*. Six persons died in the march on the U.S. Information Service in Islamabad on 12 February; another died and a hundred were injured in demonstrations the next day in Kashmir. These demonstrations were timed to protest the American publication date of the novel: bad enough that Britain had not withdrawn the novel, now America was adding insult to injury by disseminating the novel further.

Reactions in other countries were politically more contained. Bangladesh, Egypt, Indonesia, Malaysia, Qatar, and the Sudan also banned the book. In the West publishers and booksellers had to make moral decisions about whether to go forward with publication and distribution, despite bomb threats and boycott threats. Bombs did go off in two bookstores in London, four or five in the United States, and two in Italy. A Saudi Arabian imam and his Tunisian assistant imam were assassinated in Brussels for asserting on television that Rushdie should not be killed. Religious figures in Egypt and elsewhere also came out condemning Rushdie, but also condemning Khomeini's call for Rushdie's death.

Iran

> God wanted the blasphemous book of *The Satanic Verses* to be published now, so that the world of conceit, arrogance, and barbarism would bare its true face in its long-held enmity to Islam; . . . it is the world devourers' effort to annihilate Islam, and Muslims; otherwise, the issue of Salman Rushdie would not be so important to them as to place the entire Zionism and arrogance behind it.
>
> —Khomeini, 24 February 1989

> We Muslims should be as wary of the enemy's cultural front as we are of the enemy's military front.
>
> —Khamenei, Friday prayers, 17 February 1989

> . . . the author of the book entitled *The Satanic Verses* . . . as well as those publishers who were aware of its contents, have been sentenced to death. I call on all zealous Muslims to execute them quickly. . . . Whoever is killed on this path will be regarded as a martyr, God willing.
>
> —Khomeini, 14 February 1989

After Britain, Iran and its positioning in the international arena are the political settings that are most important to a reading of the novel. There are four distinct elements here: (1) the role of Shi'ism in the world and in the novel, including the competing traditions within Shi'ism of tolerating dissent versus militant, brutal suppression of all dissent; (2) the domestic politics of Iran: the defense of the revolution, and the struggle between restricted literacy keeping power in the hands of 'ulamā and other elites versus democratization of literacy and critical thought; (3) the further struggle by the Islamic state and its opponents to control the new technology of film; and (4) the international politics of Iran, and its successful playing upon the gullibility and ignorance of Westerners.

In terms of political drama and skill, Khomeini, of course, by issuing a *fatwā* calling for Rushdie's death, out-trumped and out-classed the notice achieved by the Bradford book-burning. Technically, Khomeini's *fatwā* is but an opinion issued in response to questions submitted to him by Muslims in Britain, and is not enforceable unless there is a trial under Islamic due process. In fact, however, Khomeini has transgressed normal Islamic law here as he has done elsewhere, by directly using the mass media to incite people to kill Rushdie, and by asserting that no repentance by Rushdie could be accepted (repentance can only be judged by God according to usual Muslim interpretation). Implicitly, Khomeini has thus categorized Rushdie as an apostate, subject to the death penalty without trial. The timing of Khomeini's call was not arbitrary: it was a way to seize international leadership for a cause célèbre that others had created in other arenas, and it blocked a series of moves by internal factions to normalize relations with the West. The death sentence functioned much like the seizure of the American Embassy hostages in November 1979, which helped passage of the controversial new constitution that was being opposed by Āyatullāh Shari'atmadāri and others, helped consolidate power, and enforced a break with the United States. The day after Khomeini's *fatwā,* a cleric, Hasan Sanei, head of the 15 Khordad Foundation, promised a $1 million bounty to the person who killed Rushdie, and in the next days this amount was added to by other contributors.

In the West, ignorance of the internal cultural politics of the Muslim world caused many people to accept the definitions of Islam, and of who is a proper Muslim, proposed by the fundamentalists. Within the Muslim world, the voices of progressives and liberals, and even traditional conservatives, were muted, intimidated by the extraordinary clout fundamentalism had achieved in the preceding two decades. Western intellectuals eventually defined the issue as one of illegitimate censorship and the right of expression. They did not know enough about Islam to pick up the few timid calls by moderates among Muslim traditionalists that Rushdie at least be tried before being sentenced (as muftis in Egypt and Saudi Arabia proposed), that his book be refuted, and that the bounties on Rushdie's head besmirched Islam. That is, these Muslims were trying to remind the world that Islam was being violated by Khomeini in three important ways: assassins were being encouraged to kill for money rather than for Islam; the due process legal procedures of Islam were being violated; and, most important, admission was being made that perhaps the book could not be refuted because, with one partial exception, all the stories about Islam in it, including that from which the title comes, are drawn from the ḥadīth, and thus any effort by Muslims to write a refutation would require a self-examination of precisely the sort that the novel itself engages. Moreover, Western intellectuals seemed not to be aware of the long tradition of satire in the Islamic world, including what various gate-keepers regard as blasphemy,[6] nor of the moral parables within Islam promoting tolerance in dealing with blasphemers and doubters. Several of the latter have to do with the sixth Shi'ite Imām, Imām Sadiq, one of which was invoked by the late Sayyid Mahmud Taleqani (the protector of the Islamic left during the 1977–79 revolution) in his speech at the death memorial for "Āyatullāh" Mortaḍā Muṭahhari: A young man came to the Imām and said, "*Halaktu*!" ("I am undone"). "Why?" "Because I doubt the existence of God." To this the Imām replied, "*Allah-o-Akbar!* This is the beginning of certitude and faith." Taleqani used the story as a protest against the tendency of the Islamic Republic to deal with the left by execution. Other stories have to do with Imām Sadiq and Ibn Abi al'Awja. The latter has become a hero of the left for his freethinking, and Imām Sadiq, of course, is proudly cited by Shi'ites for his philosophical acuity and ability to transcend political adversity.[7] Taleqani's sermon at Muṭahhari's death memorial is appropriate as well to Muṭahhari's own opinions:

> What, he asked, should be done with those who attacked Islam? If they attacked Islam openly, he replied, they should be answered in the same way—book against book, opinion against opinion. Only if they attacked deceitfully, intending to mislead the believers, should they be dealt with violently. But, he said, even then, if the attackers sincerely repented they should be forgiven.[8]

The furor over Rushdie's novel and Khomeini's response to it should bring into view for Westerners social cleavages that Muslims have been struggling with for well over a century. One might recall that in the 1930s, at the height of liberal constitutionalism and secularism in the Middle East, both political and intellectual elites were saying that Islam was keeping Muslim societies backward; by the 1970s no public figure dared openly assert such a position. The demographics and political sociology of different styles of religiosity have changed dramatically in the intervening period.[9] Two media of communication have also undergone revolution in the intervening time: reading and the movies.

The reading revolution in the Islamic world is, perhaps, not unlike the struggles in eighteenth- and nineteenth-century England over whether the working class (and slaves in America) should be taught to read and write. Reading is not merely an empowering device; it is (and was understood to be) a means of promoting self-reflection by externalizing, objectifying, and textualizing thought, and thus providing a distanced mirror, a space for analysis and self-critique. For nineteenth-century proponents of the spread of literacy it signified the expansion of bourgeois society, control of passion, and enlarged scope for reason. To be sure, there were worries about pulp literature, not unlike mid-twentieth-century debates over television and Hollywood films. Coleridge expressed the fears about *Lesesucht,* addiction to reading:

> For as to the devotees of the circulating libraries, I dare not compliment their *pass-time,* or rather *kill-time,* with the name of reading. Call it rather a sort of beggarly day-dreaming, in which the mind of the dreamer furnishes for itself nothing but laziness and a little mawkish sensibility; while the whole *materiel* and imagery of the doze is supplied *ab extra* by a sort of mental *camera obscura* manufactured at the printing office, which *pro tempore* fixes, reflects and transmits the moving phantasms of one man's delirium, so as to people the barrenness of a hundred other brains afflicted with the same trance or suspension of all common sense and all definite purpose.[10]

This could have been written by the ideologues of the Islamic Republic of Iran about the Rushdie novel and in fact was, in fairly similar words. In the past decades, there has been a struggle between those who would restrict literacy and those who would expand it. With the rapid spread of literacy, the authority of the clergy is threatened, and the increase of critical abilities is potentially fostered. Islam is a tradition which in general requires the individual to take responsibility for his or her own actions before God without mediation. Counterpositions have often been taken that have asserted that ordinary Muslims should follow leaders who know better. Nowhere has this struggle been sharper than in Iran, where the struggles over the issue of *taqlīd* (followership) have been recurrent. In the earlier part of the century and in the nineteenth century, the ideology of *taqlīd* was used to build up a hierarchical clerical organization that could oppose monarchy and imperialism, and also repress heterodoxy and free thought. In the past decades, the struggle has shifted to one between clerics who wish to retain authority over interpretation and judgment, and modern reformers (such as Dr. Ali Shari'ati) who urged the young people to read, interpret, and rethink Islam on their own without need for clerical authority.

If there is a reading revolution slowly emerging in the Islamic world, the revolution via movies may be faster and more powerful, particularly in more open social environments such as that of India, but also in Iran where the Islamic revolution has been very concerned to control these media (film, television, video), and to exploit them internationally (e.g., the skillful staging of demonstrations around the U.S. Embassy for nightly satellite news broadcasts in the United States). Rushdie, interestingly, is never sanguine about the revolutionary potential of the movies. In the novel *Shame,* he has a wonderful scene in which a Muslim cinema owner who refused to accept the idea of Partition, of separation of Muslims and Hindus, insists on showing double features of Hindu "masala" films and Westerns for Muslim audiences in which cowboys slaughter cows and eat them. Inevitably the movie house, aptly called "Empire Talkies," is torched. The conflagration is as violent in its microcosmic way as the massacres of the Partition. A scene in *Satanic Verses* echoes this protest against communal and religious separatism, with parallel results: Saladin Chamcha's mother throws a dinner party during the Indo-Pakistani war, and while her guests scurry for cover during an air raid, she insists on standing by her buffet and eating; she chokes and dies on a fishbone with no one around to help.[11]

There are both parallels and some interesting differences with film developments in the West. Hollywood films, it has been argued, served the function of providing people a way to think out the implications of new behavioral styles, defined by an affluent commodity-filled world, that allowed (and rewarded) individuals to break away from communal, familial, and traditional structures.[12] The Indian film industry—the largest in the world—operates similarly, dealing in love marriages, cross caste poor boy gets rich girl, and personal virtue rewarded. Various styles of cinema modify these functions, encouraging more critical, social, or political reflection and participation.[13] Tamil working-class, social-justice-oriented film in south India, for instance, provided the political basis for several state and regional political careers, including most prominently, that of the late chief minister of Tamilnadu, M. G. Ramachandran.[14] Bombay films draw upon traditional aesthetics—building art around the eight *rasas* (moods, emotions), and using drama to dispel the arbitrariness of the plots of life and a resolving of character into their underlying originary state. Thus there is a standard circular movement from village to the corruptions of urban life back to the village, and from poverty to affluence to willed poverty (renunciation, ethical development), in which negative feelings (anxiety, fear, pessimism, resignation) are explored and tamed, *dharma* (moral values) and *nivritti* (renunciation) win over *adharma* (greed, hate, suspicion, loneliness) and *pravriti* (worldliness), and the need for worldly involvement is put in perspective.[15] Among the films of the 1950s that took on this shape, *Sree 420* ("Mr. 420") was one of the most popular and is a reference point for Rushdie's opening scene, suggesting something about the shape of his novel (from a village-like outside, into the corruptions of Babylondon, and final return to India), as well as providing some specifics such as its theme song, which Gibreel Fareshta sings as he falls to earth.

Rushdie models Gibreel on the Indian movie stars M.G.R., N.T. Rama Rao, Raj Kapoor, and Amitabh Bachchan. Gibreel's playing gods on screen and eventually in real life London is modelled on the blurring between stage role and political roles of M.G.R. and Rama Rao, chief ministers of Tamilnadu and Karnataka; the hilarious scene of Gibreel's hospitalization when he is visited by Indira Gandhi and "her pilot son" (Rajiv) is modelled on a true event in the career of Amitabh Bachchan. Gibreel's world-wide appeal is not unlike that of Raj Kapoor whose 1950s movie *Awaara* (the vagabond) swept across Iran, Iraq, Syria, Egypt, Turkey, and the Soviet Union, its songs being translated into a dozen languages, even spawning an imitation in Iran, the film *Charkh-e Falak* ("Heaven's Will") with the stars Fardin and Bayk Imanverdi. The movie producer Sisodia (Whiskey-and soda), who specializes in bringing Indian film to the West, is modelled in part on Ismail Merchant.

Although there are *roman à clef* elements in Rushdie's book that deepen the amusement for those in the know, the primary concern here is the interplay of the movie medium and traditional belief systems. It is the fourth in a series of remarkable novels which together provide a comic universe of scenes, figures, emotional moods, and perceptual angles on history, geography, and social conflict that resonate from one novel to the next. There is a corpus here that ought not to be dismembered. But before turning to this corpus, we need to clear the ground on the nature of the borrowings from the Islamic tradition. Although some Muslims, mainly those who have not read the novel, charge Rushdie with blasphemy, and their distortions of events or descriptions in the novel are examples of how rumor and decontextualized excerpting can pervert reality, other Muslims acknowledge that Rushdie is all too knowledgeable about Islam, that he is essentially a traitor, exploiting real knowledge for nefarious purposes.

The point thus of identifying the Qur'anic sources of Rushdie's novel is not to prove his fidelity to Islamic traditions—that is conceded by many Muslim critics—but to provide an account of the richness of traditional grounding, the other side of the struggle between the movies and traditional religion for the hearts and souls of men and women, boys and girls.

Qur'anic Sources and A-maze-ments

> Only for you, children of doctrine and learning, have we written this work. Examine this book, ponder the meaning we have dispersed in

> various places and gathered again; what we have concealed in one place we have disclosed in another, that it may be understood by your wisdom.
> —Heinrich Cornelius Agrippa von Nettesheim, *De occulta philosophia,* epigram to Umberto Eco's *Foucault's Pendulum*

> *Hazl* (satire) is education; take it seriously
> And do not be deceived by its outer form.
> —Jalaluddin Rumi

Two sets of chapters are interbraided to form the structure of *Satanic Verses:* five chapters deal directly with the traumas of being an immigrant in Britain in the 1980s; four interstitial chapters deal with the nightmares of Gibreel Farishta ("the Angel Gabriel"), a Bombay film actor, who is one of the two lead characters in the novel. These nightmares, like videotapes that always pick up where they last stopped, enmesh the actor in the struggles of early Islam: he finds himself in the role of the Archangel Gabriel, overwhelmed by the neediness of the Prophet for further revelations to relieve the unbearable psychological pressures of being caught between the demands of Islam and those of his pagan kinsmen and townsmen (not unlike the psychological pressures of an immigrant caught between his childhood Islamic training and the sensibilities of a secular Britain—there is not only analogy but also "leakage" between the two sets of chapters).

The most striking thing about the nightmare chapters on a first superficial reading is their lack of inventiveness: they stick too close to Islamic tradition for comfort. This is the rationale for certain progressive Muslims to damn the book out of an opportunistic solidarity with their more fundamentalist brothers: irreverent fidelity, they argue, produces only mockery, not the transformative defamiliarizing-revisioning of really creative literature. At issue here, of course, is the entire parodic and satiric tradition in the Islamic world, including what various gate-keepers regard as blasphemy, which this argument would repress. More important, this argument also represses the moral parable tradition within Islam promoting tolerance in dealing with blasphemers and doubters. Several of these parables have to do with the sixth Shi'ite Imām, al-Sadiq, including the one which was invoked by the late Sayyid Mahmud Taleqani (the protector of the Islamic left during the course of the 1977–79 revolution) in his speech at the death memorial for "Āyatullāh" Murtaḍā Muṭahhari, recounted above.

But the more specific counterarguments to the charges of blasphemy are that these chapters are psychologically realistic and that they ground themselves in the psychological structures explicitly mentioned in the Qur'an and elaborated in the ḥadīth. The novel is about immigrants and the struggle in their interior psychological discourses between influences that come from the movies and those that come from traditional religion. Childhood religiosity often repeats itself obsessively; the lack of inventiveness in the novel about Islam is true to the subjects being depicted. This is not an area of easy creativity for immigrants, who feel their identity insufficiently valued by the wider society, and who further feel the interior grounds of their identity being undermined by the new lives they must lead. The point is demonstrated nowhere more clearly than in the authoritarian anger of otherwise quite pragmatic Muslims in England to burn the book, kill the author, and unleash dormant British blasphemy laws against the hard-won gains of freedom of expression. That there are quite specific sociological reasons for Muslim defensiveness and anger in an increasingly racist Britain, especially in towns such as Bradford, is something that is acknowledged in the novel and portrayed at some length in scenes set in the East End of London.

There are six, or rather three linked pairs of, primary complaints by Muslims: (1) the title story and (2) the Salman Farsi story; (3) the use of the name "Mahound" and (4) the calling of Ibrahim a "bastard" for sending Hagar into the desert; (5) the brothel scene and (6) the three uses of the name of Ayesha (the youngest wife of the Prophet) to refer to a whore in Mecca, to refer to Empress Farah of Iran, and to refer to a Pakistani (or in the novel an Indian) charismatic village girl who leads her blindly faithful followers to their deaths. Of these only the brothel scene might be said to be a Rushdie invention, but even it is only inventive in its outer form: its psychology is registered explicitly in the Qur'an, and the kernel of Rushdie's invention is present in Shi'ite uses of the name Ayesha to rhyme with "faḥisha" ("whore"), grounded in a frequently used moral parable about chaste behavior of women that Ayesha transgressed, and that is the context (*sabab al-nuzūl*) for the revelation of Sūra al-Nūr ("The Light") on female modesty, the so-called *ifk* incident. Similarly, in the other two linked pairs—the pointing out of moral failings of prophets, who in *some* versions of dogma are supposed to be models of (inhuman) perfection (3, 4),[16] and the anxieties about the text of the Qur'an not containing anything man-made, anything not revealed by God (1, 2)—there is nothing in the novel that is not explicitly grounded in the ḥadīth literature. Other parodic features have not attracted ire: the parodies of Khomeini and the Prophet's *mi'rāj* journey; the parodies of the opening of Sūra al-Najm ("The

Star," the sūra in which the title story occurs) and of the throwing down of Satan and Adam from Paradise in the brilliant opening scene of the novel. Let us examine the complaints.

(1) "Satanic Verses": The Gharānīq *Story (53:19*–23; 22:52–55):

The title alludes to a famous story in the ḥadīth literature: Muhammad, under extreme pressure from opponents in Mecca, had a revelation that Lāt, 'Uzzā, and Manāt, the most important of the three hundred and sixty goddesses of the Ka'ba, might be accepted into the Islamic belief structure as archangels like Gabriel. Almost immediately, he had regrets about such compromise. A second revelation abrogated the first, turning its suggestions into parody. Muslims debate this story under the name *al-gharānīq* ("high-flying birds," "exalted females," "angels"),[17] referring to a pre-Islamic ritual chant that echoes uncannily in the Qur'an. In pre-Islamic times, the Qur'aish used to circumambulate the Ka'ba chanting,

al-Lāt wa al-'Uzzā	Lat and Uzza
Wa Manāt al-thālithat al-'ukhrā	And another, the third, Manat
Fa innahunna al gharānīq al-'ulā	They are the high-flying birds
Minha al-shafa'atu turtajā.	May they intercede for us.

So reports Hisham ibn Muhammad al-Kalbi (d. 204) in his *al-Asnam* ("Book of Idols"). Listen to the echo in Sūra al-Najm ("The Star," 53:19–23):

> Have you seen Lāt and 'Uzzā?
> And another, the third, Manāt?

[They are high-flying birds (gharānīq), their intercession (*shafā'at*) is to be hoped for.][18]

> What! For you, the male, and for Him, the female (*'unthā*)?
> Behold such would indeed be an unfair division (*qismatun ḍīzā*).
> They are nothing but names which you have devised,
> You and your forebears without authority, for which God has sent no guidance (*hudā*).
> They follow surmise and desire although guidance has come to them from God.
> Or shall man have whatever he fancies?
> To God belongs this world and the hereafter.

The words in brackets are not part of the Qur'anic text: these are the "satanic verses" that Satan caused Muhammad for a moment to think were part of the revelation, and that subsequently were abrogated by the following lines, dripping with sarcasm.

The whole passage comes immediately after references to the Qur'an itself ("By the star when it plunges . . . this is naught but a revelation taught him by one terrible in power. . . ."), and to the Prophet's night journey (*mi'rāj*) on his high-flying winged horse, Burāq,[19] to observe the punishments and rewards of heaven and hell. That is, the Sūra opens with the three modes of communication between the heavens and the world: the descent of the divine, the ascent of the human/Prophet, and the back and forth mediating of angels.

The passage, moreover, resonates with many other passages in the Qur'an. It is another example of the funhouse a-maze-ments analyzed in chapter 2, full of echoes and mirrorings, onomatopoetic word selections, meaningful inflections and intonations, that have intrigued, puzzled, and delighted exegetes for centuries. "They are nothing but names you have devised . . . for which God has sent no authority" occurs also in 7:71 and 12:40. Phrases and warnings about those who claim (false) intercessors, either by misreading the signs of nature and of the outcomes of human trials in the world, or by deliberately tampering with the Qur'an, occur in 6:94, 7:53, 30:13, 39:43, and especially 10:18.[20] "Daughters of God," "for you the male, and for Him the female," also echo and re-echo throughout the Qur'an. References to correctly reading the signs (āyāt) of God are too numerous in the Qur'an to list. The point is that lines and passages of the Qur'an do not stand alone but are to be interpreted, clarified, and confirmed with the knowledge of other passages, elsewhere in the Qur'an.

The sarcasm of "for you the males, and for Him, the female" first of all refers to the Arab privileging of the male. The goddesses of the Ka'ba were called the "daughters of God," and this phrase reverberates through the Qur'an (53:19, 16:57; "your sons and God's daughters": 37:149, 37:153, 52:39; "those who do not believe in the hereafter give angels female names": 53:45; "are angels female?" 37:150, 43:19; "[those who] pray not except to female beings, they pray not except to a rebel Satan": 4:117). The sarcasm cuts multiple ways: Should God be assigned daughters (by men) while Arabs prefer sons? Does God prefer sons as do Arabs? Is not God above such petty discrimination? The sarcasm is directed at Christians as well: Does God have a son (Jesus)? (The Qur'an also accuses Jews of making 'Uzair [Ezra?] a son of God: 9:30.)

The Christian God has a son, and the Arab God has daughters? The sarcasm is underscored by the word *ḍīzā,* a word that is hard to pronounce, considered ugly, unpoetic, selected here as a word of derision, and given prominence as the rhyme word at the end of the line. (Contemporary repressed feminist irony is added by the circumstance that the third rhyme word, *hudā* ["guidance"], is nowadays a popular girl's name in the Arab world.) There is perhaps another anomaly: the third line ("they are nothing but names yourselves have named . . . for which God has sent no authority [*sulṭān*] . . . no guidance [*hudā*]") is extremely long relative to both the two preceding and the two following lines. Some modern scholars (e.g., Mehdi Bazargan) argue that this anomaly is a tell-tale sign of it being a later addition, a later revelation. That *ḍizā* occurs only once in the Qur'an, and is thus not a normal Qur'anic term, is further evidence for some that this passage may be a later addition. (Exegetes, of course, point out that there are a number of words in the Qur'an that occur only once. Interestingly, a number of these are Persian.)[21]

Of other passages that resonate with these lines, the most important is in Sūra al-Ḥajj (22:52–55). These are Medinan verses, that is, ones revealed some ten years after the Meccan verses of 53:19–20. They underscore the rejection of Satan's suggestion, and they respond to Muhammad's concern that he might be misled. The story is that Gabriel would periodically ask Muhammad to recite the Qur'an back to him, and in so-reciting Sūra al-Najm, Gabriel stopped him at the Satanic insertion, saying, "I did not bring that to you." Listen to the psychology of Gabriel's (God's) reassurance to Muhammad:

> Never did We send any messenger (*rasūl*) or prophet (*nabī*) before thee [Muhammad] but when he formed a desire (*tamannā, umniya*), Satan threw (*alqa*) something into his *umniya* ("desire," "recitation") but God annuls what Satan casts, and God confirms His signs/verses (*āyāt*), for God is full of knowledge and wisdom, and He may make what Satan casts a trial for those in whose hearts is sickness, and those whose hearts are hard. . . .

This is an extraordinary passage, suggesting precisely the desires of Muhammad under pressure that Rushdie attempts to portray in realistic detail. Desire, wishful thinking, is a key problem in the Qur'an: Jews in the Qur'an are often called knowers only of *amāni,* the plural of *umniya,* that is, people who learn nothing from scripture but their own "wishful thinking" ("desires") (2:78, 2:111, 4:123, 57:14). *Ummiyun,* however, is an epithet not only for Jews; Muhammad is also called *ummi.* The line between wishful thinking and righteous desire becomes an ethical puzzle, a test for the true Muslim, as it was for Muhammad, an interior struggle. (As Rushdie puts it in the novel, invoking the inimitable syntax of Indian English, Gibreel recognizing both desires contesting in himself: "it was me both times, baba, me first and second also me.") For some exegetes, the word *alqa* here indicates Satan's careless, chaotic, unsystematic thowing about that predetermines (is part of the essence of) Evil's failure in the struggle against the divine Good (a Zoroastrian conception).

The abrogration of Satan's suggestion is very clear. In Sūra al-Najm itself, the verses following say:

> How many an angel there is in the heavens whose intercession avails naught, except if God gives leave. . . . Those who do not believe in the world to come name the angels with female names. They have not any knowledge thereof; they follow only surmise, and surmise avails naught against truth.

The story that Muhammad could have used the Satanic suggestion is rejected by almost all exegetes, but the fact that the story persists as a subject of exegetes' discussions is testimony to the reality of the temptation both for Muhammad and for later Muslims in their own struggles in such "Babylons" as London, New York, Paris, or Hamburg. This is nothing invented by Rushdie.

The story appears in the early *Sīra* (biography of Muhammad) by Ibn Is-haq (A.H. 85–152), in Ṭabari's *Tārikh* ("History"), in Jalal-ud-Din Suyūṭi and Jalāl-ud-Dīn Maḥalli's *Tafsīr al-Jalālayn* ("Qur'an Commentary by the two Jalāls"), in several different versions in Suyuti's *Lubāb,* and in other source books. The first traditional question for evaluating the status of these stories would be to query their *isnād.* Their chains of narrators include such important reliable figures as Ibn 'Abbās, Sa'īd ibn Jubayr, Ḍaḥḥak, Muhammad ibn Ka'b, and Muhammad ibn Qays; there are multiple chains going back to 'Abdullah ibn 'Abbās and to several of the *tābi'īn* (second-generation Muslims), and (according to Ṭabarsī in his *Majma' al-Bayān*) from them to the Prophet. According to some exegetes, all the narration chains (*isnād*) are defective in one way or another: they are broken (*munqaṭi'*), weak (*ḍa'īf*), or missing a link (*mursal*). However, many exegetes such as Ibn Ḥajar do not rule out the possibility that the story has some foundation: after all, they argue, the fact that there are many versions and chains of narration (*kathrat al-ṭuruq*) indicates that there may be some validity. The late Allama Sayyed Muhammad Husain Tabataba'i, in his *al-Mizān* (vol. 14:396–97), also cites the numerous chains of *isnād* and the opinion of various scholars, including Ibn Hajar, that the story is *ṣaḥīḥ* (correct, valid), and finds he cannot reject it on such formal grounds, but does so instead on doctrinal grounds. Most of the extended debate, thus, turns on other reasons than the evaluation of the *isnād.*

Least impressive are doctrinal arguments: the Qur'an is the word of God, and Muhammad is a trustworthy prophet who has neither added to nor subtracted from the divine revelations. Muhammad is not merely trustworthy (*amīn*), but infallible (*ma'ṣūm*): thus he could not have mistaken the devil for Gabriel; nor as a messenger of uncompromising resistance against polytheism, could he have made such a significant concession, and even had he done so on his own accord, God would have destroyed him (e.g., 10:16, 44–46). There are, of course, counter-doctrinal lines of argument which stress that Muhammad, although a prophet, was a mere mortal and could make mistakes in recitation, of which this is an example (thus argues Abu-'Alī Jubbā'i, for instance).

Much more interesting are the speculations by various exegetes to explain how such verses might have come to be in the Qur'an. Baghawi, in his *Tafsīr,* suggests that Satan threw his suggestion not into the mouth of Muhammad, but into the ears of the polytheists, who imagined it had come from Muhammad. An alternative, more manipulative variant is the speculation that hypocrites (*munāfiqīn*) inspired by Satan threw in these verses, making others imagine it was part of the Qur'an. Shaykh al- Ṭūsi, in his *al-Tibyān* (vol. 7:292–93) reports from Mujāhid the psychological speculation that whenever there was a delay in the flow of revelations, Muhammad would begin to become anxious and desire more revelation, an opportunity which Satan would exploit by interjecting something, and which God would subsequently abrogate. Yet another possibility is suggested by Ṭabarsi: maybe Muhammad inserted these verses for the sake of argument, intended to be orally heard as silly *reductio ad absurdum* suggestions. "Are they pretty birds? Is one to pray to birds for intercession?

Ṭabarsi, in his *Majma' al-Bayān* (vol. 7:90–92), summarizes eight possibilities to explain these verses: (1) Psychological speculations: the word *umniya* can mean both "recitation" and "wish"; perhaps when Muhammad recited the Qur'an the polytheists would interrupt with verses of their own, which God subsequently abrogated; or Muhammad had wishes that Satan exploited, trying to misguide him, as he had Adam and Eve, but which God again did not allow to pass. (2) Textual evaluation: the *isnād* is weak, and the story is not to be trusted. (3) Doctrinal evaluation: the fallibility attributed to the Prophet in the story is itself evidence of its fabricated nature, since the Prophet was infallible. (4) Ironic interpretive reading: Muhammad interjected these verses as *hijāj* (for the sake of argument) thereby showing their absurdity. (5) Lexical ambiguity: *gharānīq* was metaphorically intended to refer to angels, but the polytheists mistook it to refer to their gods, and thus the verse was abrogated lest misunderstanding be perpetuated. (6) Another psychological possibility: as Muhammad recited relying on the flow of the sound of the verses, not paying much attention to the words, Satan caused him to recite the pre-Islamic poetry, which sounds very similar to the Qur'anic cadence. Or, alternatively, (7) the verse was intended to mention the three goddesses and condemn them, but Satan modified the inflection with which it was said so that it seemed to convey the opposite meaning. In any case, (8) the literal meaning of the verse asking intercession is contradicted by the rest of the sūra, and so there is little basis to give credence to the idea that Muhammad attempted to compromise with the polytheists. There is yet a ninth possibility given in the Qur'an itself, the notion that Muhammad, like all Muslims, was put through a trial so that he/Muslims might experience the devices by which the signs of God may be recognized (10:22).[22]

Finally, there has been some debate on the grounds of historical (im)possibilities. Muhammad Jawād Balāghi, in his *Ālā' al-Raḥmān,* says the whole nexus of alleged contexts of revelation linking the two sets of verses is historically suspect. After all, Sūra al-Najm, where the verses of *gharānīq* are said to have been, is a Meccan sūra, from the early period of Muhammad's prophethood, while Sūra al-Ḥajj is a Medinan sūra, revealed some ten years later. To argue for a connection between the two would be to argue that the verses of *gharānīq* were in the Qur'an for a decade before they were abrogated! On the other hand, the European scholar William Muir suggests that a group of the Muslims who fled from the oppression of Muslims in Mecca to Habasha (Ethiopia) returned some three months later. Had they not heard of some compromise between Muhammad and his opponents, there would have been no reason for them to return. (Jafar Subhani has responded to Muir, saying that they could have been deceived by false rumors, and in any case the dispute over tribal gods was not the only reason for the tension between Muhammad and the leaders of Mecca.)

The text remains ambiguous: it provides support both to those who wish to deny the Satanic verse episode ever happened and to those who wish to affirm that it did happen. The verses of Sūra al-Najm (53:21–23), if they were later additions/revelations might have been immediate corrections of (53:19–20), but they might also be temporally much later, even ten years later, in the same period as Sūra al-Ḥajj (22:52–55). (Were the abrograting verses only revealed ten years after the original event, that would mean that for ten years Muslims had been asking Lat, Manat, and Uzza for intercession! No one seriously alleges this, but it would be the result of taking literally the claim that 22:52–55 is the abrogating verse for the *al-gharānīq* incident.)

The point in all this is, first, that the debate is fully developed in traditional Muslim scholarship and that speculations of the sort engaged in by Rushdie are not his invention; and, second, that although the Qur'an inveighs against poets and spinners of idle tales (*lahw al-ḥadīth*) which distract one from the path of God, and this arguably might be opposed to all novels and other fictional genres, the Qur'an and the ḥadīth literature, are themselves full of richly didactic stories: the Qur'an calls itself the best of all stories (12:3), the most truthful of stories (3:64). The *sabab al-nuzūl* of the verse condemning idle tales is said to be condemnation specifically of Nadhr ibn Ḥārith, a narrator of the Rustam and Esfandiar stories (the epic tales of ancient Iran) and the Kalileh and Demneh stories (the fables of ancient India). Nine times the Qur'an rejects those who call the stories in the Qur'an *asāṭīr al-awwalīn* (tales of the ancients), *asāṭīr* being the Arabic pluralization of the Greek *historia* (inquiry, information, narrative, history). Rushdie's speculations in his novel, in other words, insofar as they are sincere efforts to think through the psychology of both the early days of Islam, and more directly the psychology of Muslim migrants living in the West, are no different than the debates in the long history of Islamic scholarship, which often have also drawn on humor, parables, analogies, and other devices of entertainment.

(2) The Two Salmans: Salman Farsi and Salman Rushdie:

The concern about the "Satanic Verses" is not merely about whether the incident at Mecca happened; the concern is the allegation that some, or even all, of the Qur'an might not be divine revelation, that the Qur'an is incomplete, contains material that was not supposed to be there, or has been in some other way tampered with (as Muslims claim in the case with the extant Torah and Gospels). The charge against Rushdie is that the tone or way he invokes the *gharānīq* incident, the Salman Farsi story, and the calling of the Prophet by the anti-Muslim slur "Mahound" constitutes a pattern of undermining the authority of the Qur'anic text. The counterargument, of course, is that the Qur'an itself places upon Muslims an obligation of dealing with uncertainty: Uncertainty is characteristic both for man's knowledge of the world ("They say, 'Why has a sign not been sent down upon him from his Lord?' Say to them: 'The Useen belongs only to God.'" 10:21; hence the play with *mutashābih* and *muḥkam, tafsīr* and *ta'wīl* analyzed in chapter 2), and for the moral universe in which man is placed as in a test or a trial (10:22). The story of Salman Farsi ("Salman the Persian") is an Iranian nationalist, anti-Arab one, and Rushdie merely retells it in vivid fashion. Iranians like to say that as dogma admits, Muhammad was illiterate, and moreover he was from a tradition that knew little of scriptures. How could such a person compose a Qur'an? It must have been the Zoroastrian priest, Salman, one of the first converts to Muhammad's leadership and one of the transcribers of the Qur'an, who helped the illiterate prophet compose the scripture. In Rushdie's version, Salman is a figure of desire: he desperately wants to believe in the Prophet and tests the Prophet in the hope that belief can be affirmed. Salman, thus, psychologically is a Muslim figure like so many emigrants in the West, above all the other Salman, Salman Rushdie, who wants to establish the truth value of Islam and get rid of the naïvetés, false pieties, and politically motivated perversions that make many versions of Islam unsustainable in the contemporary world. Salman in the novel tests the Prophet by changing a little word here and there, hoping the Prophet will notice, but the Prophet does not, until rather major changes are made, at which point the wrath of the Prophet is unleashed. (This part of the tale is taken from Tabari's account of Muhammad's scribe, 'Abdullāh ibn Sa'd, who lost his faith after the Prophet failed to notice a deliberate mistake in his transcription.) The figuration here is of the secular Muslim, Salman Rushdie, adapting the Islamic message to the contemporary world, and at some point becoming subject to the repressive wrath of fundamentalist brethren whose sense of Islam is violated. This is all too realistic and obvious, long before Khomeini issued a literal death sentence.

And it is in this context that the name "Mahound" must be seen.

(3) Mahound versus Muhammad: Turning Insults into Strength:

"Mahound" was a medieval Christian term of abuse for the Prophet of Islam. Rushdie adopts this name "to turn insults into strength" (p. 93), rather like defiant wearing of yellow stars to resist anti-Semites. Muslim critics find this explanation disingenuous, but what they fail to acknowledge is first of all that Rushdie problematizes this strategy in the Brickall Street scenes, when he has Jumpy Joshi and Mishal Sufiyan propose the same strategy against fascists. Joshi attempts to write poetry that takes the speeches of Enoch Powell and turns Powell's racist rhetoric against the fascists, and Mishal attempts to explain the posters and sweatshirts with the goat-devil logo as a similar gesture of defiance against the rampant racism of Thatcher in England. The tactic is recognized to be lame and ineffective in stopping racism, but important in building up the pride and will to resist among Muslims. It could be argued, moreover, that Rushdie's use of the term Mahound is a dramatically effective tactic to draw Western attention to the ways in which Western linguistic usages unthinkingly insult and degrade Muslims: after all, how many Westerners still refer to Islam as Muhammadanism, a linguistic usage that is in its implications no better than "Mahound." (Sensitivities are such that paranoid mutterings have even been voiced by Muslims in America that they suspect hostile Americans of deliberately mispronouncing Islam as Izlām, which in Arabic would mean spreading oppression (*ẓulm*) and darkness (*ẓulmat*). But see also the Iranian flashlight cartoon, chapter 6, note 12.)

Second, Rushdie uses the distinction between Mahound and Muhammad to focus attention on moral and immoral appropriations of Islam. Mahound is the name of the Muhammad of Khomeini, Zia-ul-Haq, and others, who in the name of Islam (mis)use the power of the state in morally questionable ways. The novel sets itself not only against misuses in state coercion, but also against the repressions and distortions of socialization that Rushdie and so many others in all religious traditions have seen as problematic. There is a good Muslim in the novel who lives up to the name Muhammad, and whose primary virtue is explicitly described as not being a fanatic. That person is Muhammad Sufyan, the owner of the Shandaar Cafe, the supplier of food, a place to gather and succor for the beleaguered denizens of Brickall Street. Historically, Abu Sufyan and his wife Hind are interesting figures that deepen the resonances of Rushdie's crafting. Abu Sufyan, although one of the opponents of Muhammad in the Battles of Uhud and Badr, fled when Muhammad returned to Mecca victorious, and immediately sought forgiveness through the Prophet's uncle, 'Abbās. Not only was he forgiven, and not only did he convert, but his son, Mu'awwiya was made a scribe of revelation, his house was made a sanctuary where people could seek refuge (like the Shandaar Cafe), and his daughter (Umma Habiba) married the Prophet. Moreover, Abu Sufyan is one of the first Shi'ites, since he was the first to come to Ali and offer to raise an army to restore Ali to his rightful place as the successor to Muhammad. Abu

Sufyan's wife, however, is famous as a symbol of female violence and brutality in vengeance for her menfolk. She lost her father, a son, a brother, and an uncle in the early battles against the Muslims, and swore not to sleep with Abu Sufyan until they were avenged. At the Battle of Uhud, the Muslim forces were crushed, and the womenfolk with Hind made garlands out of the noses and ears of the enemy; Hind is said to have ripped out the liver of Hamza, an uncle of the Prophet, chewed it up and spat it out. She is thus known as "Hind the liver eater," and her son and grandson, Mu'awwiya and Yezid, are cursed by Shi'ites with the epithet "son of the liver eater." But she too converted. It is said, moreover, that the Prophet was so enraged at the desecration of Hamza's corpse, that he swore to kill large numbers of those involved, at which point he received a revelation that mandated vengeance be limited to equivalence: one life for one life. Rushdie's Hind is also a hard but not evil woman, unsympathetic to the plight of Chamcha, and this fits with the Hind of early Muslim history. These were people caught in the messy reality of nasty political battles, just as are the owners of the cafe on Brickall Street. Mu'awiyya later became the founder of the Umayyid dynasty and thus has a bad reputation among Shi'ites; there are even some wild Shi'ite accusations that 'Abbās and Abu Sufyan concocted a secret alliance that would keep the caliphate in the hands of their descendants (the Umayyids and the Abbasids) rather than allowing it to go to the rightful possessors: Ali and his descendants. But Abu Sufyan's own reputation seems secure, as a sincere convert to Islam, and as the owner of a house deemed by the Prophet worthy of being a sanctuary.

(4) The Bastard Ibrahim: Basic Moral Questions:

Muslim critics claim to see in Rushdie's chiding of Abraham/Ibrahim a continuation of the disrespect toward prophets that they see in Rushdie's use of the name Mahound. But recall the analysis of the ḥajj (chapter 3). When Rushdie chides Ibrahim for having abandoned Hagar and Ishma'il, he not only mildly invokes contemporary morality (a father should not send wife and child alone into the desert), but he asks pointedly if contemporary Muslim pilgrims know why they congregate at the ḥajj. Do they in fact celebrate the survival of Hagar? That is, do they consciously reenact the dual dependence upon faith in God but also one's own skill and reason; or do they merely follow blindly rote instructions of faith? Most Muslims celebrate not the parable of Hagar, but instead (idolatrously?) worship the *maqām* (the footprint) of Ibrahim, the place he stood when he came to visit his son and grandson, or where he stood when he rebuilt the Ka‘ba. That Muslim wrath should be stirred up by Rushdie's pointing out a feminist critique of Muslim male chauvinism can only be to Rushdie's credit and to fundamentalist Muslims' discredit.

(5) The Brothel Scene: The Ifk *Incident (24:11–21):*

In the fifth or sixth year of the Islamic era, on the return from an expedition to the Banu Mustaliq, Ayesha, the youngest and most beloved wife of the Prophet, failed to reenter her closed palanquin at one of the rest stops, and was left behind. She was found by Safwan who escorted her back to the caravan. Allegations were raised about the compromising position she had allowed herself to be placed in. Muhammad had a revelation that cleared her of wrongdoing, and further proposed punishments for those who spread rumors and talk idly about chaste women. Revelations also imposed special conditions of concealment for the wives of the Prophet and even that after the Prophet's death no man would be allowed to marry his widows. Imām Ali, however, would not allow the issue to die, and he and Ayesha remained at odds. Imām Ali, and after him Muslim preachers, used the story to warn women against allowing any situation to arise in which even the appearance or possibility of misdeeds could arise. Shi‘ites in particular have seen Ayesha as a model of female transgression, rather than as a model of a good Muslim woman (Fatima and Zeinab are the models of good Muslim women); and Shi‘ites often rhyme Ayesha's name with the word for whore, *faḥisha.* No Shi‘ite names his daughter Ayesha. Sunni women who live in a predominantly Shi‘ite Iran, and who are given the name Ayesha, usually have another name which they use in public.

There is a controversial scene in Rushdie's novel. It is a scene that is set after the victorious return of the Prophet to Mecca, when he is imposing the rules and taboos of the new religion. Rules, rules, rules bring resistance and avoidance. In the brothels, people talk about the black market in pork, prayers in secret to the old gods, and especially they mutter that although ordinary Muslims are limited to four wives, the Prophet has thirteen. The resentment about the Prophet's wives and the special status accorded them, marked by their special seclusion, leads to salacious jealousy. A customer in one of the whorehouses gets excited at the idea of having the youngest whore in the brothel play the youngest wife of the Prophet. The other eleven whores decide that the same psychology may delight other customers, and they each choose the role of one of the Prophet's wives. (The madame, like Khadijeh, is not fully part of the game.) In a cute side intuition, Rushdie has the whores all marry Baal, the defeated poet that Abu Simbel had hired to vilify the Muslims, who is being hidden by the madame in the labyrinth of the whorehouse. For the whores, it is the dream marriage they would never have, and Baal is encouraged to act out the role of the Prophet. Baal becomes a drinking partner with Salman Farsi, who has by now also been forced into hiding, and Salman narrates the *ifk* story about Ayesha's indiscretion. Baal writes verses to each of his twelve wives and as they become public, it also becomes public that they have the names of the Prophet's wives. Baal is found and taken for beheading. He cries out, "Whores and writers, Mahound. We are the people you can't forgive." Mahound replies, "Writers and whores, I see no difference."

The entire scene works in terms of psychological realism, and analogically is a commentary on Khomeini's Iran. It is after all the Qur'an that originally refers to the psychology of jealousy and insinuation about the Prophet's wives, and tries to impose rules of propriety both on women's behavior and on male tongues. But the scene is also linked to the satire about Khomeini, first withdrawn to London, and then returned to Iran, where, as in Mecca centuries earlier, the whorehouses are to be closed but are given a short period of grace to phase themselves out of business. The linkage between whores and writers is a comment on the way Khomeini and other fundamentalists treat writers and intellectuals. Rushdie comments, "When Muhammad returned to Mecca in power, he was very, very tolerant. And I think, if I remember correctly, only five or six people were executed. . . . And of those five or six people, two were writers, and two were actresses who had performed in satirical texts. Now there you have an image that I thought was worth exploring."[23]

(6) Ayesha-Faḥisha:

Three Ayeshas occur in Rushdie's novel: the whore in the Meccan videotape nightmare discussed above; the Empress Farah Pahlavi; and an epileptic village girl, clad in butterflies (beautiful raiments, spiritual transformation), who leads gullible villagers on a pilgrimage to Mecca on foot into the Arabian Sea where they drown blissfully in a mirage of absolute faith (many of the images work as elaborate visual puns). (The last is based on a famous incident in Pakistan (Ahmed 1986); it also seems to be a homage to Gabriel García Márquez, who has a similar figure covered in butterflies. It, and the village Titlipur [Titlipur means butterfly village] is a reference to the song "Titli Udi" from the Hindi film *Suraj.*) The latter two occur in a chapter called "Ayesha," an interlude before the Muslims return victorious to Mecca, the interlude before Khomeini returns victorious to Iran in 1979 from his exile in Iraq and Paris. The chapter is in two parts, one about the Imām in exile (introduced by an evocative reminder that this is a nightmare: "now the dream rushes him up the outer wall"), and the other about blind faith solutions to problems in India. The parody of Khomeini is a tour de force, including among other things the Imām's radio broadcaster, Bilal (the name of the first muezzin), figured as an American convert (Bilal, the Ethiopian convert; the image of Malcolm X that the Islamic Republic tried to use to urge American blacks to rise against the Great Satan; the spokesman in Paris at his side, Ibrahim Yazdi, from Houston; but primarily, "the voice of American confidence, a weapon of the West turned against its makers") who begins the daily broadcast "with ritual abuse of the Empress, with lists of her crimes, murders, bribes, sexual relations with lizards, and so on. . . . 'Death to the tyranny of the Empress Ayesha, of calendars, of America, of time. . . . Burn the books and trust the Book; shred the papers and hear the Word, as it was revealed by the Angel Gibreel to the Messenger Mahound and explicated by your interpreter and Imām.'" The reference to the calendars is of course to the new Pahlavi calendar that the shah attempted to introduce in the late 1970s, which would have made the present, the year 2500-odd, celebrating so many years of "continuous monarchy," an extravagance that infuriated most Iranians, not only Muslims. The sexual innuendo and the use of curses is true to the rhetoric of the revolution which delighted in the language of "exposing" the shah and his regime.

We can now turn back to the novel, both to the chapters on Muslim migrants struggling to create a place for themselves in Thatcher's Britain, and to the chapters on Gibreel Farishta's nightmares in which he stars as the archangel Gabriel struggling with the Prophet in the oasis town of Jahilia, a desert town of sand and its derivatives: glass (mirrors) and silicon (chips, the electronic age). Jahilia, of course, is the name for the age of ignorance before Islam, and in fundamentalist rhetoric it applies as well to the current age of decadence, of deafness to Islam. The image of the town of sand, whose enemy is water, is not merely true to a desert oasis with its adobe buildings, a trade center whose economy was under threat from the shifting of trade from caravans to boats, but also Rushdie has named the ruler Abu Simbel, the name of the Egyptian temple whose site was drowned under the waters of Aswan High Dam, that is, by modern technology. Muslims as the enemies of the city of idolatry and false commodity religion is crystallized in the image of them constantly engaged in ablutions with water. Abu Simbel's Queen is that other great threat, Hind, India, land of female goddesses par excellence: from Kali to Indira Gandhi, exalted females, 360 idols and more, polymorphous perversity and fecundity run riot.

Reading the Novel: Highjacked Souls

> We had suspected for a long time that the man Gabriel was capable of miracles, because for many years he had talked too much about angels for someone who had no wings, so that when the miracle of the printing presses occurred we nodded our heads knowingly, but of course the foreknowledge of his sorcery did not release us from its power, and under the spell of that nostalgic witchcraft we arose from our wooden benches and garden swings and ran without once drawing breath to the place where the demented printing presses were breeding books faster than fruitflies, and the books leapt into our hands without our even having to stretch out our arms, the flood of books spilled out of the print room and knocked down the first arrivals at the streets and the sidewalks and rose lap high in the ground-flood rooms of all the houses for miles around, so that there was no one who could escape from that story, if you were blind or shut your eyes it did you no good because there were always voices reading aloud within earshot, we had all been ravished like willing virgins by that tale, which had the quality of convincing each reader that it was his personal autobiography; and then the book filled up our country and headed out to sea, and we understood in the insanity of our possession that the phenomenon would not cease until the entire surface of the globe had been covered, until seas, mountains, underground railways and deserts had been completely clogged up by the endless copies emerging from the betwitched printing press, with the exception, as Melquidades the gypsy told us, of a single northern country called Britain whose inhabitants had long ago become immune to the book disease, no matter how virulent the strain. . . .
>
> —Salman Rushdie, "Angel Gabriel," 1982 review of Gabriel García Márquez's *Chronicle of a Death Foretold*

The opening scene introduces all the major themes of the book, as well as symbols that will be unpacked or created throughout. It is one of four hijacking scenes that tease with historical allusions, but primarily serve to introduce the lead characters, Gibreel Farishta ("Angel Gabriel") and Saladin Chamcha, as psychological studies of the South Asian Muslim immigrant, and obviously as both Salman Rushdie (the Gibreel, gibbering movie reel, writer like Angel Gabriel Márquez, a schizoid personality going crazy by insisting on maintaining the continuity of his selfhood; and the Chamcha, England besotted, alien with an Oxbridge accent, thoroughly composed of discontinuous parts). Air India Flight 420 (reference to the popular film "Mr. 420"),[24] a jumbo jet named "Bostan" (a name of one of the four gardens of Paradise), is blown up by Sikh terrorists led by a Canadian-accented woman (shades of the Air India flight blown up from Canada en route to England by Sikh terrorists in revenge for the Indian government's 1984 Operation Bluestar invasion of the Golden Temple in Amritsar and killing of separatist Sikh leader Sant Jarnail Singh Bhindranwale). The two main characters, the only survivors, float down to earth, Chamcha head-first like a new born in three-piece suit and bowler hat, singing Christmas carols and "Rule Britannia," while Gibreel Farista holds himself perversely upright, singing funny songs, pitting levity against gravity. The jumbo jet is "a seed pod giving up its spores, an egg yielding its mysteries," a space of mutation; "mutation? Yessir, but not random . . . made possible by the century . . . made the century possible," a metamorphosing descent from Everest (mystical peak) of catastrophe, "down and along the hole that went to Wonderland," "debris of the soul, broken memories, sloughed off selves, severed mother-tongues, violated privacies, untranslatable jokes, extinguished futures, lost loves, forgotten meanings of hollow booming words *land, belonging, home.*" The fall from Paradise, as Daniel Defoe put it in his *History of the Devil,* which serves as Rushdie's epigram, turned fallen angel (and man) into a vagabond without fixed place. The issue for the twentieth century and the theme of the book is "how does newness come into the world? How does it survive, extreme and dangerous as it is? What compromises, what deals, what betrayals of its secret nature must it make to stave off the wrecking crew, the exterminating angel, the guillotine?" "Just two brown men, falling hard, nothing so new about that . . . those bastards down there won't know what hit them." The explosion occurs above the city named "Mahogonny, Babylon, Alphaville, London"; it is a watery reincarnation into the "English sleeve" (the Channel). As the two lead characters somersault down, a spectral figure of Rekka Merchant on her flying carpet curses Gibreel with the name Al-Lat, the ice-woman.

Some symbols: Everest (like Sinai and Mt. Qāf); the ice-woman (fair-skin, the English beloveds of the Indian men, Alleluia Cone and Pamela

Lovelace), Al-Lat the female rival of Allah from the Qur'anic story of attempts to repress the idols of Mecca; Mecca the city of sand, terrified of water.

If the opening scene introduces the problems of newness come into the world, the other three hijacking scenes introduce the themes of dreams and reality patterned after the movies, repetitions and displacements (mechanical, structural, and psychological), *déjà vu* simulacra, nightmare, and real unreality. The scene that completes the opening section of the book is constructed around the hijackers with the plane on the ground at the Zamzam (the well at Mecca) oasis, the young Sikh terrorists strutting at the doorway, playing to the satellite television newscast just the way they have seen it done on television; and the beautiful Canadian-accented woman terrorist with grenades and dynamite sticks stuck between her thighs and breasts, who means business. It is a nightmare. For Chamcha it is a *déjà vu:* he had already dreamt of the woman terrorist, Tavleen, and her Canadian accent (who terrorizes who, West the East, or East the West?); and it is a repetition ("what did they want, nothing new . . . ," "if you live in the twentieth century, you don't find it hard to see yourself in those more desperate who seek to shape it to their will," "the three men hijackers were too narcissistic to want blood, they were here to be on tv"). For Gibreel desperate to fight off sleep and his ongoing nightmare of being the archangel (it always picks up where it left off like a video, as if it is real and we are the dream), it is a time to joke about reincarnation, as if the hijacking were a second gestation creating fifty siblings born at once (like midnight's children). There are historical details, metonymic reminders of the grimly comic absurdity of reality: Tavleen shoots Jalandari first, a Sikh who has cut his hair and given up his turban (violence is sharpest against the traitors); Chamcha is afflicted with a seatmate who is an American creationist scientist who has been out to convert India. Finally, Tavleen orders them to take off, and over Europe she pulls the pin, thereby opening the stories within the frame story.

Two intermediate scenes explore the interiority of the two main characters: there's the scene inside the plane, on the way from Bombay, just before the hijacking occurs, where Chamcha is asleep, is wakened by the stewardess, and finds his English mask has slipped and the Indian-English lilt and syntax of his youth squeak out embarrassing him. And there is the scene that explains the origins of Gibreel's guilt-driven nightmare that is the source of the Muslim thematics of the novel. Chamcha and Gibreel are a pair: the one an illusionist on the Bombay film stage who has lost his faith, and has eaten pork, for which guilt he is afflicted by never-ending nightmares; the other, a would-be Englishman who pursues that other twentieth-century career, doing voice-overs for radio commercials but never showing his dark face on television, imitating both humans and commodities. Both are twice born, and go through hospital transformations:

> "To be born again," Gibreel Farishta said to Saladin Chamcha much later, "first you have to die. Me, I only half-expired, but I did it on two occasions, hospital and plane, so it adds up, it counts. And now, Spoono my friend, here I stand before you in Proper London, Vilayet, regenerated, a new man with a new life. Spoono, is this not a bloody fine thing?

Gibreel the Bombay actor is effortlessly turned into a denizen of England, only having to cope with his own psychic crises; he loses his halitosis and gains a halo, the exotic celebrity. But Chamcha is transformed by the explosion into a devil-figure with foul breath, the perfect alien, and only after his hospitalization and recovery does he lose his horns and bad breath. At the very end, their positions reverse again: Gibreel the archangel dies, leaving England and Bombay to Chamcha. It is the fall metaphor come full circle (Adam and Satan both fall from heaven; in the modern world, man survives amid the "death of God"); the discontinuous self survives in a triumph of postmodernism, while the continuous self is destroyed by its religious megalomania that overwhelms it.

Gibreel is introduced first. He was born in Poona (long before it was Rajneesh's lair) as Ismail (the sacrifice) Najmuddin ("star of the faith"),[25] and was put to work as a tiffin runner in Bombay, that fantastic occupation in which millions of hot lunches from home are delivered to offices all over town. Here Gibreel learned the skill that would allow him to do eleven movies simultaneously (a true feature of Bombay filmmaking), remembering the roles by the complex codes of tiffin running. At age thirteen, he was orphaned (his father, also a tiffin runner, ran out of his skin, pushing himself in rivalry with his son for the love of their wife/mother; she was hit by a bus), and was adopted by an uncle who hoped that a child would divert his wife's obsessive babying and controlling him. This uncle taught him to think about reincarnation, which together with his mother's stories about the Prophet helped preprogram his later nightmares. He landed a job in the film industry with the film magnate D. W. Rama, and became a star in theologicals (playing Ganesh, Hanuman, Krishna, the Buddha) until one day mysteriously he began to hemorrhage. Even Indira Gandhi and her pilot son came to the hospital to pay their respects, figuring (with the logic of Indian politics) that "if God had unleashed such an act of retribution against his most celebrated incarnation, what did he have in store for the rest of the country?"). During his illness, Gibreel prayed to God, but nothing happened; he became angry, then empty with despair, then finally prayed that God not exist, at which point he began to miraculously recover. Released from the hospital, he rushed immediately to the Taj Hotel where he stuffed himself with English pork to prove the death of God ("pork sausages from Wiltshire and the cured York hams and the rashers of bacon from godknowswhere; with the gammon steaks of his unbelief and the pig's trotters of secularism"), and there met and had an orgiastic three-day affair with a woman mountain climber of near white hair, and skin translucent as mountain ice, Alleluia Cone. Then suddenly on his fortieth birthday, the star disappears, leaving behind only a note in his Everest Villa penthouse (on the exclusive Malabar Hill), which he had decorated in the motif of a bedouin tent by a French designer recommended by the shah after he had done such a good job at Persepolis. (The allusion is to the 2500-year celebration of continuous monarchy that the shah had catered from Paris in 1971, much to the outrage of his subjects.) The note encourages his downstairs neighbor to jump out of the window with her children: her spirit floating on a carpet survives to curse him as he floats down from the hijacked plane. He had been en route to find his love, Alleluia Cone.

Meanwhile, the same fifteen years that Gibreel had spent in the Bombay movie industry, Saladin Chamcha had spent in England. (Like Saleem and Shiva in *Midnight's Children,* they are metaphorical changelings: one rich, one poor, one more Hinduized, one Muslim, one too refined, one too plebian.) Saladin too is given a childhood psychology: son of a fertilizer manufacturer ("empire of dung"), a fierce and stern (Changez Chamchawalla) disciple of Chanakaya, the monk who taught that one should practice carrying water through a crowd to learn to live in the world without being part of it. When the boy finds a wallet of money, the father takes it away; years later the father takes the son to London, returns the wallet and makes him spend the money on their food and logding, while the father sits in the hotel room fasting. At one point the lad is embarrassed carrying fast food chicken stuffed in his shirt up the elevator. Rage at his father would turn him into a secular man (p. 43). The father leaves, and the son enters a boarding school where he is presented with a kipper for breakfast, the archetype of painful learning of the immigrant. No one is willing to show him how to eat it, but he is not allowed to leave until he finishes it; it takes ninety minutes of painful mouthfuls of tiny bones. ("The eaten kipper was his first victory, the first step in his conquest of England. William the Conquerer, it is said, began by eating a mouthful of English sand" [p. 44].) On his first return home, his mother chokes to death on fishbones during the Indo-Pakistan war: while everyone else cowered under the table during the airraid, she stood in her newsprint sari munching on party food "to show that Hindus-Muslims can love as well as hate" (p. 46). Archetypically, the father remarries a woman with the same name, and father and son quarrel. The novel takes place as Saladin returns home once more to try to make some sort of peace with his father ("what Saladin had come to India for: forgiveness. But whether to give or receive, he wasn't able to say"), but the visit goes badly, and he accuses Indians of a lack of moral refinement, incapable of a sense of tragedy, using an Indian version of a Sartre parable to display differences in moral attitude.

He also visits an old friend, Zeeny Vakil, with whom he goes to bed within forty-eight hours of returning to India, but faints even before making love "because the messages reaching his brain were in such serious disagreement" (p. 51). She's an M.D. (works with the homeless, and went to Bhopal the "moment the news broke of the invisible American cloud that ate people's eyes and lungs," [p. 52]) and art critic (opposed to myths of authenticity, revels in the eclecticism of Indian culture), and tries to reclaim him for India, particularly after he tells her about his life as an unseen man of a thousand voices, and about his costar Mimi Mamoulian (the Jewish-Armenian). She takes him to heated political discussions, drives him around in a "beaten-up Hindustan, a car built for a servant culture, the back seat better upholstered than the front," and spouts tears the color and consistency of buffalo milk; as a teenager she had already boasted a Mary Quant hairstyle. Zeeny is "a siren tempting him back to his old self. But it was a dead self, a shadow, a ghost," (p. 58). Zeeny is posed as a contrast, one who revels in eclectic hybridism, while Chamcha has the dis-ease of wanting to be someone else, an Englishman. In the end he must return to England, and to his English wife, Pamela Lovelace.

City of Apparitions, Night of All Souls: The Cast

In a brilliantly titled, five-scene chapter, Rushdie portrays London as a landscape of psychological mutations. The title is "London" spelled out as in a nursery rhyme, letter by letter, "ell," "ow," "en," "dee," "ow," "en," so that it looks like "Halloween Divine" ("Elloween Deeowen"), a Holi world. Just in case one missed it the first time, a follow-up chapter is called, "A City Visible but Unseen." This pair of chapters presents the English wives/lovers of the two main characters not only as sirens of Indian males' desires, but as themselves tragicomic, mutant, changelings just like the two lead characters: Rushdie's point about Asian immigrants laying claim to a history of Huguenot, Jewish, Irish, and other immigrant/minority experiences is richly redeemed. Other characters are added to the cast who also help make the point that, psychologically, everyone is wrapped up in dreams of being other/elsewhere. The most surreal of these is eighty-eight-year-old Rosa Diamond, widow of an Argentinian, near whose house Chamcha and Gibreel land: she is the figure of the elusive "real England," the philosopher's stone, the mystical "rose stone" (of *Grimus,* Rushdie's first novel), not only herself lost in reveries of the past, but imposing these reveries on others. First of all, she sees the two figures floating down and immediately becomes the vehicle of Rushdie's conceit, iterated in several places, that this is another invasion like that of William the Conqueror, except that "whereas the Norman fleet came sailing openly, these shades were sneaky"; imagining hordes of them, she yells at them to come out into the police floodlights. Second, she frequently slips into reveries to her life in Argentina and the violent honor feuds of that colonial society, reveries which imprison and involve Gibreel so that he viscerally feels the pain of the dagger thrusts of the duel in her memory ("violent pain in his navel, a pulling pain"). Third, and most important, Rosa Diamond is a colonial analogue to the primary dream-imprisoning of Gibreel by Islam: "He was being held prisoner and manipulated by the force of Rosa's will just as the Angel Gibreel was obligated to speak by the need of Mahound."

Pamela Lovelace is Saladin Chamcha's English wife, a "voice composed of tweeds, headscarves, summer pudding, hockey-sticks, thatched houses, saddle soap, house-parties, nuns, family pews, and large dogs." She works on a community relations council, and in her social service and social radicalism tries to overrun all that her background represents for Saladin. They are thus opposites and theirs is "a marriage of crossed-purposes, each of them rushing towards the very thing from which the other was in flight." Saladin "was a real Saladin. A man with a holy land to conquer, his England" (p. 175), yet he too could dress up as "everybody's goddam cartoon of the mysteries of the East," "reeking of patchouli, wearing a white kurta," "no shame, he was ready to be anything they wanted to buy." Wanting love, he was the actor's actor: "In the theater everybody gets kissed and everybody is darling. The actor's life offers the simulacrum of love." Saladin needed someone to believe in his remaking himself as an Englishman; only after he had pursued Pamela for two years and married her did he discover that she had no self-confidence, and would periodically lock herself in the bedroom. Her parents "had committed suicide together when she had just begun to menstruate, over their heads in gambling debts, leaving her with the aristocratic bellow of a voice that marked her out as a golden girl . . . whereas in fact . . . she had no confidence at all" (p. 50).

Gibreel's English "significant other" is a similarly complicated mirror. Alleluia Cone is the daughter of a Polish Jewish émigré, wartime prison camp survivor, and art historian, who anglicized his name from Cohen, and tried to conform to an English gentry pattern. He would read no Polish literature, saying it had been polluted by history: "I am English now," he would say proudly in his thick East European accent. He would celebrate Christmas as an "English rite," but spoil it Scrooge fashion, pretending to be Chairman Mao who killed Father Xmas. When Alleluia was fourteen, and he over seventy, he committed suicide. (Shades of Primo Levi: "Why does a survivor of the camps live forty years and then complete the job?") She reacted by returning to "Cohen, the synagogue, Chanukka, and Bloom's": "no more imitation of life." She becomes a mountain climber (Cone), scaler of Mt. Everest, and subsequently appears in ads for outdoor products. Why did she climb Everest? "To escape from good and evil," she says in Nietzschean fashion. She has a sister, equally traumatized by their father's death but in different ways. Their mother assimilates Gibreel's mutterings while he is asleep to dybuks (demons of East European Jewish folklore). And the identification of immigrants is made complete by a vendor saying to Alleluia that after twenty-three years (the span of the Prophet's mission) he was being driven out by "Pakis," and Alleluia has a bizarre vision of elephants (pachys), hordes of invading pachyderms: "What's a pachy?" she asks, and is told, "a brown Jew." To Gibreel, she is a vision of the ice-woman (climber of Everest, Alleluia Cone; ice-clear skin; frigid; visionary, secular sign of the supernatural).[26] They have a stormy relationship, in which he has jealous rages, and she throws him out.

Mimi Mamoulian, the Jewish-Armenian actress, is Saladin Chamcha's female complement on "The Alien's Show": she too has a thousand voices, with a face not to be shown. Eventually she takes up with Billy Battuta, playboy Pakistani, who with the stuttering producer Sisodia (Whisky and Soda), wants to produce Hindi films in England and have stars like Gibreel cavort at Bradford Town Hall. Batutta engages in various business schemes (Batutta's Travels, named after the fourteenth-century world traveller, Ibn Batutta, is transformed into a supertanker fleet), of which the wildest scam is the day he takes Mimi to a New York furrier and picks out an expensive mink coat for her. It is Friday afternoon, and he asks if they will take a $40,000 check. They do. He goes next door and sells the coat for $30,000 cash. The second store tells the first, which calls the police and Billy is arrested for passing a bad check. Monday morning when the banks open, it turns out he has enough to cover the check in the bank, and threatens to sue the store for millions for false arrest and damage to his reputation; they settle for $250,000. When Saladin tries to warn Mimi about Billy, she retorts:

> I'm an intelligent female. I have read *Finnegans Wake,* and am conversant with postmodernist critiques of the West. . . . And as an intelligent woman, able to do fifteen minutes on Stoicism and more on Japanese cinema. . . . I am fully aware of Billy boy's reputation. Don't teach me about exploitation.

City of Apparitions, Night of All Souls: The Plot

The story line is built around immigrants being treated as mutants. While Gibreel is co-opted into Rosa Diamond's nostalgia, a bit actor in the colonial past, a benign entertainer (she dresses him in jodhpurs and smoking jacket), Chamcha, the would-be Englishman, turns into/is treated as a goat-devil and is hauled off in a paddy wagon, ending up in a hospital full of similar mutants. The paddy wagon and hospital scenes together with the later Club Hot Wax and riot scene in the East End of London, the home of generations of immigrants/mutants, provide the comic heart of the novel: both British xenophobia and immigrant insecurity are wildly parodied. The mutations are inextricably externally and internally generated.

In the paddy wagon, Saladin grows hooves, horns, and a huge phallus, he develops bad breath, and defecates small pellets. The police beat him and make him eat the pellets. "What puzzled Chamcha was . . . that his metamorphosis . . . was being treated . . . as if . . . banal." The beating is such that he ends up in the hospital, where the wards are full of transforms: a manticore (tiger head with three rows of teeth), a woman water buffalo, Nigerian businessmen with tails, Senegalese holiday makers turned into serpents, Glass Bertha with a skin of glass, partial plants and insects. Saladin learns that some of the inmates are planning to break out, and they want him to join them: "The point is . . . some of us aren't going to stand for it. We're going to break out of here before they turn us into anything worse. . . ." "But how do they do it? Chamcha wanted to know. They describe us . . . and we succumb to the pictures they construct" (p. 168). The inmates break out and Saladin tries to go home, where his erstwhile best friend, Jamshid "Jumpy Joshi," is in bed with Pamela. Terrified by the vision of the goat, they run back upstairs, Pamela wailing, "It isn't true, my husband exploded. No survivors . . . beastly dead." Saladin had tried to telephone earlier, having a flash of an English story about a man thought dead who when he returns to find his wife remarried, takes a toy as a remembrance and leaves; and the Indian version of the story in which it is his best friend who has married his wife and upon seeing this, the husband decides he too must have remarried, and leaves to search for his other wife.

Jumpy Joshi seeks help from Muhammad Sufyan, who runs a cafe nearby. How to turn Saladin back? They ruminate that once upon a time, in the case of metamorphosis into an ass (Lucius Apuleius) a kiss was required, "but old times for old fogies." Over the objections of Muhammad Sufyan's wife, Hind, who sees Saladin as the devil incarnate, they install Saladin in the attic of the cafe, gathering place for the locals of Brickall Street. Brickall Street itself is portrayed as a mythological battleground, the set for a modern Mahabharata, with epic battles between new Kurus and Pandavas. It is the scene of old battles between the Socialist Workers Party and the fascist National Front, but now there are fewer pitched battles, more vicious petty harassment under Thatcherism: skinhead whites who spit in the food of Asians; a Sikh ex-justice of the peace struck mute for seven years by a racial attack; an accountant who obsessively each night engages in a ritual of rearranging his sitting room furniture and pretending to be the conductor of a single-decker bus on its way to Bangladesh;[27] a black activist accused of being a serial murderer. Meanwhile word of the goat-devil in the attack begins to leak into the dreams of the locals. "They all dreamed him rising up in the street like the Apocalypse, burning the town like toast." A thousand and one dreams: "the non-colored dream of sulphurous enemy crushing their perfectly restored residences" while blacks and browns "found themselves cheering." Suddenly sweatshirts, posters, buttons, and rubber devil horns began to appear, and people wear them as marks of defiance.

Saladin's anger grows in the attic. At first he is angry at Sufyan's daughters, Mishal and Anahita, reacting against their kindness ("I'm not your kind, I've spent half my life trying to get away from you") and against their delight in the way people are taking up his cause in the streets ("Go away, this isn't what I wanted"). He calls Hal Vance, the creator of "The Aliens Show," and tries to get his job back ("I have a contract. . . . Don't be silly."), but is told that Prime Minister Margaret Thatcher, "Mrs. Torture . . . Maggie the Bitch . . . wants to invent a whole goddam new middle class, people without background, without history . . ." and there's no job for people like him. Seeing in the fanzine Cine Blitz (*Blitz* is a Bombay weekly) that Gibreel is making a movie comeback and will make films in London with Sisodia and Billy Batutta, Saladin becomes really angry, and this anger begins to shrink his horns. As Chamcha's anger grows, he emerges from the attic, eight feet tall, nostrils spewing yellow and black smoke, luminous red eyes, and a sizable erection. He is taken to the Club Hot Wax, where one dances amid wax figures of migrants of the past (Mary Secole, a black Florence Nightingale; Abdul Karim, munshi to Queen Victoria; an African Prince; etc.), and where during the evening a villain (Mosely, Powell, avatars of Simon Legree) are melted in a microwave to the chant of "Meltdown, burn, burn, burn." Chamcha wreaks havoc thinking of Gibreel, then is put to sleep. In the morning his spent anger has turned him back into his human form.

The denouement of the Elloween Deeoween chapters is called "The Angel Azreel," Azreel the exterminating angel. It is composed of three short scenes. Chamcha awakes in the Club Hot Wax transformed back into his former self, he returns to Pamela but realizes he is no longer in love, and moves into the lower rooms of the house, leaving the upper rooms to Pamela and Jumpy Joshi. He watches the parade of mutants on television, and goes to a meeting in defense of Dr. Uhuru Simba, the black activist accused of being a serial murderer. In the second scene, Battuta and Sisodia throw a party at the Shepperton Film Studio: the decor is a grand set of Dickens's London. Chamcha attends and sees his beloved London at the feet of his rival, Gibreel. Gibreel meanwhile is truly unstable, taking drugs to suppress his paranoid schizophrenia. During the party he goes manic, declaiming, "Prepare for the vengeance of the Lord, for I shall soon summon my lieutenant, Azreel." Gibreel and Alleluia take Chamcha to their country house in Scotland, but their differences become more obvious. They play the game of their ten favorite movies: Chamcha quotes Nabokov and lists ten cosmopolitan movies; Gibreel likes low-brow Indian films. They part, and while drunk whites harass Asians in Sufyan's cafe, Chamcha drives Gibreel wild with anonymous phone calls about his wife. Gibreel buys the trumpet Azreel from John Maslama, a looney Guyanian who claims to be a follower of Emperor Akbar's universalistic religion and who recognizes Gibreel as the Messiah.[28] In the third scene, after the death of Dr. Uhuru Simba in police custody, the serial murders start up again, generating attacks on blacks until Sikh youths catch a white Englishman perpetrating one of the murders. This then triggers riots and the unleashing of the cops and the television cameras which convey the scene unfavorably toward the Asians. Gibreel becomes an Azreel figure blowing away pimps of teenage prostitutes who bear the names of the wives of the Prophet; blowing away council housing, burning the Sufyan cafe and the Brickall community relations building. In the mayhem, Pamela and Jumpy Joshi die.

The riot scene, tragic and apocalyptic, echoes the riots of *Sammy and Rosie Get Laid,* Hanif Kureishi's film about Pakistani immigrants in third world Britain. But Rushdie's scene following out the mythic world of Brickall's Mahabharata, and the great devil scene of Saladin coming down from the attic, eight feet tall, spewing smoke from his nostrils, transforms the world into archetypes worthy of a Spielberg extravaganza.

Theological Flashbacks

Although much of the four interstitial chapters of Gibreel's nightmare of being the Archangel has already been discussed above under "Qur'anic Sources and A-maze-ments," a few comments may be in order here in the context of the novel itself.

Rushdie begins with the basic moral question of Islamic philosophy: what is the role of man? One of the central myths of Islam is the story of why Satan was thrown out of heaven: Satan refused to bow to Adam because he styled himself a strict monotheist. He was thrown out of heaven for his pride and his fanatical literalism. Muslims like to point out that human beings are superior to angels both because angels have no passion, so there is no moral struggle to overcome desire, and because angels being pure reason possess little doubt, so again no moral struggle nor achievement is possible. The human foibles of pride and arrogance in one's own reason are often spoken of as *shaiṭān,* and little boys who possess these foibles in abundance are often tolerantly called *shaiṭāni,* for their willful naughtiness. Rushdie thematizes this by having Gibreel see himself frequently as "Shaiṭān cast from the sky," and even Chamcha as a goat-devil. Gibreel's dreams often begin with falling: falling past his mother who calls him *shaiṭān* for having put Muslim meat compartments into Hindu non-veg tiffin carriers; falling as "shaitan cast from the sky" past his daughters, Lat, Manat, and Uzza, who laugh at the struggles that lie ahead for the Prophet (another role forced on Gibreel in the nightmare); and falling as that half-aware dream that one is asleep, that can lead to panic of not being in control ("Got bugs in the brain; full mad, a looney tune and a gone baboon"), a fear of being half mad that the Prophet himself must have occasionally worried about as he made his way up Mt. Ararat at age 44 (Mt. Cone in Rushdie; Gibreel is just past 40, too). Doubt is the human condition.

Rushdie does parody Islam, but much of this parody is a critique not foreign to fundamentalists like Khomeini. Both Khomeini and Rushdie make fun of ritual for ritual's sake, ablutions made endlessly: indeed this is the subject of rich humorous anecdotes by Muslims about themselves. In Rushdie's hands this subject becomes the image of Mecca as Jahilia (the term for pagan ignorance, and for the secular modern world in the lingo of fundamentalists), where water is the great enemy: "In the sand city, their obsession with water makes them freakish, ablutions, always ablutions. . . ." The image generates a series of elaborations (the watery reincarnation in the English Channel for the two brown men who fall from the egg-pod-airliner: England as maritime power versus Islam as a continental power; England as the secular West, Islam as the religious East). But water is also a purifying agent, and the lowly task of carrying water is honored in Rushdie's account in the figure of Khalid the water carrier, one of the Prophet's first converts. Water here represents the virtues of Islam against the ignorance of the pre-Islamic Mecca ruled by Abu Simbel and Hind. Abu Simbel (Egypt) and Hind (India) both became Islamicized but only Egypt fully so: India maintained its own strong Hindu traditions, just as Hind in Rushdie's fantasy city swears eternal enmity toward Mahound. Hind is also the name of the Brickall Street cafe owner, Muhammad Sufyan: she is the hard businesswoman, who has no sympathy for Saladin Chamcha's plight, seeing him as Satan incarnate, not just a fallible human *shaiṭān.* Is there replication here of the softer male, the Muslim, and the harder female, Hindu? Hind, moreover, in Rushdie's fable is the patron of the goddess Al-Lat, and while the primary story of Al-Lat is a purely Muslim one (and thus the only meaning that half-literate Muslims can see), a complementary meaning within the symbolic economy of Rushdie's novels is the goddess figure of India (think of Parvarti-Kali in *Midnight's Children,* as well as the creative-destructive sense of divinity, and also Saleen-Shiva and their parallels and crossings with Gibreel-Saladin). Rushdie makes one further jibe here which again is not out of step with Islamic tradition: he calls the Qureishi tribe, ruled by Abu Simbel and Hind (the tribe of Muhammad), the "Shark" tribe, punning on their being both shark businessmen and *shīrk* (heretics of the variety that allow God's divinity to be shared with other gods).

The story of Al-Lat's rivalry with Allah is richly worked out in Rushdie's fable: there is much more to it than reduction to the *gharānīq* story. First of all the beautiful swans of sūra 53:19–20 are changed by Rushdie into black apparition-like birds. Perhaps the white skin and hair of the female idols of desire connect with these images of Lat, Manat, and Uzza: Pamela Lovelace, Alleluia Cone, and Ayesha the prophetess of the Indian village are all so described; and all turn out to be false gods. But in any case, the story of Al-Lat is internal to Gibreel's nightmare that he is being forced to play the roles both of the archangel Gabriel and of the Prophet. Professional actor that he is, he thinks through the imagery in terms of camera shots. The scene imagining the aftermath of the first revelation (allowing compromise) is set on the last night of a masquerade carnival, the festival of Ibrahim. Abu Simbel recites Islamic prayers as if a convert, as had been agreed through the compromise formula; but behind the scenes his men are out to kill the Muslims. The assassins wear masks of manticores (scarlet lions with three rows of teeth, blue eyes, voices like a mix of trumpets and flutes, and nails like corkscrews – shades of the manticore Saladin finds in the hospital). The Muslims are worse than unprepared: Khalid the water carrier, Bilal (the black first muezzin), and Salman Farsi (the scribe) had gotten drunk in despair at the Prophet's compromise (this would have been before the revelations that completely forbade drinking), and it is only through the heroism of Hamza (uncle of the Prophet) that the manticores are routed: he kills two (both brothers of Hind), and two others run away. Meanwhile the Prophet wakes up in Hind's bed; she claims she had found him in the street drunk, but he slowly remembers fainting at the sight of his drunk disciples. They spar: "You are sand, I am water, water washes away sand." "The desert soaks up water."

In a brief interlude, Gibreel manages to rouse himself from this distressing dream ("dreams cause all the problems, movies too") and fights off sleep, "but he's only human and falls down the rabbit hole and there he is in Wonderland again up the mountain and the businessman is waking"). Gibreel and the businessman-Prophet wrestle, but the latter forces the voice, the Voice, to pour over him, while jinn, afreet, and the three winged creatures (Lat, Uzza, and Manat) watch. The Prophet now returns to Mecca to expunge the foul verses. His disciples conclude that the episode was a didactic lesson: "You brought us the devil, yes that sounds like me." (Compare sūra 22:52–55.) The Muslims to save themselves now have to slip out of Mecca/Jahilia to save themselves from the revenge of Hind. But poor Gibreel cannot get away from Lat, Uzza, and Manat so easily; his dreams continue.

There is then the two-part chapter, "Ayesha": the interlude before the

Muslims return victorious (displaced to the interlude before Khomeini returns to Iran), and the results of blind faith in village India. The Imām in exile section (displaced from Paris to London) is done with the trenchant pen of a Daumier: "unsleeping, staring into the future," "exile is a dream of glorious return . . . vision of revolution, Elba not St. Helena . . . an endless paradox: looking forward by always looking back . . . frozen in time"; "enemy of images. When he moved in the pictures slid noiselessly from the walls"; "some representations are allowed to remain: conventional images of homeland (Desh, Urdu for one's rural homeland), and a portrait of the Empress Ayesha: they plot each other's deaths;" another picture of Empress Ayesha in the bedroom drinking blood; "the curtains are kept closed so that no foreigner can creep in"; "guards disguised as women in shrouds and silvery beaks stroll the Kensington Streets;" Bilal X (shades of Malcolm X), a convert and former singer, shacked up with a redhead who turned out to be a former lover of the SAVAK chief—one needs to be vigilant in this world; his son Khalid (Ahmad Khomeini) brings him glasses of water (Khalid the water carrier), water filtered by an American machine; he wrote a famous monograph on water (i.e., his *Risāla Towzīḥ al-Masā'il:* on all the rules of purity, and other duties). Bilal is at the radio transmitter, turning Western technology against itself, as he begins with the ritual abuse of the Empress (see above). Beyond Empress Ayesha-fahisha the enemy is history herself (female), history is an intoxicant (figure of desire), and after the revolution clocks will be banned. All this is deliciously funny, and it is striking that no Muslims seem to have been in the least perturbed by the vilification of Khomeini, despite the fact that Khomeini early in the revolution made it a crime to vilify him or the revolution.

Then there is the wonderful image of the flight of Khomeini back to Iran and the final course of the revolution in February 1979. It begins as a parody of Muhammad's night journey (*mi'rāj*) on Burāq, the mystical flying horse. The Imām conjures up Gibreel, orders him to fly him back to "Jerusalem," slings his beard over his shoulder, hoists up his skirts and climbs onto Gibreel's back. As they approach the city [of Tehran] they see on the palace on the slopes of the perfectly conical mountain (Mt. Cone), and below in the city, the avenues are filled with demonstrators. Guns shoot down the people, mothers urging their children on to be martyrs. The palace bursts like an egg and the winged apparition Al Lat breaks out of Ayesha's shell. The Imām forces Gibreel to fight her till she falls. The Imām then, grown monstrous, lies with his mouth open at the gates of the palace and the people march in. Victory of water over wine.

Gibreel's nightmare then turns to India, to Mishal, a village zamindar's wife praying for a child, and an epileptic girl, Ayesha, covered in butterflies. The butterflies are familiars of a holy saint, Bibiji, whose grave once cured the impotent. Ayesha sells dolls, but loses her touch; her hair turns white at age 19, her skin becomes luminous (the same happened to Pamela Lovelace and Alleluia Cone), and the Archangel came to her (she who lies with an archangel is lost to men) and told her that Mishal has cancer and they must walk to Mecca to kiss the black stone. The chapter "The Parting of the Arabian Sea" follows this sad procession, as people die, defect, are ravished by flood and other calamity. They arrive at the Arabian Sea and march in: the sea closes over them, a few turn back, and a few bodies are recovered and revived. The survivors all claim to have seen the sea part and the promise of miracle fulfilled.

The key chapter of the four is the "Return to Jahilia" (Mecca) after the hijra, for it contains the three intuitions about Salman Farsi wanting to believe, and testing the Prophet, only to have his belief shattered; about how the imposition of rules, rules, rules brings resistance and avoidance (black market in pork, secret praying to the old gods, mutterings about the special license the Prophet has to marry so many wives; and about the resentment that is psychologically vented in the brothel satire. The stories, as noted above, are all in the ḥadīth literature; what Rushdie has done is to turn them into powerful psychological figurations, realistic analogues for contemporary psychic pressures among those caught between fundamentalist religion and secular life "in the movies."

The final chapter of the book is a modern apocalyptic, and it is Chamcha who survives, not Gibreel, whose story has dominated throughout (note that the chapter headings are all devoted to Gibreel). Chamcha has returned to Bombay to see his dying father. Gibreel has made a series of films with Sisodia but they have not done well: "The Parting of the Arabian Sea" with Ayesha played by Pimple Billimoria, a film about Mahound, and the Ramayana redone with the old heroes as evil and the villain as hero. The last seemed like a deliberate provocation of the sectarians, done by Gibreel knowing it cannot succeed. (This, of course, is a comment on Rushdie himself, but is otherwise a slip: there is a Jain version of the Ramayana which does precisely this inversion.) In the end, Gibreel kills Sisodia, Alleluia, and himself. Chamcha is left saying: let the bulldozers come, if the old refused to die, the new could not be born. It is the fall come full circle: the archangel Satan and Adam both are thrown out of Paradise: only Adam survives in today's world of the death of God, placing on man the full responsibility for (moral) creation. It is Nietzschean modernism restated in Muslim idiom.

Perhaps a stronger ending might be found, stuff for another novel, in which maybe a Zeeny Vakil–like figure in the West might star, not as a chamcha, but as a multicultural pioneer, with other issues than repression and resentment, with movies and the media thematized not just as dreams and displacements and fantasy work, but as creative/positive political forces (Max Headroom style?). But as a first portrayal of Muslim immigrants in Britain, this novel blazes a far distance.

Literature to Think With

> The novel is the privileged arena where languages in conflict can meet, bringing together in tension and dialogue, not only opposing characters, but also different historical ages, social levels, civilization and other dawning realities of human life.
>
> –Carlos Fuentes, *Guardian,* 24 February 1989

> So where do we turn, we who see the limits of liberalism and fear the absolutist demands of fundamentalism? This is ironically the central problem in *The Satanic Verses*. . . . *The Satanic Verses* is a postcolonial work that attempts the onerous duty of unravelling this cultural translation.
>
> –Homi Bhaba, *New Statesman,* 3 March 1989

Rushdie's work performs six critical functions:

(1) It attempts to block racist and narrative stereotypes, first by providing a powerful sense of the vital, humor-filled, anxious, creative imagination and interiority of several classes of ex-colonials and immigrants ("I must say I'm very taken with the idea of being a Mughal. It lends a certain tone. And it permits me to think of myself in Britain not merely as a first generation immigrant, but as a fellow ex-imperialist"),[29] and thereby blocking stereotypes created from typifications, including the "suffering victim" frame imposed by "politically correct" liberals and radicals, or the uneducated frame (be it technologically inept or democratic values and respect for Western rules of the game) imposed by well-meaning conservatives or resentful reactionaries.

Postmodern literature, such as Rushdie's, breaks with a series of traditional tropes about the past, about the third world, and about nationalism. It first of all breaks with the tropes of nostalgia for past community, seeing both past and present as deeply conflict-ridden and ideologically outrageous. Such postmodern literature attempts to reconnect in Gestalt-switching ways the ruins of the past, contemporary politics and technologies, and the emergent interreligious, intercommunal, interideological world of cultural interreferences (interreferences, interferences). There can be a political edge to such projects:

> re-describing the world is the necessary first step towards changing it. And particularly at times when the state takes reality into its own hands and sets about distorting it, altering the past to fit its present needs, then the making of the alternative realities of art, including the novel of memory, becomes politicized.[30]

Although Muslim fundamentalists are necessarily unhappy with rejections of their project to see the world as an emergent Muslim oeconome, Rushdie's work is equally disruptive to the romantic views of Britain held by most Englishmen and Americans (". . . the British are deluded about themselves and their society. They still for the most part think it the fairest, most just, most decent society ever created").[31] Rushdie, Hanif Kureishi, Farokh Dhondy, the artist Rasheed Araeem, and others, have begun portraying the harsher undersides of Thatcherite England: racist, economically pressed, class-riven, and violent.[32] Rushdie, however, goes beyond Kureishi and Dhondy's accounts by transcending the working-class genres and tropes they have applied to the newly intercultural, immigrant world of the 1980s Britain. One of the central and most powerful scenes in *Satanic Verses* is the riot scene in the East End. It is continuous with not only the motivating scene for Rushdie's preceding novel, *Shame,*[33] but also with Kureishi's films, *My Beautiful Laundrette,* and *Sammy and Rosie Get Laid.* Yet, Rushdie lays claim, as does Bharati Mukherjee in America, to the wider literary tradition:

> Indian writers in England have access to a second tradition, quite apart from their own racial history. It is the cultural and political history of the phenomenon of migration, displacement, life in a minority group. We can quite legitimately claim, as our ancestors, the Huguenots, the Irish, the Jews; the past to which we belong is an English past, the history of immigrant Britain. Swift, Conrad, Marx are as much our literary forebears as Tagore or Ram Mohan Roy.[34]

This is worked into the texture of *Satanic Verses* not only in a general philosophical way, but through the women to whom Rushdie's characters are married or paired in work settings. In similar vein, Mukherjee dedicated her first collection of short stories on life in North America to the inspiration of Bernard Malamud.

(2) Revisioning history, alternative narrative perspectives. Rushdie's novels gaily pull apart nationalist pretentions, ideological veils, corrupt disciplinary institutions (the state, the police, the media, etc.) of both third and first world authority structures. The Congress Party state of Indira Gandhi especially under the Emergency Act of the 1970s, the Sindhi-Punjabi state of Pakistan under Zulfikar Ali Bhutto and General Zia-ul-Haq, Britain under Margaret Thatcher, and Islam under the shadow of Khomeini are all equally subjected to merciless attack. But the novels are all far richer than political attacks: they revision history in unforgettable ways. Rushdie's magisterial second novel, *Midnight's Children,* breaks with the Raj and Gandhian Independence struggle epic frames of most twentieth-century Indian, Anglo-Indian, and British writing about India. It does so by a stunning revaluation of the independence movement in which the latter is all but ignored (the narrative rushes from Amritsar 1919 to Agra 1942 without comment, observes one reader;[35] and it does not necessarily remember the key moments of the anticolonialist movement complains another),[36] displacing the law, order, and progress paeans of those heroic epic narratives by attending to the bungling, the comprador authoritarianism, and the unruly vitality underneath. The narrative considers the fate of the Indian generation born in 1949, seen through a magical network ("parliament") of those born at the midnight stroke of independence, each of whom have special powers. This generation has suffered rather than been liberated. The liberation trope is that of an older generation's story. The bungling/suffering, however, is not a dirge of pessimism;[37] the novel "teems" with possibilities of renewal and rebirth as well. A complementary narrative device, used again, more fully in the novel about Pakistan, is a linking of generational perspective with family history: history as sets of stories of rivalries and conflicts told by fallible narrators with their own axes to grind. The parallels here with Günter Grass and Gabriel García Márquez are obvious. In any case, how falsely civic-bookish do standard histories of India and Pakistan seem by comparison, and how flat and unreal most sociologies of Britain.

(3) Decolonizing the English language, expanding its richness and flexibility, infusing it with new rhythms, new histories, new angles:

> The British . . . also left us this dominion of spoons. And the English language . . . is tainted by history as a result. Something of the unwashed odour of the chamcha lingers around its cadences. The language, like

> much else in the newly independent societies, needs to be decolonized, remade in other images if those of us who use it from positions outside Anglo-Saxon culture are to be more than artistic Uncle Toms.[38]

One may say that James Joyce began this task and did it in *Finnegans Wake* more richly, and certainly more intensively. But Joyce is unreadable except to the few, whereas Rushdie is available to a wider audience, and in any case Rushdie more centrally involves the mid- and late-twentieth-century Subcontinent and Muslim worlds, both of which are spilling their populations into the West, as Ireland and the margins of Europe did a century earlier. How static, sanitized, and unrealistic seem most science fiction projections of future society by comparison! As Rushdie points out, he is heir to a tradition of such play with Indian English beginning with G. V. Desani's *All About H. Hatterr,* which turned babu English against itself, and Raja Rao's experiments with the rhythms and movement of both vernacular and Sanskrit linguistic patterns.[39] And, of course, such play is nowadays no longer limited to the English from the Subcontinent: Africa, the Caribbean, and elsewhere are also contributing their resources.

(4) Expanding cosmopolitan sensibilities. An interesting undercurrent thematic in Rushdie's work is a redemption of a cosmopolitan Persian sensibility ("I must say I'm very taken with the idea of being a Mughal"), against both political or Arabicized ("pure") Islam and against European cultural colonialism. This is most explicit in *Grimus* and in *Satanic Verses.* In the latter, there is the identification (which Rushdie has acknowledged in interviews) of Salman Rushdie and Salman Farsi, the Persian scribe to the Prophet, who according to Persian nationalist satirical accounts was the behind-the-scenes author of the Qur'an for the illiterate Arab Prophet. In *Grimus,* the Persian stratum is even more central: "Grimus" is an anagram of "simurg," the mystical bird of Persian legend. The novel, although ostensibly about a vision quest of an American Indian (a play on Columbus' quest and displacement of "Indian" onto the Americas),[40] is built around Attar's mystical poem, *The Conference of the Birds* as well as images from Firdausi's *Shahnameh.* It is an inverted Dantean journey (or Prophet's *mi'rāj*) from Phoenix (a simurg-like bird), Arizona, to the Mediterranean (betwixt New World and Old, primitive and archaic, Occident and Orient), and there up an island-mountain purgatory of cosmopolitanism (Calf Island, i.e., both golden calf idolatry, and Mt. Qaf of the Qur'an, the sūra about Judgment Day), guided by an English pedant named *Virgil* Jones. The ascent to the peak is to find wisdom, Grimus, the Simurg, like the thirty

birds of Attar who eventually find out that they are the *si-murg* ("thirty birds"); compare Firdausi's line, "There is no lack of knowledge, but then it is dispersed amongst all the folk." (In Firdausi, the simurg is the mystical protector of the House of Zal and Rustam, the champions who protect the integrity of the Iranian empire.)

Midnight's Children is an encyclopedic novel, like *Finnegans Wake* or *Gravity's Rainbow,* and it too opens up cosmopolitan vistas for Indian civilization. Contained within it, as Timothy Brennan deftly points out, is a deliberate presentation of a whole literary tradition to an English-speaking readership – Vedic, Puranic, epic, television, cinema, oral storytelling, and various stages of the Anglo-Indian novel – as well as a critique of all these by parodying their misuses. There are ironic references to Raj genre writing – especially to E. M. Forster's *A Passage to India* and Paul Scott's *Jewel in the Crown* – as well as a metacommentary by the narrator on both Indian and modernist Western fictional techniques, thereby critically drawing attention to the imperial relationships that implicate them both, including worries by the narrator about the effects of his own fabulations. There are hilarious versions of historical events seen from askew points of view not unlike Günter Grass's technique in *The Tin Drum;* multiple Indian-English dialects, including the Anglo-English literalist translations of Indian language idioms, the interpolations of Urdu and Hindi, the altered spellings of Indian-English, and language as a word game drawing attention to the polyvocal linguistic strata of English as a world language drawing on multiple horizons of usage; a "teeming" of stories in the loosely connected thousand-and-one nights manner; a "postmodern" news media style of desensitized accounts of catastrophe, war, and violence; and above all, as mentioned above, a revaluation of the independence movement from heroic to bungling tones, thematizing as central the domestic collaborator, the *chamcha.* The chamcha is not only a major figure in Rushdie's novels, but is also a stock figure of other third-world literatures as well.[41]

(5) The *chamcha.* If the Persian stratum, and cosmopolitanism more generally, are central themes, a complementary critical focus is the psychological and emotional dynamics of the *chamcha* not just as a toady or collaborator, but as a range of intercultural types. As it is put prophetically in the *Satanic Verses:*

> A man who sets out to make himself up is taking on the Creator's role, according to one way of seeing things; he's unnatural, a blasphemer, an abomination of abominations. From another angle, you could see pathos in him, heroism in his struggle, in his willingness to risk: not all mutants

survive. Or, consider him sociopolitically: most migrants learn, and can become disguises. (P. 49)

Saladin Chamcha, who falls from the airliner in bowler hat and three-piece suit, singing Christian hymns and "Rule Britannia," is the fervent would-be Englishman, sent for schooling to England, estranged from his homeland and family, and embarrassed when on the plane returning from Bombay, the stewardess wakes him and he finds his voice, face, and gestures slipping back into the cadences of Indian-English he had struggled so hard to overcome:

> "Accha, means what? . . . So, okay, bibi, big give one whiskysoda only." . . . He had come awake with a jolt. . . . How had the past bubbled up, in transmogrified vowels and vocab? What next? Would he take to putting coconut oil in his hair? Would he take to squeezing his nostrils between thumb and forefinger, blowing noisily and drawing forth a glutinous silver arc of muck? (p. 34).

His very name is an orgy of transformations: Saladin Chamcha, Salad Baba, Sallyspoon, Spoono, Spoono my old Chamch, Salahuddin, son of Changeez Chachawalla. His occupation is that of actor, the man of a thousand voices who on British radio can imitate any character, but is not allowed to show his face.

Gibreel Farishta, the movie star, who plays gods (the elephant-headed Ganesh, the monkey Hanuman, becoming a sex idol when he played Krishna), is also never himself, taking on roles and finding they control him, fearing the slippage of his masks into recurring nightmares of being an archangel and prophet, fearing himself going mad because of transgressions against Muslim taboos. As he falls from the aircraft, he struggles to stay upright and awake and not slip back into nightmare; he sings an impromptu ghazal, "To be born again, first you have to die . . . Hoji Hoji . . . first one needs to fly"; and then the hit song from "Mr. 420": "O my shoes are Japanese, these trousers English, if you please. On my head, red Russian hat; my heart's Indian for all that."

There are interesting chamcha figures in *Shame* and *Midnight's Children* as well. Omar Khayyam Shakil, for instance, is named after a poet known best through an English translation; he is an illegitimate child of an unknown father who may be English, raised by three mothers, educated with his grandfather's library purchased from an Englishman, where he learns to manipulate people from a European hypnosis manual. He is said to know no shame, nor comprehend the emotions of embarrassment, shyness, modesty, or having a proper place. That is, he represents a stratum of colonial society trained to be without conscience.[42]

In *Midnight's Children,* Saleem's uncle's half-Iranian wife is driven insane by the need to be a chamcha to forty-seven wives of the "number ones" (p. 467), Pakistani leaders whose fortunes were built on the miseries of fleeing Hindus during Partition. This passing detail is blown up to full frame in *Shame.* More centrally, narrator Saleem Sinai worries about his own culpability for events as the writer of fictions, comparing his storytelling to the Bombay talkies (illusions that become less coherent the closer to the screen you come), and treating his own tale skeptically as he hopes one should the lies and ideological propaganda of the state. As Brennan points out, evil lies less in the corrupted elite or the state than in the collaboration between the masses and chamchas, the interaction between the megalomania of leaders who confuse their persons with the nation and the gullible masses impatient with history lessons or skeptical questioning. Rushdie thematizes and metaphorizes these nationalist illusions as a problem of writing in an oral folklore form that at the same time is a literary novel form, with each character having a magical folkloric function as well as a novelistic character development function. Saleem Sinai recognizes that he himself has a class position, and that to write for all India, he needs the collaboration of plebian commentators such as Padma and Shiva. Padma is his servant/mistress, his "lotus" (born in slime, but able to reach for higher beauty), crude, gullible, uninterested in the "lessons of the past"; she and Saleem have a conflictual relationship, casting doubt on the reliability of the stories Saleem tells and the way he tells them or the effectiveness of the telling for persons like her. Shiva is a changeling with Saleem: Shiva grew up poor, Hindu, sexually potent, rough, and elemental, while Saleem grew up rich, Muslim, impotent, and sterile. Brennan provides a superb reading of how these figures work as unifying recursive transforms of the Indian myths of Ganesh, Shiva, Brahma, and Parvati, and of the world of Indian politics. Shiva is the figure of the potent, destructive, rough, and violent political leaders of India, Saleem the figure of the impotent intellectuals, the critics, with their creative dreamings. Both in their own ways can be *chamchas.*

(6) Finally, Rushdie thematizes the media of communication, writing, movies, and scripture. *Grimus* deals with myth, *Midnight's Children* with plebian forms written by a scribe in the fashion of the Ramayana, *Shame* with oral stories told by elite women, and *Satanic Verses* with movies and the Qur'anic and ḥadīth literature as they reverberate through oral storytelling (of Gibreel's mother) and dream.

Satanic Verses takes the ḥadīth literature of Islam seriously, and by exposing to the outside world what normally is communal discourse challenges Muslims to develop a critical consciousness that can withstand scrutiny, or, better, that treats itself with good-humored humility. Ironically, compared to *Shame, Satanic Verses* is a much mellower book. It is a much richer, less parochial one as well. It does not parody the Qur'anic style, as Brennan for one thinks *Shame* does. But it too builds upon the repressed violence of guilt, shame, and humiliation – powerful emotions capable not merely of triggering riots in the East End, but also of death sentences against novelists.

The whole corpus of Rushdie's work gives rich food for thought for a large range of problems having to do both with the process of immigration – its strains, its class differences – and the problems of cultural transformation in milieux where intellectuals and people are often at odds, not just in their discourses but in the very media they use to express themselves.

Appendices
Notes
Glossary
Bibliography
Index

Appendix 1
Alternative Traditional Orderings of the Qur'an

IA	BQ	IS	BS	NK	SU	BZ	RY	HA	MU	GR	RL	BR
96	96	96	96	96	96	96	96	96	103	1	96	96
68	68	68	68	74	68	74	68	97	100	107	74	74
93	73	73	73	111	73	103	73	99	99	106	73	106
73	74	74	74	106	74	52	74	100	91	105	93	93
74	1	111	111	108	1	112	1	101	106	104	94	94
1	111	81	81	104	111	86	111	102	6	103	113	103
111	81	87	87	107	91	82	81	103	101	102	114	91
81	87	92	94	102	8	91	87	104	95	101	1	107
87	92	89	103	105	92	108	92	105	102	100	109	86
92	89	93	89	92	89	87	89	106	104	99	112	95
89	93	94	93	90	93	85	93	107	11	108	111	99
94	94	103	92	94	94	81	94	108	92	96	108	101
55	103	100	100	13	103	94	103	109	105	95	104	100
103	100	108	108	14	14	93	100	110	89	94	107	92
108	108	102	102	15	108	114	108	111	90	93	102	82
102	102	107	107	16	102	79	102	112	93	92	92	87
107	107	109	109	80	107	92	107	113	94	91	68	80
105	109	105	105	68	109	107	109	114	18	90	90	81
109	105	113	112	87	19	77	105	95	96	89	105	84
112	113	114	113	95	113	78	113	94	112	88	106	79
53	114	112	114	103	114	106	114	93	74	87	97	88
80	112	53	53	85	112	53	112	92	111	86	86	52
97	53	55	80	73	53	84	53	91	87	85	91	56
91	80	97	97	101	90	80	80	90	97	84	80	69
85	97	91	91	99	25	104	97	89	88	83	87	77
95	91	85	85	82	91	109	91	88	80	82	95	78
106	85	95	95	81	85	88	85	87	81	81	103	75
101	95	106	106	53	95	75	95	86	84	80	85	55
75	106	101	101	84	106	95	106	85	86	79	101	97
104	101	75	75	100	101	56	101	84	110	78	99	53
77	75	104	104	79	31	55	75	83	85	77	82	102
50	104	77	77	77	104	1	104	82	83	76	81	70
90	77	50	50	78	77	100	77	81	78	75	84	73
86	50	90	90	88	50	69	50	80	77	74	100	76
54	90	86	55	89	90	111	90	79	76	73	79	83
38	86	54	72	75	86	113	86	78	75	70	77	111
7	54	38	36	83	54	90	54	77	70	69	78	108
72	38	7	7	69	38	102	38	76	109	68	88	104

IA	BQ	IS	BS	NK	SU	BZ	RY	HA	MU	GR	RL	BR
36	7	72	25	51	7	105	7	75	107	113	89	90?
25	72	36	38	52	72	89	72	74	55	114	75	105
35	36	25	35	56	36	99	36	73	56	56	83	89
19	25	35	19	70	25	101	25	72	67	55	69	85
20	35	19	20	55	35	37	35	71	53	54	51	112
26	19	20	56	112	19	70	19	70	32	53	52	109
27	20	56	26	109	20	83	20	69	39	52	56	1
28	56	26	27	113	56	97	56	68	73	51	53	113
17	26	16	28	114	26	51	26	67	79	50	70	114
10	27	28	17	109	27	54	27	50	54	15	55	51
11	28	17	11	54	28	68	28	51	34	22	54	54
12	17	10	12	37	17	44	17	52	31	14	37	68
15	10	11	10	71	10	71	10	53	69	46	71	37
6	11	12	15	76	11	73	11	54	68	72	76	71
37	12	15	37	44	12	20	12	55	41	45	44	44
31	15	6	31	50	15	15	15	56	71	44	50	50
34	6	37	23	20	6	26	6	25	52	41	20	20
39	37	31	34	26	37	76	37	26	50	97	26	26
40	31	34	21	15	31	38	31	27	45	40	15	15
41	34	39	39	19	34	50	34	28	44	39	19	19
42	39	40	40	38	39	36	39	29	37	38	38	38
43	40	41	41	36	40	23	40	30	30	37	36	36
44	41	42	42	43	41	43	41	31	26	36	43	43
45	42	43	43	72	42	21	42	32	15	35	72	72
46	43	44	44	67	43	72	43	34	51	34	67	67
51	44	45	45	23	44	19	44	35	46	32	23	23
88	45	46	46	21	45	98	45	36	72	31	21	21
18	46	51	51	25	46	25	46	37	35	67	25	25
16	51	88	88	17	51	67	41	38	36	30	17	27
71	88	18	18	27	88	14	88	39	19	29	27	18
14	18	16	6	18	18	16	18	40	18	28	18	41
21	27	71	16	32	16	18	16	41	27	27	32	32
23	71	14	71	41	71	32	71	42	42	26	41	45
13	14	21	14	45	14	17	14	43	40	71	45	17
52	21	23	32	16	21	27	21	44	38	25	16	16
67	23	32	52	30	23	39	23	45	25	20	30	30
69	32	52	67	11	32	45	32	46	20	23	11	11
70	52	67	69	14	52	64	52	10	43	43	14	14
78	67	69	70	12	67	11	67	11	12	21	12	12
79	69	70	78	40	69	41	69	12	11	19	40	40
82	70	78	79	28	70	30	70	13	10	1	28	28
84	78	79	82	39	78	7	78	14	14	42	39	39

IA	BQ	IS	BS	NK	SU	BZ	RY	HA	MU	GR	RL	BR
30	79	82	84	29	79	6	79	15	6	18	29	29
29	82	84	30	31	92	29	82	16	64	17	31	31
83	84	30	29	42	94	34	84	17	28	16	42	42
2	30	29	83	10	30	10	30	18	23	13	10	10
8	29	83	54	34	29	12	29	19	22	12	34	34
3	83	2	86	35	93	28	83	20	21	11	35	35
59	2	8	2	7	2	40	2	21	17	10	7	7
33	8	3	8	46	8	31	8	23	16	7	46	46
24	3	33	33	6	3	42	3	6	13	6	6	6
60	33	60	3	13	33	2	33	7	29	98?	13	13
48	60	4	60	2	60	35	60	1	7	112	2	2
4	4	99	4	98	4	47	4	2	113	92?	98	98
99	99	57	99	64	99	8	99	3	114	2	64	64
22	57	47	57	94	57	61	57	4	2	62	62	62
57	47	13	47	8	47	46	47	5	47	5	8	8
47	13	55	13	47	13	62	13	98	57	47	47	47
76	55	76	76	3	55	3	55	57	8	8	3	3
65	76	65	65	61	76	63	76	58	58	24	61	61
98	65	98	98	57	93	22	65	59	65	59	57	57
62	98	59	59	4	98	59	98	60	98	3	4	4
32	59	110	110	65	59	57	59	61	62	4	65	65
63	24	24	24	59	24	33	24	62	59	57	59	59
58	22	22	22	33	103	4	22	63	24	64	33	33
49	63	63	63	63	63	13	63	64	63	61	63	63
66	58	58	58	24	58	24	58	65	48	60	24	24
64	49	49	49	58	49	48	49	66	61	58	58	58
61	66	66	66	22	66	65	66	47	4	65	22	22
5	64	61	62	48	64	49	64	48	3	33	48	48
9	61	62	64	66	61	9	61	49	5	63	66	66
110	62	64	61	60	62	110	62	24	33	49	60	60
56	48	48	48	110	48	58	48	33	60	110	110	110
100	5	9	5	49	5	60	5	22	66	48	49	49
113	9	5	9	46	9	66	113	8	49	66	9	9
114	110	?	?	47	110	5	110	9	9	9	5	5

Notes: The sūras of the Qur'an are listed here in the chronological order in which they were revealed, according to the traditional Muslim reconstructions and those of modern European and Middle Eastern scholars. See chapter 2, and especially note 12.

Headings from left to right are:

IA Ibn Abbas
BB Ibn Abbas via Biqā'i
IS Imām al Ṣādiq
BS Noman Bashīr
NK Noldeke
SU Suyūṭi
BZ Bāzargān
RY Rāmyār
HA Hashem Amir Ali
MU Sir William Muir
GR Grimme
RL Rodwell
BR Blachere

Appendix 2
The Ring, Octagon, or Eight Propositions of Political Wisdom

(1) The world is a garden the fence of which is the dynasty. (2) The dynasty is an authority through which life is given to proper behavior. (3) Proper behavior is a policy directed by the ruler. (4) The ruler is an institution supported by the soldiers. (5) The soldiers are helpers who are maintained by money. (6) Money is sustenance brought together by the subjects. (7) The subjects are servants who are protected by justice. (8) Justice is harmony and through it, the world persists. (1) The world is a garden. . . .

—The Pseudo-Aristotelian Politics [or *Sirr al-asrar, Secretum Secretorum*], cited by Ibn Khaldun [*Muqaddimah* 1:82][1]

Ancient Persian Variants

O King, the might of royal authority materializes only through the religious law . . . the religious law persists only through royal authority. Mighty royal authority is accomplished only through men. Men persist only with the help of property. The only way to property is through cultivation. The only way to cultivation is through justice. Justice is a balance set up among mankind. The Lord set it up and appointed an overseer for it, and that (overseer) is the ruler.

—Speech of the Mobeds [Zoroastrian priests] before Shah Bahram, cited by Ibn Khaldun [*Muqaddimah,* 1:80], from Mas'ūdi

[1]Franz Rosenthal, translator of the *Muqaddimah,* notes that Ibn Abī Uṣaybi'ah inscribed these eight sentences along the sides of an octagon, and that manuscripts of the *Muqaddimah* inscribed them in a circle. Serif Mardin shows Kinalizade's version in a circle. See also the lovely calligraphic version from a fifteenth century manuscript of the *Nasaylh-i Iskandar* reproduced on the opening page of the Smithsonian's catalogue of the exhibit *Timur and the Princely Vision* (Lentz and Lowry, 1989).

Royal authority exists through the army, the army through money, money through taxes, taxes through cultivation, cultivation through justice, justice through the improvement of officials, the improvement of officials through the forthrightness of wazirs, and the whole thing in the first place through the ruler's personal supervision of his subjects' condition and his ability to educate them. . . .

—Anushiravan [Shah Khosrow I, r.531–79 C.E.]
cited by Ibn Khaldun [*Muqaddimah,* 1:80],
from Masu'di

Medieval Persian Variants

Good government is secured by armed troops, armed troops are maintained with gold, gold is acquired through cultivation and cultivation sustained through payment of what is due to the peasantry, by just dealing and fairness: be just and equitable therefore.

—*The Qābūs Nāma by Kai Kavus Ibn Iskander, Prince of Gurgan,* translated and introduced by Ruben Levy, p. 213

The governor is a person endowed with divine support . . . in order to perfect individual men and to arrange (and bring about) the (general welfare). Philosophers call this person "king absolultely speaking" and call his ordinances, the art of government. The modern (philosophers) call him imam and his function the imamate. Plato calls him "world ruler" and Aristotle "statesman" . . . that is the man who watches over the affairs of the city state. . . .

—Tūsi, cited by Serif Mardin, *The Political Thought of the Young Turks,* p. 100

Turkish Variant

(1) Justice is the source of the salvation of the world. (2) The world is a vineyard, its walls the state. (3) The state is regulated by the seriat. (4) The seriat cannot take effect without the presence of land. (5) Land cannot be seized without soldiers. (6) Soldiers cannot be enlisted if there is no property. (7) Property is accumulated by the subjects. (8) The subjects pledge obedience (textually "are made slaves") to the world ruler whenever reigns justice. (1) Justice is the source of. . . .

—Kinalizade, cited by Serif Mardin, *The Political Thought of the Young Turks,* p. 100

Egyptian Nineteenth-Century Variant

> *Umma, waṭan, ḥukūma, 'adl, ẓulm, siyāsa, ḥurriyya, tarbiyya* (nation, homeland, government, justice, oppression, politics, liberty, education). (1) *Umma: jumlatun min an-nās tajma'uhum jami'a* (nation, community: a gathering assembly [of people, of coherent words in a sentence] brought together in some common bond). . . .
>
> —Husayn al-Marsafi, *Risalat al-Kilim al-Thaman* [Essay on eight words], cited by T. Mitchell, *Colonizing Egypt,* pp. 131, 142–43, 202

Appendix 3. The Imām's Blasphemystic Ghazal

Among the venerable traditions of satire and philosophical transgression of usual Islamic taboos are the traditions of Sufi and gnostic poetry. Khomeini dabbled in these traditions himself. When he died, his son Ahmad presented to the people of Iran one of Khomeini's poems as a memorial tribute. Originally dedicated and sent to a commander in the Iran-Iraq war as a token of special favor, this poem was reproduced with several others in fine calligraphy, and copies were sold to help raise money for the gold domed mausoleum constructed at Khomeini's grave. The poem attracted ephemeral interest among Western journalists impressed by the lines disdaining mosques and piety, and praising wine and love. The journalists understood neither the mystical symbolism nor that the poetry was a poor imitation of Hafez and other mystic poets, often awkwardly and inconsistently applying conventionalized imagery. Among Iranians, one reaction was to elicit a counter poem exposing Khomeini's amateurish use of this tradition, and objecting to his appropriation of the famous mystical cry of ecstatic union, *analhaq* ("I am the Truth") for which Husayn ibn Mansur al-Hallaj was executed by the clerical and political leadership of Baghdad in 309/922. The counter poem is immediately recognized by Iranians, without prompting, as a response to Khomeini, based on the same imagery turned against the first poet, the same meter, and the relation between the first person usages of the original poem and the third person of the response.

The counter poet also has pointed out some ironies in the very burial of Khomeini in the huge Behesht-e Zahra cemetery south of Tehran along with the fallen of the revolution and the Iran-Iraq war. Journalists had remarked on the temporary protective shields around the grave that gave it the appearance of the Ka'ba in Mecca. But the closer analogy, the counter poet has suggested, is the great shrine of the eighth Imām in Mashhad where the caliphs Ma'mun and Harun al-Rashid are buried along with their victims. The site originally intended as mausolea shrines of the two caliphs eventually became the great shrine of those they killed. Harun had the seventh Imām, Musa ibn Ja'far, killed, and Ma'mun ordered the death of the eighth Imām, Reza, whose shrine became the premier pilgrimage site of Iran. Pilgrims circle the graves chanting glory to Imām Reza, and curses upon Ma'mun and Harun ("*salam bar Hazrat-e Imām Reza, la'nat bar Harun, la'nat bar Ma'mun*"). Perhaps in the future, says this counter-poet, something similar will happen to the grave of Khomeini.

We present the two poems here as a reminder to those who would accept too quickly the charge that Rushdie blasphemed based on superficial readings of Rushdie and superficial knowledge of Islamic idioms of debate.

Khomeini:

Man be khāl-e labat ay dust greftār shodam	I've become possessed by the beauty spot above your lip, oh friend
Chashm-e bīmār-e torā dīdam o-bimār shodam	I saw your fevered eye, and fell ill
Fāregh az khod shodam o kus-e an-alhaq bezadam	Freed from my self, I beat the drum [with the refrain] "I am the Truth"
Hamcho Manṣūr kharīdār-e sar-e dār shodam	Like Mansur I thus bought myself the gallows
Gham-e deldār fekandast be jānam shararī	Sadness [caused by] the stealer of my heart set my soul on fire
Ke be jān āmadam o shohrah-e bāzār shodam	'Til I was overcome, and my fame spread through the bazaar
Dar-e maykhāneh goshā'īd be ruyam shab o rūz	Open the wine house door to me day and night
Ke man as masjed o az madrasa bizār shodam	For I am fed up with mosque and seminary
Jameh-e zohd o riyā kandam o bar tan kardam	I shed the garments of piety and pretention and put on
Kherqeh-e pīr-e kharābāti o hoshyār shodam	The darvish cloak of the Wine Master, and achieved consciousness
Vaeẓ-e shahr ke az pand-e khod āzāram dād	The city preacher's moralizing irritated me
Az dam-e rend-e mayaludeh madadkār shodam	I sought help from the breath of the wine besotted drunkard
Begozārid ke az botkadeh yādī bekonam	Permit me to recall the temple of idols
Man ke bā dast-e bot-e maykadeh bidār shodam	I was awakened by the hand of the idol of the wine house.

Note: The Sufi or gnostic ghazal operates on inversions of normal values, and is structured around images of initiation (being given a cloak by a master of wisdom, being allowed to put on the sacred girdle, the *zunnār* or *kusti,* achieving consciousness, detachment from preoccupation with one's self, and union with God) and images of love [of God] which since Persian has no grammatical gender may be heterosexual but often is also homosexual in imagery. Thus, typically the poet is pierced or burned by love through the sight of a small black spot, which might be as here a mole or beauty spot, or the arrow of an eyelash (*tir-e mozjan*), the bow of an eyebrow (*kaman-e abru*), the chain of a lock of hair (*zanjir-e zolf*), the pepper of a mole or beauty spot (*felfel-e khal;* pepper burns, one enjoys it but cannot stand too much of it), or the fevered/seductive eye. As one achieves spiritual consciousness one is given regalia of initiation by one's teacher: the darvish cloak (*kherqeh*), the sacred girdle (*zunnār, kusti,* originally the Zoroastrian sacred thread). Wine is the metaphor of intoxication by divine wisdom, and thus the breath of a master Sufi heals, gives life, as the breath of God gives life to human beings. Villain figures of this poetry are the preacher (*vā'ez;* who does not practice what he preaches), the *faqīh* (clerical jurisprudent, who is dry, inflexible, harsh, indifferent to human foibles or passions, and who is not deeply learned but only follows the external rules of the law), the pious ones (*zahid,* who usually are hypocrites, flaunting their piety and enforcing its rules on others, but under-standing nothing of the inner meaning and spirit of true religiosity), the police (*shahnah*) and guardians of morality (*mohtaseb*), and the *shaykh* (who usually works hand in hand with the police and guardians of morality). Good figures of this poetry include: the *kāfir* (the unbeliever, the one who challenges conventional belief); the chief Magi or Zoroastrian priest, *Pīr-e Moghān;* the *Mogh-bacce* or young disciples of this figure who seek wisdom/wine from him; the *Pīr-e Kharabat,* the great drunkard or elder of the Kharabat (the area of wine taverns in Shiraz at the time of Hafez); the beloved: *delbar* (heart stealer), *deldar* (heart possessor), *ma'shuq* (beloved), *yar* (friend), *ma'bud* (worshipped one), or *bot* (idol); and Mansur [al-Hallaj], the greatest figure executed on the charge of heresy. In Shi'ite Sufi poetry, Pīr-e Moghān or Pīr-e Kharabat is always understood to be Ali, the first Imām. (Note that the Zoroastrian resonances of the sacred girdle, and the chief Magi, are consistent with the Salman Farsi imagery in Rushdie's novel; and are also at issue in Muṭahhari's polemic [see chapter 3].)

The Counter Poem

Vāez-e shahr sūye khāneh-e khammār shodast	[If even] the city's preacher [the Āyatullāh] has headed to the wine-seller
Kār bar mohtaseb o shahnah ajab zār shodast	How difficult this makes the job of the guardians of morality and the police!
Che kamandīst sar-e zolf-e negāram ke dar ān	What a lasso is my beloved's hair that even
Zāhed-e sabheh bekaf nīz greftār shodast	The prayer bead carrying ascetic is ensnared!
Gu ke tasbih be khāk afkanad ar az sar-e ṣedq	Tell him to throw down his prayer beads if truthfully
Qātel-e moghbachegan tāleb-e zonnar shodast	This murderer of the young Magi wants to put on the sacred girdle
Shaykh-e paymāneh shekan towbeh -e dīrīn nashekast	The (wine) cup breaking shaykh has not broken his old repentance
Hazayan qūyad az an rūz ke bimār shodast	He talks in delirium since he fell sick
Hazayānash mashenow towbah-e gorgan mapazīr	Don't listen to his delirium, don't accept a wolf's recantation

Ke bedīn dām dosad galleh greftar shodast	For in this trap two hundred flocks [thousands] have fallen
Naqsh-e khod dīdeh behar āb o be nirangi now	He sees his own face in every liquid; and with a new trick
Tāleb-e ān qadah-e āyeneh kerdār shodast	That seeker wants to use the mirror cup [for his own ends]
Az pas-e rīkhtan-e khūn-e hazārān manṣūr	After shedding the blood of a thousand Mansurs
Khod be tazvīr kharīdār-e sar-e dār shodast	He deceptively pretends to claim his own place on the gallows
An setamgar ke lab-e sāghar o sāqī midūkht	The oppressor who sewed up the lips of bowl and wine drinker
Halia modda'i-ē khāl-e lab-e yār shodast	Now is claiming to love the mole on the upper lip of the beloved
Bazm-e mastan-e alastash nadahad rāh-e vorūd	The gay gathering of the drunkards of "Aren't I" won't let him in
Garche az masjed o az madraseh bīzār shodast	No matter how much he has come to despise mosque and seminary
Lāyeq-e ṣoḥbat-e rendān-e balākash nabovad	He is not worthy of the drunkards who hold suffering of the world on their shoulders
Ānke dar cheshm-e hameh ahl-e kherad khār shodast	He who is so despised in the eyes of all the fellows of wisdom

Note: Note the direct mimicking of Khomeini's lines, for instance: line 4 of Khomeini's poem and line 14 of the counter poem. The line about the wolf in couplet six draws on a Persian proverb, *towbeh-e gorg marg ast* (the repentance of a wolf is its death). The "Aren't I?" in the ninth couplet refers to the *ḥadīth qudsī* (ḥadīth from God) that at creation, God said, "Aren't I?" and creation responded, "Yes"; *mast-e alast* or *rendan-e alast* thus are those so intoxicated with the love of God that from creation, from the time of the atoms (*alam-e zarr*) uncomposed into creation, until the present, they have refused to worship anyone or anything but God. A *rend* is a drunkard or outlaw who by transgressing convention has truer insight.

Notes

Preface: Notes Toward Anthropology as Cultural Critique

1. Menocal (1987); see also Asin Palacios (1926/1968).
2. None of this is particularly novel to the authors, but for some examples of Persian and Arabic genres of expression, and the challenges they pose for the comparative method, see "Aestheticized Emotions and Critical Hermeneutics" (Fischer 1988).
3. See Harootunian (1988) and Pollack (1986).
4. For a parallel account of the mutual incomprehension between the discourse of the religious classes and that of the "enlightened" (*rowshan-fekr*) intelligentsia in the realm of stories and films, see M. Fischer (1984).
5. Buddhist is relevant both because Khorasan in northeastern Iran was an important borderland between the Buddhist and Islamic worlds, operating still in the imagination of such modern writers as Sadeq Hedayat, and because the more mystical interpretations of Islam and those of Buddhism are similar. Other comparisons are also relevant: Egyptian lore, for instance, is not only a reference point for some biblical stories (viz., the parodic Joyce epigram to chapter 3), but is also central to Greek mythology, for example, the double-entendre use of Theuth and Thamus by Plato in the *Phaedrus* (Griswold 1986:202ff.); and Greek thought in turn, of course, was a major interlocutor for Islam.
6. The pun is from Michel Serres' *L'Interférence.* Serres is a theorist who has explored in numerous areas terms that operate on dual or multiple registers. The term is put to work by Fischer (1986); see also Baumgarten (1982).
7. Firdausi, poet of the Iranian national epic, the *Shāhnāmeh,* uses a repetitive three-generation triad (grandfather-father-son) to structure the moral content of the epic (M. Fischer n.d.).
8. Sadeq Hedayat was Iran's premier modernist novella and short story writer. His masterpiece is *The Blind Owl,* a surrealist novella that blends together tropes and images from Europe, Iran, and India, and particularly plays upon notions as listed here (see M. Fischer 1984).
9. The terms used by Heidegger, as Sloterdijk (1987:195–96ff.) points out, are a "series of études in higher banality," "elevat[ing] the art of platitudes into the heights of the explicit concept." Nonetheless, many of the most eminent philosophers of contemporary Europe found that the poetic force of Heidegger's play with these terms reinvested the abstractions of philosophy with contemporary relevance. Among Heidegger's key terms are *Verfallenheit* (the Fall) into the givenness or "thrownness" (*Geworfenheit*) and caughtness (*Entschlossenheit,* a pun meaning both "being locked" or caught, having made a decision, hence "locked," and being freed from a lock and thus open to possibilities) in the Being (*Dasein*) of distractedness (*Zerstreutheit*). Being (*Dasein*) is defined in relation to truth: what is intelligible is what

is present (*Vorhandenheit, Anwesen*), what can be gathered or synchronized into a totality (the past through recollection, the future through projection), thus either a unified cosmology or an egocentric ecology (see Levinas, 1984). The danger, of course, as illustrated in Heidegger's own tainted career, is that the grounds for moral decisions can easily slide from the dilemmas of *Entschlossenheit* into being merely *dezisionistisch* ("decisionism," based on pure will). *Entschlossenheit* should refer to the dilemmas of the interchangeability of means and ends, or the unknowability of whether one is dealing with long or short chains of causation, and the need to evaluate both means and ends in context, a central problem of moral philosophy dealt with in the stories of the Qur'an (e.g., the Moses-Khizr story) as well as in other religious traditions.

10. Hans Blumenberg's phrase, *Arbeit am Mythos* (1979), translated as *Work on Myth* (1985).

11. See, for instance, the account of five generations of Islamic modernisms (Fischer 1982*b*), or the critical reevaluation of early Muslim writing by genre pioneered by Duri (1983), cited in chapter 2, as well as the efforts of three generations of European and American scholars such as Goldziher on *ḥadīth,* Wolfson on *kalām,* et al. But also within the Shi'ite seminary system, note that Ayatullah S. Husayn Borujerdi called for further codification and critical annotation of the ḥadīth literature collected in Shaykh al-Ḥurr al-'Āmili's *Wasā'il al-Shi'a.* 'Amili, as noted in chapter 2, separated correct *ḥadīth* from questionable ones. Further annotation was pursued by Borujerdi's students in *Tahdhīb al-Wasā'il.* Borujerdi himself constructed a table of generations of *rāwī*s (narrators of ḥadīth), counting himself among the thirty-sixth generation. This presumably could lead to a better appreciation of the development of the religious sciences, against the charge that the 'ulamā treated religion as totally ahistorical.

12. Blumenberg traces the long history of variants of the Prometheus myth, but focuses on Goethe's use of the metaphor of Prometheus as the world-transforming genius (Napoleon). Prometheus steals fire (enlightenment) from Zeus and is punished by being chained to the Caucasus mountains where he suffers the pain of an eagle eating his liver; with the fire, Prometheus teaches men the deceit of burnt sacrifice, keeping the cooked flesh to eat, delivering to the gods only the aroma. Zeus allows the deceit as a means of maintaining his own position: weakened but still in control. The image is of decay, each age being ended by a conflagration, and of rebirth: Napoleon too ends in defeat. Nietzsche is the last great poet to be taken with the Promethean master image. A later generation—that of Theodor Adorno and Max Horkheimer—will play with the notion of dialectic less mythically: enlightenment for them is the effort to disembed the individual from communal and cultural conventions, together with the impossibility of doing so. It is a Sisyphean or Promethean effort: the metaphor still holds, albeit in weakened, less mythic, form.

    Similar myths enthrall other civilizations. The Iranian myth of Zahāk, the demon with snakes growing out of his shoulders which demand to eat the brains of Iranian youth is an image invoked by Shari'ati at one point for the shah, and could equally well be used for the sacrifice of Iranian youth in the Iran-Iraq war. Zahāk, is finally chained to Mount Demavand, and will only break his chains for the final apocalyptic fight at the end of time.

In the Buddhist world, there is the dialectic of the encompassing, hierarchical, purifying role of the path of the Buddha, dharma, reason, called into action by the fragmenting, polluting, asocial demonic forces that has a somewhat similar structure (Kapferer 1988).

13. Charted by George Steiner (1984); see especially Hegel's use of the Antigone myth for exploring the conflict between local, familial ethics and universal ethics.
14. S. Sadraddin Sadr, father of Imām Musa Sadr (the "Vanished Imām" of Lebanon), and one of the three leaders of the Qum seminary center in the late 1930s, wrote a work entitled *Ta'sīs al-Shī'a li'ulūm al-Islām* (Shi'ites, the founders of Islamic thought).
15. In California, the English convert to Islam, Hamid Algar, was styled the "Imām of Berkeley," and pursued through his Mizan press a series of edited translations of Khomeini, Shari'ati, Taleqani, Muṭahhari, and others that tailored their works for Western sensibilities in the service of the Islamic Republic. The Iranian Foundation for the Oppressed (or Mostazafan Foundation) is said to have supported the publication of the Khomeini translations by prepurchasing ten thousand copies of the volume. Not quite so blatantly, but with similar, if slightly differently nuanced, partisanship and lack of scholarly candidness, the Houston-based "Book Distribution Center," run by close relatives of Ibrahim Yazdi, also has put out translations of Shari'ati, Muṭahhari, and others.
16. Viz. Freud's notion of deferred action (*Nachträglichkeit*) in which a primal scene is only activated and given meaning or psychic force through a later event.
17. See, for instance, the fairly devastating attack by Aijaz Ahmad (1987) on Fredric Jameson, and Jameson's meek reply. Note also the evolution of Jameson's views on "postmodernist" theories since his much cited 1984 *New Left Review* article.

1. Shi'ite Socialization in Pahlavi Iran: Autobiographical Sondages in a Postmodern World

1. For a relatively unique and picaresque autobiography of an ordinary mullā, see Fischer (1982*c*). This is not only a rare example of an autobiography from the non-Westernized, nonelite classes, but also an account much beloved by mullās, recommended to people who want to know what the life of a theological student and cleric is like.
2. On the history of pioneering irrigation systems in the valley hinterlands

of the urban oases of Iran's central plateau, see especially English (1966). On the Yazd area and its agrarian regime, see Fischer (1973, chapter 4, section 3). More generally on the agrarian regime, see Lambton (1953), Safinejad (1975), and Hooglund (1975).

3. See Moretti (1986).
4. On the periodic famines and agricultural poverty of this area, see Fischer (1973:121, 170, 179); for the nineteenth century, see Migeod (1956).
5. The tenth of the month of Muḥarram, anniversary of the martyrdom of the grandson of the Prophet, the third Imām, Husain, at Karbala. This martyrdom is the subject of the passion plays performed in the ḥusaynieh. For the story, and its centrality for Shi'ism, see Fischer (1980*a:*12–27). For its importance in mobilizing the revolution of 1977–79, see ibid., chapter 6 and the epilogue.
6. Compare the sevenfold circumambulation of the ḥajj in chapter 3.
7. The angels ask who is your prophet and what is your book; see chapter 5.
8. For a list of these floats and those of other villages, see Fischer (1980*a,* appendix 6). About *ta'ziyeh,* see Fischer (1973:306–10; 1980*a*:23, 133–34, 175–77); Chelkowski (1979); Lassy (1916); Pelly (1879); Riggio (1988).
9. On the quasi-systemic nature of such communal meals as charity and redistribution systems in both Zoroastrian and Muslim communities, see Fischer (1973:177–78).
10. On some copies, the couplet in Masnavi meter is inscribed: *masnavi-ye ma'navi-ye Mowlavi/Hast Qur'ān dar zabān-e Pahlavi* ("the spiritual verse of Mowlavi is the Qur'an in the Persian tongue").
11. The claim of a Jewish ancestor some five to seven generations back is not uncommon: the alternative pre-Islamic identity in this region would be Zoroastrian, somewhat more problematic since Muslims are ambivalent as to whether Zoroastrians count as "People of the Book."
12. Although suspected by Shi'ites of importing non-Islamic materials into the ḥadīth, for Sunnis he is an important figure. He was a major adviser to the Caliph 'Uthmān. Abu Dharr was sent into exile for hitting Ka'b al-Ahbar.
13. In Jewish *midrashim* as well as in Muslim lore.
14. Jews are identified in the Qur'an as the people of the wrath of God: see chapter 2.
15. Two ethnographic accounts of the Zoroastrian communities of Yazd in the 1960s and 1970s exist: Boyce (1977) and Fischer (1973).
16. On the legend of Bibi Shahrbānū, see Boyce (1967) and Fischer (1973:206ff.).
17. A famous story about the death of Shabdīz, the beloved horse of Khosrow Parviz, also illustrates the art of breaking bad news slowly. The king had vowed to kill anyone who brought him news of Shabdīz's death. One day the servant in charge of the stable found the horse dead. He reported to the shah that since the previous evening Shabdīz had not eaten. "Give him some water and call the vet." "He has already seen him. Shabdīz does not drink water either." "What else?" "He does not breathe." "Then he is dead!" "Your majesty said it, not I."

18. Compare the story "Moshkel goshā" (Dispel the difficulties), a women's work story and *sofreh* ritual that stresses the theme of generosity and its rewards (Fischer 1973:225–28).
19. The student is treated like a bride: tablecloth held over the head, nuts and sugar balls thrown over it into the air.
20. The word *yāsīn* is of unknown meaning. Professor Fereydun Badrehi (personal communication) suggests it might have been meant as a counter to *yasnā,* the Zoroastrian rite. Badrehi is a student of Sadegh Kia, who tried to find Pahlavi roots for many Arabic locutions. No such suggestions can be found in classical *tafsīrs*.
21. *Savād* is a term of recent usage, and it has also been suggested that it might derive from French *savoir, savant.*
22. What begins as a series of stereotype images—desert island, mermaid, Persian beauty with thick eyebrows meeting over the nose (reproduced on many miniature paintings and portraits of Qajar princesses)—takes on literary references: Sadeq Hedayat's *The Blind Owl* is a modernist masterpiece; *gharīb* has religious-philosophical overtones, being a term used for orphans and for the eighth Imām, Imām Ridā, called Imām-e Gharīb because he died in Khorasan far from home in Medina, and people therefore cry for his *ghurbat* (exile); *āvāreh* is a term for exile playwright and novelist Gholam Hosein Sa'edi contrasts with *muhājir:* the latter implies volition, like those who withdrew with Muhammad to Medina, while *āvāreh* implies force of circumstance and being caught in a purgatory not of one's own making.
23. On *mas'aleh-gū,* see Fischer and Abedi (1984).
24. A mosque built with money that is not *ḥalāl* (from legitimate sources) is not a fit place for prayer; prayers there are void. *Taṣarruf-e shar'ī* ("capturing by the law") is a procedure for purifying the premises: see Fischer and Abedi (1984).
25. Many people believed he had been blinded by the British in retaliation for *fatwās* he had issued against them.
26. The numerology of nineteen in the Qur'an has been explored at length by Shaykh Rashad Khalifa, the imām of the mosque in Tucson, Arizona. It is much discussed by Muslims except in Iran because of the sensitivity there that nineteen is a special number of Baha'i propaganda. Paknejad, for instance, said it was best not to give any publicity to Shaykh Khalifa's work. Khalifa's work has recently come under attack in the Islamic Republic. (see: *Al-Tawḥīd* #9)
27. *Rowzehs* are preachments held on various occasions, always concluding with a turning to the story of Imām Husain and Karbala. See Fischer (1980*a*) for a description of the form and its use.
28. According to a popular story Mir Dāmad (literally, "prince son-in-law") was a pious religious student (*ṭalabeh*) when one night during a storm, the shah's daughter took refuge in his *madaraseh* (theological seminary) building. Since his was the only light, she knocked at his door and he gave her refuge. She fell asleep, and his sexual interest stirred. To remind himself of the fires

of hell, he held a finger over a candle till the burning sensation quieted his lust. Sometime later, the devil whispered again, and again he held another finger over the flame. And so he passed the night. In the morning, a royal crier went about proclaiming, "Woe to him in whose house the virgin princess is found harmed." Mir Dāmad went to the authorities, and because of his burnt fingers he was arrested on suspicion that he had attacked the princess and been injured by her attempts at self-defense. The princess testified on behalf of Mir Dāmad, but her testimony was dismissed as interested in protecting her honor. Mir Dāmad then told the story of his struggle to control his passion, and Shah Abbas was impressed, gave him his daughter in marriage, and conveyed upon him the title Mir Dāmad.

29. He was one of the few *ṭalabeh*s drafted after the revolution for military service, and together with other such *ṭalabeh*s sent a plea to Khomeini for exemption. Khomeini responded that *ṭalabeh*s should learn how to use guns, they might be needed in future.

30. Some claimed that his real title was not Ṣadūqi but rather Ṣandūqi (i.e., "treasurer" for Borujerdi). He himself later claimed to be a descendant of Shaykh Ṣadūq (compiler of one of the four Shi'ite books of ḥadīth), and wanted to establish a Ṣadūq University in Qum in honor of his ancestor. He did eventually establish a Ṣadūq Foundation in Tehran.

31. This episode is recounted in his book *Shi'igari* (Kasravi n.d.).

32. I once perpetrated a similar prank in retaliation for being kicked out of the mosque when there was not enough room for all the adults, and so children were sent home. I got a dozen safety pins and slipped back into the mosque during an intermission after Saduqi had already led fifty *rak'at* of prayer. People were dozing, and I pinned their pyjamas to the *zīlū* (flat weave floor covering) of the mosque. (Yazdis did not say their prayers in dry-cleaned trousers, thinking they were *najes,* ritually impure; instead they prayed in pyjamas often worn underneath.) When the call to stand for prayer came, half a dozen pyjamas came off. Thinking that people behind them had pulled the pyjamas down, two men slapped the men behind them, and a fight broke out. I avoided the mosque. Saduqi was informed who had done the prank, and one day he caught me in the alley, and told me I was forgiven.

33. The Fateh family was from Bahrain, and had moved to Yazd before moving on to Tehran. There were two senior brothers in Tehran: Muhammad Ṣādeq Fateh, who was killed in the events leading up to the 1977–79 revolution, and who owned a series of companies called Jahan – Jahan Textiles, Jahan Tea and Oils, etc.; Abdul-Wahab, a merchant (*tājer*) and money lender (*ṣarrāf*), who was the father of my patron, Hasan. Hasan was one of four brothers and a sister. After the revolution, he moved to England and started a computer business, but it did not do well, and so he invested in bowling alleys in the United States, managed by his younger brother, Muhammad in Boston. I performed the religious wedding ceremony for Muhammad here in the States; he married the granddaughter of a man in Yazd known

as Khān-e Khar Savār ("the khan on the donkey") because he was always riding a donkey. Hasan has two sons, both now grown, the elder a pilot instructor.

34. They were accused of agitation in Turkoman country, northern Iran.

2. Qur'anic Dialogics: Islamic Poetics and Politics for Muslims and for Us

1. Āyatullāh Khomeini, for example, in his exegesis (*tafsīr*) of Sūra Fatiha says, "The Qur'an is not a book that someone can interpret comprehensively and exhaustively, for its sciences are unique and ultimately beyond our understanding" (Khomeini 1981:365).
2. Contrast the famous, frequently cited midrash on Aknai's oven (B. Metzia 59*a*, 59*b*) in which God is asked for a sign of agreement with one of the debaters about a point of law. He gives the sign, but it is disqualified on the ground that the law is "not in heaven" (Deut. 30:12): "The Torah had already been given at Mount Sinai; we pay no attention to a heavenly voice, because Thou hast long since written in the Torah at Mount Sinai: 'After the majority must one incline' [Exod. 23:2]." Elijah is asked God's reaction: "He laughed in approval, saying, "My sons have defeated Me, my sons have defeated Me." Here and elsewhere the Talmud asserts that the Torah is not in heaven, but in the decisions of the judges and sages of every generation (e.g., Yer Peah 6:2). Moreover, it is said that on Mount Sinai both the written and the oral Torah were revealed to Moses, the latter being all the interpretations that would come in future time (Leviticus Rabbah 22:1). Indeed, in another midrash, Moses finds God adding calligraphic coronets to the letters of the Torah, and is told that the great Rabbi Akiva will use each tittle to work out a new legal ruling. Moses is shown the debates that would come at the time of Rabbi Akiva, and could not follow the argumentation, but is comforted by the references to the law given to Moses at Sinai (Menahot 29*b*). Yet another midrash speaks of the thousands of laws that were forgotten during the mourning period when Moses died, and the inability to recover them by appealing to God, that instead they had to be restored by dialectical reasoning (Temurah 16*a*). Maimonides invoked these principles when he decided issues in the purity code against the views of God and the expert Rabbah bar Nahmani (Mishneh Torah, Hilkhot Tumat Tzara'at). See Handelman (1982:40–41), and Hartman (1985:33–36, 47).

   This resolute making of man responsible for the divine word contrasts sharply with the Islamic dogma that the Qur'an exists in heaven, and that perfect knowledge (for Shi'ites) resides with the Imāms. However, in practical terms the effects are similar: the ambiguity of the text requires skilled hermeneutics, and the creation of a hermeneutic tradition. Hartman points out paradoxical twists in the midrashim that remove some of God's acts from human comprehensibility: R. Akiva is martyred and God claims it as His decree; even the story of Aknai's oven has a disturbing sequel that involves God's active unpredictable intervention. The rabbis play with the tension between the Talmud's demand that man be assertive and that he submit to God's (ethical) incomprehensibility. Noah is contrasted with Abraham: Noah merely "walked with God" (Gen. 6:9), obedient, unquestioning; while Abraham stands over and against God as an other, who argues against God's plan to wipe out Sodom, holding God to his promise not to repeat wholesale destructions like the flood, as an adult moral consciousness who is consulted on God's plan, who is told, "Walk before Me" (Gen. 17:1). (Did Abraham not openly protest God's demand that he sacrifice his son, because he sensed that God could not allow him to go through with an act that would violate the covenant between them, sealed in Abraham's circumcision?)

Muslims too play with the tension between submission and self-reliant assertion (see Shari'ati on the Ḥajj in chapter 3), though they (especially fundamentalists) try to deny God's ethical inconsistencies and berate Jews for openly embracing hermeneutical play: in the Qur'an, Jews attract God's wrath precisely because of this embracing of hermeneutics.

3. Key figures are Luqmān, Hūd, and Ṣālih. Muhammad is very careful to distinguish himself from pre-Islamic Arab poets and seers. In addition to the general devaluing of the pre-Islamic period as one of *jāhiliya* (ignorance), there may have been animus against the stories of Iranian oral tradition: Ibn Abbas, among others, relates that whenever the Qur'an refers to *asāṭīr al-awwalīn* (ancient stories) or *lahw al-ḥadīth* (idle narratives), it is referring to Nadr ibn Ḥarīth, a Meccan merchant who traveled frequently to Iran, and who challenged Muhammad by saying, "I know better stories than you, I know the stories of Rustam and Isfandiar." Professor Fereydun Bedrehi (personal communication 1988) claims to have found a report of a ḥadīth in 'Abdullāh Anṣarī's *Tafsīr-e khājeh* that says Hārith knew rather the Kelileh and Dimeneh stories.
4. See especially the work of Wansborough (1977) for an effort to use Hebrew hermeneutical terms to elucidate the Qur'anic literature; more generally on theological philosophy (*kalām*), see Wolfson (1976).
5. It also is derived within Islamic reasoning from the verse, "Obey God, obey His messenger, and obey the issuer of orders" (4:62), which last Shi'ites have taken to mean the Imāms, and perhaps after them those who know the law, the clerics. Khomeini elaborated this into a doctrine of political governance, *wilāyat-e faqīh* ("guardianship by the *faqīh*/jurisconsult"), against the opposition of other *faqīh* or *mujtahid*s (like Plato's philosophers, those who exercise independent, disciplined reasoning), who pointed out that traditionally the term *wilāyat-e faqīh* applied only to the estates of orphans and widows (see Fischer 1980*a:*151–55, 221, 237).
6. These began to be introduced in the first century of Islam, but took a number of centuries to be accepted. As late as the fifth century, some jurisconsults insisted that adding any diacritical marks to the *muṣ-ḥaf* was a forbidden innovation (*bid'a*). The founder of the Malikite school of juris-

prudence, Imām Malik, allowed (*mubāḥ*) diacriticals for copies used in teaching, but would not allow them to be added to original or master manuscripts. The fifth-century A. H. Malikite jurist and reciter, "Dani" Abū 'Amrw 'Uthmān ibn al-Sirāfi (d. 444/1052), allowed them if they were added in a different color. In the seventh century, another *ḥāfiẓ*, Yahya ibn Sharaf al-Nawawi would only say diacriticals were recommended (*mustaḥabb*) insofar as they prevent misreadings (*laḥn* and *taṣ-ḥīf*). Today, jurists regard them as obligatory (*wājib*) because it is obligatory to read the Qur'an correctly, and if this can be done only with their help, then their use is obligatory: technically, they are a prelude (*muqaddima*) to an obligation, and thus obligatory. The status of diacriticals thus has moved from forbidden to permitted (*jā'iz*), to meritorious (*mustaḥabb*), to obligatory (*wājib*).

The traditions crediting individuals with introducing diacriticals are confused. Vowels and the dots that distinguish the letters "j," "h," and "kh" were first added in the time of Caliph Malik ibn Marwan (reigned 65–86/684–705) by Khalīl ibn Aḥmad, the author of the first book on Arab prosody; or by Abu al-Aswad al-Du'ali at the request of Ziyad ibn Abih; or by two students of Du'ali, Nasr ibn 'Aṣīm al-Laythi and Yaḥyā ibn Ya'mar al-'Adwāni at the order of the ruler of Iraq, Hajjaj ibn Yūsuf (d. 95/714) at the request of the caliph. Yahya was a Shi'ite, Iranian, and later grand judge of Khorasan. Yazīd al-Fārisi and Abu-Ḥatim al-Sajastāni are also credited with some of the innovations: Yazīd al-Fārisi with the letter alif (thus adding some two thousand letters to the Qur'an). Hajjaj not only ordered these innovations, but imprisoned and executed *ḥuffāz* and *qurrā'* whose recitations varied from the official ones.

7. To encourage prayer, the exact date is unknown: prayers on the night of revelation are worth a thousand prayers any other time. For differences in Shi'ite and Sunni valuation and meaning of Ramaḍān, see Fischer (1980*a*: 24–25).
8. These are aḥadīth of the Prophet Muhammad.
9. Taleqāni (n.d., p. 1) makes this suggestion. Philologically, the initial *t* is a grammatical form; *g*→*j*, *a*→*wi*, *th*→*d*. On the Vedic and Avestan traditions of enigmatic poetry contests, see Johnson (1980). See also Khomeini: (1981: 392): "The prophets are like men who have seen a dream that they cannot describe; their tongues are tied and those around them are deaf." Khomeini uses both visual and vocal imagery, equally problematic in approximations in reproducing the sound and meaning of the Qur'an without effacing them through transcription in human language, or in human visual conventions.
10. There is an alternative tradition, in Ibn Hisham's biography of the Prophet (translated by Guillaume [1955:105–6]) that Gabriel brought a brocade or silk with writing and said, "*Iqra!*" ("read"). Iranian nationalists have long been fond of agreeing that indeed Muhammad and his Arabs were illiterate and incapable of producing the Qur'an, and joking that it was a literate Persian, Salman Farsi, one of the first converts to Islam, whom the Prophet

called "one of my family" (to stress the nonethnic basis of Islam), who composed and wrote the Qur'an, passing it up in fragments from a well to his puppet, the semiliterate Arab prophet.

11. The breaking of the tablets, like the breaking of the vessels, is the making human: "'Is not My word like a hammer that breaks the rock in pieces?' [Jer. 23:29]—as the hammer causes numerous sparks to flash forth, so is a scriptural verse capable of many interpretations" [Sanh. 34a]. And Jabès: "It was necessary for Moses to break the book [tablets] in order for the book to become human" (Gould 1985:23, 66).

12. There are three traditional ways of thinking about the chronology of revelation. First, almost all editions of the Qur'an provide markings of Meccan and Medinan sūras and *āyāt.* There is a rough difference in style and general subject between the two periods of Muhammad's prophethood, e.g., warnings against disbelief in the earlier Meccan verses versus legislation for the new community in the later Medinan ones. Second, for many but not all fragments of revelation, stories exist recounting the occasions and reasons for their revelation (*asbāb al-nuzūl*). Third, seven lists of chronology of the sūras are attributed to the witnesses of the first generation (see appendix 1). In his *Itqān,* the fifteenth-century Jalaladdin Suyuti cites six of these, including those of the disciple of Ali, 'Abdullah ibn Abbas, and the son of one of Muhammad's leading disciples, Muhammad ibn Nu'mān ibn Bashīr, an important figure at the court of Mu'awiyya. The ninth-century al-Kāfi reports a chronology of the sixth Shi'ite Imām, Ja'far al-Ṣādiq. Recent European and Muslim efforts to work out the historical chronology are dependent on these older ones.

    Gustav Weil (1844, 2d ed. 1878) and Alois Sprenger (1861, 2d ed. 1869) began European efforts to establish a chronology, dividing the sūras into three Meccan and one Medinan period. Theodor Noldeke (1860, 2d ed. 1879) elaborated this into a version that became the foundation for all subsequent work. The forty-eight sūras of the first Meccan period are short, rhythmic, poetic, and escatological. The twenty-one sūras of the second Meccan period are slightly longer, are about monotheism, refer to God as al-Rahman (the most merciful), and Muhammad is told to speak out ("*qul!*") in response to emerging issues. The twenty-one sūras of the third Meccan period are less poetic, more sermonlike, moral lessons in stories of the prophets. The twenty-four Medinan sūras are long, and are about sociopolitical issues: family, marriage, divorce, inheritance, crime and punishment, jihād, and so on. Muhammad is now no longer merely a warner or messenger, but an administrator. Slightly different chronologies were proposed by Rodwell (1918), Muir (1878), and Grimme (1923). But the next conceptual step was made by Hirschfeld (1902) who constructed a chronology not by sūra, but by using groups of *āyāt.* This acknowledgment of the fragments of the sūras as the narrative units of revelation was then systematically pursued by Bell (1937, 1953). More recent efforts to work on the problem include Blachere (1947), Hartmann (1963–66), and Neuworth (1981).

European efforts stimulated renewed Muslim ones. In 1895, in Iran, I'timād al-Salṭana published a list "obtained from a European source" as an addendum to an edition of the Qur'an. In 1935 Abu Abdullah al-Zanjāni's *Tārīkh al-Qur'ān* (History of the Qur'an) was published in Cairo shortly after the translation of Noldeke's work into Arabic. In 1949 in Iran, Sayyid Muhammad Ali Taqawi published his *Tārīkh-e Qur'ān-e Majīd.* In 1967 in Iran, Mahmud Ramyar produced a *Tārīkh-e Qur'ān* based on both European and Muslim sources. In the Indo-Pakistan subcontinent there are recent efforts by Hashim Amir Ali, Abdullah Yusuf Ali (1977), and Abu'l Fazl Mirza (1955), all writing in English and all inspired by Noldeke.

Among recent Muslim scholars, one of the more innovative efforts is Mehdi Bazargan's *Sayr-e Tahawwul-e Qur'ān.* Bazargan, a professor of thermodynamics as well as an Islamic modernist, who was to become the first prime minister of the Islamic Republic of Iran in 1979, attempted to formalize Noldeke and Blachere's ideas. He tested the rule: the shorter the verse, the older it is. The chronology is harmonized with Bazargan's ideas about "step by step evolution": just as children are educated gradually, so society should undergo evolution, rather than revolution. The chronology is manipulated to show that this was God's method in early Islam. Not surprisingly, Bazargan's work came under attack in the Islamic Republic of Iran, both on grounds of traditional chronologies, and the content of the verses, e.g., Bazargan's calculations placed the *ifk aya* (revealed in response to the accusation of adultery against Ayesha, Muhammad's youngest wife) two years after the traditional account. In another example, Bazargan's rigid mathematical formalism is challenged by a mullā in the newspaper *Kayhan-e Farhangi.* The mullā asks, with this new method, what is the first verse revealed? Bazargan replies, as everyone has always agreed, "*Iqra!*" ("recite"). But, says the mullā, is not this aya too long to come first? No, says Bazargan, the verse is "*iqra*". Muhammad does nothing, so it is repeated. Bazargan is thus able to turn two commands into one, merely repeated, and to ignore the sentences which are the content of what is to be recited (Sūra 96:1–4).

13. The Qur'an counts four major scriptures: the *torah* of Moses, the (ev)*angil* of Jesus, the *zubur* ("psalm,") of David, and the *qur'an* of Muhammad. The plural form of *zubur* refers to all previous scriptures, as does the word for pages (*ṣuḥuf,* sg. *ṣahīfah;* whence also *muṣ-ḥaf*). *Lawḥ* ("tablet") is used once in the singular, with the adjective *maḥfūẓ* ("preserved"), to refer to the Umm al-Kitāb ("the mother book") or primordial Qur'an; in the plural (*alwāh*), it occurs thrice referring to the tablets of Moses, and once referring to the planks of Noah's ark—a rich metaphorical set. The word *kitāb* ("book") and its derivatives occur frequently (561 times), but it too has particular metaphorical connotations: *kitāb* means not only to write, but to decree or to prescribe, and *ahl-e kitāb* ("people of the book") is a key juridical term, demarcating those who are allowed to be second-class citizens in an Islamic polity versus those who have no legal status whatsoever, i.e., who may have writings, but who have no book. *Asfār* (sg. *sifr*), "volumes" or

"chapters," used of the Pentateuch, the five books of Moses, occurs in the famous slur on the rabbis who may read, but do not understand: they are like donkeys carrying *asfār* (Qur'an 62:5; 2:101). This slur can stand both for the alleged tampering with and loss by Jews (and Christians) of the true word of God (why otherwise would Christians have *four* Gospels?), and for all the arresting effects of writing and the deadening effects of literacy where volumes multiply but true understanding is occulted.

14. The story is about Swaid ibn Samit of the Aws tribe of Yathrib, known as *al-kamīl* ("perfect one"), whose talents included literacy. Invited by Muhammad to embrace Islam, he refused on the grounds that he had his own wisdom script of Luqman. Muhammad asked him to read it out. He did so, and Muhammad said he had something better (Abbot 1957–67).
15. Abu al-Darad and 'Abidah ibn Qays are among the Companions said to have destroyed their notes before they died, lest they mislead (Abbot 1957–67).
16. Umar also sponsored official text burnings lest confusion be disseminated. Umar was accused by Shi'ites of having burned the great libraries in Egypt (Alexandria) and Persia (Jundishapur), telling his commanders that if the information in the books agreed with the Qur'an they were superfluous, and if the books disagreed with the Qur'an they were not worth preserving. This now discredited legend has it that the libraries of Alexandria supplied fuel for the city's baths for six months. The more sympathetic story is that both Umar and Uthman only attempted to burn variant *muṣ-ḥaf*s to reduce confusion. The effort to destroy all other *muṣ-ḥaf*s, not surprisingly, was initially unsuccessful. In 398/1007, a *muṣ-ḥaf* said to be of Abdullah ibn Mas'ūd (d. 32/652) was brought to the court of the Shafi'i jurist, Abu Ḥāmid al-Isfara'ini, and was publicly burned. This so angered the Shi'ites that they rioted, chanting, "Yā Manṣūr, Ya Manṣūr" (the name of the martyr, al-Hallaj). They were put down with military force, their leader was executed by order of the caliph, Al-Qādir bi-Allah, and the Shi'ite jurist Shayk al-Mufīd was exiled from Baghdad for a time (Ramyar, 1967:180).
17. 'Abdullah ibn Sa'ib to Mecca, Mughira ibn Shahāb to Syria, 'Amir ibn 'Abd Qays to Basra, Abu 'Abd al-Rahman Sullami to Kufa, and Zayd ibn Thabit remained in Mecca (*Qanūn-e Tafsīr,* p. 175).
18. Still today, if you pick up an authoritative manuscript or printed edition of the Qur'an, you will find the following kind of note: "This *muṣ-ḥaf* was written and recorded in accord with the *riwāyat* (narration) of Hafs ibn Sulaymān ibn Mughira al-Asadi al-Kufi from the *qirā'āt* (recitation) of 'Asīm ibn Abi al-Nujud al-Kufi al-Tābi'i, from . . . Zayd ibn Thabit and Uby ibn Ka'b, from the Prophet." Encoded here is not merely the distinction between *qur'ān* (recitation) and *muṣ-ḥaf* (written text), but also that the basis of the written text is an oral dictation (*riwāyat*) from an oral recitation (*qirā'at*), and that the chain of oral transmission is from the well-known, reliable reciter Ḥafṣ ibn Sulayman back to the Prophet.
19. Like ḥadīth (classified in degrees of reliability, see p. 125 below), the

qirā'āt are classified by degree of reliability. The least reliable are called *shādhdh.* Ibn Shanbudh (d. 328/939) was tried and humiliated for *shādhdh* recitations. His student Abu Bakr 'Attār al-Naḥwi was also whipped until he recanted. A well-known grammarian, al-Naḥwī, attempted to make *qirā'āt* a subservient discipline to Arabic grammar, rather than reliant only on chains of transmission.

20. Compare the Jewish *midrash* (Menahot 29b) about the forgetting of laws after the death of Moses, but their reconstruction through dialectical reasoning rather than memory: see footnote 2. Note that both traditions insist on the indispensability of the oral tradition, though they handle it somewhat differently.
21. Zabiḥ Allah Ṣafā, *Tārīkh-e 'Ulum-e 'Aqli dar Tamaddun-e Islāmi,* p. 33.
22. Zaydan (1907, 3:434).
23. Zayd too had first to be persuaded of the need for a written text. This was not the first effort to produce a complete transcript: one of the martyrs of Yamamah, Sālim Mawla Abi-Hudhayfa is often said to have been the first to try to collect the entire Qur'an. Ali ibn Abi Talib is said to have collected a transcript in chronological order and with commentary, intended as a consolation for Fatima after the Prophet died. Abdullah ibn Mas'ūd's transcript is said to have surfaced in 398/1007, when it was burned (see footnote 16). Zayd ibn Thābit's begun at the order of Abu Bakr, the first caliph, and completed under Uthman, the third caliph, was kept, according to tradition, in a strongbox owned first by the second caliph, Umar, and inherited by his daughter, Ḥafṣah. Uthman never controlled the transcript that goes by his name, and had to borrow it from Ḥafṣah whenever he wanted to see it. After Ḥafṣah's death, her brother Abdullah presented it to Marwan ibn Ḥakam (d. 65/684) who previously had asked Ḥafṣah for it, and had repeatedly been refused, apparently with good reason: Marwān destroyed the manuscript "lest it create doubt in some hearts." Whatever the truth of this story, we do not have the original transcript of Zayd, nor of any of the original transcripts.
24. A third variant increases the collaborators to three or four: Ubyy ibn Ka'b dictates, Zayd writes, and Sa'īd ibn al-'Aṣ and 'Abd al-Raḥmān ibn al-Ḥarth provide the short vowels (*i'rāb*).
25. In Tunisia the *qirā'āt* of Qālūn from Nafi' is followed; in Morocco, that of Warsh from Nafi'; in southern Africa a version of Ibn Kathīr; in the Sudan, a version of Duri from Abū-'Amrw. Such regional differences also existed in the past: e.g., in 200/800 the people of Baṣra followed Abu-'Amrw and Yaqūb; Kufa tended to follow Ḥamza and 'Aṣīm; Mecca followed Ibn Kathīr; Medina followed Nafi'; and Syria followed Ibn 'Amrw.
26. Labib as-Said eventually conceded that he had been unduly pessimistic that the Qur'anic recitation might die: he notes that there are tens of thousands of blind reciters of the Qur'an, which should be sufficient to preserve it.
27. See Nelson (1985) for expansion.
28. Exact repetitions: 2:136 and 3:84; 2:146 and 6:20; 7:146 and 6:25; 11:82 and

15:74; 11:110 and 41:45; 15:28–40 and 38:71–82; 19:36–37 and 43:64–65; 16:43 and 21:7; 26:30–32 and 7:155. Near repetitions: 2:58–59 and 7:161–62; 17:48 and 17:98; 21:92–93 and 23:52–53. There are, of course, many phrases and epithets that are used as identifications throughout, e.g., the meaning of 1:7, "those against whom Thou are wrathful" (*al-maghdūb ʿalayhim*) is identified in traditional exegesis by its repetitions elsewhere in the text: in the story of Moses and the Children of Israel in the desert, "and they were laden with the burden of God's anger (*ghaḍab*)" (2:61); "they will be laden with the burden of God's anger" (3:108), etc.

29. "Corruption on earth" is a legal charge in the Islamic Republic of Iran carrying the death penalty. How did the angels know what Adam would be like? Both Jewish (B. Sanh 38b, Lekah Tov, Rashi) and Muslim (Tabari, Zamakhshari) traditions cite this as the ethical principle of consultation incumbent upon the greater toward the lesser in any relationship (Katsh 1954:26–29).
30. Both the Talmud and Muslim traditions provide various suggestions of what species of "tree" was involved, including the vine (inflated sense of knowledge through drunkenness), fig (used to cover their nakedness), and, perhaps most intriguingly, wheat (raw material from which to make flour, bread, civilization) (Katsh 1954:37). Compare the metaphors of wheat and flax used for the oral Torah in Seder Eliyahu Zuta 2: the wisdom of interpretation is like the making of bread and cloth, the increasing of value and utility out of what is given into one's safekeeping (Hartman 1985:35).
31. In the Jewish version, they go to a poor man who owns only a cow but receives them well, yet the next morning Joshua overhears Elijah praying that God should destroy the cow; they go to a rich man who is inhospitable, and in the morning Elijah prays God help him rebuild a collapsing wall; they go to a synagogue with inhospitable folk, and Elijah prays God make all of them leaders; they go to a generous town and Elijah prays they have only one leader. Solution: in the first case, the man's wife was going to die, and Elijah prayed that God take the cow instead; the second case is the same as in the Muslim variant: the wall contained treasure which would have been misspent; and in the last pair of cases, there is no peace when there are multiple leaders. Elijah, in the Jewish tradition, is the arbiter of all outstanding disputes at the end of time. Thus the dispute over whether the Passover Seder should have four or five cups of wine; the fifth cup is for Elijah to decide.
32. Egyptian reciters use the term *maqām;* Iranians do not, because it is associated with music, but they talk about the idea. On the theological debate about the illegitimacy of music in Islam, see Fischer (1980*a:*164–5), and Nelson (1985, ch. 3).
33. See Wansborough (1977) for a fuller account. Sources in the exegetical literature are indicated by footnote for the meanings listed below.
34. Al-Khatīb: *muḥkam* verses involve a *ḥukm* (judgment, verdict). Al-Mujāhid: *muḥkam* are those verses in which the lawful (*ḥalāl*) and unlawful (*ḥarām*)

are spoken of. Imām Ja'far al-Ṣādiq: *muḥkam* is "what we believe in, practice and rely upon" and "objects of practice," as opposed to *mutashābih* which are mistaken by the ignorant (*ishtibaha 'ala jāhilihi*).

35. Zajjāj (d. 311/923): *muḥkam* is "apparent and clear" (*ẓāhir wa bayyin*) while *mutashābih* is "subject to opinion, meditation and insight." He gives as examples of the former the stories of the prophets and of creation; and of the latter the fact of resurrection.
36. Ali ibn Abi-Talib: *muḥkam* means what it says (*ma ta'wīluhu tanziluhu,* "what is its interpretation is its revelation"), e.g., when it says "fasting is prescribed," it means just that, not something allegorical, while *mutashābih* is that which can only be understood through *ta'wīl* (interpretation, prolepsis). His disciple, 'Abdullah ibn Abbas, the father of Qur'anic exegesis (d. 68/687): *muḥkam* is "what cannot possibly be interpreted save in one way," while *mutashābih* is "open to multiple interpretations."
37. Ibn Ḥanbal (189–241/780–855).
38. Ibid.
39. Jalaladdin Suyūṭi (849–911/1445–1505) in his *al-Iqtān* cites this opinion on the authority of Ibn Zayd.
40. Mawardi (974–1058): *muḥkam* is *ma'qūl al-ma'nā* (the meaning can be rationally understood), while *mutashābih* includes rules like the number of prayers one must say or that one must fast during Ramaḍān but not during Sha'ban, which can be understood only by reference to ḥadīth and sunna.
41. Mawardi: see note 40.
42. Suyūṭi: see note 39.
43. Daḥāk; Imam Muhammad al-Baqir.
44. Said ibn Jubayr (d. 96/714); Muqatil ibn Sulaimān (d. 150/767); Muhammad bin Ṣāhib Kalibi (d. 206/819) adds the qualifications that this refers to those verses that specify prohibitions and permissions and have not been abrogated (viz. Wansborough 1977:243). For these exegetes the *mutashābihāt* were essentially the four *sigla* (independent letters, not forming words) found in thirteen of the sūras, of numerological and apocalyptic value.
45. Al-Raghib al-Isfahani (d. 502/1108) provides two typologies by verse quality and by capacity of human beings to understand. In the first, some verses may be *muḥkam,* others *mutashābih,* and others mixed. Of these last, they may be *mutashābih* with regard to their wording, to their meaning, or to extra Qur'anic data such as the circumstances of revelation, conditions of application, or degree of obligation.
46. Contemporary Shi'ite theologians often invoke this.
47. There is a strain particularly, but not only, in Shi'ite thought that acknowledges that the Muṣ-ḥaf Uthmani may be incomplete. There were the verses that may have been lost because two witnesses could not be found at the time Zayd made his collection; more darkly, Shi'ites suspect that the Muṣḥaf Uthmani may have suppressed verses favorable to the Shi'ite cause, and they have traditions that suggest that Imām Ali's muṣ-ḥaf is still extant in the hands of the Mahdi. Suyuti as well cites a tradition that scornfully says,

twenty-three years of revelations and only this much of a volume: obviously most of it has disappeared. And there is the possibility, suggested by Khomeini in his *Kashf-e Asrār* (1363/1943:130), that in the Qur'an, God was doing *taqiya* (dissimulation) in not listing openly the names of the Imāms who were to succeed Muhammad, because he knew that the Imams would have to struggle in a hostile environment, or that the Qur'an would be doctored by the usurpers. The issue periodically comes up in times of sectarian conflict: some twenty years ago a little pamphlet in Arabic was circulated in Mecca during the ḥajj accusing Shi'ites and listing their reasons for thinking the Qur'an incomplete and imperfect. The pamphlet had to be answered, and in the course of the subsequent discussions, Ayatullah S. Muhammad-Hadi Milani was put in a position in which he felt himself forced to issue a public *fatwā* (opinion) that the Qur'an was complete.

48. One of the first collections of *asbāb al-nuzūl* is reported to have been compiled by Abu al-Ḥasan Ali ibn 'Abdullah al-Madyani (d. 234/849), a teacher of Bukhari, the master compiler of ḥadīth. Most famous is *Asbabu Nuzūl al-Qur'an* by Abu al-Ḥasan Ali ibn Aḥmad al-Wahidi al-Nishaburi (d. 468/1076). Jalaladdin Suyuti (849–811/1445–1505) devoted a chapter of his *Iqtan* to this subject, and also compiled a separate volume *Lubāb al-Nuqūl.* Among the more recent collections is Sadr al-Din Maḥallāti of Shiraz's 1955 collection *Sha'n-e Nuzūl-e Ayāt-i Qur'ān.*
49. A stray ḥadīth counts nineteen months; this has been picked up with glee by Baha'is.
50. See Graham (1977) on the *aḥadīth qudsi.*
51. The first *musnad* is said to have been compiled in Basra by Abu-Dawud Sulayman ibn Dawūd ibn al-Jarīd al-Ṭaylasāni (d. 204/819). Possibly the *ṣahīfa* ("pages") of 'Abdullah ibn 'Amrw ibn al-'As (d. 65 A.H.) and Aman ibn Munabbhih (d. 131) also were early ḥadīth collections. The founders of all four Sunni schools of law also made *musnad,* and these are still extant. Imām Mālik bin Anas' *al-Muwaṭṭa',* collected entirely in Medina, contains 1,700 ḥadīth, selected, it is reported, from 10,000 considered. The Caliph al-Manṣūr, in 136 A.H., wanted to place a copy of the *Muwaṭṭa'* in the Ka'ba at Mecca to serve as a source for arbitrating disputes; Imām Mālik demurred, citing both his own fallibility and the lack of legitimacy of Mansur's Abbasid caliphate. Imām Ahmad ibn Hanbal's *Musnad* contains 3,000 ḥadīth.
52. Regional ḥadīth collections were made in Mecca (by 'Abd al-Malik ibn Jurayh, d. 144/761); in Syria (by Sufyan al-Thawri, d. 161, and 'Abd al-Raḥmān al-Awzā'ī, d. 175); in Basra (by Ḥammād); in Wāsiṭ (by Haytham); in Yemen (by Ma'mar); in Khorasan (by Ibn Mubarak); and in Ray (by Jarir ibn Hāmid).
53. The six basic Sunni collections of ḥadīth are called *al-Ṣiḥaḥ al-Sitta* (the "six correct ones"): (1) Bukhari's *al-Jāmi' al-Ṣaḥiḥ.* Abu-'Abdullah Muḥammad al-Bukhari (195–257/810–870) claimed to have spent sixteen years traveling throughout Khorasan, Iraq, Hijaz, Syria, and Egypt, examining 600,000

ḥadīth. Of these he chose 7,250, just over one percent, dismissing the rest as unreliable. He undertook the task because his teacher, Isḥāq ibn Rahawayh, wanted a "short book on the correct traditions of the Messenger of Allah." (2) Muslim's *al-Ṣaḥiḥ.* Abu al-Husayn Muslim ibn Hajjaj Nisaburi (202–262/817–875) claimed to have examined 300,000 ḥadīth, and selected 12,000. He categorized 625 narrators into reliable (*mutqinūn*), "not so well known but relatively reliable" (*masṭūrun mutawassiṭūn*), and "weak, unreliable" (*du'afā matrūkūn*). He excluded the last, and in each chapter separated the other two categories. Like Bukhari he traveled extensively, and was in Nishabur with Bukhari. (3) *al-Sunan* by Muhammad ibn Yazid, "Ibn Maja of Qazvin" (209–273/824–887) contains 4,000 ḥadīth in thirty-two chapters. (4) *al-Sunan* by Sulayman ibn Ash'ath, "Abu-Dawud Sajistani" (d. 275/889). (5) *al-Jami' al-Kabīr* by Muhammad ibn Isa Tarmadhi (209–279/824–892), a disciple of Bukhari, apparently blind. His collection contains 5,000 ḥadīth. (6) *al-Sunan* by Abu-'Abd al-Rahman Ahmad ibn Ali ibn Shu'yb al-Nasa'i (215-303/830–915), a disciple of Abu Dawūd. A summary of his work is known as *al-Mujtaba* ("the selected").

Some Sunni scholars also include here the *Sunan* of Dārimi (d. 255/868) and *al-Muwaṭṭa'* of Imām Mālik. Ḥadīth which the Six Correct Ones leave out are compiled in the *mustadrakat* books of al-Ḥākim al-Nisābūri, Ibn Khuzayma, Dārqutni, Byhaqi, Nuraddin ibn Abi-Bakr al-Haythami, Jalaladdin Suyūṭi, and Ibn Ḥajar. Several concordances were later prepared, including *Dhakhā'ir al-Mawārith fi Dilalat 'An Mawadi' al-Aḥādīth* by Abd al-Ghani ibn Ismā'īl al-Nabulusi (d. 1143 A.H.), and *al-Mu'jam al-Mufahras li Alfāẓ al-Ḥadīth al-Nabawi,* compiled by anonymous editors.

54. *'Abaqāt an Anwār* of Mir Ḥāmid Husayn Hindi Nisaburi, and *al-Ghadīr* of Shaykh 'Abd al Ḥusayn Amīnī are two such enterprises.

55. Four collections serve Shi'ites the way the Six Correct Ones serve Sunnis: (1) *al-Kāfi* by Abu-Ja'far Muḥammad ibn Ya'qūb al-Kulayni (d. 329/940), containing 16,199 ḥadīth. (2) *Man lā Yaḥduruhu al-Faqīh* (Those not in the presence of a jurist) by Muhammad ibn Ali ibn Babawayh al-Qummi, "Ṣadūq" (306–381/919–991). The title is a variant on Razi's medical handbook for laymen. "Ṣadūq" collected his ḥadīth throughout Khorasan, traveling to Nisabur, Sarakhs, Marw, Bukhara, and Farghanah. (3) *Tahdhib al-Aḥkām* and (4) *Istibṣār* by Abu-Ja'far Muḥammad ibn al-Ḥasan al-Tusi (384–460/995–1076). The former contains 13,590 ḥadīth; the latter 5,511.

Other Shi'ite collections are also well known and much used: (1) *Biḥār al-Anwar* by Muḥammad Bāqir Majlisi (1037–1110/1627–1700), the famous cleric of the Safavid period. It is notorious for its lack of discrimination between reliable and unreliable ḥadīth. Majlisi is important in the history of Iranian Shi'ism for elevating folk beliefs, including much of the stock in trade of intolerance against non-Shi'ites, into respectable orthodoxy, and his collection reflects this cultural politics. (2) *Wasā'il al-Shī'a* by Ḥurr al-Amili (1033–1104/1623–1692). By contrast with Majlisi, this work is well arranged by subject, and is often consulted by jurists. A nineteenth-century addendum, *Mustadrak al-Wasā'il,* by Haj Mirza Ḥusayn Nūri (d. 1320/1902) has recently become important because of Nuri's knowledge and care in *rijāl.* (3) *Jawami'al-Kalim* by S. Mirza al-Jazayiri (a teacher of both Majlisi and of Hurr al-Amili). (4) *al-Wāfi* by Muhammad ibn al-Murtada, "Fayḍ Kāshāni" (1006–1090/1596–1679). This is a compilation from the four "canonic" books. (5) *'Awālim* by Abdullah ibn Nurullah Bahrayni, a contemporary of Majlisi. (6) *Jami'al-Aḥadith wa al-Aqwāl* by Muhammad Qāsim ibn Muhammad Jawad (d. 1100/1688). (7) *al-Shifā fi Ḥadīth al-Muṣṭafa* by Shaykh Muhammad Riḍā ibn 'Abd al-Laṭīf Tabrizi (d. 1158/1747). (8) *Jami'al-Aḥkām* and *Jami'al-Ma'ārif wa al-Akhbār* by S. Abdullah Shubbar (d. 1242/1826).

56. From the beginning it was recognized that many fabricated ḥadīth were in circulation, and so these schools compiled biographical dictionaries of narrators (*rijāl*), giving genealogical, educational, and travel information so that one might judge the credentials of each member of narration chains, and to help differentiate individuals with similar names. Long lists of weak and fabricated ḥadīth have also been compiled: Shaykh 'Abd al-Husayn Amini, the twentieth-century Shi'ite compiler of *al-Ghadīr,* devotes much of his fifth volume to fabricated ḥadīth and their fabricators. Shi'ite historian Murtada al-'Askari, following the lead of Julius Wellhausen, similarly produced a book of *One Hundred Fifty Fictitious Companions of the Prophet,* debunking the inventions of Sayf ibn 'Amrw. Similar earlier compilations include *al-Jarḥ wa al-Ta'dīl* by Ibn Abu-Ḥatim al-Rāzi, *Tadhkirat al-Mawdū'at* by Abu al-Faḍl Muqaddasi, *Mizān al-I'tidāl* by Shams al-Din Dhahabi, *Nasb al-Rāya* by Abu-Muhammad al-Zayla'i, *Tahdhib al-Tahdhib* and *Lisan al-Mizān* by Ibn Hajar, the last part of *Sifr al-Sa'āda* by Firūzabadi, and *al-La'āli al-Maṣnū'a* by Jallaladdin Suyūṭi.
57. *Amīr* in Sunni fundamentalist political theory, *faqīh* in Khomeini's Shi'ite version.
58. On the history of the Usulis and Akhbaris from the eighteenth century on, see Algar (1969); on the institutional structure of the Shi'ite clergy in this century, see Fischer (1980*a*).
59. This difference is nicely figured in the two founders of the two schools. Vahid Behbehani (d. 1028/1793), the founder of the Usulis, forbade his followers from saying their *namāz* prayers behind Istarabari, the leader of the Akhbaris. Istarabari not only permitted his followers to say their prayers behind Behbehani, he requested in his will that Behbehani lead the funeral prayers when he, Istarabari, died. Interestingly, the Babis and Baha'is are offshoots of the Akhbaris, as befits their syncretic tolerance, while the contemporary fanatical and violent hostility of Usulis against the Baha'is is not out of tune with Behbehani and his followers.
60. Viz. the famous incident earlier this century when Shaykh Abul-Karim Ha'eri-Yazdi was dissuaded by the bazaar from sending students to Europe (Fischer 1980*a*:85).
61. "Shi'ism: A Total Party."

62. Khomeini was exiled from Iran after helping lead the 1963 uprising against the shah's White Revolution. Initially, he had been sentenced to death, but Āyatullāh Shariatmadari intervened, raising him to the rank of *marja' taqlīd* and threatening the government should they harm him. When Khomeini refused to moderate his attacks, he was exiled in 1964 first to Turkey and then to Iraq.
63. Shariatmadari made several attempts to moderate the course of the revolution in a more democratic direction. Eventually he was implicated in a plot against Khomeini's life, and stripped of his turban and put under virtual house arrest. At the end of Shariatmadari's life, Khomeini refused to allow the man who had saved his life go abroad for medical treatment for cancer.
64. On the problems of transmission and variant translations, see Fischer's commentary (1982*d*) on Algar's translation of the third Persian edition and that of the U.S. Government, Algar's bitter protest (1982), and Fischer's rebuttal (1982).
65. This rhetorical question is also to be found in Ahmad Kasravi's *Shi'i-gari.*
66. Shaul Bakhash (1987) seems to think that Muhammad Baqir Sadr's *Iqtiṣādunā* (Persian, *Iqtesad-e Ma*) was well grounded in jurisprudence. But Sadr admits very early on that the ḥadīth are so confusing as to be useless in grounding an economic argument, and contents himself with reviewing the various conclusions (*fatwā*) *fuqahā* have made. That is, one can cite authorities, but not systematically find Qur'anic or ḥadīth grounds for their reasoning.
67. Contrast for instance Meir Tamari's *With All Your Possessions: Jewish Ethics and Economic Life* (1987) with M. A. Mannan (a Pakistani)'s *Islamic Economics: Theory and Practice* (1987).
68. Tabataba'i et al. (1341/1962). See summaries by Fischer (1980*a*:164ff.) and Lambton (1964).
69. For a rich account of the struggles over fiscal policy, land rents, and agricultural capitalism in the second century of Islam, see Massignon's (1982) biography of Hallaj.
70. For example, compare the following: (1) R. Eliezar said, "If all the seas were of ink, and all ponds planted with reeds, if the sky and the earth were parchments and if all human beings practiced the art of writing—they would not exhaust the Torah I have learned, just as the Torah itself would not be diminished any more than is the sea by the water removed by a paint brush dipped in it." (2) "And were every tree that is in the earth made into pens and the sea to supply it with ink, with seven more seas to increase it, the words of Allah would not come to an end; surely Allah is mighty and wise (Sūra Luqman (37:27).
71. Islam does something similar with its insistence on prophethood, which made Zoroastrians recast Zoroaster into an Islamic style prophet, and which makes Jews in Islamic lands speak of Moses as "the Prophet" of Judaism.
72. B. Shabbat 31a: Our Rabbis taught: a certain heathen came to Shammai and asked, "How many torahs have you?" "Two," he replied, "the written

torah and the oral torah." "I believe you with respect to the written, but not with respect to the orah torah; make me a proselyte on condition that you teach me the written torah only." But he scolded and repulsed him in anger. When he went to Hillel, he accepted him as a proselyte. On the first day he taught him alef, beth, gimmel, daleth [the alphabet]; the following day he reversed them to him. "But yesterday you did not teach them to me thus," he protested. "Must you then not rely on me? Then rely on me with respect to the oral torah too."

73. Isaac Luria, the foremost of the Safed Kabbalists formulated the idea that God created the world by "contraction" (*tsimtsum*), by withdrawing into an infinitesimal point.
74. There is a Muslim saying that the whole of the Qur'an exists in the *bismillāh* ("in the name of God"), the first word of the invocation used before reading all but one of the sūras of the Qur'an; and the whole of the *bismillāh* exists in its first letter, *bā,* and the whole of the *bā* exists in its dot (which distinguishes it from other similarly shaped letters).
75. For the renewed fundamentalist stress on this wrath, see Sayyid Qutb's influential "Our Struggle with the Jews" (Nettler 1987).
76. See the suggestion that Muhammad attempted in his later career to transform the Qur'an into a book, but abandoned the effort (Bell and Watt 1970:143).

3. Fear of Différance: the Ḥajj "Rodeo"

1. The term used for the ḥajj by *moriscos* (Muslims under Christian rule in sixteenth-century Spain, legally converts to Christianity, but secretly Muslim). We have accounts of two *morisco* ḥajjīs, one a woman *anteshira* (midwife, exorcist) who settled a dispute over Islamic doctrine at an assembly of male scholars (Harvey 1988).
2. Barley and Eve: speculation in both Jewish and Islamic traditions about the identity of the "tree" in Eden includes grain, usually wheat; see chapter 2, note 30. See also the Talmudic story about the oral and written Torah, in which the latter is compared to wheat and flax, which the foolish servant merely hoards, while the wise servant makes flour and cloth (Seder Eliyahu Zuta 2; Hartman [1985:35]). Apep and Uachet are holy snakes in Egyptian books of the dead: Apep is the black, evil serpent threatening to devour Ra in clouds just before his dawn emergence; Uachet is a beneficent serpentine personification of the northern sky at sunrise (Bishop 1986: 123). Shem in Joyce is the penman, punman, riddler, shame's voice, the unconscious alter ego.
3. "For in the *Wake* [of Joyce], creation is not a historical event that happens only once, with a remote big bang in the Garden of Eden, but a 'hystorical' event (564.31 [Greek *hysteros,* "womb"]) happening constantly in the "garden of Erin" and other modern nations as people keep on waking up and children keep on spilling into the modern world" (Bishop 1986:379–80).

4. By this we mean both the submersion in the crowd of fellow ḥajjīs which generates the powerful communal feelings, reported by participants, but also more theoretically, as Tobin Siebers points out, the "unconscious does not repress as much as it represents . . . the unconscious creates the necessary space to reorient the aggressive impulses detrimental to human relations," and to defer them for as long as possible (1988:183–84). Seibers, thereby, articulates the ethics of the psychoanalytic notion of the unconscious as deferring, through linguistic and quasi-linguistic means, self-destructive and socially destructive drives or processes.
5. A trope used, for instance, by Shari'ati in his description of the ḥajj. The trope of ordinary life as oblivious repetitions, of course, has gone through many variants: repetitive rebirths (Plato, Pythagoras, Buddha, Firdausi), the animality and "false consciousness" of "the rabble" enforced by seductive ideologies and dynamics of the return of the repressed (Hegel, Marx, Nietzsche, Freud, Hedayat), and the caughtness of distracted Being in a hyper-real world of commodities and simulacra where reproductions are experienced and desired as more real than originals (Heidegger, Baudrillard, Ecco, Lasch). See the first section in this chapter, the paragraphs on work on myth.
6. These are both terms meaning moral agents. For example, the saying "*Mullā shodan, che āsān; Adam shodan che moshkel*" ("how easy to become a mull [learned]; how difficult to become Adam [a human being, a Mensch]").
7. Shari'ati suggests a connection with *umm* ("mother"), a group detached from the womb of a larger group, e.g., "Muslims are the best *umma* of mankind" (Qur'an 3:110).
8. Levinas (1970:46) notes that the biblical term *rakhamim* ("mercy," e.g., Arabic *bismillāh-e rraḥmān-e rraḥīm* ["in the name of God, the most compassionate and merciful"]) also contains a reference to *rekhem* ("uterus," "womb"). Arabic is similar. For instance, on the Arabic *raḥm* meaning both "womb/kinship" and "compassion" as used in sermons on the ḥajj, see Antoun (1988, chapter 4).
9. For example, Ali Shari'ati. Abu Dharr is said, like Abraham, to have found his father's gods impotent, and to have rejected them, to have undergone a personal search, and to have discovered Islam before Muhammad received his call. Shari'ati views Abu Dharr not merely as an early Islamic socialist, as do other Islamic leftists, but also as an existentialist. Abraham is in the Qur'an (22:78, 2:35, 4:125) and in Islamic rhetoric the founder of Islam.
10. On Middle Eastern patterns generally, see Abu-Lughod (1987), Beck and Keddie (1978), Fernea and Bezirgan (1977), Mernissi (1977), and Sadawi (1982). On Iran, see Fischer (1978, 1980*a:*160–63, 226–27).
11. Despite, as Shari'ati points out, the Qur'anic verse, "[We] made you into nations and tribes that ye may know each other" (49:13). The clearest case of denial is that of Baha'is (see chapter 4) where often there is denial that Baha'is in fact exist, or that they are anything but a Zionist-inspired political organization designed to destroy Islam. But also in the case of People

of the Book, there is dogmatic insistence that such groups and individuals be politically inactive, and that they be marked through taxation and other symbolic means as subordinate to the "protection" of Islam. On the so-called codes of Umar and the way in which they came into play in Iran during times of political stress, see Fischer (1973, appendix on religious riots). See also the story of the conversion of Abedi's great grandfather in chapter 1. Regarding class differences, there is an elaboration of the idea of Islam as based on *tawḥīd*—theologically, belief in one God, but it is elaborated as the denial of the validity of class within an Islamic society, an ideological tactic like the organicism of European fascism, intended to quash class politics. On nationalism, see below the argument (of Muṭahhari and others) that this is a European import intended to divide and rule the Muslim world.

12. On the competition over legal principles in Iran, see Fischer (1990).
13. The examples in this chapter happen to be mainly male (Bahlul, Agha-yi Bughlaneh), but it should be noted that there is an equally rich bawdy female tradition alluded to in the wedding songs in chapter 5.
14. Khomeini charges that Israeli experts were producing the celebration, that Israel had attempted to disseminate a doctored edition of the Qur'an, that Israel had set fire to the Al-Aqsa mosque, and that Israel intended to occupy all the lands of Islam and destroy Islamic shrines. He says that there have been no good kings, and that Islam is fundamentally opposed to the notion of monarchy (Khomeini 1981:200–208).
15. Compare Freud's notion that primal scenes are only activated and given meaning by later contexts (*Nachträglichkeit*); the structuralist notion employed by Marshall Sahlins that "history is a continuous and reciprocal movement between the practice of the structure and the structure of the practice" and is "powered by disconformities between conventional values and intentional values," i.e., that "in acts of reference . . . cultural categories acquire new functional values" (1981:72; 1985:137–38); and the linguistic notion of indexical functions that point to referential meanings not explicitly stated in referential form.
16. Recall the impression made most dramatically upon Malcolm X and other American Black Muslims, many of whom dropped their black separatism and joined in the world community of Islam, a movement which the Islamic Republic of Iran has attempted, without much effect, to exploit. But see the magnificent stamp issued by Iran portraying Malcolm X in the role of Bilal, the black, first muezzin (caller to prayer).
17. Al-e Ahmad (1964/1985:10). *Āftābeh*s are water pitchers used as Europeans and Americans use toilet paper.
18. The du'a Komeil is a long prayer believed to have been dictated by Imām Ali to his disciple, Komeil ibn Ziyad. It is one of the most dramatic, beautiful, and eloquent of Shi'ite prayers. During the fieldwork for "A Month among the Believers" (chapter 5) Abedi recited this prayer to the Sunni Muslims as they were breaking fast. All were impressed, some even cry-

ing. One asked for a copy of the prayer so he might learn to chant it, but changed his mind quickly when told it was a Shi'ite prayer.

19. Shari'ati sardonically played upon this verse and the phrase "justly balanced" after he was excluded from the conference of Islamic scholars at the 1968 ḥajj. He complained that the Iranian clerical establishment shunned him as a "Wahhabi," while the Wahhabi Saudi Arabian establishment shunned him as a Shi'ite extremist (*ghūlat*). Rejected from both sides must, he joked, demonstrate that he was in the "justly balanced" middle and that his witnessing was on the right track.
20. With some amusement, Al-e Ahmad recalls that he was made to feel uncomfortable about taking journal notes during his ḥajj in 1964.
21. Like "normal" science à la Thomas Kuhn.
22. For example, here faith versus reason, submission/community versus individual responsibility. The so-called Manchester School of Anthropology, led by Max Gluckman, explored in great depth this functionality of ritual.
23. Here, think of the writing of the will, asking of forgiveness from friends and relatives, and public leave taking before going on the ḥajj, as well as the visitations and sacrifices upon return. Arnold von Gennep and Durkheimeans such as Robert Hertz moved this sort of sociological analysis beyond ordinary common sense, by analyzing the ways in which classificatory schemas extended metaphorical systems, and social structures are articulated, dissolved, and reestablished through ritual.
24. Here, think of the powerful elements of the ḥajj shroudlike garb, shaving of the head, bloody sacrifice of animals, stoning, and the circumambulations, running, and trekking. Victor Turner provided anthropologists with these Freudian, Durkheimian, and Manchester School derived conceptual tools for analyzing the (re)creation of powerful, persuasive symbols and ritual forms.
25. Clifford Geertz's celebrated essay "Deep Play: Notes on a Balinese Cockfight" (1973) is a classic in this mode, but see also Victor Turner's essays in *Forest of Symbols* (1967).
26. See Hildred Geertz's (1988) analysis of a punitive ritual in a revolutionary context.
27. Amal originally was the militia attached to the Ḥarakat al-Mahrumin (Movement of the Deprived). It was an acronym for Afwaj al-Muqawama al-Lubnaniya (Lebanese Resistance Detachments). *Amal* also means "hope."
28. But compare the cognate in Hebrew, *hag,* "ceremonial day," "day" of pilgrimage.
29. One begins in Mecca (as did the Prophet's career), one withdraws to the plain of Arafat, one fights the devil, and one returns to Mecca triumphant.
30. The inverse of the story in the work of Zamakhshari and Baidawi that says that Satan hid himself in the mouth of the snake in order to enter paradise. Tabari says this snake was a quadruped and had the appearance of a camel. These stories are also found in Jewish versions: Saadia Gaon says an angel spoke out of the mouth of the snake, the snake did not itself

speak; and that the snake was like a camel is in the *midrashim* (Katsh 1954: 34–36).

31. Burton (1853) gives a list of the ten times the Ka'ba is said to have been rebuilt beginning with the angels when they were ordered to bow to Adam. God created a Bait al-Maamur of four jasper willows and a ruby roof which the angels circumambulated praising God; then they built a house for man on earth. When Adam was sent down, a tabernacle of hollow ruby went along which the angels raised on stone pillars and Adam circumambulated it. Adam, after his expulsion, lamented that he could not hear the angels pray, so God told him to take stones from five mountains (Lebanon, Sinai, Tur, Zayt, Ararat, and Hira) and Gabriel opened a way to the seventh heaven directly above the Ka'ba. This Ka'ba was removed to heaven when Adam died. The third Ka'ba was made of mud and stone by Seth, and was destroyed by the Flood. Abraham and Isma'il then built on the same foundations again with stones from the five mountains, and Gabriel restored the black stone. The Ka'ba was subsequently rebuilt six more times by the time of the Abbasids. On the various ḥadīth relating to the Abrahamic rebuilding, see Firestone (1988).
32. Katsh 1954:102.
33. Wiesel (1976:99–100) supplies the names "Aissa" and "Fatima." Aissa perhaps is "the disappointing one" (A'isah), or possibly the name is Aisha, which would make the pair an interesting coincidence from a Shi'ite perspective, since Aisha, the youngest wife of the Prophet, caught by Ali in an appearance of possible sexual indiscretion, is, for Shi'ites, a negative model, while Fatima, the daughter of the Prophet, is one of the Five Pure Souls.
34. One concern in the variant Islamic ḥadīth is to provide a link between Isma'il and an Arab tribe, the Jurhum, who raised him and taught him Arabic. Birds circling the dry wadi of Mecca attracted the Jurhum there, like the cloud which directs Abraham to the spot on which to build the Ka'ba (see Firestone 1988).
35. The legend is that when they fell from heaven, Eve landed here but Adam fell in Sri Lanka; he set off to find Eve, and their recognition (*'arafā*) of each other at Arafat gives the place its name.
36. Compare the catalogue of meanings offered by Jewish *midrashim* in Wiesel (1976:37–68): perhaps the brothers quarreled over material possessions, the one seizing real estate, the other movable wealth (animals), and the elder tried to kick the younger off his land, so the younger demanded back the animal skins the elder wore; perhaps they quarreled over a woman, either their mother (the Oedipal complex) or Abel's twin sister; perhaps Cain took domain over this world, and Abel over the next, but in this Abel overstepped himself, for the world to come is promised to all; perhaps Abel expressed no sympathy for Cain when the elder was rejected by God, and this enraged Cain: the stress on brothers is there, the theme of caring for one another, am I my brother's keeper?; or perhaps Cain killed in anger

at the injustice of God kicking their parents out of paradise, and in anger at Abel's passivity in the face of this injustice; or perhaps. . . . The list goes on. Guilt is clear, motive is not. But in any case, he is a figure eventually of remorse, of repentance, and of the possibility of redemption, atonement and pardon.

37. The Qur'an only mentions the one raven scratching the earth; but the story as popularly told involves two ravens, the one killing the other.
38. A Jewish *midrash* says that when Adam met Cain, he asked about the penalty for killing Abel, and Cain said he had repented and so his punishment had been mitigated. Thereupon Adam realized the importance of repentance (Katsh 1954:37).
39. Although, of course, Isma'il is the elder brother, Isaac the younger.
40. All the Qur'an (5:32) explicitly says is that God then introduced the laws against murder, but Yusuf Ali interprets this as an allegory of God's withdrawing his favor from the Jews and bestowing it upon a brother nation, thereby plunging the Jews into jealousy and deeper sin.
41. The Qur'an does not name the son, and there is considerable debate in the Islamic ḥadīth as to whether it was Ishma'il or Isaac (Firestone [1988] lists the variant ḥadīth).
42. Note the play between the words for sacred/forbidden (*ḥarām, iḥrām, muḥrim*) and for the normally religious state (*iḥlāl, ḥalāl*). Properly sacrificed meat is *halal;* money earned from legitimate activities is *ḥalāl.*
43. See Hartman (1985:7, 27–31) regarding the contrast between Noah, who passively obeys God and whose "covenant" is marked by a purely natural and universal sign (rainbow), i.e., a one-sided act of God, and Abraham, who is consulted by and argues with God (e.g., over Sodom) and whose convenant involves human action (circumcision) specific to each individual, and is a dialogical relationship with God. This pattern of contrast repeats in the Abraham/Isaac story, as well as in the Aknai over midrash, in both of which God takes pride that his children have "defeated" Him and kept Him to the covenant between them.
44. See Wiesel (1976:69–102) who also suggests that a suspicion lingers in Jewish thought that God pushed the test too far, and that Isaac was killed (pograms, holocaust), and that God has pangs of guilt on Rosh Hashannah, and it is Isaac who is the poet of the *minah* service and is the *melitz-yosher,* the intercessor for the children of Israel condemned for their sins. Hence also the temple was built on Mount Moriah, not on Sinai.
45. *Labbayk,* "I am coming," is technically addressed only to God during the ḥajj. Ambiguously in this slogan, it might be seen as addressed to Khomeini or merely as adding a pro-Khomeini cheer to an address to God; in either case, the intent is that Khomeini is the Husain of his time, and the people, unlike the Kufans, will follow him in the divine cause, in the return to God, against all enemies (Peter Chelkowski, slide lecture, Taziyeh Conference, Trinity College, Hartford, Connecticut, 1988).
46. On the Saudi organization see the dissertations by Makky (1981), Yafi (1983),

and Mutairi (1987); and for a historical perspective, see Khodeif (1986), Ochsenwald (1975, 1977, 1982).

47. A national ḥajj leader in the 1970s was dismissed for embezzling five million tomans. A graphic account of the situation in Ghana is given by Ibrahim Abdulai (Chernoff 1984:70): "If they don't tell you that your passport is lost, they will tell you that your injection card is lost. Maybe you paid them one thousand eight hundred as I last paid. And maybe they have collected about ten thousand or twenty thousand from someone. If they collect such an amount, they won't think about you. . . . Whatever happens they will find a way to let you remain behind so that the one who has paid ten or twenty thousand will go." The government, he explains, only has so much foreign exchange to allocate, enough for 1500 ḥajjīs the year he went, but agents collect money from many more people.
48. The first experiments with liquid nitrogen freezing were in 1982 (1402 A.H.) with 5,000 sheep. The next year 100,000 sheep (or 10 percent of total sacrifices) were so processed and 1,700 tons (64,000 carcasses) chilled to −5°C were distributed to refugee camps in the Sudan, Mali, Tanzania, Djibouti, Bangladesh, and Pakistan. In 1984, the number rose to 186,000 sheep of which 14,000 were stored for the poor in Mecca, 65,000 went by sea to Yemen, Djibouti, and Bangladesh, and the rest were airlifted to Pakistan, Yemen, and Jordan (Al-Mutairi 1987).
49. A Fort Worth Baptist went through the Tokyo training but then changed his mind and refused to convert. He sued Dynalectron Corporation for religious discrimination and pay while waiting reassignment (U.S. District Court, North Texas no. 4-79-346 K, 19 October 1983). The court rejected the religious discrimination suit on the grounds that non-Muslims caught in Mecca allegedly would be punished by beheading.
50. On the decisive changes in the numbers and organization of the ḥajj facilitated by transportation technology, see Khodeif (1986) and Cristelow (1987): the steamship turned around the declining numbers of ḥajjīs in the nineteenth century and boosted especially participation of Javanese and Malays. After World War II, the motor bus and airplane had similar effects.
51. In 1975, 25,000 vehicles congested Mina, taking up space that could handle an estimated quarter million pilgrims. Banning of private vehicles began in 1979. In 1980 there was a near total ban (Al-Mutairi 1987).
52. There were twenty-seven cholera epidemics between 1832 and 1912. In 1902, four hundred pilgrims died in one day at Mina during the peak of the epidemic. In 1893 nearly ten thousand pilgrims died (a tenth of the total), and in 1907 deaths were running a thousand a day at the peak of that year's epidemic. Today, concern is rather with such things as heat stroke.
53. The 1987 information is from "The Ḥajj: The Logistics of a Pilgrimage," *The Middle East,* August 1987, pp. 25–26.
54. Chernoff (1984).
55. Al-e Ahmad (1964).
56. "You may be ten people and there is only one place. You will see that

somebody will just squat down and use his hands to dig in the sand and ease himself there. Whether you are a man or a woman there is no shyness. If you want to see the wonders of different penises, you have to go there; and if you want to see different vaginas, it is the same thing. . . . If you feel shy, you cannot go to Mecca" (Chernoff 1984:82).

57. Trade is permitted, and the ḥajj was one of the great fairs of the Muslim world. "And take provision. . . . It is no fault in you that you should seek bounty from your Lord [during the pilgrimage]" (Qur'an 2:198).
58. On the estimates and statistics of hajjīs by country, means of travel, and totals, see Long (1979), Al-Mutairi (1987), Khodeif (1986).
59. The Wahhabis are opposed to shrines as being a form of idolatry. In Medina only the tomb of the Prophet is still marked by a mausoleum, but those of the first three caliphs are unmarked. Shi'ite popular practice is to touch and cry over the tombs of the Imāms and other saints. Money is thrown, wish ribbons are tied onto the screens around the tombs, prayers are recited, vows made, and pleas sent for divine intercession. (See note 62.) Shi'ites of Iran recite this famous Persian verse when in the shrine of Imām Ridā, the only Shi'ite Imān buried in Iran: *Aghniyā Makka ravand-o foqarā sooye to āyand / Jān be qorbān-e to Āghā ke to ḥajj-e foqarā'i* ("the rich go to Mecca [for pilgrimage], and the poor come to you / May my life be sacrificed for you, my dear, Sir, you are the ḥajj of the poor").
60. Compare Wavell (1913) at the stoning of the devils: "A man standing close to me had his cheek laid open and Masaudi got a cut on the ear" (p. 161); "[in the crush to kiss the black stone] one man lost his loin cloth and came out stark naked, much to the delight of bystanders" (p. 163); and, "the different parts of the prayer yelled out by the Mutowifs in charge of each party, the endeavors of the pilgrims to follow correctly, the complaints of women jostled in the throng, and the imprecations of the men, form a curious medley: 'Oh God, thou knowest—what we know not—Slowly, there! damn your ancestors!—keep us in the straight path'—and so on. One man, an Indian, who had seemingly lost his Mutowif, jogged along behind us for some time bleating like a lost sheep, 'Oh God, keep me among the wicked men.' What he was trying to say meant, of course, precisely the opposite" (p. 166).
61. See, for instance, Hickey and Thompson (1981) on the way becoming a ḥajjī is used to mobilize political power among Bokkos Fulani of Nigeria.
62. There is a long history of suspicion against Shi'ites: see Wavell (1913:99) and Burton (1853:51, 272, 210). Burton reports that Persian Shi'ites sometimes provoked the ill treatment and discrimination. Persians had to pay to enter the Masjid al-Nabawi in Medina, while others were allowed in free. In the southeast corner is the green domed "room of Ayesha" with the graves of Muhammad, Abu Bakr, and Umar. Burton says Persians occasionally polluted the latter two, and Arabs responded by killing Persians. He also reports the killing of a Persian who said instead of, "Peace be upon you, Ya Umar," "Peace be with thee Ya Ḥumar [oh ass]." Consider the difficulty

in aurally distinguishing between *Umar* and *Humar* and you begin to get the picture.

63. Compiled by Shaykh Abbas al-Qummi, this is a supplement to the *Biḥār al-Anwār,* an encyclopedic collection of Shi'ite sources compiled by Muhammad-Baqir Majlisi (d. 1700 C.E.).
64. See Sivan (1985) and Nettler (1987) for details about shifts in attitudes about Jews, Israelis, and Zionists due to the 1967 war.
65. Bahlul (Shaykh Muhammad Taqi Va'ez) takes his nickname from the famous Bahlul of Baghdad, brother of Caliph Haroun al-Rashid, who lived in the time of Imām Ja'far al-Sadiq, and who, like Hamlet, played crazy and dumb to escape political suspicion and imprisonment. He visited the Vaziri Library in Yazd about a year before the Algerians brokered a truce over the Shatt al-Arab between Saddam Husain and the shah, and he related his version of the events of 1936 (he was at the center of agitations against Reza Shah's campaign to unveil women and make men wear European style hats), as well as the story related here about his return to Iran after the 1967 war.
66. Revolutions often succeed through a coalition of forces that manage to sweep away the old regime. There follows a struggle for power often passing through a dual sovereignty phase in which publicly a more liberal provisional government calms fears of conservative members of the revolutionary coalition, while behind the scenes a more radical revolutionary government consolidates power and manipulates events. See Brinton (1938) for a classic account.
67. Abedi and Legenhausen (1986:89).
68. Chatterjee 1986:4.
69. Gellner 1983:124–35.
70. *Al-Kāfi,* vol. 7, p. 24; *Wasā'il al-Shī'ah,* vol. 18.
71. *Istilḥāq* marriages are those, like the levirate in the Bible, in which a widow is impregnated by a relative of her husband so that her husband may have an heir.
72. Bahram Gur (r. 421–38) is said to have imported twelve thousand musicians from India. Muṭahhari's source is Mushir al-Dawlah's (d. 1329) *Tārīkh-e Irān-e bāstan* (History of ancient Iran).
73. Nāfi', 'Aṭā ibn Abī Ribāḥ, Tawūs ibn Kaysān, Yaḥyā ibn Kathīr, Makḥul, Maymūm ibn Mihrān, Ḍaḥḥāk ibn Muzaḥim, respectively; and for Baṣra two persons: Hasan and Ibn Sīrīn; for Kūfa, Ibrahīm Nakhai'.
74. Shaykh Abu Jafar Tusi, Muslim Nishaburi, Abu Abd al-Rahman Nasa'i, Muhammad ibn Isma'il al-Bukhari, Abu Dawud Sajistani, Tarmidhi, Muhammad ibn al-Husayni Bayhaqi – all are from Khorasan. Muhammad ibn Ali Al-Ṣadūq was from Qum. Ibn Maja was from Qazvin.
75. Abū Ḥanifa was from Kabul or Nasa. Ahmad ibn Hanbal was born in Marv, although he was raised in Baghdad, and his family originally was Arab (Mutahhari's reckoning becomes tendentious here). Shafi'i is a Quraashite Arab; Malik is a Qahtani Arab.

76. The four Shi'ites are 'Aṣim who lived in Kufa; Nafi' from Isfahan who lived in Medina; Ibn Kathīr, descended from the Iranians sent to Yemen by Anushiravan; and Kisa'i, the tutor of the children of Caliph Harun al-Rashid.
77. *Islam, The Straight Path* (1958).
78. Muṭahhari gives a list of thirty names; they are somewhat suspect since almost all of them seem to be named Akhsidi, and thus belong to a single family.
79. Muṭahhari cites Minhaj Siraj Jawzayani's (d. 660 A.H.) *Tabaqāt Nāṣirī.* The main Ghaznavid court in Indian was at Lahore.
80. Khajah Mu'in al-Din Chisti (d. 634 A.H., buried at Ajmer).
81. Founded by Muhammad Sam Ghuri (r. 599–602 A.H.).
82. Both queens, Muṭahhari is careful to note, were Shi'ite.
83. Given in English translation in Fischer (1980*a*:252–54).
84. Recorded in a volume edited by Allameh Tabataba'i et al. (1341/1962); see discussion in Fischer (1980*a*:164–65).
85. The history of this struggle through 1980 is given by Fischer (1980*a*), including the silencing of Sayyid Mahmud Taleqani and Āyatullāh S. Muhammad-Kāẓem Shari'atmadari. Taleqani's last speech before his death warned of tyranny by the clergy. Shariatmadari subsequently was conveniently accused of being involved in a plot against the life of Khomeini, was stripped of his turban, placed under house arrest, and denied permission to travel abroad for medical treatment for the cancer which killed him.
86. Ali Monzer, *Shahid Mutahhari: Efshagar-e Tote'eh* (Martyr Muṭahhari: Exposer of the conspiracy), p. 417. In his lifetime Muṭahhari never directly published anything on Shari'ati. After Muṭahhari's death, Ali Monzer went through his papers and published many of his notes, including marginal commentaries on several of Shari'ati's works.
87. Safavid Shi'ism for Shari'ati is hierarchical, superstitious, and dogmatic, and thus, above all, an ideology or discursive formation that was used by a coalition of clerical and state elites to oppress the masses and true Muslims. Alavi Shi'ism was the egalitarian faith of Muhammad and Ali that requires all individuals to think for themselves and not blindly accept the authority of clerics (*taqlīd*), or of other "experts."
88. Jalal-e Al-e Ahmad's polemic *Gharb-zadegī* popularized the term. Translators have tried out various neologisms: "West-struckness," "West-toxification." Westernization seems too neutral a term: the Persian word has an active aggressive connotation.
89. The rule of marrying equals (*kufuw*) is interpreted by other jurists as meaning all Muslims are equal and may marry one another. In various parts of the Arab world, however, the rule was used locally to preserve social class differences. Muṭahhari and Shari'ati both point out that Muhammad arranged a marriage between a freed slave of Khadija (Zayd ibn Haritha) and a daughter of Muhammad's cousin (Zaynab bint Jahsh) who was the granddaughter of the chief of the Qureish tribe; i.e., the precedent of the Prophet is on the side of viewing all Muslims as equals.

90. There are a number of stories about Imām al-Sādiq's refusal of Abu Muslim's invitation to lead the Abbasid movement. The least elaborate story is that Imām al-Sādiq simply said that his time had not yet come. Somewhat more dramatic is the story that he emphatically refused by dropping the letter into the fire. This gesture is interpreted to mean both refusal and prediction that Abu Muslim would himself be consumed by the fire of the movement. A more dramatic story yet has to do with a test of loyalty the Imām administered to Abu Muslim's messenger. The Imām had an oven lighted, while he asks the messenger about his background. When the oven is hot, the Imām asks the messenger how many men Abu Muslim can muster, and is told a hundred loyal Shi'ites are ready to fight. "How loyal to me are you?" the Imām asks. "Ready to sacrifice my life." "Then jump into this oven." "That is not wise." "You question my authority, so you are not sufficiently loyal; watch!" The Imām turns to his disciple, Harun al-Makki, and commands him to jump into the oven. Harun immediately runs toward the oven. The Imām stops him and turns again to Abu Muslim's messenger: "How many men as loyal as this one do you have in your army?" The messenger replies, "None. I thought of myself as the most loyal, but I see I failed the test." "Only such loyalty do we count on," said the Imām. This last story we have on tape from a lecture by Shaykh Muhammad Javad Manaqebi, son-in-law of the renowned Allameh Tabataba'i; the lecture was delivered in Yazd in 1971.
91. See Massignon's *The Passion of al-Hallaj* (1982) for a superb account of the strategies of these families.
92. *Zindīq,* Muṭahhari notes, is a term of some dispute in the Muslim sources: some say it derives from *ṣiddīq* ("truthful"), but most now say it derives from Zand, the language of the Old Pahlavi glosses to the Avesta. Muslim scholars, Muṭahhari says, often mistakenly thought Zand was the sacred scriptures of the Manicheans, since Avesta was the scripture of the Zoroastrians.
93. "When the Lord created the sea / He set upon it a wind in motion / He set a ship on the sea / In which Muhammad and Ali sit / If you wish a place in paradise / Sit near Muhammad and Ali."
94. See Fischer and Abedi (1984).
95. From the same root as *mutashābih,* see chapter 2.
96. Abedi and Legenhausen (1986:160–61).
97. "After Shahadat" in ibid.: 248.
98. Ibid.: 247.
99. Ibid.: 245.
100. Tahirah, Qurat al-Ayn, nineteenth-century Babi leader who publicly unveiled in 1848 and declared old religious obligations abrogated.
101. Turkish author and minister of culture.
102. Egyptian physician, author, and feminist.
103. For which the Karbala story is the primary paradigmatic ritual and parable,

but control of anger is the subject of a number of parables about Moses, Ali, the seventh Imām, Musa, and others.

4. Social Change and the Mirrors of Tradition: Baha'is of Yazd

*This chapter was originally written for the Symposium on the Relation of the Baha'i Faith and Islam held at McGill University in March 1984. I would like to thank particularly Dr. Hosein Danesh and Professor Firuz Kazemzadeh for encouragement; Ahmad Farokhpay for helping translate the *Tārīkh-e Shuhadā-ye Yazd;* Mehdi Abedi for help with parts of the research; Susan Stiles for sending me her thesis and Siyavush Sefidvash's memoirs; Professor Heshmat Moayyed, Professor Amin Banani, and Secretary-General Douglas Martin for sharing corrective and supportive insights; Dr. Farid Akhtar Khavari for last minute aid during the final writing; and the many conference participants who provided insights, information, and discussion.

1. The preference of English-speaking Baha'is is "the Baha'i Faith," a locution I find (quite in line with the general thesis of this chapter) mirroring a Christian setting: viz., "the Christian faith." By contrast, to speak of "someone of the Jewish faith" marks the speaker as a Christian, not a Jew; similarly, while "the Muslim faith" is grammatically correct, it is idiomatically odd; even less likely is "someone of the Hindhu faith." "Baha'ism" is the more secular usage. I will use the two forms interchangeably.
2. *Syncretism* again is not a word preferred by Baha'is, who fear the implication that Baha'i formulations, doctrines, and beliefs be denigrated as humanly fabricated, rather than as divine revelation. *Syncretism* need not, and normally does not, carry this burden: human understanding (even of the divine) often grows by synthesis and syncretic operations, cobbling together truths wherever they be found. There is no good substitute for the word, and of course I intend to leave open the question of what is mere cobbling and what is persuasive integration. This is a key issue for the study of the spread of religions and of conversion processes.
3. The 1955 events were reported in *The New York Times* and *The Times of London,* and were raised at the United Nations. A Baha'i account is that of Muhammad Labib, interesting not only for the details of the events, but also for the conscious construction of martyrology following the style of Nabil's *Narrative* and Malimiri-Taheri's *Tārīkh-e Shuhadā-ye Yazd.* See especially the dreams and other preparations for martyrdom, the expressions of joy that "to be killed for the sake of our faith is . . . our greatest and most cherished aspiration" (p. 13; see also pp. 17, 23), and the divine retributions on all those who acted against the Baha'is.
4. See chapter 1, "*Anjoman-e Zedd-e Baha'iyat.*"
5. Paknejad was one of the "seventy-two" (actually more) members of the Islamic Republican Party killed in the bombing of the Islamic Republican

Party headquarters in 1982. Ṣadūqi was assassinated by the Mojahedin-e Khalq. The Mojahedin gave three reasons for the assassination: Ṣadūqi's speaking against the rights of women in the Assembly of Experts (*Majlis-e Khebregān*), his execution of innocent religious minority members (taken by many at the time as a veiled reference to the execution of the seven Baha'is), and his extortion of money from factory owners and other businessmen for his own projects (presumably for his long-standing dream of building an Islamic University in Qum). Suicide missions such as that which killed Ṣadūqi were called by the Mojahedin *amaliyyāt-e moqaddas-e enteḥāri* from a line by Dr. Ali Shari'ati: when one cannot live, one should choose to die taking the enemy with one. This, of course, is a variant on the much older notion that if one cannot live, one should demonstrate one's faith, dignity, and sense of purpose in the way one dies.

6. It continued crudely:

Khabar bordand be Irūn	They brought the news to Iran
Hameh goftand be kirūn	All said on my cock
Khabar bordand be Ardākūn	They brought the news to Ardekan
Hameh goftand be zardākūn	All said on my carrot (cock)
'Abbās Effendi che pīr lavandi	Abbas Effendi, what a saintly whore
Ham kos kesh o ham dayūs o ham zan lavandi.	Cunt profferer and pimp and his wife's a whore too.

Or there were various rhymed ditties:

In dalle por az barūt	This box is full of gunpowder
[or, *In hoz por-e ābe*]	[or, This pool is full of water]
Kir-e Mahmad-e Hārūt	The cock of Mahmad-e Harut [a bandit]
Bar kos-e zan-e Bābi.	Up the cunt of the Babi woman.

7. *Imām-e Zamān* and *Ṣāheb uz-Zamān* are titles for the Twelfth Imām, the Mahdi. His other titles are *al-Qāim* ("he who will arise"), *al-Muntaqim* ("the avenger"), and *Wali Aṣr* ("the guardian of the age").
8. Muhammad Reza Hakimi of Mashhad, a well-known poet and romantic writer from Khorasan, was long associated with the Islamic politics of Khomeini. Mehdi Abedi met him in 1965 or so in the Vaziri Library of Yazd. His beard was ill trimmed, and he was dressed in a small turban, knee-length coat, and loafers, i.e., a mix between clerical and lay styles. He was on a semisecret tour to recruit followers for Khomeini. When someone asked which of the *marja 'taqlīd* we should follow, he replied, "Following anyone except Ruh-e Khoda ('the spirit of God', i.e., Ruhullah [Khomeini]) is like committing adultery with one's mother or sister in Masjid al-Haram (the mosque in Mecca or one of the other major shrines)." In 1973 Abedi again met him, this time in Tehran. Stopping to exchange greetings, Hakimi asked

where Abedi was going, and Abedi joked, "To a rowzeh," to which Hakimi severely replied, "Who is preaching – Yazid?" He meant that in the absence of Khomeini, all those who continued to preach freely were no better than Yazid, the archtyrant of Shi'ite history.

9. The quotations from Akhtar Khavari are from my field notes. I am aware that they are likely to be controversial to many Baha'is, but this is what he said to me.
10. On the Yazdi Zoroastrians and their Parsi coreligionists, see Fischer (1973).
11. See Boyce (1967).
12. *Ghul-abad* means "founded by a ghoul"; *Mehdi-abad* means "founded by or for the Mahdi, the messiah."
13. Zoroastrians were long plagued by Muslims with the question of where in the Qur'an their prophet was. Their status as People of the Book depended on the answer; without such status they would have no legal rights in an Islamic polity. The compromise answer often was to make Abraham the Zoroastrian prophet, since otherwise this prophet would have no distinctive extant followers: in Muslim eyes, Moses is the Jewish prophet, and Abraham the founder of monotheism. For Jews, of course, Moses is a pivotal figure, but Abraham, Isaac, and Jacob are at least as crucial, and in any case none of these figures is defined in the nonhuman (sinless, omniscient, completely exemplary) terms of a Muslim prophet. It is for this reason, of course, that Muslims accuse Jews (as they do Christians for other reasons) of having tampered with the scriptures.
14. In good mnemonic style, he listed: (1) *idda'a kardan* (he claims to be a messenger of God); (2) *radd kardan* (he abrogates past laws, and brings new ones); (3) *istiqāmat kardan* (he stands on his word no matter what befalls him, as opposed to ordinary men, including even the Bab, who under pressure recant); (4) *kalām* (he brings a book which he says is not of his own composition, but is divine); (5) he could not remember the fifth, but was sure it was not producing miracles since these could only serve as proof to witnesses.
15. See Fischer (1973:347ff.) for dreams in conversion processes. See Labib (1981) for dreams and martyrdom.
16. The executioner of Mullā Ali in 1892 is said to have developed a worm-infested boil on his neck from which he painfully died. A less momentous but exemplary case of this Baha'i narrative topos of retribution is that of the man who burned down the door of a walled garden belonging to a Yazdi Baha'i villager, K., in 1968. K. knew who did it, but the latter would not admit it. K. would ask him, "Do you believe in God?" "Yes." "You say you did not do it?" "No." "All right . . . go on!" But that same month the man had an auto accident, running into a utility pole for which he had to pay a thousand tomas ($130) damage, and his daughter lost an eye in another accident on her way to a Muslim shrine. Baha'i Q.E.D.: God is just. But it turned out that the cause of the burning of the door was not simple

anti-Baha'ism, but that this man had owned a brick kiln near the gardens and K. had complained about the smoke to the governor's office, the mayor's office, and the police. The man had been forced to relocate the kiln six kilometers farther outside of town.

17. Sunnis interpret this verse as being the tree from which the people of hell will eat. For the Shi'ite interpretation, see the Shi'ite dictionary of the Qur'an, the *Qāmūs-e Qur'ān,* volume 4, p. 8, and volume 3, pp. 40–42.
18. According to his widow's unpublished memoir (n.d.), she was told he was the seventh. Details from her powerful, sad account include the following. A Mr. Keshmiri and "forty" uneducated villagers came at midnight to take him away. They seized all the money, silver, and books in the house. Before he left, Nurullah went into the receiving room, and took a vessel of sweets, and one by one fed them to the forty men as if he were a proper host "sweetening the mouths" of his guests. At first, for "forty days", the seven Baha'is were held in the headquarters of the Revolutionary Guards; then they were moved to a dark basement. Visits were not allowed until the last day. When his wife saw him, he could hardly open his eyes because they were so unused to the light. He told her to inform the National Assembly of Baha'is that their fate was being sealed that night. In the early morning, the phone rang and she was told to come to the Farokhi Hospital for his body. She was told that Keshmiri and a Mr. Moti'i had urged him to recant, but he had refused. "Instead he raised his hands towards the heavens, recited *ziyaratnameh*s, spoke to Baha'ullah, put sweets in the mouth of his executioners, and asked them to free him, so he could reach the presence of his beloved. So they shot him." The seven bodies, she recalls, were lying on the hot ground, on the desert, each under a shroud. When Nurullah's shroud was removed, "I saw his smiling face. There was a bullet on his chest. Mr. Moti'i ran to Nurullah's body and said, 'You see how charitable this man is? He gave us one bullet back.' Nonetheless they charged us one hundred tomans per bullet and left." The Baha'is were allowed to wash the corpses, dress them in white silk, perfume them, and do funeral rites. A Muslim man offered her some cold water with a bit of rose water, and as she took the glass, he said, "Look! Here is the desert of Karbala! Curses upon Yazid!" Mr. Moti'i ran up and seized the glass, punching the man in the face and dragging him off. Although burial was allowed, subsequent memorial rites (*porseh*) were forbidden. The next morning the widows were told to come to the court to receive their husbands' effects. Mrs. Akhtar-Khavari did not even bother to check her husband's effects, but Mrs. Faridani did and noticed that her husband's watch was missing. With some anger a Revolutionary Guard, a lad named Mobin from Mashhad, took it off his wrist and flung it at her. Some days later, Keshmiri, a Mr. Qassemi, and two mullās seized the house and its possessions, including even the bangles, wedding ring, and necklace Mrs. Akhtar-Khavari was wearing. They said if she would say she was a Zoroastrian she could have her house and possessions back.

She refused, taking off her sandals, saying, "Here, take these too." She was allowed shortly to leave the country.

19. See Farhang's article in *The Progressive* (summer 1984). His polemical style has not changed, but the content has.

5. Diasporas: Re-membering and Re-creating

1. For a registering of these differences in Iranian short stories and films over the past few decades, see Fischer (1984).
2. Fender in his book *Plotting the West* (1981) analyzes the letters and journals of those who made the overland trips across North America to the West in the nineteenth century, showing how in grasping for ways to describe their new world they oscillated between European urban imagery ("mountains like cathedrals") or a flat scientistic descriptivism; and others have commented on the complaints of early American writers that there were as yet no authentically American tropes and narratives with which to build true literary artistry. Anthony Wallace, in his now classic, *Death and Rebirth of the Seneca* (1969), illustrates how revitalization cults (of the Iroquois, but also the Great Awakening revivals among whites) take elements from both past traditions and new ways and fuse them together into new combinations that can reduce anxiety and sustain a feeling of place and competence in the world. Fredrick Jackson Turner's "frontier thesis" included the idea that a new kind of American character was created through stripping away European traits and forcing a style of self-reliance. David Riesman analyzed the sense in the 1950s that American individualism led to the feelings of atomized alienation of the "lonely crowd." Marshall Berman (1982) describes the classic European accounts of modernity in which the boulevard became an exhilarating, mysterious theater, one in which different classes were on display for each other in a new anonymous way, and in which confidence men, flanneurs, and dandies enjoyed themselves.
3. See Fischer (1984) for a description.
4. This obviously is not a comment about any lack of creativity, but instead one about the length of time it often takes for major traumas to find their conceptual form: compare the now vigorous American literary activity working through the Vietnam experience, twenty years later. It is, of course, not a matter of time alone, and definitive writing can occur during traumas, e.g., Miriam Cooke (1988) on the female poets of the Beirut civil wars. I cite Balzac and Mahfuz as figures who portrayed Paris and Cairo, respectively, so "realistically" that their readers came to view reality through the literary lenses they provided. Balzac provided powerful lenses for Karl Marx's own powerful tropes. I cite Hasek's *Good Soldier Svejk,* Heller's *Catch-22,* and Pynchon's *Gravity's Rainbow,* and Günter Grass's series of novels for providing equally powerful, but nonrealist, lenses of perception and of moral

stance for wide readerships focused on the disasters of recent and current history.

5. Islamic discourses can, of course, include many of the same analyses of social discontent as marxism. The *Crisis of the Arab Intellectual* as Laroui posed it in the late seventies was the seeming choice between a revolutionary marxism which saw Islam as obscurantist but thereby could not appeal to the masses, and a politicized Islam which while good for mobilization was ill designed for guiding political strategy, being open to multiple interpretations of the same mobilizing terms.
6. See Fischer (1973:222–31) for *sofreh*s in Yazd.
7. See Good, Good, and Moradi (1985).
8. M. Fischer (1980*a,* 1984).
9. M. C. Bateson, et al. (1977).
10. Small dealers may be caught with *boz-e shal* ("lame goat") carpets, and will sell too quickly *dokhtar-e khāneh māndeh* ("old maid") carpets. The former are carpets the seller must get rid of and does not know the real worth of, so will sell too cheaply. Often this is in a situation where he is caught in a cash flow problem where he has a good deal on a more profitable carpet, and is willing to take a loss on a smaller deal to raise the capital for the bigger deal. *Dokhtar-e khāneh māndeh* is simply a carpet whose good qualities are not evident to the seller.
11. *Kāseb* contrasts with *tājer,* a large merchant, and colloquially means someone who earns his bread, who undergoes hardship. When one is invited to a meal *kasebūné,* it means a simple meal of yogurt, *abgusht,* and *sangak* bread. There is a beloved ḥadīth in the bazaars of Iran: *al-kāsib ḥabībullah* ("he who earns his bread is a friend of God").
12. See chapter 1; Fischer (1980*a:*86); and Fischer and Abedi (1984).
13. See chapter 1.
14. See Fischer (1980*a:* 278, n. 13).
15. Big serpents (*af'i*) are said to love gold and silver. If you see a large snake, there is supposed to be treasure nearby, pictured in popular imagination as a large bucketful of emeralds, rubies, sapphires, on which coils a serpent, i.e., the moral is, if you are seduced, if you go too close, you endanger your life.
16. Since the 1965 Immigration Reform Act went into effect in 1968, replacing the Immigration Act of 1924, Asians and Latin Americans have replaced Europeans as sources of immigration into the United States. In France, North African immigrants are seen as a quite different phenomenon than previous immigrant groups such as the Poles and Jews of the past century, because they come from new nations created in a struggle against France, and because they are thought to have less desire to assimilate.
17. Of these, only Mukherjee lives in the United States, though Jamil Dehlavi was trained here. The rest live in England. One might add to the list, albeit from not quite a first-world context, the South African writer, Ahmed Essop.

18. Beeman (1986:20).
19. The Shi'ite story is that Ali refused to go to the mosque, to show his displeasure with the usurpation of the leadership of the community. Umar, insisting that Ali come to the mosque and display obedience, went to Ali's house and knocked on the door until Fatima answered it. Umar kicked the door open. It hit Fatima hard in the stomach and she (subsequently) miscarried the child, Mohsen. Umar put a rope around Ali's neck and dragged him to the mosque. Fatima was already in mourning for the recent death of her father, the Prophet Muhammad. She died shortly thereafter.

    The tragedy in Houston—one of a string of murders of female real estate agents—was particularly difficult for the husband because he had been away on a business trip in Canada when it happened. He had brought back a trinket, and Mehdi had him place the gift in the casket. The bride was laid out in her bridal dress, and in this case there was an open casket review.
20. For instance, see problem number 620 in Khomeini's *Risāleh Towzīh al-Masā'il.*
21. A Lur is questioned in the grave. *Man rabbuk* ("who is your God?"), asks the first angel in Arabic. *Man chinam Rab china* ("how do I know what Rab [God] is?"), he replies in his dialect. *Man rasūluk* ("who is your prophet?"), asks the second angel. "What?" asks the Lur, not understanding. The angels begin to beat him with a club. "Now I know why no one wants to leave the world and die: it is because of the bad treatment by these angels."
22. A much enjoyed joke under the Pahlavi regime was this version of the first night. "Who is your God?" "His Majesty, the Shahanshah!" "What is your religion?" "The White Revolution." "What is your holy book?" "His Majesty's book, *The White Revolution.*" The angels raise their clubs to beat the infidel. God stops them and asks the deceased, "What is the matter with you?" The man replies, "Sorry, God. I thought these two might be Savak agents."
23. On *mut'a* marriage in Iran under the Islamic Republic, see Shahla Ha'eri's (1985) interview materials with women who have engaged in such relationships.
24. The groom moved to Washington, D.C., where he and his wife worked in the Iranian Interests Section of the Algerian Embassy. He never criticized me directly, and in fact sent me the photos of the dancing with a warm note: "thank you for making it a memorable occasion." Later, he had a change of heart, and according to another employee of the Iranian Interests Section, he put together a "criminal file" on me, which included charges of drinking, womanizing, dancing, etc. When I heard of the allegations, I sent him the famous Omar Khayyam quatrain: "You are drunk, a mullā told a whore / That's why you do what you do / I am that, the whore replied, and perhaps worse than that / But are you really what you pretend to be?" Soon he began a telephone campaign, discouraging people from using my services in weddings. Ironically, my popularity among the Iranians in Hous-

ton rose, since people were reassured that I was not connected in any way with Khomeini's regime.

25. Research on the extreme Islamic groups (*jamā'at*) in Egypt tends to confirm this. See Ibrahim (1980), Kepel (1984).
26. A custom practiced in Egypt and the Sudan.
27. Khomeini's *Risāleh Towzih al-Masā'il* says on page 1, the very first issue: "A Muslim's belief in the fundamentals of religion must be based upon reason and he may not practice imitation in regard to the fundamentals of religion. . . . But in regard to the actions (*aḥkām*) of religion, he must either be an expert (*mujtahid*) and arrive at them through reasoning, or he imitates an expert . . . or he must practice his duties so cautiously as to be certain of having practiced according to one's duties. For example, he refrains from practicing an act which is considered unlawful by some experts and not unlawful by others, and practices an act which is considered obligatory by some and recommended by others. . . .
28. *Tirmidhi* 4:13; *Musnad,* 11:237–38; also Graham (1977:122).
29. *Wasā'il al-Shī'a* 5:5.
30. Qur'an 26:223–26.

6. Concluding Notes: Autographically Changing Iran—Minor Media and Bicultural Graphics

1. *Bicultural,* particularly for Iran, should be recognized to be a shorthand for *multicultural:* like Japan, Iran linguistically always operates at least biculturally with a language that is Indo-European and a script that is Semitic, but also a language that in its more elegant forms is often Arabicized in vocabulary and locution; in addition there is the admixure of Turkish both in general vocabulary and in the colloquial "kitchen" register of language learned from the bazaar, maids, and other service personnel in Tehran and along an isogloss that is moving eastward from Azarbaijan; and of course there are local dialects everywhere. Moreover, religiously and in terms of national identity, as was stressed in chapter 3, even in such cases as that of Muṭahhari, there is a constant tension between pre-Islamic (Zoroastrian) identity and Islamic forms and sensibilities. This then already is a complex "Iranian" side of the bicultural encounter with "Western" (an equally stratified complex of) cultural forms, be they linguistic, religious, artistic, scientific, or other. *Bicultural* is the temporal form that the *multicultural* takes in particular strategic or political polarizations, emphasizing for particular purposes binary oppositional markers and differentiations. But these are only momentary arrests or stases in a larger, mobile, hermeneutical arsenal.
2. Valid comparative work requires at least three cases to avoid dualistic better-worse judgments. Particularly in chapters 2 and 3, we have explored Jewish, Christian, and Islamic interpretations, genres, and story variants. There is a sense in which the monotheistic religious sensibility is a chordal struc-

ture which cannot be heard if the Islamic third is omitted. It would be like jazz without the blue notes. Interestingly, there has been a persistent hypothesis, primarily of Christian ecumenical persons interested in retrieving the fullness of Christian heritage and/or countering excesses of Christology, which has seen Islam as the true heir of the early Jewish Christians, who fled eastward after Hadrian's destruction of Jerusalem in 132, and who, not having participated in the development of Hellenistic Christianity, were later rejected as heretics. (Hans Küng [1987] is the most recent to pursue this thought, citing as his predecessors Adolf Schlatter, Adolph von Harnack, Hans-Joachim Schoeps, and Paul Schwarzenau. He does not mention them, but Patricia Crone and Michael Cook's controversial book, *Hagarism,* might well be reconsidered with this tradition in mind.) But one need not pursue such thoughts either in terms of the origins of Islam or in terms of transmuting Christian dogmas into acceptable "postmodern" form (e.g., Hans Küng (ibid.), much to the discomfort of his Shi'ite interlocutor, Seyyed Husain Nasr) to recognize the importance of listening for the harmonics provided by the Islamic third. Methodologically, it is a point much like the lesson that Claude Lévi-Strauss has tried to teach regarding mythology: meaning cannot be fully appreciated in any one interpretation or tradition, but only through their interplay and variations.

3. For example, the slogan that the Qur'an or Islam has rules in detail for every aspect of life. Note not only that contemporary political leaders, such as Muammar Qadhafi of Libya or the late Zia ul-Haq of Pakistan who invoke the *sharī'a,* implement Islam in opportunistic ways; but more importantly, that theorists like Sayyid Qutb of the Egyptian Brotherhood rely on a kind of existentialist interpretation of the intuitive intent of the Qur'an, which allows them latitude for reinterpreting traditional understandings. See Binder (1988) for an account of Sayyid Qutb's experience of rapture (*iltadhdh*) and desire (*ishtāq*) for the Qur'an, and the aesthetic vision (*taṣawwur*) which is actualized through a praxis of movement (*ḥarakat*); the world is not so much a place where perfection can be achieved by the application of jurisprudence as a moral field in which one must strive, where the relation between projects and the human existent (*al-kinūna al-insāniyya*) are central. Sayyid Qutb reminds Binder of Protestant theological moves that are less concerned with literal truth of revelation and more with the moral phenomenology of the message. There are interesting parallels in vocabulary, appeal to existentialism and phenomenology, between Sayyid Qutb and Ali Shari'ati.
4. See the essays by Robert Morris and W. T. J. Mitchell in *Critical Inquiry* 15(2), winter 1989. For somewhat parallel arguments about modernist styles of objective writing, including science, hegemonic ideology, and all forms of writing that assert consensus of opinion, that suppress the history of words, and that operate under the sign of nonrhetorical plain style, see Tyler (1988).
5. Sweetman (1988) traces the history of the last five centuries of mutual bor-

rowings in the influence of the flowing arabesque, the play with geometric composition, and the learning to handle the effects of light and bright colors, as well as the calligraphic. See especially pp. 19–20 for a discussion of the role of the Islamic arabesque in reworking the more static Greco-Roman grotesque, Italian "strapwork," Renaissance *rinceau,* and Celtic interlace patterns; and in turn the classical "*Rūmi*" (i.e., Greco-Roman) roots of Islamic arabesque. Sweetman describes the trade in carpets, brass work, embroidery, pottery, and calligraphy that conveyed these designs into Europe, noting in particular the collections of arabesque pattern books. In painting, he reminds us of the virtuosity of Mughal painters such as the artist of Emperor Jehangir who made five copies of the gift portrait by Isaac Oliver that Sir Thomas Roe presented the emperor, so exact that it was difficult to tell the original from the copies. In the nineteenth century, European artists experimenting in Orientalist techniques and form learned new control with light, color, and composition. While Sweetman's account is focused on Western learning from the Orient, and is not a review of Islamic art, he does pay attention to regional differences within the Islamic world.

6. Paulson (1983), also Mitchell (1986)'s chapter on Burke.
7. The theory of art, or philosophy of aesthetics, that constitutes the orthodoxy of art history departments as well as of "high culture" museums is undergoing serious critique these days from four directions: in accounts, such as Gadamer's (1977/1986), of the roots of modern art, for instance in the iconographies of Dutch still-life paintings (the half unpeeled lemon and other figures of evanescence and the fleetingness of life) that show it not to be pure compositional form; in explanations of modernist abstract, nonobjectivist art, which demonstrate its unacknowledged dependence on elaborate theories and verbalizations without which it is impossible to see; in deconstructions of the writings of idealist aestheticians such as Kant and Hegel by Gadamer (ibid.), Derrida (1987*a*), Mitchell (1986), et al.; and in the ever increasing pressure from other cross-cultural aesthetic traditions, both in the forcing of recognition of the historical roles they have played in the creation of the European high culture tradition and in their growing global constituencies and demands for recognition in cosmopolitan museums that continue to exclude them. On this last debate, see the forthcoming volume on the 1988 Smithsonian Conference on Exhibiting Culture: the Politics and Poetics of Representation (Ivan Karp and Steven Levine, eds.).
8. See Oleg Grabar's (1988) skewering of recent Islamic art shows, including the London Festival of Islam celebration of the turn of the fifteenth Islamic century, that invoke an alleged ethos of the desert, of *tawḥīd* unity in architecture, of geometry or arabesque as defining Islamic art, ignoring the chronological periods and spatial regional styles that may include quite incompatible forms.
9. Carnivalesque variant on Sassanian, "Aristotelian," and medieval Muslim Rings of Eight Propositions of Good Government (see appendix 2).
10. "(. . . the question of women, of psychoanalysis, and of politics, it brings

them all together); the question of Power, as they still say, is first of all that of the post and telecommunications . . ." (Derrida 1987*b*). Postcards, postings, the deferral/distortion/displacement of response over distance, separations between sendings and receivings ("dis-tancing"), between self and other, orderer and ordered, lover and beloved are the key metaphors in play here. Might there be an allusion as well to the Persian and Arabic *ṭanz* ("mockery," "satire") in Derrida's hyphenated *dis-tancing*?

11. The term is taken from Sreberny-Mohammadi and Mohammadi (1988).
12. There seem not to be the scatological or sexual exposure themes in Iranian cartoons that there were in French Revolution cartoons; though these themes are well developed in jokes, first about the shah, then about Khomeini, and about his successor-designate (until 1989) Montazeri. It would at some point be interesting to do a comparative analysis of cartoon themes and styles in the Pahlavi and Islamic Republic periods, as well as among pro- and anti-Khomeini cartoons. One brilliant device used during the revolution was a calligraphic one: the shah was shown literally sowing corruption (*fasād*) by throwing from a grain bag a generous shower of the words *Fasād, fasād, fasād*. . . . The same artist, Ardeshir Mohassess, also depicted the shah fleeing a cloud of words that read, "*Marg bar shāh*" ("death to the shah" or "down with the shah"). Visual puns at the time included hats on tombstones (*kola sar-e kasī gozashtan,* "putting the cap on someone," is to deceive them) and mullas turning on flashlights that shed darkness rather than light. There was also a widely admired cartoon of "Āyatullāh Ringo" (Montazeri's son) as a rock star in sombrero and six-shooters.
13. Taken to the extreme, suppression of language in the search for abstract form as a universally expressive mode of communication, as a spiritual alternative to industrial materialism, was, of course the quixotic quest of modernist art: see the essays by Morris, Mitchell, and Summers in the *Critical Inquiry* issue promoting a "New History of Art" (vol. 15, no. 2 [Winter 1989]). This modernist project was shot through with contradictions, and abstract art, as Mitchell amusingly documents, and Jonathan Borofsky lampoons, actually turned out to be "a visual machine for the generation of language" (ibid., pp. 366, 352–53).
14. In the *Phenomenology of Spirit,* taken up playfully in Derrida's *Glas.* Hegel talks of the "natural religion" of sun or light worship, where there is no figuration or representation, pure phenomenology. Then there is growth into the religion of plants and flowers, which are not quite selves or subjectivities. But the flower is a first step: it is acted upon, brought out of itself by light, by the sun, and thereby produces its own light as color. Finally, there is the religion of animals who are fully *coupable* ("guilty"), free moving, agonistic, and responsible.
15. English *tulip,* French *tulipe,* German *Tulpe,* from Turkish *tulbend,* Persian *dulband,* "turban," or from Persian *dulab,* the tulip-shaped container that feeds grain/seeds onto the millstone. German *Turkenband* (Turkish turban) is rather the tiger lily.

16. *Belated,* dialectical, always conscious of a powerful predecessor. The term is from the literary critic Harold Bloom, but see also Abdallah Laroui's comments on the dialectical condition of third-world intellectuals in his essays on *The Crisis of the Arab Intellectual.*
17. "But like all examples [Beispielen], as Hegel will have pointed out, they play, there is play in them, they give room for play" (Derrida 1978/1987*a*:79).
18. Mourning as incorporation, reactivation, performing the dead person's role or playing out his intent, thus a process of imitation, doubling, reproducing, decrypting, and putting back into the play of life. Compare the circulation of blood and tears in the martyrdom trope, where each cutting down of a martyr through tears and blood revivifies the determination of others. This is quite graphically represented in Persian posters with hatchets or bayonets (marked by U.S. insignia) cutting down either tulips, often growing at graveyards, or bodies, and drops of blood and tears irrigating newly sprouting flowers.
19. Both the linguist, Fernand de Saussure, and the author of *Journey in the Alps,* H. de Saussure, from whom Kant took a description of the wild tulip.
20. Resemblance between the emblem of the Islamic Republic and that of the Sikhs has made some opponents of the Islamic Republic attempt to denigrate the emblem as an imitative borrowing from inappropriate foreigners. Quite apart from the speciousness of the charge, the issue is not whether concrete items are borrowed from anywhere, but how a design grammar operates. It is hardly surprising that using common design grammars, the emblems should be similar.
21. "An emblem . . . is technically a composite visual-verbal form, an allegorical image accompanied by a textual gloss" (Mitchell 1989:350).
22. Melot (1988:25–26).
23. On the psychological methodism of mourning in Shi'ite passion plays, processions, and sermons, and its creation of quiet determination and stoicism; as well as on models among the Imāms that value control of rage, see Fischer (1980*a*). On the comparison between the psychological methodism and that of the Lutheran *Trauerspielen* analyzed by Walter Benjamin, see Fischer, "Becoming Mulla" (1980*c*). On the contrast between mourning in the passion plays and in funeral rites, see Fischer, Good, and Good, "Persian Passion Playing" (1978). On the operation of sadness in Iranian emigré depression, see Good, Good, and Moradi (1985); and on literary models of grief work and madness, see M. Fischer (1984).
24. On the psychic dynamics of demonstrations in Iran, see Isfandiari's novel, *Day of Sacrifice.* More generally, see also the accounts of rage and reverse Oedipal murder (of fathers against sons) in the work of Reza Barahani, the accounts of the psychological methodism of demonstrations constructed around the Karbala paradigm and their transformation of rage and grief into determination and control (Fischer 1980*a, c*), and the discussion of the dynamics of religious riots in Iran (Fischer 1973).
25. The suggestion in chapter 4 that Khomeini replayed key elements of the

Babi revolution has been spelled out somewhat more fully by Fischer (1987). Also on the dynamics of Khomeini's persona, see Fischer (1983).

26. On the different class-linked discourses of Shi'ism, and on the social stages of revolution both in long-term structural terms and in short-term processual phases, see Fischer (1980*a*). On a five-generational model of the evolution of Muslim activist movements over the past two centuries see Fischer (1982*b*).
27. The circulation of cassette tapes grew throughout the 1970s. When Khomeini was expelled from Iraq, and denied entry to Kuwait, advisers such as Ibrahim Yazdi counseled moving to Paris where cassette tape production and transmission to Iran could be efficiently organized.
28. It was alleged that Khomeini's men in Paris would announce demonstrations to be held in Iran, the BBC would report the announcements as news, and demonstrations would accordingly be held.
29. See especially Jamieson (1988), but also Wills (1987). These analyses begin to make some sense of widely discussed "postmodernist" or television politics, in which hyperreal effects are pursued, e.g., Hendrick Smith's January 1989 Public Broadcasting Service special on the new breed of Congressional politician who learns to speak in sound bites, who is constantly seeking television publicity, and constantly raising money for renewed campaigning. One of Smith's examples is the dramatic change in style and effect of Speaker of the House of Representatives, Tip O'Neill, in the last years of his career, when O'Neill changed from being a back room broker into becoming a forceful television character beating Reagan at his own game. Compare Jean Baudrillard's (1988*b*:108–9) comment: "[Americans] prefer to act as though they believed in [the merits of their leaders] on condition that their belief is not taken too much for granted. Governing today . . . is like advertising and it is the same effect that is achieved—commitment to a scenario." Richard Rose, in *The Postmodern President* (1988), argues that the resources available to a president no longer are sufficient to meet the expectations of the office, as defined by modern presidents since Franklin Roosevelt, especially because of the internationalization of the political economy; and hence perhaps the tendency to rely upon advertising tactics and effects.
30. Something that finally became particularly explicit and subject to analysis and public consciousness in the American national political campaigns of 1988.
31. In this regard, 1987–88 was a particularly interesting period. Khomeini intervened several times to ensure the étatist power of the state against conservative Islamic objections, and in so doing he seemed to push his Islamic government yet a step further along the road of disengagement from the constraints of traditional jurisprudence. There was first the response to an inquiry by the minister of labor and social welfare that the state was entitled to impose obedience to its rules in return for services rendered; i.e., the state could regulate social and medical services, imposing requirements on employers. When this was questioned by the conservative Council of

Guardians, who feared it would open the door to allowing the state to replace Islamic rulings with its own, Khomeini reaffirmed the power of the state. When President Khameneihi attempted to downplay the implications of this in a major Friday sermon, Khomeini issued a blistering rebuke, affirming that the state might even suspend such "secondary" obligations in Islam as prayer, pilgrimage, or fasting. In an interesting response to conservatives' objections about foreign films and sports coverage which allegedly displayed bodies too openly, Khomeini instructed the director of the state radio and television that actresses could be shown without veil, and soccer matches could be shown even if athletes were not fully covered. In the recent parliamentary elections, moreover, Khomeini issued a call for those to be elected who defend the interests of the poor. Like the current U.S. Congress, parliament tends to be more populist-progressive; while the Council of Guardians, like the current U.S. presidents and Supreme Court, acts as a conservative check.

32. Sreberny-Mohammadi and Mohammadi (1988) suggest the bear is associated with deceit (*makr*), but it is the fox that is deceitful in Persian folklore as it is in English. The bear licks up honey as in this cartoon. But there is an idiom, *dūsti-e khāleh kherseh* ("friendship of Auntie Bear"). The associated tale is that a man adopted a bear as his friend. One day he was trying to nap and insects kept bothering him, so he asked the bear to chase the insects away. The bear tried its best, but one fly was persistent, and the bear lost patience, picked up a stone, and smashed it on the man's forehead killing him as well. *Dūsti-e khāleh kherseh* is the archetype of foolish friendship, and not inapt to Afghanistan and Russia.
33. The Kennedy line in turn is said to be adapted from the Lebanese poet Khalil Gibran.
34. We draw from some four hundred posters, including a score in our possession; 78 from the volume edited by Ali Abulfazl (1985) issued on the sixth anniversary of the revolution; 147 from the volume issued by the Daftar Tablighat Islami (1986); 70 in the Jim Hitselberger collection, now deposited in the Hoover Library Archives, and in slide form at the Center for Middle Eastern Studies, University of Texas at Austin; other posters and images in the Hoover Archives; plus a complete collection of stamps issued by the Islamic Republic. A preliminary account of the Islamic Republic's stamps is provided by Chelokowski (1987). For some of the posters, such as those collected by Ali Abulfazl, names of the artists are given in the captions; some other posters include producer and artist names in the design of the poster itself.

    Insofar as the two volumes issued from Iran are consciously edited, a rough content analysis may be of interest. Of the 78 images in the Ali Abulfazl volume, 23 are focused on individuals (14 are prominent martyrs, 5 of these posters are devoted to Muṭahhari, and 1 interestingly claims the legacy of Mirza Kuchek Khān; 9 are of other personalities, including three clerics from earlier in the century: Fazollah Nuri, Āyatullāh Modarress, and

Āyatullāh Kashani). Of the 55 more ideographic posters, 10 are devoted to the war with Iraq, 16 to the anniversary day of the revolution (11 February), 5 to the anniversary of the declaration of the Islamic Republic (1 April), 8 to Jerusalem Day, 4 to the anniversary of 15 Khordad (1963), 2 to Students Day (4 November), 2 to Black Friday (8 September), 2 to Ashura; and 1 each to the "Days of Allah-o-akbar" (the nighttime chanting in the period leading to the victory of the revolution), Women's Day, the unity of the Kurds and the Khomeini revolution, and the martyrs buried at the now huge cemetery of Tehran, Behesht-e Zahra.

If the Ali Abulfazl volume provides some sense of the ceremonial calendar and emphasis of the Islamic republic (as well as containing quite a number of the stunning images described in our text below), the Daftar Tablighat Islami volume (1986) provides images from the war front provinces of Kurdistan, Bakhtaran/Ilam, and Khuzistan. Posters are shown in situ: on walls, on buildings, on billboards along the roads through the desert and along city streets. At least a third are directly concerned with the war; quite a number of these fuse together traditional images of Karbala or of the final battle under the Mahdi with contemporary soldiers. Half a dozen or so also specifically have images of the Dome of the Rock in Jerusalem, showing soldiers on their way to that goal. Much of the rhetoric of the war was directed toward regaining Karbala, and then Jerusalem. Thirteen of the posters are traditional Ashura or Mahdi imagery; the allusion to the war and the transcendent millenarian goals of the revolution are left implicit. Thirty or so of the posters rely completely on standardized icons and calligraphic slogans: doves, tulips, the emblem of the Islamic Republic, and so on. Some twenty-eight are portrait posters of clerical leaders; of these half are of Khomeini. Among the most interesting posters are the dozen or so murals.

35. The sublime does not exist in nature, but is beyond measure; it uses natural forces, the colossal, and the monstrous to present projections. The beautiful, by contrast, is taken from nature.
36. For a dozen examples see Daftar Tablighat Islami (1986).
37. See especially the collection in the Hoover Library Archives.
38. Michel Serres's pun on interference and interreference is used here for the idea that cultural meanings from the Islamic and from the international post-Enlightenment revolutionary tradition both block each other's hegemony and facilitate each other's transcendence of their own limitations.
39. From a story in the biographies (*sīra*) of the Prophet, that one day a worker, or poor man, felt ashamed to offer his calloused hand to the Prophet, but the Prophet grabbed it and kissed it. There is perhaps a resonance with the dispute between the Mojahedin leader, Masud Rajavi, and Khomeini: it is said that when they first met, Rajavi refused to kiss Khomeini's hand in the traditional sign of allegiance and submission; ultimately, the Mojahedin declared armed struggle against the Khomeini regime.
40. There are other humorous posters. Perhaps the next best is one of asking

President Carter to cough up the shah: two hands composed of demonstrators are around Carter's neck, his mouth opens and out pops the shah with his money bags. As if having read Derrida's *The Postcard,* there is also a postcard demanding the return of the shah with an air letter inscribed with the addresses of all the places the shah had to flee.

41. Ahriman, the Zoroastrian figure of evil, rather than the Islamic Shaitan or Iblis.
42. A few of the posters were made outside Iran, e.g., in Oklahoma by Muslim students, in Paris, and elsewhere. The Fedai'i posters are the least professional, using stars as a frequent frame for their martyrs, often in black and white, giving an air of impoverished desperation.

7. Postscriptural Parergon

1. *They Shoot Writers, Don't They?* is a collection of essays, edited by George Theiner in 1984, to which Rushdie contributed a piece called "Casualties of Censorship." It begins, "My first memories of censorship are cinematic . . ."
2. *Iran Times,* 10 March 1989, 18 (52). Merely banning or boycotting a book, he explained, does not destroy the text, and may indeed gain for it more readers, so harsher methods must be found. To my ear a second fear also resonates, as if he were saying, "We had to do something before they turned Rushdie's novel into a movie." It is worth knowing that Khamenei originally was one of the moderates who suggested Rushdie might gain clemency with the proper apology and withdrawal of the book, but Khomeini unequivocably quashed any such suggestions.
3. *Guardian,* 24 February 1989, reprinted in Appignanesi and Maitland (1989).
4. See Fischer 1984.
5. See Cooke 1987.
6. See Javadi (1988), Sprachman (1981), and Wilson (1988).
7. Ibn Abi al-'Awja used to heckle during Imām Sadiq's lectures at the mosque in Medina, calling out "Nonsense!" frequently. Students were incensed and wanted to beat him up, but the Imām told them to let Ibn Abi al-'Awja speak. Eventually the Imām asked Mofaddal ibn Umar to write a response, the well-known *Tawḥīd-i Mufaḍḍal.* One day during the ḥajj in Mecca, Ibn Abi al-'Awja came to the Imām and said, "How long will these oxen [Muslims] continue to plough this desert [barren religion]?" The Imām responded by citing the verse prohibiting disputatious argument during the ḥajj. But after the ḥajj season, the Imām came to Ibn 'Awja and said, "Let me answer with your own style of logic. If there is no God, and everything is absurd, then Muslim worshippers lose nothing by their worship; but if there is a God and Muhammad is his messenger, then woe is to you on Judgment Day." A third famous story—again relevant to a revolutionary situation when much is excused on the grounds of crisis—has to do with the first Imām, Ali, during the battle of Jamal: A man came to him and said, "How do we know God exists?" One of Ali's men drew his sword to

slay the man, saying now is no time for such debates; you endanger us all by deflecting attention from the battle. But Ali stayed the sword, saying, "On the contrary, we must clarify why we are fighting, else the fighting has no point."

8. Cited by Malcolm Yapp in the *Independent,* 22 February 1989, reprinted in Appignanesi and Maitland (1989).
9. Fischer (1982b).
10. Cited in J. Schulte Sasse (1988).
11. Within the novel itself, it is a comic comment on the earlier scene, made famous through reviews and interviews with Rushdie probing the relation between his own life and those in the novel: young Chamcha is forced to eat kippers for breakfast at public school in England. It is ninety minutes of agony: no one shows him how to eat it, and he struggles with the bones, not allowed to get up before he finishes. He swore to get revenge on England: to show them that he can conquer.
12. See Larry May (1980).
13. In the 1950s Sagyagit Ray introduced both a neorealist, social conscience-oriented film and also a sense of the analytic, intellectual possibilities of modernist film. For an insightful account of developments in the theater and its relation to film, see Karnad (1989).
14. Four chief ministers of Tamilnadu have been actors or film makers, swept to power by fan club organizations. The two best-known such political figures are M. G. Ramachandran (d. 1987), who during his acting career always played hero roles, and carefully only spoke lines that defended the downtrodden; and N. T. Rama Rao of Karnataka. M. G. Ramachandran and his D.M.K. party used films filled with party symbols and colors, disseminated through the electrification that made rural cinemas popular. See Dickey (1987).
15. See Chakravarty (1987) and also Mishra (1985) for a reading of the Bombay film against the discursive practices of the *Mahabharata* and the *Ramayana.*
16. Other versions of dogma, of course, insist that Muhammad is a fallible human being, a model precisely in the human moral struggle to attain righteousness: this is the position the Qur'an takes when it speaks in Sūra al-Najm, and elsewhere, of God setting trials for his followers.
17. The *gharānīq* are an unidentified, presumably supernatural, species of bird. The term occurs in pre-Islamic poetry in several variant forms: *ghurnūq, ghirnīq, ghurnayq, ghurānīq;* pl., *gharāniq, gharānīq, gharāniqa.* The respected Arabic dictionary, *al-Munjid,* compiled by the Jesuit Fr. Louis, describes it as a water bird with wide wings and long legs; and as a secondary meaning, beautiful, white youth or young woman. Shaykh Abu Ja'far Ṭūsi's *al-Tibyān* (7:292), citing al-Hasan [al-Basri] gives the meaning also of "angels." Other translations variously use "swans," "pretty birds," "high-flying birds," and "exalted females."
18. *Tilk al-gharānīq al-'ulā wa inna shafa'ata-hunna la-turtaja.*

19. "Burāq" is a term of uncertain origin, possibly connected with *barq* ("lightning") as in a flash of (divine) inspiration or vision. It would seem iconographically to be related to the winged horses of ancient Iran and Mesopotamia, or the classical chimera, Pegasus, and centaur figures. It is a singular image in Islamic iconography. The closest other figure is the horse of Imām Husain, *Dhu al-Janāḥ* (literally, "winged," i.e., swift), which mystically transported Imām Husain's wife (the daughter of the last Sassanian king of Iran) back to Iran after Husain was martyred at Karbala. The notion of *ṭayy al-arḍ* (the ability to be transported through space instantaneously) is a common lesser miracle (*karāmat*) in Shi'ite folklore, a power that many ulema are said to have possessed and that certainly the Imams possessed.
20. "And when Our signs are recited to them, clear signs, those who look not to encounter Us say, 'Bring a Qur'an other than this, or alter it.' Say to them: 'It is not for me to alter it of my own accord. I follow nothing, except what is revealed to me. Truly I fear, if I should rebel against my Lord, the chastisement of a dreadful day.' . . . who does greater evil than he who forges against God a lie, or cries lies to His signs? . . . they say, 'These are our intercessors with God'" (10:16–18).
21. E.g., *maqālid* (the Arabicized plural of the Persian *kelid,* "key"), for which there exists a perfectly good Arabic word (*mafātiḥ*); also *jiziya,* the Sassanian tax adapted by Islam as a poll tax on minorities of the People of the Book.
22. "When we let the people taste mercy after hardship has visited them, lo, they have a device concerning Our signs."
23. 14 February 1989, "Bandung File," Channel 4, reprinted in Appignanesi and Maitland (1989).
24. In *Midnight's Children,* Rushdie says "420" means "fraud and deception" (p. 193).
25. *Najm* ("The Star"), sūra 53, where the "Satanic Verses" are said to have occurred.
26. ". . . especially in the afternoon heat when the air turned glutinous, the visible world . . . seemed to be sticking up through the atmosphere like a profusion of hot icebergs, and he had the idea that everything continued below the surface of the soupy air . . . nine-tenths of their reality concealed from his eyes. . . . He grew up believing in God, angels, demons, afreet, djinns, as matter-of-factly as if they were bullock-carts . . ." (p. 22).
27. These are stunning figurations of what Murphy, and other ethnographers of other immigrant groups, describes in flat journalistic tones: "any group abruptly transferred from a remote corner of Asia to a European city will inevitably have quite a high incidence of 'nervous disorders' and some older Mirpuris suffer from a chronic lack of physical well-being attributable to no specific disease. But until each Brown community has produced its own professional helpers only limited aid can be given. White social workers, doctors, and psychiatrists, however kindly and well-equipped

with background knowledge, cannot have the necessary 'feel'. . ." (Murphy 1987:54).

28. Maslama is the pair to Chamcha's seatmate on the airplane from Bombay, the creationist scientist who had been to India: each is a perverted image of the main character, a creationist making nonsense of Chamcha's desire to be a modern Westerner, and Maslama a religious fanatic who cannot tell Gibreel's screen role from his actual person. Gibreel already had an encounter on the railway with Maslama in which the latter was his seatmate. The creationist turns up a second time as well late in the novel.
29. The full irony perhaps requires the preceding line, "I came to this seminar to learn; and among the many insights I've gained is Professor Narasimbaiah's view that India is a country made up of Hindus, Jains, Buddhists, Sikhs, Christians, and Mughals." Borges would love the classification scheme, the subtle but profound shift in category.
30. Rushdie, "The Indian Writer in England," in Butcher (1983), p. 78.
31. Ibid., p. 81.
32. For a stunning portrait of the underside of white British working-class violence as revealed in football (soccer) games, see Lesley Hazelton (*New York Times Magazine,* 8 May 1989).
33. In several interviews as well as in the novel's narrator's voice, Rushdie has recalled both an attack on his sister in the London underground and the intense shame this generated, such that he could well understand both the repressed violence that seethes in people subjected to such attack and the lamentable codes of honor that might cause a father to kill his own beloved daughter.
34. Rushdie, "Indian Writer," 82.
35. Brennan 1987.
36. Tariq Ali (1981) says that the massacre at Jallianwalla Bagh in Amritsar in 1919 was not as significant as the Moplah uprising in Malabar in 1921 or the Naval Mutiny and general strike of 1946; moreover Tariq Ali would have liked more stress on the Partition that traumatized so much of the middle classes.
37. Reacting to criticisms that the novel ends on a pessimistic note, with the consciousness of the narrator smashed into six hundred million fragments, Rushdie replies that he intended a contrast between form and content: although particular stories may end badly (and have done so historically for India), one need not be pessimistic about the abilities of that civilization to continually undergo transformations and generate new stories, and it is this latter mood which Rushdie intends the exuberance of the multiple plots and subplots to exemplify, and the word "teeming" to convey.
38. Rushdie, "The Empire Writes Back with a Vengeance," *The Times of London,* 3 July 1982.
39. See also Dissanayake (1985).
40. Compare the line in *Satanic Verses* (p. 54), "Columbus was right, maybe;

the world's made up of Indies, East, West, North. . . . Only thing is, we're not Indian like you. You better get used to us."

41. George Lamming's *Mr. Slim,* Chinua Achebe's *Man of the People,* Ngugi wa Thiong'o's accounts of Kenyan chamchas; but see also the essay literature by Frantz Fanon, O. Manoni, A. Mememi, and Ashis Nandy.
42. See also the account in Brennan 1987.

Glossary

abnā: Iranians who liberated Yemen from the Abyssinians in pre-Islamic, Sassanian times (short for *abnā al-aḥrār,* "sons of the free")
ādam: man, human being
aḍghāthu aḥlām: dreams which have no interpretation, bad dreams, inconsistent dreams
adhān: the call to prayer
'Aflaqī: follower of Michel Aflaq (d. 1989), one of the founders of the Ba'ath Party; derogatory nickname given to Saddam Hossain by Khomeini
āftābeh: ewer with a spout that is used for washing one's private parts after going to the bathroom
āghā: title of respect both for an ordinary male and for a person of true authority (pl. *aghayan*)
āghāzādeh: son of an *āghā,* often implies laziness
ḥadīth: stories, tales (plural of hadith)
aḥkām: decrees (plural of *hukm*)
ahl -e kitāb: people of the book, i.e., Jews and Christians, sometimes Zoroastrians
'Ajam: non-Arab, particularly Iranians (contrast with *'Arab*)
Ahrīman: Zoroastrian principle of evil; Satan
akhbārī: a Shi'ite school of jurisprudence (contrast with Usuli)
Ākhūnd: cleric; once a term of respect, now the common word for those in religious garb, slightly deprecatory
A'lā Hazrat: His Majesty
'ālem: Persian form of *alim*
'Alī Akbar: Imām Husain's 18-year-old son, martyred at Karbala
'ālim: one who is learned (pl. *ulama*), particularly those learned in Islamic jurisprudence
'allāmeh: "most learned," a title of respect
'amaliyāt -e moqaddas -e enteḥārī: "sacred suicide mission," term used by the Mojahedin Khalq
'ammeh: paternal aunt
'amū: paternal uncle
'amūd: pillar of the tent
anfāl: spoils of war, public property
angūr -e kūhi: a wild berry found in the mountains of central Iran, said to have medicinal properties; also known as *angūr -e tūreh*
Anjoman -e Āsār -e Mellī: National Heritage Society

anjoman -e khāneh va madraseh: Parents-Teachers Association

Anjoman -e Zedd -e Bahā'ī: Society Against Baha'is

Anṣār: the Muslim residents of Yathrib (later renamed Medina) who hosted those who fled or withdrew from Mecca with Muhammad (contrasts with the *Muhājirūn*).

'aqd: "contract," particularly the permanent marriage contract; contrast with the temporary or limited-term marriage contract, *ṣigheh, mut'a*

'aql: reason, rational knowledge (contrast with *naql*)

a'rāb: plural of *a'rābī* (bedouin or nomadic Arab), used in Persian as the plural for *'Arab* (Arabic speakers)

'Arab-zadegī: infatuation with Arab culture (parallel to *gharb-zadegī*)

'Arafāt: hill near Mecca, key site during the hajj pilgrimage

Arba'īn: "forty," "fortieth"; major day of mourning after a death; twentieth of the month of Safar, fortieth day after Imām Husain's martyrdom, commemorated every year as the day of mourning

Arba'ūn Ḥadīthan: "forty ḥadīth," name for collections of forty ḥadīths

'Āshūrā: "the tenth"; the tenth day of Muharram when Imām Husain was martyred. Early Muslims fasted on *'Āshūrā* before Ramadan was established as the month of fasting. Sunni Muslims continue to fast on that day as a *mustaḥabb* (meritorious) act; for Shi'ites fasting on that day is an abrogated sunna (replaced by fasting during Ramadan, when Muhammad broke with the Jews) and is *ḥarām* (forbidden). For Shi'ites fasting on 'Āshūrā amounts to *tashabbuh be kuffār* (assimilation to the practices of unbelievers), not only those of the Jews, but of Yazid's soldiers who slew Husain and also fasted on *'Ashūrā*

'atabāt: the Shi'ite holy cities of Iraq

āvāreh: homeless, vagrant

āya: sign [of God], a verse of the Qur'an

āyatullāh: "sign of God"; according to the Qur'an everything is an "āyatullāh"; a relatively new (nineteenth-twentieth century) title given to leading Shi'ite jurists. The first person to receive the title was Mirza Shirazi in his 1892 confrontation with Nassraddin Shah over the tobacco trade monopoly. Until the 1979 revolution, an āyatullāh was a mujtahid who administered religious taxes, using them to support seminary students, charity and welfare support, and other religious activities. After the revolution, the title in- flated and was applied indiscriminately to any high-level mulla in the revolution.

ayyām: stories of valor

az khod bigānegi: alienation

āzādī: freedom
āzādī -e bayān: freedom of expression
āzādī -e qalam: freedom of the pen

Bābī: a follower of the Bab; derogatory term used by Muslims for Bahā'is
Bahā'ī: a follower of Baha'ullah
Bahār -e Āzādī: "The Spring of Freedom," the gold coins minted after the Islamic Revolution of Iran to replace the "Pahlavi" gold coins
baḥth: search, particularly through dialogue: the form of debate used by theological students
barzakh: purgatory
bāṭil: void, invalid (contrasts with *ṣaḥīḥ*); falsehood (contrasts with *ḥaqq*)
bāṭin: esoteric knowledge (contrasts with *zahir*)
Bāṭinī: those who privilege symbolic interpretation of the Qur'an
bay'at: allegiance
bayyina: proof
bāzārī: shopkeeper or merchant; cultural style associated with the bazaar
bebor-nabor: a ritual performed to make a tree bear fruit
bid'a: innovation (contrast with *sunna*)
Bismillāh: "In the name of God"; the first words of the phrase which begins all the sūras of the Qur'an except one
bozkharī: (colloquial) "looking for cheap deals"

chādor: Iranian veil for women; tent
chufya: Arabian head cover for men

dabestān: elementary school
dabīrestān: secondary school
ḍa'īf: weak, unreliable (hadith)
dakhma: "tower of silence," where Zoroastrians place their corpses
dallāk: worker in a Turkish bath; barber
daqqāq: cloth finisher
dard -e del: to speak one's grievances to someone or to something (e.g., to a well, to the Qur'an)
dasteh: "group"; mourning procession for Imam Husain
dastūr: Zoroastrian priest
da'wa: "invitation," religious missionary work
dhikr: "remembrance," "reminding," ritual of invoking the name of God or a saint
Dhu al-Qarnayn: "two-horned"; mythic figure in the Qur'an, identified

by some as Cyrus the Great (from the Book of Daniel's metaphor for Cyrus as a two-horned ram) and by others as Alexander the Great (two horns referring to the adornment of a warrior's helmet)

dīn: religion

dīv: demon

dokhtar -e khāneh māndeh: "old maid"; colloquially "something hard to sell," a leftover in the shop which must be liquidated

dūsti -e khāleh kherseh: "friendship of auntie bear," stupidity done with good intentions

du'ā: prayer (contrast with *namaz*)

Du'ā Komeil: a long Shi'ite prayer usually recited melodiously on Thursday nights

eḥyā: all-night worship

ensān: moral person

ezdevāj -e Amrikāī: marriage with an American for the purpose of obtaining permanent residence in the United States

faqīh: jurisconsultant in Islamic law

farrah -e Izadī: divine powers of kinship that reside in legitimate kings

fasād: corruption

fāsiq: libertine, someone who frequently transgresses moral and religious laws

Fātiḥa: the first sūra of the Qur'an usually recited at grave sites

fatwā: opinion issued by a religious authority

fiqh: jurisprudence

fiqh -e engelābī: "revolutionary jurisprudence," reformulation of jurisprudence to meet the needs of the Islamic revolution

fiqh -e pūya: dynamic jurisprudence (contrasts with *fiqh -e sunnati*)

fiqh -e sunnatī: "traditional jurisprudence"

firqa -e nājiya: "the saved group," self-designation of Shi'ites (from Muhammad's "My umma will divide into seventy-three groups, and only one of them will enter the garden of paradise")

forū' -e dīn: the Shi'ite "ten commandments": (1) daily prayers, (2) fasting during Ramaḍān, (3) giving "one-fifth" of one's annual income to religious authorities, (4) annual charity dues, (5) *ḥajj* pilgrimage, (6) *jihād,* (7) enjoining good, (8) stopping others from committing evil, (9) love of the friends of God, and (10) keeping away from the enemies of God

fuqahā: plural of *faqīh*

Furqān: "criterion of distinguishing" between good and evil, one of the names of the Qur'an; the name of an underground terrorist group inspired by some of Ali Shariati's more extreme ideas

gabr: a derogatory term for Zoroastrians
gaziyeh: the Pahlavi (Old Persian) root for *jizya*
gelīm: flat-weave rug
gharb-zadegī: "Westoxication"
gharīb: stranger
gharībeh: stranger
gharīb-khāneh: public house for poor travellers
ghayb: "unseen"
ghayr madkhūla: "not entered into," a married girl who is still a virgin
gheirat: the sense or honor that prevents one from spoiling the honor of another man; zeal to defend one's own religion, family, or honor
ghorūb kūk: (folk term) "sunset winder," i.e., pocket watch; also, *ẓohr kūk* ("noon winder")
ghulāt: (Shi'ite) extremists, plural of *ghālī*
ghurbat: the feeling of being "homesick"
ghurfeh: the balcony of a *ḥusaynieh* where women sit
gīveh: cloth shoes with sewn cotton thread uppers and soles of pressed cotton or linen rags, held together with strong hide laces and welts; more recently, the soles are cut from used tires.
gorīz: making a connection between the main subject of a sermon and the story of Karbala
gorīz zadan: to make a *gorīz*
gowr: same as *gabr*

ḥadīth: sayings attributed to God, the archangel Gabriel, the prophets (especially Muhammad), and (among Shi'ites) the Imams
Ḥadīth -e Kisā: "Ḥadīth of the Cloak," a key Shi'ite ḥadīth according to which Muhammad, Ali, Fatima, Hasan, and Husain (the "Five Pure Souls") gather under one cloak, where the archangel Gabriel brought them the message from God that He had created the heavens and the earth for their sake. Shi'ites recite the ḥadīth melodiously in order to seek the intercession of the five pure souls at times of difficulty. Fatima's name is privileged in the ḥadīth, both in the setting (Muhammad comes into her house and asks for the cloak which he entrusted to her) and in the answers to Gabriel's query, "Who is under the cloak?": Fatima, Fatima's father, Fatima's husband, and Fatima's two sons.
ḥadīth nabawi: a saying attributed to the Prophet Muhammad

ḥadīth qudsī: a saying attributed to God not recorded in the Qur'an
Ḥāfeẓ: famous Iranian poet of Shiraz; his title derives from the fact that he was a *ḥafīz* of the Qur'an.
ḥāfiẓ: "preserver," "memorizer"; one who has memorized the entire Qur'an
ḥajj: pilgrimage to the "House of God" in Mecca during the first ten days of the month of the ḥajj (Dhi al-Hajja)
ḥajjat al-widā': Muhammad's last pilgrimage to Mecca
ḥājjī: one who has performed the *ḥajj* at least once
ḥājjī shekamī: "womb ḥajji"; one born on the day of the feast of the ḥajj, i.e., *Id al-Adha*
ḥakam: arbitrator
ḥakīm: philosopher, physician, wise
ḥākim: governor
ḥalāl: permitted, e.g., *ḥalāl* meat is meat correctly slaughtered according to religious law; *ḥalāl* money is money earned in nonsinful ways (contrasts with *haram*)
ḥalālzādeh: of legitimate birth
hālū: gullible
hamsar: spouse (literally, "same head")
ḥaqīqat: truth
ḥaqīqat al-murād: what is really meant, the true meaning
ḥaqq: truth (contrasts with *bāṭil*); truth, right (contrasts with *nāḥaq*)
ḥarakat: movement
ḥarām: forbidden, prohibited (contrasts with *ḥalāl*); sacred
ḥarb: war
ḥarāmzādeh: of illegitimate birth
Ḥarrāq al-Maṣāḥif: "Burner of the Scriptures," title given to Caliph Uthman after he burned the scattered versions of the Qur'an in order to establish a canonical text
ḥasan: a ḥadīth narrated through a connected chain of transmission, but where the reliability of one of the links of the chain is disputed
Hazrat -e Abbās: the half brother of Imam Husain, martyred at Karbala; he is the exemplar of loyalty, courage, and generosity
ḥifẓ: preservation, memorization
ḥijāb: Muslim women's dress code, the veil, modest dress
Hijra: withdrawal of the Prophet of Islam from Mecca to Yathrib in 621 C.E. until he could gather sufficient forces to conquer Mecca, the model for many later movements of Islamic activists withdrawing from society in order to bide their time to seize power
hijrat: Persian form for *hijra*

Hijrī Qamarī: the Islamic calendar. Its year (354 days) consists of twelve months, and the length of each month depends on the sighting of the moon.

Hijrī Shamsī: the Iranian solar calendar based on the *hijra* of Prophet Muhammad. Its year begins on the first day of spring (March 21). There are twelve months; the first six are 31 days each, the next 5 are 30 days each, and the last month is 29 days.

ḥikmat: wisdom, philosophy

ḥiyal -e shar'ī: "religious tricks," the cunning art of using loopholes in the religious law to one's advantage

Ḥizbullah: "Party of God"

ḥokūmat: see *ḥukūmat*

ḥowz: pond

huffaz: plural of *ḥāfiẓ*

ḥujjat: proof

Ḥujjat al-Islām: "Proof of Islam," a title once given only to a small number of top rank Islamic scholars (the first to receive the title was al-Ghazzali). Today it is a title for any mulla, whether or not a *mujtahid.*

ḥukamā: philosophers (plural of *ḥakīm*)

ḥukkām: rulers (plural of *ḥākim*)

ḥukm: decree, judgment

ḥukūma: government

Ḥulūliya: those who believe in *ḥulūl* (transmigration) of the souls

ḥusaynieh: forum or courtyard where Muḥarram passion plays and mournings for Imām Husain are done

ḥuzn: sorrow, grief

Iblīs: Satan

'īd: feast

'īd mubārak!: happy holiday!

'Id al-Aḍḥā: the Feast of Sacrifice in the month of the *ḥajj*

'Id al-F'itr: the feast on the first day of the month of Shawwal, which ends the month of fasting (Ramaḍān)

'Id al-Ghadīr: the eighteenth of the month of Dhi-Ḥajja on which, according to Shi'ites, Muhammad proclaimed Ali ibn Abi-Talib as his successor

ifṭār: breaking the fast at sunset

iḥrām: the ritual garb of the *ḥajj* pilgrim; the state of being under the special conduct restrictions of the *ḥajj*

ijāza: permission; a certificate or diploma given by a master of an Islamic discipline to his student, declaring the latter a master, an independent authority

ijtihād: the highest degree a student of jurisprudence can receive, thereby qualifying and requiring him to make independent judgments in matters of Islamic jurisprudence; the ability to make such judgment

iltadhdh: rapture

imāla: to elongate in recitation

imām: prayer leader

Imām: one of the twelve Shi'ite leaders descended from Muhammad through his daughter, Fatima, and his son-in-law, Ali. The Imāms are said to have infallible knowledge of God's intent in the Qur'an. In Arabic usage among Shi'ites of Iraq and Lebanon, "Imām" has been a synonym for "āyatullāh", i.e., the title for a *mujtahid* who administers religious funds. In Persian, Khomeini is the first to have allowed himself to be addressed as "Imām". Khomeini at first carefully had his portraits labeled "*nāyeb -e Imām*" (deputy to the Imām), but his propaganda handlers could not resist, and he did not object to, the play on the utopian resonance of being called an "Imām." Leftists initially went along with the usage, invoking Ali Shari'ati's equation of the Islamic Imām with the Weberian "charismatic leader," one who articulates the inchoate desires of the people.

imām jom'a: one who leads Friday prayers

Imām -e Zamān: "Imām of the Age," the twelfth Shi'ite Imām, believed to be in occultation for more than eleven centuries, and who will return as messiah or Mahdi

imāmzādeh: "Imām's child," the shrine of any saint from the family of the Prophet

imsāk: refraining from the acts which nullifies one's fast

inshā Allāh: "if God wills"

iqāma: a ritual formula similar to the call to prayer (*adhān*), uttered after the *adhān* and before the *namāz* prayer. With the phrase "*qad qāmat al-ṣalāt*" (the prayer has begun), it is the signal to stand up.

iqtā': land benefice or fief

'ishā: the last of the five required daily *namāz* prayers

ishkāl: criticism, question, raising an objection in a theological seminary

ishrāq: Illuminationism, a mystical school of philosophy

ishtāq: desire

isnād: the first part of a *ḥadīth,* the chain of its narrators (contrasts with *matn*)

Ithnā 'asharī: "Twelver," Shi'ites who believe in twelve infallible Imāms; other groups of Shi'ites, such as the Ismailis, believe in a longer or shorter list of Imāms, and dispute the line of succession. Eighty percent of Iranians are *Ithnā 'asharī,* as are more than half of Iraqis and Bahraynis; *Ithnā 'asharī* Shi'ites are also now the largest confessional group in Lebanon

jadal: dialogue, dialectic, debate, argumentation

jahāz: "dowry," the household items given to the bride by her parents to take to her husband's house

jāhiliya: ignorance, savagery; pre-Islamic period; in contemporary Islamic fundamentalist usage, the non-Muslim world, including nonfundamentalist, nonreligious, secular, or Westernized Muslims

jā'iz: permitted

jānamāz: "place of *namāz* prayers," i.e., the prayer rug or the handkerchief in which the *muhr* (sacred clay of Karbala or other holy site) and *sabḥa* or *tasbīḥ* (prayer beads) are carried

jihād: struggle in defense of Islam; interior struggle against evil inclinations; external war against non-Muslims

jinn: invisible creatures made of fire which have many human characteristics and may possess human beings

jin-gīr: "capturer of jinns," exorcist

jizya: poll tax paid by Jews, Christians, and Zoroastrians to an Islamic government in order to live under its protection

jom'at al-widā': "the farewell Friday," last Friday of Ramaḍān

joz': one-thirtieth of the Qur'an: the Qur'an is divided into "joz'" so that the believer can meditate on one *joz'* each day, reviewing the entire text in one month.

jūsh kardan: an illness believed to develop as a result of sudden shock from bad news or seeing a terrifying scene

juz': Arabic form of *joz'*

Ka'ba: "Cube," the cube-shaped "House of God" in the Grand Mosque of Mecca, toward which Muslims face when saying their *namāz* prayers. It is circumambulated seven times during the *hajj.*

kadkhodā: village headman

kāfir: "one who covers [the truth]," nonbeliever

kafshdārī: custodian for shoes at a mosque or shrine

kalām: dialectical theology

kalāntar: chief of police

kalima: word, logos

kalīmī: "follower of the one with whom God spoke," polite term of reference to Jews

Kalīmullāh: "the one with whom God spoke," Moses
kārt -e sabz: "Green Card," U.S. or Canadian permanent residence card
kāseb: (small) businessman
khalīfa: caliph, successor, deputy
khānaqāh: Sufi lodge
kharāj: a landtax
kharcharān: "donkey-herder," one who claims to know how to deal with stupid people
khārij -e fiqh: highest level of seminary instruction
Khātam al-Nabiyīn: "Seal of the Prophets," Muhammad
khaṭṭ: line, script
khaṭṭāshī: pictures composed of calligraphy
khums: "one-fifth"; the religious tax given to an āyatullāh, traditionally half earmarked for *sayyed*s (descendants of the Prophet) and half, called *sahm -e Imām* (the Imām's share) kept (in a cave or thrown in the sea) for the occulted twelfth Imām. In the nineteenth century, the *sahm -e Imām* became an important resource for the clergy in creating a financial base independent of the state.
Khurramdīn: follower of Babak who tried to revive the religion of Mazdak in the Islamic period
khushū': humility, awe, submission
khuṭba: sermon
al-kinūna al-insāniyya: human existant
kolāh: "hat," trick, deception
kolāh shar'ī: legal deception (see also *ḥiyal -e shar'ī*)
korsi: "chair, throne," metaphorically "the seat of Almighty God"; a traditional Iranian heater which burns charcoal
kostī: sacred thread worn around the waist by Zoroastrians
kuffār -e Ṣaddāmī: "Ṣaddām's unbelievers," term for Iraqi soldiers fighting in the Iran-Iraq war
kufr: "covering [the Truth]," unbelief
kufuw: "equal" (see *Kufuwiyat*)
Kufuwiyat: according to Abu-Hanifa, parties to a marriage must be equals, or the female may be of lower rank (i.e., a non-Arab man may not marry an Arab woman). In South Yemen, *kufuwiyat* is used to mean that people must marry within their caste rank.
kuttāb al-wahy: "Scribes of Revelation," those who wrote down what was revealed to Muhammad
al-Kutub al-Arbi'a: "The Four Books," the four main collections of ḥadīth which serve as sources for Shi'ite dogma and jurisprudence in addition to the Qur'an

Labbayk: "God! Here am I!" utterance of the *ḥajj* pilgrims as they approach the *Ka'ba*

Labbayk yā Khomeinī: "Khomeini! Here am I!" name of one of the campaigns to get volunteers to fight in the Iran-Iraq war

lafẓ: word, vocable

lāleh: tulip

Lawḥ Maḥfūẓ: "The Preserved Tablet", the heavenly tablet on which the entire Qur'an is believed to be recorded and preserved

maghḍūb 'alayhim: "those afflicted with the wrath of God," the Jews

Maghrib: the daily *namāz* prayer said at sunset

mahr: "bridewealth," property given by the groom to the bride at the wedding

maḥram: spouse and close kin with whom one cannot marry and before whom a woman need not veil: spouse, mother, father, grandmother, grandfather, brother, sister, aunt, and uncle

Majlis -e Khobregān: Assembly of Experts, the convention that wrote the constitution of the Islamic Republic of Iran

majnūn: crazy, one possessed by *jinn*

maj'ūl: invented, fabricated, false, untrue (hadith)

majūs: Qur'anic name for Zoroastrians

makr: trick, deceit

makrūh: "disliked"; religiously discouraged but not forbidden

maktab: traditional "elementary school" where one learns the Qur'an as well as functional literacy

maktab -e vāseteh: "school of the middle way," doctrine of political and economic nonalignment

mālik-mala'-mullā: "the king, the rich, the clergy," an evil trinity which, according to Ali Shariati, has always ruled history, used as a slogan at the beginning of the Islamic Revolution (see also *zar-zūr-tazwīr*)

mansūkh: abrogated

mansūkh al-ḥukm: verses of the Qur'an, which, although continuing to be part of the Qur'anic text, no longer have the force of law, having been abrogated during Muhammad's lifetime

mansūkh al-ḥukm wa al-tilāwa: verses said to have been part of the Qur'an, abrogated during Muhammad's lifetime, and no longer part of the Qur'anic text nor having the force of law

mansūkh al-tilāwa: verses said to have been part of the Qur'an, removed from the recited text during Muhammad's lifetime, but still having the force of law, e.g., the "verse of stoning" (for adultery) according to the Shafi'i school of jurisprudence.

maqām (of Ibrahim): the spot in the Grand Mosque of Mecca where Abraham is believed to have stood to build the *Ka'ba*

maqām (in music): musical mode or melody type (melodic formula with stereotyped figures, tonal progressions, ornamentations, and rhythmic patterns)

maqbūla: "accepted"; a ḥadīth on the basis of which a reputable jurist has issued a *fatwā* and which on these grounds may be regarded as valid

maqbūla of 'Umar ibn Ḥanẓala: a *maqbūla* ḥadīth which Khomeini used as the main basis of his 1971 lectures on Islamic government

ma'qūl al-ma'nā: rational meaning

marja' taqlīd: "source of imitation"; a supreme Usuli jurist whom the common Shi'ite folks follow (see also *taqlīd*)

Marwa: an important place in Mecca for the *ḥajj* ritual

al-masā'il al-mustaḥdatha: "new problems" in jurisprudence, issues without precedents

mas'aleh: problem

mas'aleh-gū: "narrator of problems," one who explains *fatwās* to the ordinary people

māshā Allah: "whatever God wills"; it is uttered against the evil eye

Mash'ar: an important place in Mecca for the *ḥajj* ritual

mashhūr: (mode of recitation of the Qur'an) "famous" but not the most preferred (contrasts with *mutawātir*)

mashraba: ewerlike water container used by Zoroastrians

masnavī: a kind of poetry with rhyming couplets; a mode of singing

masṭūrun: narrators of ḥadīth about whom nothing is known

mas'uliyat: responsibility

ma'ṣūm: infallible

matalak: repartee, aggressive humor

matalak-gū: one who engages in repartee, aggressive humor

matn: the text of a *ḥadīth* (contrasts with *isnād*)

matrūk: *ḥadīth* that experts pay no attention to because either its text is proven to be nonvalid or because its narrator has been shown to be unreliable

māzār: henna miller

Mazdayasnā: Zoroastrianism

miḥrāb: prayer niche, which marks the direction of prayer

millat: (Arabic) "religion," "ideology"; (Persian) "nation"

Minā: important place in Mecca in the *ḥajj* ritual

minbar: podium; physically a set of stairs on which a preacher or seminary teacher sits

mi'rāj: Muhammad's heavenly journey
mīrāth: heritage
mirṣād: watchtower
mirzā: one whose mother is a descendant of the Prophet
miswāk: toothbrush
mithāq: covenant
monājat: "whispering," hymns praising God
moshkel-goshā: "problem-solver"; a folk tale about the need for mutual aid as a condition for divine help, told in ritual settings while cleaning chickpeas, usually told by women at shrines; among Shi'ites also a title for Imām Ali, who, as a toddler, is made the lead character in the folk tale and rescues Khidr
movāzeneh -e manfī: "negative equilibrium," the nonalignment political ideology promoted by Muhammad Mosaddeq
mūbad: Zoroastrian priest
mūbad mūbadān: Zoroastrian high priest
mubāḥ: religiously neutral
mubaḥatha: debate, dialogue, dialectics
muezzin: he who calls believers to prayer
mufsid: corrupter
muḥaddith: narrator of *ḥadīth*
muhājir: immigrant (contrasts with *āvāreh*)
Muḥarram: the first month of the Islamic lunar year associated with the martyrdom of Imām Husain
muḥkam: clear in meaning (contrasts with *mutashābih*)
muhr: a smooth piece of clay of Karbala or other sacred site, used by Shi'ites for prostration
muḥrim: one who is observing *iḥrām* (q.v.)
mujawwad: the Qur'an recited according to regulations of *tajwīd* (contrasts with *murattal*)
mujaddid: "renewer." According to a Prophetic hadith, in every century there is a man who "reforms" or "revives" Islam.
mujtahid: a jurist qualified to express independent opinion
mullā: learned, literate; clergyman
mullā nuqaṭī: nitpicking mullā
mumayyiz: a child who has reached the age of sexual awareness
munāfiq: hypocrite
Munāfiqīn: plural of *munāfiq;* derogatory name for the People's Mojahedin of Iran
munaza'a: dispute
muqallad: one who is followed

muqallid: one who follows someone else's practice
murattal: melodious recitation
mursal: a ḥadīth with at least one missing link in its chain of narrators
murtadd: apostate
muṣannaf: a collection of ḥadīth arranged according to subject matter
musnad: a ḥadīth with a reliable chain of narrators
muṣ-ḥaf: "scripture," transcript
mustaḥabb: meritorious but not required
mut'a: limited-term marriage
muta'ahhid: engagé or politically engaged
mutakallim: dialectical theologian
mutashābih: allegorical, figurative, not literal (contrasts with *muḥkam*)
mutawātir: ḥadith or qirā'at reported through several independent chains of narrators.

nabī: prophet
nāfila: "extra"; extra prayers one says after the required daily prayers
Nahzat -e Āzādī: "Liberation Movement [of Iran]"
najes: ritually unclean, untouchable, polluting
namāz: the formal prayer involving prostrations enjoined on Muslims to perform five times a day
namāz -e jom'a: Friday prayer
naql: narrated knowledge (contrasts with *'aql*)
nāsikh: the verses of the Qur'an which are believed by some exegetes to abrogate earlier verses
naskh: abrogation
nāyeb: deputy
naẓar: opinion
nikāḥ: permanent marriage
niyat: intention
noql: sugar candy balls
noql kardan: a ceremony celebrating a child's successful passage of stages in learning the Qur'an
nowḥeh: mourning chant
nozūl-khor: usurer
nūr: "light"; mystical doctrine that Muhammad and his family were created at the beginning of time from rays of divine light

'Olyā Hazrat: Her Majesty
'Olyā Mokhaddareh: "Great and Properly Veiled Lady," a title of respect for the female members of the Prophet's family

ostokhwāndār: a businessman with considerable capital who does not need to borrow
oṣūl -e dīn: "roots of religion"; it refers to belief in (1) oneness of God, (2) prophethood, and (3) resurrection. In addition to these, the Shi'ites include (4) divine justice, and (5) imamate, i.e., belief in the infallible Imāms.

pahlavān: champion, athlete, hero
Pahlavī: a gold coin
pā-menbari: warm-up preacher before the main preacher
panīrok: an edible seed found in the mountains of Yazd
panj tan: the five pure souls: Muhammad, Ali, Fatima, Hasan, and Husain
pā-pich: leg wrapping
parhīz: warning call to the jinn
parī: fairy, angel
pesar 'ammeh: father's sister's son
pīr: saint, old person, elder
pīr -e moghān: saint, reference to Zoroastrian high priest in Persian ghazal poetry; Shi'ites construe it as a reference to Imām Ali.
purda: (Urdu, from Persian *pardeh,* "curtain") veil, modesty

qadamgāh: footprint of an Imām
qāḍī: judge
qafas -e rejīm: "cage of the regime," name for Lawrence, Kansas, given by Iranian students who opposed the shah's regime, meaning it was a cage where the regime put the students, and it was the place where the students put the regime in the cage by demonstrations and attempts to embarrass the regime
qā'im: "the one who rises up," one of the titles of the Mahdi
qalyūn: waterpipe
qaychī kardan: "to cut with scissors," pincer movement
qesmat: fate, lot, kismet
qibla: direction of prayer (Mecca, the *Ka'ba*)
qiyamat: day of judgment
qunūt: the prayer position with palms up
al-qur'ān al-nāṭiq: "the speaking Qur'an," the Imāms
qurrā: plural of *qārī,* reciters of the Qur'an
al-Qurrā al-Sab'a: "the Seven Reciters" whose names denote the seven approved ways of reciting the Qur'an

rāfiḍī: "renegade," derogatory name for Shi'ites used by Sunnis
raḥla fī ṭalab al-'ilm: "travel in search of knowledge," the trips which the collectors of ḥadīth took for collecting ḥadīth
rak'at: unit of *namāz* prayer, which includes one bow and two prostrations
rāsikhūn fi al-'ilm: "the well-grounded in knowledge"
rasūl: messenger (of God)
rāwī: narrator
ra'y: opinion
rijāl: discipline of identifying and evaluating the reliability of the narrators of ḥadīth
rowshan-fekr: "enlightened," self-designation of progressive intellectuals in Iran
rowzeh: (Persian form of *rawḍa*) preachment, homiletic sermon; from the *Rawdat al-shuhadā* ("Garden of the Martyrs") of Mulla Husain Wā'iẓ Kāshifī (d. 1504), a passionate account of the tragedy at Karbala, used to frame sermons
rowzeh-khwān: preacher
rūḥ: soul, spirit
Rūḥullāh: "Spirit of God," the title the Qur'an gives to Jesus
rūḥānī: clergyman
rūḥāniyat: the clergy
ruwāt: plural of *Rāwī,* narrators (of ḥadīth)
ru'yā: dream
Rūz -e Quds: "Day of Jerusalem," the last Friday of the month of Ramadan designated by Khomeini to be celebrated until Jerusalem is liberated into Muslim control.
rūzeh: a fast

Sab'at Aḥruf: a ḥadīth with many variations, which claims that the Qur'an was revealed in seven dialects
sabab al-nuzūl: context or circumstance under which verses of the Qur'an were revealed
ṣadāq: bridewealth (synonym of *mahr*)
Safa: an important place in Mecca for the *ḥajj* ritual
safīh: stupid
Ṣāḥib al-Zamān: "Lord of the Age," a title for the Mahdi
ṣaḥīḥ: correct, reliable (hadith)
sahm -e Imām: portion of the *khums* that belongs to the Imām of the Age and is given to his deputies, i.e., the clergy
ṣalāt a-mayyit: the formal prayer for the dead before burial

ṣalāt al-janāza: synonym for *salāt al-mayyit*
ṣalavāt: "salutations," chant that blesses the Prophet and his family
Sarbāz -e Imām -e Zamān: "Soldier of the Imām of the Age," members of the Society Against the Baha'is
ṣarrāf: moneychanger
savāb: merit
savād: literacy
ṣawāb: good deeds
sa'y: ritual act of jogging back and forth between Safa and Marwa in the *ḥajj* ritual
sayyed: descendant of the Prophet
Sepāh -e Dānesh: Literacy Corps established by the shah
Sepantā Mainū: wisdom, one of the *amshaspands*, the seven aspects of divinity in Zoroastrianism
sevvom: ceremony for the dead performed on the third day after the burial, which included visiting of the grave site
shab -e qadr: "night of power," the night the Qur'an was revealed
shabīh: "like[ness]," passion play
shabīh-gardān: passion play director
shadda: diacritical mark that stresses or doubles the sound of a letter
shādhdh: odd
shafā'at: intercession
shahāda: Islamic credo: "There is no god but God, and Muhammad is His servant and messenger."
shahādat: martyrdom, witnessing
Shāhnāmeh: "The Book of Kings," the national epic poem of Iran, composed by Abu al-Qasem Firdausi, completed 1010 C.E. (365 Q.)
sha'n al-nuzūl: references in the circumstances or contexts of the revelation of verses of the Qur'an which are said to honor the family of the Prophet and the Imams, or to bring disrepute upon the enemies of Shi'ism
shaqī: villain
sharī'a: the law of Islam
Shayṭān: (proper noun) Satan; (ordinary noun) naughty child
Shemr: the chief villain in the passion plays of Karbala
shibh: like(ness)
shirk: the heresy of attributing "partners" to God, i.e., anything contradictory to the oneness of God
shotor-gāv-palang: giraffe, anomaly (literally, "camel-cow-leopard")
shubha: obscurity
shuyū'ī: communist

ṣīgheh: limited-term marriage (synonym for *mut'a*)
al-Ṣiḥāḥ al-Sitta: the six main Sunni collections of ḥadīth
sīra: biography of the Prophet
sofreh: cloth on which meals are set; ritual setting with such a cloth
sofreh 'aqd: cloth for bridal display
soushiant: Zoroastrian messiah
sunna: tradition (of the Prophet serving as a precedent)
sūra: one of the 114 "chapters" of the Qur'an
suṭūḥ: middle level of seminary instructions

tabdīl: transformation
tabdīl be aḥsan: "transforming an endowment into something better," e.g., converting an old caravanserai into a hospital
tablīgh: propagation, propaganda
Tablīghī Jamā'at: Muslim missionary organization in India
tafsīr: exegesis (esp. of the Qur'an)
ṭāghūt: false gods, false authority; Qur'anic term used for the shah in the Islamic Revolution
tajwīd: the rules for reciting the Qur'an
takbīr: "glorification" [of God], i.e., the utterance of *Allahu Akbar* (Allah is greatest)
ṭalabeh: seminary student (Arabic plural of *ṭālib,* "student," "seeker"). In Persian *ṭalabeh* is used as the singular and *tullab* the plural
Ta'līmāt -e Islāmī: the semireligious schools established by Shaykh Abbas Ali Islami of Tehran
taqiya: dissimulation
taqlīd: "imitation," followership
tarāwiḥ: a long series of prayers which the Sunnis perform during Ramaḍān as a meritorious *sunna,* but which Shi'ites do not perform, because they regard it as an abrogated *sunna*
tārikh: history
tarjumān: interpreter
taṣarruf -e shar'ī: the temporary takeover of a property by a religious authority (*mujtahid*) in order to ritually cleanse it or transform it into something better (*tabdīl be aḥsan*)
tashabbuh: assimilation
tashabbuh be kuffār: "assimilation to unbelievers," to dress or behave like the unbelievers, a *ḥarām* (forbidden) act. A Prophetic ḥadīth has it that *man tashabbaha bi qawmin fahuwa minhum* ("one who assimilates himself to unbelievers is one of them").
Tashayyu': Shi'ism

taṣ-ḥīf: misreading of the text (of the Qur'an) or miswriting of what is being orally recited
Tāsu'ā: "the ninth" day of the month of Muharram
ṭawāf: "circumambulation" of the *Ka'ba*
tawba: repentance
tawḥīd: the oneness of God
ta'wīl: exegesis; prolepsis (contrasts with *tafsir*)
ta'zieh: passion play
thawāb: merit, reward
Tīgh -e Hazrat -e Abbās: a folk ritual used to detect thieves and liars
torbat: "dust" of Karbala or another sacred land, which is believed by Shi'ite folks to have healing power
Towzīḥ al-Masā'il: a systematic collection of a *marja' taqlīd' fatwā*s (decrees, opinions) in plain language for ordinary people
ṭughyān: rebellion
turāth: heritage
ṭuruq: legitimate "ways" of reciting the Qur'an

'ulamā: scholars; clergy
ulu al-amr: holders of authority
ulu al-'azm: a title given to five prophets who had the mission of establishing universal religion: Abraham, Noah, Moses, Jesus, and Muhammad.
umm al-kabā'ir: "mother of big sins," alcohol
Umm al-Kitāb: "Mother Book," the heavenly archetype of the Qur'an
umma: "religious community"
ummatan wasaṭan: "middle community," the Muslim community
'uṣūlī: one of the two major schools of Shi'ite jurisprudence (contrasts with *Akhbāri*)

vāe'z: preacher
vā'ẓ: preaching
velāyet -e faqīh: guardianship by the clergy (Persian form of *wilāyat -e Faqīh*)

Wa Allāhu A'lam: "And God Knows Best," a phrase uttered by pious scholars of Islam at the end of their theological disputes or following expression of an opinion
Wahhābi: a Sunni sect dominant in Saudi Arabia, the followers of Muhammad ibn Abd al-Wahhab
wāḥid: "single"; a ḥadīth which is narrated by only one chain of narrators

wājib: required
wājib al-'aynī: required for everyone individually
wājib al-kifā'i: required for the community; a duty that can be performed by one or more individuals for the whole community
walī al-amr: "guardian over the affair," the commander of believers
waqf: full stop (in recitation of the Qur'an)
waqf: endowment
waratha: heirs, inheritors (plural of *warith*)
warathat al-anbiā: "heirs of the prophets," the clergy (based on a Prophetic ḥadīth which says "The learned are the heirs of the prophets")
waṣī: executor (particularly of the Prophet, according to Shi'ites, Ali Ibn Abi-Talib)
wilāyat -e faqīh: (Arabic) guardianship by the jurist
wudū: minor ablution which prepares a Muslim for his required prayers and for touching the letters of the Qur'an (contrasts with *ghusl,* major ablution)
wulāt: governors (plural of *wālī*)
wuqūf: "staying," a ritual act during the *ḥajj*

ẓāhir: exoteric (contrasts with *batin*)
zakāt: alms
zakāt al-fiṭr: alms which every Muslim must give to the poor on *Id al-Fitr* (at the end of Ramaḍān)
Zamzam: sacred well in Mecca
zar-zūr-tazwīr: "gold-power-deception," symbolizing "the wealthy, the ruling power, and the clergy," an evil trinity that, according to Ali Shariati, has always ruled history
Zardoshtī: Zoroastrian
ẓill Allāh: "Shadow of God," royal title based on the questionable ḥadīth, "The king is God's shadow on earth"
zīlū: flat-weave rugs woven in central Iran
zindīq: atheist
ziyārat: pilgrimage, visit
zunnār: Zoroastrian sacred thread (synonym for *kostī*)
zūr khāneh: traditional gymnasium

Bibliography

Dual dates refer to original publication date, followed by date of English translation; or Iranian or Islamic calendar date, followed by Common Era date.

Abbot, Nabia

1957–67 *Studies in Arabic Literary Papyri.* 2 vols. University of Chicago Oriental Institute Publications, vols. 75, 76. Chicago: University of Chicago Press.

Abedi, Mehdi, and Gary Legenhausen, eds.

1986 *Jihad and Shahadat, Struggle and Martyrdom in Islam: Essays and Addresses by Ayatullah Mahmud Taleqani, Ayatullah Murtada Mutahhari, Dr. Ali Shariati.* Houston: Institute for Research and Islamic Studies.

Abedi, Mehdi, and A. Mirakhor

1988 *Bibliography on Islamic Banking.* Houston: Institute for Research and Islamic Studies.

Abu'l-Fazl, Mirza

1955 *The Koran, a New Translation.* 4th rev. Bombay: Reform Society.

Abul-Qasem, Muhammad

1982 *The Recitation and Interpretation of the Qur'an: Al-Ghazali's Theory.* London: Kegan Paul International.

Abu-Lughod, Lila

1987 *Veiled Sentiments.* Berkeley: University of California Press.

Ahmad, Aijaz

1987 "Jameson's Rhetoric of Otherness and the 'National Allegory.'" *Social Text* no. 17.

Ahmad, Akbar

1986 "Death in Islam: The Hawkes Bay Case." *Man* 21(1): 120–34.

Ajami, Faud

1986 *The Vanished Imam: Musa al-Sadr and the Shia of Lebanon.* Ithaca, N.Y.: Cornell University Press.

Akhtar-Khavari, Kamran

1983 "History of the Life and Martyrdom of Nurullah Akhtar Khavari." *Andalib,* spring, pp. 42–48.

Albin, Michael

1986 "The Iranian Publishing Industry." *Libri* 36(1): 1–23.

Algar, Hamid

1969 *Religion and State in Iran: 1728–1906.* Berkeley: University of California Press.

1984 "Letter to the Editor." *Iranian Studies* XX. 17(1): 138–41.

Al-e Ahmad, Jalal

1964/1985 *Lost in the Crowd.* Washington, D.C.: Three Continents Press.

A'li, Abulfazl, ed.
1985 *The Graphic Art of the Islamic Revolution.* Tehran: Publication Division of the Art Bureau of the Islamic Propagation Organization.

Ali, Tariq
1981 "Midnight's Children" *Critical Quarterly* 26(3): 87–95.

Ali, Tariq, and Howard Brenton
1989 *Iranian Nights.* London: Nick Hern Books.

Amanat, Abbas
1989 *Resurrection and Renewal: The Making of the Babi Movement.* Ithaca, N.Y.: Cornell University Press.

Amili, Shaykh Hurr al-
n.d. *Al-Wasā'il al-Shī'a.* 20 vols. Beirut: Dar Ihya al-Turath al-Arabi.

Anderson, Benedict
1983 *Imagined Communities.* London: Verso.

Antoun, Richard
1989 *Muslim Preacher in the Modern World. A Jordanian Case Study in Comparative Perspective.* Princteon, N.J.: Princeton University Press.

Appignanesi, Lisa, and Sara Maitland, eds.
1989 *The Rushdie File.* London: Fourth Estate.

Arberry, Arthur
1964 *The Koran Interpreted.* Oxford: Oxford University Press.

Arjomand, Said Amir
1981 *The Shadow of God and the Hidden Imam.* Chicago: University of Chicago Press.

Asaria, M. Iqbal
1985 "Tabung Hajji—The Malay Way to Mecca." *Inquiry,* January.

Asin Palacios, Miguel
1926/1968 *Islam and the Divine Comedy.* Edited and translated by Harold Sutherland. London: Frank Cass and Co.

Assadipour, Bidjan
1989 *Bidjan Assadipour—Calligraphy.* Upper Montclair, N.J.: Rowzan Publications.

Babinger, Franz
1909 *Stambuler Buchwesen im 18. Jahrhundert.* Leipzig: Deutsche Verein für Buchwesen und Schriftum.
1921 "Die Einführung des Buchdruckes in Persien." *Zeitschrift des deutsche Verein für Buchwesen und Schriftum* 11/12:141–43.

Baha'i Publishing Trust
1956 *The Baha'i World 1950–54.* Wilmette, Ill.
1970 *The Baha'i World 1954–63.* Ramat Gan, Israel: Universal House of Justice.

Bakhash, Shaul
1987 "Islam and Social Justice in Iran." In *Shi'ism, Resistance, and Revolution,* edited by Martin Kramer. Boulder, Colo.: Westview Press.

Balyuzi, H. M.
1970 *Edward Granville Browne and the Baha'i Faith.* London: George Ronald.

Baraheni, Reza
1977 *The Crowned Cannibals.* New York: Vintage.

Barney, Laura C.
1908 *Some Answered Questions.* London: Kegan Paul, Trench, Treubner, and Co.

Barthes, Roland
1972/1982 *The Empire of Signs.* Translated by Richard Howard. New York: Hill and Wang.

Bateson, M. C., J. W. Clinton, J. B. M. Kassarjian, H. Safavi, and M. Soraya
1977 "Safa-yi Batin: A Study of the Interrelations of a Series of Iranian Character Types." In *Psychological Dimensions of Near Eastern Studies,* edited by L. C. Browne and N. Itzkowitz. Princeton, N.J.: Darwin Press.

Baudrillard, Jean
1971/1981 *For a Critique of the Political Economy of the Sign.* Translated by Charles Levin. St. Louis: Telos Press.
1988*a* *Jean Baudrillard: Selected Writings.* Edited by Mark Poster. Stanford, Calif.: Stanford University Press.
1988*b* *America.* London: Verso.

Baumgarten, Murray
1982 *City Scriptures: Modern Jewish Writing.* Cambridge, Mass.: Harvard University Press.

Bayat, Mongol
1982 *Mysticism and Dissent: Socioreligious Thought in Qajar Iran.* Syracuse, N.Y.: Syracuse University Press.

Bazargan, Mehdi
N.d. *Saur-e Taḥawwul-e Qur'an.* Tehran. English translation. *The Evolution of the Qur'an.* Houston: Institute for Research and Islamic Studies, forthcoming.

Beck, Lois Grant, and Nikki Keddie, eds.
1978 *Women in the Muslim World.* Cambridge, Mass.: Harvard University Press.

Beeman, William O.
1986 *Language, Status, and Power in Iran.* Bloomington: Indiana University Press.
1988 "Affectivity in Persian Language Use." *Culture, Medicine and Psychiatry* 12(1): 9–30.

Bell, Richard
1937–39 *The Qur'an, Translated with a Critical Re-arrangement of the Surahs.* Edinburgh: T. and T. Clark.
1953 *Introduction to the Qur'an.* Edinburgh: University Press.

Bell, Richard, and Montgomery Watt
1970 *Introduction to the Qur'an.* Edinburgh: University Press.

Benjamin, Walter
1969 *Illuminations.* New York: Schocken.

Berger, Harry, Jr.
1987 "Levels of Discourse in Plato's Dialogues." In *Literature and the Question of Philosophy,* edited by A. Cascardi. Baltimore, Md.: Johns Hopkins University Press.

Berman, Marshall
1982 *All That Is Solid Melts into Air: The Experience of Modernity.* New York: Simon and Schuster.

Bhaba, Homi
1983 "The Other Question . . . Homi Bhaba Reconsiders the Stereotype and Colonial Discourse." *Screen* 24(6).
1985 "Signs Taken For Wonders." *Critical Inquiry* 12(1).
1989 "Down Among the Writers." *New Statesman,* 28 July, pp. 38–39.

Biesle, Megan, and Stephen Tyler, eds.
1986 Special issue on orality and literacy. *Cultural Anthropology* 1(2).

Binder, Leonard
1988 *Islamic Liberalism.* Berkeley: University of California Press.

Bishop, John
1986 *Joyce's Book of the Dark: Finnegans Wake.* Madison: University of Wisconsin Press.

Blachere, Regis
1947 *LeCoran, traduction selon un essai de reclassement des sourates.* Paris: G. P. Maisonneuve.

Blumenberg, Hans
1979/1985 *Work on Myth.* Cambridge: Massachusetts Institute of Technology Press.

Borges, Jorge Luis
1964 "Averroës' Search." *Labyrinths.* New York: New Directions.

Boyce, Mary
1967 "Bibi Shahbanu and the Lady of Pars." *Bulletin of the School of Oriental and African Studies* 30(1): 30–44.
1977 *A Persian Stronghold of Zoroastrianism.* Oxford: Clarendon Press.

Brennan, Timothy
1987 "Myths of the Nation: Salman Rushdie and the Third World." Ph.D. diss. Columbia University.

Brinton, Crane
1938 *Anatomy of Revolution.* New York: Vintage.

Browne, E. G.
1893 *A Year among the Persians.* London: Adams and Charles Black.
1918 *Materials for the Study of the Babi Religion.* London: Cambridge University Press.

Burton, John
1977 *The Collection of the Qur'an.* Cambridge: Cambridge University Press.

Burton, Richard
1853 *Personal Narrative of a Pilgrimage to El Medinah and Meccah.* New York: G. P. Putnam and Co.

Carter, Thomas F.
1943 "Islam as a Barrier to Printing." *The Moslem World* 33:213–16.

Chakravarty, Sumita
1987 "Identity and Authenticity: Nationhood and the Popular Indian Film." Ph.D. diss. University of Illinois, Champaign-Urbana.

Chatterjee, Partha
1986 *Nationalist Thought in the Colonial World.* London: Zed.

Chelkowski, Peter
1987 "Stamps of Blood." *The American Philatelist,* June, pp. 556–66.

Chelkowski, Peter, ed.
1979 *Ta'ziyeh: Ritual and Drama in Iran.* New York: New York University Press.

Chernoff, John
1984 "Pilgrimage of Mecca" *Chicago Review* 34(3): 68–93.

Church Missionary Society
1800–1970 Archives. Series G 2 PE/03-05. London.

Clifford, James, and George Marcus, eds.
1986 *Writing Culture: The Poetics and Politics of Ethnography.* Berkeley: University of California Press.

Cooke, Miriam
1988 *War's Other Voices: Women Writers on the Lebanese Civil War.* Cambridge: Cambridge University Press.

Cristelow, Allan
1987 "Political Ends and Means of Transport in the Colonial North African Pilgrimage." *The Maghreb Review* 12(3–4): 84–89.

Daftar Tabliqat Islami
1986 *Profiles of the Revolutionary Art.* Qum: Daftar Tabliqat Islami.

Derrida, Jacques
1967/1976 *Of Grammatology.* Translated by Gayatri Spivak. Baltimore, Md.: Johns Hopkins University Press.
1967/1978 *Writing and Difference.* Translated by Alan Bass. Chicago: University of Chicago Press.
1972/1981 *Disseminations.* Translated by Barbara Johnson. Chicago: University of Chicago Press.
1974/1986 *Glas.* Translated by John P. Leavey, Jr., and Richard Rand. Lincoln: University of Nebraska Press.
1978/1987*a* *The Truth in Painting.* Translated by Geoff Bennington and Ian McLeod. Chicago: University of Chicago Press.

1980/1987*b* *The Postcard from Socrates to Freud and Beyond.* Translated by Alan Bass. Chicago: University of Chicago Press.

Dickey, Sara Ann

1988 "Going to the Pictures in Madurai." Ph.D. diss., University of California at San Diego.

Dissanayake, Wimal.

1985 "Towards a Decolonized English: South Asian Creativity in Fiction." *World Englishes* 4 (2): 233–242.

Domínguez, Virginia

1989 *People as Subject, People as Object: Selfhood and Peoplehood in Contemporary Israel.* Madison: University of Wisconsin Press.

Duda, Herbert

1935 "Das Druckwesen in der Türkei." *Gutenberg Jahrbuch* 1935:226–42.

Duri, A. A.

1983 *The Rise of Historical Writing among the Arabs.* Princeton, N.J.: Princeton University Press.

Durkheim, Emile

1912/1915 *The Elementary Forms of Religious Life.* Translated by Joseph Ward Swain. New York: Macmillan.

English, Paul

1966 *City and Village in Iran: Settlement and Ecology in the Kirman Basin.* Madison: University of Wisconsin Press.

Esfandiary, Fereidoun

1959 *The Day of Sacrifice.* New York: McDowell, Obolensky.

Ettinghausen, Richard

1962 *Arab Painting.* Geneva.

Fender, Stephen

1981 *Plotting the West.* Cambridge, Cambridge University Press.

Fernea, Elizabeth, and Basima Bezirgan, eds.

1977 *Muslim Women Speak.* Austin: University of Texas Press.

Firestone, Reuven

1988 "The Evolution of Islamic Narrative Exegesis in the Abraham-Ishmael Legends." Ph.D. diss., New York University.

Fischer, Eric

1943 *The Passing of the European Age.* Cambridge: Harvard University Press.

1984 "Reminiscences and Memoirs." MS.

Fischer, Michael M. J.

1973 "Zoroastrian Iran between Myth and Praxis." Ph.D. diss., University of Chicago.

1977*a* "Interpretive Anthropology." *Reviews in Anthropology* 4(4): 391–404.

1977*b* "Persian Society: Transformation and Strain." In *Twentieth Century Iran,* edited by Hossein Amirsadeghi and R. W. Ferrier. London: Heinemann.

1978 "Changing the Concept and Position of Persian Women." In *Women in the Muslim World,* edited by Lois Beck and Nikki Keddie. Cambridge, Mass.: Harvard University Press.

1980*a* *Iran: From Religious Dispute to Revolution.* Cambridge, Mass.: Harvard University Press.

1980*b* "Competing Ideologies and Social Structures in the Persian Gulf." In *The Persian Gulf States,* edited by A. Cottrell et al. Baltimore, Md.: Johns Hopkins University Press.

1980*c* "Becoming Mulla: Reflections on Iranian Clerics in a Revolutionary Age." *Iranian Studies* 13(1–4): 83–177.

1982*a* "From Interpretive to Critical Anthropologies." *Trabalhos de Ciencias,* Serie Antropologia Social, no. 34. Brasilia: Fundaçao Universidade de Brasilia.

1982*b* "Islam and the Revolt of the Petite Bourgeoisie." *Daedalus* 111(1): 101–25.

1982*c* "Portrait of a Mullah: The Autobiography and Bildungsroman of Aqa Najafi-Quchani. *Persica* 10:223–57.

1982*d* Review of H. Algar translation of Khomeini's *Wilayat-e Faqih. Iranian Studies.* 14(3–4): 263–66.

1984 "Reply to Algar." *Iranian Studies.* 17(1): 141–143.

1983 "Imam Khomeini: Four Levels of Understanding." In *Voices of Resurgent Islam,* edited by John Esposito. New York: Oxford University Press.

1984 "Towards a Third World Poetics: Seeing through Short Stories and Films in the Iranian Culture Area." *Knowledge and Society* 5:171–241.

1986 "Ethnicity and the Postmodern Arts of Memory." In *Writing Culture,* edited by James Clifford and George Marcus. Berkeley: University of California Press.

1987 "Repetitions in the Revolution." In *Shi'ism, Resistance, and Revolution,* edited by Martin Kramer. Boulder, Colo.: Westview Press.

1988 "Aestheticized Emotions and Critical Hermeneutics." *Culture, Medicine and Psychiatry* 12(1): 31–42.

1990 "Legal Postulates in Flux: Justice, Wit and Hierarchy in Iran." *Law and Politics in the Middle East,* edited by Daisy Dwyer. Boston: J. F. Bergin.

Fischer, Michael M. J., and Mehdi Abedi

1984 Foreword to *A Clarification of Questions, An Unabridged Translation of Resaleh Towzih al-Masa'il, by Ayatollah Sayyed Ruhollah Mousavi Khomeini.* Boulder: Westview Press.

Fischer, Michael M. J., Byron Good, and Mary-Jo DelVechhio Good

1978 "Persian Passion Playing." MS.

Foucault, Michel

1979 *Discipline and Punish.* Translated by Alan Sheridan. New York: Random House.

Gadamer, Hans-Georg
1960/1975 *Truth and Method.* Translated by Garrett Barden and John Cummings. New York: Seabury Press.
1980 *Dialogue and Dialectic.* New Haven, Conn.: Yale University Press.
1986*a* *The Idea of the Good in Platonic-Aristotelian Philosophy.* Translated by Christopher P. Smith. New Haven, Conn.: Yale University Press.
1977/1986*b* *The Relevance of the Beautiful and Other Essays.* Translated by Robert Bernasconi. Cambridge: Cambridge University Press.

Geertz, Clifford
1973 "Deep Play: Notes on a Balinese Cockfight." In *The Interpretation of Cultures.* New York: Basic Books.

Geertz, Hildred
Forthcoming "A Theater of Cruelty: the Contexts of a Topeng Performance." In *State and Society in Bali,* edited by H. Geertz. Leiden: KITLV.

Gellner, Ernest
1983 *Nations and Nationalism.* Ithaca, N.Y.: Cornell University Press.

Gennep, Arnold van
1960 *The Rites of Passage.* Chicago: University of Chicago Press.

Ghafuri, Ali
1975 *Anfal.* Tehran: Enteshar.

Gluckman, Max
1957 *Order and Rebellion in Tribal Society,* Manchester, England: Manchester University Press.

Goldziher, Ignaz
1890/1971 *Muslim Studies.* Translated by C. M. Barber and S. M. Stern. London: Allen and Unwin.

Good, Byron J., Mary-Jo DelVecchio Good, and Robert Moradi
1985 "The Interpretation of Iranian Depressive Illness and Dysphoric Affect." In *Culture and Depression,* edited by A. Kleinman and B. Good. Berkeley: University of California.

Good, Mary-Jo DelVecchio, and Byron J. Good
1988 "Ritual, the State, and the Transformation of Emotional Discourse in Iranian Society." *Culture, Medicine, and Psychiatry* 12(1): 43–63.

Goodell, Grace
1977 "The Elementary Structures of Political Life: Rural Development in Pahlavi Iran." Ph.D. diss., Columbia University.

Gould, Eric
1985 *The Sin of the Book: Edmond Jabès.* Lincoln: University of Nebraska Press.

Grabar, Oleg
1988 "Geometry and Ideology: The Festival of Islam and the Study of Islamic Art." In *A Way Prepared: Essays on Islamic Culture in Honor of Richard Bayly Winder,* edited by Farhad Kazemi and R. D. McChesney. New York: New York University Press.

Grabar, Oleg, and Sheila Blair
1980 *Epic Images and Contemporary History: the Illustrations of the Great Mongol Shahnama.* Chicago: University of Chicago Press.

Graham, William A.
1977 *Divine Word and Prophetic Word in Early Islam.* The Hague: Mouton.

Great Britain, Public Records Office
1800–1960 Confidential Reports. Foreign Office Series 416.

Grimme, Hubert
1923 *Der Koran.* Paderborn: F. Schoningh.

Griswold, Charles
1986 *Self-Knowledge in Plato's Phaedrus.* New Haven, Conn.: Yale University Press.

Guillaume, Alfred
1955 *The Life of Muhammad, a Translation of Ishaq's Sirat Rasul.* London: Oxford University Press.

Guppy, Shusha
1988 *The Blindfold Horse.* Boston: Beacon.

Ha'eri, Shahla
1985 "Contracts as Models for Sexual Unions: Temporary Marriage, Mut'a, in Contemporary Iran." Ph.D. diss., University of California at Los Angeles.

Halliday, Fred
1983 *The Making of the Second Cold War.* London: Penguin.

Hanaway, William
1985 "The Symbolism of Persian Revolutionary Posters." In *Iran since the Revolution,* edited by Barry M. Rosen. New York: Columbia University Press.

Handelman, Susan A.
1982 *The Slayers of Moses.* Albany: State University of New York.

Harootunian, H. D.
1988 *Things Seen and Unseen.* Chicago: University of Chicago Press.

Hartman, David
1985 *A Living Covenant.* New York: Free Press.

Harvey, L. P.
1988 "The Moriscos and the Hajj." *British Society for Middle Eastern Studies Bulletin* 14:11–24.

Hashim, Amir-Ali
1974 *The Message of the Qur'an Presented in Perspective.* Tokyo: Charles E. Tuttle.

Havelock, Eric
1986 *The Muse Learns to Write.* New Haven, Conn.: Yale University Press.

Hedayat, Sadeq
1939/1957 *The Blind Owl.* Translated by D. P. Costello. New York: Grove Press.
1979 *Haji Agha.* Translated by G. M. Wickens. Austin: University of Texas Press.

Hickey, Joseph V.
1981 "Politics and the Emergence of Alhajis among the Bokkos Fulani." *Journal of Asian and African Studies* 16(3–4): 212–22.

Hill, Brad Sabin
1989 *Hebraica from the Valmadonna Trust.* London: Oxford University Press.

Hirschfeld, Hartwig
1902 *New Researches into the Composition and Exegesis of the Qoran.* London: Royal Asiatic Society.

Hoogland, Eric
1982 *Land and Revolution in Iran 1960–1980.* Austin: University of Texas Press.

Ibn Khaldun, Abad al-Rahman
1981 *The Muqaddimah.* Translated by Franz Rosenthal. Princeton, N.J.: Princeton University Press, 1981.

Ibrahim, Saad Eddin
1980 "Anatomy of Egypt's Militant Islamic Groups." *International Journal of Middle East Studies* 12(4): 423–53.

Jabès, Edmond
1963–65/1977 *The Book of Questions.* Middletown, Conn.: Wesleyan University Press.
1984/1987 *The Book of Dialogue.* Middletown, Conn.: Wesleyan University Press.

Jameson, Fredric
1984 "Postmodernism, or the Cultural Logic of Late Capitalism." *New Left Review* no. 146.
1986 "Third World Literature in the Era of Multinational Capital." *Social Text,* no. 15, pp. 65–88.
1986–87 "Regarding Postmodernism – A Conversation with Fredric Jameson." *Social Text,* no. 17.

Jamieson, Kathleen Hall
1988 *Eloquence in an Electronic Age: The Transformation of Speechmaking.* New York: Oxford University Press.

Javadi, Hasan
1988 *Satire in Persian Literature.* Toronto: Associated Universities Press.

Johnson, Willard
1980 *Poetry and Speculation of the Rg Veda.* Berkeley: University of California.

Joyce, James
1939 *Finnegans Wake*. London: Faber and Faber.
Kapferer, Bruce
1988 *Legends of People, Myths of State*. Washington, D.C.: Smithsonian.
Karnad, Girish
1989 "Theatre in India." *Daedalus* 118(4): 331–52.
Karp, Ivan, and Steven Levine, eds.
Forthcoming *Exhibiting Culture: The Politics and Poetics of Representation*. Washington, D.C.: Smithsonian.
Kasravi, Ahmad
n.d. *Shī'i-gari*. Tehran: Parcham.
Katirayi, Beverly A. Jensen
1987 "Oral Public Communication in the Iranian Immigrant Community." Ph.D. diss., University of Washington.
Katsh, Abraham I.
1954 *Judaism in Islam*. New York: Sepher-Hermon Press.
Keddie, Nikki
1981 *Roots of Revolution*. New Haven, Conn.: Yale University Press.
Kedouri, Elie
1960 *Nationalism*. London: Hutchinson.
1971 *Nationalism in Asia and Africa*. New York: World Publishers.
Kepel, Gilles
1984 *The Prophet and Pharaoh: Muslim Extremism in Egypt*. London: Al Saqi Books.
Khan, Mohsen S., and Abbas Mirakhor, eds.
1987 *Islamic Banking and Finance*. Houston: Institute for Research and Islamic Studies.
Khodeif, Ali Ibrahim
1986 "The Hijaz Vilayet 1869–1908: The Sharifate, the Haj and the Bedouins of the Hijaz." Ph.D. diss., University of Wisconsin, Madison.
Khomeini, Sayyid Ruhullah Musavi
1944 *Kashf-e asrār*. Qum
1978 *Ḥukūmat-e Islami: Wilāyat-e faqīh*. Tehran: Amir Kabir.
1981 *Islam and Revolution: Writings and Declarations of Imam Khomeini*. Translated by Hamid Algar. Berkeley, Calif.: Mizan Press.
1984 *A Clarification of Questions, an Unabridged Translation of Resaleh Towzīh al-Masā'il*. Translated by J. Borujerdi. Boulder, Colo.: Westview Press.
Krek, Miroslav
1976 *A Bibliography of Arabic Typography*. Weston, Mass.: Krek.
Kundera, Milan
1987 "Conversation with Milan Kundera on the Art of the Novel." *Salmagundi*, no. 73, winter.

Küng, Hans

1987 "Christianity and World Religions: The Dialogue with Islam as One Model." *The Muslim World* 77(2): 80–95.

1988 "Direction: On the Way to Postmodernity." *Theology for the Third Millennium.* New York: Doubleday.

Kureishi, Hanif

1986 "Bradford." *Granta,* 20, Winter.

Labib, Muhammad

1981 *The Seven Martyrs of Hurmazak.* Translated by Moojan Momen. Oxford: George Ronald.

Lambton, Ann K. S.

1953 *Landlord and Peasant in Persia.* London: Oxford University Press.

1964 "A Reconsideration of the Position of the Marja' Taqlid and the Religious Institution." *Studia Islamica* 20:115–35.

Laroui, Abdullah

1974/1976 *The Crisis of the Arab Intellectual.* Berkeley: University of California Press.

Lassy, Ivar J.

1916 *The Muharram Mysteries among the Azarbaijan Turks of Caucasia.* Helsingfors: Lilius and Hertzberg.

Lentz, Thomas, and Glenn D. Lowry

1989 *Timur and the Princely Vision.* Washington: Smithsonian Institution Press.

Levinas, Emmanuel

1970 "No Identity." *Emmanuel Levinas, Collected Essays,* edited by Alphonso Lingis. The Hague: Nijhof.

1984 "Dialogue with Emmanuel Levinas." In *Dialogues with Contemporary Continental Thinkers,* edited by Richard Kearney. Manchester, England: Manchester University Press.

Levy, Ruben

1951 The Qabus Nama by Kai Ka'us ibn Iskandar. New York: Dutton.

Löffler, Rheinhold

1988 *Islam in Practice: Religious Belief in a Persian Village.* Albany: State University of New York Press.

Long, David

1979 *The Hajj Today.* Albany: State University of New York Press.

Lyotard, Jean-François

1979/1984 *The Postmodern Condition: A Report on Knowledge.* Translated by Geoff Bennington and Brian Massumi. Minneapolis: University of Minnesota Press.

Makky, Ghazy

1981 "Characteristics of Pilgrim's Accommodation in Makkah." Ph.D. diss., University of Michigan.

Malcolm, Napier

1903 "Development of Schoolwork in a Persian Town." In the Church Missionary Archives, G2 PE 05:87.

1905 *Five Years in a Persian Town.* London: John Murray.

Mannan, M. A.

1987 *Islamic Economics: Theory and Practice.* Boulder, Colo.: Westview Press.

Maranhão, Tullio

1986 *Therapeutic Discourse and Socratic Dialogue.* Madison: University of Wisconsin Press.

Maranhão, Tullio, ed.

1990 *The Interpretation of Dialogue.* Chicago: University of Chicago Press.

Marcus, George, and Michael M. J. Fischer

1986 *Anthropology as Cultural Critique: An Experimental Moment in the Human Sciences.* Chicago: University of Chicago Press.

Mardin, Şerif

1962 *The Genesis of Young Ottoman Thought.* Princeton: Princeton University Press.

Massignon, Louis

1975/1982 *The Passion of al-Hallaj.* Translated by Herbert Mason. Princeton, N.J.: Princeton University Press.

May, Larry

1980 *Screening Out the Past: The Birth of Mass Culture & the Motion Picture Industry.* London: Oxford University Press.

McAuliffe, Jane Dammen

1984 "Perceptions of the Christians in Qur'anic Tafsir." Ph.D. diss., University of Toronto.

McDonnell, Mary Byrne

1986 "The Conduct of the Hajj from Malaysia and Its Socio-Economic Impact." Ph.D. diss., Columbia University.

Melot, Michel

1988 "Caricature and the Revolution: The Situation in France in 1789." In *French Caricature and the French Revolution 1789–1799: A Catalogue Issued by the Grunwald Center for the Graphic Arts, University of California at Los Angeles.* Chicago: University of Chicago Press.

Menocal, Maria Rosa

1987 *The Arabic Role in Medieval Literary History.* Philadelphia: University of Pennsylvania Press.

Mernissi, Fatima

1977 *Beyond the Veil.* New York: Schenkman.

Migeod, Heinz Georg

1956 "Über die persische Gesellschaft unter Nasiru'd-Din Shah 1848–96." Ph.D. diss., University of Göttingen.

Mills, Margaret
Forthcoming *The Mullah and the Mason.* Philadelphia: University of Pennsylvania Press.

Mishra, Vijay
1985 "Towards a Theoretical Critique of Bombay Cinema." *Screen* 26 (2-3): 133–46.

Mitchell, Timothy
1988 *Colonizing Egypt.* Cambridge: Cambridge University Press.

Mitchell, W. J. T.
1986 *Iconology: Image, Text, Ideology.* Chicago: University of Chicago Press.
1989 "Ut Pictura Theoria: Abstract Painting and the Repression of Language." *Critical Inquiry* 15(2): 348–71.

Mohasses, Ardeshir
1989 *Closed Circuit History.* Washington, D.C.: Mage Publishers

Monzer, Ali Abolhasan
1972 *Shahid Mutahhari: Efshagar-e Toṭe'eh.* Tehran.

Moretti, Franco
1986 "The Moment of Truth." *New Left Review,* no. 159.

Morgan, Kenneth W., ed.
1958 *Islam, the Straight Path.* New York: Ronald Press.

Morris, Robert
1989 "Words and Images in Modernism and Postmodernism." *Critical Inquiry* 15(2): 337–47.

Mottahedeh, Mildred
1956 "Report of Baha'i Activities in Relation to the United Nations." *The Baha'i World 1950–54.* Wilmette, Ill.: Baha'i Publishing Trust.

Mottahedeh, Roy
1985 *The Mantle of the Prophet.* New York: Simon and Schuster.

Muhammad Ali
1963 *The Holy Qur'an.* 6th ed. Lahore.

Muir, William
1878 *The Coran: Its Composition and Teaching and the Testimony It Bears to the Holy Scriptures.* New York: Pott and Young.

Mukherjee, Bharati
1988 *The Middleman and Other Stories.* New York: Grove Press.
1989 *Jasmine.* New York: Grove Wiedenfeld.

Murphy, Dervla
1987 *Tales From Two Cities: Travels of Another Sort.* London: Penquin.

Muṭahhari, Murtaḍā
1962 "Ijtihād dar Islām." In *Bahthi dar bāreye marja'iyat va ruḥāniyat,* edited by S. Muhammad-Husain Tabataba'i et al. Tehran: Enteshar Press.
1971 *'Ilal-e gerayesh be maddīgari.* Mashhad, Iran: Tus.

1975 *Khadamat-e mutaqabel-e Islam va Iran.* 7th ed. Tehran: Daftar-e Nashr-e Farhang-e Islami (*Mutual Services of Islam and Iran,* Translated by Mehdi Abedi. Houston: Institute for Research and Islamic Studies, forthcoming).

1978 *Nezam-e huquq-e zan dar Islam.* Tehran: Sadra Publications.

Mutairi, Hezam Mater, al-

1987 "An Islamic Perspective on Public Service with Reference to the Hajj Research Center." Ph.D. diss., State University of New York at Albany.

Nabil-i-Azam, Mohammad Zarandi

1932 *The Dawn Breakers.* Translated by Shoghi Effendi. New York: Baha'i Publishing Committee.

Naficy, Hamid

1988 "Culture in Exile: Fetishized Iranian TV in the U.S." MS.

Nelson, Kristina

1985 *The Art of Reciting the Qur'an.* Austin: University of Texas Press.

Nettler, Ronald L.

1987 *Past Trials and Present Tribulations: A Mulsim Fundamentalist's View of the Jews,* Oxford: Pergamon Press.

Neuwirth, Angelika

1981 *Studein zur Komposition der mekkanischen Suren.* Berlin.

Noldeke, Theodor

1860 *Geschichte des Qorans.* Göttingen: Verlag der Dieterichschen Buchhandlung.

1909–26 *Geschichte des Qorans.* 2d ed. Leipzig: Verlag der Dieterichschen Buchhandlung.

Noqaba'i, Hesam

1983 *Tahireh (Qurrat ul-Ayn).* 2d ed. N.p.

Ochsenwald, William

1975 "Ottoman Subsidies to the Hijaz 1877–1886." *International Journal of Middle East Studies.*

1977 "The Financial Basis of Ottoman Rule in the Hijaz 1840–77." In *Nationalism in a Non-National State: The Dissolution of the Ottoman Empire,* edited by William Haddad and W. Ochsenwald. Columbus: Ohio State Press.

1982 "Commercial History of the Hijaz Vilayat 1840–1908." *Arabian Studies.*

Paulson, Ronald

1983 *Representations of Revolutions.* New Haven, Conn.: Yale University Press.

Pedersen, Johannes

1984 *The Arabic Book.* Princeton, N.J.: Princeton University Press.

Pelly, Lewis

1879 *The Miracle Play of Hasan and Husain.* London: William H. Allen.

Pliskin, Karen
1987 *Silent Boundaries: Cultural Constraints on Sickness and Diagnosis of Iranians in Israel.* New Haven, Conn.: Yale University Press.
Politzer, Georges
1946 *Principes élémentaires de philosophie.* Paris: Editions sociales.
Pollack, David
1986 *The Fracture of Meaning.* Princeton, N.J.: Princeton University Press.
Qurashi, S. Ali
1973 *Qamus-e Qur'an.* Reza'iyeh.
Radi al-Sharif, Muhammad ibn al-Husayn, al-
1967 *Nahjul al-Balagha.* Beirut.
Ramyar, Mahmud
1967 *Tārīkh-e Qur'ān.* Tehran: Andisheh.
Riggio, Milla Cozart, ed.
1988 *Ta'ziyeh: Ritual and Popular Beliefs in Iran.* Hartford, Conn.: Trinity College.
Rodwell, J. M.
1918 *The Koran, Translated from the Arabic.* New York: E. P. Dutton.
Rose, Richard
1988 *The Postmodern President.* New York: Basic Books.
Rosen, Stanley
1987 *Hermeneutics as Politics.* New York: Oxford University Press.
Rumi, Jalalu'ddin
1926 *The Mathnawi of Jalau'ddin Rumi.* Translated by Reynold A. Nicholson. Cambridge, England: Gibb Memorial Trust.
Rusche, Georg, and Otto Kirchheimer
1939 *Punishment and Social Structure.* New York: Columbia University Press.
Rushdie, Salman
1975 *Grimus.* London: Victor Gollancz.
1980 *Midnight's Children.* New York: Alfred A. Knopf.
1982*a* "The Empire Writes Back with a Vengeance." *Times of London,* 3 July,
1982*b* "Angel Gabriel." *London Review of Books,* 16 Sept.–6 October.
1983*a* *Shame.* New York: Alfred A. Knopf.
1983*b* "Casualties of Censorship." In *They Shoot Writers Don't They?,* edited by George Theiner. London: Faber and Faber.
1983*c* "The Indian Writer in England." In *In the Eye of the Beholder,* edited by Maggie Butcher. London: Commonwealth Institute.
1983*d* "Outside the Whale." *Granta* vol. 2, pp. 123–41.
1985 "The Location of Brazil." *American Film,* Sept., pp. 50–53.
1988 *Satanic Verses.* London: Viking.
Saadawi, Nawal El-
1982 *The Hidden Face of Eve.* London: Zed.

Sadr, S. Muhammad-Baqir

1971 *Iqtiṣād-e Ma.* Persian translation by M. Kazem Musavi. Tehran: Aftab.

1981 *Iqtisaduna.* 14th ed. (1st ed. 1961). Beirut: Dar al-Fiqh al-Islami.

Safinejad, Javad

1972 *Boneh.* Tehran: University of Tehran.

Sahlins, Marshall

1981 *Historical Metaphors and Mythical Realities.* Ann Arbor: University of Michigan Press.

1985 *Islands of History.* Chicago: University of Chicago Press.

Said, Edward

1988 "Representing the Colonized: Anthropology's Interlocutors." *Critical Inquiry* 15(2): 205–25.

Said, Labib as-

1975 *The Recited Koran.* Princeton, N.J.: Darwin Press.

Schulte-Sasse, J.

1988 "Mass-Produced Narratives." *Cultural Critique,* No. 10.

Seery, John E.

1985 "Political Returns." Ph.D. diss., University of California at Berkeley.

Sefidvash, Siyavush

132B/1975 *Memoirs.* Tehran: Moasseseh-ye Melli Matbusateh Amri.

Serres, Michel

1972 *L'Intereférence.* Paris: Editions de Minuit.

Shamas, Anton

1989 "The Shroud of Mahfouz." *New York Review of Books,* 2 February, pp. 19–21.

Shari'ati, Ali

1334/1955 *Maktab-e Vasateh* (The Middle Way School of Thought). Mashhad, Iran (n.p.). reprinted in *Collected Works,* vol. 31, Tehran: Chapakhash, 1982.

1349/1970 *Kevir.* Mashhad, Iran: Tus.

1350/1971*a* *Ḥajj.* Tehran: Husainiyya Irshad. English translation, Bedford, Ohio: FILINC, 1978.

1351/1971*b* *Ummat va imamat.* Tehran: Husainiyya Irshad.

1350/1971*c* *Return to Self.* English translation by Mehdi Abedi, Houston: Institute for Research and Islamic Studies, forthcoming.

Sharkawi, A. R.

1962 *Egyptian Earth.* London: Heinemann.

Shoghi Effendi

1952 *God Passes By.* Wilmette, Ill.: Baha'i Publishing Trust.

Siebers, Tobin

1988 *The Ethics of Criticism.* Ithaca, N.Y.: Cornell University Press.

Sivan, Emanuel

1985 *Radical Islam: Medieval Theology and Modern Politics.* New Haven, Conn.: Yale University Press.

Siyuti, Jalal-ud-Din, and Jalal-ud-Din Mahalli
1974 *Tafsir al-Jalālayn.* Beirut: Dar al-Arabiyya.

Sloterdijk, Peter
1987 *Critique of Cynical Reason.* Minneapolis: University of Minnesota Press.

Slyomovics, Susan
1987 *The Merchant of Art: An Egyptian Hilali Oral Epic Poet in Performance.* Berkeley: University of California Press.

Sprachman, Paul
1981 "The Comic Works of 'Ubayd-Zakani: A Study of Medieval Persian Bawdy, Verbal Aggression, and Satire." Ph.D. diss., University of Chicago.

Sprenger, Alois
1861 *Das Leben und die Lehre des Mohammad.* (2d ed. 1869). Berlin: Nicolaische Verlagsbuchandlung.

Sreberny-Mohammadi, Annabelle, and Ali Mohammadi
1988 "The Islamic Republic and the World: Images, Propaganda, Intentions and Results." In *Post-Revolutionary Iran,* edited by Hooshang Amirahamdi and Manouchehr Parvin. Boulder, Colo.: Westview Press.

Steiner, George
1984 *Antigones.* New York: Oxford University Press.

Stiles, Susan Judith
1983 "Zoroastrian Conversions to the Baha'i Faith in Yazd, Iran." M.A. thesis, University of Arizona.

Subhani, Jafar
1979 *Raz-e Bozorg-e Risalat.* Tehran: Kitab Khaneh Masjid Jame'.

Summers, David
1989 "Form, Nineteenth-Century Metaphysics, and the Problem of Art Historical Description." *Critical Inquiry* 15(2): 372–406.

Suyuti, Jalal al-Din abd al-Rahim
1980 *al-Itqān fi 'ulūm al-Qur'ān.* Lahore: Suhayl Academy of Lahore.

Sweetman, John
1988 *The Oriental Obsession: Islamic Inspiration in British and American Art and Architecture 1500–1920.* Cambridge: Cambridge University Press.

al-Tabarsi, Faḍl ibn al-Hasan
1960 *Majma' al-Bayan.* Beirut: Dar Ihya al-Turath al-Arabi.

Tabataba'i, S. Muhammad Hosain, et al.
1341/1962 *Bahhth-i dar bara eh-e Marja'iyyat ya Ruḥāniyyat.* Tehran: Enteshar Press.

Taheri-Bethel, Fereshteh
1984 "A Psychological Theory of Martyrdom: A Content Analysis of Personal Documents of Baha'i Martyrs of Iran Written between 1979 and 1982." Ph.D. diss., U.S. International University, San Diego.

Taheri-Malamiri, Muhammad
1342/1923–24 *Tarikh-e Shahada-ye Yazd.* Cairo: n.p.

Taleqani, S. Mahmud
N.d. *Partovi Az Qur'an.* Tehran: Enteshar Press.

Tamari, Meir
1987 *With All Your Possessions: Jewish Ethics and Economic Life.* New York: Free Press.

Taqawi, S. Muhammad Ali
1949 *Tarikh-e Qur'an-e Majid.* Tehran.

Taylor, J. M.
1982 "The Politics of Aesthetic Debate: The Case of Brazilian Carnival." *Ethnology* 21(2): 301–11.

Tedlock, Barbara
1987 *Dreaming: Anthropological and Psychological Interpretations.* Cambridge: Cambridge University Press.

Traweek, Sharon
1988 *Beamtimes and Lifetimes.* Cambridge, Mass.: Harvard University Press.

Turner, Victor
1957 *Schism and Continuity in an African Society.* Manchester, England: Manchester University Press.
1967 *The Forest of Symbols.* Ithaca, N.Y.: Cornell University Press.

al-Tusi, Shaykh al-Taifeh
n.d. *al-Tibyan.* Najaf: Maktab

Tyler, Stephen
1977 *The Said and the Unsaid.* Philadelphia: Academic.
1987 *The Unspeakable: Discourse, Dialogue, and Rhetoric in the Post-modern World.* Madison: University of Wisconsin Press.

Virilio, Paul
1984/1989 *War and Cinema, The Logistics of Perception.* New York: Verso.

Wallace, Anthony F. C.
1969 *The Death and Rebirth of the Seneca.* New York: Alfred A. Knopf.

Wansborough, John
1977 *Qur'anic Studies.* Oxford: Oxford University Press.

Wasserstrom, S. M.
1985 "Species of Misbelief: A History of Muslim Heresiography of the Jews." Ph.D. diss., University of Toronto.

Wavel, A. J. B.
1913 *A Modern Pilgrim in Mecca.* London: Constable and Co.

Weil, Gustav
1844 *Historisch-kritisch Einleitung in den Koran.* Beilefeld, W. Germany: Velhagen and Klasing.

Williams, Raymond
1989 *The Politics of Modernism.* New York: Verso.

Williams, Raymond Brady

1988 *Religions of Immigrants from India and Pakistan: New Threads in the American Tapestry.* New York: Cambridge University Press.

Wiesel, Elie

1976 *Messengers of God.* New York: Random House.

Wills, Garry

1987 *Reagan's America.* New York: Doubleday.

Wilson, Peter Lamborn

1988 *Scandal: Essays in Islamic Heresy.* Brooklyn, N.Y.: Autonomedia.

Wolfson, Harry

1976 *The Philosophy of the Kalam.* Cambridge, Mass.: Harvard University Press.

Yafi, A. A.

1983 "Management of Some Large-Scale Logistical Problems of the Hajj." Ph.D. diss., University of Texas at Austin.

Yusuf Ali, Abdullah

1977 *The Holy Qur'an: Translation and Commentary.* Houston: Muslim Students Association of the United States and Canada.

Zanjani, Abu Abdullah

1935 *Tārīkh al-Qur'ān.* Cairo.

Zaydān, Jirjī

1907 *History of Islamic Civilization.* Translated by D. S. Margoliouth. Leiden: E. J. Brill.

Index